R&D Collaboration on Trial

R&D
COLLABORATION ON
TRIAL

The Microelectronics and Computer Technology Corporation

DAVID V. GIBSON
IC^2 INSTITUTE
THE UNIVERSITY OF TEXAS AT AUSTIN

AND

EVERETT M. ROGERS
UNIVERSITY OF NEW MEXICO

HARVARD BUSINESS SCHOOL PRESS
BOSTON, MASSACHUSETTS

98   97   96   95   94   5   4   3   2   1

Library of Congress Cataloging-in-Publication Date

Gibson, David V.
    R&D collaboration on trial: the Microelectronics and Computer Technology
Corporation / David V. Gibson and Everett M. Rogers.
    p. c.
    Includes bibliographical references and index.
    ISBN 0-875484-364-6 (alk. paper)
    1. Microelectronics and Computer Technology Corporation. 2. Computer industry—
United States. 3. Microelectronics industry—United States. 4. Strategic alliances—United States—
Case studies. I. Rogers, Everett M. II. Title. III. Title: R and D collaboration on trial.
HD9696.C64M524 1994   93-1374
338.4'7004'0973—dc20   CIP

To
George Kozmetsky and William C. Norris,
visionaries for enhanced U.S. technology competitiveness,
and
to those champions who have helped implement these visions

CONTENTS

LIST OF TABLES AND FIGURES

TABLES

ix

FIGURES

PREFACE

R&D Collaboration on Trial describes the formation and first decade of operation of the United States' first major, for-profit R&D consortium: the Microelectronics and Computer Technology Corporation (MCC).

MCC was launched in 1982 with high expectations by a select group of U.S. computer executives to help save their industry from Japanese competition. They collaborated in planning, implementing, and funding MCC. This private-sector initiative did not seek U.S. government funding. No foreign-owned firms were allowed to join. MCC challenged U.S. antitrust law and encouraged the passage of the National Cooperative Research Act in 1984, under which more than 350 U.S.-based R&D consortia have registered.

In 1983, the national competition for MCC's headquarters motivated city and state governments to realize that the process of regional economic development had changed from one of "chasing smokestacks" to one of creating conditions for high-tech entrepreneurship. The MCC site-selection process was a high-stakes political and economic development contest that involved 57 cities in 27 states, including four finalists: Raleigh-Durham, North Carolina; San Diego, California; Atlanta, Georgia; and Austin, Texas. MCC chose Austin, but the losing locations also won by gaining public/private support for regional investment in microelectronics R&D, educational excellence, and a renewed appreciation for quality-of-life considerations in community-based economic development.

During MCC's first ten years of operation, more than $500 million of member-company funds have been invested in the consortium. Leading researchers from U.S. industry, universities, and federal laboratories were hired to work at the state-of-the-art facility. Research priorities were set by the member companies in four program areas: computer-aided design, packaging/interconnect, software technology, and advanced computer architecture. Structure and process were put in place to facilitate the timely transfer of MCC-developed technologies to the funding companies whose job it was to commercialize the research.

The answer to whether MCC is judged a success or failure depends on the perspective of the evaluator. On one hand, the consortium has not "crashed and burned" as some predicted it would. MCC has maintained its size at 20 plus shareholder companies while dramatically increasing other forms of membership. MCC has been awarded or allowed 117 U.S. patents, licensed 182 technologies, and published and distributed more than 2,400 technical reports and 400 technical videotapes. On the other hand, while a wide range of technologies has been transferred to member companies, MCC has not produced "silver bullet," leapfrog technologies to beat back Japanese advances in the microelectronics and computer industries. MCC has not been vital to the economic competitiveness of its member companies.

MCC has contributed to U.S. industrial competitiveness in ways not originally imagined. The consortium has been a useful impetus and model for many U.S. (and foreign-based) R&D consortia. Important lessons have been learned—lessons about collaborative alliances and technology commercialization. MCC's member companies have learned to collaborate in ways not considered feasible before they joined the consortium. But the consortium's most important initial legacy may have been to demonstrate the barriers and facilitators to achieving successful commercial applications from R&D produced in an organization that is at arm's length from technology users. This is a critically important challenge faced by U.S. research universities and federal labs as well as hundreds of consortia and alliances.

During MCC's first decade, the consortium has gone through three distinct management eras under the leadership of retired Admiral Bobby Ray Inman (1983-1986), former Texas Instruments executive Grant Dove (1987-1990), and former DARPA (Defense Advanced Research Projects Agency) director Dr. Craig Fields (1990-present). The challenges to commercializing MCC-developed technologies have been substantial, and by 1991 the consortium was encouraging its researchers to become more entrepreneurial and to spin out companies. Funding for the consortium has shifted from highly leveraged corporate support of long-term, goal-directed research to single– and few–company, division-level research projects. U.S. government funding has increased substantially and technology collaboration with foreign counties has been initiated.

MCC is an important experiment that clarifies issues fundamentally important to the realization of public/private collaboration to enhance U.S. industrial competitiveness. The consortium's first decade has demonstrated just how difficult it is for U.S. corporations to collaborate in pre-competitive R&D leading to successful product/process commercialization. These lessons contain important "management technologies" for other U.S. consortia, government laboratories, and research universities.

Here we tell of visionaries who inspired new ways of collaborating to compete in worldwide high technology. We base our story on the personal accounts of those whose task it was to implement these visions.

DVG
EMR

ACKNOWLEDGMENTS

Our ten years of research on MCC have been conducted with the cooperation and assistance of a number of individuals and organizations. We thank:

Executives and others who were involved in the planning and early formation of MCC, most notably William C. Norris, Robert M. Price, Phillip W. Arneson, and Robert G. Rutishauser, all of Control Data Corporation, as well as Palle Smidt, vice president, Sperry Corporation, and consultant Jess Rifkind, for their valuable insights concerning the birth of MCC. We are especially grateful to Phil Arneson for allowing us to reference his personal records on MCC's formation.

MCC officials and researchers, including the consortium's CEOs, Bobby Ray Inman; Grant Dove; and Dr. Craig Fields and MCC's early senior managers: Palle Smidt, senior vice president, programs and plans; Robert G. Rutishauser, vice president, finance and administration; Dr. John Pinkston, vice president, chief scientist; and George Black, vice president, human resources. We are especially grateful to Bill Stotesbery, director of communications, and Meg Wilson, vice president for business development, who patiently worked with us over the years and who provided valuable comments and insights on MCC's operations. We are also indebted to former and current managers and researchers at MCC and at MCC's shareholder companies, especially Laszlo Belady, Bill Curtis, Katherine Hammer, Mary Kragie, David Misunas, Charles Petrie, Jerry Werner, and the others who are listed in Appendix B. During our extended study of MCC, the personnel of the consortium and member companies have been most cooperative in sharing information and insights with us so that we might capture the most important events in MCC's history.

Those public and private leaders who were central to Austin and Texas' 1983 campaign for MCC, especially John Watson,

Austin real estate developer; Pike Powers, executive assistant to Governor Mark White; Harden Wiedemann, governor's assistant for economic development; Meg Wilson, special assistant to the governor; Neal Spelce and Harold Falkenberg, of Neal Spelce Communications; Herb Woodson and Ben Streetman, professors in the College of Engineering, and Clif Drummond, associate director for energy studies, all of The University of Texas at Austin; John Gray, director of economic development, Austin's Chamber of Commerce; and Henry Cisneros, mayor of San Antonio.

Dan Pegg, president of the San Diego Economic Development Corporation, and other California leaders who led San Diego's 1983 campaign for MCC; their North Carolina counterparts, including Governor James Hunt, Joe Herbert, director of the Research Triangle Institute, and Bill Friday of the University of North Carolina; and our respondents in Atlanta, who described Georgia's campaign for MCC, especially Professor Robert McMath of Georgia Tech.

Dr. William J. Murphy III, whose 1987 dissertation at the Harvard Business School, "Cooperative Action to Achieve Competitive Strategic Objectives: A Study of the Microelectronics and Computer Technology Corporation," was an important reference document for our analysis of MCC's early years.

We thank Elizabeth Lopez and Jean Campbell of the Annenberg School for Communication, University of Southern California, for their help with preparing this book, and also Peter Clarke, former dean, Annenberg School, who had faith in the present research since its beginnings a decade ago.

Our research on MCC led to involvement with the University of Texas' IC^2 (Innovation, Creativity, and Capital) Institute and its director, Dr. George Kozmetsky. Over the years, the institute's research fellows and associates have provided valuable input to our study of MCC and to technology commercialization, and regionally based economic development. Most notably these colleagues were Bert Cunnington, Kunio Goto, Laura Kilcrease, Kiyoshi Niwa, Fred Phillips, Nikolay D. Ragalyev, Syed Shariq, Raymond W. Smilor, Sten Thore, Fred Williams, and Francis Wu. We are indebted to the institute's staff, including Christine Brown, Tom Harlan, Ophelia Mallari, Chris Lake Marcum, Nancy Richey, and Patricia L. Roe. We thank Leanne Beaver, administrative assistant, who was most cooperative in helping type this manuscript. Most important, we thank Linda Teague who tirelessly, efficiently, and with good spirit worked with us to prepare our manuscript and to format the figures and tables. Linda deserves much credit for helping us bring this project to a successful conclusion.

Dr. Christopher M. Avery and Dr. Nan Muir, who assisted us in our data collection as they completed research for their dissertations on MCC: "Organizational Communication in Technology Transfer between an R&D Consortium and Its Shareholders: The Case of the MCC" (Avery, 1989) and "R&D Consortium Technology Transfer: A Study of Shareholder Technology Strategy and Organizational Learning" (Muir, 1991).

Mark P. Strain, for allowing us access to his research notes and tapes of personal interviews that he conducted for his 1989 University of Texas senior honors' thesis, "The Decision of SEMATECH to Locate in Austin." For our chapter on SEMATECH, we also appreciate the helpful comments of Turner Hasty, Miller Bonner, David Smith, Elias Zachos, Andy and Alison Cohen, and Michael Harper.

We wish to thank our many friends, colleagues, and students (too many to mention by name) for their insights and suggestions for R&D Collaboration on Trial. Special thanks are due the following scholars who read our book in manuscript form: Dr. Rolf T. Wigand, School of Information Studies, Syracuse University; Dr. James W. Dearing, Department of Communication, Michigan State University; and Dr. Arvind Singhal, School of Interpersonal Communication, Ohio University.

We thank the Harvard Business School Press acquisition editors Richard Luecke and Scott Mahler, editor Alistair D. Williamson, production editor Natalie Greenberg, copyeditor Susan Cohan, and the reviewers of our manuscript for their useful comments and suggestions. Natalie was especially helpful in guiding our manuscript through to completion.

Finally, we thank those who supported our research with funds and other organizational resources: the Annenberg School for Communication at the University of Southern California and its dean, Peter Clarke; the IC^2 Institute and its director, George Kozmetsky; William D. Livingston, vice president and dean of Graduate Studies, and the University of Texas Research Institute for summer research funding; and John Pinkston at MCC for funding the IC^2 Institute's survey on technology transfer. Most important, we thank the management and researchers at MCC and the member companies for allowing us unfettered access to archival materials and personnel during our decade-long study.

PROLOGUE BY GEORGE KOZMETSKY

For more than 40 years, U.S. science and technology policies focused on competition with the nation's enemies primarily in the Eastern European bloc. Current issues concern the viability of U.S. economic policies, the strength of U.S. industry, and the effectiveness of firms to compete technologically. The problems go beyond shifting from military to commercial demands and delineating science and technology policies for bridging such a transformation. The profound science and technology issues concern moving from political leadership to socioeconomic political participation with other nations in establishing science and technology commercialization directions for the twenty-first century.

Leadership for transformation spans all institutions of society—government, academia, labor, and business. A critical mass of leadership is needed to transform the United States and all nations if we are to compete technologically in a world at peace, ensure jobs for all people, and increase the world's standard of living. Shorter term issues are: (1) how to change attitudes toward the science and technology achievements of other nations; (2) how to share science and technology knowledge in a meaningful way; (3) how to utilize dual technologies for both national and economic security; and (4) how to share, within and among nations, the wealth created by science and technology.

The traditional and still current strategy for commercializing technology is that industrial laboratories concentrate on shorter-term R&D developments, government laboratories concentrate on mission-oriented projects, and universities confine themselves to basic research. During the past decade, advocates for changing this strategy recognized security gaps and loss of global markets. Consequently, they concentrated on mechanisms to encourage long-term commitments for research and development by both government and industry. They agree that our industries should have greater involvement with government labs and university research.

For much of the period from the 1950s to the 1980s, it was generally assumed that scientific research would, in one way or another, be transferred automatically into viable technologies and be subsequently commercialized. Little attention was paid to how science was actually transformed into technology, then employed for specific commercial purposes, and ultimately diffused regionally as well as internationally. The traditional paradigm was that basic research innovations would occur when R&D results were not only economical but also better understood. The utilization of technology as a resource was perceived as an individual institution's responsibility. Economic developments would flow from this process because of American ingenuity and entrepreneurial spirit. It was expected that all regions of the United States would, in time, enjoy the benefits of the new innovations from research.

The end of the cold war has made peace and shared economic prosperity possible. Science and technology are the key resources and enablers. Never before has such an opportunity been possible in human history. At the end of a hot war the world struggled over political systems and the use of war for economic purposes. Now democracy and the market economy are available to all nations. How we build a better, peaceful, sharing world is the real basis of science and technology policies. It is the exploitation of knowledge and intellect for the benefit of all people that is a humanistic challenge. It is more than one country counting its Nobel prizes, the number of patents issued, the sophistication of its infrastructures, or the accumulation of material things. It is the maximization of people's potential for the general welfare of everyone in the world that needs to drive science and technology policies.

The Reagan and Bush administrations left the Clinton/Gore administration with a three-way polarization for commercializing science and technology. One is championed by laissez faire conservative politicians and neoclassical economists. They recommend that the government play a minor role—let the market dictate. They would limit federal R&D to basic research, leaving applications and commercialization to private industry.

The second approach, promulgated by many high-technology industry executives and consortia as well as liberal economists, is to develop an industrial policy. They urge the government to intervene in strategic technology and to manage trade.

The third approach is to develop U.S. technology policy apart from an industrial policy. The technology policy involves assisting U.S. firms—large, medium, and small—to find and put rapidly to use the best technology available through collaboration. The leadership for this concept comes primarily from those who have studied global markets and the commercialization of technology. They believe cooperation and collaboration among business, government, labor, and education are necessary to maximize the potential of America and her citizens. The congressional Committee on Science, Space, and Technology refers to this kind of collaboration as a competitive tool. Under this approach, U.S. science and technology policy focuses more on the downstream phases of application and commercialization.

To prepare for the twenty-first century, countries and communities as well as companies will have to implement new strategies that will take into account globally competitive market systems. The next millennium must be a round of collaboration and competition between different forms of market-driven economies. Shared prosperity at home and abroad must be the goal of twenty-first century science and technology national policies.

PROLOGUE BY WILLIAM C. NORRIS

This comprehensive review of the first ten years of operation of MCC is a significant contribution to the process of learning how to benefit from R&D consortia. Importantly, the study was placed in the broader context of U.S. public/private collaboration to expand regionally based economic growth and improve industrial competitiveness.

The title, *R&D Collaboration on Trial,* and the fact that MCC has been, and continues to be, an important experiment in clarifying how to work together on research and development imply that the experiment is singular. In fact, public/private collaboration is as much a part of the experiment as MCC.

The authors note that community-based public/private collaboration for economic development is difficult to establish and sustain. My experience with many such collaborative efforts is similar. Decision makers often lack an understanding of the complex factors that drive the development of the economy. They lack the insight on how to stimulate the growth of companies that use sophisticated equipment run by technically educated workers to make high value-added products for a global market.

For example, a community of 50,000 people with an urgent need for better jobs will enthusiastically invest $2 million in a skating rink, yet quibble over a $100,000 allocation for collaborative economic development for job creation. Members of the board of directors of public/private partnerships are loath to support long-term programs that promise to create more and better jobs because of fear of criticism when results are not quickly evident.

However, even more than R&D collaboration and public/private collaboration, the U.S. social and economic system is the critical focus of this "trial." Some of the problems of MCC and other public/private collaboratives for economic development reflect the shortcomings of the social and economic system itself. Most notable is the failure to provide a technically literate society, which results in a lack of understanding of the pivotal role of industrial innovation in determining our social and economic well-being. Industrial innovation is the source of most good jobs.

This lack of understanding of how to develop and sustain an environment that promotes good jobs is pervasive. It includes executives and professionals in business and government. It includes political leaders as well as the public at large.

The degree of state and federal support for collaborative efforts to create jobs at any given time is primarily a function of who is president, who is governor, and who are the legislative leaders. Support in normal times can vary widely. When budgets are tight, it is disproportionately reduced. The result is a "behavioral challenge," noted by the authors, that makes it difficult for technology transfer to be accomplished by MCC or any other organization, be it a government laboratory, university, or company.

Improving the behavioral environment for collaboration is largely dependent on achieving widespread technical literacy, and this will require education on a massive scale. Education stressing the pivotal importance of technology in the process of innovation should be lifelong and should commence with middle school. Kids at that age can readily grasp the concepts involved. It is a challenge of enormous proportions, but it can be accomplished in a timely and economic manner through the use of interactive, multimedia computer-based equipment.

Meanwhile, MCC must cope in a technically illiterate society. Its increased emphasis on technology transfer is a practical adaptation to that reality. MCC's current priority on transferring product-oriented, short-term technologies to shareholders and on spinning out technologies into new companies is consonant with growing federal government support for collaboration in research.

MCC shareholders benefit in several ways from this strategy of technology transfer. They can benefit from their financial relationships with the new spin-offs as those companies prosper. They also can obtain preferential access to new and proven products in areas of interest and that entail little risk. With the breathtaking rate of technological advancement and escalating cost of research and development, the latter may prove to be the most important benefit for the shareholders.

The U.S. social and economic system, public/private collaboration, and research and development cooperation are all on trial in the MCC experiment. The critical question, however, is not whether to collaborate, but HOW.

Technology-based companies are the source of most new and good jobs, which buttress a healthy social and economic system. MCC's efforts are significant in helping its shareholders, its observers, and the public to understand how industrial innovation determines our social and economic well-being. MCC's collaborating organizations (both public and private) can provide important leadership across the nation in meeting its most urgent need—the creation of good jobs.

1

INTRODUCTION

When you look back at history, you'll see that new technologies build new civilizations. Technology determines the quality and quantity of the human economy. . . . Japan is the only country that is developing practical uses of superconductivity, and, I believe, will master the technology in ten years. Then Japan will be at the center of industry. . . . In fact, the U.S. can't make reliable one-megabit chips. Japan is the only country that can mass-produce high-performance semiconductors. When I said this at the [Washington, D.C.] party, the Americans turned pale.

Shintaro Ishihara, Japanese legislator and co-author of
The Japan That Can Say No,
quoted in *Time,* November 20, 1989, pp. 81–82

Nobody's sitting here predicting that we'll survive. We may not. There's no regulation saying that we must survive. Purely voluntary. . . . We can rise from the ashes like a Phoenix, but it will take a transformation to do it.

Dr. W. Edwards Deming,
quoted by Lloyd Dobyns (1990)

Deep in the heart of the Lone Star State, there exists an important, ten-year experiment in R&D collaboration. This first-of-its-kind organization is headquartered in a massive modern building that stands alone in a grove of cedar trees in the hill country at The University of Texas at Austin's Balcones Research Center. At the entrance, a modest blue sign reads "MCC." There is little to indicate that this four-story building was built to house the United States' best and brightest researchers in microelectronics and com-

1

puter technology—the first major attempt to have U.S.-owned corporations collaborate on long-term research while competing in the marketplace. The technologies invented here were to be key to the United States' winning global computer and software battles.

In 1982, a group of concerned U.S. executives from the computer and electronics industries launched the first salvo of a new collaborative strategy to compete in the global marketplace. They formed MCC (the Microelectronics and Computer Technology Corporation). This watershed event marked the creation of a new form of alliance to jump start U.S. industrial competitiveness and beat back Japanese competition. MCC's mission was to:

- Establish and maintain a reputation for technical excellence.
- Enhance the structural competitive position of U.S. companies by sponsoring and engaging in technology programs that would:
  –Enable the design of the next generation of computing structures.
  –Provide design tools to increase productivity.
  –Enable step-function increases in microelectronics and computer factory yield and productivity.
- License the results of cooperative technology efforts.
- Provide broad participation in MCC through an Associates Program that would include all interested parties who had a stake in the computer and microelectronics industries (MCC planning document, July 1, 1982).

Over the years, MCC has undergone many structural, cultural, and operational changes as it has attempted to fulfill its mission. By mid-1993, MCC could best be described as a consortium of consortia made up of 100 member companies (22 shareholders and 48 associates as well as 18 small business associates and 12 university affiliates) with 340 full-time researchers working in areas argued to be key to U.S. global competitiveness in the computer and semiconductor packaging industries. During its first decade, the consortium spent approximately $500 million of its members' funds, transferred more than 200 technologies, was issued or assured 117 patents, licensed more than 182 technologies to universities and corporations, published more than 2,400 technical reports, and produced more than 400 technical videotapes.

On the one hand, critics call MCC a failure, or at best a major disappointment. Their position is based on the belief that MCC in particular and U.S. consortia in general have produced minimal results that have enhanced member company competitiveness and that the money spent on these alliances could have been more profitably invested in the member companies' own R&D. Funding collaborative R&D ventures, they argue, smacks of a national industrial policy, which goes against the competitive and adversarial traditions that helped make the United States the world's greatest industrial power of the twentieth century.

As T.J. Rodgers, the 47-year-old chief executive of Cypress Semiconductor, observed: "It's best to go it alone because when the government meddles in the fast-paced world of electronics, you get a dime's worth of benefit for every dollar spent" (Richards, 1989). Similarly, Harvard Business School Professor Michael Porter states:

> Slowly and almost imperceptibly, over more than a decade, America has been retreating from one of the most fundamental principles that has distinguished our nation from others: our faith in competition. . . . What is needed today in American industry is not less competition, but more. Instead of relaxing antitrust enforcement, we should be tightening it. Mergers and alliances between leading competitors should be prohibited— they are good neither for companies nor for America. (Porter, 1990)

On the other hand, R&D consortia and other forms of alliances among businesses, government, and academia have become increasingly common during the 1980s and the early 1990s. Public and private leaders contend that the "go it alone" strategy will be the downfall of U.S. business. In response to global competitive challenges, alliances are argued to be important for maintaining scientific preeminence; to leapfrog foreign technology advances; to establish new technology-based, fast-growth entrepreneurial firms; to create high-value jobs; and to enhance U.S. industrial competitiveness.

R&D Collaboration on Trial illustrates important lessons about the challenges of (1) forming and managing R&D alliances, (2) technology transfer across organizational boundaries leading to successful product commercialization, and (3) public/private collaboration to spur the creation of jobs and regional economic development. How to effectively use the resources of advanced technology-based research to benefit U.S. industrial competitiveness is a major challenge faced by U.S. managers, scientists, academics, and government officials. MCC is presented as a laboratory useful for achieving a better understanding of the structure and process of R&D collaboration leading to successful technology commercialization. We base our account of MCC's first decade of existence on the experiences of the scientists and managers who formed and managed the consortium.

MCC and the collaborative philosophy that this R&D consortium represents are ideas still on trial in the United States. Mistakes have been made. Successes have been achieved.

THE BIRTH OF MCC

MCC was launched in 1982 to enhance the industrial competitiveness of U.S. computer and electronic industries; yet, IBM was not a founding member, and neither was AT&T. All foreign-owned companies were excluded, especially the Japanese. MCC was a contravention of almost a century of U.S. public and business policy. It was, some said at the time, an illegal and ill-conceived organization—a conspiracy to choke off competition and restrain trade.

MCC was born out of the vision of the respected computer industry leader William C. (Bill) Norris, founder, CEO, and chairman, Control Data Corporation (CDC). It was an American first; nothing like it had ever existed in the United States. Motivated by Norris, and worried about their own corporate survival, senior-level executives from 16 leading U.S. computer and semiconductor firms came together to explore how to compete more successfully with Japan. The objective, as described by one of the participants, was: "To keep the discussion above the trivia about competition in the marketplace, and to discuss where the industry would be in 10 to 12 years. And if we didn't like what we saw, to discuss how we might do things differently."

MCC's founders were committed to funding long-range (five to ten years), pre-competitive research aimed at important advances in computer and semiconductor technologies. This new "national resource" was to bring together the nation's most talented scientists and engineers into teams to conduct complex, multidisciplined research. MCC was to leverage the resources of its member companies to develop breakthroughs in advanced technology and development tools and to transfer these research advances to the funding companies in a timely manner. It was the responsibility of the consortium's corporate sponsors to commercialize MCC-developed technologies.

Bobby Ray Inman—a retired four-star admiral, former director of the National Security Agency, and deputy director of the Central Intelligence Agency—was selected to be MCC's first president, CEO, and chairman of the board. At the time, to many observers, Inman seemed an unusual choice. The admiral's first task was to find a suitable location for the consortium's headquarters. MCC's site-selection process evolved into a national competition that took on the aura of a mega–media event, which had a profound impact on how the nation's public and private leaders would thereafter view regional economic development. Corporate leaders, university presidents, governors, senators, and congressional representatives as well as regional community leaders from 57 cities in 27 states competed to have this revolutionary R&D consortium locate in their region. The stakes were high. It was a dramatic surprise when, in 1983, Austin, Texas, was selected as the home for MCC. As one well-known electronics company executive in Silicon Valley, California, said in reaction to the announcement: *"Austin?* Where the hell is Austin?"

In the early 1980s, key leaders in Texas government, business, and academe believed that their state should be less dependent on oil, agriculture, and ranching for its wealth and jobs. These leaders were concerned about declining resources from energy and agricultural products as they explored how their state might successfully compete in the coming global economy. They were concerned with how Texas might develop technology-based businesses in order to lessen migration of the state's most valuable resource, its educated sons and daughters. And they were concerned about how best to employ Texas' booming population with high-value jobs in manufacturing and service industries.

R&D Collaboration on Trial tells how Texas' public and private leaders collaborated to bring MCC to Austin and how the loss of public/private collaboration contributed to the region's economic downturn in 1985. Other finalists for MCC—San Diego, California; Atlanta, Georgia; and Raleigh-Durham, North Carolina—actually benefited by losing the consortium. These regions re-evaluated and improved their public/private initiatives for accelerated technology-based economic development.

Dr. George Kozmetsky, director of the IC^2 Institute at The University of Texas at Austin (UT), has an international reputation as a key facilitator in forging public/private alliances to accelerate the growth of high-tech development within Texas and the nation. Kozmetsky was a cofounder of Teledyne Inc., former dean of UT's College and Graduate School of Business, and he is science and technology advisor to UT's Board of Regents. He was an early visionary behind the collaborative strategy to bring MCC to Austin, and several years later, he championed the formation of the Austin Technology Incubator, which in 1990, accepted MCC's first spin-out company. Austin's boom to bust to slow, steady growth (from 1983 to 1993) provides important lessons about U.S. industrial competitiveness and the creation of high-paying jobs through regionally based technology commercialization and economic development.

METHODOLOGY

If one is to investigate organization and community change, data should be gathered over time. *R&D Collaboration on Trial* chronicles a decade of change in an organization (MCC) and a community (Austin, Texas). This chronicle of events is based on interviews, survey data, archival documents, scholarly publications, mass media accounts, and the personal files and records of informants (see Appendix A).

Interviews were conducted with individuals most knowledgeable about the formation of MCC and the consortium's site-selection process, and with those involved in MCC's management and on-site research activities. A smaller number of interviews were also conducted with people knowledgeable about SEMATECH, another major R&D consortium that located in Austin, Texas, in 1988. (See Appendix B for a list of all interviews.) These data were collected over a period of nine years and include contrasting views and opinions from a range of individuals representing the nation's research universities; businesses; and local, state, and national government. (See Appendix C for a glossary of the main characters.)

Our methodology of viewing organizations as relational networks embedded within communities, allowed us to: (1) get beneath superficial accounts of the dynamics of public/private collaboration, (2) analyze how important decisions are really made and implemented while decision makers were constrained by organizational and environmental contexts, and (3) analyze the results of collaborative activities in a variety of situations over time.[1]

THE MOTIVATION FOR MCC

In the early 1980s, the top ten Japanese imports from the United States were: soybeans; corn for fodder and feed; saw and veneer logs (Douglas fir and hemlock); coking coal; wheat; cotton; turbojet airplanes; rawhide and skins of bovine animals; and waste and scrap metal for smelting other than alloy steel. The top U.S. imports from Japan were: passenger cars; iron and steel plates and sheets; radio receivers; motorcycles; audiotape and videotape players and recorders; iron and steel pipes, tubes, and blanks; still cameras and parts; nails, screws, and other fasteners; TV receivers; office machines; metal-cutting machine tools; calculating machines; automotive trucks; microphones, speakers, and audio amplifiers; and iron and steel angles, shapes, and sections. Reviewing these data, a U.S. congressman from the House Subcommittee on Trade commented:

> A comparison of our leading exports to Japan versus our imports from her is devastating. The data seem to indicate that (aircraft excluded) we are a developing nation supplying a more advanced nation—we are Japan's plantation: Haulers of wood and growers of crops, in exchange for high-technology, value-added products. (Melman, 1983)

American steel, shipbuilding, auto, and consumer electronics industries had illustrated what Japanese companies could do to their

U.S. competitors. By the early 1980s, the nation's once proud automobile industry was being humbled by superior Japanese products,
despite the fact that the industry was born in America and embodied Yankee know-how. Japanese dominance of U.S. consumer electronics was evident in most American homes. Color TV was invented by RCA but was manufactured almost exclusively in Japan for
worldwide distribution. The microwave oven was invented by U.S.
scientists but was largely produced in Japan and South Korea. The
videocassette recorder (VCR) was invented in the 1950s by Ampex
Corporation in Redwood City, California, but by the early 1980s,
the VCRs purchased by U.S. consumers were being manufactured in
Japan, Korea, and other Asian countries. The semiconductor chip
was invented in the United States in 1959, but by the mid-1970s,
the nation's once immensely profitable chipmakers were beginning
to lose their worldwide dominance of this important industry. By
the early 1980s, Japanese companies had seized world market share
in dynamic random access memory (DRAM) semiconductors, a key
technology in the computer industry (Figure 1.1).

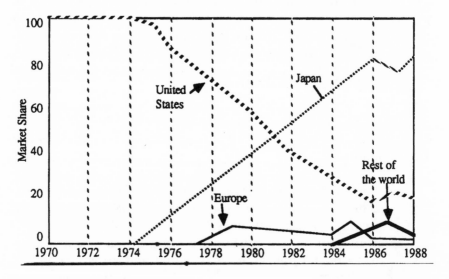

Source: National Advisory Committee on Semiconductors (1989, p. 10),
based on data from Dataquest.

**Figure 1.1 U.S. semiconductor companies lose world market
share in DRAM semiconductors to Japanese companies**

In industry after industry, including some of the most power-ful U.S.-owned and -operated firms, many of which were based on technologies invented in the United States, companies were going out of business or were losing market share and profitability to the Japanese. Something was wrong here, seriously wrong—at least from the U.S. point of view. In a 1981 speech titled, "Microelectronics—The Crude Oil of the 80s," Robert (Bob) Price, president of CDC, concluded:

> Essentially there are only two or possibly three efforts in microcircuits that have sufficient scale and coordina-tion to effectively cope with the changing environment: Japan, Inc.; IBM; and possibly Bell Labs. The other efforts, which include Control Data's, are fractionated, uncoordinated and over time will not be productive enough.
>
> Either the U.S. computer industry will adopt a strategy of technological cooperation on a broad basis—or it will not. If it does there will be vitality and growth. If it does not, then there will be isolation and sickness—IBM will be the General Motors of the 90s—the rest of us won't even have to worry about it.

Japan's VLSI (Very Large Scale Integration) Project (1976–1979) was credited by many industry observers with helping move Japanese semiconductor companies toward a dominant world mar-ket share. The VLSI Project had facilitated Japanese technological innovation, and it had helped get participating companies to agree on standards for semiconductor manufacturing equipment (see Chapter 2). By the early 1980s, CDC's Bill Norris was keenly aware of the important role R&D consortia were playing in Japan's increased competitiveness. A large U.S.-owned research consortium of national scope had been Norris's objective since the late 1970s. But his vision did not receive much industry support until the 1981 announcement of the Japanese Fifth-Generation Computer Project (ICOT). This event, combined with the success of Japan's VLSI Project, provided Norris with the cue-to-action that was needed to convince a key group of U.S. electronics executives to found MCC. As Norris (interview, August 10, 1990) remembered: "I worked on setting up MCC long before the Japanese appeared on the horizon. But what made [the consortium] possible was the Japanese threat."

Antitrust constraints were a major concern of MCC's founders, but, during the early 1980s, the federal government was most concerned with U.S. industrial competitiveness. Semiconductor and computer technologies were considered essential to (1) increasing U.S. productivity and (2) maintaining the superiority of the nation's armed forces. The White House and the Department of Defense shuddered at the thought of having to depend on foreign suppliers (i.e., the Japanese) for essential semiconductor and computer components. Given these critical defense concerns and the growing Japanese industrial threat, a strict interpretation of U.S. antitrust policy did not seem appropriate.

COLLABORATING TO COMPETE

"Coordinate," "cooperate," "collaborate," and "synergy" are words commonly used to describe what the U.S. public and private sectors must do in the 1990s in order to compete effectively in the global marketplace.[2] At various times, each of these terms is used in this text; however, our focus is on business collaboration within R&D consortia and public/private collaboration within U.S. communities. We emphasize that organizations and institutions that collaborate together to coordinate activities, cooperate on tasks, and perhaps achieve synergy in selected instances are indeed often competitors (i.e., enemies) in the marketplace or they are competitors for personnel, funding, and other scarce resources. We chose the word "collaboration" to heighten the reader's awareness that for many public and private organizations to achieve cooperative and perhaps synergistic effort, they must work closely with and trust their competitors.

Collaboration is the process of working together with competitors for a common purpose. Collaborators do not lose their separate identities. *Collaborative individualism* is a process in which individuals remain competitive while collaborating on specific tasks (Cunnington and Gibson, 1991). Each unit in a collaborative system does not own or control any of the other units. Rather, the collaborating units agree to a limited form of cooperation, to achieve a desired objective. If one company acquires another company, control is achieved, not collaboration. William Ouchi (1984a) argues that an interdependent collaboration of public/private organizations (which he labels an "M-Form society") needs to be adopted by the United States in order to compete effectively with Japan. An M-Form society maintains a tenuous balance between competition and cooperation.

Much of classic economic theory, starting with Adam Smith's concept of the "invisible hand," and most of what is taught today in U.S. business schools, rests on the nature of unrestrained competition between individuals, business firms, and nations. It is assumed that "free market forces," unhindered by government policies, are the most efficient mechanisms for setting the price of a product, determining supply, and deciding which firms will survive and which should die. Infant industries are not to be protected or nurtured. Market forces should determine which firms grow and prosper. Such values rest on the belief that the Darwinian struggle for survival is a natural ideal. The market is served by the competitive process, with customers benefiting from lower-priced, higher-quality, and more innovative products than would otherwise be available. Everyone, it is argued, is best served by unrestrained competition.

There are many excellent accounts of U.S. industrial competitiveness that discuss trade and financial data at aggregate levels of analysis and provide snapshots in time of specific industries and organizations.[3] R&D Collaboration on Trial benefits from a longitudinal, in-depth look at the dynamics of public/private collaboration from the perspective of individual participants and the organizations and institutions that they represent. Collaborative relationships can be (1) formal, as expressed in an official pact between the two units detailing the scope and nature of the collaboration; or (2) informal, in which one individual exchanges information with another individual over a period of time without any written or official authorization to do so. R&D consortia are an example of formal collaboration, but within such an official context, informal collaboration occurs at the level of individual research scientists and managers. The power of informal networks to move information across organizational and institutional boundaries is central to the collaborative activity associated with technology commercialization and regional economic development (Rogers and Kincaid, 1981; Aldrich and Von Glinow, 1992).

The value of competition and individual excellence is highly prized in American business culture. The value of collaboration or cooperation is less well understood and rewarded. As Norris stated: "In our society, which glorifies the rugged individualist and emphasizes confrontation, cooperation is the recourse of last resort. . . . You cooperate when nothing else works." (Zonana, 1988)

Perhaps more than any other state, Texas—the locale of much of our analysis on public/private collaboration—has embodied the heroic value of the rugged individualist and the desire for a minimum of government intervention in individual or corporate activities. In *R&D Collaboration on Trial*, we describe how the Lone Star State enacted academic, business, and government collaboration at the regional level to win MCC and to commercialize the consortium's technologies through the Austin Technology Incubator. We stress the importance of a unifying and well-articulated vision as well as competition from sources external to the system in leading to collaboration among the members within the system.

Collaboration among units in a system to obtain one type of benefit may lead to other, related types of collaboration and additional benefits by the same units. Intellectual returns-to-scale can occur when information is being exchanged among creative and diverse individuals. In an R&D consortium like MCC, member companies collaborate in conducting research but they benefit in many other ways through sharing information as they continue to compete in the marketplace. Participants cannot demand compliance, but each can influence the others toward collaborative action. Such pre-competitive collaboration encourages the leveraging of resources at the front end of the technology transfer process so that individual organizations can be more competitive at the back end of the process by focusing their unique efforts on value-added marketplace competition.

Synergy centers on the notion that the simultaneous action of separate agencies has a greater total effect than the sum of individual effects. Synergy is evident when the right mix of individuals passionately explores a scientific breakthrough, where individual comments spark others to respond in innovative ways, and where the end result reflects the "magic" of a creative collaboration. In such situations, collaborating individuals should possess a certain degree of diversity, but not too much. If all the participants were virtually identical, they would have few resources to leverage and the information exchanged would be of little value. At the other extreme, if the critical mass of participants was completely diverse, there would be little basis for common discourse. So an important cause of synergy in a system is for it to be composed of participants that are somewhat (but not too) different. One way to obtain such synergy is through a larger total volume of activity by collaborators than is represented by each separate participant. Ideally, such synergy would allow an R&D consortium with many researchers and state-of-the-art resources to enjoy certain benefits that each of its member companies acting alone could not achieve.

THE WORLDWIDE RISE OF R&D CONSORTIA

Collaborative research projects come in many different sizes and forms and have many different objectives, depending on the reasons individuals and organizations have for coming together, and the nature of the technologies and the industries involved. The rational for consortia is heavily influenced by the industrial structure into which the technology will be transferred and the public policies for industrial promotion. The motivations to form R&D consortia include efficiencies of shared cost and risk, exploration of new concepts, pooling scarce talent, sharing research or manufacturing facilities, desire for research synergy, diversification of a technology portfolio, developing frameworks into which other technology modules or tools can fit, setting standards, marketing products, pre-competitive sharing of research results, industrial organization and accelerated technology development, big science and large projects, infrastructure development, and facilitating technology transfer or partnering, whether domestic or foreign. (Peck, 1986; Ouchi and Bolton, 1988; Eaton, 1993)

The United States borrowed the idea of R&D consortia in the early 1980s from Japan, but the underlying philosophy of intercompany collaboration can be traced to England (Table 1.1).[4] Dr. Masao Sugimoto, director of MITI's (Ministry of International Trade and Industry) Mechanical Engineering Laboratory, played a major role in promoting the idea of R&D consortia in Japan. In 1953, he read about English research associations that had been in existence since 1917. Each of these associations was typically composed of small and medium-sized companies in the same industry.

Table 1.1
Key events in the worldwide development of R&D consortia

	Europe	Japan	United States
1917	Research associations are founded in England, out of fear of German competition.		
1950		1953—Japanese study group investigates research associations in England 1956—First R&D consortium of auto parts manufacturers formed.	
1970		Several R&D consortia of Japanese electronics companies are organized by MITI to compete with IBM/Japan. VLSI Project, 1976–1979.	Bill Norris, CDC president, implements two relatively small, company-based R&D consortia. EPRI, 1972-present, electric power research GRI, 1976-present, natural gas research MCNC, 1980-present, micro-electronics research.
1980	Alvey Project, 1983–1987, a British effort. ESPRIT, 1984–1994, a European Economic Community effort. RACE I, formed in 1985. JESSI, 1989–present, semiconductor research.	Japanese Fifth-Generation Computer Project (ICOT), 1982–1992.	SRC, 1982-present, semiconductor research. MCC, 1982-present, computer research. SEMATECH, 1987-present, semiconductor research.
1990	RACE II, formed in 1992, more applied than RACE I.	Sixth-Generation Computer Project for a ten-year period with U.S. and European participation.	

The companies were motivated to collaborate by the fear of increased industrial competition, primarily from Germany. The British government's Department of Scientific and Industrial Research provided partial funding for these associations, with the rest of the financing coming from member-company contributions (Sigurdson, 1986). Thinking that this approach might be a useful "technology" for Japan, Sugimoto headed a study group of Japanese who went to England to visit several of these research associations. The visitors wrote a report recommending that MITI experiment with this new organizational form.[5]

The first Japanese research association was organized in 1956 by companies that were manufacturing air filters for cars. This initial effort at collaborative R&D was not successful. However, MITI continued to push the idea, and from 1956 to 1961 five additional research associations were organized. Most were formed by companies that were manufacturing car parts such as radiators, engine components, springs and instruments, in addition to cameras and high-molecule material (Sasaki interview, July 27, 1993). In 1961, the Japanese Diet passed the Engineering Research Association Law, which allowed the nation's major companies to form collaborative research organizations to conduct joint R&D without fear of antitrust action. As an added incentive, the law provided tax benefits to companies joining such consortia. So the Japanese had been working at R&D consortia for about 30 years before MCC came along. The Japanese law allowing such activities was passed 23 years prior to its U.S. counterpart, the 1984 National Cooperative Research Act (see Chapter 7).

There are many different models for the organization of research consortia as well as strategic alliances and other forms of teaming. Each structure motivates its own particular management and technology transfer challenges. These models are not mutually exclusive. Examples are:

- Research that clusters around a technology source such as a national lab, university, or geographic region.
- Research dispersed at a range of facilities and sometimes in different countries as is common in Europe.
- Pooled investment in a start-up company or other unique technology source.

- A shared central research lab such as MCC.
- A shared prototype facility or research program.
- Mission-oriented research such as putting a man on the moon or building a fifth-generation computer. (Eaton, 1993)

Compared to Europe and Japan, the United States spends less of its research dollars on funding consortia: Europe spends 6 percent, with half coming from government; Japan spends 4 percent, also with half coming from government; and the United States spends less than 1 percent with about a quarter of 1 percent coming from government. (Dove, 1990; Rifkin, 1990; Zorpette, 1990)

JAPANESE CONSORTIA

After the Japanese Diet passed the Engineering Research Association Law, 13 research associations were formed by 1970. Membership in each consortia ranged from 3 to 45 companies. Thirty-one Japanese research associations were formed in the 1970s, 68 in the 1980s, and 18 by early 1993. Most of the research associations formed in the 1970s had start and stop dates, but beginning in the 1980s and increasingly in the 1990s, designated stop dates are not as prevalent. (Sasaki interview, July 27, 1993)

MITI pressured the major Japanese electronics companies to form research associations or R&D consortia. The companies were also motivated by their fear of IBM, the U.S. competitor that had dominated their domestic computer market for many years. With each major IBM technological advance, MITI reacted by forming a consortium. The most frequent members of these consortia were Japan's largest computer companies: Fujitsu, Toshiba, Hitachi, NEC, and Mitsubishi. Nippon Telegraph and Telephone (NTT) also established joint R&D projects for the development of specific product prototypes such as a number of key semiconductor devices, including the 64K and 256K DRAM. Depending on the evaluation criteria used, many of Japan's initial attempts at consortia could be considered failures, but over time companies learned to overcome their suspicions and to collaborate in research while competing in the marketplace.

Japan has established consortia in such industries as computers, semiconductors, lasers, biotechnology, and chemicals. Japanese electronics consortia include the following:

- The VLSI (Very Large Scale Integration) Project (1976–1979) formed to produce manufacturing technologies that would allow Japanese industry to catch up with IBM and other U.S. semiconductor manufacturers in large-scale and very-large-scale integration. The project was funded at $312 million with half coming from government and half coming from industry. The VLSI Project built on research that was started at the Electrocommunciations Labs of NTT (see Chapter 2).
- The Institute for New Generation Computer Technology (ICOT) had eight members plus NTT, was formed by MITI in 1982, and ended in 1992. ICOT was funded at $1.35 billion with one-third provided by the Japanese government. The consortium researched advanced computer architectures, hardware, and software for artificial intelligence. ICOT's formation spurred the formation of MCC (see Chapter 2).
- The Realtime Operating Nucleus (TRON), which has 142 members, was formed in 1984 and researches computer software, hardware, and architecture. The members, without government involvement, coordinate their R&D fund allocation.
- Synchrotron Orbital Radiation Technology Center (SORTEC) was formed in 1986 as a ten-year project and has 14 members. SORTEC is researching synchrotron optical radiation technology, which is needed to produce semiconductors with a density of 16 or more megabits. SORTEC has an annual budget of $12 million with 30 percent coming from government sources.
- Optoelectronic Technology Research Corporation (OTRC) has 14 members and was formed in 1986 as a ten-year project to develop manufacturing techniques for optoelectronic materials. Seventy percent

of OTRC's budget of $77 million is being furnished
by Japan's Key Technology Center, an agency affiliat-
ed with MITI that funds high-risk advanced technology projects.
- The International Superconductivity Technology
  Center (ISTEC), formed in 1988, has over 100 members including 97 Japanese, 2 U.S., 1 U.K., and 2
  U.S. affiliates. It is funded annually at the level of
  $17 million (33 percent from government sources).

In March 1991, MITI launched the Sixth Generation Project,
which is also known as the Real World Computing (RWC) or the
New Information Processing Technology Program, or the Four-
Dimensional Computer Project for an ultraparallel supercomputer
that can process real space (three-dimensional) data in real time (the
fourth dimension). Overall, the consortium is focusing on leading-
edge basic research that realizes "soft" or flexible information-
processing functions—the capabilities of humans—for the twenty-
first century. The project has four objectives: (1) to build a massively
parallel computer that consists of upwards of one million separate
processors, (2) to research neural network machines based on how
the brain is believed to function, (3) to use optical signals to transmit data within or between computers, and (4) to develop software
to manage these yet-to-be-developed computers. The project is
targeted to sustain long-term research that might otherwise lose out
to more immediate projects in the internal budget battles of
Japanese companies.

Members of the RWC Partnership (New Information
Processing Development Institute) include 17 corporations and
industry groups such as Fujitsu, NEC, Hitachi, Toshiba, Sumitomo
Electric, NTT, Mitsubishi Research Institute, and the German
National Research Center for Computer Science. The budget is projected to be over ¥70 billion through 2001. Approximately ¥880
million were appropriated for the fiscal year starting in 1992.

RWC research is being conducted in parallel by five groups of
30 researchers and assignees in the Mitsui Building, an office complex in the center of Tsukuba Science City, and 32 distributed
research groups (with about three to five researchers each) within
the member organizations. The research groups are relying on U.S.
technology such as high-end Macintoshes, Sun workstations, a
Thinking Machines CM-5, and an Intel Paragon X/MP. Each group

is working on its own distinct theories and principles rather than on a "straight line toward a single goal." A framework is in place to encourage research cooperation with the universities and research institutes of other nations. Professor Takemochi Ishii, Keio University, summarized the approach: "The age when we made development of a single machine a national project is over. It may even be unnecessary for the RWC project to produce a computer itself." (Senda, 1993, p. 4)

EUROPEAN CONSORTIA

Like the Americans, Europeans were motivated to form their own R&D consortia by the success of Japan's VLSI Project and by the threat of ICOT. The European experience is somewhat unique, however, since many of these consortia involve companies based in different countries.

- Founded in 1984, ESPRIT I (the European Strategic Programme for R&D in Information Technology) was funded with $2 billion and has grown into a ten-year program sponsored by the European Economic Community (EEC) and a number of European companies. The consortium includes more than 400 members and is conducting large-scale, pre-competitive research as well as smaller projects in technology integration, microelectronics, information processing, advanced business and home systems, and computer-integrated manufacturing and engineering. ESPRIT is intended to get European electronics companies working together rather than with U.S. or Japanese partners. The European subsidiary of IBM is a member of ESPRIT but had to apply 12 times before being accepted. ESPRIT II (1987–1991) was funded at $4.2 billion and ESPRIT III (1990–1994) received an additional $3.7 billion with roughly 50 percent of all funding coming from the European Commission.
- The Alvey Project, formed in 1983, was a five-year, $360 million collaborative research effort. It was funded by the British government to improve Britain's semiconductor manufacturing through a

consortium of 50 companies and 41 universities. Alvey was disbanded in 1987 (see Chapter 2).

- RACE I (Research and Development in Advanced Communications) was formed in 1985, has about 90 members, and is funded at $1.6 billion (with less than 50 percent from government sources). RACE I is researching broadband local network technology, high-definition television (HDTV) switching, mobile telecommunications, integrated broadband communications, and advanced telecommunications for manufacturing. The objective of RACE is to generate R&D collaboration among manufacturers and research institutions within Europe. More than 300 organizations take part in some 92 projects, with an average of nine participants per project. RACE II began in January 1992 and is intended to provide a more practical, less theoretical approach to the development of a European broadband strategy and market.

- EUREKA (European Research Cooperation Agency) was formed in 1985, has more than 370 members, and is funded to the level of $8 billion (with about 30 percent from government sources). EUREKA is conducting research in the Joint European Submicron Silicon Initiative (JESSI), Prometheus (automotive technology), and HDTV.

- Basic Research for Industrial Technology in Europe (BRITE), formed in 1985, and European Research in Advanced Materials (EURAM), formed in 1986, have about 490 members and are funded at $1.3 billion (with 50 percent from government sources). These consortia are conducting research in superconducting materials, testing techniques, computer-assisted techniques in manufacturing, advanced mathematical modeling of industrial processes, advanced materials, and aeronautics.

- Chip 1995 is a consortium of large European electronics companies. Chip is funded by the French and German governments to develop a 64 megabit DRAM semiconductor chip by 1995.

- Mega-Project is a five-year consortium of Siemens and Philips. The German and Dutch governments provide $150 million of its $2 billion funding. The effort is targeted toward developing advanced memory chips using as much European manufacturing equipment as possible.
- JESSI is a research consortium of European semiconductor firms, led by Philips, Siemens, and SGS-Thompson Microelectronics. JESSI was launched in 1989, is headquartered in Munich, and will spend $4 billion over eight years. The EEC provides about one-fourth of the funding. JESSI is similar to SEMATECH in its objectives, although it is somewhat broader. Because of IBM's strong presence in Europe, where it produces about 35 percent of its semiconductor chips, JESSI's member companies will not allow IBM to become a member until SEMATECH allows European companies to participate (which SEMATECH refused to do as of 1993).

U.S. CONSORTIA

After the passage of the National Cooperative Research Act (NCRA) in 1984, 50 consortia had registered with the U.S. Department of Justice by the end of 1985; the number of new registrants fell to 17 in 1986 but then increased to 25 in 1987, 31 in 1988, 27 in 1989, 44 in 1990, and 61 in 1991. By December 1992, 325 R&D consortia had registered under the NCRA. These U.S.-based consortia included a mix of 3,372 U.S. companies; 635 foreign members; 187 associations, institutes, and councils; 218 universities; 33 federal government agencies; and 84 state government agencies. Ranked by frequency, most consortia are involved in microelectronics and computing, telecommunications, the environment, energy, chemicals, automotive, materials, manufacturing, building and construction materials, health care, and biotechnology (see Figure 1.2).

As of late 1992, most U.S. consortia (29 percent) were two-member organizations, while 20 percent had 3 to 5 members, 22 percent had 6 to 10 members, 18 percent had 11 to 25 members, 7 percent had 26 to 75 members, and 4 percent had more than 75 members (see Figure 1.3). About one-third were engaged in pre-competitive research and were industry-, university-, and national laboratory-based; one-third were engaged in noncompetitive research such as industry trade associations; and one-third were involved in joint research ventures.[6]

U.S. consortia include the following:

- The Electric Power Research Institute (EPRI) was founded in 1972 as an independent, nonprofit R&D organization on behalf of the U.S. electric utility industry and the public. EPRI is located in Palo Alto, California, and is staffed by 550 research and supporting professionals. Public and private utilities furnish support in proportion to their electricity sales. EPRI's R&D budget has grown from about $200 million in 1973 to over $700 million in 1992. A strong emphasis on power generation and delivery systems in EPRI's formative years has evolved to research activities in environmental science and controls, customer end-use technology, and such projects as electric vehicles, advanced light water reactors, high-speed electronic transmission networks, and on-line technology transfer links to the utility research community. EPRI recently accepted international affiliates.

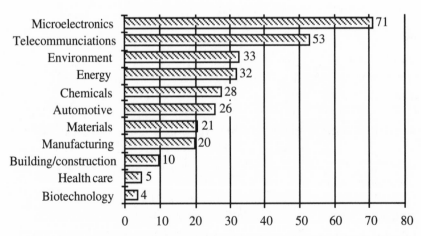

Figure 1.2 Industry focus of consortia registered with the U.S. Department of Justice, as of October 1992

- The Gas Research Institute (GRI) was founded in 1976 by the board of directors of the American Gas Association of America as a nonprofit R&D organization of the natural gas industry. GRI's purpose is to plan, manage, and develop financing for comprehensive cooperative R&D programs for the development of new technologies designed to benefit all segments of the natural gas industry and consumers. GRI's member companies—including equipment manufacturers, service companies, major energy users, and government agencies—provide funding and program direction. GRI is headquartered in Chicago, has a staff of 140 technical/analytical personnel, and an annual budget of about $215 million. No research is conducted on site. The institute prioritizes research that is then contracted out to universities, institutes, and private companies.
- The Microelectronics Center of North Carolina (MCNC), founded in 1980, is annually funded at $30 million (with 65 percent from the state of North Carolina). The MCNC has 70 company members, 9 universities, and 1 research institution. This state-led consortium conducts research in microelectronics, telecommunications, and supercomputing.

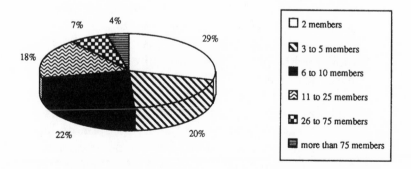

Figure 1.3   Size of consortia registered with the U.S. Department of Justice, as of October 1992

- The Semiconductor Research Corporation (SRC) was created in 1982 by 11 U.S. semiconductor companies with a $7 million budget to enhance the competitiveness of the North American semiconductor industry through support of generic, pre-competitive research and educational initiatives in areas relevant to industry needs, and through the timely transfer of research results to its participants. By 1993, the SRC had a $36 million budget and was funded by 24 members, 4 associates (including MCC and SEMA-TECH), and 34 affiliate participants as well as seven U.S. government agencies. SRC's revenue apportionment was 69 percent industry, 28 percent SEMA-TECH, and 3 percent government. SRC has funded and coordinated 111 research contracts at $28.2 million. These contracts include 37 microstructure sciences, 31 design sciences, 24 manufacturing process sciences, 11 packaging sciences, and 8 manufacturing sciences involving 345 faculty and 733 students from sixty universities and research institutes. During the past decade the SRC has funded over $200 million in semiconductor research, published 8,000 research reports, and has been issued 41 patents with another 38 filed.
- The Center for Advanced Television Studies (CATS), headquartered at MIT, was begun in 1983 to develop new television technologies (especially high-definition TV) and to increase the number of U.S. researchers studying television. CATS, which was motivated by government but is directed by industry, has nine members, which include ABC, NBC, Eastman Kodak, Ampex, and HBO.
- Thirty-six utility, appliance, and supply companies formed Smart House in 1984 under the sponsorship of the National Association of Home Builders. The consortium is located in Rockville, Maryland. Included among its 116 members are Apple Computer, AT&T Network, Black and Decker, Sears Roebuck, Texas Instruments, and Westinghouse. The

consortium conducts research on safer, more efficient home wiring to build a house of the future with one electrical wiring system and with all appliances controlled by a central computer.

- The Plastics Recycling Foundation (PRF), founded in 1985, is located in Kennett Square, Pennsylvania. This consortium investigates problems of solid waste management and thus seeks to head off restrictive government regulations on using plastics. PRF has 20 members, including Coca-Cola, Union Carbide, and 7-Up.

- The National Center for Manufacturing Sciences (NCMS), which is headquartered in Ann Arbor, Michigan, is an industry-led, not-for-profit collaborative organization. Publicly supported at federal and state levels, NCMS's budget is between $10 and $15 million per year. NCMS, which was launched in 1986, has 160 member companies that are located in 25 states. The overall objective of the consortium is to aid member firms in becoming internationally competitive in manufacturing by sponsoring research and transferring results to its members. Collaborative research projects include manufacturing processes and materials; production equipment design, analyses, testing, and control; and strategic issues.

- SEMATECH (SEmiconductor MAnufacturing TECHnology initiative) was formed in 1987 as an industry-government consortium to restore the United States to preeminence in semiconductor-manufacturing technology. In 1988, after a national site-selection competition, SEMATECH established its headquarters in Austin, Texas. An overview of SEMATECH's formation and operation is presented in Chapter 7. SEMATECH's annual funding of $180 to $200 million comes from a congressional appropriation and its member companies.

- The Consortium for Superconducting Electronics (CSE), founded in 1989, is funded at the level of $15 million (with 50 percent coming from government

sources). CSE has four members plus two subcon-
tractors and is conducting research on electronics
applications of superconductive films.

A good example of the organizational learning that takes
place across consortia is the Council of Consortia that was formed
in April 1990 by Dr. Robert Noyce, president and CEO of SEMA-
TECH; Grant Dove, president and CEO of MCC; and Larry
Sumney, president and CEO of the Semiconductor Research
Corporation. Council members include CEOs from North American
consortia who come together to discuss lessons learned and issues of
concern. Working groups, composed of the consortia's practitioners,
are formed to study such topics as technology development, transfer,
and application; human resources; and research management. The
council strives to share best practices among its members, which
include such consortia as Bellcore, Electric Power Research Institute,
Gas Research Institute, MCC, MCNC, National Center for
Manufacturing Sciences, SRC, Ohio Aerospace Institute, Software
Engineering Institute, the Software Productivity Consortia, and
SEMATECH.

OVERVIEW OF THE BOOK

CHAPTER 2: THE FORMATION OF MCC

Examples are provided from Tsukuba Science City, the VLSI
Project, and ICOT to show that the Japanese have a long and somewhat troubled history of learning about how to manage consortia
and about interfirm collaboration. The success of Japan's VLSI
Project and the threat of Japan's Fifth-Generation Computer Project
were important antecedents to the formation of MCC and other
U.S. and foreign consortia. On February 19, 1982, a group of U.S.
computer industry executives from 16 companies met in Orlando,
Florida, to consider whether they were ready to collaborate in the
formation of a large R&D consortium. An interim board of directors planned MCC's formal structure and research focus. The board
concluded its activities with the hiring of MCC's first CEO and the
recruitment of the consortium's ten founding shareholders.

CHAPTER 3: MCC COMES TO TEXAS

The success or failure of an R&D consortium like MCC is linked to the political-social-economic context in which it is embedded. As MCC's shareholders were learning how to collaborate, the site-selection process for the consortium caused the nation's business, government, and university leaders to think differently about how to use public/private alliances to spur regional economic development. Chapter 3 describes how information was gathered and plans were implemented in the complex, unstructured decision-making process through which Austin, Texas, won and San Diego, Raleigh-Durham, and Atlanta "lost" the MCC competition. The discussion focuses on how business, academic, and government sectors can collaborate on targeted tasks of national importance. Appendix 3.1 provides a chronology of the main events in the 1993 selection of Austin as MCC's headquarters.

CHAPTER 4: MCC IN OPERATION

Chapter 4 chronicles the first decade of MCC's evolution in terms of governance, personnel issues, organizational culture, funding challenges, and research programs through three periods of leadership: (1) Admiral Bobby Ray Inman (1983–1986), (2) Grant Dove (1987-1990), and (3) Dr. Craig Fields (1990–present). MCC's basic mission—to strengthen and sustain the competitiveness of its member companies—has remained fairly constant over the years, but management strategies have changed considerably. After ten years of struggling to get its technologies commercialized by its member companies, MCC has become more involved with near-term, project-based R&D, received increased government financial support, fostered more research projects in small companies, and encouraged more entrepreneurial activities.

Appendix 4.1 is a chronology of MCC's evolution in operations and organizational structure. Appendix 4.2 reviews MCC's research activities and productivity over its ten-year history. Appendix 4.3 uses a bibliographic survey of published research articles as an indicator of MCC's collaboration with member companies, universities, and corporations worldwide.

CHAPTER 5: TECHNOLOGY TRANSFER AND MCC

Technology transfer is defined as the application of knowledge, which includes moving ideas and products from the research laboratory across organizational boundaries into process and commercial applications. Timely, efficient technology transfer from the research base of U.S. universities, federal laboratories, and R&D consortia to successful commercial applications is a challenge of national importance. Chapter 5 details the barriers to technology transfer faced by researchers and managers at MCC and at the consortium's member companies. For over a decade, MCC has struggled with how to achieve effective technology transfer. The consortium has moved from passive and broad-based strategies to more active and focused technology transfer, and to increased reliance on third-party licensing, entrepreneurship, and spin-out activities. Valuable lessons have been learned—lessons that are central to strengthening U.S. industrial competitiveness.

CHAPTER 6: LOSERS AND WINNERS: REGIONAL IMPACTS OF MCC OVER TIME

MCC was launched with a flash of publicity as the United States' best hope for competing with the Japanese in computer-based R&D. The consortium was valued for its high-tech jobs and as an important symbol of state-of-the-art development in the high-tech age. While winning MCC contributed to an economic development boom for Austin, Texas, the loss of MCC by San Diego, Atlanta, Raleigh-Durham, and other sites caused public and private leaders from these regions to enhance their commitment to technology-based economic development. It took ten years of structural and cultural change at MCC and the formation of the Austin Technology Incubator (ATI) for Texas to begin to benefit from entrepreneurial spin-out activity from the consortium. The ATI was formed in 1989 through public/private collaboration to help bring cutting-edge research to commercial applications, fill vacant office space with fast-growth firms, and create high-value jobs.

CHAPTER 7: THE POLITICS OF R&D CONSORTIA: MCC AND SEMATECH

Some would argue that R&D consortia are mainly a political response to the lack of U.S. international competitiveness and that

Austin, Texas, won two of the nation's prime R&D consortia—
MCC and SEMATECH—largely through political means. Chapter 7
discusses the politics of overcoming U.S. antitrust law in the formation of MCC and the politics surrounding the formation and operation of SEMATECH. The case of SEMATECH is used to generalize
our research on MCC, in terms of the formation and management
of R&D consortia.

CHAPTER 8: LESSONS LEARNED

Over the years, increased public and private attention has
been directed toward enhancing U.S. industrial competitiveness and
the creation of high-value jobs. We offer lessons learned from MCC
to better understand meaningful ways to overcome challenges to
R&D collaboration and to the profitable commercialization of
U.S.-developed technologies from federal laboratories and research
universities as well as R&D consortia. Chapter 8 uses the case of
MCC to highlight and summarize lessons learned about
public/private collaboration and the commercialization of
pre-competitive R&D.

NOTES

1. We studied unstructured decision processes that involved actions not previous-
    ly encountered in the same form and for which no predetermined, explicit set
    of ordered responses existed (Mintzberg, Raisinghani, and Theôrét, 1976). In
    this way our present research is similar to Graham Allison's (1971) *Essence of
    Decision,* in which he identified "the game in which an issue will arise, the rel-
    evant players, and their relative power and skill." Allison focused on the 1962
    Cuban missile crisis and specifically on how President John Kennedy's
    "kitchen cabinet" responded to this Russian threat (also see Allison, 1969;
    Anderson, 1983). Here we analyze the 1982 decision to form MCC, the 1983
    site-selection process, and the decisions and actions taken concerning the for-
    mation and operation of this first-of-its-kind organization during its first ten
    years. The present study is one step toward correcting for the overwhelming
    tendency of scholars to investigate routine, structured decision making, often
    at a high level of abstraction, out of context, and with little analysis of the
    impact of decision implementation and consequences over time.
    Among the few studies of unstructured decisions by a city are Cude's
    (1987) investigation of the nondecision process through which Austin consid-
    ered relocating its municipal airport and Chen's (1987) study of how the city
    of Palo Alto, California, engaged in a lengthy decision process to grant a cable
    TV franchise while federal policy and other events complicated the process.

2. "Coordinate" means to bring into proper order or relation; to harmonize; to adjust. "Cooperate" means to act or work together with others for a common purpose; to combine in producing an effect. "Collaborate" means to cooperate treacherously with an enemy; to be a collaborationist or to cooperate in a literary or artistic manner. "Synergism" is the simultaneous action of separate agencies which together have a greater total effect than the sum of their individual effects (*Webster's New World Dictionary*).

3. For example, see Scott and Lodge (1985).

4. The idea of the English research association may have been adapted from a Swedish counterpart organization, the *Jernkontoret* (the executive body of the Ironmasters' Association), which was founded in 1774. The organization collected a fee on all Swedish iron exports and used these funds to sponsor R&D on iron making (Torstendahl, 1989). While there was extensive contact between England and Sweden, especially concerning industrial technology, we know of no definite evidence that the English research associations were direct copies of the *Jernkontoret*.

5. The Japanese have a long tradition of taking a "process technology" developed in another country and adapting it to their national purpose. A different but perhaps better known example of such "national learning" also occurred in the 1950s when the Japanese imported W. Edwards Deming's philosophy of quality control at the same time that Deming was having difficulty transferring this process technology to U.S. organizations and institutions. Indeed, while Deming's quality control concepts were largely being ignored by U.S. business schools and American industry, the Japanese considered them so important to their strategy for improved industrial competitiveness that they instituted the annual, nationally recognized Deming Award for the most important quality-improving idea/program. The late Emperor Hirohito awarded Deming Japan's Second Order Medal of the Sacred Treasure, accompanied by a citation attributing the rebirth of Japanese industry and its worldwide success to Deming. Some 30 years after the Japanese embraced Deming's philosophy, the United States launched its own drive for quality with the Malcom Baldrige Quality Awards, and U.S. business schools began to see the wisdom of offering courses in quality control concepts.

6. A prior analysis conducted in 1988 by IC^2 research associate Tom Harlan produced similar statistics on the composition and size of U.S.-based R&D consortia indicating that these percentages are rather consistent.

2

THE FORMATION OF MCC

Kyōdō *wa Zen de Aru* (Collaboration Is Everything).

Slogan of the Japanese VLSI Project, 1976–1980

MCC represents a cooperative effort to develop a broad base of fundamental technologies for use by individual members who will add to their own value and compete against each other in individually chosen markets with products and services of individual conception and design.

William Norris (1982), chairman of Control
Data Corporation and visionary for MCC

In my opinion, your contemplated conduct is an unequivocal combination in violation of the antitrust laws of the United States. The effect that your agreement will have upon competition and innovations in the otherwise dynamic and exponentially expanding electronics industry is obvious—not to mention the destructive impact on the establishment of new submarket industries and jobs. . . . If your company nonetheless chooses to proceed with the combination, then at least you do so with full knowledge of the legal consequences.

Joseph M. Alioto, former mayor of San Francisco
and noted antitrust lawyer, in a July 27, 1983, letter
sent to the presidents of 12 MCC member companies
and to Senator Howard Metzenbaum,
quoted from Bower and Rhenman (1985)

When MCC was founded, it was a unique organization. What were its crucial antecedents? How did intensely competitive U.S. electronics and computer companies agree to mitigate their belief in freewheeling competition, push against antitrust law, and organize for collaborative R&D?

In October 1981, on the heels of its successful VLSI Project, Japan announced the Fifth-Generation Computer Project (Table 2.1). The threat of a new Japanese R&D consortium directed at "their" industry caused the presidents of U.S. computer companies to think: "Maybe we need to look at [the threat of Japanese competition] a little differently." There was a mood of concern, even fear. U.S. electronics executives felt that they had to continue to fund high-cost research in order to keep up with international competition and rapid technological advancements in the increasingly competitive global economy, but the price tag for this "bet-your-company" R&D was higher than most firms could afford. One solution was to form a cooperative of companies, with each company funding a share of the consortium's budget. It had worked for the Japanese. The U.S. computer industry had to do something. So MCC, the nation's first, for-profit collaborative R&D consortium, was launched largely out of self-interest and fear on the part of U.S. executives who believed they had to take action if their companies were to survive Japanese competition.

JAPANESE ANTECEDENTS TO MCC

Japan is the world's great economic success story of the twentieth century. During the 1960s, 1970s, and 1980s, the annual rate of increase in Japan's gross national product was consistently higher than that of Europe or North America. The island nation's strategy was to import technologies from the most scientifically advanced nations (primarily the United States) and then commercialize these technologies in new and improved products. This "fast-second" strategy had the advantage of bypassing the expensive, high-risk prior stage of basic research (Peck and Goto, 1981). In order for this strategy to be effective, Japanese companies had to excel in (1) identifying promising technologies worldwide and (2) being able to quickly improve, commercialize, and market these technologies globally.

Table 2.1
Chronology of the main events in the formation of MCC

1976–1979	The VSLI Project, involving five Japanese electronics companies and two government organizations, becomes one of Japan's most successful R&D consortia. The Japanese dramatically increase their world market share of DRAMS (dynamic random-access memory semiconductors).
1981 April	Control Data Corporation (CDC) President Bob Price gives a speech titled "Microelectornics — the Crude Oil of the 80's." In the speech, Price describes the Japanese threat to the U.S. computer industry. He argues that unless U.S. companies learn to share technology, there will be just three survivors: IBM; Japan, Inc.; and AT&T.
October	The Japanese Fifth-Generation Computer Project, a new R&D consortium, is announced in Tokyo, with participation by the Ministry of International Trade and Industry, Nippon Telegraph and Telephone (NTT), and eight major Japanese electronics companies.
December	CDC's William C. Norris and President Bob Price lead the effort to form some kind of industry consortium and appoint Phil Arneson to supervise the CDC activities.
1982 February	Norris invites industry leaders from 16 U.S. electronics companies to a one-day conference held near Orlando, Florida, to consider an industry-led response to Japanese competition.
April– December	Chaired by Price, MCC's steering committee and subsequent interim board of directors meetings are held monthly in Denver, Colorado. Phil Arneson and his team work on MCC's business plan, form technology program task teams, and facilitate a pro-MCC action plan.
August	MCC is legally incorporated in Delaware.
December	Ten companies agree to found MCC. Recently retired Admiral Bobby Ray Inman is interviewed for the job of the consortium's top manager.
December	The U.S. Department of Justice gives a yellow light to MCC by stating that the R&D consortium will not be prosecuted for violation of U.S. antitrust policy.
1983 January	Admiral Inman is appointed as chairman, president, and CEO of MCC.

MITI (the Japanese Ministry of International Trade and Industry) and keiretsu (Japanese business groups) have been key to Japan's successful economic strategy. MITI aggressively seeks technological information from abroad, channels it to Japanese companies, and directs the nation's competitive thrust. Keiretsu like Mitsubishi, Mitsui, and Sumitomo have their origins in zaibatsu that existed in the Meiji period, long before World War II.[1] Each zaibatsu was controlled by a single family through a central holding company. Zaibatsu were outlawed in 1945 by General Douglas MacArthur's occupation government.

Keiretsu include horizontally and vertically integrated groupings of firms such as a bank, an oil company, an automobile manufacturer, suppliers, a computer company, and a trading company. Firms within a keiretsu are linked through stock ownership, interlocking boards of directors, executive associations, and through the buying and selling of products. Most important, keiretsu act as "information clubs," with member companies sharing technical and business information that they obtain worldwide. A tradition of trust is part of the culture of keiretsu, as the collaborating companies work together over the long term to find efficient solutions to challenges involving supply ordering, manufacturing, and sales. While the keiretsu structure facilitates cooperation within one's business group, it promotes fierce competition across keiretsu, especially across companies in the same industry.

In the latter twentieth century, Japan has been moving toward conducting more basic research, in part, because other nations' markets and technologies have been diminished by Japan's commercial success. However, many of Japan's academic, business, and government leaders have not been enthusiastic about enacting strong promotion policies for basic science (Onda, 1988, pp. 51–52). These Japanese officials referred to *kiso* (which means "basic research") as being little more than *kuso* (which means "crap"). They argued that MITI was essentially a commerce-oriented ministry.[2] However, the attitudes of Japanese R&D administrators are changing, and the view that MITI can only lead the country to industrial success through a fast-second strategy is being transformed, by necessity, to an awareness that MITI must find new ways for Japan to be competitive globally in R&D. Beginning in the late 1960s and continuing into the 1990s, under MITI's guidance, Japan has been engaged in four major research programs: large-scale industrial projects that are finite (such as the VLSI and ICOT projects); sunshine or new-energy projects; moonlight or energy conservation projects; and research in next-generation basic technologies such as new materials, biotechnology, new types of semiconductors, 3-D technology, chemicals, the separation of gases, and high-efficiency permeable membranes. (Goto interview, summer 1992)

The tradition of collaboration within keiretsu, which was central in the era of the fast-second strategy, made the formation of R&D consortia a seemingly natural development for Japan as the nation moved into a new era of conducting basic research. However, despite Japan's success with keiretsu, collaboration across interest groups, organizations, and institutions in the pursuit of advanced R&D has not come easily to the Japanese. Initial attempts at R&D consortia were problematic. Companies within the same industry were such bitter enemies that they resisted working collaboratively.

TSUKUBA SCIENCE CITY

We use the case of Tsukuba—Japan's first large-scale, planned science city to exemplify the point that while being relatively homogeneous, Japanese society is *not* innately predisposed to be cooperative across groups and institutions.[3] Tsukuba, planned and developed by the public sector, was first envisioned, in the metropolitan area development plan of 1958, as a satellite city about 70 miles north of Tokyo. This plan was an adaptation of the Greater London Area Plan, consisting of existing urban areas, greenbelts, and outer areas for later development (Onda, 1988). A second metropolitan area reform plan was presented in 1968, and in the third plan, completed in 1976, the greater metropolitan area of Tokyo was defined as a center city with a number of urban areas to be developed around its perimeter. These outer areas were planned as independent and self-sustaining. Tsukuba was to be a "knowledge generation" city. Since Japan's 1983 technopolis law, MITI has approved over 20 designated areas as "knowledge consuming" cities. (See Chapter 3 for more on the concept of the technopolis.)

By 1990, with funding from MITI and other government agencies, Japan had moved over 47 government basic research laboratories to Tsukuba. The Tokyo University for Education was moved and established as Tsukuba University. In addition, a two-year college of library and information science was moved from Tokyo to Tsukuba and turned into a four-year college, and the new Institute of High Energy Physics (KEK) was also established in the science city. Because of a general lack of consensus among Japanese educators, politicians, and businessmen, even with substantial funding from the government and pressure from eight national ministries, these Tsukuba-based projects progressed slowly.

Long-term planning is a characteristic for which the Japanese are well known; however, according to Goto (interview, summer 1992), Tsukuba suffered from a lack of "software" (people issues) planning, and while the "planners were competent in urban construction, they had no idea about science and technology of the future." As Dearing (interview, June 3, 1993) commented, "People issues were designed in the plan but were gradually excluded by jealous and opportunistic ministries." While being efficient and orderly in its design, the city lacked many of the cultural and social amenities that the transplanted researchers and their families had enjoyed in Tokyo. Early complaints were that Tsukuba did not have a sense of permanence and history.[4] Suicide rates were high in the city, even for Japan, and some residents developed a skin rash called "Tsukuba syndrome." The city was planned for a population of 200,000, but it was not until after the World Science and Technology Exposition of 1985 and the crunch of population overflow from Tokyo that Tsukuba's population increased beyond 60,000.

Tsukuba was planned to function as a large consortium where researchers would collaborate across organizational and institutional boundaries, but the social characteristics and individual preferences of Tsukuba's researchers, especially those who were well established, resisted such an ideal. The city has three emerging cultures—a public and university research culture, an administrative culture, and a private research culture—set within the traditional farming culture of a centuries-old agricultural valley. There is a disparity between public researchers, who are accorded traditional academic freedom in deciding on research topics and in arranging their schedules, as contrasted with private researchers, whose topics of inquiry and schedules are more restricted. Public and university researchers tend to have diminished respect for the work being done by private researchers and vice versa. Neither side believes that what the other side is doing is of much relevance to its own work: "Public researchers perceive that the work of private researchers is too applied and thus of little theoretical utility; while private researchers perceive that the work of public researchers is too theoretical and thus of little practical utility" (Dearing, 1991). Self-interest, jealousy, secrecy, and dogmatism are exhibited by Tsukuba's research scientists. There are feuds between top researchers; between competing government research labs; and between public, private, and university research activities.

> Where there are government research laboratories, there are government bureaucrats and science administrators and Tsukuba Science City is no exception. Administrators in Tsukuba are very loyal to their respective ministry or agency, so long-standing hatred and competition between the employees of rival national ministries are carried over to Tsukuba. (Dearing, 1991)[5]

As a result of such cultural and personal characteristics, many officially sanctioned boundary-spanning organizations have failed to operate effectively in Tsukuba Science City. For example, in the early 1980s, the Research Institute Directors Association decided that there should be more collaboration among researchers. Memos were sent to scientists recommending that they make a sustained effort to meet with colleagues in other Tsukuba-based laboratories. This suggestion was largely disregarded. As noted by Dearing (1991): "[Japanese] scientists dislike being told how to behave by administrators whom the scientists perceive to be peripheral to the mission of their work."

In Tsukuba, there is a conspicuous lack of boundary-spanning organizations (1) between the laboratories of rival ministries and (2) between public and private laboratories. Cultural differences and competitive pressures inhibit the formation of formal linkages, and attempts to bridge these chasms have been largely unsuccessful. An electronic-mail network for all Tsukuba researchers failed soon after the pilot system was installed connecting only university and government researchers. Private researchers perceived the network to be biased and of no utility. They declined to participate. Tsukuba's administrators attempted to create a shared electronic data base among all government research laboratories. The attempt failed because of cultural animosity and the fear of researchers and administrators that to open data bases to their counterparts from other ministries would imperil proprietary information. As of early 1992, no viable interministry data base existed in Tsukuba Science City.

One can conclude from the experiences of Tsukuba Science City that Japanese academic, business, and government sectors are not predisposed to collaborate. The most efficient mechanisms to bridge researcher/administrator gaps within Tsukuba have been emergent, highly transient, informal groups and interpersonal networks through which relatively high-value knowledge is exchanged. As Dearing (1991) concludes: "Such private interpersonal relations often bridge (1) academic or government scientists with corporate scientists, (2) government scientists with academics, and (3) occasionally lead to meaningful collaboration between corporations."[6]

THE VLSI PROJECT

The Japan Electronic Industry Development Association (JEIDA) was founded in 1958 by major Japanese electronics companies for the purpose of advancing the industry. In early 1975, JEIDA organized a small discussion group to consider how Japan might become more competitive in the design and production of very large-scale semiconductor devices. Japanese computer firms were hard at work figuring out how to make the 64K RAM, as was NTT and the Electro Technical Laboratory (ETL) of the Agency of Industrial Science and Technology (AIST), an arm of MITI. But these companies could not successfully compete with IBM and other U.S. producers. Professor Shoji Tanaka of the University of Tokyo, a member of a JEIDA discussion group, suggested that NEC, Toshiba, Hitachi, Mitsubishi Electric, Fujitsu, and Oki Electric collaborate on VLSI research (Ouchi, 1984b). The companies resisted, preferring direct subsidies without government interference or the requirement of collaboration. They were leery of this new MITI initiative. Previous attempts at collaboration had been largely unsuccessful, and some of those involved in the current discussions had vowed never again to collaborate with certain competitors. At the same time, the government was unwilling to make direct subsidies to the companies. MITI officials, supported by NTT, which was a major customer of all six of the computer companies, insisted that such a large subsidy must take place through a joint laboratory, if for no other reason than to give the appearance of synergy, thus justifying in the public's mind the large cash outlay. In addition, there were some critical areas of research in which no single company had sufficient numbers of specialists to be able to move ahead quickly enough to keep up with IBM. (Ouchi, 1984b; Sigurdson, 1986; Sakakibara, 1989)

It took a year of discussion to set the framework for the VLSI Project, which was to last four years. The companies disagreed on the focus of research activities, whether the work should be more basic or applied, and where the research would be conducted. Giving up hard-won know-how and expertise in product design and manufacturing to a domestic competitor did not come easily. As one Fujitsu manager commented: "Of course, to some extent each firm wanted to get the most technology while contributing little as possible to the project" (quoted in Ouchi, 1984b, p. 23). In spring 1976, the project set up temporary headquarters on the twenty-ninth floor of the Kasumigaseki Building, in the heart of downtown Tokyo and, after a fierce debate about its permanent location, the facility was finally moved to a then-vacant NEC laboratory located in Kawasaki (Japan's Silicon Valley), a suburb south of Tokyo. The project's initial staff included two key leaders of different types: Masato Nebashi, executive director and former senior MITI official, and Dr. Yasuo Tarui, a highly respected engineer, from ETL. As the top scientist, Tarui directed the consortium's joint laboratory. Nebashi's great interest in the organization was the human problem: how to coordinate the researchers from different companies and have them interact. As he stated: "I wanted them [the researchers] to become good friends, communicate with each other, and open their hearts" (quoted in Sakakibara, 1989, pp. 16, 17). It was considered important that neither Tarui or Nebashi had come from any of the private companies.

Over one-third of the project's $312 million funding was in the form of an interest-free loan from MITI, part of which the five companies had to pay back after a four-year grace period. The funding involved was two to three times greater than the total investment in semiconductor R&D by all the private member companies. While the VLSI Project was being initiated, rumors were circulating in Japan about a new line of IBM computers that would use VLSI chips. So the "carrot" of ample funding from MITI and the "stick" of IBM competition combined to provide the necessary motivation for these domestic competitors to try to collaborate, one more time, in an R&D consortium.

VLSI was governed by two executive committees that were made up of presidents, vice presidents, and executive directors of each of the five private companies and a technology committee and an operations committee each consisting of division general managers. Deciding who was to head the technology and operations committees, which were to work closely with the laboratory scientists, resulted in heated debate among the collaborating companies. Technology transfer was to be facilitated by 100 "loaned" young scientists (most were under 40 years of age), who would work at the lab and then rotate back to their home companies after two years. There was the fear that some of the companies would not send their top people, which would doom the project before it began. To deal with this potential problem, Tarui announced that he would personally interview each scientist sent to Kawasaki. He did not imply that he would refuse anyone, but in the context of the many overlapping joint efforts among the collaborating companies, the knowledge that Tauri "would serve as a memory of who had sent its best and who had not, was sufficient to deter any thoughts of sending unqualified scientists" (Ouchi, 1984b, p. 24). Tauri's professional networks also helped recruit 20 or so core researchers. On the part of the individual scientists who were to be transferred, there was the concern that they might be "forgotten" by the parent company. As Nebashi commented:

> Thinking that the best way to dissolve this kind of fear would be to retain close contact with the parent company, we held all of the meetings for the executive committee, council, committees, and committee sections at the lab's Kawasaki location. I think it lent special emotional support to a researcher when, after a conference, the directors and the president of his company took a tour of the lab. (quoted in Ouchi, 1984b, p. 26)

The laboratory was divided into six projects: micromanufac-
turing technology, crystal technology, design technology, process
technology, test evaluation technology, and device technology. Each
of the five companies nominated a project head, and one came from
ETL. All basic research was to take place in the joint laboratory,
and final product development was to be done by each company on
its own. After numerous meetings, patent ownership rights were
finally settled in 1980, after the project had ended and the joint lab
had been disbanded. The final decision was in keeping with the initial objective that all parties would have equal-use rights. More
specifically, any patent that government scientists developed alone
was held by the government; a few government-business patents
were jointly owned by the research association and the government;
and any patent on which government scientists had not worked was
held by the research association. (Ouchi, 1984b)

Despite Nebashi's best efforts at team building, the walls
remained thick between the companies and between lab projects.
Initially, collaboration was fostered once or twice a month by formal meetings that were held to promote communication among the
scientists, despite the fact that scientists from each company physically shared each project area. Groups of researchers would present
their work, which was followed by discussion. Nebashi was disturbed by the limits of the formal communication that was taking
place at the lab. Important team building and collaboration, the
very reason for the joint laboratory facility, were not taking place.
To break down the walls between the research projects and to
enrich the communication among the scientists, Nebashi finally
resorted to *yoma atsumari* (whiskey operations), taking small
groups of scientists out for drinks. Meetings between sections were
held each Saturday, and in the evenings, informal conversations
would go on late into the night. Follow-up meetings would define
and solve the problem areas that had been revealed during the *yoma
atsumari*. As Nebashi commented: "So, what I did was the typical
Japanese way: All I did this four years was to drink with them as
frequently as I could. I wanted to understand their complaints on
those occasions and try to eliminate the problem" (quoted in
Sakakibara, 1989, p. 17). Over an extended period of time and
after many *yoma atsumari*, suspicion and mistrust gradually
decreased among the researchers, and they began to work as a team

(Sigurdson, 1986). Researchers who were initially reserved with each other became good friends. After the VLSI graduation party, which was held in March 1980, an alumni association was organized and alumni newspapers were issued.

The VLSI Project was completed ahead of schedule in 1979, the laboratory was dissolved, and the 100 or so scientists returned to their home companies. The project filed 1,000 patent applications; about 600 were granted. The member companies began to produce 64K random-access memory chips, which ushered in the era of the fourth-generation computer. But the most important benefits of the VLSI Project are argued to be that it focused Japanese semiconductor firms on a common research agenda and that it facilitated the standardization of Japanese manufacturing technologies for DRAM production. Japanese equipment companies were now able to sell the same manufacturing tools to each of their country's semiconductor companies. The dependence of Japanese companies on foreign equipment dropped from 75 percent in 1977 to 50 percent in 1980. (Sakakibara, 1989)

Swedish scholar Jan Sigurdson (1986, p. 62) concluded from his analysis of VLSI that: "The Project resulted in firmly raising the level of the VLSI manufacturing technology of the five participating companies . . . [which was] a contributing factor for the increasing shares taken by these companies in the world market for memory circuits." For example, Japanese companies increased their worldwide production in 1976 to 70 percent of 64K RAM production in 1981 and to 85 percent of 256K RAM production in 1986 (see Figure 1.1). The VLSI Project convinced many Japanese policy makers of the important benefits that could be derived from R&D consortia.

Why did Japan's VLSI Project succeed to a greater degree than the 40 or so high-tech R&D consortia that had previously been organized by MITI? First, the $312 million funding represented a major escalation in R&D semiconductor research. Unlike its predecessor consortia, the VLSI consortium established a collaborative research laboratory rather than having each member company carry out its part of the total research program in its own facilities. The young scientists were physically present in the Kawasaki building, which allowed Nebashi to build team spirit. Furthermore, the timing of the project was just right. The five Japanese electronics companies had gained useful experience from their participation in the previous R&D consortia. The VLSI consortium also benefited from good timing from a technological point of view. X-ray and electron beam lithography, which replaced photolithography, had just become available for use in producing VLSI semiconductor chips. The consortium was well timed to capitalize on this technological opportunity. (Sakakibara, 1989)

But perhaps the most important reason for the VLSI Project's success was the socio-emotional leadership of Nebashi and his strategy of "management by whiskey." Nebashi had just the right personality for this task. He was generous, warm, respected, and well liked by the researchers. On a daily basis, he urged the scientists to appreciate the unique nature of the consortium and to appreciate the worldwide attention it would bring if they were successful (Sakakibara, 1989). Nebashi managed the scientists so that everyone lived up to the VLSI Project's slogan: Kyōdō *wa Zen de Aru* (Collaboration Is Everything).

Some analysts question whether the contributions of the VLSI Project might have been just as great had the $312 million been spent independently by the five electronics companies. We think not. A considerable synergy was achieved among the researchers during the four-year project when research results from each of the five specialized laboratories were exchanged. Standardization of Japanese semiconductor manufacturing equipment had not occurred prior to the formation of the consortium.

THE FIFTH-GENERATION COMPUTER PROJECT

Japanese leaders planned for the Fifth-Generation Computer Project before the VLSI Project was completed, and after three years of negotiation, MITI announced the new R&D consortium at a conference in Tokyo in October 1981. A new organization, the Institute for New Generation Computer Technology (ICOT), was created to carry out the collaborative project, which would have a total budget of $1.35 billion for ten years, with one-third of this money coming from the Japanese government. At about $130 million per year, the budget for the Fifth-Generation Computer Project was considerably larger than the budget for the VLSI Project. ICOT's objective was to use cutting-edge research in developing parallel inference machines and artificial intelligence to create a new breed of computers that would be more human-like in their functioning.[7]

ICOT was located on the top floor of the 22-story Mita Kokusai office building in Minato-ku, a section of downtown Tokyo near the Tokyo Tower. The scientists who worked at ICOT came mainly from the eight computer companies that MITI invited to join the consortium: Hitachi, Fujitsu, Toshiba, Mitsubishi Electric, NEC, Oki Electric, Matsushita Electric, and Sharp (the first five were also members of the VLSI Project), plus NTT, Japan's privatized telecommunications company, which was regulated by the Ministry of Posts and Telegraph.[8] In addition to the 100 ICOT scientists and their support staff working in five laboratories in the Mita Kokusai building, another 200 scientists worked on related research projects in the facilities of the eight computer companies. However, less than half of ICOT's 1,200 technical reports and memoranda were authored or co-authored by these 200 off-site scientists.

The managing director of ICOT, Dr. Kazuhiro Fuchi, was a highly respected computer scientist with 24 years of experience at the ElectroTechnical Laboratory. Fuchi's number-two man was Takashi Kurozumi, who joined ICOT from the NTT Research Laboratory (the Bell Labs of Japan). Dr. Fuchi commented that it was important that he and Kurozumi did not come from one of the eight ICOT companies. As "neutrals," they could better adjudicate disputes over funds and personnel among the member companies.

Fuchi's unusual (by Japanese standards) professional background led to his being chosen to direct ICOT. He had previously quit a prestigious position in a national ministry, an unthinkable action for a respected Japanese professional. Fuchi was considered by his peers to be something of a pariah who had taken on Western ways. It was thought that this "black sheep" would have the necessary qualities to understand how to manage ICOT in keeping with the mandate of making it open to Western scientists. (Rifkind interview, November 11, 1992)

Fuchi insisted that ICOT, unlike previous R&D consortia organized by MITI, should disclose its research results in international journals and at international conferences (Uttal, 1982). Most U.S. observers have interpreted this policy in one of two ways. One view holds that the Japanese, with MITI in the lead, were simply targeting another U.S. industry, as was the case with the VLSI

Project. Bill Norris held (or at the very least used) this view to increase the sense of crisis and urgency in his call for U.S. computer executives to form their own, privately funded R&D consortium. Some academics also used the threat of ICOT to pressure the U.S. government for more federally funded R&D in such areas as artificial intelligence.

An alternative interpretation of Japan's founding of ICOT was offered by two of MCC's early planners, Phil Arneson and Jess Rifkind (both of whom are discussed later in this chapter), who visited Dr. Fuchi and ICOT in 1982. Fuchi explained to them that his island nation had been stung by U.S. and world criticism that Japan was only a user and not a contributor to the world's basic science. According to Fuchi, Japan was using ICOT as a way to "redeem Japan in the eyes of the world's scientific community." In support of this latter view, ICOT was open to foreign scientists, and the world's scientific journals published ICOT research.[9]

Based on a 1986 agreement, ICOT received U.S. research visitors selected by the National Science Foundation (NSF). ICOT demonstrated its technologies at research symposiums in Japan and in the United States, and technical information exchange took place with 26 U.S. research institutions. The *ICOT Journal* was distributed to 550 overseas locations. By 1989, 51 researchers from around the world had participated in ICOT: from the United States (13), France (4), the United Kingdom (13), Israel (5), Sweden (4), Canada (3), and Germany (5), among other nations. ICOT technical reports and memoranda were sent regularly to research institutes and universities worldwide (Kurozumi, 1992). Despite such collaboration and information dissemination, some observers contend that the project, which ended in June 1992 and cost over $1 billion, was not successful. The critics focused their complaints on the fact that the program had made few contributions in terms of new Japanese products—but most agreed that it did contribute to science.

ICOT was a high-risk activity, far out on technology's cutting edge. The MITI order establishing ICOT had seven goals: five focused on technology diffusion and setting technology standards throughout Japan; and two focused on research and technology development (Eaton, 1988). The typical scientist stayed at ICOT for about three years before returning to his or her home company. These researchers embodied the main technology transfer strategy employed by ICOT. Returning scientists were to become leaders of product design teams, thereby utilizing the technology acquired at ICOT. Perhaps it is too early to judge ICOT's ultimate impact; since the consortium focused on basic research, product commercialization is not expected to occur until the late 1990s. One unanticipated problem for ICOT was that the computer industry shifted from the technological path taken by the consortium, one that had seemed a wise choice when ICOT was launched.[10]

ICOT did succeed in developing prototype computers that could perform reasoning and functioning at high speeds, and the consortium also developed software. Some useful technologies have been produced such as the PSI (personal sequential inference) machine and the Pegasus PROLOG processing chip. In June 1992, MITI announced that it would release the fifth-generation software to all interested parties, without charge.

Even if ICOT did not reach the original technical goals of a fifth-generation computer, it has gotten Japanese electronics companies under way in basic research in artificial intelligence and in other aspects of advanced computing, a very valuable legacy. As Mark Eaton, director of MCC's International Liaison Office, commented:

> [Through ICOT] MITI has helped create a new industry on what is really a very small investment. Japan probably would have gotten around to AI and advanced computer architectures without MITI help, but there would not have been the "AI Boom" of the early 1980s. These, by the way, are exactly the types of industries which a decade ago MITI and MITI advisory organs were saying would be good for the future of the Japanese economy. (Eaton, 1988, p. 19)

ICOT's questionable success as of 1993 should not lessen the reader's appreciation for the anxiety with which ICOT's announcement was received by the world's government officials and computer industry executives in 1982. Then the implication was clear to policy makers and corporate planners in the United States and Europe: after winning a key segment of the integrated chip market, the Japanese were likely to pick off the computer market by redefining computing in artificial intelligence terms. The prevailing view was that fifth-generation technology would be a thousand times faster than existing computers. It would be especially useful in scientific applications like meteorological forecasting and aerodynamic analysis. If Japan could beat the United States in the race for the fifth-generation computer, it would most likely leapfrog U.S. competitors in many technological fields that would benefit from such advanced computing power. The success of the VLSI Project was in the minds of many U.S. executives. ICOT was in its formative stages. Together these Japanese initiatives stimulated U.S. and European business and government leaders to try something radically different.

The United Kingdom's Alvey project—a five-year, $360 million government-sponsored collaborative research effort—was launched in 1983. It involved the establishment of a MITI-style directorate, with staff coming from major information technology firms. Collaborative research rather than the traditional national champion approach (one main company competitor) was the major distinction of Alvey as it pursued the development of generic, pre-competitive information technology (Dowler and Brown, 1991). Not long after the formation of the consortium, however, pressure built within Prime Minister Margaret Thatcher's government for the Alvey directorate to produce marketable results. Alvey was disbanded in 1987. Many observers call it a failure. On the other hand, some Alvey participants believe that the consortium has been judged unfairly by using criteria that differed from its original intent—basic research. As Brian Oakley, former Alvey director, said in 1991: "The United Kingdom was foolish enough to think that prosperity could be based simply on research." (*Science*, 1991)[11]

THE MAVERICK WHO FOUNDED MC

William C. Norris is in some ways typical of many U.S. electronics executives. He has lived the life of an entrepreneur. He looks at a particular situation and then says: "Whoa! That isn't right. Let's do it this way." Norris's biography is appropriately titled *William C. Norris: Portrait of a Maverick* (Worthy, 1987). He is fond of saying: "Whenever I see everybody going south, I have a great compulsion to go north." His contrariness evidently has worked; Norris is a highly respected (especially within the electronics industry) self-made multimillionaire.

CDC had, by 1982, experienced moderately favorable results with two relatively small R&D consortia that spread R&D costs across a larger volume of products than were being produced by a single company. Each of these consortia was founded at a time of stress in the computer industry: (1) Computer Peripherals, Inc. (CPI), which was founded in 1972, and included three member companies; and (2) Magnetic Peripherals, Inc. (MPI), formed in 1975 by CDC and two other companies. To avoid antitrust restrictions, CDC kept the U.S. Department of Justice (DOJ) fully informed during the operation of both consortia. So for CDC, the idea of an R&D consortium was not just an abstract notion; it was the product of actual experience, most of it positive. "We weren't preaching something theoretical; we were preaching something that worked," commented one of the CDC employees who worked on MCC's organizational design. Originally, CDC officials were thinking about a consortium of 4 or 5 companies, which might later be expanded to 10 or 15. But Norris said no to this type of small-time thinking: "That's going after walleyes; I [Norris] want to fish for lake trout." (interview, August 10, 1990)

Norris's MCC initiative benefited from the concern, if not fear, that existed among U.S. computer and microelectronics company executives in early 1982. Bob Price, CDC's president, gave his "three computer companies" talk at an April 1981 trade association conference. The image of IBM, Japan, Inc., and AT&T as the only major global computer companies was unnerving to high-tech executives whose firms would be the ones to disappear. Then, in late 1981, when the Japanese announced the creation of the Fifth-Generation Computer Project right on the heels of the highly successful VLSI Project, Bill Norris sensed that the time was ripe for a bold, new initiative. Perhaps a collaborative R&D center, sort of "an American MITI," would be the appropriate response. It should be aimed at basic research, he thought, to develop processes and techniques rather than product-oriented technology (Warsh, 1983b).[12] As Norris commented: "I tried to set up the equivalent of MCC almost 20 years ago, but it wasn't until these companies had the hell scared out of them by the Japanese that they were willing to give it a try." (Davis, 1985)

Throughout early 1981, Norris and Price visited and communicated with the top management of Honeywell, National Semiconductor, Fairchild Semiconductor, and Motorola. Exploratory dialogue with Fairchild Semiconductor did not lead anywhere. A former vice president from Honeywell was brought in to champion the idea, but he was unsuccessful in getting a consortium started. Norris was losing patience and wanted results. Price called on Phillip W. Arneson, vice president and group executive at Control Data. As Arneson (correspondence, October 6, 1992) remembered:

> I felt a certain mount of concern when I was called to Bob Price's office to meet with him about taking the assignment to form a consortium. I had witnessed a considerable amount of failure and poor results [concerning Norris's previous attempts]. Price explained that Norris was determined to put a consortium together . . . they wanted me to make it happen. It was also clear that there wasn't any opportunity for me to decline the assignment. So I would characterize my feelings as reluctant acquiescence.

As Price remembered:

> Gordon Moore of Intel visited us [Norris and Price] in Minneapolis in the summer of '81. We were talking about beating the bushes for this thing when Gordon asked us what we thought of getting all the players in one room—together at the same time. (interview, May 12, 1993)

Norris, Price, and Arneson agreed that what was needed was a high-level meeting of top representatives from leading U.S. electronics companies. They realized that the success of their venture hinged on getting the right people to attend, ideally the president or chairman of each targeted company. Briefings were held with executives from such companies as General Electric, Rockwell International, Mostek, IBM, Xerox, Digital, and North American Philips as well as the Department of Defense and the Electronics

Industry Association. There was general support for Norris's initiative that the planned R&D consortium should be large with a narrow to moderate range of activities, to do a few things extremely well. It was agreed that technology transfer was of central importance. The inclination was toward including a "few big guys with big bucks" versus "[giving] everyone a little bit." There was broad support for creating a response to the Japanese threat, and that the response should be of sufficient magnitude and direction so as to help neutralize it (notes on pre-Orlando briefings).

WILLIAM C. NORRIS

William C. (Bill) Norris was born on a farm near Red Cloud, Nebraska. He graduated from the University of Nebraska in 1932 with a degree in electrical engineering. His first job with Westinghouse Corporation was followed by five years of service in the U.S. Navy during World War II, where he became involved in electronic equipment, the forerunner of today's computers.

After the war, Norris helped found Engineering Research Associates, Inc. (ERA), in St. Paul, Minnesota, which was a pioneer in the development of the digital computer. ERA later was merged into Sperry Rand Corporation. Norris headed the Univac Division of Sperry Rand through mid-1957, when he left to found Control Data Corporation (CDC). His understanding of how business and government can leverage each other's strengths was a cornerstone of the development of CDC's computers and systems. Norris was chairman and CEO of Control Data Corporation until he retired in 1986.

High on Norris's list of concerns in the late 1970s and early 1980s was the ability of U.S. electronics companies, including CDC, to compete successfully with the Japanese. He felt that part of the solution might be collaborative research: "That's the only way we're going to be able to solve this goddamned situation with Japan, where they are getting a cheap ride on our technology" (quoted in Worthy, 1987, p. 220). Norris often referred to dramatic cases in which the United States invented technologies only to have Japanese companies commercialize the resultant products for sale in the United States and worldwide. One of his favorite examples was the videocassette recorder (VCR), which was invented by Ampex, then a small high-tech company in Redwood City, California.[1]

In order to inhibit the outflow of technology from the United States to Japan, Norris proposed a variety of national policies, most of which were not well received at the time. In late 1982, when he proposed the need for collaborative R&D by U.S. companies, his own engineers at CDC were "aghast" (Norris, interview, August 10, 1990). Later, in 1983, he floated the idea of closing the doors of U.S. university laboratories to the Japanese. "It aroused howls of protest here and abroad and nothing ever came of it" (Worthy, 1987, p. 220). Concurrent with his leadership in the establishment of MCC, Norris implemented smaller and more regional versions of similar concepts in his home state, Minnesota, during the 1980s, including:

- The Midwest Cooperation Organization, a 12-state consortium for cooperative sponsorship by midwestern businesses and state governments of multi-university research teams in special areas of opportunity.
- Minnesota Wellspring, a coalition of state labor, business, government, and education, with the mission of improved business infrastructure and competitive environment.
- The Microelectronic and Information Science Research Center, an interdepartmental research center at the University of Minnesota, sponsored by CDC, Honeywell, 3M, Sperry, and other regional corporations for basic research of interest to industry.
- The Minnesota Advanced Manufacturing Technology Centers and the Greater Minnesota Corporation, public-private corporations, initially sponsored by the state of Minnesota through appropriations and proceeds of the Minnesota State Lottery; now Minnesota Technology, Incorporated, with sponsorship from federal and state governments as well as business. (Russell interview, February 25, 1993)

In addition, Norris has helped organize several successful cooperative venture groups, including Norwest Growth Fund, Minnesota Seed Capital Fund, and Minnesota Cooperation Office. The latter organization assists technology-based companies in their start-up and growth stages with both investment financing and seasoned executive guidance.

In 1986, Norris was awarded the National Medal of Technology by President Reagan. He is also a recipient of the Institute of Electrical and Electronics Engineers' Founders Medal and of numerous other awards and honorary degrees. In the past decade, Norris has focused his concern about the lack of U.S. competitiveness in two areas: collaboration for expanding innovation via small business, and the need to improve the technological literacy of all U.S. citizens. As chairman of the William C. Norris Institute since 1988, he has devoted his time and the foundation's resources to catalyzing large-scale public/private collaboration to address major unmet or poorly met societal needs.

Current activities of the William C. Norris Institute include three consortia; K-12 Transforming Schools Consortium, the Technology-Based Engineering Education Consortium, and the Academic Quality Consortium. In addition, the institute has two joint ventures with Russian organizations for the development and delivery of computer-based instruction courseware. The institute also fosters public/private collaboration to expand innovation by assisting technology-based start-up companies to provide low-cost, computer-based education in order to increase public understanding of the pivotal role of technology in job creation. (Russell interview, February 25, 1993)

Norris's interest in the educational use of technology, especially for science and math engineering, began in the 1970s with the introduction of computer time-sharing and the development of CDC's Plato Systems, a forerunner of computer-based, interactive learning.

Norris still lives within walking distance of CDC's Minneapolis-based headquarters and the nearby headquarters of the William C. Norris Institute.[2]

NOTES

1. Ampex sold large-sized VCRs to television broadcasting stations but did not think that a consumer market existed. Mr. Morita, president of the Sony Corporation, thought otherwise. Sony acquired the Ampex-developed technology and designed the Sony Betamax in the 1970s (Lardner, 1987). According to Goto (interview, summer 1992), Toshiba developed the "helical" single recording head, which permitted the development of the consumer model VCR. Japan's initial marketing strategy was not successful because of the lack of a common standard, poor software, and relatively high price. While Sony's Betamax did not turn out to be the preferred standard, today more than 80 percent of U.S. households have at least one VCR, most of which were made in Japan.

2. Norris was the visionary behind the founding of MCC. George Kozmetsky was an early visionary and strategist in the Texas bid for MCC and in the formation of the Austin Technology Incubator, which accepted MCC's and SEMATECH's first spin-out, technology-based companies. Both men champion increased industrial competitiveness for their home states and the nation. A less visible similarity between these two is exemplified in the historic concept of the "grandfather house." In early Pennsylvania Dutch communities, a family's grandparents often lived in a small house within walking distance from the second- and third-generation family. The children and grandchildren would visit their elders for comfort and advice and to ease the transition of the farm's management from generation to generation. A path winds from CDC's headquarters building, which sits on the banks of the Mississippi River, across a street to Norris's bungalow, commonly called "bluff house" by those who came for advice and to pay their respects. Similarly, Kozmetsky's IC^2 Institute is a short walk from The University of Texas at Austin, where he was dean of the business school.

On November 6, 1981, Norris sent a letter to the president or chairman of major companies in the semiconductor and computer industries, inviting them to attend a February meeting in Orlando to discuss how "to achieve the broad-scale technological cooperation which is necessary to meet the Japanese challenge facing us in microelectronics." The letter continued:

The brightest star in U.S. economic performance for the past quarter century has been the entrepreneurial growth of the semiconductor and computer industries. Now it is up to us to see that that opportunity remains open in the future. Unless action is taken, it will not. The extent and nature of the changes in our industry have been well documented in recent months . . . .

What matters more is what we do. The Japanese challenge has served the beneficial purpose of raising awareness generally. The status quo in our industries will not suffice. Various responses have been proposed, and while all are important steps in the right direction, we must go further to successfully meet this challenge.

We all know the fate of those industries who did not respond vigorously to similar challenges in the past.

A broad based, cooperative approach is required to help assure U.S. leadership in the future and maintain that leadership position thereafter. Such a cooperative program can be constructed, which at the same time will maintain the basic competitive climate which has fueled the growth of the past.

The initial planning for the meeting took place from December 1981 through January 1982, and involved Norris and Price, CDC's chief of staff, John W. Lacey, and Arneson. The basic plan was twofold: (1) to emphasize the Japanese threat, and (2) to set forth an invitation to create a business plan that would stand the scrutiny of capable businesspeople and technologists. Arneson emphasized that presentation of a business plan at the meeting "would turn the participants off." Therefore, only a general verbal concept of the proposed R&D consortium was presented. (correspondence, September 24, 1993)

THE ORLANDO MEETING

The February 19, 1982, meeting was held at the Greenlefe golf and tennis resort near Orlando, Florida, and it had the atmosphere of a secret get-together of Mafia dons. The invitation to attend the history-making meeting was followed by a telephone call from Norris or Price. The dialogue continued for several weeks: "We tried to have a first-class meeting in a place that would be easy to get to. We used every trick in the book to get senior participation from the invited companies. . . . If you had ever spent much time in Minneapolis in February, you'd know why the meeting was held in Orlando." (Rutishauser, interview, January 23, 1987)

Present at Greenlefe were chairmen, presidents, and other high officials from 16 of the nation's leading electronics, computer, and merchant semiconductor companies, including Norris, Price, Lacey, and Arneson from CDC; Dr. Jacob E. (Jack) Goldman of Xerox; Jerry Sanders of AMD; Charles Sporck of National Semiconductor; Harold Ergott of Mostek Corporation; Gerry

Probst of Sperry; Gordon Bell of Digital Equipment Corporation (DEC); Dr. William G. (Bill) Howard of Motorola; Charles Exley, Jr. of NCR Corporation; Gerald (Gerry) Dineen of Honeywell; Charles Phipps of Texas Instruments; and representatives from Harris, North American Philips, United Technologies, Rockwell, and Signetics. IBM, General Electric, Intel, and Hewlett-Packard declined Norris's invitation.

Also present were representatives from two trade associations (the Electronic Industries Association and the Computer and Business Equipment Manufacturers Association); Professor Mike Dertouzos, director, MIT Laboratory for Computer Science; Dr. Richard DeLauer, undersecretary of defense for research and engineering; Dr. Michael Boretsky, undersecretary for international trade, Department of Commerce; and the Pentagon's chief of research and engineering. Norris's general strategy in CDC's two previous R&D consortia was to keep the government's antitrust watchdogs fully informed. He continued this "tell-all" policy by informing the Federal Trade Commission in advance about the meeting and giving it a summary of the proceedings. As Price remembered:

> We worked on the legal clearance right from the start. We would not talk about markets or prices but we would talk about technology. We had lawyers present from the first meeting in Orlando through the steering committee and interim board meetings. (interview, May 12, 1993)

Norris began the meeting with a warning: "Before starting, we should all remind ourselves that whenever competitors meet for any purpose, certain topics may not be discussed. None of us need to be reminded about the specifics of those rules, but it doesn't hurt to mention their existence."[13] The objective was to explore the feasibility of founding Microelectronics & Computer Technology Enterprises (MCE).[14] Bob Price gave a short speech in which he tried to set a tone of looking for ways to encourage collaboration among the meeting's participants. He said:

> I want to emphasize first that the proposal [to achieve needed collaboration] itself can only be meaningful if it is always kept in the context of a very specific question:

What is the greatest need—at least the greatest technical need—facing each of our individual companies?—I
say, "need"—but you can just as easily substitute
"threat" or "opportunity" and arrive at the same point.
That is just another way of saying that "enlightened
self-interest" has got to be the byword of any successful
cooperation. Lord knows, there is plenty of
territory in which we can seek common technical needs if
we put our minds to it. (quoted in Arneson, 1982, p. 1)

Japan was on the minds of the participants, but there was a
wide divergence of opinion about the causes for the island nation's
considerable success in technology commercialization. Bell of DEC
spoke on Japan's fifth-generation computer project. Howard of
Motorola gave a presentation entitled "Perspectives of the Foreign
Challenge in High-Technology Industries," in which he discussed a
range of issues that were troublesome to U.S. industry, including the
Japanese system of government, zaibatsu, America's 5:1 debt to
equity ratio with Japan, patent-filing trends, semiconductors and
telecommunications, the 256K DRAM, Kyoto Ceramics, robotics,
and prospects for the future. Probst of Sperry commented that
Japanese technological success was the result of a leakage of technology information from U.S. universities and labs. He was immediately shouted down by Bell, who said that Japan's success had nothing to do with technology leakage but rather was due to investment
level, organization, and determination:

I thought we were past these archaic views of the
Japanese. . . . The non-innovative Japanese model is 10
years obsolete. . . . Anyone who feels the model is right is
ready for retirement. They [the Japanese] are incredibly
innovative. (G. Bell, as quoted in Arneson, 1982, p. 3)

Sanders of AMD chimed in: "The only reason I'm here is
because of the Japanese. They are competent, and they will kill us if
we don't do something. We must do something different in coordination." Sporck of National Semiconductor agreed: "Our lack of a
U.S. industrial policy is our biggest problem. . . . Somehow the
country has to be rallied to meet the cooperative effort here like

MITI. We must focus on how to survive—it's overwhelming."
DeLauer, the undersecretary of defense, challenged the group: "I
don't know if you are looking far enough ahead. . . . Do you want
to beat Japan? You have to beat them like we did before. . . . Take
major steps. Take the long-term view and invest. The short-term
view did it to autos and it'll do it to computers."

In order to support the proposal to form a consortium, the
executives felt that they needed a definitive agenda of R&D activities. How would the consortium be different from universities and
the recently formed SRC?[15] "We all sponsor university research. If
it was the answer to everything, we wouldn't be here," noted Price.
Sporck emphasized: "The research must be targeted and in the
hands of industry." "Half of the graduate students here [in the
United States] are foreign, most of them are full-paying—universities love 'em," commented DeLauer. Bell interjected: "DOD is pour-
ing money down a rat hole. The faculty isn't in place to do the
work, their research is undirected and undisciplined." Goldman,
vice president of research at Xerox, stated:

> Innovation is the process of transferring knowledge
> into meaningful products. Universities don't do that
> except rarely when staff leave to form their own com-
> pany, and then they suffer all the ills of every small
> company. We need what the universities have—but
> inside [an organization like MCC] so it gets a market
> focus. (quoted in Arneson, 1982, p. 7)

Price presented the strawhorse proposal for the MCE (later
called MCC), which covered eligibility, mission, organization, governance, personnel, financing, legal and tax issues, and next steps.
He noted that the basic mission of the consortium was to:

- Preserve and enhance U.S. predominance and
  preeminence in microelectronics and computing.
- Cooperate at the basic-technology level and leverage
  R&D to provide long-term benefit to the industry
  and nation.

"I'm hopeful, not confident. . . . If we are to win, we
must draw closer to the Japanese not further apart . . . for better

negotiations with Japan and get the technology flow reversed," said Goldman. "Think broadly about what can be done to save our - - - - - ten years from now. This is a declaration of war, and we must respond."[16] Randall agreed. "Now that we have brought high technology to our economy, we need an industrial policy. I feel this is a very good approach." Sporck emphasized:

> What will our children and grandchildren do? They won't be part of the information industry. IBM and AT&T R&D expenditures aren't enough to stem the Japanese—the gap is widening. We've been talking about this now for years. The [MCC] proposal may be imperfect, but we will learn and then we can evolve into something really meaningful. I'm in favor of proceeding. (quoted in Arneson, 1982, p. 3)

Dineen commented: "The problem of technology transfer is the key issue." Sporck agreed: "They've beaten us on the application of technology—quality, productivity—not the technology itself." Norris concluded that if they were to proceed, they would need high-level people who could represent the personality of their company and speak for it with tenacity and flexibility. Exley suggested that in order for NCR to support MCC, there had to be a more definitive agenda.

A vote was taken not on whether or not to form a consortium but rather on whether or not to proceed with studying the possibility of forming one. The votes for continuing were counted: 14 for yes, 0 no, and 2 maybe.[17] The Orlando meeting planted the seed for MCC, and this time Norris's vision took hold.[18]

> Bill Norris wasn't certain what to do but he was sure of several things; doing nothing was wrong; the seven dwarfs[19] would never make it on their own; running to Washington wasn't the answer. Somehow the answer to fighting off the Japanese threat lay in technology. From the outset, we who planned and created MCC understood the design constraints that needed to be satisfied:
>
> •   The U.S. government would have to view the resulting organization as legal.

- The governance structure would have to be saleable to the highly suspicious co-venturers.
- The initial set of research programs had to be specific enough to get people to sign up and yet general enough not to overly constrain the researchers.
- The real importance of MCC would not be simply the technological results, but finding a way for U.S. companies to "level the playing field" without compromising the precious principles of competition and free markets. (Arneson correspondence, April 8, 1993)

ORGANIZING MCC'S FORMAL STRUCTURE AND RESEARCH FOCUS

A survey taken of those present at the Orlando meeting showed that the desire to cooperate in forming a consortium was directly related to the degree of the perceived Japanese threat to company survival (Figure 2.1). Table 2.2 was compiled by Arneson to speculate where the Japanese and the United States were in 1982 and where they were likely to be in 1990, with and without MCC, on such criteria as manufacturing costs, quality, architecture, software, design tools, cost of capital, technology cooperation, and government encouragement.

MCC's steering committee was made up of two individuals from each company who were generally the second, third, or fourth highest-ranked executives from 17 companies interested in MCC's formation.[20] While such "tall timber" facilitated MCC's progress, it was still a real balancing act to nuture the growth of MCC through the steering committee meetings. As Price emphasized:

In 1982 it wasn't in the nature of people [U.S. computer executives] to cooperate. I started each steering committee meeting with a statement putting down the fear of antitrust . . . company lawyers were always present. . . . I made it clear that what we were interested in was greater competition not collusion. (interview, May 12, 1993)

The nation's first for-profit R&D consortium had to be conceived of as a strongly independent entity that would attract and serve its shareholders. It was extremely important that no one company have undue influence in MCC's formation. As Arneson emphasized: "Even the perception of influence was dangerous. . . . We had the task of doing the nearly impossible, to get a bunch of intense competitors to work together toward a common goal and, by the way, finesse your own company's wishes along the way." (Arneson correspondence, June 15, 1993)

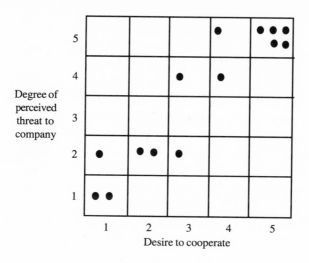

Source: Arneson's CDC file, 1982.

Figure 2.1 Survey of Orlando meeting attendees, indicating a high correlation between desire to cooperate and degree of perceived threat to company

Twelve of the 17 companies represented on the steering committee ultimately agreed to contribute the time of a senior executive plus $10,000 as a pro rata share of the expected costs of preparing a business plan for MCC. To the large computer companies: "It was worth $10,000 and some staff time not to be left out, just in case something good would happen. It was a trivial cost" (Rutishauser interview, January 23, 1987). However, the $10,000 contribution by each of the dozen interested companies was a token gesture compared to the actual costs to CDC of close to $1 million for providing legal and administrative support for the new organization.

Table 2.2
United States and Japan: relative competitive positions as perceived by MCC's steering committee

| | | | 1990 | | | |
| | 1982 | | Without MCC | | With MCC | |
	Japan	U.S.	Japan	U.S.	Japan	U.S.
Manufacturing Costs	A	B	A	B	E	E
Quality	A	B	E	E	E	E
Architecture	B	A	A	B	B	A
Software	B	A	E	E	B	A
Design Tools	B	A	A	B	B	A
Cost of Capital	A	B	A	B	A	B
Technology Cooperation	A	B	A	B	E	E
Government Encouragement	A	B	A	B	A	B

A = ahead, B = behind, and E = even.

Source: Arneson's CDC file, 1982.

Figure 2.2 shows MCC's steering committee's planning schedule from the February 1982 meeting in Orlando through MCC's planned founding in January 1983. Task groups were formed on (1) organization, governance, and facilities; (2) charter and dimensions including R&D, licenses, and fees; (3) selection of MCC's president; and (4) government relations including tax and antitrust issues.

One of the early significant challenges facing the steering committee (which later became MCC's interim board of directors) was determining the focus of MCC's research activities. As Bob Price who chaired the committee and later, the interim board meetings, put it:

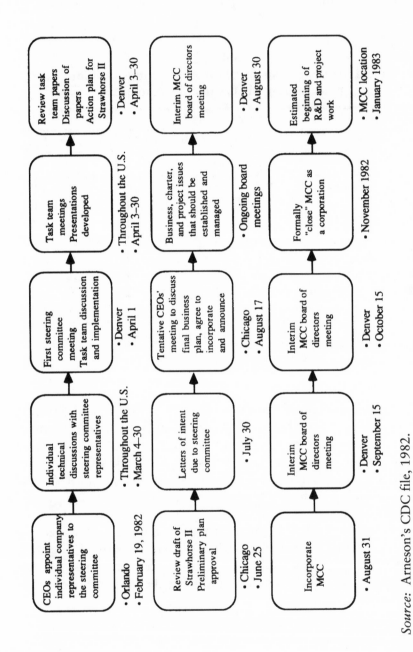

Source: Arneson's CDC file, 1982.

Figure 2.2 MCC steering committee's planning schedule, 1982

There was a concern at the top of the companies that
they didn't want to be screwed in the marketplace. It
took nine months to determine what was pre-competitive. We understand the concept now but at the time we
sweated blood to decide MCC's research priorities that
we all could agree to. (interview, May 12, 1993)

Arneson, who was responsible for much of the day-to-day
coordination and planning for the consortium, formed a small, but
key advisory group of two close associates: Robert H. Price (a technologist and engineer with whom Arneson had worked at Control
Data, referred to here as "technical Bob Price" to distinguish him
from Bob Price the president of CDC) and Jess Rifkind (a long-time
business acquaintance who had recently left Xerox Corporation,
where he headed research efforts in Southern California). Technical
Bob Price advised Arneson on technical matters. Rifkind was
Arneson's *éminence grise*.[21] Additional members of Arneson's team
were Bob Rutishauser, a CDC accountant who helped with financial
modeling, and a couple of Control Data attorneys (Steve Olson and
Bob Hibbard) who helped construct MCC's legal documents.

MCC's steering committee proposed and debated a list of
advanced technology projects it considered crucial to its industry,
including electronic CAD, semiconductor packaging, gallium
arsenide, and advanced computer architecture. Arneson and technical Bob Price rented a Lear jet and flew coast to coast, visiting as
many as four companies a day to solicit the opinions of potential
shareholders concerning the research focus of MCC. As Arneson
remembered:

The visits that Bob [technical Bob Price] and I had with
the prospects were extremely useful in being able to
"distill" a set of projects that appeared to have widespread support. These projects were basically those that
an individual company could not afford to fund at a
level sufficient to generate "critical mass," but by
investing with others could put in funds and get high
leverage from the total investment of the group.
(Arneson correspondence, June 15, 1992)

A chart was compiled that showed the average degree of support for 19 technologies (Figure 2.3). Five research areas were then culled down to four: CAD/CAM, packaging, software, and advanced computer architecture. Factory automation was discussed, but this fifth research idea was shelved in spring 1982. Each company did not enthusiastically support all of these projects; however, they did represent the lowest common denominator.

> MCC's planning task force visited the technical people in each of the companies to try to figure out what things were ripe for cooperation . . . what things were sufficiently generic that a cooperative approach would be meaningful and not get the shareholders all uptight about risk and jeopardizing their family jewels and all that, and yet would have a major impact on the companies. (Rutishauser interview, January 23, 1987)

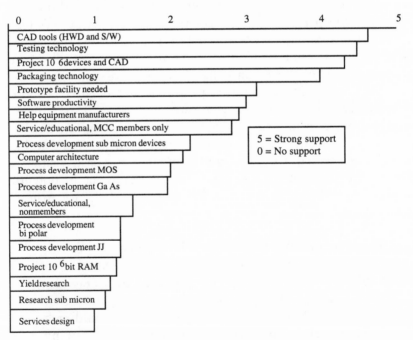

Source: Arneson's CDC file, 1982.

Figure 2.3 Ranking of shareholder support for 19 possible MCC research programs

Four subcommittees were formed, with members representing the companies that might be interested in joining each research program. The CAD/CAM subcommittee was chaired by technical Bob Price, packaging by an official from Harris, software by an NCR executive, and advanced computer architecture by a DEC employee. The objective was to conduct microelectronics-based R&D in areas essential to future computing systems and to the competiveness of MCC's funding companies.[22] MCC was charged with taking projects from basic research to advanced development. The shareholder companies were responsible for carrying the research through product development, preproduction, and production (Figure 2.4).

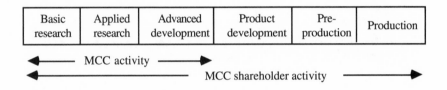

Source: Arneson's CDC file, 1982.

Figure 2.4 Envisioned MCC and shareholder responsibilities concerning technology commercialization

MCC was motivated by the goal of individual company survival and of beating back Japanese competition in the computer industry, particularly the threat posed by Japan's Super Computer Association, the Fifth-Generation Computer Project (ICOT) and new-function "next-generation" devices (Figure 2.5). MCC was to emphasize technological and research areas where it was not beneficial for U.S. firms to go it alone in competition with Japan. Needed financial resources and research talent were increasingly scarce and costly. Product development cycles were shrinking dramatically as new technologies were proliferating rapidly. As Price commented:

> In the late 1970s there was an incredible rate of change and investment in R&D, what used to be a $100 million investment was approaching $1 billion . . . collaboration on a different scale was needed. (interview, May 12, 1993)

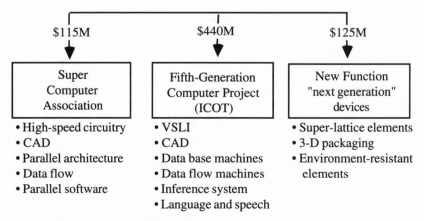

$115M	$440M	$125M
Super Computer Association	Fifth-Generation Computer Project (ICOT)	New Function "next generation" devices
• High-speed circuitry • CAD • Parallel architecture • Data flow • Parallel software	• VSLI • CAD • Data base machines • Data flow machines • Inference system • Language and speech	• Super-lattice elements • 3-D packaging • Environment-resistant elements

Source: Arneson's CDC file, 1982.

Figure 2.5 Japan's strategy for the 1980s as perceived by MCC's planners

MCC's longest and most complex technology project was initially dubbed Alpha/Omega—later to be called the Advanced Computer Architecture (ACA) Program. This project was closest to a head-to-head competition with ICOT and was to develop and transfer prototype technologies for future generations of computers and smart peripherals in four areas: (1) AI architectures and a prototype system capable of 100,00 inferences per second, (2) data base machine architecture with a tenfold performance improvement over present processing architectures, (3) a user interface incorporating a speech- and image-recognition system, and (4) one or more parallel-processing architectures. Initial work in all these areas was to be followed by a second phase in which the prototypes would be implemented as large-scale integrated circuits. In a third phase, the LSI chips would be incorporated into the basis of a complete computing system (Barney, 1983). This eight-to-ten-year program was to involve 80 to 90 scientists and engineers and have an estimated annual budget of $18 million.

On November 30, 1982, R.E. Wagner, a CDC technician charged with looking into the Alpha/Omega project, wrote a memo to John Lacey with a copy to Bob Price, in which he commented on the research activities being planned for MCC. In his visits to academic and research institutions, Wagner became convinced that CDC was not a force in these domains; either as system suppliers or as a source of ideas or people with ideas. DEC, on the other hand, has seemingly unbounded involvement in these same institutions . . . . [Given the above realization] I am very concerned as to how CDC can take advantage of results produced by Alpha/Omega. We don't seem to have the internal mechanisms required to gather, disseminate and/or utilize [these] new technologies as they are developed. . . . CDC needs an internal technology transfer center that mirrors the MCC Alpha/Omega technology center in its project organization. . . .

To realize any benefit for MCC and/or such an internal center, CDC must improve its ability to rapidly produce products and services based on new technologies. If we don't and MCC succeeds then we will have been our own worst enemy; DEC and/or Japan will be the benefactors. . . . Aside from sticking our technical heads into the sand it seems to me our worst problem is having too many diverse projects, each with too little support to succeed. (memo, November 30, 1982)

The CAD/CAM project initally attracted the largest number of company sponsors (perhaps because it demanded the smallest investment, $1.2 million a year per company for an initial commitment of three years). This project focused on reducing design cost and improving quality by allowing the layout of mixed-technology chips incorporating from 1 million to 10 million devices. This eight-year program was expected to ramp up to about 80 people with an annual budget of $11 million after the third year.

The third research project, was initially called software productivity, but was renamed software technology, because the productivity label implied tweaking conventional approaches to get more out of them (Barney, 1983, p. 90). This research effort was to use intelligent systems to gain an order-of-magnitude improvement in the effectiveness of both the systems and application software development processes. The seven-to-eight-year program was estimated to cost $60 to $70 million.

The fourth research effort, microelectronics packaging, was expected to be the smallest in professional manpower, with an estimated 25 technicians for a five-to-six-year effort. The project was to have five phases: (1) die-preparation techniques for automated mass bonding that were feasible for pin counts of over 400; (2) equipment automation to handle device lead bonding, burn-in, and attachment to substrate; (3) device encapsulation to facilitate direct, reliable attachment to a printed-circuit board; and (4) reliable manufacturing and test ability for volume production (Barney, 1983). The program was expected to cost $3 to $4 million per year and was MCC's most short-term research activity. (As we describe in Chapters 4 and 5, the Packaging/Interconnect Program turned out to be the most productive in patents, technologies licensed, technologies transferred and used, and in terms of sustained shareholder and member company support.)

There were at least four relatively obscure components of MCC's initial business plan that proved to be especially problematic. As noted by Arneson (correspondence, July 19, 1993): "These 'barrier ideas' posed enormous problems for us because we knew that no one would join MCC under such conditions. We eliminated those ideas one-by-one by interacting with potential MCC member companies. . . ." First, it was proposed that MCC would have no permanent employees. The consortium's employees would all be on loan from the member companies, and they would be the best and the brightest. As discussed subsequently, from the moment he was hired as MCC's first CEO, Admiral Inman was uncomfortable with the emphasis placed on securing MCC's research personnel from the shareholder companies. Second, Norris wanted some kind of arrangement for small companies that could not afford to join MCC. Under the concept of an Associates Program, small companies were to get technology and technology services (e.g., silicon foundry, testing, and lab analysis) from MCC at affordable rates. While such a program helped mitigate antitrust concerns, it was not actively promoted during MCC's formative years. The full-paying shareholders were concerned that associates would get MCC's technology on the cheap.

Third, it was initially thought that MCC, as a for-profit organization, would be able to stand on its own within a few years. As discussed in Chapter 4, it took about six to eight years for the consortium to have the technologies and to initiate the policy for licensing and spin-out strategies that might one day begin to provide

MCC with meaningful operating capital. Fourth, those planning for MCC's research programs realized that an international liaison office, which would monitor technological developments around the world, would help make sure that MCC's research efforts were consistent, competitive, and compatible with what was going on globally. Out of concern for antitrust issues, it was decided that a similar office for scanning domestic technology could not be designed into MCC's operating plan even though such domestic scanning would have been extremely useful.

Benefits were expected to accrue to MCC's participants (e.g., leveraging of R&D investment, access to state-of-the-art technology, and less duplication of effort), U.S. industry (e.g., broadening the scope of R&D work that would otherwise not be done), and the nation (e.g., retaining technology leadership in computers and microelectronics). Shareholders were expected to add value to MCC-developed pre-competitive technology by producing their own products for markets of their own choice. It was also expected that MCC would stimulate other technological activity (e.g., equipment suppliers), which would also contribute to each shareholder's ability to develop products (Figure 2.6). As Bob Price emphasized:

> Pre-competitive collaboration can actually increase interfirm competition. Resources are leveraged in terms of R&D activities. This sharing of costs allows the individual companies to focus their own resources on producing added value and uniqueness in product design, manufacturing, marketing, and sales. People didn't naturally think of sharing necessary technologies in order to be able to concentrate more on those absolutely key value-added technologies that would make them more competitive. (interview, May 12, 1993)

According to its planners, MCC was not set up to produce "silver bullet technologies" that would save the U.S. computer industry. MCC was organized to be engaged in goal directed, long-term research, but less ambitious research than that being conducted

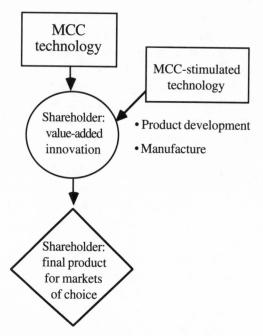

Source: Arneson's CDC file, 1982.

Figure 2.6 MCC and shareholder conception of technology transfer
responsibilities, as of 1982

at U.S. universities, Xerox PARC, DuPont, IBM, and Bell Labs.
Product development belonged to the companies. The initial set of
research programs was chosen because it was felt that it satisfied
the dual requirements of being needed and falling into the
applied science/technology categories. (Arneson correspondence,
April 8, 1993)

As Price emphasized:

> Nothing like MCC had existed, so people had their
> own image of what we were talking about. Some
> viewed it as a giant cartel, a project to produce a one-
> megabit DRAM or to answer the Japanese Fifth-
> Generation, a new EPRI, or a new research institute.
> Collaboration between supplier and user was di6
> fficult; there was fear of vertical integration. Some
> viewed [MCC] as a threat to the U.S. economy and way

of life that would have a devastating effect on innovation, industrial growth, and competitiveness.

MCC was set up as a framework to facilitate collaboration among various organizations and institutions; however, no one realized just how difficult successful collaboration would be—people thought in terms of projects/outputs rather than process or a way to focus and concentrate resources. (paraphrase of presentation to MCC PartnerMart, at the consortium's tenth anniversary, May 12, 1993)

RECRUITING MCC'S FIRST CEO

During MCC's formation, participating executives from the shareholder companies exhibited a strong antigovernment philosophy. They thought microelectronics technology was critically important to the United States, but they did not want the federal government actively involved in interfirm collaboration or competition. They made it especially clear that they did not want the U.S. Department of Defense (DOD) as a member or even as a contributor.[23] The government agency most on the minds of the shareholders was the Department of Justice and its pending ruling on antitrust.

Bob Price chaired the subcommittee that was charged with hiring MCC's first chief executive officer. The interim board of directors agreed that the consortium's chances of success would improve dramatically with the selection of an outstanding, visionary, and trusted leader. After a nationwide search, it decided (although not unanimously) that MCC's first CEO should be Bobby Ray Inman, the recently retired deputy director of the U.S. Central Intelligence Agency (CIA), former director of the National Security Agency (NSA), and a former four-star admiral. Given the strong antigovernment attitudes of MCC's founding members, it seemed rather odd, at the time, that a career government official was selected to be the consortium's first CEO.

Inman had no previous experience in managing a private company, nor was he an expert in computer technology. He had high-level connections in Washington that might prove useful, and it was considered an asset that he was not formally associated with any of MCC's founding companies. In his high-level government position, the admiral had purchased supercomputers, so he was somewhat known by top management at CDC, Burroughs, Honeywell, and Sperry. About a year before MCC was formed, Inman had made a particularly positive impression on electronics industry leaders when he gave a luncheon speech at the Commonwealth Club, an elite businessmen's association located in San Francisco. Inman declared that the gradual loss of U.S. leadership in microelectronics to foreign competitors represented a grave threat to national security. In essence, he implied that it was the patriotic duty of Silicon Valley's semiconductor companies to successfully compete with the Japanese. When a top government intelligence officer like Inman articulated such a message, it created waves of enthusiasm from U.S. electronics executives. Inman indicated that the government cared about what Japan was doing to the nation's semiconductor companies. Wisely, he said little about what the federal government should do to assist these same companies, a topic about which there were ambivalent feelings in the government as well as in Silicon Valley.

ADMIRAL INMAN AND MCC

After his retirement from the navy, Inman considered several executive positions with U.S. corporations, one of which was with American Express, where he was asked to head international strategy. On October 4, 1982, Bob Price called to inquire if Inman had already committed to a job. "No, I haven't yet," was the response. Price continued (interview, May 12, 1993): "Would you at least listen to something totally new and different, that's never been done before? A lot of people keep telling us that you might be the right guy for the job." MCC was not only a brand new organization; it was a new type of organization. This appealed to Inman, so when he was approached by Price about becoming MCC's first CEO, he was receptive. A handful of finalists were invited to visit each of the shareholder companies. Inman had not yet completed his swing of visits when he was invited to MCC's interim board of directors meeting in Denver on December 4, 1982.

On 11 October 1982, I went out to Minneapolis to

hear what this was all about. This was the first that I
was exposed to the concept of MCC. I was intrigued.
On 4 December, I went to an interim board meeting of
MCC in Denver. I was interviewed by several of the
companies. . . . I levied two conditions that evening
before I left. That if I would consider the position at all,
I would have to be chairman of the board as well as
president and chief executive officer, to deal with questions of equity and fairness among the member companies. Second, I wanted absolute authority in personnel
matters. (Inman interview, January 26, 1987)

Inman believed that he needed absolute authority as head of
MCC to contend with disputes that were likely to arise among the
consortium's shareholder companies. He was also concerned about
hiring quality researchers to staff the consortium. Inman had been
told that the research talent could be recruited from the member
companies, but he knew from his Washington, D.C., experiences
that such a policy could lead to MCC's becoming a "turkey farm"
for member-company castoffs.

Inman had already traveled to Minneapolis, where he had
interviewed three potential shareholder companies, and to Silicon
Valley, where he had interviewed three or four more. He talked to
the remaining member companies in Denver. Most of the executives
liked what they saw, but Inman was not so sure. Rutishauser, who
was at the meeting, recalls:

It was a stormy meeting. . . . Fish or cut bait time for
the member companies. They weren't really sure about
this new venture. . . . They were concerned about this,
and they were concerned about that. . . . It was our
most difficult meeting in terms of cohesiveness and
working together. . . . Inman told me afterward: "I
went home from that meeting and I wasn't sure
whether this was something that I wanted to get
involved in. But then, for all those years, I had been trying to convince the air force and the army that the
enemy was the KGB, and not the U.S. intelligence services of the other military branches." There are analo-

gies between getting government agencies to work
together and getting competitive companies to work
together. It takes very similar skills. (interview, January
23, 1987)

Inman was acquainted with Steven Jobs, founder and chairman of the board of Apple Computer, and while he was considering
the MCC offer, he was approached by Jobs about the presidency of
Apple. On the first of December 1982, Inman flew to Cupertino in
Silicon Valley to be interviewed, but he doubted that he wanted to
manage an established company. "The salary, the stock options, and
other things that Apple was offering were dazzling by comparison
to the MCC offer, but I was convinced that what they needed was a
marketing guy, not a strategic planner. They weren't ready to diversify." (Inman interview, January 26, 1987)[24]
MCC's board of directors officially offered the job to Inman
on December 21, 1982. Inman tells what happened next: "On 4
January, I called Apple and then accepted the MCC offer on 17
January. On the twenty-first, I flew up to Minneapolis to pick up
the reins of this fledgling company as its first employee. . . . I indicated that I was going to put the temporary office in Washington,
while we decided where to locate the consortium." (interview,
January 26, 1987)
Inman's intellect, razor-sharp mind, unquestioned integrity,
and ability to handle the press were useful qualities as the CEO of
the nation's first high-tech R&D consortium. In his Washington
days, the admiral had a reputation for being "squeaky clean."
MCC's top executive would need such a reputation, as well as considerable abilities in negotiation and persuasion, in order to handle
the federal government and MCC's member companies.

He picks up things very quickly. . . . In spring 1983, he
asked the heads of each of the technology teams [who
were planning MCC's research programs] to come to
Washington and give him a briefing. Inman started one
of these briefings by saying to the team leader: "I probably won't understand a whole lot about your program
by the time we're finished this afternoon. But if you'll
be patient, perhaps I will be slightly less ignorant."

BOBBY RAY INMAN

Bobby Ray Inman was born in the small east Texas town of Rhonesboro on April 4, 1931. From childhood he had demonstrated a phenomenal ability to recount a stunning array of facts and calculations (Hilts, 1984). He graduated from high school at age 15 and earned his B.A. in history from The University of Texas at Austin in 1950. After one year of teaching junior high school, Inman enlisted in the U.S. Navy. After graduating from officers candidate school, he began his military career decoding messages on an aircraft carrier and was shifted to intelligence in 1957. Inman proceeded to hold a variety of increasingly important administrative, operational, and intelligence posts as he rapidly rose through the ranks from ensign to admiral, a very difficult achievement for an individual who did not attend the U.S. Naval Academy and who had a degree in history. Indeed, Inman was the Navy's first intelligence specialist to reach the rank of four-star admiral.

Inman's military career benefited from a key, fortuitous event that provides some insight into the man. In 1958, the U.S. Navy was concerned that the People's Republic of China might invade Taiwan. On one particularly tense morning in the Pentagon, Admiral Arleigh Burke, chief of naval operations, was briefed by a Navy commander about the increasingly threatening situation with respect to Taiwan. The commander recommended immediate action, and Admiral Burke began dispatching warships; however, it was soon realized that the information about China's threatening moves was incorrect. By this time, the senior intelligence officer who had originally advised Burke was unavailable, and so were intelligence reports. Inman happened to be on duty and was called before the admiral the following morning. "Blessed with a nearly photographic memory, Inman was able to recall each of the hundreds of dispatches that he had read that night. Inman answered Admiral Burke's questions and he was promptly chosen to replace the disgraced commander" (O'Reilly, 1986).

In 1972, Inman graduated from the National War College and then served as executive assistant and senior aide to the vice chief of naval operations. He received added distinction for his unique and correct analysis of Arab and Soviet moves during the Yom Kippur War of 1973. In 1974, he was selected for promotion to rear admiral and director of naval intelligence; two and one-half years later, he was promoted to vice admiral and in 1981 was promoted to four-star admiral. Inman finished his military career as director of the National Security Agency in 1977–1981 and deputy director of the Central Intelligence Agency in 1981–1982. On July 1, 1982, at the age of 51, Inman retired from government service. He did not discuss with us why he resigned from the CIA, but he is reported to have opposed the Reagan administration's attempts to broaden domestic spying (Day, 1984). At the time, it was officially reported that he quit over "policy differences." *The Nation* (May 8, 1982) claimed Inman resigned because he disagreed with a proposal to create a single intelligence agency that would have included both the CIA and the FBI. In any event, when William Casey stepped down as CIA director in 1986, Inman was sounded out about returning to the CIA as top man. He said: "No thanks."

During his 31 years of military service, Inman felt that he had grown out of touch with the United States. "When I retired on 1 July 1982, I wanted my sons to see more of their country. My wife was an easterner who didn't know very much about the United States, so we took a lengthy car trip. Eleven thousand miles in eight weeks. Circled back and forth, all over the West. We did it in a Riviera. One suitcase and one small baggage each. . . . We were also looking for places in which we'd like to live" (Inman interview, July 21, 1987). The family tour included a visit to Austin, where the admiral had attended the University of Texas three decades earlier. He was impressed with how beautiful the city was and how much it had changed over the years. It was Nancy Inman's first visit to Austin. It looked like a nice place, with trees, hills, and lakes; not at all like the sagebrush image of Texas.

Forty minutes later, Inman was asking the team leader questions that he could not answer. . . . The team leader went out of the meeting just amazed. He had thought he was going to give a tutorial to a military man with a degree in history. (Rutishauser interview, January 23, 1987)

In summary, Inman brought several important qualities to MCC:

- A national identity, which was important in attracting mass media attention and public recognition to the consortium. This high visibility was leveraged by Inman's ability to "use the press."
- Insider know-how and know-who regarding the Washington scene. Such knowledge was especially useful when MCC lobbied to reduce the risk of federal antitrust concerns.
- A reputation for integrity and an "intelligence" point of view that influenced how MCC's site-selection process was conducted and how MCC was managed during its early years.

After he was appointed MCC's first CEO, Inman gave frequent talks on the consortium's activities and technology plans. He made one such presentation in March 1983 at the CompCon meeting in San Francisco. He stated that he envisioned two main problems for the new cooperative: how to keep his staff from being raided by MCC's shareholders and how to transfer MCC-developed technology to the corporate sponsors. He saw the raiding problem as especially touchy since MCC was doing all it could to hire the sponsoring companies' most highly qualified technical and research personnel. Technology transfer activities at MCC would be reviewed semiannually by a technical advisory board of high-level personnel from the shareholder companies; however, Inman commented that:

> The real trick will be to ensure that only those companies that have actually invested in a project will benefit from it. . . . The real success of MCC will be determined by whether or not the sponsors themselves profit from projects they have underwritten. . . . We will not abandon market competition, but we will share research. (paraphrased in Barney, 1983, p. 90)

ANTITRUST AND MCC

The Sherman Antitrust Act (named after U.S. Senator John Sherman, who proposed the legislation) was aimed specifically at breaking up Standard Oil (John D. Rockefeller's quasimonopoly) into 30 smaller companies.[25] The act of July 2, 1890, established the following prohibitions: "Every contract, combination in the form of trust or otherwise, or conspiracy, in restraint of trade or commerce among the several states, or with foreign nations, is hereby declared to be illegal (a felony punishable by fine or imprisonment)" (Gelhorn, 1981, p. 21). Section 7 of the Clayton Antitrust Act of 1914 strengthened these antitrust provisions. Together these laws established a hallowed government policy that had ruled U.S. business for 100 years. U.S. antitrust legislation was designed to control the exercise of private economic power by preventing monopolies and by encouraging interfirm competition. Companies in the same or related industries were prohibited from talking together, even informally, about the restraint of trade, setting prices, and/or the allocation of markets, resources, capacity, and R&D effort (Bower and Rhenman, 1985). If the Justice Department's Antitrust Division found a company guilty of anticompetitive practices, it could impose fines with triple damages. Furthermore, the company could be tied up with frivolous antitrust suits that were relatively inexpensive to file and could keep the company mired in a web of legal entanglements. It is easy to see why the executives on MCC's interim board of directors and their company lawyers were nervous about even talking with one another about collaborative R&D.

Motivated by President Reagan's Innovation Task Force, lawyers of the Antitrust Division were sending signals to U.S. industry that cooperative research programs were not necessarily illegal. Of ten joint R&D proposals reviewed by the DOJ since 1972, eight had been fully cleared (Werner, 1980). Ky Ewing, Jr., deputy assistant attorney general, Antitrust Division, said in 1980:

> I believe there may be misperceptions of the reach of anti-trust laws in relation to cooperative research—particularly with smaller and medium-sized businesses. . . .
> A company should be careful not to be put off by their

> corporate counsel's necessarily cautious words. . . . It's
> the ultimate analysis that counts. . . . The basic issue in
> anti-trust analysis of a proposed joint research project
> is whether it will produce more or less innovation. . . .
> Basic research usually involves general principles that
> no one makes a trade secret of anyway. Joint efforts in
> the development end of the spectrum—product differ-
> entiation—are more likely to be anticompetitive.
> (Werner, 1980, pp. 1–2)

Steve Olson, CDC's legal counsel, played a key role in influencing the DOJ to rule in favor of MCC. CDC dealt with the Justice
Department on a full-disclosure basis, explaining exactly what it
was going to do before doing it. CDC did not ask for DOJ
approval; it just told the government's antitrust lawyers that if they
wanted to disapprove of the consortium, this was the time to do so.
Representatives of DOJ's Antitrust Division attended MCC's steering committee and interim board meetings. Reports of what tran-
spired at these meetings were sent to Washington. However, despite
these communication efforts with the DOJ, by late 1982, MCC's
member companies were becoming increasingly nervous about the
antitrust implications of what they were proposing. A concerted
effort was made to get Justice to make a public statement regarding
MCC. On December 28, 1982, the DOJ issued its yellow-light decision, which stated that it would not object to the creation of MCC
but would review each research program as required.[26] As noted,
MCC's board of directors had voted to offer the top leadership position to Admiral Inman at its December 21, 1982, meeting in Denver.
The December 28 announcement by the Department of Justice came
at just the right time to help convince Inman, who was officially
appointed MCC's CEO on January 25, 1983.

If the December 1982 statement by the DOJ was a cautionary
go-ahead for MCC, the National Cooperative Research Act
(NCRA) of 1984 was a green all clear. The NCRA, which unanimously passed Congress, clarified existing antitrust standards
regarding cooperative research. So MCC was officially legalized
after the consortium had been in existence for about two years.[27]
While the NCRA does not grant immunity from antitrust actions, it
does lessen the danger of prosecution:

In any action under the antitrust laws, or under any
state law similar to the antitrust laws, the conduct of
any person in making or performing under a contract
to carry out a joint research and development venture
shall not be deemed illegal *per se:* such conduct shall be
judged on the basis of its reasonableness taking into
account all relevant factors affecting competition,
including, but not limited to, effects on competition in
properly defined, relevant research and development
markets. (NCRA legislation, Section 3)

WHO JOINED MCC?

According to MCC's bylaws, member companies had to be
"Domiciled in the United States and ultimately controlled and
substantially owned by citizens of the United States." Four
main categories of U.S.-owned companies initially joined the
R&D consortium.

1. Among the first companies to join MCC were mainframe computer manufacturers Sperry, NCR, CDC,
   and Honeywell; Harris (an electronics conglomerate
   that was heavily involved in computers); and DEC,
   primarily a minicomputer company (Figure 2.7).
   What these companies had in common, in addition
   to fear of the Japanese Fifth-Generation Computer
   Project, was ongoing competition with IBM. A 1986
   survey of MCC member companies showed that
   while the Japanese were clearly the main threat, IBM
   and other domestic companies were also seen as
   important competitors. (Murphy, 1987)[28]

2. Four semiconductor manufacturers (AMD,
   Motorola, National Semiconductor, and Mostek in
   the spring of 1983) were also instrumental in launching MCC. These companies had been hurt badly by
   Japan's success in capturing the RAM market. The
   Japanese threat to their continued survival was very
   real indeed.

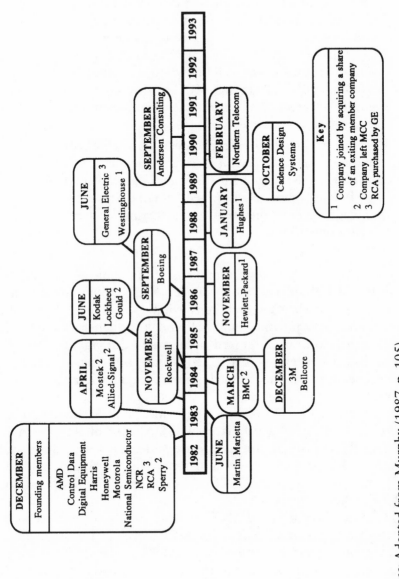

Source: Adapted from Murphy (1987, p. 105).

Figure 2.7 Shareholder company participation in MCC

3. A third category of early MCC shareholders was made up of four aerospace manufacturers: Boeing, Rockwell International, Martin Marietta, and Lockheed Missiles and Space. These companies, each doing several billion dollars of defense contracting per year, joined MCC in the months just after Admiral Inman took charge. Although none of the four had attended the February 1982 meeting in Orlando, Inman was well known to their executives. Undoubtedly the fact that MCC was overcoming the antitrust threat also helped sway the minds of the aerospace executives.

4. A fourth category of shareholders consisted of conglomerates (e.g., General Electric, which in 1986 acquired the share of MCC's founding member RCA; 3M; Westinghouse; and Allied-Signal) that were engaged in computer, semiconductor, and/or aerospace operations.

In addition to these four groupings of shareholders, two other early MCC shareholders were (1) Bellcore (Bell Communications Research, Inc.), itself a research consortium of the seven Bell telephone operating companies; and (2) Kodak, which had acquired several small computer-related companies during the 1980s. Kodak's R&D strategy was affected by the blurring distinction between chemicals-on-paper imaging and computer imaging. With time, the cost of becoming an MCC shareholder increased from the original entry fee of $150,000 to a one-time fee of $1 million. The consortium also added a surcharge of 25 percent of the previous cost of an R&D program for new shareholder members. However, no shareholder paid the $1 million fee or the surcharge, and in 1985, the cost of joining MCC as a shareholder dropped to $250,000, where it remains today.

Cadence, which joined MCC in 1989, was a software design company and a potential vendor for MCC-developed technologies. Two companies became shareholders in 1990. Andersen Consulting was engaged in large system integration for its customers and thus represented the interests of information technology consumers.

Northern Telecom, the giant Canadian telecommunications company, joined MCC after the consortium's restriction against non-U.S. members was changed to allow North American companies to become shareholders. This change in MCC's bylaws was motivated by the U.S.-Canadian Free Trade Agreement.

During MCC's first decade, six shareholders left the consortium as a result of mergers and acquisitions as well as dissatisfaction with its performance. Other shareholders have exercised their option to go on inactive status by keeping their MCC membership while not funding research or otherwise participating in the consortium's programs. Lockheed, Westinghouse, and General Electric went on inactive status in the late 1980s and then returned to active status by the early 1990s. Currently, Honeywell, Martin Marietta, National Semiconductor, and Westinghouse are on inactive status.

1. BMC Industries, Inc., of St. Paul, Minnesota, was near bankruptcy in 1986 when the company sold its MCC share to Hewlett-Packard.
2. Mostek was bought by United Technologies Corporation (UTC) in 1985. Later, Thomson-CSF of France purchased Mostek from UTC, which precluded Mostek's membership in MCC. Mostek's MCC share was sold to Westinghouse in 1986.
3. Burroughs Corporation acquired Sperry to form Unisys in 1986 and then dropped out of MCC in 1987. Hughes purchased Unisys's share in 1988, and Unisys rejoined MCC as an associate.
4. RCA was acquired by General Electric in 1986.
5. Allied-Signal dropped its shareholder membership status and became an associate in 1987.
6. Gould dropped its MCC membership in 1987 and is currently owned by Japanese interests.

BMC Industries, Mostek, and Gould are the three shareholders that have permanently left MCC and not returned as associate members of the consortium. MCC's 10 founding shareholders and 22 shareholders as of 1993 are shown in Table 2.3.

THE DIVERSITY OF MCC'S SHAREHOLDER COMPANIES

MCC's shareholder companies are diverse on such dimensions as size, markets, R&D expenditures, geographic location, and involvement in defense contracting. Figure 2.8 shows the wide range in annual sales of MCC's member companies. Another point of comparison is the percentage of a company's R&D budget going to MCC. For most MCC shareholders, this has been less than 5 percent, ranging down to 1 or 2 percent for the big conglomerates and up to 6 to 10 percent for several of the semiconductor manufacturers. With $79 million in annual sales, BMC Industries was furthest out on the small end of company size. Fifty percent of BMC's R&D funds went to MCC, a dubious investment given that the consortium's activities consisted of long-term research. BMC did make a world competitive CAD/CAM plotter and fine-line masks, and so MCC's CAD and packaging research programs were directly related to its product lines. Still, the relatively small size of BMC led to its early withdrawal. It was just too diverse a fit with the much larger electronics and aerospace companies that made up the majority of MCC's members.

Figure 2.9 shows the geographic clustering of the headquarters locations of MCC's shareholders. There is a concentration in California, especially in Silicon Valley; another cluster in the New York/New Jersey area; and a grouping in Minneapolis–St. Paul. These three clusters include about two-thirds of the corporate offices of MCC's shareholders, with others scattered around the United States, mainly in the Midwest and East. Austin is about as distant as possible, on the average, from the headquarters of each of its shareholder companies.

Table 2.3 MCC shareholder companies in 1983 and 1993

Ten Founding Shareholders in 1983	Shareholders in 1993
1. Advanced Micro Devices	1. Advanced Micro Devices
	2. Andersen Consulting
	3. Bellcore
	4. Boeing Company
	5. Cadence Design Systems, Inc.
2. Control Data Corporation	6. Ceridian Corporation
3. Digital Equipment Corporation	7. Digital Equipment Corporation
	8. Eastman Kodak Company
	9. General Electric
4. Harris Corporation	10. Harris Corporation
	11. Hewlett-Packard Company (HP)
5. Honeywell Corporation	12. Honeywell Corporation *
	13. Hughes Aircraft Company
	14. Lockheed Corporation
	15. 3M Company
	16. Martin Marietta *
6. Motorola Incorporated	17. Motorola Incorporated
7. National Semiconductor Corp.	18. National Semiconductor Corp.*
8. NCR Corporation	19. NCR Corporation
	20. Northern Telecom Limited
	21. Rockwell International
	22. Westinghouse Electric Corp.*
9. RCA (share sold to General Electric)	
10. Sperry (share sold to Hughes)	* Currently on inactive status

The market focus of MCC's shareholders is also very diverse. While together MCC's shareholders represented about one-fourth of the 1985 total U.S. defense contracts of $153 billion, this ranged from none (for such companies as 3M, AMD, Bellcore, and National Semiconductor) up to $5 or $6 billion per year (for companies like Lockheed, Boeing, General Electric, Hughes, and Rockwell). MCC's defense contractor shareholders initially wanted the Pentagon to fund the consortium's research, but the other shareholders were opposed, fearing that the Department of Defense might influence MCC's research in directions that would restrict the nonmilitary application of the resulting technologies.

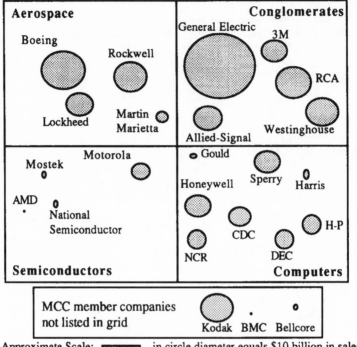

Approximate Scale: ▬▬▬ in circle diameter equals $10 billion in sales.

In 1983, IBM had $34.4 billion in sales.

Source: Adapted from Murphy (1987, p. 107).

Figure 2.8 Approximate relative size of MCC's shareholders by annual sales revenue

Competitive pressures are quite different for MCC's share-holders. For instance, Boeing operates in an international market-place with only a few other companies of comparative strength. Boeing's competitive situation contrasts with that of AMD, a rela-tively small semiconductor company headquartered in Silicon Valley. AMD had been "eaten for lunch" during the 1980s by Japan's giant electronics companies. One could easily imagine that what AMD would want from MCC would likely be quite different from what Boeing would want. This heterogeneity in MCC's mem-bership led to divergent objectives and measures of success for the consortium, and it posed significant challenges for MCC's management.[29]

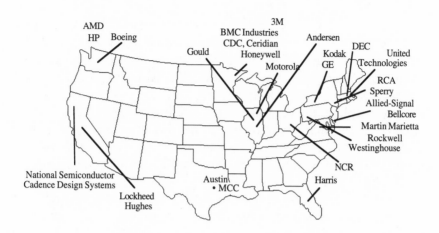

Not Currently a Shareholder
Allied-Signal Corp., Morristown, NJ
BMC Industries, Inc., St. Paul, MN
Gould Inc., Rolling Meadows, IL
RCA Corp. New York, NY
Sperry Corp., New York, NY
United Technologies Corp.,
    Hartford, CT

Currently a Shareholder
Advanced Micro Devices (AMD),
    Sunnyvale, CA
Andersen Consulting, Chicago, IL
Bell Communications Research
    Ind. (Bellcore), Livingston, NJ
Boeing Co., Seattle, WA
Cadence Design Sys., San Jose, CA
Ceridian Corp., Minneapolis, MN
Digital Equipment, Maynard, MA

Currently a Shareholder (cont.)
Eastman Kodak Co., Rochester, NY
General Electric Co., Rochester, NY
Harris Corp., Melbourne, FL
Hewlett-Packard, Palo Alto, CA
Honeywell, Inc., Minneapolis, MN
Hughes Aircraft Co., Culver City, CA
Lockheed Corp., Burbank, CA
3M, St. Paul, MN
Martin Marietta, Bethesda, MD
Motorola, Inc., Schaumberg, IL
National Semiconductor Corp.,
    Santa Clara, CA
NCR Corp., Dayton, OH
Northern Telecom, Nepean, Ontario
Rockwell International Corp.,
    Pittsburgh, PA
Westinghouse Electric Corp.,
    Pittsburgh, PA

Source: Adapted from Murphy (1987, p. 114).

**Figure 2.9 Location of the headquarters of MCC's
shareholder companies**

WHY JOIN MCC?

Why did intensely competitive companies in the same industry, as well as such a broad range of industry types, join MCC? According to Inman: "The Japanese, to be blunt, provided the inspiration and the impetus, the 'shotgun' as it were, for the marriage" (Inman, 1984, p. 150). Underpinning this impetus was a desire to try a more collaborative, less competitive business strategy. Murphy concluded from his survey of MCC member companies: "The participants in MCC view the microelectronics industry as having excessive inter-firm competition and insufficient inter-firm cooperation." (1987, p. 237)

MCC focused on long-term R&D, the kind of research that many of the member companies could not, or would not, conduct. By sharing cost, they could ostensibly obtain multiple dollars worth of research for each dollar invested. In the face of sharply increased costs, such leveraging was one way to pool resources and avoid unwanted duplication. Another prime motivation for joining MCC was the chance to agglomerate a critical mass of quality R&D talent. Well-trained scientists and engineers capable of working in state-of-the-art research on microelectronics were expensive and in short supply. The idea of each of MCC's shareholders lending research talent to the consortium, to form a critical mass, was argued to be a win-win situation. By offering a range of research projects, MCC allowed its member companies to diversify their research interests while leveraging risk and cost. Furthermore, in an age of increasingly short product development cycles, MCC would help the member companies monitor the rapid proliferation of advanced technologies worldwide. In short, MCC would enable member companies to compete with giants like IBM, AT&T, and NEC.

Other less salient reasons for joining MCC were to (1) monitor the technological activities of the other member companies, (2) participate in this new venture just in case the consortium was successful, and (3) enhance corporate image and reap the positive public relations of being a good corporate citizen by enhancing U.S. industrial competiveness in critical industries.

MCC'S ASSOCIATE MEMBERS

Bill Norris felt strongly that MCC should not be just a rich man's club, but it was Arneson's éminence grise, Jess Rifkind, who developed the idea of an associates' program. Accordingly, the consortium's business plan included a provision for associate member companies that could not afford the several million dollars to join MCC as full shareholders. Associates were nonvoting members of MCC and did not receive proprietary technology. Early in MCC's formation, the Associates Program hit a high of 13 firms, but interest waned and associate members dropped to 5 in 1986. Shortly after Grant Dove took charge of the consortium, the number of associate members grew steadily to 50 by 1991 and, under the leadership of Craig Fields, to 55 by May 1992 (Figure 2.10 and Table 2.4).

CONCLUSIONS

When MCC was formed, it went against a century of U.S. governmental and legal policy and a long-standing business tradition of unfettered competition—institutions and values that were associated with the nation's economic strength. Japanese success in dominating many established U.S. industries and the threat of such dominance in the computer industry spurred federal officials to relax antitrust legislation and industry leaders to invest in a collaborative R&D enterprise.

Japan's economic competitiveness benefited from the national direction and worldwide information gathering by MITI and Japanese industry groups. The prewar tradition of zaibatsu and the more modern keiretsu, while facilitating Japan's "fast-second" strategy, did little to pave the way for collaborative R&D. While benefiting from advanced urban planning and construction, Tsukuba Science City suffered from a lack of human planning. While the VLSI Project benefited from propitious timing in terms of organizational and technical considerations, it was the inspired and team-oriented leadership at the level of the individual researchers that led to the ultimate benefits of this R&D consortium. The Japanese had difficulty repeating the VLSI success in their more distributed and open ICOT Project, which focused more on basic research.

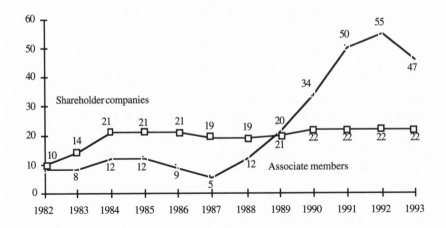

Figure 2.10 Number of MCC's shareholder and associate member companies from 1982 to 1993

MCC—America's first attempt at large-scale, collaborative R&D—was inspired by Bill Norris of CDC. However, until the Japanese threat to the U.S. computer and semiconductor industries had been made salient to the nation's corporate leaders, Norris's calls for a major collaborative R&D effort fell on deaf ears. By early 1982, a critical mass of computer industry leaders was ready to commit to Norris's vision of a privately funded R&D consortium. High-level managers and technologists worked for about one year to organize and plan a collaborative research effort that would meet U.S. industry needs. MCC's structure and research focus reflected the desires of the consortium's initial shareholders to leverage their financial and intellectual resources to beat back the Japanese threat—the motive was individual company survival and the continuation of U.S. leadership in cutting-edge computer and software research.

Despite the fact that MCC's founding companies were adamant about keeping the federal government out of the consortium, they chose a career military and government official as its first CEO. The choice of Admiral Bobby Ray Inman served MCC well in meeting the early challenges of (1) getting a favorable ruling on antitrust, (2) gaining shareholder support from U.S. areospace

Table 2.4 Current and past MCC associate members

Advanced Packaging Systems *	National Security Agency
Aerojet Electronics	National Starch & Chemical Co.
Allied-Signal, Inc.	Ablestik Lab.
American Express Co.	Northrop Corp. *
Amoco Production Co.	Occidental Chemical Corp.*
AMP, Inc.	Olin Corp.
Apple Computer, Inc.	Optical Imaging Systems *
AT&T	Photonics Imaging, Inc. *
BroadBand Technologies, Inc.	Planar Systems *
Cherry Display Systems, Inc. *	Plasmaco, Inc. *
Conner Peripherals, Inc. *	Plasma-Therm *
Corporate Memory Systems, Inc.	Projectavision, Inc.
Cypress Semiconductor	PROMEX *
DSC Communications Corp.	Raytheon Company
EDEN International Corp. *	Rogers Corporation *
E.I. Dupont Denemours	RTB Technology, Inc.
E.I.T. Corp. *	SAIC
Electronics Manuf. Prod. Facility *	Sandia National Laboratory
Electro-Plasma, Inc. *	SEMATECH *
Embedded Computing Institute,	Shipley Company
Naval Air Warfare Center	Software Engineering Institute *
Weapons Division	Space Systems Loral
E.M. Warburg, Pincus & Co.	Sprint Corp.
ERIM	Standish Industries *
E-Systems, Inc.	State of Texas
Fairchild Space and Defense Corp.	Sun Microsystems, Inc. *
FBI	Tandem Computers, Inc.
IBM Corporation	Tektronix, Inc. *
ITASCA Systems, Inc. *	Teledyne Microelectronics
Lawrence Livermore Labs	Teradyne, Inc. *
Limited Inc./Express	Texas Instruments
LTV Missiles and Electronics *	The Markle Foundation
Magnascreen *	Tracor
Mars, Inc. *	TRW, Inc.
Mentor Graphics Corporation	Unisys Corp.
Microsoft Corporation	United Technologies Corporation
The MITRE Corp.	University at Albany, SUNY
Multichip Technology, Inc.*	Valid Logic *
NASA	VLSI Technology, Inc.
NASA JSC *	Western Technologies Automation *

*No longer an associate member as of November 1993.

companies and other industries, (3) gaining national and international visibility in locating MCC's headquarters, and (4) keeping the consortium at the forefront of public/private leaders' attention in general and MCC's shareholder CEOs' attention in particular.

As it was being formed in 1982–1983, MCC enjoyed the advantage of being a bold, new, and "patriotic" organization. Industry, government, and academic leaders became caught up in the vision of a privately funded, collaborative R&D consortium that would sustain U.S. leadership in industries deemed critical to global competitiveness. A second main advantage was the immediacy of the Japanese threat, which inspired and united public and private leaders to a common purpose.

However, there were also constraints, which limited what MCC's founders were capable of implementing in terms of the consortium's operating procedures and these constraints contributed to management and technology transfer challenges during MCC's first decade of operation. Antitrust and competitive concerns motivated MCC's planners to focus on pre-competitive R&D or, as some MCC planners would prefer, long-term goal-directed research. It later became apparent that private firms were not all that receptive to commercializing such pre-competitive technology.

The challenge of meeting the technological and research interests of a broad range of shareholders and the concern of transferring technology only to the program sponsors, led to a "cafeteria strategy" of research offerings. However, this strategy came to pose lasting organizational consequences for MCC in terms of (1) establishing research leveraging and synergy across research programs and (2) transferring technologies to the companies funding the research. Admiral Inman later commented that he regretted MCC's decision to mount separate research programs, but he probably had little choice in 1983. Some of MCC's founding shareholders had large internally funded R&D activities; others had none. Some shareholders were represented by industrial statesmen who were interested in long-term benefits, others were more interested in short-term results. None were interested in contributing to the technological competitiveness of their fellow shareholders if they were not full partners in funding the research.

National and international publicity facilitated MCC's start-up in terms of gaining shareholder support, recruiting qualified researchers, and motivating a highly competitive site-selection process. However, this same publicity also built very high (some would say unrealistic) expectations for MCC. Despite the fact that MCC was an experimental organization dedicated to long-term (five to ten years), pre-competitive research, it was not long before critics began asking for the "silver bullet" technologies that would beat back the Japanese. MCC was stung by critics who questioned the lack of specific, measurable results.

NOTES

1. Some important Japanese companies—such as Matsushita, Toyota, Honda, Sony, Hitachi, New Japanese Steel, and Nissan—did not belong to prewar zaibatsu. (Goto interview, summer 1992)

2. According to Goto (interview, summer 1992), Japan's prewar basic research was of a higher level (especially in accelerator and particle physics, magnetism, and electrical networks) than generally thought by Western observers. On the other hand, such technologies as precision manufacturing, machine tools, and materials research were not very advanced even into the early 1900s. The commercialization of this research base was restricted because of Japan's prewar concentration on weapons development. For example, Japan's prewar quality control was generally poor except for the development of such weapons systems as the Zero fighter plane by Mitsubishi.

3. Much of our material on Tsukuba Science City is based on the research of our colleague James W. Dearing, assistant professor, Department of Communication, Michigan State University. Dr. Dearing lived in Japan in 1988–1989 while he collected interview, survey, and archival data for his doctoral dissertation (Dearing, 1989). Dearing's book about Tsukuba, *Growing a Science City*, is published by Routledge Publishers, London (1994). We also thank IC^2 Institute's visiting research fellow Dr. Kunio Goto for reviewing our discussion of Japan and Tsukuba Science City.

4. Dearing quotes E. Takayama, the chief designer of Tsukuba Science City: "My only regret in planning Tsukuba is that I forgot to plan a cemetery. The cemeteries in the area belong to the old-time residents, and they don't want newcomers [scientists] buried in their cemeteries. In Japan, we have a saying that you should be buried where you do your life's work. There is no place to bury the first-generation science city people." (Dearing interview of E. Takayama, April 12, 1989)

5. Dearing provided us with pointed examples demonstrating the lack of collaboration among Japanese ministries located in Tsukuba. Workers in the different ministries were opposed to sharing library resources and expensive equipment. As a result, equipment was often over-ordered and under-utilized. For example, 35 wind tunnels were purchased by numerous labs located in Tsukuba because the technicians representing the various ministries were unwilling to share these facilities.

6. The Tsukuba experience is being studied in detail by the Japanese who are currently planning and building Kansai Science City, located between Osaka, Nara, and Kyoto, about 300 miles from Tokyo. Lessons learned at Tsukuba are being used to the benefit of Kansai.

7. The basic technology underlying each of the first four generations of computers, in which U.S. technology was dominant, is as follows: first-generation computers used vacuum tubes (for example, ENIAC, the world's first computer, which was developed in 1946); second-generation computers were built with transistors; third-generation computers used integrated circuits; and fourth-generation computers had very large scale integrated (VLSI) circuits. In each instance, the new technology totally revamped existing systems and paved the way for computers to perform increasingly complex tasks. The United States dominated the world computer markets with fourth-generation machines and software. Fifth-generation computers were to be built with information-processing systems that could converse with humans in natural language, learn, draw inferences, and make decisions.

8. When Rogers visited ICOT late in 1989, he was struck by the youth of the ICOT scientists. Their average age was about 30 when ICOT began. About half had Ph.D.'s, many from U.S. universities.

9. The openness of the Fifth-Generation Computer Project surprised Americans who visited the consortium. When Rogers toured ICOT in 1989, he encountered European and American scientists at work in ICOT's research laboratories. MCC's International Liaison Office (ILO) has generally found the Japanese to be quite willing to share information. As Meg Wilson, vice president for Business Development, said: "We can find incredible amounts of information. We just have to ask in their language" (interview, November 15, 1993). MITI may have been willing to open ICOT to the world out of concern about Japan's image in the world research community and because of trade friction with the United States and Europe. Or this openness may have been stimulated by the desire to acquire foreign technology by having world-class researchers come to Japan for an extended period of time. A feeling that has persisted as commented by Edward Malloy, counselor for scientific and technical affairs at the American embassy in Tokyo: "Companies are understandably cautious these days about giving up technology in return for some loose change for research." (quoted in Sanger, 1991)

10. This MITI-directed effort stayed the course with its chosen technology PRO-LOG software and logic programming, for a long-term payoff that did not occur. A similarly MITI-directed effort concerns high-definition television (HDTV). With two decades of development invested, Japanese HDTV is based on analog technology. Many experts believe that a shift to digital television technology will favor U.S. research and subsequent product commercialization. (Pollack, 1992)

11. In *Science* (May 1991, vol. 252), "Britain Picks Wrong Way to Beat the Japanese," Alvey planners were criticized both for misunderstanding the Japanese programs they were trying to imitate and for overvaluing the strength of research in helping the British information technology industry. Sharing precompetitive research among rival companies was also seen as a major challenge in the successful operation of the Alvey Project.

12. While this "processes and techniques" orientation made sense to Norris in

1982 and would be less of a direct challenge to U.S. antitrust law, it also resulted in significant technology transfer problems for MCC.

13. The material and quotes from the Orlando meeting are based on the transcribed notes and files of Phillip W. Arneson (1982).

14. Norris had originally proposed to name the consortium "MCE, Inc.," for Microelectronics & Computer Enterprises. The word "technology" was used to broaden the scope of "computer," as noncomputer companies were likely to be involved. The consortium was incorporated under the name "Microelectronics and Computer Technology Corporation." The initials "MCC," rather than "MCTC," were used to avoid confusion with an existing organization and because MCC was easier to pronounce than MCTC.

15. Nine of the original 12 MCC shareholders were among the 33 companies that had formed the Semiconductor Research Corporation (SRC) in February 1982. SRC, a subsidiary of the Semiconductor Industry Association (SIA), is a nonprofit cooperative research center made up primarily of U.S. semiconductor and computer system manufacturers. It is headquartered in Research Triangle Park, North Carolina. Like MCC, SRC was formed to deal with Japanese competition in microelectronics. But rather than conducting in-house research, SRC funds research projects that are proposed and carried out primarily by university scholars. Both Norris and Price believed that the SRC did not go far enough, but as Price remembered (interview, May 12, 1993): "Noyce argued that we needed to walk before we could run, so CDC committed to the SRC even while we were working on forming an R&D consortium more like MCC." Prior experience with the SRC predisposed several of MCC's member companies to the idea of a research consortium.

When MCC was first announced to the U.S. public, there was some confusion as to how it differed from the SRC. The main differences were (1) SRC was a nonprofit organization, while MCC was for-profit; (2) SRC research was conducted by universities, while MCC research was to be conducted on site; and (3) MCC was able to keep its research confidential and proprietary, while the SRC operated in the public domain. The SRC avoided the antitrust issue because universities are open research settings. MCC softened the antitrust concern by focusing on pre-competitive research. It was the function of the funding companies to turn MCC's long-term (five to ten years) research into competitive products.

16. Goldman was an early and strong proponent of MCC, but Xerox chose not to join the consortium. As Jess Rifkind (interview, November 11, 1992) commented: "Corporate staff members at Xerox beat it to death."

17. Texas Instruments' (TI) headquarters are in Dallas, and the company has often distanced itself from the other semiconductor companies clustered in Silicon Valley. TI did not join MCC as a shareholder even after the consortium located in Austin, Texas; however, TI did become an associate member in 1989. By 1993, under the leadership of CEO Jerry R. Jenkins, TI had abandoned its go-it-alone strategy and had formed joint ventures in Europe and Asia. Jenkins commented: "We're looking for shared dependence." *(Business Week,* "TI Is Moving Up in the World," August 2, 1993, pp. 46–47)

18. Once MCC was launched, Norris withdrew from being directly involved, perhaps because of his age. He was then 71. Norris continues to be involved in the William C. Norris Institute and such projects as expanding innovation

through small businesses and the need to improve the technological literacy of all U.S. citizens.

19. Seven of the ten companies initially joining MCC were dubbed "the seven dwarfs" for their practice of frequently joining in competition against IBM. Soon there were 12 dwarfs joining MCC with the combined potential of becoming a giant in their own right.

20. These firms were: AMD, Burroughs, Control Data, DEC, Harris, Honeywell, Mostek, Motorola, NCR, National Semiconductor, RCA, Rockwell, Signetics, Sperry Univac, United Technologies, Westinghouse, and Xerox.

21. During the reign of Louis XIII (1624–1642), Cardinal Richelieu (1585–1642), a favorite of the Pope, advised the king on how to eliminate the feudal barons and consolidate the power of his throne. For Richelieu, the interests of the state overrode religion, ordinary morality, and constitutional procedures. Louis was a weak king who followed the advice of his cardinal. What is not often appreciated is that Richelieu received valued advice from a monk of the Capuchin order, François Le Clerc du Tremblay, or as he was called, Father Joseph. Cardinals wore red (*éminence rouge*). Father Joseph's order wore gray (*éminence grise*). For more on Louis XIII, Richelieu, and Father Joseph, see Aldous Huxley's *Grey Eminence* (1969).

22. See Appendix 4.2 for a more complete description of the development of MCC's research programs as well as a listing of some of MCC's most significant technological developments. MCC's current research divisions and projects are described in Chapter 4.

23. This prohibition of federal government involvement softened a few years later when MCC sought U.S. Department of Defense approval to charge MCC research costs against the defense contracts of its shareholders that were conducting defense-related work. By 1988, MCC was accepting DOD contracts from DARPA (Defense Advanced Research Projects Agency). The subject of MCC's increased government funding is discussed more fully in Chapter 4.

24. Later, Apple did indeed hire a marketing expert as president: John Scully, from the PepsiCo Company. They paid him an annual salary of $1 million, plus a signing bonus of $1 million. At MCC, Inman received a rather modest salary by industry standards.

25. One hundred years ago John D. Rockefeller, then about 40 years old, was the wealthiest individual in America. He more or less owned the oil industry.

26. The yellow-light decision by the Department of Justice was also facilitated by the return of Professor William F. Baxter to Stanford's School of Law. Baxter had been on a two-year leave to serve in Washington, where he was the assistant attorney general in charge of the DOJ's Antitrust Division. He was the Reagan administration's leading opponent of modification of the Sherman Antitrust restrictions, even for an R&D consortium like MCC.

27. This weakening of U.S. antitrust law was the result of extensive lobbying by Bill Norris, Steve Olson, Admiral Inman, MCC's member companies, and Texas' Washington politicians (most notably, Congressmen Jake Pickle and Jim Wright), as we detail in Chapter 7.

28. IBM did not need to join MCC to achieve a critical mass of R&D activity. In 1982, IBM had an annual research budget of $2.1 billion, in contrast to MCC's expected annual budget of $70 million or the Japanese Fifth-

Generation Computer Project's expected annual budget of $1.35 billion. In fact, Big Blue's R&D budget was approximately equal to that of all the microelectronics companies in Silicon Valley. What benefit would IBM obtain from pooling research talent with its lesser R&D-endowed U.S. competitors?

Given the dubious antitrust status of MCC in 1982, IBM had another reason to be leery of joining the new consortium. Shortly before MCC's initial planning meeting in Orlando in February 1982, the U.S. Department of Justice dropped a massive, 13-year antitrust suit against IBM. So Big Blue had gone a few rounds with Justice. IBM's executives were hardly eager to mix it up with DOJ lawyers again. Furthermore, if IBM or AT&T had joined MCC, the consortium would have faced more serious antitrust problems, since it would have lost its main U.S. competitors (Peck, 1986). IBM became an associate member of MCC in 1992 after previously joining SEMATECH in 1988 and the ill-fated attempt to launch U.S. Memories in 1989 (see Chapter 7).

About 20 U.S. companies that are roughly the size of MCC's shareholders (R&D budgets of $100 million or more) have not joined MCC (Peck, 1986). This means that the consortium's members can potentially use MCC research results to gain market share at the expense of nonmember U.S. companies.

29. Most recently, MCC is beginning to view member company diversity as a unique competitive advantage, especially in research areas such as enterprise integration and technology commercialization. By expanding horizontal (e.g., customers) and vertical (e.g., suppliers and manufacturers) integration, as of 1993 MCC was approaching the form and function of a keiretsu, without the banking function.

3

MCC COMES TO TEXAS

I gather that Texas bought it.

Andrew Young, mayor of Atlanta, when informed that
Austin won the competition for MCC (May 17, 1983)

Texas did not buy MCC. I can guarantee that.

Palle Smidt, member of MCC's interim board of directors
(May 5, 1986)

Before the final stage of the site-selection process for the
Microelectronics and Computer Technology Corporation (MCC)
began early in April 1983, Admiral Inman asked representatives
from the consortium's ten shareholder companies to rank the four
finalist cities as the preferred site for the consortium's headquarters.
The results were: Raleigh-Durham, first; San Diego, second;
Atlanta, third; and Austin, fourth. This ranking was "based on
impressions and images from afar," commented Inman. (interview,
January 26, 1987)

Shortly after the jet carrying MCC's site-selection team took
off from the airport at Raleigh-Durham (the last site visited, on May
12, 1983) en route to Washington, D.C., Inman again asked the
team members how they ranked the four finalists. To minimize hier-
archial pressures, he called on the lowest-ranked MCC staff members first, working up to the higher officers. The admiral voted last.
Everyone put Austin ahead of the other three sites, although for
somewhat different reasons; Atlanta was second; Raleigh-Durham,
third; and San Diego, fourth.

This chapter describes the series of decisions and events that
moved Austin from being ranked last to first in a matter of four
weeks, as MCC's choice for its headquarters. We explain how infor-

mation was gathered, decisions made, and plans implemented by public and private actors working across institutional and organizational boundaries. As MCC's founders were learning how to collaborate with each other during the formation of MCC, the site-selection process would cause the nation's business, government, and university leaders to think differently about how public/private collaboration could foster educational excellence, create jobs, and accelerate regional economic development. An important theme emerged: for geographic regions to compete effectively (nationally and internationally), they must collaborate at the local level across public/private sectors.

Because MCC was a new type of organization, the site-selection process represented a series of unstructured decisions, with events being defined over time by the participants. Decision makers were not able to follow established routines, as nothing quite like MCC had existed previously in the United States. This chapter focuses on the various actors' contrasting viewpoints regarding the same series of events: different perceptions of how Austin won and how the other three finalists lost MCC. We give meaning to these perceptions through the words and insights of participants who were personally involved. We identify key individuals to add credibility and meaning to our analysis.[1]

THE TECHNOPOLIS FRAMEWORK

New kinds of relationships/alliances between public and private sectors—especially government, business, and academia—are having far-reaching consequences for the way people think about and implement economic development. This emerging reality is captured in the term "technopolis."[2] The modern technopolis interactively links technology commercialization with public and private sectors to promote regional economic development and technology diversification. Four factors are fundamental in the development of a region as a technopolis: (1) the achievement of scientific preeminence in technology-based research, (2) the development of new technologies for emerging industries, (3) the attraction of major technology companies, and (4) the creation of home-grown technology companies. (Smilor, Gibson, and Kozmetsky, 1988)

We use the "technopolis wheel" as an organizing framework for our discussion of technology-based regional economic development in general and the MCC site-selection process in particular. As depicted in Figure 3.1, the technopolis wheel emphasizes seven sectors: education, with particular emphasis on the research university; large corporations; emerging companies; federal, state, and local governments; and support groups. The framework also emphasizes the key role that individuals play in linking the seven segments of the wheel in collaborative activity. While the specific labels of each of the sectors of the wheel may vary across national boundaries, the framework is useful for analyzing technology-based economic development worldwide.[3]

On the one hand, a great deal of competition takes place among a region's companies, universities, and public- and private-sector entities. On the other hand, collaboration is essential for a technopolis to develop and provide a high quality of life for a region's populace, over time. Segments of the technopolis wheel must find ways to collaborate while competing. We use MCC's site-selection process to focus on the ability of first- and second-level influencers—in Austin, Atlanta, Raleigh-Durham, and San Diego—to link public- and private-sector entities to effect change.[4] First-level influencers, whether from a national or regional perspective, have a number of criteria in common (Smilor, Gibson, and Kozmetsky, 1988):

- They provide leadership in at least one segment of the technopolis wheel because of their established success in that segment.
- They maintain extensive personal and professional communication linkages to their counterparts in the other segments of the wheel.
- They have high credibility and function effectively within all segments of the wheel.
- They are visionaries who inspire others to action.

While first-level influencers set the vision, inspire, and get things started, it is the second-level influencers who carry through and enact these visions. Second-level influencers have the confidence and support of the first-level influencers in their own sector of operation, which facilitates their linkages with influencers in the other sectors of the technopolis wheel.

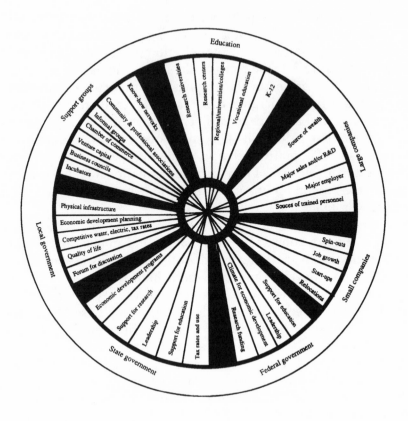

Source: Adapted from Smilor, Gibson, and Kozmetsky, 1988.

Figure 3.1 The technopolis wheel, emphasizing public/private collaboration across the academic, business, and government sectors

The linkages of first- and second-level influencers that cut across the sectors of the technopolis wheel are usually not formally organized. Influencers are commonly not formally rewarded for their boundary-spanning activities. Cross-institutional linkages are activated on a volunteer basis as required for specific projects or key events such as a particular economic development project (like the MCC site-selection process) or other regional projects such as improved education, environmental concerns, and other quality-of-life issues. Such influencers tend to see the connections, the possible synergy, that can be achieved in accomplishing tasks that require collaborative effort. Activities leading to such collaboration cannot be forced. We use the term "collaborative individualism" to identify the process by which individuals with disparate organizational affiliations voluntarily come together to accomplish specific tasks of limited duration. (Cunnington and Gibson, 1991)[5]

THE ANNOUNCEMENT THAT AUSTIN WON MCC

At a press conference on the state capitol lawn in Austin, Texas, on May 18, 1983, Governor Mark White; the chancellor of the University of Texas system; the presidents of The University of Texas at Austin and of Texas A&M University; the mayor of Austin; and Bobby Ray Inman announced that after an intense national competition, the nation's premier R&D consortium would locate in the capital city of the Lone Star State. This announcement was greeted with disbelief by many observers prominent in the U.S. high-tech industry. As Inman conceded in 1983: "There were some gulps" over the decision not to locate near any of the academic big three in electronics and computer science research: Carnegie Mellon, MIT, and Stanford (Walsh, 1983). Austin was not perceived as a major crossroads on the map of electronics centers in the United States. The public image of Texas tended to be projected by such media as the television prime-time series "Dallas" and, prior to that, by the movie *Giant*. But by the early 1980s, there was another, dynamic high-tech side of Texas, and Austin was on its way to becoming an emerging technopolis.

Admiral Inman announced to the press, just after the MCC competition, that any of the other three finalists—San Diego, Atlanta, and Raleigh-Durham—would have been an excellent choice, but Austin was selected after an intensive, exhaustive analysis. Governor White predicted glowingly that MCC would prove to be a turning point in the economic history of Texas. The event held great symbolic meaning for Texans, who wanted their state to be able to compete in the global, technology-based economy of the future. MCC's coming to Austin was compared to "Santa Rita #1" and the discovery of oil on university lands in 1923.[6] Indeed, "winning" MCC set off a dramatic two-year real estate boom in the city, which was followed by a steep downward plunge (see Chapter 6).

MCC was most valued not just for its projected $75 million annual budget and the 500 scientific and administrative jobs that it would add to the local economy but for the high-tech firms that were expected (by local community leaders) to follow MCC to Austin and to spin off from the R&D consortium.[7] As the competition for MCC progressed during the spring of 1983, expectations grew that the winning site would also become an important global center of high-technology microelectronics, perhaps someday rivaling northern California's Silicon Valley. Texans saw MCC as a means of creating high-value-added jobs and of diversifying the state's economy from its heavy dependency on agriculture, ranching, oil, and gas. Important state and community leaders (first-level influencers) saw winning MCC as a "must" event, essential for Texas' high-tech future.

EXPLODING MYTHS ABOUT WHY TEXAS WON

Numerous accounts of the 1983 MCC decision to locate in Austin appeared in the popular press and in scholarly publications (for example, Butler and Myers, 1984; Farley and Glickman, 1986; and Myers, 1987). Our present analysis, based on in-depth personal interviews with key participants, disputes several of the explanations provided to the public. For example, the media often quoted the mayor of Atlanta, Andrew Young, who stated dryly (as we quote at the top of this chapter): "I gather that Texas bought it." While Texas' financial incentives for MCC were considerable, the funding was only one of several reasons for MCC's site decision. It was not the most important reason why Austin won.

Most of the financial incentives were raised by the private sector and they went to Texas' two flagship universities: The University of Texas at Austin and Texas A&M University. Essentially, Texans gave the MCC incentives to themselves, as an investment in their future. As Admiral Iman said in May 1983: "What brought MCC to Austin more than any other single factor was the conviction that the investments which are now being accelerated by the University of Texas System and the Texas A&M System will make them absolute world-class leaders in computer science and electrical engineering at the graduate level. That was the magnet" (quoted in Coggins, 1983). We conclude that Austin did not win MCC because

Texas gave a large cash incentive to the consortium but rather because of the planned-for excellence of its research universities in microelectronics research and graduate education, which coincided with MCC's research agenda.

A second reason given by the popular press for MCC's selection of Austin was that the key decision maker concerning MCC's location was "a good ol' Texas boy." Inman was indeed born in Texas, and he had graduated from The University of Texas at Austin. But throughout most of the MCC decision process, he favored San Diego. Inman was raised south of Los Angeles. "I'm from Orange County. Everyone talks about me being from Texas. In fact, my family moved to Orange County when I was a teenager. That's where my voting residence was all my adult life" (Inman interview, January 26, 1987). At the time of the MCC site-selection process, one of Inman's sons was a student at the University of California at Irvine. Inman had strong friendships with several retired navy colleagues who lived in San Diego, and he was on the board of directors of a high-tech defense company (Science Applications International Corporation [SAIC]) located in the San Diego area. So in 1983, Inman had much stronger ties to San Diego than to Austin.

When it came down to the final vote by MCC's site-selection team, the members all favored locating in Austin before Inman cast his vote. He then made the decision unanimous and the site-selection team's recommendation was accepted by MCC's interim board of directors. We conclude that Austin did not win MCC because Admiral Inman personally favored the Texas location but rather in spite of the fact that he preferred another site, San Diego.

BREEDING IN A FISHBOWL

Because it was so public, MCC's site-selection process was highly unusual when compared to the traditional corporate selection of a plant site. Inman decided to conduct the process publicly for two reasons: (1) to ensure that regional leaders competing for MCC would fully understand and be committed to its purpose and (2) to guarantee sustained support for MCC from its shareholders.

At the December 6, 1982, MCC board meeting in Denver (at which the initial ten companies had agreed to form the consortium),

Inman observed the deep suspicions that existed among the share-holders. MCC represented an important shift for these firms from a position of total, if not hostile, competition toward R&D collaboration on cutting-edge technologies. Mass media coverage of MCC's site-selection process, Inman felt, "Would help nail down the support of the ten companies who had privately committed and of the two others who were wavering but were probably going to join." Inman realized that media coverage of MCC would bind the companies to the consensus they had agreed upon in private. "If they were 'breeding in a fishbowl,' they would be less likely to go back to their old mode of [competitive] operation," commented Inman. (interview, January 26, 1987)

Bob Rutishauser (interview, January 23, 1987) described the following scenario, which occurred in March 1983:

> I sat in his [Inman's] office [in a deserted Sperry building in Arlington, Virginia] one afternoon. It was about the middle of the site-selection process, and it was just incredible. About every ten minutes there would be a governor, a senator, a congressman, the president of some university, or the president of some big company calling. I sat in his office three hours and spent maybe fifteen minutes with him between calls trying to get some business done.

Why did MCC's site-selection process attract so much attention? Rutishauser (interview, January 23, 1987) noted: "There's always some excitement in a contest. We got an awful lot of ink because of this ex-spy starting this big venture to turn back the Japanese. The newspapers loved it. They had a ball." The level of public interest in MCC initially came as a surprise to the consortium's founders and to Inman. Governors were accompanied by mayors and other high-level officials and representatives from their states' most prestigious universities. Other cities, not to be outdone, then invited their governors and high-ranking officials to participate in their presentations. Such "tall timber" motivated the national media to give increased attention to MCC's site-selection process, which had by then become a national political and economic development competition.

This high level of public attention helped MCC reverse the nature of the usual industrial site-selection process from one of giving incentives to a city to one of being offered incentives by the competing sites, a phenomenon that has since become quite common. Thus, MCC, thanks in part to the media attention that it received, was able to shape the meanings involved in the location decision so as to become the "customer." MCC was courted in lavish style by many sellers. According to Inman:

> None of the reaction to the MCC contest was preconceived when I set out to do the site-selection process. Some of it was instinctive, and some of it developed as it went along. It was not part of a "grand strategy plan." A lot of the things which were forecast (e.g., . . . as job creation) were greatly blown out of context. But what was fascinating to me was that it picked up a life absolutely of its own. And that has continued. (interview, January 23, 1987)

MCC'S SITE-SELECTION PROCESS GETS STARTED

MCC arranged the site-selection competition so that (1) it generated favorable publicity about MCC (an objective to which the U.S. media enthusiastically contributed) and (2) each finalist was encouraged to offer maximum incentives. MCC was the central node in the network of competing cities (Figure 3.2). Finalist-to-finalist contact was discouraged. MCC's location decision process was, in part, a competition for information as well as a struggle by each competing city to keep its incentive package secret so as not to give competing sites any advantage.

Inman and MCC's headquarters staff drew up a list of seven cities that they thought would be desirable sites: Raleigh-Durham, San Antonio, Boston, San Francisco, San Jose, San Diego, and Austin. Each city was sent a letter inviting it to make a brief presentation at one of the hearings, to be held in Rosslyn, Virginia; San Francisco; or Chicago. A similar letter went to the directors of economic development in most states. Information about the site competition also appeared in computer magazines and electronics industry newsletters.

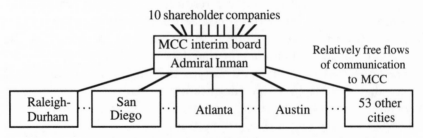

Figure 3.2 The main sites and information flows in the 1983 competition for MCC

Some states coordinated their offering to MCC and some did not. Pennsylvania's state officials sent a letter of support for Philadelphia's presentation, but as a result of poor communication failed to endorse Pittsburgh's bid (Metzenbaum, 1991). As Jan Schaffer of the *Philadelphia Inquirer* commented (May 29, 1983, p. 10-F): "The appearance of two cities from the same state battling for the headquarters left both feeling uncomfortable and MCC with the sense that the state government didn't care as much as it should about capturing the company." But the Keystone State did learn valuable lessons.

> The city [Philadelphia] offered to assist MCC in getting financing and it offered the fledgling company the orphaned Port of History Museum at Penn's Landing as a possible location. . . . The reasoning . . . was that because MCC's president . . . was a sailor, "he might like to be in the port museum. . . [one official commented]. There were a lot of questions they asked that we didn't really think about before." What became particularly apparent was the city's need to get a better grasp of its academic resources and to embellish its support for such resources. (Schaffer, 1983)

The primary reason that most of the cities and states jumped into the fray was to win prestige and to gain what was perceived to be an important foothold as a high-tech center. Local employment and a large company payroll were not the major inducements. Rather, MCC was seen to be a quick way of getting into the big leagues with Silicon Valley and Boston.

> By attracting a pure research firm, it could engineer the kind of coup that a city—even an entire state—could build its economic future around. . . . Publicity aside, the long-term benefits of such an enterprise look enormous. At the least, dozens of applied research and manufacturing facilities were sure to spring up around it. . . . here was one of the surefire launching pads to the marketplace of the twenty-first century. (Kahn, 1983)

Universities often got involved because they saw increased funding and prestige. Winning MCC would attract quality faculty and students to their institutions, which would translate into increased research funding. Community business leaders and developers saw increased profits and escalating real-estate prices, some even offered free land as an inducement to MCC. Government officials saw enhanced re-election prospects flowing from moving their state from traditional sources of wealth and jobs to high tech. And at times, state politicians and community leaders seemed to revel in the contest, trying to outdo each other for increased national attention and recognition. Other public and private leaders, however, decided MCC was not worth the time or effort.

Regional first- and second-level influencers were not usually activated through MCC's formal, planned announcements, but rather through unplanned, often serendipitous events and personal contacts—very tenuous "switches" for an event as important as the MCC site-selection process, which grew to national and international importance.

Dan Pegg, president of San Diego's Economic Development Commission, headed his city's campaign for MCC. Early in the process, San Diego (along with San Antonio, which did not make the final four) was the best-informed of the competing sites. Pegg first became aware of MCC in late 1982 through news items in the computer trade press. Pegg expected that MCC would soon be looking for a location. Then, on February 10, 1983, Pegg read a news story that Admiral Inman had been selected to head the consortium. This news triggered Pegg to action. San Diego was a navy town, and Pegg reasoned that a retired admiral, such as Inman, would have to have been stationed in San Diego sometime during his career. Pegg began checking around.

> San Diego is a bastion for retired admirals. We got hold of an Admiral Sharp, who turned us on to a couple of other admirals. We had a quick meeting with Herb Klein [a former White House official in the Richard Nixon era, who lived in San Diego], who gave us names of people who knew Inman. Admiral "Red Dog" Davis was a good old buddy of his. We had to network through several people to get Inman's unlisted home phone number in Arlington, Virginia. I called him, tracked him down, and found out that he was right here in San Diego! He's on the board of directors of SAIC, a high-tech defense contractor right up here in La Jolla. Inman was staying at the La Jolla Village Hotel. I said: "Look, we want to be involved in this."
> (Pegg interview, July 14, 1986)

Admiral Inman and Pegg discussed San Diego as a possible site for MCC. Their conversations continued by telephone for the next several months, and the information that was exchanged was valuable to San Diego's campaign for MCC. Dan Pegg explained his successful use of personal networks by stating (interview, July 14, 1986): "Look, it's an incestuous world."[8]

Atlanta just barely made it to the Chicago presentations on March 18, 1983. The state government had somehow ignored or lost the February letter inviting it to apply for the MCC site. Governor Joe Frank Harris called MCC's temporary office in Arlington, Virginia, at the very last minute, on the morning of the day of the Chicago presentations. Governor Harris said that Georgia had an important story to tell. The day's schedule for presentations was already filled, with plans to end at 3:00 P.M. However, Governor Harris was told that "There might be a few [MCC] people who would stick around for a little while."

If individuals could contact Admiral Inman or others involved with MCC, and if they knew what to ask, a city's official could become well informed. However, many potential site locations did not even learn of the contest until after the preliminary competition had been decided. How Austin learned about the MCC competition, and became actively engaged in it, is a rather fascinating set of stories. We elaborate this point because of its crucial importance to understanding how public/private influencers are activated. If an actor (individual, city, state) is not activated to move on an opportunity or a problem, little can happen.[9]

THE SAN ANTONIO CONNECTION

The state of Texas initially got into the MCC competition through the initiative of Dr. Henry G. Cisneros, mayor of San Antonio, the nation's tenth largest city, located 80 miles south of Austin. In 1983, Cisneros was the only Spanish-surnamed mayor of a major U.S. city. A Texas A&M- and Harvard-educated native son, who grew up in a barrio in San Antonio, Cisneros led his city through a coalition of the Hispanic and Anglo power structures. Democratic party presidential candidate Walter Mondale seriously considered Cisneros as his running mate in 1984. Cisneros served on Governor Clinton's presidental campaign committee in 1992, and in 1993, he was appointed Secretary of Housing and Urban Development.[10]

In early 1983, as San Antonio's mayor, Cisneros completed a city planning document called "Target 90," which provided San Antonio's public and private leaders with a vision of the city's future. It stressed high-tech economic development as a means to create jobs and wealth, so that both Hispanics and Anglos would benefit from economic progress. Cisneros was ready for something like MCC to come along, perhaps more than any other mayor of a U.S. city.

How Cisneros learned about MCC tells something about the value of having public officials who are well connected (i.e., cosmopolites) in formal and informal communication networks that span public/private sectors and geographic regions (Figure 3.3).

> I first heard about MCC from William Norris of Control Data, when I met him in his office. I had given a talk to an employees' group at CDC [in Minneapolis]. Norris told me about the Japanese fifth-generation

computer threat, and about forming the consortium. . . .
He told me to keep my ear to the ground, and later he
sent me some material about MCC. [CDC had a manufacturing facility in San Antonio.]

When I heard that Inman was hired, I called him
at his home on a Saturday. . . . I called him from
Austin, where I was speaking at the LBJ School. Inman
told me about Chicago. We went to work on our [San
Antonio's] presentation right away. (Cisneros interview,
February 16, 1987)

Admiral Inman described the same event from his perspective:

There were never any formal announcements from us
[that is, except for the initial letters from the consor-
tium] about the MCC site selection. We relied entirely
on calling from community leaders who had read what
was in the national news media. . . . A lot of the people
called from the various cities to ask questions. The
most focused and the most thoughtful questions came
from Henry Cisneros. I didn't have an MCC office in
Washington yet. He called my residence, introduced
himself to my wife as to who he was. Very polite, very
concise. He'd be grateful for a return call. I did return
the call. He knew exactly what to ask about the nature
of MCC. He absolutely understood what we were looking for and why. (interview, January 26, 1987)

Narcisso Cano, director of economic and employment development for the city of San Antonio and Cisneros's boyhood friend
and college chum at Texas A&M, first heard of MCC when the
mayor called him into his office and showed him a Minneapolis
newspaper clipping about the forthcoming MCC competition.
Norm Berg, a CDC vice president and Bill Norris's right-hand man
on such issues, had mailed the newspaper clipping to Cisneros (see
Figure 3.3). "Through all this, Henry [Cisneros] was talking by
phone to Bill Norris [about MCC]. Bill was not giving away the
store, but he was kind of cueing Henry as to what to do, what to
say." (Cano interview, February 16, 1987)

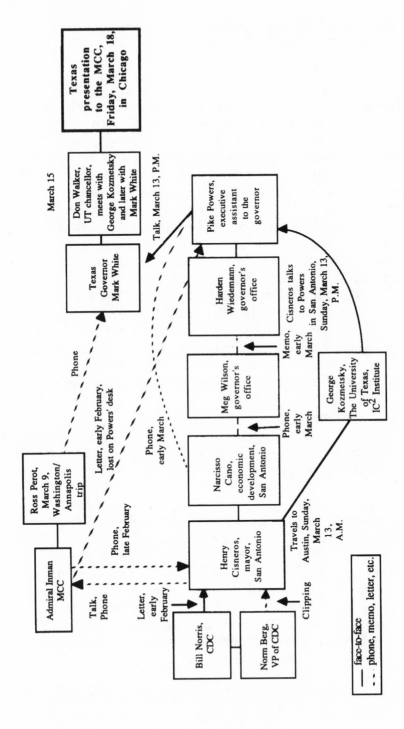

Figure 3.3 Communication flows in activating Governor Mark White to attract MCC to Texas

THE SERENDIPITOUS ACTIVATION OF AUSTIN AND
THE STATE OF TEXAS

Even though San Antonio was actively pursuing MCC, the city of Austin slumbered. That situation changed as the result of two important "switching events" that occurred on February 27, 1983, just after Admiral Inman had given a public lecture at the LBJ School of Public Affairs at The University of Texas at Austin.[11] Dr. Bill Livingston, vice president for graduate studies at the university, attended the presentation and talked with Inman about MCC. The next day Livingston called Ben Head, president of the Austin Chamber of Commerce, to alert him to the importance of MCC (Figure 3.4). Another exemplar of informal network activation was Bernard Goss, who worked for Austin's Department of Water and Wastewater. Goss also attended Inman's presentation, and he also approached the admiral to ask whether Austin had indicated an interest in MCC. Inman said he didn't think so. Goss was surprised and vowed to do something about it.[12] The next morning, he telephoned his friend John Gray, who managed economic development activities for Austin's Chamber of Commerce. It was only 18 days until Austin would make its presentation to MCC at the O'Hare Airport Hilton in Chicago. That is, if Austin were to make a presentation.

As Gray remembered:

> My first warning of the whole thing [MCC] came from a personal friend by the name of Bernard Goss, an analyst in the Department of Water and Wastewater, a very energetic, activist-type person. That [Goss's] phone call gave me at least a two- or three-day jump on getting into action. . . . Formal notification came down through the University of Texas, from Dr. Bill Livingston. He called the Austin Chamber of Commerce president, Ben Head, a banker. But during those three [extra] days that Goss gave me, I was bustin' my buttons. One of the first things I did was call Del Asmussen [a CDC executive] in Minnesota, and he told me the deal. (interview, January 22, 1987)

After Gray had obtained the list of MCC site-selection criteria from Del Asmussen, he penciled a page of notes showing how well

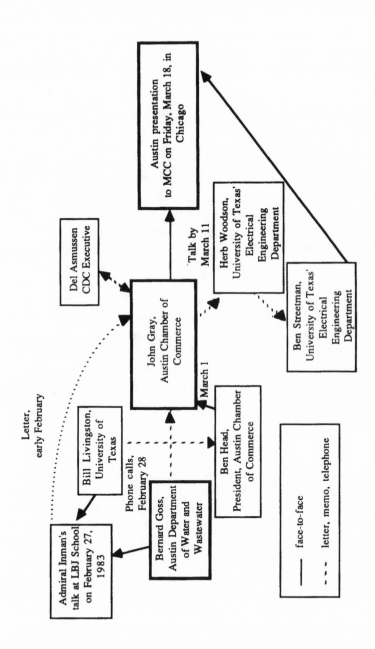

Figure 3.4 Communication flows in activating the city of Austin to enter the competition for MCC

Austin fulfilled each point. These notes were to become the outline for his presentation in Chicago. Gray particularly noted the MCC criterion concerning university excellence in electrical engineering and computer science. The March 18 presentation was to consist of a scheduled one and a half hours for the state of Texas, with 20 minutes allocated to each of three cities: Dallas, Austin, and San Antonio.

REGIONAL COLLABORATION THROUGH VISIONARY LEADERS

On March 13, 1983, an important turning point concerning MCC occurred for Texas when Mayor Henry Cisneros drove from San Antonio to Austin to discuss the forthcoming competition with Dr. George Kozmetsky, director of the IC^2 Institute at the University of Texas. It proved to be an eventful meeting (see Figure 3.3).

Kozmetsky was familiar with MCC from its media coverage and through his network of high-technology friends. In fact, he had known of the consortium since the initial meeting in Orlando a year previously. So when Cisneros phoned to discuss San Antonio's bid for MCC, Kozmetsky knew that it was important. He arranged for a 6:30 A.M. Sunday meeting. Cisneros, accompanied by a couple of San Antonio's leaders, drove the 80 miles to meet with Kozmetsky at the IC^2 Institute building in Austin. Kozmetsky is well known for his early-morning work habits; in any event, he and his wife, Ronya, had a social event later that morning and he was scheduled to fly to New York that afternoon.

Cisneros wanted advice on how he might position San Antonio to make an effective bid for MCC. The mayor knew that San Antonio's Achilles' heel was the city's lack of a nationally prominent engineering school. He asked Kozmetsky to help him obtain engineering expertise for San Antonio, from the University of Texas and Texas A&M. He asked about the possibility of setting up academic and telecommunications linkages with the state's two flag-ship universities. Kozmetsky told him that other Texas cities were going to try for MCC and it was essential to make a Texas presenta-tion to Inman and the MCC committee. That meant both The University of Texas at Austin and Texas A&M University had to get on board the MCC campaign. The logical route to that end was to activate the governor of Texas, Mark White.

Donald Walker, chancellor of the University of Texas system, telephoned Kozmetsky in New York on Monday, March 14, to request a briefing about MCC, prior to his forthcoming Tuesday meeting with the governor. Kozmetsky flew back from New York on Monday evening so that he could meet Walker early Tuesday morning. Kozmetsky told Walker that many of Texas' young people, educated at state expense by the University of Texas system, were migrating to California in order to find employment in high-tech electronics jobs. MCC represented one means of keeping these talented young people in Texas, so that they could repay the state for its investment in their education.

Walker and Kozmetsky discussed the basic strategy underlying Texas' bid for MCC: raise funds to endow professorships in computer and electrical engineering at the University of Texas in order to improve microelectronics research. This strategy amounted to Texans throwing a forward pass and then running out to catch it.[13] That Tuesday evening, March 15, George and Ronya Kozmetsky attended a dinner party (hosted by Austin lawyer Sam Winters) with Dr. Peter T. Flawn, president of the University of Texas; Bill Hobby, lieutenant governor; a wealthy Austinite who was a big donor to the university; plus other academic and business leaders. The guest list was carefully orchestrated to ensure that several MCC enthusiasts were present. Several guests emphasized the importance of MCC as a means of expanding Texas' microelectronics industry. President Flawn expressed reluctance about involving the University of Texas in such a for-profit enterprise. But gradually, his objections faded somewhat in light of the others' enthusiasm. Eventually, the university was to become the cornerstone of "The Texas Incentive for Austin."

HOW A KEY "SWITCH" GOT ACTIVATED

The first link between San Antonio and the Texas state government took place in Phoenix, Arizona, at a weekend workshop of the Small Business Technology Insitute. This serendipitous personal connection occurred on February 8, 1983, Saturday morning, during the conference when Meg Wilson, an official in the Texas governor's office, met Narcisso Cano. They talked about high-tech public policy and realized that they saw eye-to-eye on most matters. Then in early March, Cano phoned Wilson at the Texas state capital (see Figure 3.3) and told her about the forthcoming MCC site-selection competition. Wilson sent a memo about MCC to her boss, Harden Wiedemann. Cano also telephoned Pike Powers, to alert him about MCC.

Pike Powers (interview, March 27, 1986) takes full blame for being unresponsive to several attempts to alert him to the crucial significance of MCC:

> The original communiqué came from somewhere [it was MCC] about how important MCC was. . . . It came to my desk in the governor's office, and I put it in a big stack. Bill Livingston called me to say that I'd better get the governor interested. I still failed to do so. February 1983 was extremely busy, hectic. Mark White was sworn in on January 18, and we went immediately into a full-tilt fray about whether 200 appointments ought to be recalled from the Texas Senate. We were busy on a lot of things. We were brand new, with all hell breaking loose on all fronts. This is all rather strange, given that Mark White got me to come to work as his executive assistant in order to do some innovative economic development things. White had asked, "Would you help me develop a game plan like what Jim Hunt has done in North Carolina and what Henry Cisneros is doing in San Antonio?" I had said that I would.

Cisneros tracked Powers down in San Antonio, where he was vacationing with his family at the Four Seasons Hotel (see Figure 3.3). He explained the high-stakes nature of MCC and that it was essential to get Governor White behind the effort. Powers canceled his short-lived vacation and drove back to Austin. He talked to the governor that night. Monday morning, Governor White called a breakfast meeting at the governor's mansion to launch the state of Texas' push for MCC.

So the governor's office got in late, quickly, and accidentally. "Henry [Cisneros] was the catalyst behind the whole thing. He energized the state. Then he transformed that energy over to the governor, who ran like a son of a bitch with it." (Cano interview, February 16, 1987)

ENTHUSIASM AND LUCK

Governor White canceled his appointments for March 18 so that he could lead the Texas delegation at Chicago. Realizing that the quest for academic excellence at his state's research universities was important to MCC, he asked the chancellor of the University of Texas system, Donald Walker, and the chancellor of the Texas A&M system, Arthur Hansen, to accompany him to Chicago. Three Texas cities made their bids as part of the state's presentation:

- Dallas' presentation was made by an official from the city's chamber of commerce.
- The San Antonio group was led by Mayor Cisneros and included his economic development coordinator, Narcisso Cano, and General McDermott, founder and CEO of USAA, the huge insurance company that serves military people throughout the world and is one of the largest employers in the city.
- Austin was represented by John Gray of the Austin Chamber of Commerce and Dr. Ben Streetman, a professor of electrical engineering at the University of Texas.

As Gray (interview, January 22, 1987) recalled:

I didn't hardly sleep the night before I was to make the Chicago presentation, running it over and over in my mind as to just how to best use the brief amount of time. Twenty minutes to sell the city, to tell them all about it, to convey in words the uniqueness of Austin. I felt a heavy weight on my shoulders. . . . I just had to wing it. I handed out our thick, colored brochures about the city at the end of my presentation. I never talked so fast in my life. . . . I had told Ben Streetman to prepare for five minutes, but I short-potted him. Nevertheless, he made a valiant effort in two minutes to tell about electronics research at the university. . . . How he was trying to attract the top talent.

In Admiral Inman's opinion, Ben Streetman's presentation in the O'Hare Airport Hilton saved the day for Austin. "Thank God they had added Ben Streetman. For a couple of minutes, Ben Streetman talked about the nature of [microelectronics] research at UT. He struck sparks and created excitement" (Inman interview, January 26, 1987). Gray had invited Streetman on something of a fluke. When Gray realized what MCC was looking for, he had phoned someone at UT with whom he had worked previously on economic development matters, Professor Herb Woodson of the Department of Electrical Engineering (see Figure 3.4). But Woodson was tied up the day of the Chicago presentation. Gray remembered:

> Herb said: "We've got a young man by the name of Ben Streetman that we just recruited and he's great, but he's in New York for a meeting. . . ." As luck would have it, he was coming home from New York that day [March 18], and agreed to return via Chicago. I met him in the lobby of the O'Hare Hilton Hotel, and we had just a minute to get acquainted. Then we made our presentation to MCC in that tiny hotel room. (interview, January 22, 1987)

Room 200-1 at the O'Hare Airport Hilton Hotel was spartan and packed with Admiral Inman and his six-member MCC committee plus several Texas officials. Some sat on the hotel's hideaway bed. UT Chancellor Donald Walker and the Texas A&M System Chancellor, Arthur Hansen, made their presentations. Inman remembered: "The only humor during the Chicago presentations occurred when I stopped the proceedings to tell my MCC colleagues that they were watching a minor miracle. . . . It [the University of Texas and the Texas A&M promise of collaboration] was a big hit" (interview, January 26, 1987). While scheduled for one and a half hours, the Texas presentation was allowed to run somewhat longer. The Texans took that to be a good sign. It was, for Austin.

Inman (interview, January 26, 1987) gave high marks to the San Antonio presentation in Chicago:

> Henry [Cisneros] came in and told us what they would do to help us get settled if we came to his city. He had gotten bankers to commit to a package of guaranteed lending below FHA mortgage rates, set up a relocation

office, things like that they would do to help us. The only thing he did not have was a graduate-level university. But it was, without anyone else [being] even close, the best-focused presentation, directly tailored to the needs of our new organization.

Rutishauser (interview, January 23, 1987) remembered:

Henry Cisneros made the San Antonio presentation come alive. He did a beautiful job of creating a vision and [showed] enthusiasm and credibility that they could fulfill the role [as the site for MCC]. But San Antonio had a fatal flaw. Cisneros did not have the basic materials [a strong university program in microelectronics].

When San Antonio was not chosen as one of the four MCC finalist sites, Cisneros' strategy for his city became the Austin and Texas strategy for winning MCC.

Inman:	When I called Governor Mark White on April 5 with the good news about Austin, he instantly zeroed in on the Chicago presentation, analyzing exactly what the strong points were . . . what the weaknesses were . . . looking for my reaction. What Governor Mark White was doing was creating a statewide group to essentially duplicate and broaden Henry Cisneros' plan.
Interviewer:	What Austin did in the final site competition was pretty much what San Antonio did in Chicago?
Inman:	You've got it. If San Antonio had had academic excellence, we probably wouldn't have gone any further. We would have settled on San Antonio. (interview, January 26, 1987)

If Austin had not been successful in Chicago, MCC would have been lost to Texas. How Austin did it was a matter of luck and timing, committed first- and second-level influencers communicating across public and private sectors—plus San Antonio's lack of a major research university.

SELECTING THE FOUR FINALISTS

During the first preliminary presentations that were made in Rosslyn, Virginia, on February 23, 1983, six sites told their story: Baltimore; Boston; Fairfax County, Virginia; Philadelphia; Pittsburgh; and Research Triangle, North Carolina. At the presentations in San Francisco on March 3, five California cities were on the agenda (San Diego, Orange County, the San Francisco area and minipresentations on San Jose and Sacramento) along with Phoenix and Tuscon, Arizona; Portland, Oregon; and Salt Lake City, Utah. MCC suggested that the governor's office of economic development coordinate the state's presentation. Lieutenant Governor Leo McCarthy came to San Francisco, along with several other state officials. News of this participation by high state government officials spread quickly and inspired Arizona Governor Bruce Babbitt to introduce the Phoenix and Tuscon presentations. Lt. Governor McCarthy scheduled a press conference following the San Francisco presentation. By the end of the day, the Arizona media were also on the scene, interviewing Governor Babbitt, who commented:

> Admiral Inman and his associates toured the country like an imperial court, as mayors and governors extolled the virtues of their respective sites and offered up such tangible inducements as real estate, research facilities, and endowed professorships. . . . The great MCC bidding war marks a special chapter in American industrial history. (Babbitt, 1984)

Admiral Inman describes what happened next, in Chicago on March 18: "We had huge delegations. Governors from five of the six states: Ohio, Minnesota, Michigan, Colorado, Texas, and Georgia. . . . And there were television cameras. By this point, it [the site-selection process] had taken on a major public life of its own" (interview, January 26, 1987). As the media buildup continued through March, additional states and cities insisted that they also be considered. So a fourth round of presentations was scheduled in Washington, D.C., on March 28, with New Hampshire, Illinois, Missouri, and Florida sending delegations. Several other states and cities mailed their proposals directly to Inman.

During February and March 1983, Inman and MCC's representatives heard or read presentations from 57 cities in 27 states. At MCC's board of directors meeting on April 6, 1983, they began to work on cutting the candidate sites down to a short list of finalists. MCC had initially identified six criteria for the site-selection process:

- a supportive state and local government,
- a high quality of life to support the recruitment of top-notch research personnel (including reasonable housing costs and quality schools for the children of MCC's employees),
- existing high-tech industry and a supportive business environment,
- a large potential employee base,
- a quality transportation infrastructure, which included both commuting time for high-tech employees and airline connections to the headquarters of MCC's founding members, and
- overall cost of operation.

To this list, Inman had added a seventh factor: proximity to centers of academic excellence at the graduate level in computer science and electrical engineering. Inman emphasized that MCC's site should be more than just a location that would allow MCC to get under way rapidly; it should also be a sustaining kind of environment, where the consortium could continue to prosper and hire its own talent locally if needed.

While MCC wanted to be located near a leading research university with quality programs in computer science and electrical engineering, it was decided not to locate the consortium near the top-tier schools. There was concern with "saturation" at existing research centers such as Silicon Valley and the Boston area, and there was concern about the high employee turnover rate in these areas. MCC wanted to grow with a strong research university and benefit from a long-term flow of fresh talent, and the consortium wanted to be located in an area where it could be a major player and not have its activities fade into the background (Metzenbaum, 1991). As Inman stated in 1983:

> We would clearly have had to pay a premium for being there [near Carnegie Mellon, MIT, Stanford] and it was a conscious judgment by the board that we were ultimately better off in a long-term building process if we could find the right climate and place at the next level, but still with a very established base of computer science and electrical engineering. (Walsh, 1983)

Close ties with a major research university were important to MCC for three other reasons. First, the consortium could leverage its research activities with university faculty and graduate students as well as university-based laboratories. Second, MCC could begin its research activities more rapidly by not having to wait the approximately two years that it would take to build and equip a permanent headquarters faculty. Third, recruiting outstanding researchers could be facilitated with the lure of an adjunct university professorship and collegial ties with researchers working in common areas of interest.

Fifteen candidate cities emerged from this preliminary scoring process. The committee then narrowed the field down to seven and then to four finalists by eliminating sites on the basis of their most negative aspects. Many of the 57 sites did not make the final 4 because they lacked one fundamentally important resource: a major research university with the capacity to be in the top tier in the near future. While none of the four finalists was ranked highest on all seven criteria, not having access to one or more research universities that were strong in microelectronics and computer science caused otherwise excellent candidates to be dropped from the list.

Eliminations were also made on the basis of subjective criteria, like quality of life. About half of MCC's shareholder companies had facilities located in the Sunbelt, and MCC planned to recruit many of its employees from these locations. MCC's founders believed that getting the "best and brightest" to move north would be difficult. So in terms of climate, the Sunbelt cities had an advantage. The personal views of MCC's shareholder participants were also given considerable weight. One potential site was eliminated from being a finalist because a member of the committee was quite outspoken about his unpleasant memories of having lived there. "He was so eloquent about the strength of his views that [the Sunbelt city] fell off the list." (interview, January 26, 1987)

According to Inman, a main reason for the Sunbelt location of all four finalists was a result of the major problems then being experienced by the older industrial areas in the North. Rustbelt sites that might have been on the list were at the time in a serious economic downturn that limited what they could offer MCC. For example, Ann Arbor, Michigan, was almost a finalist, but as Inman explained: "Governor Blanchard left his MCC presentation [on March 18 in Chicago] to announce cuts in the state government's investments and in public education to meet a large state budget deficit. Frankly, if that had not occurred, we might have had five finalist sites instead of four." (interview, January 26, 1987)

MCC's founders also tried not to give a special location advantage to any particular shareholder company. The headquarters of MCC's ten founding member companies were clustered in California, Minneapolis, and the Northeast (see Figure 2.9). If a neutral site were to be found, Silicon Valley was out, as were the Twin Cities of Minneapolis–Saint Paul, Boston, and the Big Apple. Palle Smidt (interview, June 2, 1993), one of MCC's interim board members, countered that such an objection was nonsense. What was of some concern, he commented, was wanting MCC to be a major player in the area in which it located. Furthermore, proximity to the operating divisions of a number of shareholders was not an issue. "We were to be concerned with long-term, goal-directed research at MCC. It's only when you are involved in project-based research that you need to be close to services of supply and manufacturing."

The four finalists almost went to three by dropping Atlanta. But the positive impact of Dr. Joseph Pettit's presentation in Chicago, three weeks earlier, swung MCC's board to include Atlanta. Pettit was the president of Georgia's prestigious Institute of Technology. Research Triangle was solidly supported by several MCC shareholder companies who knew that area through the Semiconductor Research Consortium (SRC) and had investigated the area as a possible site for their own companies' operations.

Existing collaboration among the area's three universities was a plus, as was Governor Hunt's drive to foster science and technology education in North Carolina.

So getting to the final four was largely a matter of (1) "can't-change criteria," at least in the short run, as well as (2) subjective evaluations such as a perceived high quality of life.

Each of the four finalist locations had the basic infrastructure to serve as MCC's national headquarters, so from there on out, winning was a matter of accessing and evaluating information to overcome weaknesses and to provide MCC, the customer, with what it wanted. The four finalists were given two weeks in April–May 1983 to ready their final offer. MCC's shareholder companies were concerned about the speed with which the Japanese ICOT Project was moving. They felt pressed to quickly identify a headquarters location so the consortium could begin recruiting employees and get its R&D activities under way. Participants in the competing cities and states often interpreted this rush for a location as a "test" by ex-CIA deputy director Inman to determine how well they could operate under pressure with limited information. Indeed, under such time pressure, the chances of winning depended directly on the degree to which finalists could (1) rapidly obtain detailed information about what MCC was looking for in a site, (2) construct their offer so that it would give MCC's decision makers what they wanted, and (3) learn crucial information about the strategy and offerings of the competing sites while keeping secret the details of their own MCC incentives.

On April 12, MCC telephoned, then mailed site-selection criteria to the four finalist sites. Austin had 15 days before MCC's fact-finding team was to arrive (Table 3.1). This was to be a "one-stop shopping process." There would be no second chances, no opportunity to make up for the lack of a critical component or for coming up short with an offer to MCC.

HOW AUSTIN AND TEXAS WON MCC

Austin was more successful than San Diego, Atlanta, and Raleigh-Durham in attracting MCC because Texas' first- and second-level influencers more accurately perceived what MCC was looking for and fulfilled these expectations through statewide

Table 3.1 Information flows between MCC and the governor's and Austin task forces

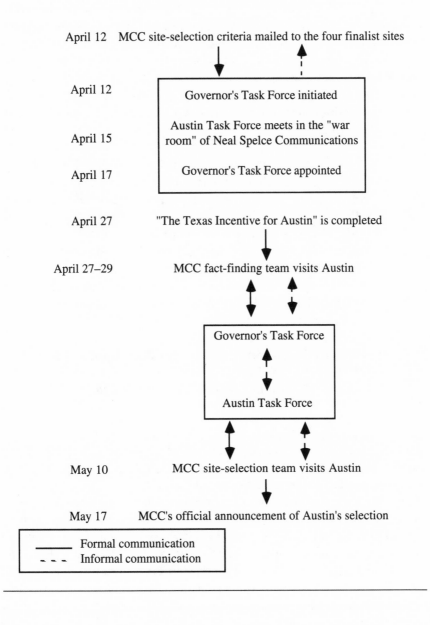

public/private collaboration. There were two MCC site visits at each of the four locations: the first by a preliminary four-person fact finding team and the second (about two weeks later) by a six-person site-selection committee who were all members of MCC's board of directors. The second group was chaired by Inman. When forming both the fact-finding and the site-selection groups, Inman asked for volunteers who would represent geographic spread and the diversity of MCC member companies.

The fact-finding team visited each of the four finalist sites to inspect possible facilities for MCC's headquarters and to collect information on:

- Access to a local university that was considered to be a leader or potential leader in graduate teaching and research in electrical engineering and computer science
- Quality of life in such areas as primary and secondary education facilities, affordable housing, and recreational and cultural amenities
- Airline connections to the major metropolitan areas where MCC member companies were headquartered
- State and local government support for MCC's operations
- Overall cost of operating MCC at the proposed site

THE GOVERNOR'S AND AUSTIN TASK FORCES

On April 12, 1983, Pike Powers began to appoint the Governor's Task Force for MCC, which included individuals with financial and political clout, business and government expertise, and academic prestige (Table 3.2). Ross Perot, then chairman of Electronic Data Systems (EDS), and EDS company president Mort Myerson were the only two individuals from the private sector who did not live in Austin. Business representatives on the Governor's Task Force included developers John P. Watson (The Watson Group) and Daron Butler (Austin Industrial Interests); Ed Hanslik (partner, Arthur Andersen), and two bankers, Ben Head (chairman and CEO of RepublicBank Austin and chairman of the board of Austin's Chamber of Commerce) and Robert Lane (chairman, InterFirst Bank, Austin).

Table 3.2 Members of the Governor's Task Force for MCC

I. Business
    • John Watson, president, The Watson Group, Austin
      developer, chair of both the Governor's Task Force and
      Austin Task Force for MCC*
    • Daron Butler, Austin Industrial Interests*
    • Ed Hanslik, partner in Austin's division of Arthur
      Andersen, Inc., economic development VP, Austin Chamber
      of Commerce*
    • Ben Head, CEO and chairman, RepublicBank Austin and
      president, Austin Chamber of Commerce*
    • H. Ross Perot, chairman, Electronic Data Systems
      Corp., Dallas
    • Mort Myerson, president, Electronic Data Systems
      Corp., Dallas
    • Robert Lane, chairman, InterFirst Bank, Austin
II. Government
    • Mark White, governor
    • Pike Powers, partner, Fulbright and Jaworski law firm, and
      executive assistant to Governor White*
    • Harden Wiedemann, director, governor's office of planning*
    • Henry Cisneros, mayor of San Antonio
    • Narcisso Cano, director of economic development, city
      of San Antonio
III. Academia
    • Jon Newton, chairman, board of regents, University
      of Texas system
    • Robert Baldwin, vice chairman, board of regents, UT-Austin
    • Donald Walker, chancellor, University of Texas system
    • Skip Porter, director of the Engineering Experiment Station at
      Texas A&M University

*These six individuals also served on the Austin Task Force for MCC.

State government was represented by Governor White and his executive assistant, Pike Powers (managing partner, Fulbright and Jaworski) and his director of the office of planning and intergovernmental relations, Harden Wiedemann. The Governor's Task Force also had participation from Mayor Henry Cisneros of San Antonio and his director for economic and employment development, Narcisso Cano. The strategy and style of San Antonio's presentation for MCC that had so impressed MCC representatives in Chicago were adopted and used by Austin. "It was a formal transfer in substance and process," remembered Meg Wilson, then assistant to the governor (interview, August 8, 1993). "Henry [Cisneros] and Narcisso [Cano] came and told us, and we listened."

The academic sector was represented by Jon P. Newton, chairman, and Robert B. Baldwin, III, vice chairman of the University of Texas system's board of regents; the chancellor of the University of Texas system, Donald Walker; and the director of the Engineering Experiment Station at Texas A&M University, Skip Porter. Six who served on the Governor's Task Force for MCC—Watson, Butler, Hanslick, Head, Weidemann, and Powers—also served on the Austin Task Force. Watson was the chair of both groups.

The Austin Task Force for MCC (Table 3.3) had a core group of 12 public and private influencers who represented business, state, government, and academia. In addition to Watson, Butler, Head, and Hanslik, business representatives on the Austin Task Force included two public relations specialists: Neal Spelce, chairman and CEO, and Howard Falkenberg, president, Neal Spelce Communications, an Austin-based public relations firm. Falkenberg was largely responsible for coordinating, writing, and editing "The Texas Incentive for Austin." Powers, Weidemann, and Meg Wilson (assistant to the governor) represented the governor's office on the Austin Task Force. The academic sector was represented by two midlevel administrators: Mary Roberts from Texas A&M and Clif Drummond from UT-Austin. Other volunteers on the Austin task force came and went as needed. Fourteen-hour work days were volunteered and support equipment and supplies were donated.

As volunteers coming from the state's public and private sectors, the "Texas team" (which included both the governor's and Austin task forces) brought together a broad range of business and professional expertise as well as an expanded network of personal contacts—statewide—in business, academia, and government. A few of the first-level influencers—like Governor White, Ross Perot, Jon Newton, Robert Baldwin, and Donald Walker—enjoyed considerable statewide clout. As a team, these individuals could personally access a broad network of resources.[14]

Table 3.3
Members of the Austin Task Force for MCC

I.   Business
   • John Watson, president, The Watson Group, and chair*
   • Daron Butler, Austin Industrial Interests*
   • Ed Hanslik, partner in Austin's division of Arthur Andersen, Inc.*
   • John Gray, manager, economic development, Austin Chamber of Commerce
   • Neal Spelce, chairman and CEO, Neal Spelce Communications
   • Harold Falkenberg, president, Neal Spelce Communications
   • Ben Head, CEO and chairman, RepublicBank Austin and president, Austin Chanber of Commerce*
II. Government†
   • Pike Powers, executive assistant to Governor White*
   • Meg Wilson, assistant to the governor
   • Harden Wiedemann, director, governor's office of planning*
III. Academia
   • Mary Roberts, Texas A&M University
   • Clif Drummond, research coordinator, Center for Energy Studies, The University of Texas at Austin

* These six individuals also served on the Governor's Task Force for MCC.
† In addition, San Antonio Mayor Henry Cisneros and Narcisso Cano, San Antonio's director of economic and employment development, joined the Austin Task Force for several sessions.

INMAN'S SECRET VISIT TO AUSTIN

In interviews with key players involved with MCC, we frequently received different interpretations of the same event. To help deal with this methodological problem, we used multiple sources of data to formulate accounts of key events. We provide examples of different explanations of the same event when such multiple interpretations are informative.

Inman's NSA and CIA background colored how people perceived his involvement with MCC. During our interviews with public and private officials from Texas and other states, several respondents mentioned a "secret visit" to Austin by the admiral and his wife. One individual told us that the Inmans had mysteriously slipped into the city, looked around, and then disappeared without the mass media's being tipped off. Someone else insisted that it was during this secret visit that the admiral actually decided to locate MCC in Austin; the rest of the selection process was just a façade. No one could tell us the exact date of the secret visit, but several individuals insisted that it was just prior to the first MCC site visit to Austin on April 27, 1983. Others claimed that it was months before, perhaps thinking of Inman's visit to Austin during his family's tour of the United States, after he retired from the navy in July 1982.

We provide two accounts of this "secret visit" to Austin: Inman's (the visitor) and John Gray's (the host). These contrasting versions of the same event provide a Rashomon-like story, showing that reality is indeed in the eye of the beholder.

By the time of MCC's site-selection process, Gray had accumulated several impressive successes during his 17 years as manager of economic development for Austin's Chamber of Commerce. He had helped to recruit Houston Instruments in 1965, Texas Instruments and Burroughs in 1966, IBM in 1967, Motorola in 1974, and then, in fairly rapid succession, Data General, AMD, Tandem, ROLM, Schlumberger, and Fisher Controls.

Gray was a 1942 graduate of The University of Texas at Austin. When we interviewed him on January 22, 1987, in his office at an Austin real estate company (he left the chamber shortly after MCC came to town), his Longhorn loyalty was on display. John (Jack) Gray was a former basketball All-American at The University of Texas and he was a proud alumnus. He bled burnt orange (UT's school color). His office was wallpapered in burnt orange and contained several UT sports trophies, such as a wrinkled, prune-like football from a long-ago "Bevo" victory in the Cotton Bowl. The shriveled football occupied a place of honor. His leaving the chamber represented the passing of the small and rather informal "one-man show" of economic development activities, which had existed until the the arrival of MCC. In his way, John Gray played a very important role in selling Austin to MCC.

As Gray remembered it, Inman's secret visit occurred on March 21, 1983, the Monday just after Gray's March 18 presentation to MCC's representatives in Chicago and just prior to the announcement of the four finalist sites on April 5.

I was at the chamber that afternoon when the phone rang. It was Admiral Inman. He said, "John, this is Bob Inman." I thought, Who in heck do I know named Inman? Then a light came on. "Oh, Bob!" He said: "John, I'm down here making a speech to the Cattlemen's Association over at the hotel, and I've got two or three free hours. Nancy is with me. After the speech, could you show us something of Austin?" I said, "Bob, is the Pope Catholic?" I dropped everything and went over to the hotel in my old 1974 Pontiac, a real clunker. I've always had a reputation for driving fast. In those three hours, I showed them the whole town. Inman was just delighted. But he was worried about getting back to the Austin airport in time. I got them there with five to ten minutes to spare. Nancy had never seen bluebonnets. So after they left, I mailed her a packet or two of seeds. (interview, January 22, 1987)

Admiral Inman remembered his tour a bit differently:

Ann Armstrong [an heir to the King Ranch, a member of LBJ's team in Washington in the 1960s, a former chairperson of the President's Foreign Intelligence Advisory Committee, and a leader in the Southwest Cattleraisers Association] had been after me for a long time to come down here and do a speech. So Nancy and I came to Austin in late March to the Texas Southwest Cattleraisers Association convention at Palmer Auditorium. Oh, man, the ride in John Gray's car, getting carsick, whipping up and down the hills. And John talking endlessly. I'll tell you, we got a fast look at Austin in the process. We barely made it to our plane.

> Interviewer: Did that visit sway your wife or you at all on Austin?
>
> Inman: Well, what it did was help remove some of the "Texas? Yech," which had been sort of her reaction. (interview, January 26, 1987)

There were no Austin government representatives on either task force. At the time of MCC's site selection, Austin's no-growth mayor had resigned, an interim mayor was in office, and an election campaign was under way. Newly elected pro-growth Mayor Ron Mullen was later defeated by a no-growth mayor and city council who took office in 1985. If the no-growth slate of candidates had been in office during the site-selection process, there would likely have been strong resistance to Austin's participation in the campaign for MCC (see Chapter 6). As Admiral Inman (interview, July 21, 1987) commented:

> Timing meant everything. The timing was such that the rallying causes against growth were preoccupied with getting candidates elected. So they were not involved in the MCC decision. Then they were bypassed entirely in 3M's decision to move to Austin [which came right after MCC]. They reacted [to MCC and 3M] by writing to the top 500 U.S. companies saying: "Don't plan on coming to Austin unless you contact us first."

ACHIEVING REGIONAL PUBLIC/PRIVATE COLLABORATION

Despite instances of provincialism and resistance to statewide cooperation, the Texas team generally brought a high level of collaborative individualism to the focused task of selling Austin and Texas to MCC. Pike Powers (interview, March 27, 1986) remembers the MCC competition:

> I still get kind of a special tingle about the people that were involved. Nobody ever said "no." Nobody ever

complained. Everybody just did what they were supposed to do, and more. There was a sense that we were
on a special mission. The MCC competition was more
important than anything that most people had worked
on before. We couldn't flub it. We wanted to do it
right, and we didn't want it all over the street. It's still
amazing to me that, in Texas, 300 plus people were in
and out of the transaction and we never had a leak to
the press. I really attribute that to the special mission—
a special sense of what was there and how uniquely
people perform in a special circumstance when they
have to. People just rose to the occasion. . . . It was one
of those once-in-a-lifetime situations where people did
more than they probably thought they were capable of
doing, and they exceeded their own capacity. You know
that there are just some times like that where people
perform better. . . . You have an incredibly good performance by human beings who are otherwise very flawed
and very normal and very ordinary. I'm not trying to
describe it as a superhuman, death-defying flip off the
backboard. It's closely akin to wartime, when people
do things far beyond what they normally can do. . . . It
was a public competition, which helped excite the
adrenaline. We knew the MCC story was being written
up on the front page of *The Wall Street Journal.*

The Texans used various terms to express the feelings they
experienced during the MCC competition: "the right chemistry
among us," "the magic," and "Camelot." "Jamming," a term from
music and sports, is defined as "fluid behavioral coordination that
occurs without detailed knowledge of personality" (Eisenberg,
1990). When jamming occurs, individuals "play over their heads,"
lose their sense of time, and work together with a nearly perfect (but
unspoken) sense of coordination.[15] In Austin, the jamming experience lasted several weeks and included a core group of first- and
second-level influencers from academia, government, and business
(this experience has been repeated in subsequent economic development efforts, such as the case of SEMATECH; see Chapter 7).
    How did a small group of public/private individuals come
together in Austin and in Texas to facilitate a high level of

public/private commitment and collaboration (1) for the two weeks just before the MCC site-location visit and (2) during the fulfillment of Texas' commitment to MCC? How was such public/private synergy initiated, and how was it maintained? How did the Governor's Task Force and the Austin Task Force develop a feeling of jamming, an "M-Form" (Ouchi, 1984a) spirit across all sectors of the technopolis wheel?

The answers to these questions concern focus and commitment, cultural and geographic proximity, effective information gathering, and coordinated power and influence from the top levels of both the public and private sectors.

FOCUS AND COMMITMENT: THE VALUE OF A
PERCEIVED CRISIS

In 1983, MCC provided a positive economic alternative to Texas' dependence on oil and gas, agriculture, and ranching. Key Texas leaders (first-level influencers) believed that technology-based companies that had located in the state (such as IBM, Texas Instruments, and Motorola,) provided a premier route to economic growth. MCC was seen as a means of jump starting and further diversifying the Texas economy by creating jobs and wealth in high-tech industry. Winning MCC was a way of proving that the Lone Star State could successfully compete in the coming global economy.

Texas' overall economic strength had been slipping for several years prior to the advent of MCC. The state's agriculture and ranching industries were in an economic downturn in 1983, the result of a severe drought. A devaluation of the Mexican peso had a negative impact on south Texas. Most important, the state's oil and gas resources were diminishing. By 1984, Texas pumped one-third less oil and gas than it had in 1972, even though drilling had increased threefold (O'Reilly, 1985). Oil prices were then escalating, but Texas leaders were uncomfortable with the state's heavy reliance on this volatile industry.[16] Texas needed to create jobs, specifically high-paying jobs, for its educated youth who were migrating to high-technology industries on the east and west coasts. Key Texas leaders who were represented on the governor's and Austin task forces for MCC felt that they *had* to have the consortium.

On the other hand, key public and private leaders in San Diego did not really feel that they had to have MCC, at least not to the degree that Texas leaders did. San Diego's economy rested on tourism, the military, and defense industries. Local leaders questioned why the city should provide financial incentives to an R&D consortium composed of some of the richest electronics companies in the United States. Nevertheless, San Diego's economic development officials did everything possible to attract MCC, knowing that the other three finalist sites were also making an all-out effort.

> Right up to the last minute, we were digging for more gold. All the way down the line. . . . We didn't understand how significant incentives were going to be. I'm not sure MCC did either, until Austin put so much on the table. It got to be like a feeding frenzy in a shark tank. We tried to be as responsive as we could. We wanted MCC badly, but once you arrive at a brick wall, what more can you do? . . . We took the MCC team up in helicopters. It got down to such trivia, they told us that Texas had nicer helicopters. That's how crazy it got. (Pegg interview, July 14, 1986)

As John Gray remembered (interview, January 27, 1987):

> None of the fact-finding committee had even been to Austin. We were worried about MCC's perception of Texas as nothing but cowboys, cattle, cactus, and sagebrush. Top-flight intellectuals and researchers wouldn't want to come to such a place. So, we got the committee members up in the air to let them see the trees, hills, and lakes. Their eyes opened up real fast when we landed on top of the Hyatt right by Town Lake.

CULTURAL AND PHYSICAL PROXIMITY

While being diverse in talent and experience, the Texas team was relatively homogeneous on several other criteria. Almost all the participants were young professionals, longtime Texas residents, and graduates of either UT-Austin or Texas A&M.[17] And they were united by a common vision, the desire to do Texas proud in the national competition for MCC. As Meg Wilson, one of the key players in "The Texas Incentive for Austin," remembered (interview, April 8, 1993):

> It was more than a collaborative spirit. . . . The team truly and deeply believed in the mission of MCC, wherever MCC went. . . . The selflessness of the team was apparent even though we [the Texas team] were all selling [Austin] like hell.

While most of the dozen or so key leaders were old friends who respected one another and who enjoyed instant rapport, some were not. Perot, for example, did not personally know Governor White or other members of the Austin Task Force, and he was a graduate of the Naval Academy at Annapolis. In general, A&M and UT professors and administrators were more comfortable competing with each other than collaborating. But all of the participants (or at least most) united, for a brief period of time, behind one goal—the desire to win MCC for Texas.

> In Texas they lined up something like 40 people [statewide] to sign "The Texas Incentive for Austin," giving a very clear sense of collaboration between business, academic institutions, and government to build a better future for Texas. At almost every other [finalist] location, you would see the university people being introduced to the businesspeople, and they would say: "Hello, Mr. So-and-So." In Texas, the president of the university would be talking to a banker or somebody— "Hello, Charlie. How are the kids? Is Jane enjoying her trip to Waco?" You could just see that they were all part of a cohesive community. (Rutishauser interview, January 23, 1987)

Perception was key for the MCC fact-finding and site-selection teams, each of which only briefly visited Austin. Compared to other states, Texas' easy style, friendly smiles, and first-name familiarity enhanced MCC visitors' impression of statewide collaboration. But it was not all style and form. The Texans were voracious information gatherers. They planned their actions in detail. They thought through how best to present "The Texas Incentive for Austin." They rehearsed each aspect of their presentation to MCC's fact-finding and site-selection committees.

Austin's successful bid for MCC was also facilitated by the spatial proximity of its centers of academic, business, and government leadership. The governor's office, the office of the chancellor of the University of Texas system, The University of Texas at Austin, and a number of the state's largest high-tech companies are located in and around Austin (Figure 3.5). The president of The University of Texas at Austin can look out his office window in the UT Tower and see the sunset red granite state capitol (which Texans swear is one foot taller than the U.S. Capitol in Washington, D.C.) several blocks away. It is a 20-minute drive to Tracor, IBM, Motorola, and the other high-tech companies on Austin's city limits. This propinquity greatly facilitated communication and coordination among key government/ academic/business leaders who made up the Texas team for MCC.[18]

But it was more than the physical proximity of key influencers in Austin that fostered the spirit of public/private collaboration in "The Texas Incentive for Austin." Texas first demonstrated its statewide initiative during the initial site presentations of Dallas, San Antonio, and Austin in Chicago on March 18, 1983. As an MCC representative recollected:

> It was very interesting because, in some of the states, the different cities were pretty much "every man for himself." You know, they'd make their pitch, and they'd also make subtle innuendos about how some other city in their state wasn't nearly as good as they were. But not so in Texas. Governor Mark White led the delegation of three very good presentations: San Antonio, Austin, and Dallas. And it came across as a "Texas Presentation" with three options, but Texas wants you. (Rutishauser interview, January 23, 1987)

Again, perception was key, for despite such a visible collaborative spirit, there was dissension and foot dragging. Meg Wilson (interview, April 8, 1993) commented that Dallas was "furious

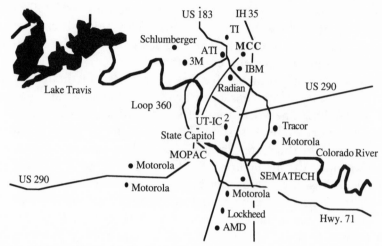

Source: Adapted from Farley and Glickman, 1986. Used by permission of the *Journal of the American Planning Association,* vol. 52, no. 4, Autumn 1986.

Figure 3.5 Map of the Austin area showing the state capitol, MCC, SEMATECH, UT-Austin, the IC^2 Institute, the Austin Technology Incubator (ATI), and major high-tech companies

about giving up two to three minutes of their time to Governor White" during the Chicago presentation. Dallas representatives even called the state capitol and "made vague, onerous threats if [the governor] tried to sway the bid to Austin or San Antonio. . . . They even suggested that the governor not go to Chicago. But we successfully hid that problem [from MCC] and went straight over their heads. . . . Thanks to Ross [Perot]."

COMPETING FOR SCARCE INFORMATION

Our analysis of MCC's site-selection process shows the crucial nature of (1) the type of information considered important, (2) how such information was collected and analyzed, and (3) how such information was used. The MCC location process can be understood as a competition among the main actors for scarce information about MCC and about the expectations, activities, and decisions of the other key competitors. Success in MCC's site-selection competition depended on the ability of each competing city to quickly obtain and use relevant information in a context of high uncertainty.

After Inman was appointed to the top job at MCC in January 1983, he opened a temporary headquarters in Arlington, Virginia. Sperry, one of MCC's initial shareholders, donated office space for the admiral on the top floor of an almost-deserted building at 1501 Wilson Boulevard. MCC did not have a publicly listed telephone. To get to MCC's temporary headquarters a visitor had to take an elevator to the building's vacant and unfurnished twelfth floor, where a small, hand-lettered sign said "MCC." An arrow pointed up a staircase. On the thirteenth floor, a visitor encountered 5,000 square feet of empty space. In the far corner of this barn-like area were the desks of the admiral and his secretary. The total effect on a visitor to MCC's headquarters in early 1983 was that of a James Bond spy movie. (Murphy, 1987, p. 158)

Powers stressed the crucial role of intelligence work by the Austin Task Force:

> We read every shred of paper written on Inman. We got 10Ks and annual reports for the member companies back seven to eight years and tried to analyze their management. We analyzed the board of director connections with MCC's member companies. I spent hours on the phone with our MCC contacts—we made lists of questions, page after page—that I would ask over the phone. We went to a lot of trouble to do our intelligence homework about who these people were so we could make our best sale. For example, who on the site-selection team was married, where did they go to school, how many dogs did they have, and what were their hobbies and interests? We tried, wherever possible, to match Texas people with [MCC visitors] of like interests. If we knew [an MCC site visitor] was a sailor, we made sure we talked about sailboats as we flew over Lake Travis. If he liked dogs and hunting, we made sure we matched him up with Texans of like interests. (Powers interview, March 27, 1986)

Because the Texas leaders were particularly adept at obtaining a variety of hard-to-get information, they gained an important advantage over their counterparts in San Diego, Atlanta, and Raleigh-Durham. This information was transformed by the Texas team into strategies for winning MCC. Obtaining such information, however, was not easy. "We had two weeks until MCC's first visit to Austin. And we had almost no guidance from MCC as to what they wanted. The normal questions that you ask in an [industry] recruitment effort are: 'What interests them? What is important to them?' The information available from MCC was sparse. It became clear early-on that it was on purpose sparse." (Drummond interview, March 26, 1986)

COORDINATED POWER AND INFLUENCE FROM THE TOP

Capable "foot soldiers" (second-level influencers) were inspired by capable leaders, some of the most powerful public and private (first-level) influencers in Texas. The Governor's Task Force had an important network advantage in that Ross Perot had a personal relationship with Admiral Inman. As Ed Hanslik, a member of the Austin Task Force, explained (interview, January 22, 1987): "Early on, we tried to think of who in the hell in the state of Texas knows Bob Inman. It turns out there was just one person: Ross Perot. Because he had been supporting [appropriations] efforts for the National Security Agency, the CIA, and all of that. That was our 'Deep Throat,' Ross Perot."

Perot made himself available to the Texas officials spearheading the MCC drive, no matter how busy he might be. Often, he would not return a call from Powers until late at night, but these nocturnal chats provided a direct pipeline to Inman. The admiral was equally willing to convey information to the other cities, but they didn't have such an energetic and perceptive source of information. John Watson emphasized that: "Perot . . . gave the whole [Texas] process stature. Inman would use Ross as a sounding board on some questions about MCC." Watson wasn't sure who called whom, but he did know that Perot stayed on top of MCC. Perot could also obtain information about the other finalist cities: "Ross said: 'If you need some information on San Diego, tell me what you need and I'll have it in the morning.' You never know how, but he gets it done." (Watson interview, January 23, 1987)

According to Narcisso Cano (interview, February 16, 1987) "Ross Perot is classified. He thinks completely differently than anyone I've ever come across. Just at a different level." Neal Spelce (interview, December 18, 1985) thought that Perot (in addition to

H. ROSS PEROT

Ross Perot was born on June 27, 1930, in Texarkana, East Texas. By 1989, Perot had amassed a personal fortune of $3 billion, which made him the second wealthiest individual in the United States, second only to Sam Walton, founder of Wal-Mart stores. Perot graduated from Annapolis in 1953. After serving in the navy, he worked as a salesman for IBM for five years. In 1962, only three weeks into the year, he earned IBM's maximum allowable annual commission.

Perot left IBM to start his own company, Electronic Data Systems, a firm that designed computer software for such tasks as clearing bank checks, processing health care claims, and handling airline tickets. When EDS went public in 1970, Perot became a millionaire. In 1984, Perot sold EDS to General Motors for $2.5 billion plus a seat on GM's board of directors. His critical evaluation of GM in particular and the management of the U.S. auto industry in general was prominent in the media for the next several years. The auto industry was largely unmoved by his suggestions; in fact, Roger Smith, CEO of General Motors, found Perot to be a rather large irritant. GM ultimately paid Perot $700 million to sever his ties with the auto giant and with EDS. In 1988, Perot launched Perot Systems, an EDS competitor.

Perot is an individualist. His Dallas office has numerous carvings of eagles, his favorite bird. One of his pet sayings is: "Eagles don't flock." In 1979, Perot organized a commando unit to rescue two EDS employees from a Tehran prison during the beginning of the Iranian revolution. This escapade was popularized in a book and a made-for-TV movie. With such media exposure, Perot became a very public figure. In his acceptance speech, upon receiving the Winston Churchill Foundation leadership award from England's Prince Charles in 1986, Perot likened himself to a grain of sand in an oyster. It irritates the oyster to produce a pearl. An irritant for positive change, that's how Perot sees himself.

Ross Perot first became impressed with Admiral Inman when Perot served on the presidential advisory committee on foreign intelligence. After Inman retired from the CIA, Perot tried to hire Inman to succeed him as president of EDS. Inman described what happened on March 9, 1983:

> Nancy [Mrs. Inman] took a call from Ross, who was coming up to Washington. He wanted to take the two of us to dinner. . . . When Nancy told him that we couldn't go because I was going to Annapolis to speak to the banquet of the Society of Military Operational

Research, Ross said: "Well, I think I'll go over there
with him." When I said "Fine," he asked me to pick
him up at the Old Executive Office Building. We set the
time. I had planned to write my speech in my mind
while driving to Annapolis. I swung by and there's Ross
standing on the curb. All the way to Annapolis, he asks
me: "Do you know what you're doing? Why get yourself tangled up with MCC? It's never going to work.
You really ought to junk it and come join me at EDS."

We arrived at the Holiday Inn in Annapolis just as a
thunderstorm hit. Ross ate dinner in the Holiday Inn
restaurant. He didn't want to join me at the banquet.
He sat in the lobby reading a book for three and a half
hours while I went through dinner and the speech.
When we came out, the thunderstorm had passed and
we started back to Washington. You would never have
known that our previous conversation had ever taken
place. The moment we got in the car, Ross asks: "How
are you going to recruit the people? How are you going
to do this or that?" All the way to Washington. I wheel
up to his hotel, and he gets out of my car. Then he asks
a final question: "Do you have any reasons—personal
reasons—why you would be unwilling to live in Texas
again?" I said: "No." He said: "Well, that's where
you're going to live." Then he slammed the car door
shut. (interview, January 26, 1987)

During the 1992 presidential race, Perot inspired a grassroots campaign that got him on the ballot in all 50 states. Perot
earned 18.9 percent of the popular vote, a strong showing for
an independent candidate. Perot's contribution to his run for
the White House totaled $63 million. After the election, Perot's
campaign group—United We Stand, America—formed a lobby
and signed up many of the more than 19 million people who
voted for him on November 3.

Governor Mark White) was key to bringing MCC to Texas: "The guy
seems to get a big 'S' on his chest, coming out of a phone booth and
all. Perot deserves the applause. He was a motivator. He said: 'We can
do it. It's worth it. I'll do this. Why can't you do that?'" As Powers
(interview, March 27, 1986) recalled: "We just kept listening to him.
We were never cut off. He would talk to us [by phone] forever."

Governor Mark White actively participated in the Governor's Task Force for MCC, and he championed the actions of the Austin Task Force. He emphasized to Powers (interview, March 27, 1986): "I don't want to finish second, and I don't want to win by an inch. So you do everything necessary. I don't care if you have to quit doing everything else connected with being an executive assistant to the governor. Whether you totally ignore the Legislature, this is the most important thing that you are working on." Powers (interview, March 27, 1986) noted:

> I ostensibly was supposed to be responsible for 435 people in the operation of the governor's office, but it was more important to him that I give my undivided attention [to MCC], and grab him any time that he was needed, than it was to finish second or win by an inch. He was there from beginning to end. He'd greet them [the MCC fact-finding and site-selection representatives] at the plane. He'd put them on the plane. He'd have every meal with them. He'd walk them all around the grounds of the governor's mansion talking to them with his arm around them. He didn't miss a trick. I mean, every time we saw them or talked with them or whatever, there was a personal note immediately behind it in the mail with some kind of book, package, autographed picture, or program or something. Mark White made the commitment to cross every "t" and dot every "i" with all the force of his office and personality.

Respondents at other finalist sites for MCC emphasized the difficulty they had in getting top state leaders to devote time and effort to their MCC recruitment drive. As one San Diego respondent stated: "While there was no starting Duekmejian [the governor of California], there was no slowing White down." Dan Pegg, who led San Diego's campaign for MCC, commented: "Our California governor is not personally inclined to do these things [recruit MCC]. He had a state official or two in charge of economic development and assigned the MCC thing to them. But when Inman had been stroked by the governors of other states, our California officials just didn't draw the water." (Pegg interview, July 14, 1986)

George Black, who served as chair of the MCC fact-finding team, identified one variable that predicted which site would win MCC:

> If you had a single measure, only one criterion with which to measure the serious commitment of each of the finalist sites, it would be the amount of time spent by the governor of the state with us. People from a chamber of commerce or an economic development council or whatever, that was their job. The California governor spoke to us at the University of California at San Diego chancellor's mansion on a spectacular cliff overlooking the Pacific. He walked in with an entourage, moved immediately to the podium, made a formal presentation, and then walked out. That's all we saw of the governor. (interview, May 5, 1986)

As Admiral Inman (interview, January 26, 1987) commented: "We were cooling our heels for half an hour before Governor Duekmejian came in. He read a speech and left. No visiting, no chatting, no anything. It would have been much better for him never to have been there at all."

North Carolina Governor James Hunt was directly involved in the MCC site-selection committee's visit to his state. As Inman recalled:

> At Research Triangle, we had breakfast with the governor and then had presentations. What stood out to us was that there were no business leaders there. Strong representation from the academic community and from the government sectors and the Research Triangle and Don Beilman, who had just set up the MCNC [Microelectronics Center North Carolina]. But no other business leaders from the state.
>
> The other issue in North Carolina was "Who after Hunt?" Research Triangle began under [Governor] Luther Hodges and had great growth under [Governor] Terry Sanford. Then it went into a sort of somnolence for some time. There had been another surge under Jim

Hunt. But the question was: "Who's going to sustain [the Research Triangle] after Hunt?" If he goes, where is the supporting infrastructure that gives you confidence that it's going to continue? (interview, January 26, 1987)

George Black (interview, May 5, 1986) compared the attention that his MCC fact-finding team received from the Texas governor with that from his counterpart in North Carolina:

In North Carolina, we had breakfast at the governor's mansion with a very large group of people. Almost immediately after breakfast, he said good-bye. Grabbed you by the arm, shook your hand, ushered you out the door. Getting eyeball-to-eyeball commitments from a top official is important. You know that you can count on their promises. In Austin, we were whisked by helicopter to the Hyatt when we arived. Then we were told that the governor is waiting with a late supper for you at the mansion. Virtually every breakfast, lunch, and dinner. . . the Texas governor was present. As if he didn't have other pressing matters. That was very impressive to us. It was a strong message.

Governor White realized that he was making a statement to MCC by his continued presence. For instance, when he met Black and the other fact-finding team members upon their arrival in Austin from having just visited North Carolina, White asked with a grin: "Say, how's my good friend Jim Hunt?" He knew full well that the MCC team had hardly met him.

Inman felt that Atlanta made a mixed impression on MCC's site-selection committee:

Governor Harris had just done a beautiful job. Mrs. Harris got them out to the governor's mansion and toured them around, and her charm just exuded. She made a smash hit on the fact-finding team. We [the site-selection committee] had a business luncheon on top of one of the [downtown] buildings. It seemed like the

first time they had ever gotten together to talk about
economic development . . . the business leaders
of Atlanta, along with the political leaders of the state
and city. . . . Then the mayor of Atlanta [Andrew
Young] made this speech at the end of the luncheon
saying that if we came to Atlanta, he'd help us market
our products all over the world. It was very clear then
that he didn't have a clue what we were or what we
did. . . . It was a real sour note of that occasion. (interview, January 26, 1987)

FINANCIAL INCENTIVES

Did the Texas financial incentives influence MCC's decision
to locate in Austin? They did. According to Inman and other members of MCC's site-selection committee, the cash incentives were one
important reason for Austin's selection. Georgia's package most
closely approached the Texas incentive in size. North Carolina, on
the other hand, declined to offer MCC any form of sizable subsidy.
North Carolinians didn't see why they should subsidize a for-profit
R&D consortium that was founded by some of the nation's wealthiest computer and microelectronics firms. However, what won for
Texas was *how* its incentives were structured, which reflected how
well the Texas leaders obtained and used information about MCC.
The Texas incentive package came largely from the private sector,
statewide, not from state or local taxes, and the incentives were
structured so as to be an investment in the future of Texas as a state,
its universities, and business development rather than funds given to
MCC. According to San Diego's Dan Pegg (interview, July 14,
1986): "Once the numbers correlated with the spirit, there was no
stopping Texas."

About one-third of the Texas financial incentives ($20 mil-
lion) were to build MCC a building, which would be owned by the
UT-System, on land belonging to the University of Texas at the
Balcones Research Center. In an attempt to broaden the financial
appeal of the campaign for MCC, contributions were made to "The
University of Texas System High-Tech Fund," and the MCC facility

was advertised as available to both UT-Austin and Texas A&M for use in their respective academic endeavors. "It is the location of the facility in Austin and specifically at the Balcones Research Center which dictates that contributions at this time be made to the University of Texas system, although benefits from the project will unquestionably inure to Texas A&M University as well." (MCC solicitation brochure, January 9, 1983)

On April 26, 1983, Jon P. Newton, chairman of the board of regents, wrote to Governor White that the UT system "enthusiastically supports your efforts to bring MCC to the State of Texas. . . . We are pleased to join with you in supporting this important development effort, because it enables the University to develop and expand its teaching and research capability in this most critical field at a much accelerated pace." The value of the combined commitments from the UT system totaled $49.5 million, which consisted of:

- A lease of 20 acres of land located at the Balcones West Tract to MCC at a nominal rental ($1 per year) for ten years.
- Five million dollars from Permanent University Fund (PUF)[19] bond proceeds or other sources for the construction of a $20 million building (of approximately 200,000 square feet), which would be available to MCC at a nominal rate ($1 per year) for a ten-year period. The private sector was responsible for the remaining $15 million contribution toward the building.
- The establishment of endowed academic positions in electrical engineering and computer science with $15 million, $5 million of which would be raised by the private sector through the efforts of the Governor's Task Force for MCC. UT would also create 30 new faculty positions in microelectronics and computer science over a period of three years, specifically for younger scientists with research potential.
- Two million dollars, during the 1983–1985 biennium, for the purchase of new equipment in support of university research and teaching in areas of interest to MCC.

- Supplemented through the special efforts of the
  Governor's Task Force for MCC, $9.5 million in
  additional funds were made available to UT-Austin
  for the 1984–1985 biennium. These funds, which
  complemented MCC's efforts in computer science
  and microelectronics, were used in research support
  ($2 million), academic and research equipment ($3
  million), graduate fellowships ($1.5 million), and
  faculty positions ($3 million). Seven hundred and
  fifty thousand dollars was to be made available to
  support 75 graduate students annually in microelectronics and computer science.

Texas A&M made similar but more general commitments,
without mentioning specifics on money and faculty positions, such
as:

- Establishing additional endowed chairs in microelectronics and computer science.
- Completing an engineering research building, which
  included additional space for microelectronics and
  robotics research.
- Offering adjunct faculty status for members of
  MCC's research staff.
- Offering MCC opportunities for remote research
  sites at A&M's campus.
- Offering research sabbaticals so that A&M professors could spend time in Austin at MCC, career-
  development courses for A&M students that would
  be geared toward the needs of MCC, and internship
  programs and graduate student support.

The Texas business community emphasized the inherent economic advantages of operating in Texas, including a low cost of living and the lack of state and local income taxes. MCC's professional
employees were expected to make between $50,000 and $100,000
per year. It was pointed out to MCC that the net annual pay for a
single person with no dependents earning $50,000 was $28,905 in
San Diego, $26,766 in Raleigh-Durham, $30,348 in Atlanta, and
$33,008 in Austin.

The Austin business community put together a $20 million package to subsidize single-family mortgage loans (at two points below the Federal National Mortgage Association's prevailing rate of about 13.5) for MCC employees. Each lending organization was responsible for a loan amount determined by its 1983 market share of Austin home mortgages. The banks and savings and loan associations absorbed 1 percentage point on each mortgage, as did the home builders. Loans were made available until a savings of $20 million total mortgage lending was reached. The financial institutions also provided $3 million as a bridge loan for MCC personnel who sold homes to buy in Austin. Relocation expenses incurred by MCC personnel (e.g., car rentals, airfare, temporary housing), up to $500,000, were also underwritten. An additional $3 million was made available, at below prime rate, for MCC personnel who needed assistance with moving costs.

Austin-based institutional lenders participated in "The Texas Incentive for Austin" out of a mixture of their responding to personal requests from Texas influencers, enlightened self-interest, and the momentum of the event. Economic gain was to be achieved through the increased volume of car loans and other banking services that would likely accompany the home mortgages of MCC employees. In fact, the loan package proved to be so successful from the point of view of both MCC and the banks that it was extended.

The first meeting of the MCC Leadership Steering Committee, the group responsible for raising the funds for MCC, was called by Governor White—five months after the MCC competition—on October 25, 1983. High-level business representatives were present from 12 Texas regions representing five cities (Houston, San Antonio, Austin, Dallas, and El Paso) and seven geographic areas: East Texas (Longview, Tyler), Fort Worth, the Golden Triangle (bounded by Dallas–Fort Worth, San Antonio and Houston-Austin, and Bryan–College Station), the Panhandle (Lubbock, Amarillo), Permian Basin (Midland, Odessa), South Texas, and the Rio Grande Valley. The committee was made up of some of Texas' most prominent business leaders, including Lloyd Bentsen of Houston, Ross Perot and H.R. (Bum) Bright of Dallas, and Perry Bass of Fort Worth.[20]

Each area's contribution for MCC was based on (1) established giving patterns, (2) the size and strength of a region's econo-

**Table 3.4 The Texas campaign to raise $23.5 million to attract
MCC to Austin, as of June 30, 1986**

Region	Total Goal	Total Pledges and/or Cash Received as of 6/30/86	Balance Remaining to Be Raised Amount*	Percentage of Goal
Amarillo	$ 500,000	$ 60,950	$ 439,050	88
Austin	2,400,000	3,156,880	0	0
Dallas	5,800,000	2,229,517	3,570,483	62
East Texas	900,000	63,750	836,250	93
El Paso	900,000	17,875	882,125	98
Fort Worth	1,500,000	2,020,000	0	0
Golden Triangle	500,000	12,500	487,500	98
Houston	6,200,000	6,309,950	0	0
Lubbock	400,000	14,000	386,000	97
Permian Basin	1,100,000	1,285,450	0	0
Rio Grande Valley	500,000	9,100	490,900	98
San Antonio	1,800,000	605,850	1,194,150	66
South Texas	600,000	45,000	555,000	93
Totals	$23,100,000	$15,830,822	$7,599,178	32

* The sum of numbers in this column does not add to the total because
some regions exceeded their goals.

my (e.g., how many *Fortune* 500 headquarters were located in the
area), and (3) the leadership factor. Houston banker Ben Love
(interview, August 10, 1992) commented that "The leadership factor was key. We had to target, in each region, the guy who had the
influence and clout to make it happen." Austin was seen to be the
main beneficiary of MCC, and some of Texas' other regions wondered why the capital city's contribution was relatively low com-

pared to Houston's and Dallas' (Table 3.4). Love's response was that MCC would benefit all of Texas. Austin would become a research headquarters, but high-tech manufacturing growth would spread throughout the Lone Star State. As a banker, Love was well aware of each region's ability to give, and he combined this criterion with the estimated benefits of MCC to arrive at each region's targeted amount. Austin was not a corporate headquarters city, and its fund-raising did not have the benefit of large foundations as did Houston and Fort Worth.

At the Houston kickoff of the campaign to redeem Texas' MCC pledge, Houston banker Lee Straus observed in his remarks: "I don't think any of this money is going to walk in the door. . . . It's going to take a big effort." Texas foundations were targeted for $13.8 million; businesses, $7.6 million; and individuals, $2.1 million. Houston's quota of $6.2 million was the largest of any region and was filled mainly by The Houston Endowment, Inc., a philanthropy endowed by Mr. and Mrs. Jesse H. Jones, which contributed $5 million to Houston's and the Permian Basin's fund-raising efforts. The Sid Richardson Foundation of Fort Worth committed $2 million to the MCC project, an amount that exceeded the region's assigned goal. Contributions could be made in three-year segments because some of the funds were not to be spent until the MCC building was completed.

The MCC Leadership Steering Committee was fearful of the negative consequences of the perception by potential Texas contributors that (1) the owner-corporations should be funding MCC themselves, (2) UT/Texas A&M were constantly asking for money, (3) foundations would have an "escape hatch" by saying: "We already give to UT/A&M," and (4) they would lose the pressure point of urgency to meet the state's commitment to MCC. To counter these concerns, the committee attempted to:

- Broaden the base of MCC's geographic appeal by creating excitement about Japan's fifth-generation technology and concern about national security implications and by portraying MCC as an investment in a Texas (not Austin) effort—a United States against Japan effort that represented a "call to arms" by the entire state

- Focus on Texas' premier educational institutions
  as recipients of the private-sector support rather
  than MCC
- Use Silicon Valley as a positive example of economic
  development and job creation flowing from the electronics industry[21]

Governor White and Admiral Inman traveled throughout
Texas to assist in the local fund-raising activities. They presented
MCC as an important "turning point in the economic history of
Texas and the U.S. . . . . This combined effort of 13 companies
[MCC's first shareholders] represents our country's best effort at
maintaining world preeminence in the increasingly critical field of
information processing and computer technology." (from the
brochure for the MCC fund-raising campaign)

The solicitation material stated that the U.S. Justice
Department had given tentative approval for the formation of R&D
partnerships like MCC and that Japan had committed more than
$250 million a year to a crash course to develop a fifth-generation
computer. The brochure emphasized that "the development of a
machine with true artificial intelligence will be nothing short of
revolutionary for society. Failure to maintain the lead in this crucial
area of research has broad business and national defense
implications. The goal of MCC is to see that the United States
stays on top."

Local steering committees were formed to meet the designated
financial goals for the MCC campaign. Fund raising, however,
became more difficult as time passed and other concerns began to
occupy Texas' leaders. Adding to the challenge of collecting the
pledges, Texas was hit by a serious financial downturn soon after
the consortium came to Austin. In order to keep the matter "upper-
most in all of our minds," on March 22, 1984, Governor White
chaired a breakfast for Austin's fund-raising steering committee.[22]

A July 18, 1984, letter to Larry Taylor, president of Taylor
Petroleum, Inc., from George P. Walsh, of the Amarillo/Panhandle
MCC Steering Committee, stated:

The Amarillo area can take advantage of a statewide
economic development effort. No one knows better

than you that Texas must replace some of the oil and gas related income with which we've been blessed. An event occurred last year which can provide this needed diversification. Governor White led an effort that won our State the location of the Microelectronics and Computer Technology Corp. (MCC). This was accomplished in spite of the best sales ability of officials of 26 other states. . . . The ultimate production of the world's first "fifth generation" computers and all the needed components—some of which could be manufactured in our area—will add another major element to our economy . . . and provide additional benefits for current and future generations of Texans. . . . Successful achievement of our $500,000 goal will certainly help establish our area favorably in the minds of the folks in Austin.

When he toured the state, Governor White spoke on the future economic and business climate of Texas and the development of a high-technology industry to position Texas as a national and international business site in the coming decade. By the end of June 1986, Amarillo, East Texas, El Paso, the Golden Triangle, Lubbock, the Rio Grande Valley, and South Texas had each contributed less than 10 percent of their targeted amount for MCC. Austin, Fort Worth, Houston, and Permian Basin fulfilled the targeted commitments of the MCC Steering Committee (see Table 3.4). When asked to comment, Powers said, "What can I say? We were beaten down by the path of reality. No, I didn't think it would be this hard" (quoted in Sullivan, 1986). Given the severity of Texas' economic downturn, officials at the University of Texas decided later in 1986 not to pursue collection of the remaining $7,599,178. As Jim Crowson (interview, February 28, 1993), former vice chancellor and general counsel for the UT-system said: "Texas' economy went south and we decided not to pursue collection on the outstanding pledges."

THE KEY ROLE OF THE RESEARCH UNIVERSITY

As previously stated, a very important criterion for MCC's deciding where to locate its headquarters was the proximity of a major research university. While the university would not have to be at the top of the national rankings in electrical engineering and computer science, it was considered important that it have the potential for world-class excellence. Such a university was envisioned to be an important source of talented faculty and graduate students, research facilities, and future employees.

NORTH CAROLINA

Governor Hunt, as had his predecessors, strongly supported collaboration among the state's research universities (Duke, the University of North Carolina, and North Carolina State) in Research Triangle. The Microelectronics Center of North Carolina (MCNC), an R&D center founded by Governor Hunt in 1981, had favorably impressed MCC's site-selection teams. However, one particular event negatively affected MCC's perceptions of North Carolina's commitment to excellence in education.

During the site visit to Research Triangle, Inman asked the head of the computer science department at one of the universities how he recruited topflight academic talent. The department chair divulged that he had two vacancies that he could not fill with the current salary cap of $68,000 per year. By lunchtime, he had the authority to offer $90,000, but it was too late to prevent a strong negative influence on MCC's site-selection team. Inman and his colleagues wondered whether the state government's commitment to high-technology development and educational excellence would continue once Governor Hunt left office.

GEORGIA

Dr. Joseph Pettit, president of Georgia Institute of Technology, made an outstanding presentation to the MCC representatives at the Chicago meeting. He told MCC how he was going to make Georgia Tech "the Stanford of the South." He created a compelling vision of all the exciting activities under way in Georgia to create another Silicon Valley. Pettit had been the dean of engineering at Stanford University and was a protégé of Frederick E.

Terman, the "godfather" of Silicon Valley. The Georgia governor also made an effective presentation, but it was Pettit who dazzled the technologists on MCC's site-selection committee. Georgia Tech offered MCC a building for immediate occupancy. MCC's site-selection teams were impressed by their tour of Georgia Tech's semiconductor and microelectronics research facilities.

The Texas team was aware of the strength of Georgia's proposal to MCC, especially the importance of Georgia Tech and Joe Pettit. So whenever possible, they attempted to undermine its value. As George Black (interview, May 5, 1986) remembered: "The people in Austin were kind enough to tell me at one point that we shouldn't rely on anything related to Joe Pettit's presence because he intended to go back to Stanford. You must measure Georgia Tech as if he were not there, they emphasized. Obviously, Austin thought that Atlanta was a worthy opponent."

Atlanta learned about the full scope of the Texas incentive when MCC's site-selection team was listening to Georgia's proposal. Georgia's leaders asked for a recess, after which they told MCC's representatives that they had an elastic clause in their offer. "'We're prepared to do more, if you'll just tell us what you want. We have additional yardage that we can go.' But they did not know where to put their chips, and in terms of total value, they just misjudged it. But not by much, not by much." (Black interview, May 5, 1986)

CALIFORNIA

In order to compete effectively for MCC, it was obvious to San Diego's leaders that they needed to capitalize on the strong academic programs of the state's prestigious universities. The University of California at San Diego (UCSD) was not strong in microelectronics research, but some sort of linkage with Stanford, Berkeley, and UCLA might overcome this weakness. Inman worked with San Diego's team to try to pull together a consortium of California universities centered in San Diego. But the state's universities were not all that supportive of the idea. For example, administrators at the University of California at Berkeley feared that UCSD's gain would be their loss and would negatively affect Berkeley in its future funding battles with University of California system regents. As Dan Pegg (interview, July 14, 1986) concluded: "Berkeley didn't want to give up anything to San Diego, even though they didn't have a chance of getting it [MCC] themselves."

The lack of enthusiasm for the proposed California University Engineering Consortium (CUEC) became transparent to the MCC site visitors when the consortium's spokesperson stated that he would consult with MCC wherever it decided to locate. Pegg (interview, July 14, 1986) remembered seeing Admiral Inman shudder when that statement was made. Both Inman and Pegg realized that San Diego's chances of attracting MCC had dropped. Inman (interview, January 26, 1987) remembered: "What they said to us was how much they each would look forward to working with us bilaterally. They were unwilling to work together."

A second negative perception concerned California's continued commitment to academic excellence. As one MCC site-selection team member stated: "That issue [continued excellence in California's education] was very unclear in the spring of 1983." California was going through the tax limitations of Proposition 13. The state's budget surplus had shrunk from $6 billion to $2 billion in three years. Future funding for UCSD was very unclear in the spring of 1983—at least in the minds of MCC's site-selection team.

TEXAS

Texas, on the other hand, was making a major investment in education in 1983. The state was celebrating its sesquicentennial, and The University of Texas at Austin was celebrating its centennial. These were heady times for higher education. Matching funds from the Permanent University Fund were being used by UT to double private gifts to the university for endowed chairs, professorships, lectureships, and scholarships. In the eyes of MCC's site visitors, the university component of the Texas incentive represented a brilliant strategy. It wasn't just "what we can do for MCC," but it was "what we can do together with MCC to improve university research in microelectronics." The University of Texas said it wanted to partner with MCC. Administrators and professors outlined an aggressive program for improving research and teaching at the university—where they could work with MCC.

Universities are by nature rather ponderous and cautious organizations. It was no small miracle then that The University of Texas at Austin, a state-supported school, agreed to triple the size of its microelectronics research program and establish 30 new endowed professorships in electrical engineering and computer science. Usually, such a major change at a university would require years of planning, involve faculty committees and administrators in the decision process, and demand complicated budget maneuvering. In spring 1983, the University of Texas had two weeks. How did UT do it? All of the usual procedures for making such a sea change in a large educational institution were ignored. No faculty committees. No detailed budget planning. The university's offer to MCC did not even originate with high-level university administrators.

SQUEEZING THE ELEPHANT

Professor Herbert Woodson of UT's Department of Electrical Engineering (EE), played a key behind-the-scenes role in the recruitment of MCC to Austin.[23] Since fall 1982, his department, under the chairmanship of Edward J. Powers, had been working on a strategic plan for achieving world-class excellence with a visiting committee made up of engineers and executives representing a broad section of electrical, electronic, and computer companies. The consensus of the committee was that UT should focus the department's resources on microelectronics and computer engineering. The plan was in the early stages of implementation when Woodson was asked by his old friend John Gray at Austin's Chamber of Commerce to take the lead in developing the university's position on MCC. Woodson saw how the selection of Austin as the site for a major R&D consortium in microelectronics and computer research would fit nicely into the university's long-range plans. To help him formulate and sell a plan for the university's involvement in the MCC competition, he recruited the help of two trusted friends and colleagues: Professor Ben Streetman and Clif Drummond.

Woodson had recruited Streetman from the University of Illinois in 1982. It was Streetman who helped sell Austin to MCC during the site presentations in Chicago in 1983.[24] Drummond was the associate director of the Center for Energy Studies and associate director of the Fusion Research Center.[25] Together, these three people provide an excellent example of how second-level influencers can be the key to forming institutional alliances that might not be achievable through more formal and standard bureaucratic procedures, especially given a short time-frame, as was the case in the MCC competition.

Table 3.5 Academic quality of doctoral programs in electrical
engineering at U.S. universities in 1983

Place	University
First	MIT
2.5 (tie)	Stanford University
	University of California at Berkeley
4th	University of Illinois at Urbana
5.5 (tie)	UCLA
	USC
7th	Cornell University
8th	Purdue University
9th	University of Michigan
11.5 (tie)	Princeton University
	California Institute of Technology
12th	Carnegie Mellon University
13th	Polytechnic Institute of New York
14th	*University of Texas at Austin*
16th (tie)	Ohio State University
	University of Maryland
	University of California at San Diego
21.5 (tie)	University of Colorado at Boulder
	Columbia University
	University of Florida
	Georgia Tech
	University of California at Santa Barbara
	University of Minnesota
	Northwestern University
	University of Wisconsin at Madison
	—
47th	*Duke University*
(tie among 20 universities)	*North Carolina State University*
	—

Note: The five universities whose names are italicized in the table are located at the four MCC finalist sites (the University of North Carolina had a department of computer science but no department of electrical engineering and so is not included in this table).

Sources: An Assessment of Research-Doctorate Programs in the United States: Engineering (Washington, D.C.: National Academy of Sciences, 1981); and the Jones-Lindzey Report, *An Assessment of Research-Doctoral Programs in the U.S. Engineering* (Washington, D.C.: National Academic Press, 1982).

Woodson, Streetman, and Drummond studied the Jones-Lindzey Report, which ranked the quality of U.S. doctoral programs in electrical engineering (Table 3.5). The four sites chosen by MCC were associated with universities in the second rank, not the top-tier universities. They reasoned that MCC wanted to pair up with a second-level university and grow with it to excellence. UT's administration had indicated support for the Electricial Engineering Department's long-range plan for growth in size and quality, so the train was already moving in the right direction. MCC just accelerated these objectives from 15 years down to 5 years.

Woodson and his colleagues made a list of the number of professorships, graduate student fellowships, and laboratory research equipment that the University of Texas would need to escalate its microelectronics research program into the top tier of U.S. universities. Schools like Stanford, MIT, Berkeley, and Illinois each produced 40 to 50 Ph.D.'s in electrical engineering/computer science per year. The University of Texas was then turning out from 10 to 15 Ph.D.'s per year. The plan was to get that number up to about 50 by dramatically increasing professorships, graduate student stipends, and research facilities. This objective, with only minor changes, became the heart of the university's incentive to MCC. Once the plan was roughed out on paper, it was Drummond's job to sell it, first to Governor White and then to UT President Dr. Peter T. Flawn. White would be easy, Flawn would not.

President Flawn earned his Ph.D. from Yale University, where he had specialized in the geology of oil deposits. His "kitchen cabinet" of informal advisors were oil-minded businessmen, who were not well oriented to computers and semiconductors. As president of the flagship institution of the UT system, which had about 48,000 full-time students—most of them Texans—Flawn operated under the constant scrutiny of the Texas legislature. MCC was a new type of for-profit organization. In Flawn's mind, things were moving too fast. As one high-level university administrator recounted:

> MCC was not brought to Flawn's attention by his own and trusted advisors, so he didn't trust it from day one. His first questions were: "What in the hell is MCC? How do I know they're not a bunch of con men who are trying to fool us?" The MCC thing happppened over Flawn's objections. Flawn would have preferred that

MCC never happened, that it would just go away and not bother him. The MCC exercise occurred in spite of Flawn. But Vice President Fonken was very supportive.

Gerry Fonken, vice president for research and academic affairs, could see that MCC fit nicely into the long-range plans for expanding the university's Balcones Research Center, but he could also appreciate President Flawn's apprehension about the university's role in "The Texas Incentive for Austin."[26] UT was being asked to make several million dollars of up-front commitments, with Governor White promising to make up these funds later on by appealing to the state legislature and private donors. Despite the governor's promise, what if these funds were subsequently counted against UT's annual budget? Further, what would the other academic departments at the university think about the sudden expansion of electrical engineering and computer science? Then there was the joint involvement of Texas A&M University in the MCC incentives. It was understandable why A&M had to be included. Lots of powerful Texans such as Henry Cisneros and George Mitchell, the Houston energy millionaire, were Aggies. If you don't have A&M along, you don't have political support in Texas.

The fact that Clif Drummond was representing the Texas push for MCC also made Flawn nervous. Drummond was not a high-level University of Texas official. He was not a tenure-track faculty member. He did not even have a bachelor's degree. Why was a department-level employee like Drummond playing such a key role in UT's effort to attract MCC?

Drummond was a key link between (1) the main players on the governor's and Austin task forces, and (2) the University of Texas. Drummond not only had broad political contacts and instincts (including having run Congressman Jake Pickle's Austin office), but he had another useful quality: he was relatively "invisible" and expendable if something went wrong. Drummond had previously been used as a stalking horse in several ventures involving the University of Texas. If the venture went sour, Drummond took the heat.

Just how astutely Drummond orchestrated the University of Texas' role in the MCC competition is illustrated by a key meeting in the governor's office at the state capitol on April 22, 1983.

Present were Pike Powers, Drummond, John Watson, Governor White, Jon Newton, Don Walker, and Gerhard Fonken. Peter Flawn had the flu and could not attend. Prior to the meeting, Drummond had lunched with Powers at Austin's Capital Club. They went over his one-page list of resources needed by the University of Texas to improve its program in microelectronics research. Drummond warned Powers to expect resistance from UT's leadership. The university was a $1 billion enterprise, and it would not react favorably to the rush of the Texas campaign for MCC.

Governor White began the meeting with his "I don't want to win by an inch" speech. Then he asked Fonken: "Gerry, how many faculty positions do we need to win MCC by a mile? How many in electrical engineering? How many in computer science?" Drummond (interview, March 26, 1986) remembered Fonken's reply like this:

> [Fonken] gave a very slow answer, a lot of filler up front, before he ever got to any numbers. He would say: "Several, uh, uh,..a few dozen, uh, a small number of tens." White let him run on for a while and then patiently asked: "Well, do we need 20?" "Well, yeah, certainly 20 would be. . . ." "Could it be 30?" 'Thirty would not be bad." "How about 50? Wouldn't 50 be the best? Isn't that what we really need?" The governor led Fonken through this lengthy process. Professorships, research equipment, and so forth. Pike Powers had briefed the governor on my numbers, and I had briefed Gerry Fonken. So they wound up agreeing on the numbers every time. Fonken would sit on the couch and look over at his chairman and his chancellor, to see if what he was saying suited them. They said: "You're right, Gerry, that's what it's going to take." At least two levels of communication were going on in that room: the spoken word and the mental telepathy. A lot of eye contact and a lot of people moving very rapidly through some very tall grass. The agreements were in words of gentlemen, and that's as good as they come. Fonken smokes a lot, but he didn't light up a cigarette until the meeting was over. It ended when the

governor said: "Look, you don't need to be cashing in your chits on this. I'll cash my chits. I'll go ask for the new lines." You could see a sigh of relief go up from the university. Audibly. Absolutely audible. Then people crossed their legs and smiled. The governor said that he had already talked to private leaders for contributions. And he would go to the legislature to raise the money.

Both parties at the negotiation were mentally referring to the same script, so Drummond knew in advance what was to be agreed upon. Pike Powers (interview, March 27, 1986) gives Drummond high praise for his efforts:

> As Drummond told me then: "We squeezed the big elephant more in six days than ever before in the hundred and some odd years of the history of the University of Texas. . . ." The reason that I give Drummond a lot of credit is that he was really a man without a title. By all accounts, on the basis of what he was doing, he should have been some vice chancellor or something. He was a corporal running around with a bunch of generals. Without having Clif Drummond on the university side, I don't think we would have pulled it off.

So to the members of MCC's fact-finding and site-selection teams, higher education was on the move in Texas. They believed that the Lone Star State was committed to making a major investment in its future through increased funding of university education.[27] As Rutishauser (interview, January 23, 1987) remembered, Texans were saying:

> Not only do we have the resources, but we will commit them . . . to put UT in the first rank of world-class universities. . . . All we have to do is to get Don over there and Charlie and Mark and Bill. We'll have a meeting this afternoon and make the decision. . . . In Texas all you had to do was get the people to decide to write a check, and "boom" it was done.

UT AND TEXAS A&M COLLABORATION

The University of Texas at Austin has an enrollment of about 48,000 students. Texas A&M has an enrollment of about 34,000 and is located in College Station, about 95 miles to the east of the capital city. These two flagship universities have a long, broad, and deep history as competitors in such areas as state funding, academic prestige (e.g., recruiting prestigious faculty and national merit scholars), sports, and alumni loyalty. To a UT Longhorn, an A&M Aggie is a relatively unlettered individual, militarily inclined, although perhaps technically well trained. Aggies disdainfully describe someone from the Austin campus as an effete "tea-sipper." So indeed it was a memorable event when Inman stopped the March 18, 1983, Texas presentation in Chicago and told MCC's board: "What a historic moment this is when these two [UT and A&M] stand together."

While UT and Texas A&M collaboration with regard to MCC has not occurred as broadly and deeply as predicted in 1983, Texas presented the vision of such cross-institutional collaboration in a very meaningful way for MCC's fact-finding and site-selection committees. The spirit of university collaboration was symbolized at the highest levels (first-level influencers) by the chancellors of the University of Texas system and the Texas A&M system. This collaborative spirit was enacted at the operational level during faculty presentations to MCC. Pike Powers (interview, March 27, 1986) remembered the practice session on May 9, which included senior faculty from both UT and Texas A&M. In Powers' mind, this was a crucial event:

> We asked them [the university faculty] to all stand in a particular place. We videotaped and critiqued their presentations. We didn't want any one participant to talk too long and be boring or dull. They resented being told all that stuff. They're typically stars in their respective fields in microelectronics, electrical engineering, computer science, and all that. This really flipped them out that day, but they all showed up and did their bit. What happened unexpectedly is that as they all got over there and started practicing, they all started talking and working with each other and they became a

team of their own even though they were from A&M and UT. They sort of said: "Hey, we're in this together. We've got to look good as a team, as a unit." So a lot of the provincial turf guarding fell by the wayside the day that we got them over there to practice. I'm satisfied that if we hadn't made them practice, they would have been on different sides of the room [during MCC's site visit], and they wouldn't have cooperated as fully.[28]

SELLING AUSTIN TO MCC

The Texas leaders had a formidable marketing task regarding their competition with San Diego, Raleigh-Durham, and Atlanta. They knew that a straw poll of MCC shareholder representatives showed that Austin ranked last among the four finalists in terms of quality of life. How the Texas team sold MCC on Austin is an excellent example of "social marketing," the application of marketing strategies from for-profit selling of commercial products to the selling of ideas like good health, safety, and a clean environment (Kotler and Zaltman, 1971). Table 3.6 lists key marketing aspects of "The Texas Incentive for Austin."

QUALITY-OF-LIFE ISSUES

Pike Powers (interview, March 27, 1986) stated:

On the flight to California [on April 21, 1983] with Watson and the others, we started realizing that the quality-of-life thing was pretty important. Del Asmussen of MCC mentioned that they had done some kind of poll at Control Data and asked MCC member companies what they liked about the various finalist cities. Austin didn't rate very well on some things. The clear import of that message was that you need to tackle the quality of life issue, and you need to tackle air transportation. Here are some of your problem areas that you've got to nail up front.

Table 3.6 Key marketing strategies in the
Texas campaign for MCC

1. A Texas proposal, not just an Austin proposal, through the involvement of government, business, and academic sectors
2. Synergy of the Austin Task Force and the "war room" strategy meetings
3. Strong commitment of the Texas governor
4. Involvement of professional public relations personnel
5. Involvement of Texas business leaders in a statewide funding campaign for UT-Austin
6. UT and Texas A&M collaboration
7. Intensive data collection about MCC and the competing cities
8. Keeping the Texas incentive package confidential
9. The nurturing of positive perceptions of Austin by means of:
    a. The Texas incentive briefing book
    b. A logo, which emphasized government and academic cooperation with MCC, using the official seals of the state of Texas, the city of Austin, UT, and Texas A&M
    c. A quality-of-life survey
    d. A helicopter tour of Austin's lakes and hill country
    e. A specially commissioned five-minute film touting Austin's quality of life
    f. Securing the services of a Lear 35 jet for MCC officials for two years
10. Attention to detail in the site-selection process, exemplified by:
    a. Only one typo in the briefing book
    b. The piano player in the Performing Arts Center at UT-Austin
    c. The fountain's being turned on outside the LBJ Library
    d. Career planning for spouses of MCC employees

The Semiconductor Research Corporation (SRC), headquartered in Research Triangle, had been formed in 1982 as an association of U.S. semiconductor companies to fund research projects carried out by university scholars. Several of MCC's original shareholder companies belonged to the SRC. A couple had located manufacturing facilities in Research Triangle Park. So North Carolina was a known quality to several MCC member companies. This was one reason why North Carolina ranked first in the straw poll of MCC's board of directors prior to the 1983 site visits.

MCC's site-selection team was impressed by the pleasant climate of San Diego, but they were put off by the attitude they encountered during their visit. MCC was offered a three-acre plot of land at the University of California at San Diego. The view of the Pacific Ocean was breathtaking, but the emphasis in the presentation to MCC was on what a wonderful place it was for recreation. San Diego's considerable assets were not presented well to the MCC representatives. For example, during their visit, the MCC fact-finding team was driven inland to the Scripps' Ranch housing development to see the type of home that a typical MCC employee might purchase. After inspecting one model home, an MCC visitor noted that the main criterion that set the house apart from similar homes in other parts of the United States was its high cost.[29]

Inman personally preferred San Diego. He felt that at least one California site ought to be a finalist. He had even looked at housing in the area. But Inman had to work at selling MCC's shareholders on this idea. During the first evening of the site-selection visit to San Diego, the committee members caucused in the admiral's hotel room after dinner.

> The site-selection team had really come down very cool on San Diego as a prospect. A lot of that opinion was cost [of housing] and the Californians' general attitude that "Gee, you ought to be willing to pay to come to California." So I had to do a lot of work that night and early the next morning. I had to turn that around to at least keep it [San Diego] open for them during the presentation. (Inman interview, January 26, 1987)

THE MCC SITE-SELECTION TEAM VISITS AUSTIN

As an MCC site visitor stated:

> Most of us who had not been to Texas had the image that most people had. You go to Dallas or to Houston, and you watch "Giant," and you think that's the state. In the brochure that Austin's Chamber of Commerce had prepared to sell the city, there is water in every scene. It's a picture of Town Lake, or it's a picture of Lake Travis. . . . When I took the helicopter ride over Austin, I looked down at Lake Travis, and I thought: "Boy, that would be a beautiful place to have my boat." (Rutishauser interview, January 23, 1987)[30]

The Governor's Task Force for MCC commissioned Shipley and Associates, Inc. (a local independent market research agency) to conduct a telephone survey of the quality of life in Austin, San Diego, Raleigh-Durham, and Atlanta. The study utilized 16 scientifically replicable measures among demographically equivalent subsamples of 150 randomly selected respondents in each city. Survey questions focused on (1) the quality of schools, parks, playgrounds, and outdoor recreational activities; (2) entertainment activities and cultural events; (3) community ambiance, safety, and cleanliness; (4) ease of transportation and airport access; (5) housing costs; (6) availability of jobs for spouses; (7) desirability as a place to live and raise children; and (8) climate and air quality. All the cities were considered a desirable place to live by the respondents; however, the objective of the survey was to quantify the relative differences among the four locations. The survey was conducted in the two weeks before MCC's site visit to Austin. Survey results were not to be used unless they favored Austin, but the statistically valid results, as it turned out, did document that Austin, when compared to the other three finalist sites, had a very desirable quality of life on the specified criteria. The notable exception was climate.[31]

However, how the quality-of-life survey was presented to MCC may have had more influence than the actual results. An employee of Neal Spelce Communication, Monty Roberts, presented the results. Roberts (who had honed his marketing skills working for Anheuser-Busch) turned out to be a good choice for the task. He was a loyal, although recent, Austinite who had the distinction of having lived in the other three finalist cities. He worked his own living experiences into his presentation and when he got to the section on crime, he spontaneously blurted out: "You know, I've got a sister that lives in San Diego, and I was talking to her just a couple of weeks ago. Some guy got killed out in her front yard" (Powers interview, March 27, 1986). It would not have mattered what the exact crime statistics were: the rug was pulled out from under San Diego's feet on the crime factor. "When he said, 'My sister told me this guy was killed right out in her front yard,' that little coincidence could not have been planned. He just was getting into it, and out it came." (Black interview, May 5, 1986)

It was during the April 28 meeting with MCC's fact-finding committee and Austin's business leaders that the "tree-hugger" incident occurred.

> We had no idea that the IBM guy was going to say out of the blue (he was not programmed for this) that this was a "tree-hugger town"—that once you get an employee here, they put their arms around a tree and you can't get them to go anywhere else. That came out very spontaneously. Of course, we deliberately got local electronics company people who we knew were going to be very favorable, but we didn't know the IBM official was going to say what he did that day. We knew "Y" of Lockheed would be great because the company had just gone through this extensive computer profile of all these communities and, after 75 or 80 cities, picked Austin. So we knew that having a guy like him in the room wasn't going to be bad. But the tree-hugger metaphor made a big impression on the MCC visitors. (Powers interview, March 27, 1986)

OVERCOMING FATAL FLAWS

Mort Myerson, president of EDS, and Ross Perot attended a Sunday, April 24, noon meeting of the Governor's Task Force. Myerson observed: "These guys are going to want to recruit from all over the country, and Inman's going to want to get around. I think we ought to have a Lear 35 for them." Perot responded: "Has any other state offered a plane yet? No? Well, Dave, can we have your plane for a month or two? Trammel, how about you? OK, now we've got a Lear jet for MCC. What else do we need?" (Cano interview, February 16, 1987). While the Texas offer of a Lear jet for a period of two years took on tremendous symbolic value, its use actually proved to be of little importance to MCC's operations.

The Research Triangle officials who first became aware of the MCC competition did not contact their governor's office until the very last minute. Nor did they bring North Carolina business leaders into the drive for MCC. The lack of significant private-sector involvement in the MCNC and in North Carolina's microelectronics initiative in general was one of the reasons why MCC selected Austin, Texas, rather than the Research Triangle (Whittington, 1985). Research Triangle officials played the MCC game alone, at least in the early stages of the competition. They saw MCC as another high-tech company that they wanted to recruit. Such a go-it-alone approach was to doom their efforts, as MCC was looking for a candidate site that demonstrated a spirit of collaboration among academic, state and local government, and business interests.

Perot was concerned that Texas business leaders were not being involved closely enough with Admiral Inman. So Perot phoned Governor White, urging him to organize a meeting for April 21, but Inman had to be in California that same day. Perot had the solution. He sent a plane to pick up Inman after his speech in Washington at 11:00 o'clock on the night of April 20. The half-day meeting in Austin included breakfast with Perot, Watson, Powers, and UT Chancellor Donald Walker, which was followed by a meeting with high-level executives from some of Austin's more prominent high-tech firms. As Inman remembers (interview, January 26, 1987):

> I got to Austin at about 3:00 o'clock in the morning, slept a few hours at the Hyatt, had breakfast and met with the Texas business leaders to talk about the whole concept of MCC, and then flew on to the West Coast in Ross's plane for my noontime speech. . . . I had passengers on the plane . . . John Watson, Gerry Fonken, and Ben Love. It was a working two and one-half hour trip.

They wanted to squeeze out every detail about what our needs were, what our interests were. . . . The business community in Texas really did play a very big role. I should underline that. For the executives on the MCC site-selection committee much more than for me. Businessmen talking about how it was to do business in the state was a significant plus.

One MCC site-selection committee member, John Lacey of CDC, had a schedule conflict and could not attend the planned visit to Austin on April 28. The Governor's Task Force worked to turn this potential problem into an opportunity. Perot flew his Lear from Dallas to Austin to pick up Powers and Fonken and then to Houston to meet Lacey as he got off a flight from Baltimore. "We had 24 hours with him, and every minute was precious—he was a voting member of the site-selection committee—it gave us an extra hour in the plane from Houston to Austin, and we were also able to taxi Perot's plane next to the Governor's and have Lacey meet Governor White at the Austin airport as he [Lacey] got off the Lear." (Powers interview, March 27, 1986)
     Powers stated:

We were given credit for being geniuses, but a lot of it was coming right to us straight from MCC. One of the reasons we didn't let any of those people fly in here [Austin] on commercial aircraft, if we could avoid it, was that we didn't want them snagged up at the Dallas/Fort Worth airport. Part of the reason that we picked up Lacey, other than wanting to have him for an extra hour, was that we didn't want him being jacked around in an airport and having a bad experience changing planes getting to Austin. We didn't want anybody left with the wrong impression or experiences. What we did was try to take all of our negatives we were hearing from MCC and overcome them.

ATTENTION TO STRATEGIC ISSUES

Texas was the only finalist site to promise assistance in resolving MCC's potential antitrust problem with the federal government. The Governor's Task Force knew that MCC was concerned about possible antitrust prosecution by the U.S. Department of Justice. So Texas' senior Congressmen Jake Pickle and Jim Wright and other influential Washington leaders were recruited to work with MCC and its shareholder companies to secure federal legislation in order to counter the antitrust threat to MCC (see Chapter 7).

ATTENTION TO DETAIL

Powers (interview, March 27, 1986) remembered how he and John Watson were continually monitored by Perot to make certain that no detail was left unattended:

> He [Perot] used to phone me in the middle of the night and ask: "Have you done this? Have you got that covered?" Finally, one day he turned to John Watson and me and said: "I'm not going to ask you about paying attention to detail ever again." And he didn't. Talk about a guy who pays attention to detail. He is incredible.

Pegg was taking a shower at his home when Admiral Inman telephoned from the San Diego airport to inquire how MCC's site-selection team was to get to their hotel. At first, Pegg couldn't understand how Inman and the team had arrived three hours early. Later, he found out that his secretary had gotten confused about the three hours' difference in time zones between Washington, D.C., and San Diego. This type of goof did not happen in Texas, where every detail was checked and rechecked.[32]

In Austin on May 10, 1983, MCC's site-selection committee was treated to a breakfast of quail in Lady Bird Johnson's suite at the LBJ Library on the University of Texas campus. Mrs. Johnson made a cameo appearance, and a wonderful little exchange occurred between Governor White and Admiral Inman, who inquired whether it was quail season. Inman recalled: "It wasn't quail hunting season. But they were serving it for breakfast that morning.

Nobody ever quite explained where the quail came from." (Inman interview, January 26, 1987)

Just before the MCC site-selection committee arrived at the library, Pike Powers happened to look out across the UT campus from the fourth-story window of the library. He was disturbed to see that the massive fountain at the entrance was shut down, drained, and being cleaned. As Powers remembered (interview, March 27, 1986): "I look out there, it's a pretty day, and the fountain is dead." The site-selection committee would soon be walking by that fountain. Powers made a hurried call to a UT official and requested that the fountain be turned on. So while the site-selection committee ate dove, the cleaning crew was removed and the fountain turned on just in time to add to the ambience of the beautiful Texas morning as the visitors walked past the shimmering fountain on their way to UT's Peforming Arts Center.[33]

The Performing Arts Center—just across the street from the LBJ Library—is a beautiful, five-story, state-of-the-art facility. The Texas team thought it would serve as an important symbol to MCC that Austin was more than just a small country town. They realized that the R&D consortium had to attract the best and the brightest researchers from such culturally rich areas as Boston, San Francisco, and Minneapolis. While inspecting the center in preparation for MCC's site visit, John Watson, the chair of the Austin team commented (interview, January 23, 1987): "Well, if there's nothing going on in it, the center is not too exciting." Someone else suggested: "Let's get a Juilliard School pianist playing up on the stage, like he's practicing." Admiral Inman (interview, January 26, 1987) later recalled: "We walk in there and they [MCC's site-selection committee] look down, and there's this guy playing a Steinway on the stage. They were totally in awe. It was amazing, the effect of it."

Not only would MCC have to recruit highly educated employees to Austin, but the consortium would also be recruiting the employees' spouses. As Meg Wilson remembered (interview, April 8, 1993): "We went to such detail that we even had a plan to help MCC spouses find jobs or otherwise get acclimated to Austin. . . . I believe that was a unique feature . . . the demographics indicated that many young researchers would have professional working spouses." The Austin Apartment Association agreed to provide a pool of 100 apartments near what would be MCC's temporary headquarters site. The apartments were made available on a floating basis without deposits and served as temporary housing for MCC personnel.

While MCC's fact-finding team actually exercised great influence in the final decision, San Diego, Atlanta, and Raleigh-Durham perceived that they played a much less important role than the voting members of MCC's site-selection committee. So while these finalist sites wined and dined the site-selection committee, they tended to treat the advance fact-finding team with much less attention. Austin was the only one of the four finalist sites to treat both teams as being equally important.

Interviewer:	Four years later, please remember what impressed you and the MCC site-selection committees most about Texas?
Inman:	It was the mix of talent, the mix of people; it was the warmth. Where they [Texas] really scored was in all the things they did with the fact-finding team. The other three finalist sites tended to say: "Well, gee, a fact-finding team. These are sort of low-level guys, so don't bother." So frankly they [Texas] made many points with the fact-finding team. Like swooping them around in the helicopters and so forth. And then the little things like the concert pianist [in the UT Performing Arts Center] have become sort of a folklore.
Interviewer:	And being attended to by the governor . . . .
Inman:	And dinner at Ellen and Alfred King's residence. A lot of things like that clearly had an impact. (Inman interview, July 21, 1987)

CONCLUSIONS

During the early months of 1983, the most pressing challenge for MCC's founders was to successfully launch the nation's first major for-profit R&D consortium. The Japanese were rapidly moving ahead with their ICOT program. The threat to the U.S. computer industry seemed imminent. MCC's steering committee elected to conduct a national competition to select the best site for MCC's headquarters, one that would allow the consortium to get off to a rapid and successful beginning and to sustain the consortium over the long term.

The consortium was to be a state-of-the-art facility staffed by the nation's brightest computer scientists and engineers. Fifty-seven cities representing 27 states made a bid for MCC's headquarters. MCC was courted by business leaders, university presidents, and federal and state government officials. National media attention raised the stakes and motivated interest. MCC representatives believed that the consortium should be located (1) in an area that had a high quality of life to facilitate the recruitment of top researchers and (2) near a major research university that had the potential to become world-class in microelectronics and computer science and could provide a resource pool of highly qualified talent. These and other criteria narrowed the site-selection competition to four sites, which had the initial preference ranking of Raleigh-Durham, San Diego, Atlanta, and Austin.

After a brief but intense site-selection process, Austin became MCC's top choice for its headquarters location. In this chapter we identified the following key factors that moved Austin from last to first in the competition for MCC:

- Austin did not win MCC simply because Texas gave a large financial incentive to the consortium but because of how these funds were to be used—primarily, the planned-for excellence in microelectronics and computer science research and graduate education of the state's two premier research universities.
- Austin did not win MCC because Admiral Inman personally favored the capital city but rather in spite of the fact that he preferred San Diego.
- Success in MCC's site-selection competition depended on the ability of the competing cities to obtain relevant, crucial information in a context of high uncertainty. Austin was more successful than San Diego, Atlanta, and Raleigh-Durham in accurately perceiv-

ing what MCC was looking for and fulfilling those expectations.

The Texas team used its intelligence about MCC to meet the strategic and operational needs of the consortium. For example, Texas was the only finalist site to promise high-level political support in resolving MCC's potential antitrust problems with the U.S. government. The Texas team also made sure that the state's incentives to MCC targeted personal levels in terms of the smallest details.

- Texas' successful bid for MCC was facilitated by the commitment of key public/private leaders who believed that Texas had to have MCC, by the cultural proximity of key participants, and by the spatial proximity of centers of academic, business, and government leadership.

- Texas displayed considerable statewide collaboration and a local, focused synergy to achieve a united Texas incentive for Austin. Public/private collaboration was facilitated by strong leadership from a few committed first-level influencers and visionaries from business, academic, and government sectors who were able to motivate capable and resourceful second-level influencers.

Most important, Texas' bid to MCC did not suffer from the type of fatal flaw that characterized the recruitment efforts of San Diego, Atlanta, and Raleigh-Durham. In each MCC visit to the three unsuccessful finalist sites, a seemingly small but symbolic incident occurred that became an important marker event in the site's losing bid to attract MCC.

In Atlanta, a key negative event occurred when Mayor Andrew Young remarked that his city could serve as a hub for the transportation of MCC's products. Such a comment by an important city official signaled, to the site-selection committee, a lack of understanding of MCC's purpose

Dan Pegg and his team of San Diego leaders had to overcome three main handicaps in their race for MCC: (1) the lack of high-quality university research and graduate programs in microelectronics and computer science, (2) the high cost of housing, and (3) the questionable commitment of California's leaders to educational excellence.

In Research Triangle, the salary cap of $68,000 for top professors in the University of North Carolina's Department of Computer Science created the impression on the part of MCC visitors that North Carolina universities were not really serious in striving for world-class academic excellence. Governor Hunt and Georgia Tech President Pettit were reassuring to MCC, but MCC was concerned about who would follow Hunt and Pettit. A lack of participation by local business leaders in the recruitment effort was also noticed by MCC personnel during their brief visit to North Carolina.

These fatal flaws provided MCC site visitors with a way to give meaning to the complex offers being made by each of the finalist sites. Using such simplified marker events is a common practice when a group must make a decision in the face of a high level of complexity and uncertainty. In this sense, Austin had an important advantage because of its extremely thorough preparation, which prevented the emergence of a fatal flaw in its presentation of "The Texas Incentive for Austin." The lack of direct commercial flights from the Austin airport could have been a serious disadvantage in the eyes of the MCC visitors. But such complications were circumvented and turned into the positive attribute of providing MCC with a Lear jet. Austin increased its stature as the site for MCC's headquarters because the Texas team successfully marketed the city's assets to meet MCC's needs while not making a fatal mistake in its presentation of the Texas incentive.

NOTES

1. We analyze the 1983 MCC location decision from a variety of perspectives in order to learn useful lessons about unstructured decision making across public/private sectors. We concentrate on the individual level of analysis, at which collaborative activity ultimately succeeds or fails. Some of the identified participants are nationally prominent, many are well known in their respective regions, and a few are not well known even within the regions where they live. However, all these participants were important actors in the national competition for MCC, and all add a richness of perspectives and varied viewpoints about what can facilitate or inhibit public/private collaboration on projects of national and regional importance.

2. "Techno" reflects an emphasis on technology; "polis" is Greek for city-state and suggests a balance between public and private sectors. The plural form of the word "polis" is "poleis"; therefore, we use the plural "technopoleis" rather than "technopolises" or "technopoli." For further information on the technopolis concept, see Tatsuno (1986); Smilor, Kozmetsky, and Gibson (1988); and Gibson, Kozmetsky, and Smilor (1992).

3. Some technopoleis are the result of long-term planning and varying degrees of public/private collaboration, such as Tsukuba and Kansai Science Cities, Japan; Bari, Italy; Sophia-Antipolis, France; Pyramids Technology Valley, Egypt; and Raleigh-Durham, North Carolina. Two of the oldest and most famous U.S. technopoleis—Silicon Valley, California, and Route 128, Boston—were not based on long-term planning. This is not to say that these areas did not have visionaries and champions of high-technology development, such as the important role played by Frederick Terman of Stanford University in the development of Silicon Valley (Rogers and Larsen, 1984). Some technopoleis have benefited from varying degrees of visionary planning and sporadic public/private collaboration, such as Austin, Texas; Troy, New York; Phoenix, Arizona; Cambridge and Oxford, England; and Bangalore, India (see Tatsuno, 1988; Morita and Hiraoka, 1988; Onda, 1988; Segal, 1988; Lafitte, 1988; Bozzo and Gibson, 1990; and Singhal et al., 1990).

4. First- and second-level influencers are identified in the communication literature as (1) cosmopolites (individuals who have a relatively high degree of communication with a system's external environments), (2) opinion leaders (individuals who are able to influence other individuals' attitudes or overt behavior), and (3) liaisons (individuals who connect otherwise separate communication networks). The personal communication networks of first- and second-level influencers tend to be outward looking and global, as opposed to closed and provincial. We focus our analysis on the actions of such influencers from different sectors of the technopolis wheel (see Table A.1).

5. This chapter's in-depth analysis of the MCC site-location process focuses on first- and second-level influencers who networked across the technopolis wheel's seven segments to bring MCC to Austin, Texas. Chapter 6 discusses (1) the fracturing of Austin's public/private consensus and (2) the emergence of new kinds of institutional developments—in Austin and other sites that competed for MCC—to create technology-based jobs and spur regional economic development.

6. Santa Rita #1 was the first producing oil well located on Permanent University Fund (PUF) lands, see note 19. The oil rig's memorial plaque states that on May 28, 1923: "It [Santa Rita #1] blew in to launch a new era in the development of the University of Texas and the Agricultural and Mechanical College of Texas [Texas A&M]. The well was named by its drillers for Santa Rita, the saint of the impossible, because of the popular notion that there was no chance of success in this location." The land was initially given to the universities when it was fairly desolate and of little value, before it was discovered that there was oil beneath the barren, dry plains of sagebrush, mesquite, and grazing longhorns.

7. The perception of MCC's being an engine of regional economic growth was not deliberately fostered by MCC officials. MCC was to pursue long-term research. If economic development were to result from MCC-produced technologies, it would take many years and would most likely occur at the sites of the shareholder company divisions that used the technology.

8. Inman's ongoing dialogue with Pegg was not considered unfair to the other three finalists. Inman had told representatives of all potential sites that he would be happy to visit them to help shape their final package to MCC. But he would not tell any site about any other site's offer. Inman briefly visited Austin and North Carolina as well as San Diego. Atlanta did not ask for Inman's assistance.

9. Some public and private leaders in both the United States and Japan suggest that the two countries are engaged in an economic war. If the reader accepts this metaphor, it is interesting to compare (1) the difficulty in activating, or switching on, Washington's political and military leaders concerning warnings or visible signs of the impending surprise attack on Pearl Harbor with (2) the difficulty in activating national and local public/private leaders to meaningful action concerning the seriousness of the economic threat that Japan posed to U.S. industrial competitiveness.

10. In 1993, Cisneros was confirmed as President Clinton's HUD secretary (the Department of Housing and Urban Development). During his confirmation hearings, Cisneros described himself as an advocate of the cities, a skeptic of the status quo, and a believer in experimentation, federalism, and the need to provide people with hope. Cisneros is fond of quoting Woodrow Wilson's observation that the most important human discovery is not fire or the wheel but that people can work together as a team.

11. Communication network theory emphasizes the importance of "weak ties" in connecting otherwise separate communication cliques (Granovetter, 1973). This example shows how crucial triggering information is transferred across separate communication networks through weak ties and circuitous routes.

12. Goss saw himself as a community activist but was sometimes regarded by the city's political leaders as a busybody. Nevertheless, he played an important catalytic role for Austin regarding MCC, just as Henry Cisneros did for San Antonio. After Austin won MCC, Goss was cited in a resolution by the Texas State Senate for his Paul Revere–like role.

13. We emphasize this point because none of the other finalist site delegations thought of such a strategy, or at least none acted on a vision to improve university education and research the way that the Texas task force did.

14. In communication network theory, these individuals are called cosmopolites and opinion leaders. They each had extended communication network ties to key leaders from the academic, business, and government sectors throughout the state of Texas and nationwide.

15. Professional basketball center Bill Russell spent his career searching for the jamming experience. He stated in his memoirs: "Every so often a Celtic game would heat up so that it became more than a physical or even mental game. It would be magical. . . . It came rarely, and would last anywhere from five minutes to a whole quarter or more. The game would just take off, and there'd be a natural ebb and flow that reminded you of how rhythmic and musical basketball is supposed to be." (Russell and Branch, 1979, pp. 156–157)

16. Oil prices began their dramatic plunge from $40 to under $10 per barrel in 1983, soon after MCC came to Austin.

17. In Texas, the importance of one's ties to the Lone Star State and to the region's two premier universities (UT-Austin and Texas A&M) is not trivial. The authors were raised in the east and midwest and both spent more than ten years on the West Coast. Texans exhibit a pride in their state, a "can-do" attitude, which contributes to statewide collaboration in economic development and political activities.

18. Compare the geographic proximity of key players in the different sectors of the technopolis wheel in Austin with the situation in California, where the state's government is located in Sacramento, about 600 miles from San Diego. The office of the chancellor of the University of California system is located near UC Berkeley, about 500 miles from UC at San Diego.

19. The Permanent University Fund (PUF) is a public endowment contributing to the support of the University of Texas system and the Texas A&M system. The Texas constitution of 1876 established the PUF through the appropriation of land grants that comprise over 2.1 million acres of agricultural and desolate land in West Texas. Higher education got a significant boost in the Lone Star State when oil was discovered under this largely barren land in May 1923. By April 30, 1992, the book value of the PUF was about $3.6 billion. Interest comes to nearly $145 million annually. Two-thirds of the income goes to the University of Texas system and a third to the Texas A&M system.

20. The MCC Leadership Steering Committee was chaired by Ben Love (chairman of the board and CEO, Texas Commerce Bancshares, Inc., Houston), with the assistance of Lee E. Straus (senior vice president and chief administrative officer, Texas Commerce Bancshares, Inc., Houston), and composed of the following with their regions of responsibility:

G. D. Anderson, Jr., Bovina	Perry Bass, Fort Worth
Donald Bentsen, Edinburg	Lloyd Bentsen, Houston
Jack Blanton, Houston	H.R. (Bum) Bright, Dallas
Edward A. Clark, Austin	James Clement, Kingsville
B.W. Crain, Longview	Robert Duffey, Jr., Brownsville
Tom Frost, San Antonio	Travis Johnson, El Paso
Dee J. Kelly, Fort Worth	John T. Kelley, El Paso
Ken Kelley, Amarillo	Lowell Lebermann, Austin
W.D. Noel, Odessa	George Mitchell, The Woodlands
Jack Rains, Houston	Ben J. Rogers, Beaumont
Wayne Showers, McAllen	Warren Woodward, Fort Worth
Sam Young, El Paso	

21. Considerable care was also taken to secure an IRS ruling covering the income-tax deductibility of the contributions to be used for MCC's research building and laboratory. The favorable tax ruling regarding private gifts and foundations came from the IRS on March 19, 1984: "We conclude that bona fide contributions and gifts [and foundations] made to 'W' for the construction and equipping of the new facility in 'X' will be charitable contributions within the meaning of section 170(c)(1) [4945 for private foundations]."

22. Austin's steering committee was headed by Ben T. Head, chair and chairman of RepublicBank of Texas and included Robert T. Present, chairman of the board and CEO, Texas Commerce Bank; John Tolleson, president, American Bank; Robert Lane, chairman, InterFirst Bank; Jack Collins, president, First City Bank; Frank McBee, chairman, Tracor; John Watson, The Watson Group and head of the governor's and Austin task forces; Ed Hanslik, partner, Arthur Andersen and member of the Austin Task Force; and Lee Cooke, president, Austin Chamber of Commerce. All the major industries of Austin—a total of 22 categories, including banks ($225,000), developers ($300,000), home builders ($250,000), major landowners ($200,000), realtors ($200,000), savings and loans ($100,000), attorneys ($150,000), CPAs ($75,000), auto dealers ($100,000), hotels/motels ($75,000), restaurants ($50,000), retailers ($40,000), utilities ($35,000), brokers ($40,000), airlines ($40,000), communications ($150,000), and so forth—were reviewed in order to identify a key contact person to serve on the local executive committee (called "Friends of MCC" in Austin) and to secure the financial allocations from each business group. Of the 22 groups, only the home builders (with a $280,413 contribution) met their funding goal. The attorneys, construction companies, restaurants, and major landowners did not pledge or give any funds to the MCC fund-raising effort.

23. Woodson received his Ph.D. in engineering from The University of Texas at Austin in 1942. His distinguished career earned him a position at MIT and a membership in the prestigious National Academy of Engineering. In 1971, he was recruited back to UT. Woodson had represented the university in previous efforts by Austin's Chamber of Commerce to recruit electronics companies to the city.

24. Ben Streetman was a Texan and had attended The University of Texas at Austin where he earned his B.S. in electrical engineering. He left Texas to pursue his Ph.D. and made an academic name for himself at the University of Illinois. In 1982, he was recruited back to UT. Streetman was a world-class specialist in semiconductors and had the right expertise for talking bits and bytes with the MCC committee in Chicago and during the national site competition process.

25. Clif Drummond was born in Jones County, near Abilene, Texas, close to where Woodson was raised. Drummond came to UT in the 1960s to major in pharmacy. He soon became involved in student politics and was elected student body president. He switched his major to political science. After six years of study, he left UT to become Congressman Jake Pickle's administrative assistant, heading his Austin office. After several years of business experience (running a small high-tech firm), Drummond returned to the university at the invitation of his friend and mentor Herb Woodson.

26. Indeed, when MCC's headquarters building was constructed at West Balcones, it opened up one whole side of the research park, which had previously been undeveloped acreage. With MCC as the magnet, it proved feasible later in 1983 to convince the UT board of regents to approve $52 million for building construction and improvements for the west tract of Balcones.

27. This perception of strong momentum for higher education turned out to be paradoxical in light of the downturn in such support a short 18 months after MCC located in Austin. But in spring 1983, MCC site visitors were impressed with how much Texas wanted to improve the quality of education in general and in electrical engineering and computer science in particular.

28. According to one respondent, it was also important that Ross Perot, a major donor to both universities, sat through the practice session. His presence added a sense of importance and bipartisanship to the event.

29. A San Diego leader observed in retrospect that it may have been a mistake to drive the MCC team inland about 30 minutes to the Scripps' Ranch area, away from the beautiful coastline and beaches. "Why pay $200,000 for a tract house and a view that was not that distinctive?" The MCC site-selection team could have been shown houses overlooking the Pacific Ocean, which were available for $200,000 and up. Then the MCC visitors might at least have felt that the high housing costs in San Diego were more justified.

30. When the MCC site-selection team arrived in Austin, they were flown by heli- copter over the lakes and the green Texas hill country and were assured that this scenery was quite affordable.

31. Of course the survey could have been more of a reflection of the respondents' propensity to be critical or favorable within different geographical regions. Texans are known to be proud of their home whether it is Lubbock, Waco, or Austin. Furthermore, there were no statistics on how many of the respondents had actually lived in or visited each of the four regions. As one observer noted, ". . . the study showed respondents didn't always know what they were talking about. While Austinites rate theirs the second safest community [of the four sites], crime statistics . . . show Austin had the second highest crime rate." (Marks, 1983)

32. For example, whenever MCC visitors were to be transported around Austin, the inflation of the limousine's tires was tested and retested. Extra limousines stood in waiting and then followed the convoy, in case one of the vehicles had a problem. Several Austin respondents commented that certain city and state leaders had vivid memories of their experience in preparing for visits by President Johnson to Austin during the years when he was in the White House. Many of the lessons learned during the LBJ years became part of the operating procedures for the MCC site visits.

33. MCC's facilities were never expected to be located on the UT campus. MCC employees were not likely to stroll around the LBJ Library's fountain on their lunch break. So what was the connection? In decision analysis terms, how much weight should be given to such details—the breakfast of quail and the operating fountain—concerning the site-selection committee's decision to locate MCC in Austin? We let the reader judge.

APPENDIX 3.1

Main events in the 1983 selection of Austin
as MCC's headquarters

February   MCC sends letters of invitation to state economic
                development directors and to seven cities especially
                selected by Inman and MCC.

February 8   Narcisso Cano (director of economic and employ-
                ment development for the city of San Antonio) meets
                Meg Wilson (on the governor's staff for planning
                and development for the state of Texas) at the Small
                Business Technology Institute weekend meeting
                in Phoenix.

February 10   Dan Pegg, president of the San Diego Economic
                Development Corporation, arranges to meet Admiral
                Inman while he is in San Diego for a board of direc-
                tors meeting of SAIC.

February 27   UT Vice President Bill Livingston and Bernard Goss
                talk to Admiral Inman after his lecture at the LBJ
                School of Public Affairs at the University of Texas.
                They both learn from Inman that Austin is not yet
                actively involved in the MCC competition. The next
                morning, Livingston calls Ben Head, president of
                Austin's Chamber of Commerce. Goss calls his
                friend, John Gray, manager of economic develop-
                ment for Austin's Chamber of Commerce.

March   Cano calls Wilson and encourages her to activate
                Governor White concerning MCC. Wilson sends a
                memo to her boss Harden Weidemann, director of
                Planning and Intergovernmental Relations.

March 9   Memo from Wiedemann to Governor White, asking
                him to lead the Texas delegation to Chicago for the
                presentation to MCC.

March 13   Mayor Cisneros of San Antonio drives to Austin to
                talk with George Kozmetsky, director of the IC^2
                Institute, about MCC. He then drives back to San
                Antonio to talk with Pike Powers, who is vacation-
                ing in San Antonio.

March 14	Pike Powers briefs Governor White about the importance of MCC. Four days of frenzied preparation follow.
March 18	Governor White leads the three-city Texas delegation (Austin, Dallas, and San Antonio) to Chicago for its presentation at the O'Hare Airport Hilton Hotel from 11:00 A.M. to 12:30 P.M. John Gray and Ben Streetman present for Austin and The University of Texas at Austin.
March 21	Inman and his wife Nancy visit Austin on a so-called secret visit. Inman gives a luncheon talk to the Southwest Cattleraisers Association. After the presentation, John Gray gives Inman and his wife an automobile tour of Austin.
March 25	Governor White writes a follow-up letter to Admiral Inman promising that he will learn more about microelectronics.
April 12	MCC announces the four finalists: Austin, Atlanta, San Diego, and Raleigh-Durham. Pike Powers starts putting together the Governor's Task Force for MCC.
April 13	John Gray learns of MCC's site-selection time schedule from MCC's Del Asmussen. Governor White takes over control of the MCC campaign from the Austin Chamber of Commerce.
April 14	An Austin Chamber of Commerce meeting with the governor's staff is attended by Professor Herb Woodson of UT's College of Engineering.
April 15	Ed Hanslik, vice president, economic development, of the Austin Chamber of Commerce, calls the first meeting of what is to become the Austin Task Force, which meets in the "war room" at Neal Spelce Communications. Governor White meets in his office with UT officials.
April 17	Governor White chairs a meeting at the governor's mansion and appoints the Governor's Task Force.

April 18   The San Antonio MCC team visits the capital city to advise the Austin Task Force how it should structure its offer to MCC.

                The idea of conducting a telephone survey of quality-of-life factors in the four competing sites is considered.

April 19   Asmussen informs Pike Powers, in an hour-long telephone conversation that the MCC fact-finding team will visit Austin on April 27–29. A midnight meeting is held at John Watson's home to plan for the visit. A key question that Powers was asked by Asmussen concerned whether The University of Texas at Austin was determined to become a leader in microelectronics.

                Top UT officials continue discussion of their plans.

                Drummond agrees to contact author James Michener, who is currently living in Austin, to ask for a quote describing the capital city's favorable quality of life. The quote is to be used in the final report to MCC's site-selection committee.

April 20   Telephone interviews begin for the four-city, quality-of-life survey. Staff members of Neal Spelce's firm conduct the survey.

April 21–30   The MCC fact-finding team visits the four finalist sites in the following order: (1) Raleigh-Durham, (2) Atlanta, (3) Austin, and (4) San Diego.

April 21   Harold Falkenberg of Neal Spelce Communications begins drafting "The Texas Incentive for Austin." Ross Perot brings Inman in his Lear jet from Washington, D.C., to Austin for a half-day visit. Inman breakfasts with UT system Chancellor Don Walker, Pike Powers, Ross Perot, and John Watson, and then meets with Houston banker, Ben Love, and 35 Texas business leaders at the governor's mansion. They stress Texas' advantage in corporate tax law. Powers, Watson, and others fly on to California with Inman in Perot's jet.

April 22   The Austin Task Force decides to make a five and a
                half-minute video about Austin that will be ready by
                Monday, April 25.

                University officials meet with Governor White in his
                office and adopt the UT plan for increased effort in
                microelectronics research.

April 24   The Governor's Task Force meets all day. Results are
                available from the quality-of-life survey. The
                decision is made to lend a Lear jet to MCC for
                two years, to counter the lack of Austin's direct
                airline connections.

April 26   A City of Austin resolution of support is signed by
                all city council members. The Austin Task Force
                reviews a draft of "The Texas Incentive for Austin."

                UT officials meet from 7:15 A.M. to 7:00 P.M. in the
                board of regents room, chaired by Jon Newton. The
                group includes Regents Vice Chairman, Robert
                Baldwin, Chancellor Walker, UT President Peter
                Flawn, Vice President for Academic Affairs and
                Research Gerhard Fonken, the deans of engineering
                and natural sciences, chairmen of computer science
                and electrical engineering departments, and Clif
                Drummond.

April 27   MCC fact-finding team arrives from Atlanta late in
                the day on a Lear jet provided by Perot, tours the
                city by helicopter, and has dinner with the governor
                at 8:15 P.M. Falkenberg arrives at the back door of
                the governor's mansion with the 2.5-inch-thick
                leather-bound report of "The Texas Incentive for
                Austin," minutes before the arrival at the front door
                of the MCC fact-finding team. The 250-page report
                is later found to contain only one typo.

April 28   Austin presents to MCC's fact-finding team.
                Breakfast with the governor and task force members.
                Lunch with leaders of local industry. Dinner at the
                ranch of Alfred and Ellen King.

April 29	MCC fact-finding team visits Texas A&M before flying to San Diego in the Lear.
May 8–12	The MCC site-selection committee visits the four finalist sites in the following order: (1) San Diego (May 9), (2) Austin (May 10), (3) Atlanta (May 11), and (4) Raleigh-Durham (May 12), the reverse order of the visits by MCC's fact-finding team.
May 9	Dry run of the Texas presentation.
	The MCC site-selection team is flown in a Lear jet from San Diego so that the Texas leaders can spend a few more hours with MCC's visitors.
	MCC site-selection committee arrives in Austin late in the afternoon and tours the city and Lake Travis by helicopter. Dinner with the task force at the governor's mansion.
May 10	Breakfast of quail on the eighth floor of the LBJ Library and a multimedia presentation with taped messages from Senator John Tower and Representative Jim Wright.
	Lunch at UT's Littlefield House.
May 12	The MCC team votes to select Austin as the site for MCC's headquarters, while flying from Raleigh-Durham to Washington, D.C.
May 16 (evening)	After approval of the team's choice by MCC's board of directors, Inman telephones the news of Austin's selection to the governors of the four finalist states.
May 17	Inman makes the official announcement of MCC's Austin location at the National Computer Conference in Anaheim, California.
May 18	Inman flies to Austin to address the Texas House and Senate, and holds a news conference on the lawn of the capitol.
July	MCC moves its office from Washington, D.C., to Austin and begins recruiting personnel.

4

MCC in Operation

In reflecting on the decisions taken in 1982 to get MCC launched, one must resist the temptation to measure the appropriateness of those choices against the realities of 1993. In 1982 the computer and related industries were in a state of shock. The floppy disk business was gone, consumer electronics was gone, the DRAM business was going. Japan, Inc. was viewed as an impregnable giant controlled by a super-brain, MITI, with a voracious appetite for swallowing up industries and ultimately dominating the world's economy. Furthermore, the U.S. government had recently convicted a number of GE and Westinghouse executives of illegal collaboration. With IBM to contend with on one side, and the Japanese on the other, computer and semiconductor industry executives felt increasingly helpless.

> Phillip W. Arneson, President, Financial Services,
> National Computer Systems and CDC contributor
> to MCC's formation, in personal correspondence
> with the authors, April 8, 1993

A formula for disaster. . . . I'll start a central lab in Austin, Texas, to do long-range research, interacting with the R&D staff of the member companies—in particular the chief technical officers—on a common technical vision. . . . Almost every phrase is enough to sink you.

> Craig Fields, MCC's third CEO, in a
> personal interview with the authors,
> March 1, 1991

189

MCC is an important experiment. It is the United States' first major attempt to get private corporations to collaborate in research while they compete in the marketplace. In 1983, MCC went up against U.S. antitrust law and a long-standing belief in the value of free enterprise and unfettered competition. As of 1993, MCC is still on trial as a symbol of an emerging paradox in U.S. economic development: the belief that for U.S. corporations to compete effectively in the international marketplace, they must collaborate with their domestic competitors.

As described in Chapter 2, during late 1982, an interim board of directors, composed of executives from MCC's ten founding companies, met monthly to negotiate how to design an R&D consortium that could develop generic, cutting-edge, pre-competitive computer hardware and software to enhance the worldwide competitiveness of its shareholders. It was considered essential that the research be carried out in a central laboratory that would encourage close communication with the shareholders. Key areas of concern were: (1) getting MCC up and running; (2) staffing the consortium with high-quality researchers; (3) focusing on appropriate research projects; (4) handling intellectual property and confidentiality issues; and (5) planning how to achieve equitable, timely, and efficient technology transfer to the companies funding the research.

These were challenging tasks. Not only was MCC to be the United States' first large-scale, for-profit R&D consortium, but it was to be funded by a diverse group of highly competitive U.S. computer and semiconductor firms. MCC was an important test to see if U.S. managers could transcend their competitive instincts and provincial concerns to learn how to collaborate in goal-directed, long-term R&D. The goal was to help regain or sustain their technological advantage and beat overseas competitors, particularly the Japanese, in industries considered crucial to U.S. military security and economic strength. The stakes were high, and so was the glare of public and private scrutiny. Harvard professor Robert Reich, a consultant to MCC, stated (quoted in Warsh, 1983b, p. c-1):

> It has been a very delicate task to bring these companies together. You have to understand that there is a very deep suspicion about such working together. . . . The central issue has been designing [MCC] so that

everybody feels they get benefits from the work that is
done, and so that it meets the test of the law.

Since its birth in Orlando, Florida, in 1982, MCC has dramatically changed its structure and process in response to internal and
external forces (see Appendix 4.1 for a chronology of MCC's evolution in operations and organizational structure). Initial operational
decisions—made to accommodate the economic, organizational,
and political realities of 1982–1983—became liabilities to effective
management and technology transfer. One of the hallmarks of MCC
is that the consortium is continually enacting new operational alternatives, areas of research, and methods of technology transfer. On
the one hand, this dynamic nature adds to the challenge of managing and working within the organization, and it makes the consortium difficult to portray accurately at any one point in time. On the
other hand, MCC has served as an excellent laboratory for assessing
the management and operational challenge of commercializing pre-
competitive R&D.[1]

Despite dramatic changes in MCC's structure, organizational
culture, and research activities, the consortium's basic mission has
remained essentially the same: to strengthen and sustain the competitiveness of its member companies—to collaborate to win. Although
a private, for-profit consortium, MCC has traditionally emphasized
technology development and transfer, not profit. Shareholder and
associate member companies are to use MCC technologies to produce products and services of their own design and to compete in
markets of their choice.[2] The for-profit and self-sustaining aspect of
MCC's operations have been increasingly emphasized since 1990.

MCC's most dramatic operational and strategic changes have
occurred during three distinct phases of leadership: (1) a honeymoon era, from 1983 to 1986, under the leadership of Admiral
Inman; (2) a reassessment phase, from 1987 to 1990, under the
leadership of Grant Dove, a 28-year veteran of Texas Instruments;
and (3) a major restructuring phase from 1990 to the present,
directed by former DARPA executive Dr. Craig Fields (see Figure
4.1). During each era, MCC has been confronted with different
challenges and opportunities. Important lessons have been demonstrated about public/private alliances and about learning how to collaborate in research and related activities in order to compete effectively in the world's marketplace.

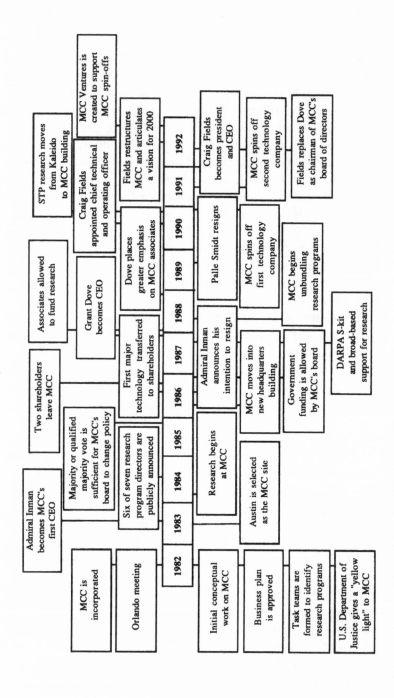

Source: Adapted from Murphy (1987, p. 138).

Figure 4.1 Important changes at MCC during its first decade

We believe that the challenges that have confronted MCC and its member companies foreshadow challenges that confront participants of many other interorganizational alliances (e.g., among government, universities, and private participants as well as other new organizational forms, such as networked or virtual organizations) that formed nationally and internationally during the late 1980s and early 1990s. When it was launched in 1983, MCC was argued by some to be the prototypical organization of the future— i.e., an organization without boundaries composed of strategic alliances with public/private organizations. In this chapter, we document the operational and strategic highlights of MCC's first decade of operation. Appendix 4.2 describes MCC's research program history and output. Appendix 4.3 uses a bibliographic search of co-authored research papers as a means of assessing university, corporate, and government collaboration with MCC.

THE INMAN ERA: 1983–1986

The early Inman years at MCC, from 1983 to 1985, were basically the consortium's honeymoon period.[3] Research programs were getting started with three years' guaranteed funding and a five- to ten-year time frame before concrete results were expected. Corporate chief executive officers and other high-level managers from the shareholder companies generally supported the consortium and attended MCC's regularly scheduled meetings. There was the unifying theme of a common vision and a sense of purpose in being associated with an important, revolutionary, and innovative initiative to spur U.S. industrial competitiveness in cutting-edge technologies. National and international media were generally supportive.

Addressing the issue of whether MCC would integrate the results of its programs into a single computer to combat the Japanese fifth-generation project, Inman commented: "We may end up designing the fastest computer or the largest computer or a substantial series of multiple processing computers or all of the above, depending on the market for it" (Ladendorf, 1983b). Inman and the board believed that MCC's broader approach to research was the best way to proceed.

It may be that some of our best ideas are not in the design of an overall computer, as they are in the appli-

cations (of artificial intelligence, or human interaction
with computers or computer aided design). . . . It may
turn out to be applications in those areas (that are
important) as opposed to something that actually
thinks. (Inman quoted in Ladendorf, 1984)

Despite such optimism, at times, MCC's honeymoon was
strained. Inman used his negotiating skills to fight to save the consortium from the competitive instincts of the member companies,
which had to unlearn old ways and practices in order to learn how
to collaborate. According to Inman (interview, January 26, 1987),
while some shareholders enthusiastically plunged into the process,
"others leaned back and sipped through a long straw."[4] In contrast
to Inman's recollection, an MCC board member during the Inman
years commented: "This is grossly exaggerated. As an involved player, I feel that Inman sat in the cabin of his flagship and waited for
the companies to beat his door down."
One of the first major challenges Inman faced in his effort to
successfully launch MCC was to encourage the rapid recruitment of
a number of shareholder firms that were significant players in the
computer and microelectronics industries. MCC's interim board of
directors established the cafeteria style of research offerings to allow
individual shareholder companies to choose which of the four
research programs they wished to fund. The decision to go for a
cafeteria-style approach helped attract another ten or so companies,
which further increased MCC's shareholder diversity (see Chapter
2). While some potential shareholders (e.g., CDC, Harris, and
Sperry) were committed to funding all four of MCC's research programs, the majority were planning to fund three programs (e.g.,
DEC and NCR), two programs (e.g., AMD and Honeywell), or one
program. The shareholders funding several programs were adamant
that other shareholders should not get benefits from research programs that they did not fund. Such "free-rider" concerns led to
MCC's being structured as a set of four "watertight" compartments
(Figure 4.2).
Access to MCC's facilities and research findings by the general public has always been restricted; however, over the years an
interesting transformation has taken place concerning the value
placed on secrecy and researcher collaboration within the consor-

tium. During the early years (1983–1986), when all the research programs were located at one site, key cards were issued to MCC employees to restrict their access to the different programs. When MCC moved into its new headquarters building in 1986, research was conducted at three different locations, and physical distance acted as a barrier to interprogram collaboration. However, over the years, "leakage of research activities" across research programs has been inhibited mostly through technological barriers (e.g., computer passwords, and different hardware and software platforms) and organizational and cultural barriers (e.g., management styles, research priorities, and technological orientations) of the different research programs. Indeed, the main concern of information sharing moved from one of secrecy and protecting research advancements from unauthorized personnel to the challenge of how to get the researchers, within and across the program areas, to collaborate (more on this later).

MCC was formed to benefit the competitive competencies of the shareholders funding the research, not to disseminate research

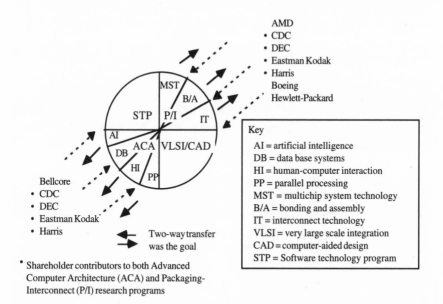

Figure 4.2 Program-specific R&D funding and technology transfer
at MCC, 1983–1986

results to the public. Yet Inman and the research program directors were inundated with a flood of requests for interviews and information. Harking back to his CIA and NSA days, Inman appointed MCC's director of government and public affairs, Bill Stotesbery, as MCC's single point of contact for the press. Within the consortium, Inman encouraged MCC's researchers to use professional judgment and discretion. As remembered by Stotesbery (interview, April 8, 1993): "The marching orders were if you hear it as confidential, keep it confidential. Research information was to be shared on a need-to-know basis only. But we never turned down an interview or a visit to MCC."

MCC's computer systems were not compatible across the four research programs or, at times, even within a research program area. This incompatibility was due to two main reasons. First, each program director was encouraged to select the researchers and support technology that would maximize research excellence. Each research specialist was able to order the equipment he or she preferred. The desire to maximize autonomy for each research program overshadowed the desire for control. Second, in 1983 open systems and enterprise integration were not receiving the level of attention that these philosophies received in the early 1990s. While such systems incompatibility was in accord with the cafeteria-style mode of research program support, it later frustrated the in-house use and sharing of MCC-developed technologies across research programs. The downsizing of MCC in the early 1990s and cost-cutting considerations motivated the establishment of an MCC-wide computer network in late 1991.

Inman later regretted MCC's decision to mount separate research programs; however, MCC's founding executives remain convinced that the consortium could never have been launched if all shareholders had been required to fund all four research programs. Furthermore, antitrust concerns would have increased with a united R&D effort in which 20 of the nation's largest computer, electronics, and semiconductor companies would share information. As Phil Arneson remembered (interview, October 6, 1992): "There is absolutely no question about it. If we had not conceived the 'four programs' concept, there would have been *no* MCC. The concept allowed us to 'coalesce' the merchant semiconductor companies with the systems companies."

Serving on the search committee that hired Inman, Palle Smidt (then the vice president of business strategy at Sperry) worked hard to convince the admiral to take the helm of this important U.S. experiment. As he listened to "all the good reasons" why Inman should join MCC, he convinced himself to leave Sperry to become MCC's highest-ranking official (senior vice president for programs and plans) with extensive industry experience.

Three committees were also formed by high-ranking share-holder executives to set MCC policy in the areas of personnel and compensation, audit, and governance. Under the leadership of Smidt, the governance committee formed a task force on procedures and policy for technology transfer. This committee took nine months to establish MCC-wide policy concerning technology trans-fer between the consortium and the shareholders and another nine months to determine the policy regarding technology transfer among the research programs within MCC.

In the mid-1980s, Smidt was somewhat prophetic about the importance of the speed with which MCC needed to transfer its research into commercial applications: "Because profitability cycles are so short these days and revenue life cycles are so short, we have a tremendous . . . requirement for doing things appropriately with the right content, but also at the right time." Smidt (interview, May 5, 1986) emphasized that

> What [will ultimately be] important is how did we structure it [MCC]. . . . Did we create an environment where highly talented people would be motivated to work, and did we create an environment in which you actually could get jobs done on a timely basis? . . . Don't forget that industries spend most of their time on product development and applied research; therefore, when you go beyond what is driven by market require-ments and spend a lot of dollars, . . . if [they're] not spent correctly, you end it immediately. Just before we signed Sperry to MCC, we canned a long-term research center because we couldn't see what it gave us. If you can't see the benefits, and there is no historical evidence of benefit, you stop things immediately, right?[5]

Smidt (interview, May 5, 1986), speaking in his authoritative Danish accent, pressed the point that in a competitive environment, you have one objective: superior performance:

> If anybody tells you anything else, I think they are kidding themselves. Long-term research has to stack up in that environment, even in national programs, or you can end up with no return. I'm not suggesting that's what's going to happen, but I'm just saying that there [have to] be very specific questions and activities for something like MCC to be really meaningful. I wouldn't exclude that further down the line MCC could do very viable product development, but you have to understand under what circumstances. Right now we can't . . . but it [MCC] can force a lot of issues that were not considered in the past. In my view, MCC's a super vehicle to highlight a lot of meaningful things where we [the United States] need to take a stand.

Another early challenge facing Inman and MCC's founders was the task of quickly attracting highly qualified researchers to the consortium and to Austin. During its first year of operation, MCC was not very successful in hiring the needed numbers of researchers from the shareholder companies. The strategy was to staff the research programs from the top down: to start by hiring highly qualified research program directors and then let them use their professional networks and prestige to hire qualified researchers and technicians to staff their programs.

By December 1983, MCC had hired only 17 researchers. One main reason for this slow start was the perceived low quality of the scientists nominated by the consortium's member companies to head MCC's research programs.[6] The admiral turned thumbs down on 95 percent of the job candidates sent by the member companies for the consortium's top jobs. Of MCC's seven original research program directors (including the four separate research activities in the ACA program), four came from nonmember companies, two from universities, and one from a member company. "Some [shareholders] reportedly offered raises and bonuses to their top engineers if they promised *not* to join MCC" (Sanger, 1984). Clearly, something had to be done.

An MCC board of directors meeting in late 1983 was a major turning point concerning employee recruitment. According to one perspective, Inman told the shareholders that they had to start acting in a more cooperative manner and that he wanted their authorization to hire scientists from outside MCC's member companies. Remembering things a bit differently, an MCC board member stated that "Inman always had the authority to go 'outside,' and he was admonished in that meeting for not having moved faster." Regardless of these different recollections, immediately after the board meeting, Inman began to invite talented researchers and technicians to Austin. He had been building a data base of qualified researchers at universities and nonmember companies. He had also identified young researchers who were employed by MCC shareholder companies but who had not been nominated for an assignment at MCC. Not all accepted the invitation to visit Austin, but of those who did visit MCC and were offered a job, about 90 percent accepted.

MCC was not intended to operate in the sunshine. Some MCC shareholders hoped that the research consortium would be a hush-hush skunkworks type of operation. During 1982, when MCC was being formed and the fear of antitrust prosecution loomed in the background, most media coverage of MCC consisted of short newspaper or magazine articles about U.S. electronics companies' joining to meet the Japanese competitive threat in computer technology. MCC did not even disclose which companies had joined each of the research programs, nor how much each company paid to do so.

In 1983, after Admiral Inman signed on as CEO, after the U.S. Department of Justice issued its yellow-light ruling authorizing a cautious go-ahead, and as MCC's national site-selection process unfolded, the press coverage accorded MCC increased dramatically. The issue of Japanese competition ranked high on the national agenda. By the time Austin was selected as MCC's hometown in May 1983, national and international media coverage had peaked. But by fall 1983, however, press coverage began to slump. Inman started making more frequent public appearances and granting more interviews. Why? In order to give MCC the needed visibility to facilitate the recruitment of top research talent.

Bob Price and the interim board of directors designed MCC to avoid obstructing bureaucracy, to allow the organization to focus its resources on research, and to encourage personnel to make faster and better decisions. MCC's first business plan called for three hier- archical levels: executive managers, program managers, and researchers (Figure 4.3). MCC's board of directors was (and still is) composed of one representative from each shareholder company plus MCC's CEO who has traditionally served as chairman. In 1983, the consortium's rather thin administrative hierarchy included Senior Vice President for Programs and Plans Palle Smidt; Vice President and Chief Scientist John Pinkston, formerly deputy chief of the U.S. National Security Agency's research group; Vice President for Human Resources George Black, formerly with RCA; Vice President for Finance and Administration Bob Rutishauser, for- merly with CDC; and Director for Government and Public Affairs Bill Stotesbery, formerly with Peat Marwick Mitchell.

A technical advisory board (TAB) was to serve as an outside review group. The TAB was to review research plans and budgets, to articulate changes in MCC's objectives, and to advise MCC on long-term, strategic research by giving advice to the consortium's board of directors, CEO, and research program directors (the evolu- tion of MCC's governance is discussed later in this chapter).

> We try to do things as simple, as straightforward, and as informal as you can. We have a very low overhead, four percent of total expenses. We try to keep it that way. We have only three layers of management. . . . We have delegated extensive authority throughout our staff based on the notion that if you have excellent people, you can let them loose, so to speak; if you have weak- ness, you centralize control. . . . But then it takes longer, and you have to educate amateurs in the process. We are not afraid to give our people authority to call the shots. Of course, there are limits, you know: they can't sell the company or things like that. (Smidt interview, May 5, 1986)

At the second level of MCC's relatively flat hierarchy were the vice presidents and directors for each of the research programs. Research program directors enjoyed considerable autonomy in such matters as how research funds were spent and the hiring and pro- moting of personnel. Laszlo Belady, the first program director of

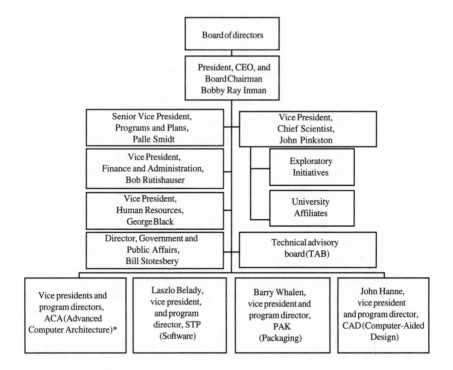

* ACA was divided into four separate research programs: artificial intelligence (directed by Woodrow Bledsoe); data base methods (directed by Eugene Lowenthal); user-machine interaction (directed by Ray Allard); and parallel processing (directed by Peter Patton).

Figure 4.3 MCC's organizational structure, 1983–1986

MCC's Software Technology Program, remembered how it was for someone coming from IBM: "where every new idea must be presented to, and approved by, numerous organizations, experts and executives before anything can happen. . . . How refreshing was Admiral Inman's inspired leadership, with significant decisions delegated to the program directors and bureaucracy held to a delightful minimum!" (Belady, 1992, p. 12)[7]

Up until the end of 1985 each of MCC's research programs had been adding corporate sponsorship: packaging increased from six sponsors to eleven; CAD from ten to twelve; STP from six to ten; and ACA from six to eight. However, despite MCC's charter of long-term, pre-competitive research, there were signs of early impatience for technical results on the part of some of the shareholders that were funding the research. As Belady remembered:

> In [the end of] our [STP research program] sixth month of existence I was courageous enough to call our first Program Technical Advisory Board meeting. . . . In the true tradition of short-term thinking and in a rather massive misunderstanding of our research vision, one delegate stood up and asked: "Where are the deliverables?" We had a hard time answering the question. (Belady, 1992, p. 13)

MCC's headquarters building has a large atrium that encircles an open-area cafeteria. During the consortium's early years, MCC staff and researchers gathered in the dining area for "all-hands" meetings every three months to listen to progress reports by the admiral. Such a meeting was scheduled on the afternoon of the September 3, 1986, board of directors meeting, at which Inman had announced his resignation effective at the end of December 1986. Two members of the board, George Scalise of AMD and Joe Boyd of Harris, decided to attend the meeting "to calm the troops" after Inman announced his intention to leave MCC. Inman made his announcement and asked if there were any questions or comments. At first, the employees sat quietly in stunned surprise, then a researcher rose to ask: "Bob, what progress have we made in getting a stoplight installed on Braker Lane [where one turns off 183 to get to MCC's entrance]?" The audience exploded in laughter and relief.

Inman had been the chief national and international representative of MCC. Public and private leaders saw his departure as a serious blow to the consortium. Inman was matter of fact about his leaving. He had originally agreed to a three-year contract. He had stayed four years. "I'm a builder, not a sustainer," he commented. (interview, July 21, 1987)

By the end of the admiral's tenure as MCC's first CEO, each of the four research programs had reached a peak of shareholder and funding support: Advanced Computer Architecture, with its four research projects, was being funded at $22 million per year; Computer-Aided Design at $20 million per year; Packaging/ Interconnect at $14 million per year; and Software at $8.5 million per year. However, there were also signs that the consortium was headed for trouble. The Japanese Fifth-Generation Computer Project was perceived to be less of a threat. Many of MCC's shareholders were undergoing financially hard times. Three companies had recently left the consortium—BMC Industries, Mostek, and Gould—and three had announced their intention to leave at the end of 1987—Sperry/Unisys, Allied-Signal, and Lockheed Missiles and Space. The media sensationalized these departures (as they did Inman's) as nails in MCC's coffin. Little attention was paid to the variety of reasons for the shareholders' leaving, which included corporate mergers and restructuring, and shifting priorities as well as dissatisfaction with the payback received from the consortium (see Chapter 2).

With the departure of Inman, the loss of shareholders, and rumors of additional departures, MCC was receiving increasingly frequent and heavy criticism from the media as well as the public and private sectors. Commentators asked: "Where are the technological breakthroughs, the silver bullets?" "Where are the technological advances that will help the United States beat the Japanese?" "What is wrong with MCC?"

THE GRANT DOVE ERA: 1987–1990

When I came [to MCC], I took time to go around and visit with all the companies. . . . It was a listening mode. I thought that was very important at that point in the development of MCC, to calibrate how the companies felt about our positioning, particularly the value of MCC to their operation. That was a very useful thing to do and it really tempered the changes we put into place. It brought more emphasis to my phrase "evolution on the way to revolution." (Dove interview, March 1, 1991)

MCC's second chairman, president, and CEO was Grant Dove, a 28-year veteran of Texas Instruments. As Bob Rutishauser (interview, January 23, 1987) remembered: "We needed someone with a lot of national visibility to get things started. Then we needed an industry person." When Dove took charge, the consortium employed 473 technicians and staff, had 19 shareholders (with 3 shareholders announcing their intention to leave), four major research programs, and a projected annual budget of $73 million. MCC was feeling the strain of decreasing financial support, increasing overhead, and a growing impatience among its membership. The consortium needed a midcourse correction. To restabilize MCC's funding, Dove encouraged (1) the recruitment of new shareholders, (2) the unbundling of research programs, (3) a renewed emphasis on the Associates Program, and (4) the solicitation of government funds.

Dove was aware that some shareholders were becoming increasingly uncomfortable with MCC's expensive, long-term research orientation. Inman had talked long and hard about programs having five- to ten-year horizons, and "Please don't expect early results. . . . On the other hand, the troops in the companies weren't listening" (Dove interview, August 15, 1990). Dove tried to understand who MCC's customers really were and the specific operations in the shareholder companies that could put MCC's technology to work. As Dove emphasized, the "kings" who helped form MCC (the CEOs of the shareholder companies) were drifting away from direct involvement in the consortium and were off setting up new programs while "dukes" and "barons" (the division heads) had the job of gaining value out of MCC.

Inman, commenting on the problems he experienced with technology transfer, said as he handed MCC over to Dove:

> Some companies pick up the pieces [of research] pretty quickly. Some don't move at all. It's not just an MCC problem. It's a larger U.S. problem. The issue is clearly going to draw a lot of [Dove's] energies. This one I wish him good luck on. (quoted by Barnett, 1987)

Dove encouraged the "opening up" of MCC's research programs:

> Initially, there was great concern that there was going to be leakage across the walls—between the projects. So Bobby agreed and was urged to put these big walls up and not have any interchange. I found that there had been enough trust developed by the time I got here that we could break those walls down for the benefit of

MCC. And we did indeed. The results are not spectacular, but at least we have some sharing, and there has been some transfer of technology between programs and projects. (interview, March 1, 1991)

In September 1985, MCC's board of directors had agreed that the consortium could share technologies across research programs if it would benefit MCC. For example, if a computer software program developed by STP could be used by CAD researchers to improve their productivity, that was acceptable. But if CAD delivered the technology to its research program's participants, then CAD would have to work out a licensing agreement with STP. But as one of our respondents commented: "Simply allowing MCC's researchers to use each other's technologies was not enough. MCC did not develop a culture of transferring and using its own technologies in-house." (Werner interview, March 30, 1992)[8]

From MCC's board, Dove heard: "Don't go and start up a whole lot of new programs. Let's get value out of the ones we have." It was no longer possible to get the CEOs of the shareholder companies excited about a major new research thrust. Central R&D labs at the shareholder companies were becoming an endangered species. As Dove observed (interview, March 1, 1991):

One of the reasons you are seeing R&D labs being decentralized . . . is because CEOs are sick and tired of hearing those group managers—and I used to be one of them—bitching about all this damn money going in and nothing coming out. They feel that if the group and division managers do the investing, it's their money going into it, and they're going to be much more committed to take the technology and put it to work.

It was becoming increasingly clear that MCC would have to market the consortium's research to division-level managers and group managers and to their R&D departments.

Interviewer: But isn't that a catch 22 in that by having researchers meet the needs of division- and group-level managers, you also drive

> the research more to the short term,
> thereby frustrating the original purpose
> of MCC?

Dove: You're right on target. That's exactly
        what's happening. (Dove interview,
        March 1, 1991)

"Our biggest challenge at MCC," continued Dove, "is that our focus is on a three- to ten-year horizon. Even with evolutionary steps along the way, it is . . . that region of R&D that now has the lowest priority in U.S. companies and has one of the highest priorities in Japanese companies."

For some of MCC's programs, it was a $10 million decision to bring in a new company. The difficulty in recruiting new shareholders led Dove to champion the unbundling of MCC's research programs into smaller, more affordable "satellites" so that MCC shareholders and associate members could buy into single technology projects without contributing to the funding an entire research program (Figure 4.4). As Dove commented (interview, March 1, 1991): "We tried to get the decisions down in the half million to $1 million range per year with a three-year commitment." In 1987, the ACA and P/I research programs were the first to reorganize so that shareholders could choose to fund the projects that most clearly matched their technology requirements. While unbundling the research programs facilitated the recruitment of new associate member companies, it also allowed the shareholders to reduce their funding and commitment to MCC, a strategy that several shareholders were advocating. Furthermore, as an MCC manager commented:

> Some degree of unbundling may be desirable in consortia programs, since it allows more companies and divisions to be eligible for participation. But unbundling also carries risks for consortia, such as the fracturing of a coherent research vision and possible friction among participants with very specific and perhaps divergent interests.

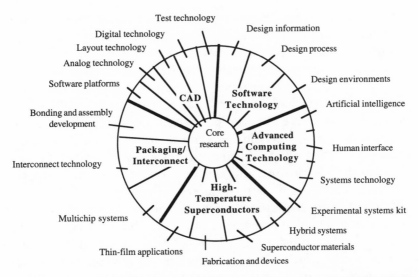

Figure 4.4 Unbundling of MCC's research programs, 1987–1990

Under Dove's leadership, MCC researchers were encouraged to deliver interim technologies to the shareholders while they continued to pursue long-term research objectives. As one long-time MCC staff member commented:

> When Dove came on board as CEO, the relationship between MCC and the shareholders changed in a subtle but significant way. In the original concept, MCC was considered to be an extension of the R&D staffs of its shareholders. Dove saw MCC as a technology supplier and the shareholders as customers.

In 1987, the first well-publicized result of MCC's emphasis on technology deliverables was the transfer of an artificial intelligence software package from the Advanced Computing Technology (ACT; formerly ACA) Program to a commercial product produced by NCR (this technology transfer case is described in detail in the section of Chapter 5 entitled "The Case of Proteus"). In 1988, the CAD research program was organized into a core and five satellites. In 1989, Cadence Design Systems joined CAD to become MCC's first vendor shareholder, and MCC issued its first technology license

to a third-party vendor.[9] A new Exploratory Initiatives research program—the Computer Physics Lab—was formed, and the Advanced
Computing Technology and Software Technology programs were
merged under one director, Laszlo Belady.

MCC had been in existence four years when Grant Dove took
charge. Technology had been transferred to the shareholders, but
these occurrences were not well publicized. For competitive reasons
the shareholder recipients did not want their use of MCC-developed
technology made public and many transfers were rather modest,
incremental applications and not considered very newsworthy.
MCC was secretive about proprietary technology, and the shareholder companies encouraged such a strategy. They did not want
their Japanese or U.S. competitors informed about the consortium's
activities. So the bright media-generated flash about MCC's launch
was followed by a lack of publicity concerning the consortium's specific research activities. At the same time, the media as well as some
observers of MCC were becoming increasingly impatient for tangible results. As Bill Stotesbery stated (interview, January 23, 1987):

> There are relatively few public disclosures of technolo-
> gy transfer from MCC by the shareholders. Technology
> transfer is ongoing; MCC is transferring things that
> they [MCC researchers] sometimes don't know they are
> transferring. Continuous transfer doesn't make very
> interesting copy. Also, shareholders do not want to tell
> what they are using [or even not using] because some-
> one [a competitor] can tell a lot about research priori-
> ties from this.

From the birth of MCC, the consortium's management had
realized the benefits of good public relations to maintain shareholder support and to facilitate the recruitment of quality researchers.
But maintaining a positive public perception of MCC over the long
term, five to ten years, until research results were expected was
problematic. As one observer from the press noted:

> By 1986 MCC had begun to squirm under the glare of
> the outside world, from the budget-conscious compa-
> nies that support it, from the community that held such

high hopes for what MCC would bring to town with it, and from the dozens of other newly-formed research ventures that viewed the MCC as a model. (Walters, 1986)

MCC's sometimes negative media image began to influence the consortium's ability to carry out its mission. More favorable coverage was needed to (1) maintain shareholder support, and (2) facilitate the recruitment of qualified researchers and new member companies. A positive public image was especially important for MCC's shareholder companies that had joined the consortium to be associated with what was perceived to be an important research organization at the forefront of U.S. technological advancement in the competitive struggle with Japan.

MCC's penchant for secrecy made it difficult for shareholder executives to justify their investment in MCC, especially when they were being forced to cut back, because of financially difficult times, on their own operations. Furthermore, there were member company complaints about MCC's going ahead with its own research agenda while not listening to its shareholder companies. As observed by Tom Schwartz, a technology industry consultant in Mountain View, California: "MCC is saying they have a technology leadership position in the country, but nobody knows about it. . . . You have here an organization that for many years has been purposely secretive. They are finally learning that being super-secretive doesn't get you very far" (quoted in Pope, 1989h). "It has been just a vacuum of information," said John Kelly, a senior analyst with Boston-based Seybold Office Computing Group. "People heard the word consortium and they heard something about the Japanese, then the whole thing kind of went underwater. . . . What it's going to take is a greater revelation of details about success stories." (Pope, 1989h)

To have an effective marketing campaign, MCC needed to be able to publicize its technology transfer successes—more than one or two, but a string of success stories. It was an uphill battle to convince MCC's shareholders to be open about how they were using the consortium's technology. "In the beginning, the members said they were willing to pay more to have fewer companies," stated Steve Maysonave, director of marketing and business development for the Advanced Technology Program. "There was a real concern that if you're going to share research, how broadly do you share it? There has been a complete change to the opposite. They now say they would rather pay less and have more companies participate" (Pope, 1989h). As observed by Barry Whalen: "The number one myth is that MCC hasn't accomplished anything. The bottom line is we have decided to be a lot more aggressive in getting our message across. There is a lot of ignorance about MCC, and ignorance is dangerous" (Pope, 1989h).

As part of its more aggressive marketing strategy, MCC hired Regis McKenna, a Silicon Valley public relations agency, as a consultant and it hired marketing, business development, and technology transfer personnel for the consortium's headquarters and for the research programs. MCC's executives and managers embarked on a kind of traveling high-tech road show pitching the advantages of MCC membership. Management pressured the consortium's researchers to get out of their labs and to meet with industry analysts and consultants as well as current and potential member companies. Jerry Sullivan, director of CAD, commented: "[Researchers] now realize that they have to be able to explain what they are doing and illustrate why it's good to do it that way. It's very easy for a research organization not to pay attention to that" (Pope, 1989h). In 1990, MCC's board of directors appointed Barry Whalen as vice president for marketing and customer services to oversee business planning and marketing, communication, the international liaison office (ILO), requirements analysis and competitive assessment, and the office of government programs (Figure 4.5).

MCC was achieving some success in leveraging shareholder resources for technological advancements. Cost savings and accelerated time to market were achieved. For example, the laser bonder, a device that provides high-speed inner lead bonding for computer chips, was developed in five years at a cost of $2.5 million. Risk and cost were spread across 14 research participants interested in advanced technology for building integrated circuits. AMD served as a beta testing site for the technology that offered a significant breakthrough to the fundamental limitations of conventional bonding tools. As Phil Spletter, an assignee from Harris Corporation and head of the laser bonder project, stated: "It was definitely faster to do the project here. . . . If an individual company had started this they probably would have given up." (quoted in Rifkin, 1990)

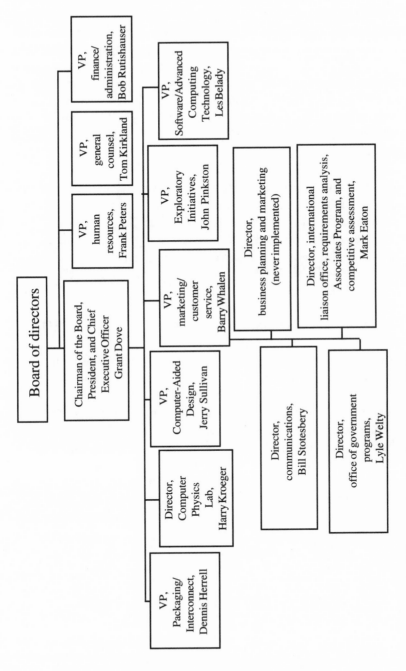

Figure 4.5 MCC's organizational structure, 1990

In 1990, MCC admitted its first Canadian shareholder, Northern Telecom, and its first consulting company shareholder, Andersen Consulting. These two additions brought the total number of MCC shareholders to 22. MCC's Associates Program had grown to 35 companies under the leadership of Meg Wilson (the same Meg Wilson who had served on the Austin Task Force to recruit MCC back in 1983). Still, there was concern over MCC's lack of a clear, attainable mission. As observed by one of MCC's then most recent additions to the board of directors, Joseph Costello, of Cadence Design Systems:

> I don't think there's a clear mission about what the hell [MCC] is going to do in the 1990s. If there is no bold new agenda introduced to the world in the next year, you've got a lame duck here. My guess is probably one-third of the people still have hope, a third don't care, and a third think it's a bunch of crap. (quoted in Ladendorf, 1990b)

As Dove remembered in 1991 (interview, March 1, 1991):

> As we've gone through these eight years when the fifth generation was the clarion call, each year it has become less of a priority and has had much less intensity in terms of corporate worry and concern. *This* Japanese threat has not really materialized. . . . During my reign here, I asked them [the shareholders]: "Do you want to keep this thing going? We can phase out what we've got. Do you want permanence?" The answer was: "Yes! Write a ten-year plan for us. Tell us what the new thrust should be. Write a vision 2000. We believe in it. We want to keep it."

THE CRAIG FIELDS ERA: 1990–PRESENT

> I remain convinced that consortia are in principle a good idea, and that's irrespective of the fact of whether they have met expectations or not. That's important,

because if the principle is flawed, then you'd just want
to give up. But the principle isn't flawed. It's the execution that's flawed. . . . Everything is possible, but nothing is probable. (Fields interview, March 1, 1991)

Dr. Craig Fields was appointed chief technical and operating
officer of MCC on July 9, 1990. He became MCC's president and
CEO in March 1991. Grant Dove continued to serve as MCC's
chairman of the board into 1992. The consortium wanted to exe-
cute a gradual transition of leadership. With 28 years' experience as
a senior executive at Texas Instruments, the 63-year-old Dove provided a calming, reassuring presence to MCC's corporate constituents, while the 43-year-old Fields implemented dramatic
changes in the consortium's structure and operation.

Fields was described by our MCC respondents as "intense,"
"hard-driving," "not afraid of controversy," and "someone who has
little time for fools." He grew up in New York, where he attended
the Bronx High School of Science, and went on to earn a bachelors
degree in physics from MIT and a Ph.D. in mathematics, psychology, and physiology from Rockefeller University. In contrast to Dove,
Fields had minimal corporate experience. Fields came to MCC after
serving as director (from 1989 to 1990) of DARPA (the Defense
Advanced Research Projects Agency), a $1.3 billion a year U.S.
Department of Defense R&D funding agency for military technology. While at DARPA, Fields had championed a strong federal government role in strengthening U.S. industrial competitiveness.
"When I first knew Craig," commented Dove (interview, March 1,
1991), "he was managing about 800 million of dual-use technologies." DARPA has two missions: one of them is specific military
solutions, and the other is technologies that can have an impact on
the military and civilian sectors. Dove continued:

At DARPA, Fields was working with similar challenges.
. . . He has put together programs that have called on
the best talents in the United States whether they were
in industry or universities. He's been on the firing line
for a billion-five, world-renowned R&D laboratory.
His credibility with researchers is very, very high. He
had the challenge of trying to look at what defense
needed and to try to anticipate those needs and get

technologies ready for them. He had to get customer inputs in terms of needs and problems and worry about technology transfer. (Dove interview, March 1, 1991)

In April 1990, after 16 years at DARPA, Fields ran afoul of the White House. President Bush's conservative economic policy opposed giving government aid to specific industries, such as DARPA's research funding and support of selected technologies.[10] MCC moved quickly to offer Fields the presidency of the consortium.

In the same blunt manner that won him both friends and foes as DARPA's director, [Fields] has dissected the challenges facing MCC into their logical parts. Fields is a ruthlessly organized man who seems to divide topics into mental file drawers. As often as not, he will describe an organizational problem at MCC with a scientific metaphor. He thinks of member firms as "meteorites" traveling on independent paths. He describes one dilemma as "a closed loop missile tracking problem." (Richards, 1991)

Soon after taking command of MCC, Fields traveled 200,000 miles in six months, visiting MCC shareholder corporate and division management and R&D staff. He studied consortia in the United States, Europe, and Japan as well as research centers like SRI International and the National Center for Manufacturing Sciences. He conducted a review of MCC's structure and research activities. His conclusion was that U.S. consortia had started out with a disastrous recipe, which was based on (1) giving competitive advantage to member companies, (2) helping the United States, (3) advancing science, and (4) advancing industry.

Twenty years ago . . . these four criteria were reasonably aligned. The way the world has gone, that correlation is much, much lower. Almost all large companies that are part of consortia are multinational, so helping the company doesn't necessarily create high-value jobs in the United States. For many companies, business success is only modestly related to technology advance-

ment; it's more closely related to issues of good marketing, closeness to the customer, and continuous small
incremental gains and improvements rather than some
breakthrough technology. (Fields interview, August 15,
1990)

Fields sees two categories of reasons for R&D consortia: efficiency reasons and multicompany, multi-industry reasons. The first
category involves such considerations as the reduction of duplication in R&D spending; the execution of high-risk, high-cost R&D
projects; and leveraging resources and talent. The second category
involves doing those things that only consortia can do, irrespective
of money, such as laying the foundations for data structures and
protocols and expanding markets.

Fields's other main impression gained during his initial visits
with MCC's member companies was the noticeable lack of a long-
term vision among U.S. industry leaders. "When I ask them [the
CEOs] where are you going, so I can help you get there, that was
often the end of the conversation. . . . If you don't have a destina-
tion, it's hard to produce a road map (Fields interview, August 15,
1990). Dove noted that "Craig's weakness is that he is a bit idealis-
tic in terms of how companies actually operate. . . . He'll ask them
for their vision and no vision comes, or if it does, it doesn't make a
lot of sense to him." (interview, August 15, 1990)

In 1982–1983, Norris and Inman could point with emphasis
to Japan's success with the VLSI Project and to the threat of ICOT,
which had helped motivate the shareholder CEOs to support MCC.
"That's my biggest problem," said Fields. "The lack of a crisis is a
pain in the neck."

When you look at our members, we have computer
guys, semiconductor guys, and aerospace guys. For the
aerospace guys, I show them the shrinking DOD budget and emphasize that they are increasingly subject to
foreign competition. . . . For the computer guys, I show
them their declining share of the world market compared to the Japanese. For the semiconductor guys, it's
the same declining curve, just [a few] years older.
(Fields interview, August 15, 1990)

By mid-1991, Fields had begun to terminate projects in MCC's research programs. His reasoning was that the projects were not being supported by the shareholders, or support had dwindled to one or two funders. In order to survive Fields's review, MCC research programs had to have active corporate champions that funded the research, and there had to be "a concrete plan" for transferring the technology into application. Some current and former MCC researchers were of the opinion that Fields was overzealous in his termination of research projects, especially software research. Others emphasized that he had no choice but to cut the projects since shareholder support was not there in terms of funding and/or commercializing the research results.

> Overall, the research has been quite spotty. . . . But that's the nature of research. Researchers tend to hold the founders hostage. Craig Fields knows how to select people. He's not interested in running an old folks' home. . . . (Gordon Bell, DEC's vice president of engineering who in 1983 helped form MCC, quoted in Rifkin, 1990)

Human interface research in the ACT Program was one of the first projects canceled by Fields. He noted that while the technology was interesting, it would have little useful application:

> In my model of management, all programs should end, because otherwise, we get in a rut. It's just a question of sooner versus later, and when the press calls me up and says: "Are you ending any programs at MCC?" I say: "Yes—all of them at some time." If you look at our budget projections, they all go to zero. . . . And to me that's exactly right. But you also have to have a renewal program for setting up new things. (interview, March 1, 1991)[11]

MCC's board met in Austin in early March 1991 to review and approve the consortium's program for the next ten years. The perceived need was to tighten the consortium's focus, improve efficiency, and move emerging technology more quickly into the private sector. Fields was appointed CEO; Dove would continue as chairman of the board into the next year. MCC's "Vision for the '90s" was based on a new business model and predicated on better cooperation with government and universities. The consortium was to move more toward research application, preparing new technologies with the expectation that they be transferred to the private sector to be used in promising applications. MCC was to be run like a business with special attention paid to technology transfer, business impact, and schedules (Table 4.1). Such business practices, Fields argued, need not hurt creativity.[12] Irwin Dorros, executive vice president of technical services at Bellcore and an MCC board member, admitted that the "work has been good, but MCC has drifted from one project to the next, a reason why it has been static in growth and prominence. [But now] I'm excited, and so are many board members." (Baker, 1991)

Table 4.1
MCC's outline of disciplined project management, 1992

Standard Project Plan Format in Sequential Ordered Stages

Project name	Business impact
Project manager	Competitive assessment
Start and stop dates	Marketing plan
Budget profile and current members	Implementation plan
Problem addressed	Intellectual property plan
Technical idea	Milestones/deliverables schedule
Technical impact	Documentation plan
Technology transfer plan	Licensing plan

Source: MCC, 1992.

MCC's first operational focus was to develop an awareness of new business opportunities for its members. The new strategy called for MCC to be a partner in enabling technologies, applications, and the accelerated creation of new standards. "You can't just do one or two and succeed. . . . You must do all three," commented Fields

(Baker, 1991). "It's dangerous to develop standards without having the technologies, and you can't do the applications without technology and standards." In Fields' view, MCC was the best place to share the risks of market testing of the possible integration of diverse technologies and businesses. "That takes new protocols, interfaces, and frameworks, and for that the consortium is the only game in town." (Baker, 1991)

The second operational focus of MCC's vision referred to increased cooperation with the research elements of MCC's members, government, universities, and foreign institutions. MCC was to serve as a model for how to bring multidisicplinary tasks together and to interface with the government. And Fields continued: "[And there is] the very yeasty brew of venture capitalists and startups. We have to work with them. And not everything will be in the U.S." (Baker, 1991)

> First of all, absolutely, unambiguously we're here to give competitive benefits to our 52 member companies [shareholders and associates] . . . and if we end up with substantial federal funding, we will have to add the public interest, too. . . . Mostly, I think it's good management not to linger on forever and get disappointing returns. But there is another reason, and that is companies change their plans a lot. So it has to be fixed-term. . . . and I want to have somebody in charge because I really believe in line management. (Fields interview, March 1, 1991)

The key motivation for an MCC project under Fields' reign is whether there is a high business impact on a set of companies that want to collaborate to carry it out.

> And that has to be calculated. . . . If the balance sheet will change, then it seems like a pretty good thing to me. . . . It's not necessary that all companies benefit equally, but it is necessary that all companies benefit a lot. Some unusually small technology impact may have a very large business impact and vice versa, which is why a technologist's intuitions are not always so hot. (Fields interview, March 1, 1991)

By summer 1992, MCC was striving to provide two types of value added for its participants. The first was technology management, which includes technology transfer, technology maturation, consortia management, intellectual property protection, financial management, and finding technology breakthroughs. "That takes about 30 people," said Fields. "The other value added, which takes about 400 people, is doing R&D, the classical central lab kind of things." (All-hands meeting videotape, June 18, 1992)

In early October 1992, Fields was asked by *New York Times'* reporter Peter H. Lewis, "What is your biggest challenge?" Fields responded (Lewis, 1992): "Mutating scientists and engineers into businessmen and entrepreneurs."

> Lewis: Does this mean the basic concept of MCC has evolved? The original mandate was for companies to pool research resources and develop technologies, without pressure to contribute immediately to the members' bottom lines. Was the original idea naive, or did the climate change?
>
> Fields: Yes, yes, and yes. It's really two issues and it's important to separate them. Time scales are shorter everywhere. Our time scales are longer than most, but everything is compressed. The real issue is more the transfer of the work. The ivory tower has closed its doors for a while, and one has to not only do good work but also attend very directly to getting it commercialized.

A NEW DIRECTION FOR MCC

During the transition of MCC's leadership from Dove to Fields, there was considerable turnover of top management personnel as well as researchers.[13] One of Field's first high-level appointments was Major General Alan Salisbury as executive vice president and chief operating officer in June 1991. In 1987, General Salisbury had retired from the U.S. Army, where he was in charge of the

Information Systems Engineering Command (USAISEC), a world-wide organization of more than 4,500 computer scientists and communication and systems engineers responsible for the acquisition and support of state-of-the-art information systems. After leaving the army and before joining MCC, Salisbury served as president of Contel Technology Center, an advanced technology research and development division. Contel was the nation's third-largest independent telephone company before being acquired by GTE in 1991.

As COO, Salisbury shared responsibility for the day-to-day operation of MCC with Fields. According to Fields (MCC press release, June 4, 1991):

> Alan has . . . particularly excelled in the management and application of information technology and research as strategic weapons. . . . Alan's proven ability to manage research and technology transfer, and his extensive experience in information and communications management, make him ideally suited to the task of operating MCC.

Neither Fields nor Salisbury established permanent residence in Austin, each preferring to keep his primary residence in the Washington, D.C., area. During 1991–1992, both Fields and Salisbury spent about 50 percent of their time in residence at MCC's headquarters, and when they were not in Austin, they kept in touch with MCC managers and researchers through phone, fax, and two-way video. (By late 1992, Salisbury was permanently assigned to MCC's Washington office, which employed about six administrative staff and no researchers. By mid-1993, he had left MCC.)

In the June 18, 1992, "all-hands" quarterly meeting/video conference from the auditorium of MCC's headquarters, Fields introduced Brian Kushner, MCC's recently hired VP for corporate development. He also planned to keep his permanent residence in Washington, D.C.; however, by summer 1993, Kushner was living in Austin. Kushner stated that he wanted: "To build on the inherent capabilities that we [MCC] have but take them in new directions working with new clients and looking at applications that might not have been previously considered." (All-hands meeting videotape, June 18, 1992)

Fields noted that the June 18 all-hands meeting marked his second year as MCC's CEO. He complemented MCC's staff for being supportive of the "tremendous change in MCC personnel in the last two years" and emphasized several future trends for the consortium (all-hands meeting videotape, June 18, 1992):

- It was clear that MCC's members valued MCC for its technology. MCC's technical staff was its greatest resource.
- Single-company development activities coupled with consortia R&D was a "magic formula." Consortia R&D gave MCC "the stuff to transfer," and single-company activities gave MCC the transfer opportunity.
- Recent spin-off activities had worked well for both MCC and the member companies (see Chapter 5). The spin-offs provided career opportunities for MCC staff, technology transfer to member companies, and financial stability for MCC.
- It was abundantly clear that the federal government would continue to play an important role in MCC's operation. As of 1992, 30 percent of MCC's funding was coming from government sources.
- While Fields had no intention of trying to change MCC's bylaws concerning foreign members, he thought that in the global marketplace, MCC should welcome foreign partners if such alliances benefited MCC and the member companies.
- MCC would continue to welcome member companies that were rich but did not have technological expertise. Such companies were preferred to those that were poor but had lots of technology. (Fields wanted to increase the number of technology users and diversity of MCC.)
- MCC would continue to expand its foreign technology assessment, since MCC's member companies would increasingly face a world where advanced technologies were being produced in Asia and Europe.

At the conclusion of the all-hands meeting, Fields emphasized that MCC's impact depended on three things: "Our performance, the performance of our members, and our structure." According to Fields, MCC's member companies had no complaints about MCC's performance; it was not a limiting factor. In assessing the performance of the member companies, one had to ask: "Do they tell us what they want, do they plan to pick up our technology and use it wisely—do they act as real partners?" Here, Fields commented that things could be better. U.S. business culture had not yet reached the point of supporting consortia. Fields commented that he was working with MCC's board to change MCC's structure so there would be more opportunities to take technologies further downstream in service and development.

MCC'S INTERNATIONAL LIAISON OFFICE

Mark Eaton, MCC vice president for strategy and development, was also director of the International Liaison Office (ILO), which employs Japanese, European, and technical information specialists. MCC's ILO services have proven to be of considerable value to MCC's member companies which often have inadequate resources dedicated to global technology assessment. When one recruit into the ILO, who was fluent in Japanese but had little technical knowledge, questioned his value to MCC's member companies, Eaton responded: "Remember, in the land of the blind, the one-eyed man is king."

ILO's mission is to track high-technology R&D primarily in Japan and Western Europe, but also in Eastern Europe, Russia, and Asia. ILO informs MCC's membership of important trends and developments in such areas as semiconductor packaging and interconnect, computer component technologies (including batteries, displays, and mass storage devices), computer architectures and systems, distributed software systems and development environments, and networking and telecommunications.

Services of the ILO include a monthly technical report, the *Global Technology Monitor,* which covers technology developments overseas; in-depth technical reports on particular areas of interest; presentations and briefings at member-company sites; response to queries from MCC researchers and member companies; translation of articles; and assisting member companies with their own technology tracking efforts. ILO maintains two data bases: one that indexes Japanese trade publications, technical journals, and conference proceedings, and another that is a combination bibliographic and full-text file that covers Japanese and European research activity in microelectronics, computing, software, and telecommunications.

MCC's associate members receive limited copies of the *Global Technology Monitor,* technology reports, and translated articles, and they have access to ILO's data bases. MCC's shareholders receive these services in addition to being able to identify technical report topics and literature for translation, request technical briefings at member sites, organize fact-finding missions abroad, and request ILO assistance in seeking foreign technology partners and in-house technology monitoring.

MCC'S RESEARCH

Shortly after Fields took charge, MCC's research programs were reorganized as follows: the Packaging/Interconnect Program was relabeled the High Value Electronics (HVE) Division, surviving research projects from MCC's Advanced Computing Technology Program were placed under the Distributed Intelligent Information Systems (DIIS) Division, the Computer Physics Laboratory (MCC's most recent research effort) remained largely the same, and the research projects that were not cut from MCC's Computer-Aided Design and Software Technology programs were listed under the newly formed Enterprise Integration (EI) Division.

As of mid-1992, MCC's research activities were again reorganized and placed under two divisions: High Value Electronics (which included most of the Packaging/Interconnect Program as well as the Computer Physics Lab) and Information Systems (which included selected projects from the former Distributed Intelligent Information Systems and Enterprise Integration divisions). As of late 1993, MCC had about 35 separate research projects grouped in these two divisions (see Figure 4.6). (The following is an overview of MCC's most current research activities; see Appendix 4.2 for a review of research activities from 1983 to 1990.)

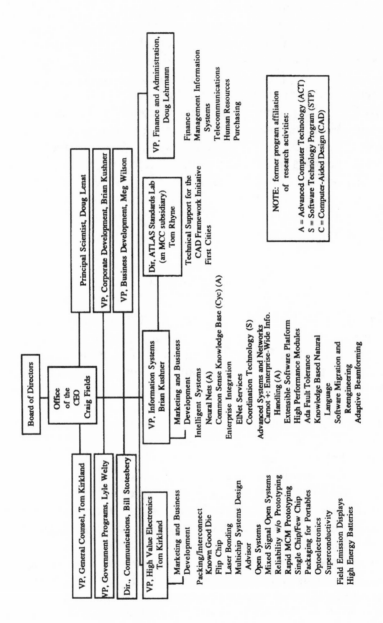

Figure 4.6   MCC's organizational chart, late 1993

HIGH VALUE ELECTRONICS DIVISION

The High Value Electronics (HVE) Division absorbed MCC's Packaging/Interconnect research projects, such as enabling technologies (key packaging technologies for use in a variety of applications); low-cost interconnect substrates for multichip module applications; advanced tape-automated bonding; flip-chip technology, which bonds chips with contact pads face down by adhesive or solder bump connections; laser bonding; open systems; and reliability without hermeticity, funded jointly by industry and the air force. Enabling packaging technology research involves basic materials and their potential applications as adhesives, dielectrics, and encapsulants; investigates liquid metal ion cluster sources as a technique for the direct physical deposition of metal; and studies optical interconnect technologies for applications with optical communications paths as alternatives to electrical interconnects.

MCC's Power Sources research program has focused on a review of electrochemical power sources for portable electronics (such as laptop and notebook computers) and is attempting to develop a series of lightweight, reliable, high-power, solid-state battery technologies. MCC's Displays research program is working to fill gaps in existing display technologies while seeking government and industry support for further technology development and licensing technologies developed by MCC in order to speed manufacturing and commercialization.

MCC's Computer Physics Lab was formed in 1989 and remained largely unchanged when it moved into the HVE Division, except for spinning out a start-up company called Tamarack Storage Devices, Inc. in 1992, a topic discussed later in this chapter. The lab includes the superconductivity and optics in computing projects, which require the integration of multiple technologies such as holographic storage technology, commercialization of volume holographic storage, low-temperature superconducting circuits and systems, and high-temperature superconductor components and process technology.

Holographic storage allows access and transfer speeds that are 100 to 1,000 times faster than magnetic disk and with significantly greater density. Since it has no moving parts, this form of data storage is potentially more reliable and maintainable than traditional magnetic media. This research project has collaborative agreements with Stanford University, the University of Colorado, and the University of Rochester. In March 1991, MCC received an award from the Advanced Technology Program of the U.S. Department of Commerce (administered by the National Institute of Standards, or NIST) for its work in the commercialization of volume holographic storage. Among the technology commercialization objectives are a volume mass storage subsystem with the electro-optical components of the system and low-cost designs and processes for producing crystallite arrays. To achieve its objectives, MCC created a vertically integrated joint venture that included companies from the following industry segments: materials, components, subassemblies, subsystems, and high-performance computer systems.

A few months before he left MCC to work for Tamarack Storage Devices, Inc., David Misunas, an HVE business development manager, commented (personal correspondence, April 2, 1993):

> HVE is undergoing a shift from technology development projects (TAB, Flip Chip, Laser Bonding) in which MCC develops and transfers technologies to technology overview projects in which external technologies are surveyed and analyzed and the trade-off results are reported back to the members (Open Systems, Known Good Die).
>
> Technology development projects tend to be the 4-5 member projects (it is hard to get a larger group to agree on specific development goals). . . . The survey projects are the larger ones. . . . But small projects receive higher satisfaction ratings from the member companies than large projects (10 members), an interesting comment on how it's more feasible to find common goals in a group of 4 or 5. However, such a small project is not necessarily cost-effective for MCC.

HVE is increasingly coordinating research projects and hiring out MCC's technical expertise and testing facilities. It takes about 12 to 18 months and four group meetings to organize a technical project, which lasts two to three years. At the first meeting, there is usually a lot of distrust among the attendees who represent a range of participants and competitors, including equipment suppliers, component technicians, and users. A proposal normally comes out of the second meeting. At the third meeting, participants commonly "gang up" on the proposal, which is finalized in the fourth meeting. In between these meetings, MCC project leaders make frequent visits to the participating companies to work out differences on such things as the priority and location of tasks, technical specifications, intellectual property, financial concerns, and technology transfer. At times projects are completed before the lengthy and complex contract has made it through the bureaucracies and legal departments of the participating companies. A technology interest group that might start with 45 organizations would commonly decrease to about five participants by the time the project begins. If the project is successful it might be followed by a renewal process with follow-up goals.

After a contract is signed, project groups normally get together about every two months for a review. Organizational meetings are often held at the Hyatt at Dallas–Fort Worth Airport while the project meetings are held at MCC's headquarters. The meetings, especially the technology transfer and marketing activities, benefit tremendously from the involvement of a strong, if not dominant, project leader who acts as technology champion. Projects are graded according to an MCC-generated customer-satisfaction rating system, which is taken quite seriously by MCC's management. "A poor project review would mean off with their heads," commented one project manager. "There is a lot of time and expense in staff reporting and communication, but it does usually result in defined and tangible results."

By 1993, HVE was coordinating 15 projects, about 15 percent of which had some government funding. The division had a staff of 110 and an annual income of about $25 million, about double the size of that of the Information Systems Division. Equipment and staff overhead costs are high so the division hopes to launch about 7 to 8 projects a year. Project leaders are each responsible for 3 to 4 contracts and HVE technicians are commonly employed across several projects. This high volume of work has led to a complex accounting system. Some specialists use as many as 20 different charge codes per week on one timecard. As one of the project leaders commented in 1993: "The process is frustrating for the technical staff. The academics generally leave and those that stay usually don't put in heroic efforts."

An example of one of HVE's more recent projects is MCC's partnership with SI Diamond Technology Inc., which began in September 1993. The objective is to develop and market a new generation of flat-panel displays—the lightweight, low-power screens used in laptop computers and other devices. SI Diamond is leasing space from MCC and is using the consortium's lab facilities and researchers. Working together, MCC and SI Diamond technicians are developing the technology for diamond-based field emitter displays, which are expected to deliver better performing computer screens than current technology of active-matrix liquid crystal displays (LCDs). Initial production, to demonstrate cost levels and yields, of 6-inch-square screens is expected to occur at MCC by 1994. The technology will be used in computer applications for medical instruments, automobiles, and avionics.

SI Diamond had 42 employees and raised $5 million in a public stock offering in February 1993. The Houston-based company will pay MCC about $9 million in cash and stock over the next three years to cover the costs of using the consortium's space, equipment, and people. SI Diamond will have exclusive license to use the technology for two years. MCC can issue two technology licenses in the third year and subsequently license the technology to others with the consortium and SI Diamond splitting the royalties. Dennis Herrell commented: "We believe the diamond FED [field emitter displays] technologies included in this pooled package have the potential for gaining a significant price/performance lead over future active-matrix, liquid-crystal and all other flat panel display technologies now under development" (MCC press release, September 8, 1993). According to Fields, the partnership has three distinct advantages: (1) it speeds the commercialization of an advanced U.S. microelectronics technology, (2) it gives companies belonging to MCC preferred access to advanced systems, and (3) it provides MCC with a potentially lucrative investment in SI Diamond stock and licensing rights.

INFORMATION SYSTEMS DIVISION

MCC's Information Systems Division (ISD) is developing and testing technologies to facilitate the intelligent, seamless acquisition, management, and delivery of services and information across networks. Several projects are aimed at technology development for distributed, heterogeneous, user-friendly, multimedia (particularly graphics and images), multinational, scalable, customized systems. The impact of these technologies is expected to be in network-based systems of electronic commerce, new ways of delivering consumer products and services, and advanced processing technologies.

The STP research program had its last review by its funding companies in summer 1991. By 1992, all of STP's research activities were ended except the project on coordination theory and technology, which had funding through 1993 from Motorola. With the end of this program, MCC's STP research activities—once one of the major worldwide centers of exploratory, long-term research projects in software development—came to an end. As Stotesbery commented in 1993: "Much of the research was completed. Much of it wasn't used, but MCC had to look at what's next." (interview, April 8)

ISD absorbed the surviving research projects from MCC's Computer-Aided Design (e.g., PRISM system-modeling tool kit), Software Technology (e.g., requirements modeling and coordination technology), and Advanced Computing Technology programs (e.g., neural nets, knowledge-based natural language, and Carnot). These projects were grouped under ISD's Intelligent Systems, Enterprise Integration and Advanced Systems and Network programs (see Figure 4.6).

MCC's Enterprise Integration effort focuses on activities that can best be accomplished cooperatively among companies. The overall objective is to provide a commercial information infrastructure that connects people and systems within and across enterprises and to enable them to develop, manufacture, sell, deliver, and support products and services with speed, flexibility, quality, security, and economy. The EINet Services Project, which was the foundation of MCC's EI Program, was formed to create synergy among the other projects and to provide important services to guide and complement these activities. The project has emerged as a nearly commercial service that is offered to external customers.[14] In November 1993, the Texas Department of Commerce received a $2.5 million federal grant from President Clinton's Technology Reinvestment program for its Texas-One Project. The project will use MCC's EInet technology to create an electronic network for the state's small- and medium-sized manufacturers. The system will enable companies to exchange information on contracts, purchasing, and inventory.

In 1984, Doug Lenat, a computer scientist and leading AI researcher from Stanford, was hired by MCC to begin a ten-year project, Common Sense Knowledge Base (Cyc—short for encyclopedia), the consortium's most heavily funded, long-term software project. Cyc is a knowledge base filled with millions of pieces of information and intelligent reasoning capabilities with the understanding of such concepts as time and spatial relationships. By reaching beyond today's domain-specific artificial intelligence approach, it is hoped that Cyc will help resolve the limitations associated with expert systems and intelligent software. Millions of Cyc rules enable "sanity checking" and verification of data consistency and accuracy. The vast amount of information required for such a knowledge base has been entered by researchers at MCC, several U.S. universities, and MCC member companies.

By 1990, Cyc had seven company sponsors each paying $500,000, and by 1991, $15 million had been invested. Member companies had used parts of Cyc in prototype systems. Digital Equipment Corporation, for example, used Cyc to help size and configure information systems. MCC's Carnot Project—a technology for accessing and maintaining information databases distributed across a network—has used Cyc as a key component of its distributed information-management system. Microsoft Corporation is exploring product applications using Cyc.

In early 1992, Lenat and Cyc were featured in a public television series called "The Thinking Machine." Jon Palfreman, the executive producer of the series, observed that the Cyc research project may be the last, best hope for a large-scale research breakthrough in artificial intelligence. As he stated: "I was glad [Lenat] was there, otherwise the story of AI is a very down beat story." (Ladendorf, 1992d)

As of 1993, 30 Cyc programmers (with a core group of 6) worked long days, nights, and weekends at MCC's headquarters. They are described as compulsive "software hackers," and they commonly show up for work in shorts and T-shirts. As commented by the spouse of one of the researchers (Millea interview, June 6, 1993): "Their job is their life. They are addicted to their work. They all go through a two-year learning curve to become creative 'knowledge engineers.'" Cyc is generally seen as pushing "the edges of the envelope" in software development. Members of the team teach at Stanford and at UT. At times, they feel constrained by MCC's more formal, rigid culture; they resent being (in their opinion) the "cash cow" of the Information Systems Division; and they complain that MCC's marketing staff does not really understand Cyc.

By 1994, the goal is for Cyc to have acquired sufficient knowledge and natural language to "learn on its own," receiving information on-line. More than any other MCC software project, Cyc has been able to maintain sustained corporate support over an extended period of time based on the promise of future applications. The ultimate value of Cyc is a much debated topic. Brian C. Smith, a researcher at Xerox Corporation, wrote a scathing critique of Cyc in an 1991 issue of *Artificial Intelligence*. Bledsoe suggests that the arguments come down to a battle between the "scruffies" and the "neats." Neats are theorists who want roadmaps for everything they do, and scruffies, such as Lenat, want to get on with it. (Stanley, 1991)

MCC's First Cities Program is a national initiative for interactive high-performance and intelligent systems and is envisioned as an environment for testing member-company technologies and for identifying technology or standards gaps that may impede value-added product and service delivery. On July 7, 1993, MCC made a First Cities presentation in Albuquerque, New Mexico. MCC was presented as a catalyst for First Cities by bringing together companies, universities, and the local community for collaboration to lessen the risks and increase the wins of establishing an interactive, multimedia information system. Chosen sites will be testbeds for advanced information technologies and services emphasizing impartial, market-driven approaches at the local level. MCC representatives note that previous trials in establishing such interactive networks, by individual industries, have had problems with user interfaces, inappropriate applications, and inadequate trials.

MCC established the ATLAS Standards Laboratory as an independent subsidiary to help speed the creation and adoption of a wide range of electronic information standards. Rather than seeking to define the standards themselves, ATLAS has positioned itself to provide such services as coordination of technical evaluation activities related to draft standards, performance of technical evaluations, verification and certification services for users of new standards, and assistance in publicizing new standards. Non-U.S. firms may participate in certain ATLAS activities, since effective standards development is considered an inherently international activity.

MCC'S PHYSICAL PLANT

Shortly after Austin won the national competition for MCC's headquarters, Admiral Inman moved into an unpretentious set of offices in the Littlefield building in the capital city's downtown. About six months later, MCC leased space for its headquarters in a new, four-story, steel and glass building (called Echelon I) in North Austin and a year later rented additional space in adjacent buildings called Kaleido and Echelon III. It was about two miles from these initial corporate facilities to the 475-acre Balcones Research Park, where the University of Texas was building MCC's headquarters, which was completed in 1986.

> A massive new building hulks in the forest at the north end of this Texas city, its top three stories jutting out like a furrowed brow over the entrance. An as yet unfilled trough sidles up to the clay-brown structure, more suggestive of a moat than a pond. Inside, beyond the locked doors that flank the security desk, an atrium reaches to the ceiling, its blank white walls dividing the 200,000-square foot building lengthwise. Along the other side of it, columns of computer-filled offices march down inner halls, progressively numbered but otherwise mute to the identity of their occupants or purpose. This is the home of the Microelectronics & Computer Technology Corporation, or MCC as it calls itself in a cryptogram to the outside world, a $23.5-million fortress in the battle for technological superiority. (Walters, 1986)[15]

The hugely successful interstate competition for MCC resulted in an unexpected financial windfall for the consortium in addition to the income from a larger-than-expected number of shareholders. Inman was able to increase MCC's research activities, hire additional researchers, and purchase more advanced computer hardware. The decision was made to split the consortium's research activities into three sites: (1) Software Technology (STP) would remain in the Kaleido building; (2) the Packaging/Interconnect (PI) Program would set up its clean rooms and offices about four miles north, just off Route 183; and (3) MCC's new headquarters building, which housed the CAD and ACA research programs, would be located about halfway in between. By 1984, the Packaging/Interconnect Program completed construction of its semiconductor packaging laboratory, with over 2,000 square feet of class 100 clean rooms and 8,000 square feet of class 10,000 clean rooms.[16]

MCC's headquarters building, called the "BRC," is located on the west track of the university's Balcones Research Center about ten miles north of The University of Texas at Austin campus.[17] The modern 210,000-square-foot building has four floors of private offices that surround the large atrium area with a cafeteria at one end of the first floor. MCC leases the facility along with 20 acres of land at $2 per year for ten years from UT-Austin. MCC has an option to continue leasing the building at a commercial rate beginning in 1996. The Kaleido building, where the STP research program was located, and the buildings for the P/I Program were leased from commercial vendors.

During MCC's early years, the interior of the BRC was replete with the requisite signs of high corporate culture: a state-of-the-art exercise room, library, indoor greenery, and a cafeteria that prepared quality, health-conscious meals served in a well-appointed and spacious dining area. Inman saw the cafeteria as an important communal space where the researchers could meet and talk. To encourage the researchers to eat at the cafeteria, the meals were heavily subsidized. Inman's wife selected poster art to hang on the walls. Just outside the front door, a jogging trail wound through cedar trees. As George Black, MCC's vice president for human relations, noted in 1986 (interview, May 5): "These things are not add-ons—we are consciously creating an environment which is satisfactory to bright people who can change the face of the world."[18]

With MCC's downsizing, which began in 1990, what was left of the Software Technology Program moved from the Kaleido building to the third floor of the BRC. While the sunk costs of the High Value Electronics (HVE, formerly Packaging/Interconnect) laboratory and clean room facility prevented these research activities from moving, HVE's office and support staff were moved to the BRC in late 1993. Overhead and other expenses could be saved by selling the labs or spinning them out, but then MCC would lose control of one of its most significant technological capabilities. The Texas Institute for Computational Mechanics, which is part of The University of Texas at Austin, moved into the third floor of the BRC building, and significant blocks of offices were occupied by MCC's spin-out companies.

As of late 1993, MCC has two main facilities in Austin: (1) the BRC headquarters building that houses the Information Systems Division and (2) the High Value Electronics Division (including the clean room and laboratory) located in a leased building three miles northwest of the BRC. MCC's Washington, D.C., location contains offices for a staff of about six. MCC-West is located in Palo Alto and provides facilities for researchers working on the Cyc project.

> Interviewer: Given the possibilities at the time, what is your feeling in retrospect about the decision to bring MCC to Austin?
>
> Dove: I think it's better than Atlanta or North Carolina would have been. It's certainly a lower-cost operating environment than San Diego, much lower-cost than Silicon Valley. Boston is isolated in a way. . . . Now, I would say that we probably have missed getting some world-class people by being here . . . but I think this is a good place for our kind of shop; I don't think I would change what Bobby did there at all. (Dove interview, March 1, 1991)

Some of MCC's founders were in favor of the consortium operating as a distributed enterprise, where the research would be conducted on-site at the member companies. But this idea met with stiff resistance by the shareholder companies who were operating within the same industry. Price commented (interview, May 12, 1993):

Their reactions were, "There is no way I'm going to let [company X] researchers into my labs." And those companies with weak or modest R&D efforts would say, "There is no way I'm going to fund research in [company Y] who is already a leader in this technology." MCC provided a neutral site—which no one member company could own. The concept of a central lab in neutral turf helped get the fiercely competitive companies to begin to think about collaboration with their competitors.

Inman commented in 1992 (interview, October 22): "I remember discussing the point of a centralized versus a decentralized research operation. I pressed for a single location to try and get synergy among the researchers. I think this is especially important in long-term research when you are not sure what will come out of your effort." Palle Smidt commented (interview, June 2, 1993): "Locating in Austin gave us the added challenge of providing quick evidence of doing world-class research so we could attract quality people."

The value of centralized versus distributed R&D is an ongoing debate in the consortia world. MCC (as was Japan's VLSI Project) was set up as a central laboratory to do on-site R&D. European models such as ESPRIT in information technology, BRITE in advanced materials manufacturing, RACE in advanced communications, JESSI in semiconductors, and JFIT in information technologies all favor R&D being distributed at several sites rather than consolidated in a central lab.[19] Under Fields' leadership, MCC has attempted to move toward a more distributed R&D environment.

Fields does not envision MCC's beginning any major basic research programs in Austin; as he emphasized (interview, March 1, 1991): "There is a world of basic research out there, free of charge." Fields thinks efforts toward agglomeration are an obstacle—that it is unrealistic to try to recruit to Austin all the best researchers in MCC's range of research projects. Under Fields' vision, MCC seeks out the needed technology, the researchers, and technology users wherever possible (Figure 4.7).[20]

Interviewer: With distributed R&D, aren't you back-
                ing the technology transfer problem up to
                the research side? You now have to get
                these distributed research projects
                coordinated to share ideas. Now you've
                got multiple sources and multiple
                destinations.

Dove: Yes, it's not natural . . . to let people
                come into their shop, and they have to
                agree to share results. . . . Getting the
                technology transfer, the piece that each
                company has to share with the other two
                or three, that's a difficult task. I believe
                that technology transfer is much easier
                for the central lab concept that Bobby set
                up and that I fundamentally followed.
                (Dove interview, March 1, 1991)

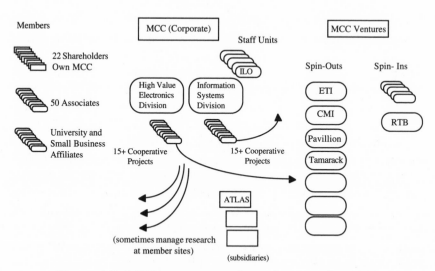

Figure 4.7 MCC as a consortium of consortia, 1993

Fields (interview, March 1, 1991) responded:

There's been an unspoken assumption for the last seven or eight years that the most instrumental means of doing cooperation among members was to join together to pay the salaries of researchers in Austin. And I'm calling that into question. There's no reason why MCC staff shouldn't go elsewhere if recruitment and retention is an issue. So one of the things we're doing is expanding our offices in San Francisco [Palo Alto] at a rapid rate. Not because that's our goal, but because that's a consequence of our willingness to manage a distributed enterprise, and we need to have the world's best people. We may well be expanding our offices elsewhere, all centered around groups of people.

As an HVE technician commented in April 1993:

It's [distributed R&D] slowly happening that way in HVE, but mostly by market pull rather than MCC push. There is resistance to encouraging outside work when there is a need to support existing staff. [On the other hand] . . . Some of the best results for both MCC and a member [Motorola] have been achieved recently in the Single/Few Chip Packaging project due to the close interaction allowed by being in the same town. The Motorola people stop in on their way to work and we go over to do experiments in their labs, and both sides are very pleased with the relationship and the results.

Smidt commented (interview, June 2, 1993):

Distributed versus centralized research is not the issue. It's whether the research is short or long term. Long-term research has no bearing on co-location with manufacturing, but the closer you get to project-based research, the more important it is to be co-located with development and manufacturing. Revenue and life cycles are so short—decentralized development is doomed to fail. . . . Who in the hell wants a remote development organization?[21]

MCC'S GOVERNANCE

During the Inman and Dove years, MCC had four layers of shareholder governance, with some differences across each of the four research programs (Figure 4.8). The desire for a board of directors and a technical advisory board came from MCC's founders. The impetus for the program technical advisory boards (PTABs) and program technical panels (PTPs) came from MCC's management and research program directors in 1985. This relatively flat hierarchical structure was formed to provide ample opportunities for communication between MCC and its shareholders at policy, strategy, and technical levels.

The governance of MCC's research programs was designed to establish a system of research management and incentives more similar to corporate R&D than to academic research or to a government laboratory. Program technical advisory board members were usually senior-level engineering or research directors from the shareholder companies who served as technical advisors. PTABs were intended to ensure that research programs were responsive to the needs of the shareholder companies. They reviewed general program direction, objectives, and progress. They decided the qualifications of research personnel, the program's annual budget and technical plan, incentive payments, licensing plans, and royalty rates for the program's technologies.[22]

According to one MCC researcher, the main purpose of the TAB and PTABs was to ensure that MCC researchers were engaged in problem-driven research. A major barrier developed when these governance committees "provided glowing feedback about the research per se, but failed to link it to specific customer groups or problems [in the shareholder companies]." However, as one MCC researcher noted, this was not surprising since the TABs and PTABs had neither the accountability or power to see that MCC technologies were applied in the shareholder companies. This technology transfer problem was further complicated by MCC researchers

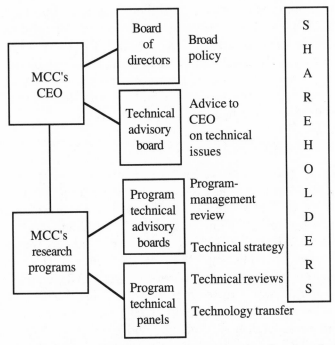

Figure 4.8 Four levels of MCC governance by the shareholder companies, 1983–1991

working on technologies that were "new to the world," and for which the shareholders, their customers, were unprepared (see Chapter 5).

Program technical panels (PTPs) were composed of hands-on researchers and engineers. PTP personnel were to evaluate program technical requirements and get involved in technology transfer activities. They were charged with understanding the research at MCC in which their company participated and determining where these technologies might fit into their company's operations.

Some shareholder companies sent no personnel to PTAB/PTP meetings, but most sent three or four company representatives. MCC researchers made presentations and provided demonstrations at these technical briefings. These visits were viewed as a high-pressure review by MCC scientists. As one MCC researcher stated in 1987: "When the shareholders finally get on their ——— plane and get the ——— out of here, a big sigh goes up. But it is something that the [MCC] people have to accept as part of the job. They may not like it, but they get it done and they do a damn good job of it."

MCC's board of directors, the consortium's top governing body, continues to meet quarterly in Austin. MCC's CEO serves as chairman of the board. Each shareholder company appoints one board member who has one vote on MCC policy considerations. The board appoints corporate officers, approves new members, and decides the scope of research programs and new strategic directions.[23]

MCC GOVERNANCE UNDER CRAIG FIELDS

By his second year at MCC, Fields believed that the TAB and PTABs were "totally unnecessary. . . . The last thing we need is technical advice. . . . However, we could use some requirements advice on what the members want from MCC" (all-hands meeting, videotape, June 18, 1992). Project management, Fields argued, did away with the need for PTPs. By 1992, MCC's TAB and PTABs had been replaced by a requirements advisory board (RAB), whose purpose, in Fields words, was: "to see that we [MCC] get the best data possible on what our members actually want from MCC rather than our having to guess." (all-hands meeting, videotape, June 18, 1992)

The RAB meets quarterly and is composed of the senior vice president for strategic planning, and engineering or research directors from the shareholder companies. Different RAB members host the quarterly meetings. Past meetings have been held in Atlanta; Washington, D.C.; Albuquerque, New Mexico; and Palo Alto, California; as well as Austin. The RAB focuses on major national initiatives. As of spring 1993, four working RAB groups were focusing on: medical information systems with 53 partner companies; the environment with 13 member companies; intelligent vehicle and highway systems (IVHS) with 6 partner companies; and software/systems integration with 6 partner companies.

The RAB's mission is to advise MCC management, the board of directors, and the membership concerning shared strategic technology needs and long-term requirements in order to enhance corporate and national competitiveness and maximize the value of MCC to the members and the nation. The RAB is to:

- Provide effective means and encouragement for members to participate in MCC program formulation

- Identify with MCC, multicompany, global, target technology areas and formulate associated long-term requirements through which potential MCC programs can help create and maintain competitive advantage for the members
- Recommend technology areas for MCC to develop as its core competencies
- Establish measures of MCC strategic success and periodically benchmark MCC's progress

SHAREHOLDER PARTICIPATION

In MCC's early days, when the consortium's board of directors and TAB were populated with CEOs and other high-ranking executives from the shareholder companies, the agreed-upon strategic emphasis for MCC was long-term (five to ten years) pre-competitive research. MCC's founders had high expectations for the research benefits to be provided by the consortium. CDC Chairman Bill Norris stated that he hoped to get $114 million worth of research in return for his company's $17 million investment over the first five years of MCC. Lockheed Group President Robert Fuhrman expected a greater return on "several million dollars" worth of investment in MCC than if Lockheed were doing the research itself. Fuhrman also expected MCC to "force" Lockheed to adjust its marketing strategy: "We're looking for the long-term payoff. We'll join together for the basic research, but we'll still be competing on how we apply it." (Day, 1984)

By the mid-1980s, it was common for shareholder companies to be represented on the board and TAB by division-level managers and managers of technical services. As Admiral Inman stated (interview, January 26, 1987): "What has happened over time . . . is that there are more short-term expectations. . . . The high-level executives who first organized MCC were looking at mountains, but MCC is now being directed by people at the member companies who are looking at what's going to make their profit centers profitable." As their funding increasingly came from the "the dukes and barons," MCC was pressured to deliver usable technologies that would have a direct impact on a division's bottom line. By 1988, MCC research program directors and managers were spending significant amounts of time on the road selling MCC research to member-company divisions in order to obtain $50,000 to $100,000 chunks of a shareholder company's annual contribution.

Early in his tenure as MCC's CEO, Fields became resigned to "can't-change categories." One such category was that everything was becoming shorter-term and that, within companies, the locus of power was shifting to division line managers rather than the CEO and chief technical officers. These line managers tended to want shorter-term R&D. They did not want process, they wanted products. "That's just the way it is," said Fields. (interview, February 29, 1991)

MCC'S EMPLOYEES

By 1984, MCC employed 72 researchers, managers, and staff. The consortium rapidly grew to 260 employees by 1985, to 400 by 1986, and to a peak of 473 in 1987, the year that Grant Dove took over MCC's leadership (Figure 4.9). From 1988 to 1991, the consortium held relatively steady at about 430 employees, dropping to 372 employees in 1992. By 1993, MCC had downsized to 340 employees. [24]

MCC researchers can be classified into three categories: direct hires, shareholder representatives (called "liaisons" until 1988), and assignees. Direct hires come from industry, university, and government backgrounds. They are full-time MCC employees paid by the consortium. Direct hires have traditionally made up the largest percentage of MCC's employees—about 65 percent in 1986 and about 85 percent in 1992.

Shareholder representatives were about 20 percent of MCC's workforce in 1986, 15 percent in 1990, and 10 percent in 1993. Shareholder representatives are paid by the shareholder companies and have traditionally been charged with the responsibility of transferring MCC's technology back to their companies. Some MCC member companies have had as many as three representatives in residence at MCC at one time, and some have had none in residence.

Assignees are maintained as employees at the shareholder company while being assigned to MCC to work on a particular research project. MCC reimburses the company for their salary.

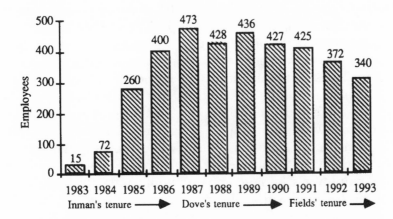

Note: The number of MCC employees includes shareholder personnel, but not temporary employees.

Figure 4.9 Number of MCC employees at the start of each year

Shareholder representatives and assignees work on the research projects that their company funds. Visiting researchers are also paid by the shareholder company. They visit MCC over an extended period of time for a specific purpose—such as the transfer of the Proteus technology to NCR (elaborated on in Chapter 5).

During MCC's planning phase, it was believed that if the consortium's people did not move, neither would the technology. Shareholder representatives were expected to be the primary carriers of technologies. They were to divide their time between transferring technology via periodic trips to their home companies (about 20 percent) and conducting research at MCC (about 80 percent). After a two- or three-year residence at MCC, the shareholder representative was expected to permanently return to his or her company. Thus, "people transfer" was to have been a main means of technology transfer.

The original plan was for MCC to get about 65 percent of its researchers from the shareholder companies. However, within the first year of MCC's operation, Admiral Inman realized that the expectation of staffing the consortium with quality researchers borrowed from shareholder companies was not going to work.[25] Inman rejected about 95 percent of the scientists initially offered by the shareholder companies to serve as MCC's research program directors. As he (Inman interview, July 21, 1987) exclaimed in frustration: "I did not want to preside over a turkey farm. . . . The reality was that the talent was not in the companies, or [else] they didn't make it available, and I think it was the former."

Although Inman had the authority to hire the researchers he wanted, the shareholders could veto his selections for program managers. At times when he attempted to appoint a qualified researcher from a particular shareholder company as a program manager, he found that the other companies would reject the choice out of fear that the employee's home company would unfairly benefit. To counter this fear, and without much effect, Inman suggested that the complaining companies send him their best people to head the research programs.

Since research talent was not forthcoming from the shareholder companies, MCC set out to attract quality scientists from research universities, federal laboratories, and nonshareholder corporate laboratories.

> When I understood early on that we were going to get a very attractive offer from Austin in regards to getting in business there [that is, the offer of a free building], I went back to the member companies and locked up a deal in which I could use the money that we had budgeted for facilities to hire more researchers and buy more research equipment. Then, as additional companies joined MCC, I also managed to move these extra funds [to hire more researchers and to buy equipment]. So instead of the initial ceiling of 350 to 360 researchers originally planned, we got on up to 475 researchers. We were, in our first couple of years of operation, the largest single purchaser of Sun workstations. . . . The equipment and the three-year guaranteed funding [for research projects] helped us recruit the talent we needed. We hired 90 percent of the individuals to whom we made an offer. If we got them to visit our labs, and see the research facilities, they would usually decide to join MCC. (Inman interview, December 12, 1989)

Inman and Black (MCC's first vice president for human resources) used Austin's high quality of life as a recruiting incentive. Rutishauser recalled (interview, January 23, 1987): "For recruiting purposes, Austin is just marvelous. There's just an ambiance about the community that makes it very easy. . . . For a while, we were saying that if we can just get them off the airplane, we've got 'em." Smidt remembered things a bit differently when he stated (interview, June 2, 1993):

> It was difficult to attract academic and research super-stars to Austin. UT was considered too dogmatic and conserva-tive. . . . We also had to contend with a poor incentive plan at MCC. There was no stock plan, no equity participation. A move to Austin did not favor long-term career planning for the young researchers who were the best in their fields. It was better for them to stay close to where things were happening. Furthermore, most of the shareholder superstars were in development not research and the researchers we did hire often brought their own tailor-made research agendas.

Factors that facilitated MCC's recruiting researchers to Austin were: (1) high salaries (usually 10 to 20 percent above the industry average) and attractive bonuses, (2) state-of-the-art computer equipment (e.g., Symbolics and Sun workstations), (3) guaranteed long-term (three-year) research funding, and (4) the freedom to concentrate on one's research in a very pleasant work environment. MCC researchers could earn an annual bonus of up to 50 percent of their base rate for spectacular performance and for technology applications. However, overtime bonus payments (as much as $38,000 for a senior researcher) tended to become a common, if not expected, practice. (The average burdened cost for an MCC researcher approached $175,000 in 1988.) MCC hires coming to Texas from the East and West Coasts also were attracted by low housing costs, subsidized mortgages, and no state income tax. MCC was by most measures a dream come true for the researchers that were hired. In the end, these "ideal" working conditions contributed to what some observers called a "candy store" mentality at MCC. This mind-set had important implications for technology transfer.

By the mid-1980s, the "world's" perception of MCC's on-site research talent was generally quite favorable.[26] As John McCarthy, a well-known computer scientist at Stanford University, said: "Those [MCC researchers] I have seen and know are very good and are capable of advancing the goals of MCC. . . . It is a part of the total U.S. effort in artificial intelligence. . . . From that point of view, MCC is very important" (quoted by Krishnan, 1987). In 1986, 46 percent of MCC's scientists had doctorates and possessed an average of 15 years' research experience. The remaining researchers (54 percent) had an average of 12 years' industry experience, and over half of them had masters degrees. About 65 percent came from non-MCC companies. About 20 percent came from universities and government laboratories. The rest came from the shareholder companies (Murphy, 1987).

Over the years, MCC continued to have difficulty in attracting quality personnel from the shareholder companies. Don Wiersma, manager of electronic products at Eastman Kodak commented in 1990 that staff members were not beating down his door to request transfers to the consortium. Of the nearly 3,000 R&D personnel at Kodak, only three were currently at MCC. "There are both family issues and career issues for people," stated Wiersma (quoted in Rifkind, 1990). As of 1990, only 15 percent of the consortium's staff were from the member firms, the rest were MCC employees.

During MCC's "honeymoon" years, the consortium's high quality of research life resulted in a very low turnover rate—only about 3 percent per year, compared to around 10 percent in the average U.S. organization. Additionally, a high percentage of the shareholder representatives elected to become permanent assignees to the consortium rather than return to their home organizations. Establishing a meaningful career track for returning assignees was a challenge. The typical MCC shareholder representative enjoyed considerable freedom and resources. A return to the researcher's home company would often lead to a less-stimulating position and one having little to do with the research that he or she had pursued at MCC.

MCC employees who bought homes in Austin during the boom years from 1983 to 1985 had another strong inducement to remain at the consortium. These recruits commonly earned high profits when they sold their East and West Coast homes to purchase a larger home in Austin at substantial savings. However, selling their Austin home during the late 1980s and early 1990s involved a substantial loss. So Austin's real estate bust of 1987 helped dissuade some MCC researchers from leaving town. Furthermore, many of MCC's employees and their families enjoyed living in the area. Their children were enrolled in Austin's schools. The prospect of moving to the more crowded and expensive East or West Coast was not all that attractive. So the desire to "go native" and remain at MCC was tied to several strong motivations.[27]

Hiring researchers from nonshareholder companies and other sources allowed MCC to reach full staffing more quickly while rejecting the "turkeys" that the shareholder companies wanted to dump on the consortium. However, this heavy dependence on direct hires was later to cause problems in terms of establishing a coherent and company-focused research agenda and in facilitating technology transfer (see Chapter 5). Furthermore, the liaisons/shareholder representatives who were assigned to MCC were often not up to the task. Inman realized that he had made a mistake by exercising quality control over the full-time research staff but not over the liaisons. "Many of the liaisons were not first-rate and didn't command attention in their own companies." (Inman quoted in Rifkin, 1990)

THE CRITICAL MASS OF INTELLECTUAL TALENT

In the early years, some MCC researchers commented that they missed being at what they considered the center of research action for their area of expertise, which they perceived to be on the West and East Coasts. Despite the software and microelectronics research going on at The University of Texas at Austin and Texas A&M University, and the presence of major R&D activities at IBM, Motorola, 3M, Texas Instruments, and other high-tech companies, the level of technology-based information exchange that characterizes Silicon Valley and Route 128 did not exist in Austin throughout the 1980s.[28]

Fields believed that no matter how effective he might be, he would never be able to recruit all the needed technical talent to Austin. He cautioned:

You can wind up with an installed base of high-quality people with the wrong skills for the next generation of technologies, and then what do you do? No place should say they have all the key people. Some of the hottest work in formal methods documentation of hardware and software is going on in England and France, so why should I try and recreate that? Technology import, to me, is very legitimate . . . scan, assess, bring it in, benchmark, reverse engineer, integrate, harden, distribute—it's a very legitimate thing to do. (interview, March 1, 1991)

Under Fields' tenure, MCC is conducting more contract research with companies and universities, via licenses, by making equity investments in small firms or through agreements for preferential technology access. As Fields stated (interview, March 1, 1991): "So suddenly, you've opened the whole world, and when you're doing things by contract, you have greater flexibility. . . . I want our project managers to realize that the job is to get the work done, not add head count."

With his philosophy of distributed R&D, Fields has encouraged more assignees but with an important difference:

I'll let the assignees stay in Rochester or in Palo Alto. I'll pay a price for that. It's harder to manage a distributed enterprise, but I'll get their involvement. I also want reverse assignees. I want MCC staff to physically spend three, six, nine months in the member companies. And I've identified 25 of my best people and said: "You guys are consultants. You're here to consult with our member companies, not for profit but in order to get more closely tied." (interview, March 1, 1991)[29]

MCC'S CULTURE

Establishing an MCC-wide corporate culture has been a seemingly impossible task. In 1983, there were few existing U.S. models of R&D consortia from which MCC management could learn. MCC was a new type of organization, which quickly ramped up from 15 employees in 1983, to 400 by 1986, and to 473 by

1987. Employees came from a diverse group of shareholder and nonshareholder locations, including aerospace companies, computer companies, electronics companies, and conglomerates. They came from the nation's universities, and they came from federal laboratories. With each MCC recruit came a somewhat unique set of research preferences and values. As one MCC researcher noted: "Before coming to MCC, I would not have believed how diverse corporate cultures could be."[30]

The pressure was on MCC's management to quickly build a critical mass of research talent.

> This resulted in somewhat lower quality [of researcher] than a slower starting process might have, [and] it made later "team building" more difficult. The newcomers were mutual strangers, each looking for something meaningful to do since there were no existing projects to fit the typical researcher we hired. . . . Communication was a continual problem. . . . Many researchers tended to continue their old line of research. While program management put lots of energy into keeping all efforts well aligned and synergistic with each other, some individuals spent too little time in understanding and discussing [program] research beyond their own efforts. (Belady, 1992, p. 13)

During the mid-1980s, many of MCC's hires believed that they would be at the consortium for two to three years. They were grouped in one of four research programs in one of three different Austin locations. Given such circumstances, George Black understood the challenge of establishing an MCC identity. He emphasized (interview, May 5, 1986): "One of the things we need to build is a sense of permanence. . . . I think we have something very special happening here. . . . But it has to be made clear that . . . this is just the beginning of a very long and exciting adventure."

Black scheduled regular events to help build a common culture at MCC. Employees took weekend field trips to San Antonio and other Texas tourist spots. Social events and meetings were regularly scheduled at MCC's BRC headquarters building in the central eating area. Black believed that Inman was pleased with the kind of things that he had scheduled and tried to institutionalize such events as the spring fiesta, the summer picnic, the Christmas party, and the arts and crafts show. "We get levels of participation that other companies only dream about," said Black.

> Friday is the day for boots. This Friday particularly. This is our annual spring fiesta, where we come to work dressed as cowboys, get on buses at noon, drink a Lone Star on the way to San Antonio and margaritas when you get there . . . take over the plaza at a little place called . . . La Villita, have a private party that night, and pour everybody back into the buses on Saturday. (Black interview, May 5, 1986)

Adding to the challenge of establishing an MCC culture in a rapidly growing organization was the reality that the consortium was itself in a state of constant change as MCC managers and scientists—from academic, business, and government backgrounds—were joining and leaving MCC, launching new research projects, and experimenting with ways to manage the consortium. With each of the consortium's CEOs—from Admiral Inman to Grant Dove to Craig Fields—MCC has assumed a decidedly different character.[31] As Inman observed (interview, October 22, 1992): "I was focused on accomplishing MCC's mission, not with keeping the companies happy. Grant was most concerned with the shareholders. Craig, he's Machiavellian and fast-moving."

Inman emphasized the values of long-term pre-competitive research and the responsibility of the shareholders to commercialize the technology. It was not until the late 1980s that it became apparent just how difficult it would be to have the shareholders transfer MCC technologies to commercial applications. As Dove recollected (interview, March 1, 1991): "Bobby had them [MCC's researchers] believing that U.S. industry leaders were basically giving them tenure. 'Here comes the money. You've got ten years.'"

> Interviewer: Sit in your office and think good thoughts.
>
> Dove: Exactly. (interview, March 1, 1991)

MCC's culture changed during Dove's tenure, and employee dissatisfaction increased, as did turnover. Dissatisfaction among MCC's researchers centered around two important changes: (1) the need to spend increasing amounts of time—up to 50 percent in some cases—on technology transfer and (2) the need to be actively involved in fund raising for MCC's research programs. MCC's management considered both activities crucial to the survival of the consortium, but neither task was perceived to be a particularly enjoyable endeavor by the technologists who were, after all, recruited to MCC to pursue long-term research.

Under Fields' leadership, MCC emphasized distributed R&D, early buy-in of project-based research activities, technology transfer through specific plans, the value of member-company diversity, entrepreneurial behavior, and spin-out companies. By early 1991, MCC management was emphasizing two- to four-year research projects, which had their own directors and start and stop dates. Such changes were difficult for some of MCC's researchers to accept.[32] As Dove commented (interview, March 1, 1991):

The idea that we were under pressure to deliver really took them [the researchers] a while. And the idea that we have to work with those dirty old group and division managers took them a while. We thought [in the late 1980s] that to have start and stop dates on projects would have been too much for them to take, and then Craig came along.

After studying consortia, during his first few months at MCC, Fields concluded that almost all went through two phases—phase I is: "We're going to do long-term basic research"; phase II is "Whoops, we didn't mean it." Consortia that can successfully transition their culture and personnel from phase I to phase II will survive and thrive, and those that can't, will not. (Fields interview, March 1, 1991)

Turnover at MCC was about 3 percent during Inman's era of leadership. It increased to about 20 percent under Dove, increased to 30 percent under Fields in 1990, and settled down to around 17 percent by 1993. About six months after Fields took charge of MCC, the following sign appeared on the office door of one of the

staff: "The beatings will stop as soon as the morale improves."
Fields is pushing for each MCC activity to be a profit center, includ-
ing research activities as well as such staff functions as the ILO and
public relations. "If everybody is a profit center, why stay at
MCC?" commented Eaton (interview, August 5, 1993). Indeed,
Eaton left MCC in fall 1993.

In summary, during its first decade of existence, MCC has *not*
established an organizationwide culture and/or mythology of its
founding and history. As one MCC researcher said in 1992: "When
I joined MCC [in 1990], there was no induction course, no explana-
tion of what MCC's goals were. My perceptions [of MCC] are
totally self-developed."

SECRECY VERSUS COLLABORATION

In 1982–1983, MCC was a revolutionary idea. Never before
had major U.S. high-tech companies funded such a massive effort in
long-term research collaboration. As Admiral Inman observed, the
suspicion was palpable among MCC's ten founding companies at
the November 1982 Denver meeting at which they decided to "fish
or cut bait." The clandestine nature of MCC grew out of the consortium's prime objective: to enhance and maintain U.S. leadership
in computer and semiconductor research for its member companies.
During his tenure at the National Security Agency and the Central
Intelligence Agency, Inman had been troubled by the loss of U.S.
technology to economic competitors and political enemies of the
United States. The nation's computer and semiconductor companies
needed help in sustaining their industrial competitiveness. MCC
was in business to aid its shareholders, not to generally inform
U.S. business and the public and certainly not the nation's
foreign competitors.

During MCC's formative years, the basic operating notion
was that if the shareholder companies were paying for research in
areas that they considered important, they would be competitive
about transferring and using MCC-developed technologies.
Supporting this contention was the fact that the shareholders had
encouraged the admiral to insulate the four research programs so
that only those companies funding the research would benefit. This
partitioning meant that considerable attention had to be given to
ensuring the secrecy of each research program from the other three

as well as from the outside world. In short, protecting as well as transferring MCC's technologies seemed to be on the minds of MCC's personnel and the consortium's shareholders.[33] There were differing opinions on the importance of protecting MCC's technologies. Smidt expressed little concern about technology's leaking from one research program to another or even out of MCC. As he stated (interview, May 5, 1986): "Effective competition comes not from trying to capture and monopolize a technology, but from being the first to produce, market, and deliver a quality product."

To preserve a sense of fairness, MCC's original technology transfer plans incorporated the concept of the standard technology package, which released an MCC-developed technology at the same time to all shareholder sponsors of the research. An appropriate analogy is the starting gate at a racetrack. All shareholders would be starting at the same time in their race toward technology commercialization. Two major problems frustrated this initial strategy: (1) it was often difficult to get MCC scientists to say that their research was ready to be released (they always wanted to do more), and (2) after the announced technical release to all funding shareholders, "the technology just seemed to lie there" rather than being actively commercialized by the funding companies.

Under Grant Dove, MCC began to move from being a relatively closed and secretive organization in terms of its research activities to being more open and collaborative across its research programs. There were powerful internal and external motivators for this change. The threat of ICOT had receded. MCC's annual funding was becoming increasingly difficult to obtain from the shareholders. Several shareholders had left the consortium, and others were expressing dissatisfaction. As problems with technology transfer became more apparent, concern about interprogram secrecy within MCC gradually decreased to the point where, in February 1989, the STP research program hosted MCC's first "research program open house." MCC researchers from the CAD and ACT research programs (located at MCC's headquarters, about two miles north) and P/I researchers (from their MCC buildings about four miles north) visited with STP researchers in the Kaleido building. Maps were distributed to MCC researchers to help them find the building and to locate specific STP researchers and projects through the maze of offices within Kaleido. As the announcement stated,

"To catch your attention and leave you with an impression of the STP way of life," short presentations, videos, networked Sun computers and "stashes of tech reports" were provided. The event was informal and interactive. Gourmet ice cream and cookies were served. For many MCC researchers, it was the *first time* that they had toured the STP Program facility and talked with STP researchers about their work.

By the end of 1989, each of MCC's research programs had held an open house. These informal get-togethers were viewed as one means of facilitating intra-MCC technology transfer. Modest successes at cross-program cooperation did occur. For example, in April 1990, MCC announced a joint effort between the STP and CAD programs to investigate the simultaneous design of systems composed of hardware and software, called CoDesign. Still, according to several MCC researchers, MCC had done a poor job of using its technologies in-house—within and between program areas—while these technologies were being developed for shareholder use.

Perhaps the most challenging secrecy barrier, which inhibited effective technology transfer, was for MCC researchers to be able to learn how their research was being used by the shareholders. As an ACA program researcher commented in 1989:

> Shareholders built applications without consulting us. Not only did we not get the benefit of the feedback, but shareholders could not fully exploit the novel elements of the technology. When we did visit to prospect, secrecy kept us from seeing the right people. (E-mail, July 18, 1989)

In mid-1990, Jerry Werner, director of technology transfer for CAD, proposed a new MCC corporate function, which he called "Exploratory Applications," to use MCC technology in-house. MCC would serve as an "alpha test site" and work to make the technology more usable for its shareholder customers. STP's gIBIS (graphical Issue-Based Information System) software was proposed as the first Exploratory Application, and EXTRACT (modified for incremental data translations rather than large batch translations) was proposed as the second. Werner's proposal went to John Pinkston, director of MCC's Exploratory Initiatives program, who liked the concept but declined to fund it out of funds that were earmarked for "front-end" rather than "back-end" tasks. (It is interesting to note that both gIBIS and EXTRACT were among the first technologies to be spun out of MCC, in part because of shareholder reticence to adopt technologies that were not developed to product applications.)

Despite early setbacks and disappointments, through trial and error, R&D collaboration did increase over time (1) across MCC's research programs, (2) between MCC and its member companies, and (3) among MCC's shareholders and associates. As a shareholder researcher told us in 1990:

> I was involved with the MCC back in the formative stages, when they were just putting this project together. I never believed that the companies would ever work together close enough to accomplish anything like this. I was amazed, when we actually started, at how much cooperation there was. But it is all relative, because as I look back, the kind of cooperation they are showing now is so much more. There really wasn't much [cooperation] then. It has definitely grown steadily with time.

MCC-facilitated collaboration with particular shareholder companies also benefited other shareholders. For example, 3M (a shareholder member of the P/I Program) supplied MCC with the high-quality tape needed to bond semiconductor chips by laser. The company stated that it wanted to improve the technology and raise the standards of the semiconductor industry. It was also looking to increase market share, as a 3M vice president remarked:

> We've been working on tape-automated bonding [TAB] for well over ten years. . . . Our work at MCC has advanced the state of the art in TAB, and it gets a much broader exposure to major customers. Now they are incorporating it into their processes, and we become the supplier to other [MCC] members.[34]

Belonging to MCC has also facilitated collaboration across divisions within member firms. In an effort to coordinate sharehold-

er demands, the P/I research program initiated a technical requirements panel (TRP). The TRP, composed of shareholder technicians
and researchers, established industrywide technical requirements for
MCC researchers. As an unexpected benefit, shareholder companies
realized that through TRP meetings, they became more aware of
their own companies internal technical requirements. As an MCC
shareholder representative told us:

> Out of these technical requirements panels, a few peo-
> ple developed an enthusiasm and vision for what MCC
> was trying to do, and they realized that finding out
> their companies position on these requirements was
> difficult. So they went back and convinced their man-
> agement that they should be assigned full-time to worry
> about this MCC requirements business and that they
> should be dedicated to going around and ferreting out
> the requirements in the various divisions in their
> companies to establish some kind of companywide
> requirements consensus.

After ten years, are MCC's member companies moving
toward increased collaboration? "Some member companies are
more open to this than others," said Fields. "Some are saying it's
about time. Others are saying it's un-American, an unnatural act—
it'll never happen." Fields believes that the members of U.S. consortia have never known or have forgotten that the principal reason for
belonging to a consortium is to collaborate to win.

> You say that's the whole idea and it's pretty obvious,
> but let me tell you it's not so obvious. For one thing, in
> many consortia, the member companies treat the con-
> sortium not as an instrument of collaboration but as a
> vendor which they send money to [while they] sit back
> and wait for results and products. That's not true coop-
> eration. (Fields interview, February 29, 1991)

Bob Price, who chaired the steering committee and interim
board of directors meetings that gave birth to MCC, delivered a

keynote presentation at MCC's tenth anniversary in which he stated:

> It's difficult to imagine, now, just how much of a chal-
> lenge it was [in 1983] for people to accept the idea for
> a major collaboration like MCC. There was the fear of
> antitrust. People held different visions of MCC. . . .
> Intuitively we knew how to structure MCC as a frame-
> work for facilitating collaboration. . . . The real
> technology to come out of MCC is the technology of
> partnering; however, nobody realizes just how
> difficult that is. (paraphrased comments of Price's MCC
> PartnerMart remarks, May 12, 1993)

MCC'S FUNDING

During the late 1980s, MCC's $60 to $70 million annual research budget allowed shareholders to engage in long-term, large-scale research activities that they would not, or could not, carry out on their own. Although MCC's shareholders were major U.S. companies, each firm's total R&D expenditure—little "r" (for "research") and big "D" (for "development")—was relatively modest (about $5 to $20 million per year), when compared to IBM's annual research budget during this time period of over $1 billion. Bell Laboratories had a yearly research budget that was even larger than IBM's.[35]

By early 1993, MCC had spent over $500 million of its member-companies funds (Figure 4.10).[36] These funds have traditionally come from one major source: annual fees for the research programs or projects to which the shareholder companies belonged. When a company becomes an MCC shareholder, it purchases one share of MCC stock and agrees to participate in at least one of the consortium's major research programs or projects. The price of a share of stock is set by MCC's board of directors.[37] During MCC's early years, funding from the shareholder companies was a multimillion-dollar line item signed off by the CEO. By 1988, the average MCC shareholder was paying about $3 million annually to the consor-

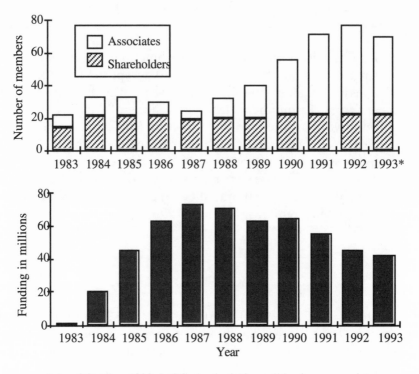

*As of October 1993, MCC also had 18 small business associates
and 12 university affiliates.

**Figure 4.10 MCC shareholder and associate membership and finan-
cial support, 1983 to 1993**

tium. However, companies that belonged to all four of the consortium's research programs were paying from $12 to $13 million for a
three-year commitment.

The more member companies participating in a research program or project, the less the cost to each. For example, if an MCC
research program cost $10 million per year, and ten companies
joined, each member would pay $1 million while ostensibly receiv-
ing the benefits of $10 million worth of research. Such resource
leveraging was one of the advertised benefits of joining MCC.

In 1987, Dove was concerned about R&D leverage for
MCC's member companies. It had decreased in two of MCC's
research programs to 5 or 6 to 1. "That was not enough," reasoned

Dove: "The companies themselves need to invest in terms of tech-nology transfer resources, and you have to decalibrate it in terms of its [the research's] not being exactly on target for any one company, so you've got to degrade it from that standpoint, and pretty soon you're down to maybe 2 to 1. So if you have only six companies in it [the research program], that's not good enough" (interview, March 1, 1991).[38] Responding to the issue of leveraging, Smidt commented: "The question is what's being done and what does it cost, what is the ROI [return on investment], and can you do it yourself, what is the value added. This is a much bigger issue." (interview, June 2, 1993)

In the late 1980s, aerospace, computer, and semiconductor industries were downsizing. Shareholder managers were making hard financial choices that included laying off employees. Cutting back on expenditures to MCC became an increasingly attractive alternative. However, the shareholders wishing to leave MCC found it difficult to sell their memberships to another company as BMC, Mostek, and Unisys had done a few years earlier.

Many U.S. microelectronics and other high-tech companies were not convinced of the viability of R&D consortia, and they declined to join MCC or any consortium. Other U.S. companies joined recently formed R&D consortia such as the Semiconductor Research Corporation and the Microelectronics Center of North Carolina in Research Triangle Park, North Carolina; the Microelectronics and Information Sciences Center in Minneapolis, Minnesota; the Software Engineering Institute at Carnegie-Mellon University in Pittsburgh; or the Software Productivity Consortium in Washington, D.C. Although the intent of these consortia was to at least coordinate, if not share, the results of their work and to elimi-nate duplication, they often became competitors for financial sup-port, prestige, and researchers. As Smidt commented:

> MCC does not try to fit into a collection of research activities. . . . Our focus is to understand what can drive the potentially biggest revenue opportunities and profit for our shareholders, irrespective of what the rest of the world does. . . . National objectives and compa-ny business objectives are not necessarily the same. . . . People form businesses to increase wealth. If they in the

process also meet national objectives, it's wonderful.
(quoted in Fischetti, 1986)

Initially, MCC was a big-company club. When Dove took
charge, AMD at about $300 million sales was the smallest MCC
shareholder. Dove initiated an "unbundling" of the consortium's
research activities, so that smaller companies could afford to join
particular research projects as associate members. At the same time,
shareholders could become more selective in the programs that they
funded, so a net gain in MCC funding was not realized (see Figure
4.10). Dove also increased U.S. government funding and welcomed
new shareholders. As he recollected (interview, March 1, 1991):
"It's taken all that effort to keep our size and technical research
roughly constant with quite a few shutdowns of projects and quite a
few start-ups. We've spread the load across more companies."

Dove lamented (interview, March 1, 1991): "So we are run
like a private enterprise. If there is one thing I would have [had]
Bobby [Inman] change at the start, it would have been to have a
small tax of some sort. We are about the only major consortium
that says: 'O.K. here's what we're going to do and this is what the
price is, and do you want to do it or not?' The rest of them have a
tie to a percentage of semiconductor billings or something like
that." Smidt commented (interview, June 2, 1993): "The problem
was there was nothing to tax. MCC was always entitled to royalty
payments on specific projects, but there was no license revenue."

As of late 1992, some of MCC's shareholder companies were
electing to contribute a flat rate in order to hold a sustaining membership in the High Value Electronics and Information Systems
Divisions. Their objective was to gain more leverage on their investment by coordinating across several research projects. Fields cited
the example of Motorola, which had agreed to be a sustaining member of the Information Systems Division. He hoped that other MCC
shareholders would support the "rebundling" of separate research
projects to keep costs down. "It's better for them, and it's better for
us. . . . It gives them better leverage, and it makes our costs for just
keeping things going go down dramatically." (all-hands meeting
videotape, June 18, 1992)

In 1992, MCC reactivated the royalties issue in an arrangement with Microsoft (an MCC associate and single-client member),
which planned to employ MCC's Cyc technology in a future prod-

uct. This single-company development was leveraged off MCC's cooperative R&D, and Fields hoped that more such arrangements would result from the other single-company projects currently under way at MCC.

Despite increased amounts of funding from the federal government (to about 30 percent of MCC's budget) and associate members (to about 20 percent) as of 1993, the consortium was still wholly owned and governed by its shareholders. Eighteen shareholders (not counting the four companies on inactive status) provided about 50 percent of MCC's funding. Funding from associate members had increased to the point where some were paying more for specific research projects than the annual contribution of some shareholders to the consortium.

FOREIGN MEMBERSHIP

MCC was designed to bolster U.S. international competitiveness in key semiconductor and computer-related industries. According to the consortium's bylaws, shareholders and participants had to be at least 51 percent owned by U.S. interests. In October 1987, Grant Dove made a presentation to the U.S. Council on Research and Technology in which he stated: "I have enough on my agenda, concentrating on U.S. interests and U.S. problems. . . . We must operate in an international industrial competition, and we must be sure that the tools and the talent which we bring to that competition are as good as, or exceed, that of the other players."[39]

The initial breach of the "U.S. companies only rule" for MCC came in 1989, after the passage of the Free Trade Agreement with Canada, when membership was opened to accommodate Northern Telecom (a Canadian telecommunications company). Fields continued the momentum toward being increasingly open to working with non-U.S. companies. He emphasized that international collaboration was an effective way to forge ties with U.S. allies and that given the increasingly global operations of most large U.S. companies, it was difficult to talk meaningfully about national competitiveness from the standpoint of particular U.S. firms. He noted:

> There is some concern with Europe, but it's not high on people's list. Also, all these [European] companies are multinational. Just as there are a lot of Siemens, Schlumbergers, and Philips in the United States, there's

a lot of Motorola, TI, and DEC in France and
Germany. Japanese company behavior does have a
nationalistic component of substance. But that's the
special case. The principle I have to revert to is
companies, not countries. (all-hands meeting videotape,
June 18, 1992)[40]

By summer 1992, Fields stated that he had no intention of
trying to change MCC's bylaws to allow foreign memberships, but
he was negotiating with Korean and Taiwanese companies about becoming partners with MCC in terms of (1) licensing MCC technology and (2) having MCC accept foreign contracts. Benefits to MCC
and its member companies included improved financing, access to
low-cost manufacturing, and technology know-how for joint technology development. An example of this emerging philosophy of
international collaboration is provided by MCC's relationship with
Samsung. Since December 1992, Samsung has been a partner in
MCC's portable electronics research project, and a Korean technician has worked in the HVE facilities. The collaborative research
agreement also allows the U.S. partners in the research project to
visit Samsung's laboratories in South Korea.

MCC has faced an interesting dilemma with its strategy to
involve foreign collaborators in specific research projects; interest
from Japan, Taiwan, and Korea has often overshadowed U.S. member company interest. The potential of such heavy non-U.S. funding
of MCC research is difficult to rationalize with MCC's board. As a
result, such international R&D collaboration has not yet fully materialized. Fields noted:

There is a very different atmosphere toward consorting
in the Far East, including the "Little Tigers," than there
is in the United States. . . . Much more positive, acceptance, understanding of what it means to be in a consortium . . . a very different atmosphere. . . . The business culture there is not the same as our business culture. . . . We are edging toward that model, but we
have a long way to go. (all-hands meeting videotape,
June 18, 1992)

MCC ASSOCIATES AND OTHER MEMBERS

Bill Norris had always felt strongly that MCC should not be a rich men's club. That is why, early in 1982, MCC's interim board of directors made provisions for an MCC Associates Program, which would allow at least limited participation by companies that could not, or did not want to, pay several million dollars a year to participate in the consortium. For $25,000 per year (which can be paid quarterly), a company can become an associate of MCC.

During MCC's early years, the Associates Program was relatively undeveloped. MCC's shareholders were concerned that relatively large companies might elect to become associate members instead of shareholders, receive MCC technology cheap, and avoid the substantially larger research fees. From an associate company's point of view, the consortium's research programs were just getting started, and there was little technology to transfer. MCC was getting the funding it required from the shareholders, and the consortium's managers and researchers had more than enough to do with keeping these owner/customers content.

Wilson (interview, April 8, 1993) commented: "In the mid-1980s, there was little to give associate members other than non-confidential reports and they could attend selected workshops. Beginning with the research unbundling in 1987, associates could become active participants in research projects, receive confidential information, and participate in ILO." The opening up of MCC's research programs laid the groundwork for many of the changes that were subsequently implemented within the consortium such as project-based research, vertical integration, and MCC Ventures. With the launch of the superconductivity and ES-Kit programs and DARPA funding, it became more important to have broad-based participation of MCC's members (shareholders and associates) in the consortium's research activities.

MCC associates must be substantially U.S.- or Canadian-owned and operated. When any division of a company becomes an MCC associate, all parts of the company are included in that membership. Asociates (1) can influence and plan new research efforts, (2) receive nonconfidential technical reports from MCC's research programs and regular updates on research efforts, (3) are granted all proprietary technology monitoring and forecasting products of MCC's international liaison office, (4) are invited to take take part in seminars and conferences at MCC, and (5) can meet with MCC researchers to obtain a more in-depth assessment of a technology (Table 4.2). The basic difference between shareholders and associates is that the former have a seat on MCC's board, they exercise technology rights over MCC, and they receive distributions of royalty income from such activities as third-party technology licensing and dividends. Associates have technology rights only for those projects they help fund.

In early 1993, MCC created two new classes of members that can join the consortium for discounted fees (see Table 4.2). Businesses with sales of less than $25 million can become small-business associates for an annual fee of $5,000. University affiliates pay $2,500 per year. The motivation for these new classes of memberships is more for access to advanced technologies than research funds. As Fields stated: "Nationally, small businesses have proven to be major innovators that can rapidly implement advanced technologies, and universities are excellent sources of technologies" (Ladendorf, 1993b). Partnering benefits large companies who want smaller, nimble partners as well as access to technology. Small companies get access to the resources, manufacturing capability, and markets of the large companies.

In May 1993, MCC hosted its first PartnerMart exhibition, in which members of the consortium displayed a variety of partnering opportunities from seeking expansion support to licensing technology. The exhibit was held at the Austin Convention Center and involved about 30 companies and organizations linked to MCC. The hope was that dialogues would be established among MCC members, technicians, and nonmembers that might culminate in business relationships. About 400 executives from MCC's 77 member companies and potential member companies attended discussions and observed technology demonstrations of the consortium's research. There was no charge for MCC members; others paid from $300 to $500 to attend.

GOVERNMENT FUNDING

During MCC's formative days, the majority of the shareholders thought it best to keep the intrusive hand of government out of the consortium. Inman tried twice to get permission from MCC's

Table 4.2 MCC membership categories and benefits

When any division of a company joins MCC, all parts of the company are included in that membership	Shareholder	Associate	Small Business Associate	University Affiliate
Equity ownership in MCC	x			
Governance rights: a seat on the MCC Board of Directors	x			
Rights to plan new initiatives, research projects, and joint ventures: a seat on the MCC Requirements Advisory Board (RAB)	x			
Right of first refusal to invest in MCC ventures companies	x			
Right to license MCC technology 36 months after project completion	x			
International Liaison Office (ILO) Consulting	x	for a fee	for a fee	for a fee
Global Technology Monitor, an ILO monthly publication	x	x	for a fee	
Electronic assess to MCC	x	x		
Eligibility to participate in any MCC project	x	x	x	
Opportunity to jointly bid with MCC for consortial research contracts	x	x	x	x
Participation Requirements Advisory Board (RAB) Working Groups	x	x	x	x
Access to over 1,000 non-confidential technical reports and over 65 videos from MCC's research projects	x	x	for a fee	for a fee
Attendance at MCC Membership Workshops	x	x	for a fee	for a fee
Access to partnering opportunities	x	x	x	x
Membership Update, a monthly newsletter and Collaborations, a quarterly report	x	x	x	x
Yearly membership fee	$50,000	$25,000	$5,000	$2,500

Source: MCC.

board of directors to accept government funding for research. His efforts were rejected until two key events happened during his last year as CEO. First, the board accepted a change in the consortium's governance so that a unanimous vote would no longer be required to change MCC's policy; two-thirds of the board or three-fourths of the participants would suffice for large-scale changes. Second, MCC shareholders who were major defense contractors became eligible for Independent R&D (IR&D) credits for research that benefited their government contracts. In 1986, MCC's board voted to accept government funding, with two shareholders opposing this policy change.

Dove encountered two sources of opposition to seeking increased funding from the federal government. First, the aerospace companies did not want MCC competing with them for large government contracts. In response to this concern, MCC set up a government business committee to oversee MCC's government contracts, and MCC agreed not to respond to federal RFPs (requests for proposals). As Dove stated: "The policy I set up is that we would not go after government grants. That's what SEMATECH is doing. We [MCC] would go after task contracts." (interview, August 15, 1990)

The second group opposing the possibility of government funding was composed of MCC shareholders that "did not trust the federal government, did not want to work with the government, and . . . thought that the government was a terrible customer. . . . Because the government always wants to get in on a cost basis and doesn't want to deal at a commercial arm's length" (Dove interview, August 15, 1990). But by 1988, in order to increase the leveraging for some of MCC's research programs, Dove and the board decided to "go ahead . . . where it made sense, with dual technologies in particular, and where it did not detract from our [MCC's] strategic thrust in the programs. We didn't want to just shoot at ducks as they jumped up in the defense world."

In April 1988, MCC signed its first government contract, a three-year, $6.3 million research grant from DARPA to study the use of rapid prototyping hardware and software modules for the design of parallel processing systems. Under this research agreement, ACT was to develop an "Experimental Systems Kit" to cut the time that it takes to build prototypes of high-performance computer systems from two to three years to six to nine months. Another DOD contract funded MCC to fabricate critical components of semiconductors from superconductors. And in 1990, DARPA funded MCC to conduct research on HDTV flat panel displays.

In 1991, MCC negotiated a government partnership involving the U.S. Air Force that provided $4 million for a period of three years, and 20 companies each contributed $60,000 per year. The leverage for an individual company was about 40 to 1. The research project, called "Reliability Without Hermeticity," centers on putting semiconductor chips on multichip substrates with a conformal protective layer rather than on expensive hermetically sealed packages. The goal was to lower cost and improve reliability.

In May 1991, MCC's optics in computing research received a $10.3 million Advanced Technology Program (ATP) award for a period of five years from the U.S. Department of Commerce. The objectives were to establish a technology infrastructure for components and subsystems aimed at the commercialization of holographic storage. A syndicate of companies representing a vertically integrated chain, from materials and component suppliers to holographic storage subsystem device manufacturers to system vendors and users, are providing 122 percent matching funding of at least $12.6 million over the life of the program. In addition to the ATP award, the optics research also received an Advanced Research Projects Agency (ARPA) contract for the development of High Definition Systems (e.g., a VCR for HDTV) using holographic storage technology. Total spending for this project will be approximately $0.8 million over 15 months. This project is focusing on the development of tape-format holographic storage media and a transport mechanism for reading and writing. In 1992, MCC's optics technology was spun out as Tamarack Storage Devices, Inc. (see following discussion).

Such leveraging through MCC (or other consortia for that matter) makes sense from the federal government's point of view for several reasons. First, it obtains more research for each dollar spent. Second, if the government puts R&D money into a single company, and if that company succeeds and the technology is put into production, then the government's intervention is considered successful. But if the company does not utilize the technology, it can very easily die on the vine. "There are very few cases where companies take defense technology and put it to work commercially," reasoned Dove (interview, August 15, 1990). "Whereas an investment at MCC with [the involvement of several] companies increases the chances of both defense and commercial application, which is very important. We've got a magic formula, if you wish, and it's being recognized in Washington." MCC and other U.S. consortia are getting a boost from federal legislation that states that in some government contracts, bidders must specify their plans to work with consortia or other forms of strategic alliances. Dove championed this legislation, and he believes that this change will be very important to consortia. As of 1991, government funding constituted 16.5 percent of MCC's revenue, and it was growing steadily in importance. It approached 30 percent in 1993.

INTELLECTUAL PROPERTY

MCC holds all intellectual property rights to technology developed at the consortium. For the first three years after project completion, the member companies that participate in a given research area have exclusive and free access to the technology produced by that project. During this three-year period, these companies can choose to license the technology to other MCC members as well as nonmember companies. After three years, the board of directors must allow nonparticipating shareholders the right to license the technology and the board can vote to license the technology to non-MCC members.

Until 1991, 70 percent of the royalties from an MCC-produced technology were returned to the shareholders participating in the research program that produced the technology; 25 percent were used to support future research at the consortium; and the remaining 5 percent were allocated to the technology's key researchers and/or patent holders. As of December 1991, royalties from an MCC-produced technology were split one-third to the funders of the research, one-third to support future research at MCC, and one-third is retained by MCC to be used for individual technical contributor awards and other purposes. Associate members receive no royalty payments unless specified in a project R&D agreement or contract.

THIRD-PARTY LICENSING

During the mid- to late 1980s, MCC struggled with the challenge of how to get Beta-testable tools used by one or two shareholders. "That gave us a heck of a challenge," commented Dove, "because the users of the technology look at it as paying twice: they pay for the research, and then they pay again for the tools and the support" (interview, March 1, 1991). Through a third-party licensing arrangement, MCC funders of the research become the preferred customer of the firm that productizes and supports the technology, and the funders receive special pricing arrangements and royalty returns.

MCC-produced technology can be licensed to a third party at any time with approval of MCC's board and the companies participating in the project. For example, in February 1989, the consortium licensed a nonshareholder company (Electro Scientific Industries, Inc., a Portland, Oregon–based semiconductor equipment company) to make and sell a P/I-developed laser-bonding technology. MCC had announced that the technology was ready for transfer, but the funding companies did not want to manufacture it even though they expressed a desire to use the technology. So the companies agreed to license the technology to an outside vendor. Electro Scientific paid a royalty fee for the use of the technology. MCC shareholder companies that funded the research receive royalties. When the bonders were ready for sale, MCC member companies had the option of being first buyers of the equipment.

MCC SPIN-OUT COMPANIES

In 1983, when MCC came to Austin, local community leaders were quick to cite the example of Silicon Valley and to predict rapid economic growth in the Austin area through entrepreneurial spin-out activity.[41] MCC officials were careful to emphasize that such spin-out activity was not an objective of MCC. The goal of the consortium was long-term research and to transfer these pre-competitive technologies to the shareholder companies. If spin-outs were to occur, it would most likely happen at the divisions of MCC shareholders, which were spread throughout the United States.

Years would be required for economic growth benefits. MCC was engaged in goal-directed research, not product development.

During MCC's early years, two qualified spin-outs did occur. Both were founded around technology that the entrepreneurs had worked on prior to their employment at MCC. Emory Garth, a 17-year veteran of Texas Instruments, left MCC at the end of 1984 (after just six months with the consortium) to found XeTel Corporation, a provider of printed circuit boards using surface-mount technolgy. Garth worked at MCC while he obtained seed funding for his start-up company. Soon after leaving MCC, XeTel had a team of eight workers, and by 1987, the company had 150 employees and $20 million in sales by sustaining a 30 percent annual growth rate. In 1986, Rohm Co. Ltd. (a Japanese firm) bought a 63 percent interest in XeTel for about $3.3 million. Japanese banks provided needed funds to XeTel at lower interest rates than could be obtained at U.S. banks. As of 1993, XeTel employed 395 people in Austin, had sales of $58 million, and ranked among the top 30 North American contact manufacturers. Garth left XeTel in 1991. The second early MCC spin-out occurred when Steve Stach left MCC in May 1986, after one year of employment, to found Austin American Technology Corporation. Stach's company grew to several dozen employees and several hundred thousand dollars of sales in its first years of operation.

ADMINISTRATIVE SPIN-OUTS

Administrative spin-out activity has also occurred at MCC's headquarters. These spin-outs resulted from senior-level managers leaving MCC to form start-up service-based companies in the Austin area.[42] One of the first and most visible MCC administrative spin-outs occurred when Admiral Inman left MCC in 1987 and formed Westmark Systems Inc., a defense electronics holding company. Another highly visible administrative spin-out occurred when Palle Smidt left MCC in 1989. Smidt founded and became chairman of the board and CEO of Mercantile Holdings, Inc., a worldwide management consulting and merchant banking company. In 1993, Mark Eaton left MCC and launched an international technology brokering company and Bill Stotesbery also left to form a consulting company based in Austin.

TECHNOLOGY SPIN-OUTS

During Admiral Inman's tenure as MCC's CEO, technology spin-outs were not encouraged. During Dove's tenure, several MCC scientists did attempt to spin their technologies out of MCC. These researchers were frustrated by MCC's inability to get the shareholder companies to commercialize the technologies they had developed and championed. Resistance to the spin-out idea came from MCC's board and some of the consortium's managers who were uncomfortable with this major change in the consortium's basic mission. Furthermore, in contradiction to the board vision of enhancing U.S. industrial competitiveness, the firms that funded the research did not want nonfunders to get profits from "their" technology, even if they were not interested in commercializing it themselves.

The Austin Technology Incubator (ATI) opened its doors for business in 1989 (see Chapter 6). The purpose of ATI was to accelerate the development of new technology-based companies in the Austin area. The first MCC link with ATI came with the incubator's acceptance of the Donoho Publishing Group (DPG), in late 1990. DPG markets plug-in accelerator boards that enhance the performance of Apple Macintosh computers, making them capable of parallel processing. The technology was licensed from MCC's Experimental Systems Group. MCC wanted two things from this technology licensing agreement: royalties and favorable publicity.

At the time Craig Fields was taking command of MCC, Kay Hammer, a data base researcher in MCC's ACT research program, was actively championing her entrepreneurial venture, Evolutionary Technologies Incorporated (ETI). To spin out ETI, she knew she had to gain the support of MCC's management as well as the member companies funding her research. With the assistance of Dove and Fields, she was successful, and in June 1990, ETI became MCC's first official spin-out company. After completing a business plan, ETI was accepted into the Austin Technology Incubator in November. (We detail this case in Chapter 5.)

During 1991, MCC terminated several of its research projects, most of which were in the Software Technology Program. One of these technologies was gIBIS, a software technology that records and displays the evolution of issues and arguments made in group design discussions and meetings. gIBIS was based on the IBIS method developed in the 1970s by the late Professor Horst Rittel while he was at the University of California at Berkeley. IBIS supports the formulation of issues, positions, and arguments as the fundamental "moves" in a decision-making conversation. MCC researchers worked to apply these principles to the software-engineering process by adding a graphical interface and hypertext capabilities.

Several shareholder companies used gIBIS in exploratory software products. Software designers at NCR used the technology to locate "hidden" design errors in 2,300 decisions made in constructing a large program. But none of MCC's members wanted to develop the technology to market strength nor did they want to support the product. Jeff Conklin and Michael Begeman were the primary researchers for gIBIS, and as a result of their championing, in September 1991, Corporate Memory Systems became MCC's second spin-out technology to move into the ATI. The company's first product release, CM/1, allowed users to state an issue and represent it graphically as a node in a shared hypertext space on the computer screen. The history and rationale behind the decision are captured for future reference and analysis. The technology was especially intriguing for large companies, such as utilities, who wanted to have a record of the decision-making process on big complex projects. As of early 1993, Corporate Memory Systems had ten employees and Southern California Edison and Nabisco as customers.

MCC's third technology spin-out, Pavilion Technologies, Inc., occurred in early 1992. The company is based on MCC's research on neural networks, advanced software structures that are designed to sort through data looking for identifiable patterns rather than following a sequence of predetermined operating steps. Ronald Riedesel, director of MCC's Advanced Computing Technology program, became Pavilion's president and CEO. Three other ACT researchers joined the spin-out and became stockholders. The company occupies subsidized office space and receives business support from MCC. Fields has a seat on the company's board.

Pavilion's first software product, called Process Insights™, helps optimize unit- and plant-level production operations in the petroleum-refining and chemical-manufacturing industries. Process Insights™ is based on a combination of neural network, fuzzy logic, and chaotic systems technologies and allows the use of historical production data to operate facilities at higher efficiency. In early 1993, Pavilion Technologies won a $200,000 award from the Texas Department of Commerce's Product Commercialization Fund. These funds were to be used to adapt Pavilion's software to increase efficiency and reduce pollution of the state's electric power industry.

In September 1992, MCC's board unanimously approved the creation of MCC Ventures, Inc. as a for-profit subsidiary to support the licensing and commercialization of new technologies whether developed at the consortium or elsewhere. MCC Ventures was organized to reduce market risk, increase infrastructure support, and help secure seed funding for MCC spin-outs. The new subsidiary was also to seek out technologies and companies that were expected to spin into the consortium. In presenting their case for MCC Ventures, MCC's management argued that many new business ventures fail not because of inferior technology, but because the CEO is not investible, poor market access, lack of customer satisfaction, and cost. MCC Ventures was set up to leverage in-house expertise and resources as well as potential alliances with MCC member companies to provide the start-up with facilities and support activities such as media production, purchasing, legal issues, marketing, finance, manufacturing capabilities, and human resources management.

In October 1992, RTB Technology, Inc. became the first start-up company to spin into MCC Ventures. RTB's co-founders, Emory Garth (the founder of XeTel) and Clive Lankford, received a small amount of investment capital from MCC plus rent-free space, and the use of MCC laboratories and expertise to help with the development of their product, a memory "cube" that stacks computer chips on top of one another. RTB is working with MCC to produce small numbers of the memory modules for evaluation and demonstration while the company seeks additional capital for expansion. In return, MCC owns a share of RTB and will have access to the technology. RTB claims that its memory modules will deliver a high-performance cluster of memory chips that will weigh less and use less space at a competitive cost than current technology where chips are lined up tightly side by side on small circuit cards. Because of size and weight reduction, RTB technology is predicted to have strong appeal for the growing notebook and palmtop computer markets as well as high-performance computers and high-definition television.

On November 10, 1992, MCC announced its fourth spin-out company, Tamarack Storage Devices, Inc., which began as a research project in the Computer Physics Lab in 1986 and was later transferred to HVE. The founder and engineering vice president for the company is former MCC researcher, Steve Redfield. John Stockton, a former MCC research administrator, became president and CEO of Tamarack. The start-up company is working to commercialize the consortium's holographic storage technology, which uses low-power lasers to store information on holograms recorded on a low-cost film or crystal medium using a multiplexing scheme for stacking multiple holograms in the same physical space. This technology is a potential replacement for floppy disks, tapes, and CD-ROMs in existing applications such as backing-up image and record storage as well as emerging markets such as multimedia computing that require the storage and interchange of large amounts of data.

The three-dimensional storage aspect of this technology will ultimately allow for data-storage densities, approximately ten times greater than existing magnetic or optical recording technologies. In addition to funding from ATP and ARPA (see section on government funding), Tamarack received seed funding from MCC Ventures in return for an equity interest. The company's 30 employees are housed in MCC's headquarters building. In early 1993, Projectavision, Inc. (a New York developer of advanced projection and display systems and an MCC associate) agreed to enter a joint development effort with Tamarack. Projectavision purchased 33 percent of Tamarack's stock for $3 million and is helping the start-up to arrange for outside investors to put as much as $30 million into the company over a period of years. In December 1993, Tamarack Storage Devices was named a "Technology of the Year" by *Industry Week* magazine. The start-up company hopes to commercialize and introduce its first product in the second quarter of 1994. MCC will receive royalties from the sale of Tamarack's technology.

So from the early 1980s to the early 1990s, MCC's culture changed from one of not permitting spin-out activity to actively championing spin-outs. Alliances are structured so that (1) the companies that funded the research can retain equity in the venture, which might include licensing fees and royalty income; (2) MCC companies interested in the technology can get preferential treatment; and (3) MCC can become less financially dependent on the shareholders as a result of licensing fees and royalty income.

The strategy of spin-out activity made sense for the consortium, because transferring MCC-developed technologies to the member firms had proven to be extremely difficult; the member companies wanted market strength products and services; and funding for MCC was becoming increasingly difficult to obtain from the shareholders. Job security and guaranteed research funding had diminished at MCC by 1990. MCC needed to have visible commercial "wins." With the termination of research projects beginning in 1991, more and more MCC-developed technologies were left "sitting on the shelf" or abandoned after millions of dollars of investment. MCC researchers believed in their technologies and wanted them used. As Craig Fields commented to the press in February 1991: "This approach [spin-outs] is one of many ways to effectively transfer technology, and it is one that is of benefit to our participants and, closer to home, the Austin community. . . . The members' interest is not only equity appreciation but also the availability of the technology," says Fields. "The private source sees a lower risk for the investment, so it is more appealing. The net effect is to leave equity for the actual workers who started the [spin-out] venture, which means better workers. Now, that's a good model." (MCC publication)

MCC's initial start-up companies were based on research conducted on site and funded by MCC's shareholders since the mid-1980s. As MCC becomes more of a distributed enterprise, access to such technology may become more problematic, or, as Fields asserts, given the rich resource of technologies available at federal labs and universities as well as small businesses, more technologies may become available. The consortium's most immediate challenges in pursuing a strategy of rapidly growing spin-out and spin-in technology-based companies are to be able to (1) have access to a sufficient volume of marketable technologies, (2) secure adequate financing to fund the start-ups, and (3) be able to establish the necessary entrepreneurial culture to foster fast-growth start-ups.

An important step in MCC's evolution toward a distributed enterprise came in August 1993, when MCC Ventures was awarded a $1 million six-month contract with Los Alamos National Laboratory to assess the lab's computer-related and electronics technologies and to develop strategies for commercializing technological breakthroughs, with an emphasis on small-business opportunities. MCC opened offices at Los Alamos and at nearby Santa Fe, New Mexico. Sig Hecker, director of Los Alamos, commented that:

> Technology transfer has been an explicit mission of the national laboratories for several years. . . . A wide range of vehicles for accomplishing this technology transfer has been established (i.e., CRADAs, sponsored research agreements, user facility agreements). However, no mechanism has been established that systematically identifies those national laboratory technologies with the potential for commercialization and then matures those technologies into effective successful enterprises. (MCC press release, August 25, 1993)

Perhaps the most daunting challenge for MCC Ventures will be to foster the culture and business know-how networks needed to nurture entrepreneurs and to transfer quality research to successful commercial applications. (See Chapter 6 for a discussion of the success factors critical to the Austin Technology Incubator.)

CONCLUSIONS

Two major themes emerge from MCC's first decade of operation: first, many of the actions that were deemed necessary to successfully launch the consortium contributed to subsequent operational difficulties; second, rapid and efficient technology transfer (i.e., adoption, application, commercialization) to the companies funding MCC's research has proved to be much more difficult than originally thought. A major contribution of MCC has been to exemplify just how difficult it is for U.S. firms to collaborate in research leading to successful product commercialization.

MCC's founders successfully launched the United States' first major, for-profit R&D consortium in 1983. Admiral Inman's credibility and visibility resulting from his high government positions, coupled with his relative lack of official ties to any one shareholder company, inspired the high level of credibility and trust needed to launch the consortium. During his tenure as MCC's first CEO, Inman was challenged to build alliances across organizational boundaries, alliances which centered on the high-risk, high-cost, and vitally important task of R&D leading to new products and services for the shareholder firms. MCC was in the unique and challenging position of trying to successfully implement the new process technology of R&D collaboration while providing adequate ROI to its owners.

The vision/crisis that launched MCC did not sustain it over the years as the world changed and the shareholder companies faced new and different challenges. Most important, MCC was never seen by the shareholders (the owners and customers), as being vital to their survival and prosperity.

In order to be perceived as a success, MCC had to rapidly recruit a number of shareholders that were major players in the microelectronics industry. MCC was in no position to select member companies that were most adept at technology commercialization. Indeed, the companies that elected to join MCC were themselves not doing a very good job at technology transfer and development. To make it attractive for a diverse set of companies to join this experimental, quasi-legal organization, a cafeteria style of research offering was devised. While this policy facilitated the recruitment of shareholders, it also contributed to technology transfer challenges within MCC and between the consortium and its member companies. Watertight compartments inhibited the leveraging of research resources that might have led to a greater realization of MCC-wide synergy.

Researchers—from universities, federal labs, and industry—were lured to MCC by high salaries, sophisticated research equipment, a great deal of research autonomy and financial support, and Austin's affordable and high quality of life. However, this research environment contributed to an elitist culture that was buffered from the product development and marketplace realities of the shareholder companies. MCC was to produce state-of-the-art pre-competitive technologies. It was the job of the funding companies to use these technologies in their own products and processes. Accordingly, MCC channeled most of its resources toward knowledge creation. MCC researchers were hired on the basis of their reputations for research excellence, not their proficiency in technology transfer.

About five years into the experiment of R&D collaboration, funding for MCC was pushed down corporate hierarchies to the operating division levels. While such decentralized funding was construed as an attempt to get division-level managers to value and use the research they were paying for, it also caused these managers to push MCC to deliver more near-term results, and it accentuated the competition for R&D funds between MCC and member-company researchers. The emphasis on shorter-term research results has moved MCC away from the consortium's original mission of goal-driven, long-term research.

Craig Fields ushered in dramatic changes concerning MCC's structure and management. Under his direction, MCC moved toward a project-based research organization where research and staff activities were viewed as profit centers. MCC has become more of a coordinating organization—a consortium of consortia—that seeks out the technology it needs through flexible partnerships with universities, government, and vendors as well as its member companies. As MCC's research has become more project based to the point of single clients with R&D conducted off site and licensed from other sources, the consortium's coordination and integration challenges have increased.

When MCC first came to Austin in 1983, there was excitement over envisioned economic growth and job benefits to the local community through spin-out activity, even though such entrepreneurial activity was not the mission of the consortium. But by the 1990s, MCC was encouraging a culture of entrepreneurship through MCC Ventures and by spinning-out and spinning-in start-up companies.

NOTES

1. Working with two doctoral students (Christopher Avery, College of Communication, UT-Austin, and Nan Muir, College of Business, UT-Arlington), we interviewed MCC staff and researchers and member-company representatives over a period of nine years (Appendix B). Numerous research documents, publications, and the personal files of respondents were used to evaluate and cross-check these personal interviews. Selected respondents often remembered the same event in different ways. Published records also reflect biased viewpoints. We present a variety of perspectives on MCC's first decade so that the reader is left with a full, rich account and not one that has been narrowed by a particular point of view (Appendix A).

2. When MCC was formed, and during its first five years of operation, the consortium was primarily funded by shareholder companies. Beginning in 1987, the number of MCC associate members increased dramatically. While there continue to be important distinctions that differentiate shareholder and associate status (e.g., voting privileges on MCC's board), as of 1993, both groups were commonly referred to as "member companies."

3. A "honeymoon" phase seems to characterize most of the important, revolutionary U.S. consortia/alliances that have been formed since MCC and that are also targeted to beat back Japanese and other foreign and domestic competition. Unfortunately, in our opinion, little meaningful organizational learning (i.e., getting beneath the rhetoric and labels of collaboration) has taken place from the nation's early experiments with R&D consortia, learning that would benefit later attempts at new organizational forms and alliances. Each new attempt was thought to be just unique enough and endowed with such exceptional leadership, that little could be learned from preceding attempts. A noteworthy exception is the Council of Consortia, which was formed in 1990 by the CEOs of MCC, SEMATECH, and the SRC (see Chapter 1).

4. As one of our MCC respondents noted: "In 1983, the idea of 'partnering' was a new and strange concept in America's management circles, where going it alone had been the only way to operate." Indeed, it is difficult to find many references to strategic alliances among U.S. companies in pre-MCC days, at least not at the level of the late 1980s and early 1990s.

5. MCC was not established with a definite life span. In contrast, Japan's VLSI Project lasted four years, and the Fifth-Generation Computer Project lasted ten years. The issue of MCC's permanence has been discussed at MCC's board of directors meetings. The preference has been to change and evolve MCC, rather than to terminate the consortium. However, with the arrival of Craig Fields in 1990, research programs were ended, and individual research projects were assigned start and stop dates.

6. Another opinion was offered by an MCC board member: "Since I had opposed hiring Inman, allow me another comment. . . . I had recommended hiring a CEO with industrywide prominence, such as Jack Goldman, Xerox chief scientist [then retired]. Top people would have readily joined a team led by Jack." While Goldman did attend the 1982 meeting in Orlando, Xerox declined to become a shareholder.

7. In 1991, after almost seven years as head of MCC's Software Technology Program, and more recently the Advanced Computer Technology Program, Belady left the consortium. He came to MCC after a 23-year career at IBM where he was manager of software engineering at IBM's Japan Science Institute and program manager for software technology at IBM's corporate headquarters. For a more detailed description of the demise of MCC's Software Technology Program, see Appendix 4.2 and Belady (1992).

8. Indeed, several MCC personnel indicated that MCC's overall technology transfer effort suffered from the failure to encourage—if not mandate—the use of MCC-developed technologies in-house. Advocates of using MCC researchers and managers as lead customers for MCC technologies stated that such local users would have provided valuable feedback for technology developers (see Chapter 5). A counter view offered by other MCC personnel emphasized the lack of in-house technology transfer and usage was the result

of: (1) a lack of platform and software compatibility across MCC's research programs, and (2) the lack of MCC-developed technology that was at sufficient industrial or market strength so that it could be used by other MCC researchers. Complicating this issue was the realization that MCC was prevented from setting standards by U.S. antitrust law. Shareholders were commercial competitors and were they to set standards through MCC, they could be found guilty of collusion. As chief scientist Pinkston commented in 1986: "But we can provide data on which standards decisions could be based, although we cannot be part of that decision process." (quoted in Fishcetti, 1986, p. 78)

9.   Cadence's membership was somewhat unusual in that the company paid most of its fee by "in-kind" contributions of computer code. CAD's membership fee was $1.3 million per year. Cadence paid $200,000 plus code.

10. In early April 1990 under Fields' direction, DARPA invested $54 million in Gazelle Microcircuits, Inc., a small Silicon Valley gallium arsenide manufacturer that a Japanese firm was interested in buying. Defense Secretary Dick Cheney was not pleased with this development. The White House had also quashed Commerce Department efforts to support high-definition television (HDTV). As Fields' boss, Deputy Defense Secretary Donald J. Atwood, told the National Security Industrial Association: "We cannot retain our manufacturing, technological, and scientific leadership by selectively supporting particular sectors of industry." (quoted in Haas, 1990)

11. In the words of one of the ACT Program researchers: "He killed an interesting set of technologies just as the Japanese began flooding human interface research with money." But as another MCC staff person in charge of technology transfer stated: "These are the comments that I heard at a TAB meeting in mid-1990 from Bellcore's TAB member, summing up the consensus view of the STAC [Software Technology Program Advisory Committee]. 'First, we are convinced that the STP is addressing the right problems. Second, we all feel that the research to date is first class—bordering in many cases on world-class. Third, STP technology is not having any impact on our companies and we are facing a tough time justifying our continued participation.' The only way I could rationalize these three comments was that the STAC members had very little political clout within their home organizations and that they were facing a hard time selling STP technologies internally." (Werner interview, December 4, 1992)

12. As of early 1992, some shareholders and associates were beginning to find the project-specific funding a bit tedious and light on leverage. Furthermore, such a strategy placed heavy burdens on MCC personnel who had to manage several research projects and their customers. Some of MCC's member companies preferred to go with multiproject funding within MCC's research divisions, a rebundling of MCC's research on an optimal basis. However, during the Craig Fields era, such "flat commitments" were to last a specific period of time, and they were to involve project-to-project coordination with specific plans for technology transfer.

13. Chairman of the Board Grant Dove left Austin in 1991 to join Technology Strategic Alliances (TSA) in Menlo Park, California. Chief Scientist John Pinkston also left MCC in 1991. Barry Whalen, who had been director of MCC's Packaging-Interconnect (P/I) Program, became senior vice president of

MCC in 1989. By the end of 1990, Whalen and Belady were the only MCC research program directors remaining from the Inman years. Both left in 1991. Belady became chairman and director of Mitsubishi Electric Research Laboratories, Cambridge, Massachusetts. Whalen became president of a small advanced technology company (Conductus) in Silicon Valley, California. Under Whalen's leadership, the P/I Program had by far MCC's best record of transferring technologies to member companies (see Chapter 5 and Appendix 4.2).

14. MCC's Enterprise Integration (EI) research program centers on the operational core of the consortium—collaborating across public and private sectors. EI research and standards activity emphasizes the technological aspects of linking people through enhanced E-mail using directory and security services as well as remittance. For the previous decade, MCC had struggled to learn how to collaborate effectively with its broad base of member companies from a variety of industries, including both users and suppliers of electronic products and services. As we continue to describe MCC's first decade of operation (Chapter 4), and with specific reference to the interorganization, collaborative activity of technology transfer and commercialization (Chapter 5), we see just how difficult the behavioral and managerial challenges are to realizing the benefits of such enterprise integration despite superior technological advancements.

15. Several respondents told us that the fortress-like design of MCC was intentional. The stone pillars ringing the circular drive at the building's entrance were to form a permanent barrier to possible gate-crashers. The moat and fountain surrounding the outdoor eating area were to stifle conversations that might be recorded by sophisticated listening devices. Video cameras mounted in the parking lot and exterior lighting were used to identify and illuminate unwanted visitors who could be obscured by the cedar trees that surround the headquarters building. Whether this design philosophy was more myth or reality, the feeling persisted that MCC needed to go to great lengths to protect its research.

16. A clean room is a specially constructed facility that is kept dust-free and is used to conduct research on, and produce, semiconductor chips. Tolerances are such that a speck of dust on a chip looms like a boulder on a highway. MCC does not produce chips; rather, it studies how they are packaged for installation in a product.

17. "BRC" stood for "Balcones Research Center," or at times, "Bobby Ray's Condominium," depending on whom you talked to during MCC's formative years. Researchers in the P/I program also referred to the BRC as "Intergalactic Headquarters."

18. In 1991, as part of MCC's cost-cutting measures, the white linen table cloths and napkins were eliminated, as were the free coffee and cookies and the numerous refrigerators filled with free juice and soda that were placed at various locations throughout the BRC. These changes were part of Craig Fields' cost-cutting policy and served as a symbol of the new austerity at MCC.

19. Europeans favor such a distributed model largely because of a lack of alternatives. First, the political and economic barriers to a central R&D location seem insurmountable. Getting political and scientific leaders from the various countries to agree on a central location for a prestigious research facility in one country is problematic. Second, the logistical and cultural challenges of cycling

researchers and technicians, for a period of two to three years, through such a country-based facility would result in a high-cost operation. Indeed, the cultural and emotional barriers to getting several researchers (and their families) to move from different countries (e.g., Italy, England, and Germany) and to communicate, collaborate, and conduct advanced research in a laboratory in another country (e.g., France) are considerable. Consequently, Europeans adopted the distributed model in which different companies and research laboratories in different countries would "cooperate" on large research efforts. As one European researcher commented, in 1992, at a U.S. conference on technology transfer: "We use brute force to make it [the distributed system] work."

20. As pointed out by several critics of this policy, Fields may be attempting to employ the DARPA model in an inappropriate environment. Whereas DARPA had megafunds to entice and reward research participants, MCC has traditionally relied on member-company funding of its research activities. In short, the critics argue: "What does MCC bring to the table as a coordinator of research projects? Where is the value added?" In fall 1992, Fields created MCC Ventures to (1) pull technologies into MCC, (2) provide support services such as marketing, business, and financial planning, and (3) help locate venture financing.

21. Since its founding, MCC has continued to host a considerable number of visitors, but over the years the character of these visits has changed. While more R&D is done off-site, member companies continue to visit the consortium for the research projects they are involved with, for ILO (International Liaison Office) activities, and for general updates. MCC still hosts quarterly board meetings and Program Advisory Board meetings for the HVE Division (the Requirements Advisory Board commonly meets off-site). The increase in a new type of visitor to MCC comes from companies that are prospecting for technologies and partners, and professionals who are working with MCC's spin-out companies. Such visitors include small business managers, entrepreneurs, bankers, underwriters, and intellectual property lawyers. Foreign visitors continue to visit MCC, and this has proven to be beneficial for MCC since the value of the ILO to MCC's member companies depends, in part, on access to foreign researchers and publications, and this access comes, in part, through being receptive hosts to foreign researchers, executives, and government officials. For example, in late 1993, a German minister, who was head of a government technology transfer committee, visited MCC. Germany wants to strengthen its software industry and to do this they want to establish partnerships with U.S. firms and R&D organizations as well as focus on key market niches.

22. As of early 1993, only the High Value Electronics Division continued to have a PTAB.

23. Several shareholders have elected to go on inactive status and not fund MCC research or sit on MCC's board of directors. Lockheed and Westinghouse exercised this option in December 1991; General Electric and Honeywell went on inactive status in 1992. Lockheed, Westinghouse, and General Electric were reactivated as funding shareholders in 1992–1993. As of late 1993, Honeywell, Martin Marietta, National Semiconductor, and Westinghouse were on inactive status.

24. At any one time during its first seven years, MCC also had as many as 85 part-time employees, who were made up of visiting researchers, faculty, and graduate students.

25. Indeed, Inman had never been comfortable with the arrangement of member companies' supplying MCC's research talent. This is why he had insisted on having absolute authority over MCC's personnel matters in terms of direct hires. As described in Chapter 2, this hesitancy had its roots in Inman's frustrations in trying to staff federal intelligence programs with people "donated" from existing government agencies. Inman later regretted that MCC did not have the authority to also select shareholder liaisons/representatives.

26. Some of the researchers that MCC brought to the Lone Star State were rather eccentric. For a point of illustration, one of the CAD researchers who had the reputation of being especially brilliant was known for walking the halls of Kaleido while giving off a "howl" or two on his way for a stroll outside, and then standing in the parking lot in white socks and no shoes, with his head tilted far back staring at the sky—for extended periods of time.

27. On the other hand, during 1991–1992 when many of MCC's software programs were terminated or downsized, many researchers and staff did leave Austin, despite a relatively poor housing market, to pursue their careers in other states. So, in the late 1980s, despite economic and personal considerations that kept them in Austin, MCC employees could have pursued career options in other regions of the United States if they had so desired.

28. Rogers and Larsen (1984) emphasized the importance of the agglomeration of a wide variety of research and technology talent in the mature technopolis of Silicon Valley. For example, Austin has yet to have a networking institution like Silicon Valley's famous Wagon Wheel Bar, where Bay Area scientists/technicians meet to informally exchange industry gossip and technical information. The bar has oversized white place mats for note taking and technical drawings. Many ideas and technologies were exchanged and entrepreneurial ventures begun over lunch and drinks at the Wagon Wheel Bar. It is also interesting to note that, in the 1960s, scientists and entrepreneurs in northern California also perceived that area as lacking the concentration of high-tech stars and infrastructure then found in the northeastern United States.

29. While this program of reverse assignees has not worked out as expected, Fields continually emphasizes that it is important for MCC's technologists and staff to get out of MCC and regularly visit with "the customers," the consortium's member companies. As Fields mentioned during a June 18, 1992, all-hands meeting: "Kodak's management team has gone through three major changes since I've been here [at MCC]. . . . You need to meet the customer, go to dinner, talk, and listen. Companies that don't, won't succeed." In 1992, MCC was installing a user-friendly data base to try to help its personnel track key management turnover in the member companies.

30. In the process of conducting on-site interviews and other data collection, we made numerous visits to MCC over a period of eight years. During these visits, we rarely saw MCC researchers or administrators engaged in informal conversation in one of MCC's "conversation areas." MCC's structure seemed somewhat sterile, with rows of closed office doors surrounding the atrium. There were few indications of skunkworks or other forms of informal, cross-program research activity. The most predominant and visible enactment of informal

gathering was at the communal dining area, which did not generally serve MCC employees from the STP and P/I research programs, which were housed in separate locations.

31. Inman has been described by MCC researchers as having exceptional relations with the consortium's external constituents. He could get the attention of, and inspire, academic, government, and corporate leaders. Although not one to socialize with MCC researchers, when he would "pass you in the hallway, he would acknowledge you by name and ask about your family. . . . And when he called the quarterly all-hands meetings, just about everybody showed up." Dove enjoyed high credibility with his industry peers, but he was less able to inspire and lead MCC's researchers. Fields, the most able technologist of the three, is described as being the most detached of all of MCC's managers—living in Washington and frequently managing by two-way video. None of MCC's CEOs seem to have assumed the socio-emotional role of Masato Nebashi and his "management by whiskey" among the collaborating VLSI Project scientists (see Chapter 2).

32. As one MCC researcher commented: "Why would talent want to continue into year three of a three-year research project knowing that their job goes away? . . . Just as a project comes to fruition . . . they'll start bailing out."

33. MCC research reports have covers in three different colors: dark blue for highest security, light blue for proprietary, and white for open distribution. According to some MCC researchers, such coding was a largely symbolic effort. However, as Stotesbery (interview, April 8, 1993) countered: "We are strict about who gets which reports at the point of distribution, but it's impossible to control who sees what as the reports get disseminated throughout MCC's member companies." One MCC staff member commented that some researchers selected dark blue covers more for enhanced research credit and status than because of security concerns.

34. 3M's transition is an interesting case. According to one MCC researcher, 3M initially joined projects not to learn about technology but to learn the needs of the users who were also members of the research project. In 1992, the company decided that this benefit was not worth the expense, and MCC created a materials company membership at reduced rates and with limited or no rights to the technologies developed. (Misunas correspondence, March 10, 1993)

35. IBM's T.J. Watson Research Center in Yorktown Heights and associated labs have, during the past few years, enjoyed a yearly budget of around $1.2 billion with $600 to $700 million coming from the divisions and $500 to $600 million coming from corporate. In the coming years, IBM's plan is to reduce corporate support for the labs by 20 percent per year until the base budget is zeroed out. The labs are to recover this portion of their budget from the operating divisions and other sources. At a May 1–2, 1993, conference held in Tarrytown, New York, several researchers from IBM's T.J. Watson Research Center expressed great interest in our discussion of MCC's evolution from long-term goal-directed research to research projects being funded at the division level, because they saw the "hand writing is on the wall," that IBM was moving in the same direction.

36. By mid-1984, MCC had a budget of $20 million and research was fully under way in several research programs. Member companies had committed to three years of funding. So it took about two and a half years from the meeting in Orlando for MCC to ramp up to full speed.

37. MCC's shareholders fee is not based on size of company or percentage of sales. The ten original members paid $150,000 each for their shares. MCC's shareholder fee rose to an asking price of $1 million from 1985 to mid-1986—no shareholders were recruited to MCC during this period. By late 1986, the fee for joining MCC as a shareholder had dropped to $250,000.

38. In STP, ACT, and CAD, the research leveraging became so marginal that the programs barely survived to the end of 1991. In an attempt to increase leverage, MCC tried to recruit more shareholders; however, as MCC was experiencing a drop in the number of its funding companies, it was difficult to market the research to others.

39. The Council on Research and Technology was founded in 1987 and had over 124 members (as of October 1987), including 8 research institutes, 41 companies, and 75 universities. The council's goals are to develop and implement policies that foster basic and applied research.

40. To "buy American" is increasingly an exercise in futility. Japanese products are produced in the United States, and American products are produced all over the world. Corporate alliances that cross national boundaries are increasingly common. For example, in March 1991, IBM, announcing a new international strategy, joined with 11 Japanese computermakers in a concerted attack on NEC, the corporation that dominated Japan's highly fragmented computer market. In April 1991, AT&T announced that it would join with NEC to explore better ways to make advanced semiconductors. In July 1991, IBM and German electronics giant Siemens AG announced that they would build a $700 million chip-making factory in France to produce the world's most advanced computer chips. In November 1991, Texas Instruments and Hitachi Ltd. announced plans to form a joint design group in Japan to develop the technology needed to make 64-megabit memory chips. TI and Hitachi had previously shared technology in the development of 16-megabit memory chips. In July 1992, IBM, Toshiba, and Siemens announced they would work together to develop new, more powerful computer chips. An official from Toshiba was to lead a group of about 200 engineers from the three companies, who were to work at IBM's East Fishkill, New York, lab. In the same month, AMD and Fujitsu Ltd. announced that they would cooperate on a $700 million joint venture to build a chip plant in Japan to make flash memory chips that can remember computer data after the electricity is shut off. In May 1993, Kaleida Labs, a joint venture of Apple Computer and IBM, announced that Hitachi, Mitsubishi Electric, and Toshiba would become charter members in an alliance to use Script X, Kaleida's computer language for the creation and playback of multimedia programs.

41. These expectations were hyped by developers who were becoming wealthy as a result of the economic boom mentality that existed in Austin in 1983–1984. Land and building prices were flipping two to three times a day, and talk of technology spin-outs from MCC fueled such real estate speculation (see Chapter 6). Austin's public and private leaders were well aware of how Silicon Valley, a 10- by 20-mile area between Stanford University in Palo Alto and San Jose, got its start in 1960. By 1991, 350,000 high-tech employees worked in the valley's microelectronics companies. While the public is most familiar with such large companies as Fairchild, Hewlett-Packard, and Apple Computer, most of the area's 3,000 microelectronics companies have fewer

than 15 employees. Many of these smaller companies spun out of "parent companies" or from Stanford University. Some spin-outs became large companies: Intel spun out from Fairchild, and Apple, Tandem, and Rolm are entrepreneurial offspring of Hewlett-Packard, which, in turn, spun out from Stanford University. Silicon Valley spin-outs are often organized around a new technology. While companies commonly seek to prevent technology transfer by departing employees, technology transfer via such entrepreneurial activity is fairly common.

42. One of the major, but less advertised benefits of MCC's coming to Austin was that it brought senior-level managers as well as technicians to live in the area. This talent tended to remain in Austin after leaving MCC. These professionals have benefited the local community in many public and private activities, and they have contributed to Austin's emerging high-tech infrastructures and know-how networks; see Chapter 6.

APPENDIX 4.1

Evolution of MCC's Operations and Structure

1982

February William C. Norris, chairman and CEO of CDC, invites 16 major electronics companies and several government agencies to Orlando, Florida, to discuss the creation of a joint research venture.

July The steering committee/interim board of directors approves MCC's business plan.

August MCC is chartered as a Delaware corporation by 10 U.S. semiconductor and computer companies.

December The U.S. Justice Department announces that it will not undertake an antitrust challenge to MCC.

MCC's founding shareholders identify the consortium's first four research programs in advanced computer architecture, computer-aided design for very large scale integrated circuits, software technology, and microelectronics packaging.

1983

January MCC's first employee is hired: Admiral Bobby Ray Inman, president, chairman of the board, and chief executive officer.

April Mostek and Allied-Signal join MCC, to make 12 shareholder companies.

May MCC locates in Austin, Texas, after a nationwide competition.

June Martin Marietta joins MCC.

October Austin research facilities open in leased buildings.

Eugene Lowenthal named director of data base system research program.

November	Rockwell joins MCC, to make a total of 14 member companies.
	John Hanne named director of VLSI-CAD research program.
December	Raymond Allard named director of human factors technology research program.

1984

January	MCC employs 72 individuals, and research begins, with a $20 million research budget, and by mid-year is fully under way in all four research programs.
March	BMC Industries, Inc., joins MCC.
	Barry Whalen named director of semiconductor packaging and interconnect research program
May	Woodrow Bledsoe named director of artificial intelligence/knowledge-based systems research program.
June	Eastman Kodak, Lockheed, and Gould join MCC.
	Research is underway in six of MCC's programs.
September	Boeing joins MCC.
	Laszlo Belady named director of software technology research program.
October	The National Cooperative Research Act is signed into law by President Reagan.
November	The Packaging/Interconnect Program moves into its Austin microelectronics laboratory.
December	3M and Bellcore join MCC, for a total of 21 shareholders.

1985

January	MCC has 21 shareholders, 12 associate members, employs 260 individuals, and has an annual budget of $45 million.
June	The Exploratory Initiatives Program is approved by MCC's board of directors on a yearly basis and

funds research in optics, neural networks, and high-temperature semiconductors.

July

Stephen Lundstrom replaces Peter Patton as director of parallel processing research program.

September

MCC's board of directors permits policy changes at the consortium to be approved by a three-fourths, rather than a unanimous vote.

MCC's board approves means for conducting formal agreements between shareholders in related programs.

December

MCC has produced more than 190 technical reports.

MCC transfers its first technologies: (1) Tape-automated bonding from P/I and (2) Proteus from ACA.

Research contracts awarded to U.S. universities.

Three shareholders announce that they will leave MCC at the end of 1986: BMC Industries, Mostek, and Gould.

1986

January

MCC has 21 shareholders, 9 associate members, employs 400 individuals (340 in research, 60 administrative) and has an annual budget of $65 million.

June

Westinghouse purchases Mostek's MCC share (Mostek had been purchased in 1985 by United Technologies, which then shut down Mostek's operations).

General Electric buys RCA and assumes the company's MCC share.

August

MCC moves into its new headquarters building in the west tract of UT's Balcones Research Center.

September

Inman announces his resignation (effective at year-end) at the quarterly staff meeting.

November

Hewlett-Packard purchases BMC Industries' MCC share.

December	Inman resigns from MCC.

MCC has 20 shareholders.

More than 460 technical reports are delivered to shareholders in 1986.

Technologies transferred include: P/I—TAB, air cooling and power regulation systems form chips; ACA—Proteus, Cyc, SEMNET, LUCY, and ORION; and STP—RADDLE and extended PROLOG.

Three shareholders announce intent to leave the consortium at the end of 1987: Sperry/Unisys, Allied-Signal, and Lockheed Missiles and Space.

1987

January   MCC has 19 shareholders, 5 associate members, employs 473 individuals, and has an annual budget of $73 million.

March   Grant Dove appointed CEO and chairman.

MCC's board of directors agrees to consider methods of obtaining federal government funding for some research projects.

MCC appoints a director of business development, who is charged with finding replacements for departing shareholders.

Honeywell incorporates the Proteus technology into PLEX.

Boeing announces that its laboratories will support tape-automated bonding, wafer bumping, and thin- and medium-film MCC technologies.

June   NCR's DesignAdvisor, based on Proteus software, is announced as the first commercial product based on licensed MCC technology.

The ACA research program is reorganized (in order to increase shareholder flexibility and cut costs) into a core research area with satellites in artificial intelligence, human interface, and systems technology, which includes parallel processing and database management.

July   Grant Dove becomes chairman and CEO of MCC.

September   P/I is reorganized (so that shareholders can select research areas that most clearly match their technology requirements) into a core research area with satellites in multichip systems, interconnect, and bonding/assembly.

              The board of directors approves the creation of a fifth research program in the electronic applications of high-temperature semiconductors.

October   Dove rules out the possibility of foreign membership in MCC in the near future.

December   Allied-Signal sells its semiconductor division and drops its MCC shareholder membership; Lockheed exercises its membership option and goes into inactive status.

              MCC implements its high-temperature superconductor research program with 13 participating companies, in cooperation with the University of Houston.

1988

January   MCC has 19 shareholders, 12 associate members, employs 428 individuals and has an annual budget of $71 million.

              Hughes Aircraft purchases Unisys's MCC share (Unisys was formed in 1986 when Burroughs acquired Sperry).

              MCC's ACA Program is "unbundled" into separate research projects.

April   MCC acknowledges setback in computer-aided design program. Four years of effort in writing computer code in Lisp is left in doubt as the consortium moves to using the computer language C.

June	First federal funding of MCC research: the Experimental Systems Kit Project is awarded a contract by DARPA.
	MCC commissions an IC^2 Institute research project on technology transfer.
August	MCC establishes annual awards recognizing outstanding graduate research at UT.
December	CAD is reorganized into a research core and four satellites in physical design, test design, digital design, and systems design.
	MCC celebrates its fifth anniversary.

1989

January	MCC has 20 shareholders, 21 associate members, 436 employees, and an annual budget of $63 million.
	MCC votes to accept Canadian members in response to the U.S.-Canada Free Trade Agreement.
	Under special terms and conditions, associate members are permitted to participate in MCC's research programs.
February	The Software Technology Program hosts MCC's first open house to encourage communication and cooperation across research programs.
	First licensing of MCC technology to an outside vendor, Electro Scientific Industries, Inc., Portland, Oregon, to produce a laser bonder.
March	MCC reaches a cooperative agreement with the University of Houston to accelerate the transfer of superconductivity technology to the private sector.
May	MCC begins Optics in Computing Program.
June	An MCC-wide technology transfer study group formed.

Palle Smidt leaves MCC to head an international merchant banking and consulting firm based in Austin.

Barry Whalen, head of the P/I research program, becomes senior vice president of MCC.

August   Advanced Computing Program is restructured to allow shareholders and associates to choose which of the programs' nine projects they want to fund.

The Advanced Computing Technology Program is unbundled.

September   MCC's Open Systems Satellite is formed in the P/I Program.

October   Cadence Design Systems Inc., a CAD vendor, becomes MCC's first vendor shareholder.

November   The CAD research program forms a CAD Framework Lab to verify and validate CAD industry design guidelines, separate from MCC.

December   Apple Computer becomes one of MCC's first associate members to actively fund research projects.

1990

January   MCC has 20 shareholders, 34 associate members, 427 employees, and an annual budget of $65 million.

February   Northern Telecom, the Canadian telecommunication giant, joins MCC as its twenty-first shareholder.

MCC identifies four key technolgy areas: visualization, high-definition systems, large-scale distributed networks, and quick time-to-market technologies.

May   ACT Program Director Bob White becomes the undersecretary of technology in the U.S. Department of Commerce.

The P/I Program begins two new research satellites, involving (1) the establishment of an infrastructure for the development of multichip modules and (2) laser bonding.

June

MCC announces its first spin-out company, Evolutionary Technologies, Inc.

July

Craig Fields, formerly director of DARPA, is appointed president, chief technical officer, and chief operating officer of MCC.

Grant Dove remains as MCC's chairman and chief executive officer.

MCC wins $1.9 million, three-year research contract from the Office of Naval Research for work on superconductors.

The Software Technology Program explores the possibility of partnerships in application research (PAR) to develop site-specific application software.

August

Sun Microsystems becomes the first company to establish a PAR in STP.

MCC has 48 patents.

September

Andersen Consulting joins MCC as the consortium's twenty-second shareholder and the first service-based company, making the largest number of shareholders since MCC's founding.

MCC's Computer Physics Lab is created as a "center of excellence," to conduct research on superconductivity and optics in computing.

MCC's Associates Program expands to become the membership services office to ensure better corporatewide member services.

1991

January

MCC has 22 shareholders, 36 associate members, 425 employees, and an annual budget of $56 million.

February	MCC joins UT's Institute for Advanced Technology and Sandia National Laboratories to use MCC technology in driving networks of computers applied to difficult problems.
March	Craig Fields is appointed president and CEO of MCC, and Grant Dove continues as chairman of the board.
	MCC adopts a "Vision for the 1990s" that reflects rapid advances in information technology products and services.
	Some MCC research programs are ended; the remaining programs are reorganized under four new research divisions with an emphasis on project management.
April	Jay Tanenbaum, president of Enterprise Integration Technologies Corp., Palo Alto, California, is hired to help develop MCC's enterprise integration research division.
	John Pinkston, MCC's chief scientist 1983–1990, leaves the consortium.
	Exploratory Initiatives program canceled.
May	Les Belady leaves MCC.
June	Alan Salisbury is appointed executive vice president and chief operating officer of MCC.
	Barry Whalen leaves MCC.
	Grant Dove remains as chairman of the board but moves to his Dallas residence.
July	MCC announces its second spin-out company, Corporate Memory Systems.
December	MCC researchers have been awarded 72 patents, most are generated by the packaging/interconnect program.

1992

January   MCC has 22 shareholders, 59 associate members, 11 government sponsors, employs 372 researchers, and has an annual budget of $45 million.

               MCC announces its third spin-out company, Pavilion Technologies.

               MCC begins EINet, a cross-country computer network, with four other research organizations: UUNET, SEMATECH, National Center for Manufacturing Sciences, and the Industrial Technology Institute.

February   MCC has a total of 73 member companies: 22 shareholders and 51 associate members.

May   Texas becomes the first state government to join MCC as an associate member.

June   Fields is elected chairman of MCC's board of directors.

               MCC reorganizes into two research divisions: High Value Electronics (HVE) and Information Systems Division (ISD).

               Thirty-five research projects are designated with start and stop dates.

               Surviving CAD, STP, ACA, and P/I research projects are allocated to the HVE and ISD divisions.

               MCC implements Requirements Advisory Board, doing away with the technical advisory board and program technical advisory boards.

September   MCC Ventures is established as an independent company to foster technology company spin-outs and spin-ins.

October   RTB becomes MCC's first spin-in company.

November   MCC announces its fourth spin-out company, Tamarack Storage Devices, Inc.

More than 180 technologies transferred since 1985.

2,200 technical reports published since 1984.

400 plus videotapes produced since 1985.

In total, MCC has received 95 patents, with another 17 awaiting final issue.

1993

January   MCC has 22 shareholders, 46 associate members, and 340 full-time employees.

March   MCC creates discount memberships for small businesses associates and for university affiliates.

May   MCC celebrates its tenth anniversary and holds first MCC PartnerMart in conjunction with the consortium's annual membership workshop.

June   MCC and Sprint (the nation's third-largest long-distance carrier) form an alliance to create a new business link in the information superhighway.

July   During its first decade, MCC has transferred more than 200 technologies, been issued or assured 117 patents, licensed more than 182 technologies, published over 2,400 technical reports, and distributed more than 400 technical videotapes.

	Original Member Company/Successor	ACT	PAK/I	ST	CAD
●	3M Company		■		
●	Advanced Micro Devices F		■		■
○	Allied-Signal Corporation		■		
●	Bell Communications Research (Bellcore)	■		■	
○	BMC Corporation		▨		
●	Boeing Corporation		■		
●	Control Data Corporation F	■	■		■
●	Digital Equipment Corporation F	■	■	■	
●	Eastman Kodak Corporation	■			
○	Gould, Inc.				▨
●	Harris Corporation F	■			■
●	Hewlett-Packard		■		■
●	Honeywell, Inc. F	■			■
○	Lockheed Missiles and Space Co.			■	
●	Martin Marietta				■
○	Mostek Corporation/CTU		▧		▨
●	Motorola, Inc. F			■	■
●	National Semiconductor Corp. F				■
●	NCR Corporation F	■			■
●	RCA/General Electric Corp. F	■		■	■
●	Rockwell International Corp.				■
○	Sperry/Burroughs/Unisys F	■		■	■
●	Westinghouse			■	

■ Program participation
▨ Program participation transferred to new member
▧ Remains inactive participant
F Founding member company
● Current member company
○ Had left or announced intention to terminate membership

Source: Adapted from Murphy (1987).

Figure 4.2.1 MCC shareholder company research program participation, 1986

APPENDIX 4.2

MCC'S Research Program History and Output

During 1983–1984, MCC began long-term (five to ten years) research in four program areas: Advanced Computer Architecture (later called Advanced Computing Technology), Software Technology, Semiconductor Packaging (later to be called Packaging/ Interconnect), and Very Large Scale Integration/Computer-Aided Design (later called Computer-Aided Design).[1] Each research area was established as a highly independent and secretive program. Such autonomy was encouraged by the different mix of shareholder companies funding each program and the different technology and research orientations of the program scientists. From 1984 to 1990, each of MCC's research programs evolved differently, reflecting program-management styles, the mandates of shareholder constituencies, relative success in technology transfer, and changing technology.

As of 1986, three shareholders (CDC, Harris, and Sperry) funded research in all four MCC programs; 2 (DEC and NCR) funded three research program areas; 6 (AMD, Bell, Kodak, Honeywell, Motorola, and RCA/GE) funded two program areas; and the rest of the shareholders funded one research program. The MCC research program with the most shareholder support was CAD (with 11 shareholders), followed by P/I and ST (with 10 each) and ACT (with 8) (see Figure 4.2.1).

Resource allocation decisions for MCC's research programs, satellites, and projects were made on the basis of shareholder input largely from MCC's advisory boards and from MCC's research program management and scientists. Program directors could approve expenditures of up to $100,000 and enjoyed a high level of administrative discretion. MCC researchers and managers, in conjunction with shareholder representatives on the TAB and PTABs, periodically met to set the research agenda for each program. There was conflict within MCC, and between MCC and its shareholders, about research priorities. These conflicts were settled in negotiations, with decisions being weighted toward the most influential scientists and managers from MCC and the largest shareholder companies funding the research.

As MCC matured, research programs were increasingly faced with the challenge of balancing long-term, basic research with shorter-term projects that had sufficient commercial promise to attract and hold shareholder and associate member funders of the research. This ongoing challenge caused MCC to eliminate some research projects, merge others, and add exploratory initiatives.

ADVANCED COMPUTING TECHNOLOGY

In 1983, the goal of the Advanced Computing Technology (ACT) Program was to develop technologies that would help MCC shareholders build "intelligent systems" so that they could compete in the global markets of the 1990s and beyond. Of all the research being conducted at MCC, ACT researched technologies that were closest to a head-to-head competition with Japan's ICOT Program.

ACT was divided into four subprograms: (1) parallel processing, headed by Peter Patton (and later Stephen F. Lundstrom, formerly with Stanford University); (2) data base systems, headed by Eugene Lowenthal, formerly with Intel Corporation; (3) human-computer interaction, headed by Raymond Allard, formerly with CDC; and (4) artificial intelligence (AI), headed by Woodrow Bledsoe, on leave from The University of Texas at Austin. The data base project developed an object-oriented system called ORION, which included a formal specification of Logic Data Language (LDL); an optimizing compiler for LDL; and a scalable, parallel data base machine for executing LDL object code. The parallel processing project focused on a parallel LISP environment and a simulator for multiprocessor systems. Two of the more publicized AI research projects were (1) Cyc, a very large "commonsense" knowledge base (described in Chapter 4), and (2) Proteus, an expert system environment incorporating forward and backward chaining of rules, truth maintenance, and an object-oriented data base. (Proteus is the subject of the technology transfer case described in Chapter 5.) ACT also developed a knowledge-based natural language interface and other underlying technologies for enhanced interfaces.

In mid-1987, MCC's board of directors approved a restructuring of the ACT Program into a core research effort and three satellites: AI, Human Interface, and Systems Technology (which included both data base systems and some parallel processing). Each shareholder funded the core research plus one or more satellite research projects of its choice.

Honeywell was one of two MCC shareholders (Boeing was the other) to make the first public announcement regarding the use of MCC technology. Honeywell announced that it had incorporated MCC's Proteus technology into an internal product called PLEX, an expert system designed to place components on a multilayer printed circuit board. Later in 1987, NCR announced the development of DesignAdvisor, an expert system for designers of integrated circuits. This software was also based on MCC's Proteus technology and was the first well-publicized example of a technology's being transferred and licensed from MCC to a commercial application.

In addition to shareholder utilization of Proteus by NCR and Honeywell, two other ACT technologies were being used by shareholders by 1989: (1) Plane Text, MCC's hypertext system, was being used by Rockwell to develop on-line documentation for AI applications, and (2) Cyc, the large, commonsense knowledge base, was being used by Digital Equipment Corporation in its Sizer system.

In an effort to make MCC more accessible to smaller-sized companies, ACT's PTAB voted to allow shareholders to select particular research projects rather than subscribe to the entire research program. Companies, or even divisions of companies, could now pay for the ACT projects that best fit their needs. The objective was to customize MCC research offerings, to focus more clearly on the requirements of MCC shareholders and associates, and to encourage new MCC memberships. However, this strategy also allowed shareholders to decrease their financial commitment to MCC by picking particular projects to fund.

By 1990, ACT focused on three areas of research: (1) system functionality, or expert-system development environments and large-scale knowledge bases; (2) usability, or knowledge-based human interface tools; and (3) performance, or advanced languages and object-oriented data base technologies, especially for distributed systems.

COMPUTER-AIDED DESIGN

As chip components get smaller and smaller—as part of the effort to fit more capacity into smaller areas—there are incredible shifts in their physics, including the vastly increased effort of the atmospheric surroundings. Conventional wisdom is that such components will not be available in the 1990's unless you buy them from Hitachi. (John Hanne, MCC vice president and CAD Program director, formerly with Osborne Corporation and Texas Instruments, quoted by Reed, 1987)

In the mid-1980s, an important near-term goal of the Computer-Aided Design (CAD) research program was to develop an advanced software platform for tool development that would allow designers to access design information easily and uniformly. Longer-term objectives included development of methods for circuit and systems design and other CAD tools that advanced the state of the art. Early research areas of CAD included test technology, analog technology, digital technology, layout technology, and software platforms. By 1986, the CAD Program concept of "fast prototyping" was emphasizing the development of an integrated design environment that led to new circuit simulation algorithms and editing tools.

CAD researchers initially made the decision to use the computer language LISP because of the powerful artificial intelligence characteristics and the software-development efficiencies offered by the LISP workstation environment. LISP was considered an especially good, rapid prototyping support language. An integrated LISP system was released to the shareholders but it was painfully slow to operate. By 1988, LISP machine manufacturers were either going out of business or were in jeopardy of doing so. Many of the shareholder companies had in-house C programming resources, but little or no LISP resources. C, based on the UNIX operating system, was slowly but surely becoming an industry standard as workstations improved in price, performance, and functionality. All 11 shareholder companies participating in the program complained about CAD's research activities and direction. In March 1988, after a review by CAD's technical advisory committee and MCC's board of directors, the decision was made to revamp the CAD Program and to change from LISP to C and C++. This decision was made at considerable expense and necessitated the reworking of thousands of hours of computer code written by CAD's 100 employees.

MCC's problems with LISP-based CAD systems illustrates the importance of the consortium's understanding the shareholders' deployment environment. On the other hand, the need to reorganize the CAD Program could be seen as one of the hazards of MCC's attempt to build a complete set of tools for a whole spectrum of CAD applications. In the early 1980s, it was not clear that UNIX would prevail. Indeed, one of the supposed advantages of having such a research "failure" happen at MCC was that it would cost each shareholder only one-eleventh of what it would have cost if an individual shareholder had funded the entire effort.

By 1989, CAD was divided into separate research groups so that smaller high-tech firms such as Cadence Design Systems could afford to join and so that participants could selectively fund those research areas that most clearly reflected their technical requirements. The new structure included a core research effort and four "satellite" research areas: Physical Design, Digital Design, Test Design, and Systems Design.

In September 1989, the CAD Framework Laboratory (CFL) was established to support an industry effort to standardize CAD system interfaces. The CFL operated as a separate enterprise, but with MCC management and participation, to test and verify software interfaces between CAD tools and the specialized software environments that support their use. By November, seven companies had joined the laboratory (including both MCC shareholders and nonshareholders). This effort later evolved into MCC's Atlas program.

PACKAGING/INTERCONNECT

> We're the "blue collar" section because we're the only people who produce hardware—we're closer to an industrial company. . . . We will bring out a new technology every year for the next 50 years. (Barry Whalen, vice president and director of the P/I Program, formerly with TRW Corporation, quoted by Reed, 1987)

In 1983, the objective of the P/I Program was to develop advances that would yield substantial cost and performance improvements over current packaging and interconnect technologies and to enable the shareholder companies to keep pace with the rapid progress in chip integration and speed.

In 1987, the P/I Program was restructured into (1) Bonding and Assembly Development, (2) Multi-Chip System Technology, and

(3) Interconnect Technology, in order to allow the shareholders to select research areas that most clearly matched their technical needs. Boeing announced that its electronics company would establish four advanced laboratories in Seattle to support MCC-transferred technologies: a tape-automated bonding/chip-on-board laboratory, a wafer bumping processing laboratory, a thin-film lab, and a medium-film lab.

In 1988, the P/I Program was awarded a patent for an advanced testing system for electronic components. The system tested a component, such as an integrated circuit, using an electron beam as the test probe. MCC began research on the electron beam tester in 1986 in response to needs posed by trends toward more complex electronic components that were incorporated into larger electronic systems.

By 1989, the P/I Program refined its tape-automated bonding (TAB) technologies and continued research into novel air-cooling systems for semiconductor chips. The automated bonding technique used hair-thin adhesive tape, instead of dozens of lead wires, to attach computer chips to their ceramic casing. While tape-automated bonding was not a new technology, MCC demonstrated a considerable advance by increasing the number of leads on a chip from an average of 45 to 350.

In February 1989, in what was a first for MCC, the consortium licensed a nonshareholder company, Electro Scientific Industries, Inc. (a Portland, Oregon–based semiconductor equipment company), to make and sell the MCC-developed laser-bonding technology. In August 1989, Digital Equipment Corporation stated that it would incorporate P/I's tape-automated bonding technology in its VAX 6000 Model 400 mainframe computer systems. So this technology, which was targeted by the P/I Program in 1983, at the beginning of the consortium, continued to find applications in the shareholder companies.

In June 1990, the P/I Program launched the Open Systems Satellite to build an infrastructure that would allow for growth and to bring in small vendor companies. Research focused on developing open systems support infrastructure for the "multi-chip module market." A satellite was formed to deal with small vendors. As Program Manager Marshall Andrews stated: "It's kind of a departure for MCC. . . . There is less pure research involved and more application and market-driven concerns." (quoted in Ladendorf, 1990a)

SOFTWARE TECHNOLOGY

These [large, complex, networked] systems cause major problems; they are very difficult to design and put together. . . . But our market is huge, because this is the next step in business automation. (Laszlo A. Belady, formerly with IBM Corporation, quoted by Reed, 1987)

Research in the Software Technology Program (STP) was not fully engaged until the last few months of 1984, after the director, Laszlo Belady, was hired. Since both MCC's management and the participating companies (Bellcore, DEC, CDC, Lockheed, NCR, Sperry, Rockwell, RCA, and Harris) offered little and sometimes contradictory advice, Belady determined that he and his researchers would take the initiative for research direction. Rather than theorize about how software engineers should carry out systems analysis and design, STP researchers collected data about how shareholder design and development groups actually performed their tasks. Then they set about performing research to address the shareholders' problems. STP research focused on the early (upstream) stages of software development, when requirements often were not clearly articulated. The objective was to develop tools and methods that would improve the productivity of the shareholders' software-development process and the quality of the software product.

STP believed that the program's strength would be in exploiting an intimate involvement with its ultimate customers (the shareholder funders of the research) and "the capability of establishing a set of coherent projects, sharing a vision and feeding on each other's results" (Belady, 1992, p. 12). In 1985, STP organized a workshop in interdisciplinary design, which included software researchers and practitioners, design theorists, and chief designers of complex projects. STP enacted an open policy to incorporate solutions from outside MCC and to benefit from software research from a variety of disciplines. STP's early vision was to integrate its research into a design environment called Leonardo, which would computer assist much of the early phases of designing large, complex systems. Team-based technologies, such as groupware and coordination technology, were to facilitate collaboration even when a system's designers were geographically separated.

In 1986, STP transferred several software system design tools to program participants, including RADDLE, a tool to aid in the design of distributed systems, and an extended PROLOG language for object-oriented programming. In the same year, STP hosted the nation's first conference on computer-supported cooperative work, which set the stage for much of the groupware research that was to follow. By 1988, NCR's System Engineering Plant in Copenhagen was experimenting with the STP technology VERDI, a visual design language that allowed designers to visually simulate design aspects. NCR's redesign, which was made available to MCC, allowed VERDI to be used on a personal computer. Rockwell's Switching System Division in Downers Grove, Illinois, continued using Plane Text (a hypertext system released by STP in 1987) to develop on-line documentation for artificial intelligence applications such as a set of network routing tables for a telephone switching system involving multiple PBX switchboards. Shareholder support for STP peaked in 1986 with ten companies. An example of an STP technology that was transferred to MCC's member companies was gIBIS (graphical Issue-Based Information System), which was also MCC's second technology spin-out (after Evolutionary Technologies, Inc., from the ACT research program).

In August 1990, the existing STP staff of 50 software professionals moved from the Kaleido building to the third floor of MCC's headquarters building. STP had always been MCC's smallest research program, and it was the only program to remain "bundled" (not segmented and separately funded), ostensibly to protect the components of the elaborate software development. STP was committed to making an integrated design environment a reality at one shareholder organization by the mid-1990s. In early 1991, STP became the first research program to come under the budget cutting/research accountability of Fields. By October 1991, fragments of what remained of MCC's Software Technology Program were distributed into the consortium's new research divisions, putting an end to one of the most coherent and innovative of all major software technology efforts in the United States.

Why did STP have so little direct impact on the U.S. software industry? Belady (1992) offered his reply: (1) we underestimated the time scale of a new research effort, leading to shareholder impatience; (2) there were insufficient budgets for absorbing MCC's technology at the shareholder companies, resulting in a "technology transfer gap" between research results and finished (market strength) software tools; (3) STP failed to understand the extent of marketing necessary to secure sufficient and patient funding; (4) shareholder-company structural changes such as mergers and acquisitions inhibited the STP research effort and technology transfer; and (5) changes in management resulted in decision makers who were unfriendly to software research and the concept of consortia in general.

COMPUTER PHYSICS LAB

Prior to 1991, MCC initiated a major research program involving high-temperature superconductivity that later merged with the Computer Physics Laboratory. Research in this lab focused on high-risk and potentially high-payoff projects in collaboration with established centers of excellence. The Computer Physics Lab and the P/I research program were the two MCC programs to survive largely unchanged during Fields' restructuring in 1991. The Computer Physics Lab had two areas of concentration: superconductivity and optics in computing.

High-Temperature Super Conductivity

In September 1987, MCC announced a new High-Temperature Superconductivity (HTSC) research program.[2] Research was initially funded to the amount of $1.3 million by 13 member companies (each of which paid $100,000). Funding grew to $3.5 million per year by 1991. The support of E.I. dupont de Nemours & Company was an early example of MCC opening up one of its research programs to a nonshareholder. Grant Dove, MCC's chairman, stated that the program would be enhanced by the diversity of the participants, which included computer, materials, semiconductor, and aerospace companies.

The HTSC Program aimed to capitalize on recent breakthroughs in superconductivity by applying these technologies to semiconductor chip operations. The program explored how superconducting materials could link the internal components of a chip and connect chips to each other. It modeled key technical issues such as hybrid semiconductor/superconductor systems; evaluated progress in superconductor materials, fabrication, and devices; and experimented with high-temperature superconductors in thin-film applications.

In 1989, MCC teamed with the University of Houston (UH) to create the Texas Superconductivity Center, a $10 million research consortium that included cooperative agreements with federal labs in Argonne, Illinois; Los Alamos, New Mexico; and Oak Ridge, Tennessee. Under the terms of the agreements, MCC and UH researchers would swap findings with the national labs. This was to represent a sharing of knowledge, resources, and activities on a scale that would make the center one of the world's largest joint research ventures in superconductivity. The project ended in 1991.

In 1990, MCC launched a second major push into the area of superconductivity research. This initiative was a joint development project with the Superconductivity Pilot Center at the Argonne National Laboratory, a research lab run by the U.S. Department of Energy. MCC and Argonne each contributed $228,000 to the project. Argonne built a vacuum chamber for the project to research new forms of tapes and wires used to transmit superconducting materials. In 1991, MCC's superconductivity research was folded into the Packaging/Interconnect program.

Optics in Computing

In May 1989, MCC unveiled a new Optics in Computing Program to test ways to use lasers to store information in tiny crystal fibers. The program was under development at MCC for three years as an exploratory initiative and it had developed a proprietary technique that enabled data to be stored and retrieved billions of times without disintegrating. The storage of data in the form of holographic images had been under investigation for over 20 years; however, a limiting factor was the degradation of data retrieved from the disks. The program began with $1 million in funding from four MCC shareholders and an associate member. This group included a computer systems vendor, a disk drive manufacturer, an electronic imaging firm, and an aerospace contractor. This program became part of the Computer Physics Lab in 1990.

MCC scientists worked with scientists at Stanford University on optics research to enable information to be stored in the form of holographic images in order to speed transfer by more than 10,000 times. Steve Redfield, director of the program, predicted that what the system could transmit in one second would take magnetic disk five hours to transfer. Such speed would be especially useful in industries that process large amounts of information, such as publishing, medical systems, and computer-aided design. Tamarack Storage Devices spun out of this research program in 1992.

SUMMARY OF MCC'S RESEARCH OUTPUT

By late 1991, MCC had published more than 2,000 technology reports, created more than 400 technical videotapes, and delivered more than 185 new technologies to its shareholders. According to MCC documents, approximately 100 MCC technologies were being applied in research, internal processes, or products of the shareholders and associates, and another 500 were under evaluation. The consortium had been allowed 70 patents, and been issued 54. Most of the patent activity had come from the P/I research program. MCC had been issued 56 technology licenses.

According to MCC publications, shareholders had:

- Made multimillion-dollar equipment investment decisions based on MCC research results.
- Created internal manufacturing and design capabilities based on knowledge and tools from MCC.
- Used MCC research to determine technical directions for their companies. Often, MCC's research "failures" provided useful information to the shareholders about technology paths *not* to take.
- Used MCC as a model for a consortium within a company between its research and application groups.
- Caught up with international competition in the area of semiconductor packaging/interconnect.

As of 1993, MCC had 117 patents (issued and assured), for an average of about 20 patents per year (allowing two years for research start-up and two years for filing). The University of Texas at Austin (including Balcones Research Center) was granted 14 patents in 1991. (For comparison purposes, the UT system as a whole, with its 15 campuses and research centers, ranked third among all U.S. universities, with 87 patents in 1991.) SEMATECH has been granted 15 patents since its formation in 1988. IBM-Austin was granted 23 patents in 1990, 58 in 1991, and 71 in 1992. IBM's Austin-based patent activity centered on the RS/6000 family of workstations and its proprietary UNIX software. To make such comparison data meaningful, we would need to analyze the resource expenditure required and the ultimate economic impact of these patents. A most important consideration is the degree to which R&D and patent activity has contributed to the launching of successful products, increased market share, and increased global competitiveness. Patents that sit on the shelf or that are most successfully used by foreign competitors do not enhance the industrial competitiveness of MCC's member companies or the United States.[3]

One sign of the impact and quality of an R&D organization is the degree to which other workers cite its research work.[4] In the case of patents, examiners (rather than inventors) assign the cited references. These references, both in patents and in other publications, represent prior art. As of December 31, 1991, 43 patent documents cited MCC patents. Of these, 10 represented MCC's building on its own research, and 1 patent was jointly held by MCC and Digital Equipment. Of the remaining 32 patents citing MCC's work, 25 organizations were represented: 1 U.S. university (CalTech), the air force, 1 German company, 7 Japanese companies, 8 MCC shareholder companies, and 7 U.S. nonshareholder companies. Only 3 organizations are represented more than once: DEC twice, Rogers Corp. twice, and IBM six times. Of these companies, only DEC is an MCC shareholder. (Rogers Corp. was an MCC associate and IBM currently is an associate.) The citation of MCC's patents compares very favorably with the low citation rate for all U.S. patents, especially when one considers that a large number of MCC patents are relatively young and that 70 percent of all U.S. patents are either never cited or cited only once or twice in the first eight years after issue (Narin and Olivastro, 1988).

NOTES

1. As described in Chapter 4, under the leadership of Craig Fields, MCC has become a federation of loosely coupled research projects, a holding company, or a consortium of consortia. This appendix provides an overview of MCC's research activities prior to the restructuring of 1991. As discussed in Chapter 5, there are many ways to measure research output. Here we present some of the more quantifiable and visible indicators of MCC's research output. No independent attempt has been made to evaluate the scientific quality or market potential of MCC's research.

2. Superconductivity is the phenomenon in which materials, when cooled, become completely free of resistance to electricity. This means that electricity can move through the materials at much higher speeds and not lose energy in the form of heat, as is the case with other conductors. The principle of superconductivity was discovered in 1911, but interest in the concept was renewed after the 1986 discoveries of Dr. Paul Chu at the University of Houston.

3. The support structure and awards available to researchers are also important contextual variables to consider when assessing patent filing rates. MCC's culture encourages the filing of patents. There is an on-site patent office to facilitate applications as well as provide bonuses and other awards for filing.

4. This patent search was conducted by Ms. Cindy Kehoe, Ph.D. candidate, Graduate School of Library and Information Science, The University of Texas at Austin (Kehoe, 1993).

APPENDIX 4.3

University, Corporate, and Government
Collaboration with MCC

We do have the finest research base in the world in our university establishment. Much more so than what's to be found in industry. It's much broader in the universities, not as much depth as IBM or GE in a specific area, but those tend toward application as opposed to pure research.

Admiral Inman, in a personal interview, April 18, 1989

I don't see us [MCC] starting up any basic research. There's a world of basic research out there free of charge. Everybody, by and large, is living on a federally supported university base that's generally of high quality and open so those that can exploit it are the winners.

Fields, in a personnal interview, August 15, 1990

MCC'S TIES WITH TEXAS UNIVERSITIES

One of the primary site-selection criteria for MCC was the presence of a major research university with high-quality programs in computer science and electrical engineering. MCC's site-selection team believed it was crucial to locate the consortium near a strong university with the momentum to become an academic leader in microelectronics research. Inman "wanted to be at the end of a pipeline of talent," home grown at the local university. MCC decided not to locate in Silicon Valley or along Route 128, despite the excellent regional university programs in computer science and electrical engineering, in part because of a desire to have MCC be the star recruiter of research talent in its area of location. (Other reasons for this decision are detailed in Chapter 3.)

Over the years, The University of Texas at Austin faculty and graduate students have received numerous MCC research grants and contracts. UT faculty have served as consultants to the consortium, and UT graduate students have worked on a range of MCC projects.

> I think the place that the University [of Texas] helps us [MCC] most is with graduate student labor. Most people's honest opinion is that if we were near Stanford or MIT, we would have benefited a lot more. . . . Some of the researchers feel that isolation is a real problem. In some cases researchers don't want to locate here because of the lack of a critical mass of people doing research in their particular area. (MCC researcher, 1990)

Specific MCC-UT linkages have depended on MCC's research needs and the talents and desires of UT faculty and students. For example, in the mid-1980s, the ACT Program had about 25 to 35 UT graduate students each spending from 15 to 20 hours per week at MCC. These students came mostly from UT's Departments of Computer Science and Electrical Engineering, with a few from the Linguistics Department.

An early and rather dramatic example of the indirect impact of MCC on UT's pursuit of excellence in research and teaching occurred shortly after MCC came to Austin, when the university benefited from a $32 million gift for endowed chairs in computer science and electrical engineering: $8 million came from a private donor who wanted to have a positive impact on the quality of Texas education, $8 million came from private matching funds, and $16 million in further matching funds came from the Permanent University Fund (PUF) in celebration of the university's centennial (see Chapter 6).

Other less dramatic examples of MCC's indirect and beneficial impact on The University of Texas at Austin concerned student quality and support. The year after MCC came to Austin, graduate student applicants to the Computer Science and Electrical Engineering departments increased in quality (GRE scores rose by about 200 points) and numbers. In 1988, MCC established an annual award program that recognized outstanding graduate research at UT-Austin. Awards of $500 recognized student researchers who published their research in refereed journals or conference proceedings. Furthermore, MCC researchers served as adjunct professors in UT's College of Engineering, Department of Electrical Engineering; College of Natural Sciences, Department of Computer Science; and the Graduate School of Business, Department of Management Science and Information Systems.

Admiral Inman said:

> Part of the deal that got MCC to Austin, was a proposal for $750,000 a year for ten years in grant aid to graduate students in computer science and electrical engineering. In May of 1985, I took part in the commencement ceremonies [at UT]. Half of those getting their Ph.D.'s in computer science were from East Asia, and most of them were going back . . . that fall's entering class was the first for which that $18,000-per-person grant was available. Every vacancy was filled by a U.S. graduate student, and their GREs were more than 200 points above the previous year. (interview, January 26, 1987)

MCC'S TIES WITH THE NATION'S UNIVERSITIES

Geographic distance has not proved to be a significant deterrent to MCC's establishing a range of research links with the nation's preeminent research universities. Such ties began in 1984, when MCC sent letters to 22 institutions of higher education inviting their participation in the University Affiliates Program. Through the program, MCC offered U.S. universities (1) a forum for addressing current unsolved research problems and lines of research, (2) a forum for establishing collaborative research efforts, and (3) access to MCC researchers and nonconfidential research results and equipment. MCC also encouraged university interaction through the utilization of faculty consultants, adjunct professorships, symposiums, visiting committees, workshops, and summer employment.

Texas A&M played an important role in MCC's location decision, and there have been research ties between the consortium and A&M; however, these ties have decreased over the years, and they were never as broad and deep as MCC's ties to The University of Texas at Austin. In 1984, Texas A&M submitted a proposal to MCC for a study of data base management for a distributed VLSI design. A&M had established a high level of expertise and a large data base of such designs, as well as CAD tools covering the hierarchy of design. MCC awarded Texas A&M $25,000 to investigate data organization and protection methods to enhance free access to data while maintaining data integrity.

MCC's Artificial Intelligence/Knowledge-Based Systems (AI/KBS) Program became a participant in a joint research project with Texas A&M. The AI/KBS Program provided A&M with six Xerox 1108 LISP workstations. (These were the same LISP workstations which proved to be of little use to MCC after the CAD program switched to C.) The university provided the research staff to work in (1) cognitive models of the systems development process, (2) cognitive skills in modeling and simulation analysis, and (3) analog integrated circuit design.

In 1985, research grants were awarded to faculty and graduate students at (1) Southern Methodist University (in Dallas, Texas) in artificial intelligence, (2) UT-Austin in data base machine concepts and logic, (3) Stanford University in research on parallel processing, (4) the University of Pennsylvania, and (5) Yale University.

In 1986, MCC awarded 48 research grants, totaling approximately $852,000, to UT-Austin, the University of Southern California (USC), Carnegie-Mellon University, Case Western Reserve, MIT, Stanford, the University of California at Berkeley, Yale University, and the University of Illinois. Research focused on such areas as:

- The support of functional languages
- The development of systems performance presentation techniques and software
- The development of a communication interconnect simulator
- Discourse understanding
- The development of a grammar formalism that would be useful to natural language processing
- Human-computer interaction, parallel distributed processing, and intelligent systems

In 1987, 22 research grants totaling approximately $550,000 were awarded to UT-Austin, Texas A&M, Stanford, UT, Berkeley,

MIT, USC, the University of Wisconsin, and Carnegie-Mellon in such areas as design data bases, stochastic simulation, the use of analogy to aid automatic proof discovery, and human interface with intelligent systems. Forty-seven consultants were employed from 18 different universities, 52 graduate and undergraduate students were hired for the summer, and 72 students held yearlong part-time positions with MCC. By 1987, 34 universities had participated in MCC's University Affiliates Program though such means as adjunct professorships, departmental visiting committees, scholarships, speakers, and workshops.

As Dove commented (interview, August 15, 1990):

> It's difficult for universities to transfer technology to the companies. It's difficult for universities to figure out what to do, or when they have something how to get the companies to pick it up. There is a tremendous impedence match and, because of this, a strong [opportunity] for MCC to play a conduit role between universities and industry.

By 1991, Craig Fields had rejected the strategy of trying to recruit to Austin research talent of the necessary quality and in the necessary numbers. His policy of seeking out talented researchers and going to them to collaborate promised to expand MCC's ties with universities. As an example of such a policy, in November 1991, Lehigh University's Iacocca Institute became a charter participant of MCC's Enterprise Integration (EI) Program. The objective of the program was to enhance U.S. competitiveness by developing business practices and technology that would enable organizations to share information and coordinate their people, activities, and resources. The Iacocca Institute joined with MCC and others throughout the United States working toward the common methods and technologies required to enable widespread integration of manufacturing efforts.

MCC'S IMPACT ON RESEARCH COLLABORATION
ACROSS BUSINESS, GOVERNMENT, AND ACADEMIC
ORGANIZATIONS

To what degree has MCC facilitated collaborative research with its member organizations as well as with government and academic institutions? Reliable, meaningful measures of such interorganizational collaboration are difficult to obtain. In the present discussion, a bibliographic search of a select sample of co-authored research papers is used to analyze the impact of MCC on collaborative research across university, government, and business sectors.[1]

Of 195 MCC-authored articles identified in the Science Citation Index from 1984 to 1990, interorganizational collaboration increased during the early years of the consortium's formation, and it has remained fairly constant to 1990 (Table 4.3.1). However, whereas MCC-only-authored and MCC-collaborative publications were relatively in balance from 1985 to 1987, MCC-only-authored articles dominated interorganizational collaborations from 1988 to 1990.

Table 4.3.1 Number of MCC-authored papers published by year

	1984	1985	1986	1987	1988	1989	1990	Total
MCC author(s) only	1	8	13	15	26	26	27	116
Interorganizational collaboration		8	10	13	18	13	17	79
Total	1	16	23	28	44	39	44	195
Percentage/ organizational collaboration	0	50	43	46	41	33	39	41

Note: Identified by the Science Citation Index in 1991.

Source: Gibson, Kehoe, and Lee, 1994.

Universities, corporations, research institutes, and federal laboratories—in the United States and 12 other nations—have collaborated with MCC researchers (Table 4.3.2). Surprisingly, according to the SCI sample of 79 co-authored research publications, MCC researchers collaborated more frequently with nonshareholder corporations than with shareholders. Of the 31 corporate research collaborations, 7 involved shareholder companies and 24 were with nonshareholders (Table 4.3.3).

IBM (was not an MCC shareholder but became an associate in 1991) is listed in 7 MCC collaborations: 3 times for its Israel Science Center and 4 times for its New York research labs (Table 4.3.2). Digital Equipment (an MCC shareholder) is listed 5 times: twice for its Paris Research Lab and 3 times for its research activities in Massachusetts. Such a high number of collaborations co-authored by MCC researchers and nonshareholders may reflect the fact that a high percentage of MCC's direct hires came from non-shareholder locations—i.e., that MCC research collaborations are based on long-term, previously formed social and professional ties.

The university with which MCC has collaborated the most in co-authored publications (as recorded by the SCI) is The University of Texas at Austin (Table 4.3.2). Stanford University, Carnegie-Mellon University, the University of Wisconsin, and MIT collaborated with MCC scientists more than have other more proximate universities. Non-U.S. universities and research institutes collaborating with MCC researchers are located in Canada, Denmark, England, France, Finland, Germany, Israel, Italy, Sweden, Switzerland, South Korea, and Japan.

Proximity is also not a strong indicator of MCC-industry collaboration. Centers of research exellence and professional ties play a stronger role than geographic and even cultural proximity in determining patterns of scientific collaboration at MCC. The Austin offices of five shareholder companies are each included once as collaborating with MCC researchers. On the other hand, the two most frequent corporate collaborators with MCC are IBM and DEC. While Texas-based universities and corporations have collaborated most with MCC researchers (27 times), researchers in California and Massachusetts as well as the New York/New Jersey area and the Northwest have also collaborated quite frequently with MCC researchers (Table 4.3.4).

Table 4.3.2 Organizations that have collaborated with MCC researchers in published research papers, according to SCI, 1984–1990

U.S. universities
  18 The University of Texas at Austin
   7 Stanford University, California
   5 Carnegie-Mellon University, Pittsburgh, Pennsylvania
   4 University of Wisconsin, Madison
   3 MIT, Cambridge, Massachusetts
   2 Cornell University, Ithaca, New York
   2 University of California at Berkeley
   2 University of Massachusetts, Amherst
   2 University of Minnesota, Minneapolis
      U.S. universities that collaborated once—17
U.S. companies—shareholders
   3 Digital Equipment Corporation, Hudson, Massachusetts
   2 Bell Communications Research, Inc. (Bellcore), Livingston, New Jersey
      Shareholders that collaborated once—5
U.S. companies—nonshareholders
   4 IBM, Thomas J. Watson Research Center, Yorktown Heights, New York*
   3 AT&T Bell Labs, Murray Hill, New Jersey, and Naperville, Illinois*
   3 Texas Instruments, Austin, Dallas, and Lewisville, Texas*
   2 Ashton Tate, Walnut Creek, California
      Nonshareholders that collaborated once—20
      (* became associate members of MCC)
U.S. government laboratories
   2 USN, Research Laboratory, Washington, D.C.
      U.S. government laboratories that collaborated once—1
U.S. research institute
      U.S. institutes that collaborated once—1
U.S. companies, non-U.S. office
   3 IBM, Israel Science Center, Haifa, Israel
   2 Digital Equipment Corporation, Paris Research Laboratory, France
Non-U.S. universities
   4 Technion Israel Institute of Technology, Haifa, Israel
   2 University of Calabria, Rende, Italy
   2 University of Lund, Solvegatan, Lund, Sweden
      Non-U.S. universities that collaborated once—11
Non-U.S. companies
   2 Nippon Telegraph and Telephone Public Corp., Japan
Non-U.S. government institutes
      Non-U.S. institutes that collaborated once—2

Table 4.3.3 Types of institutions collaborating in
research publications with MCC

	Each Organization Counted Singly	Each Occurrence Counted
U.S. universities	27	64
U.S. companies (shareholders)	7	10
U.S. companies (nonshareholders)	24	32
Non-U.S. universities	14	19
U.S. government laboratories	2	3
U.S. institutes	1	1
U.S. companies, non-U.S. office	2	5
Non-U.S. government institutes	2	2
Total	79	136

Table 4.3.4
Proximity of MCC collaborators by organizational type

	University	Corporation	Others	Total
Austin	18	4		22
Other Texas	2	3		5
California	11	8		19
Massachusetts	5	6		11
Minnesota	2	3		5
New York and New Jersey	4	10		14
Central, North Central, and Northwest	9	2	1	12
West and Southwest	2	1		3
Northeast	7	1		8
East and Southeast	3	3	3	9
Other countries	19	7	2	28
Total	82	48	6	136
	(60%)	(35%)	(4%)	(100%)

Given the U.S. bias of MCC, it is surprising that 19 foreign universities and 7 foreign corporations collaborated with MCC researchers in research publications as cited by the SCI from 1984 to 1990 (Table 4.3.4). Of course, it could be argued that MCC shareholders are the ultimate beneficiaries of these extended U.S. and foreign research linkages of MCC scientists.

COLLABORATION AMONG MCC SHAREHOLDERS

Has MCC facilitated research collaboration among its shareholders? Of 166 articles identified by SCI, 68 were before MCC was operating, from 1980 to 1983 (68/4 = 17 per year); and 98 were after the shareholders joined MCC from 1985 to 1990 (98/6 = 16 per year)—indicating that the yearly volume of research publications has remained fairly constant.[2] In some cases, collaboration increased after MCC membership (e.g., GE, Lockheed, Hewlett-Packard, Martin Marietta, and DEC), and in some cases, it decreased (e.g., Boeing, Westinghouse, Honeywell, Hughes, and Kodak) (Table 4.3.5). The total amount of collaboration among MCC shareholders from 1980 to 1990 (as indicated by SCI references) ranged from 67 articles with GE researchers to 2 articles with Control Data Corporation authors. The less frequent MCC-shareholder collaborations generally involved computer and semiconductor firms, while the most frequent collaborations involved aerospace firms and conglomerates.

The articles involving collaboration among noncomputer firms often were about such topics as nuclear energy and aerospace research—areas involving large projects and several companies. Companies in such industries tend to become each other's customers and collaborators in their primary missions. Government research labs and institutes (e.g., NASA) are frequent third parties to collaboration in the aerospace industry. Computer and semiconductor firms, on the other hand, are often in direct competition and have fewer joint contracts.

Of the 79 research articles involving interorganizational collaborations (Table 4.3.3), 15 percent involved only corporations; 29 percent included authors from universities, corporations, and MCC; and 49 percent involved only university researchers and MCC. Universities play an important bridging role for MCC research activities. Universities were involved most frequently when computer and semiconductor firms collaborated.

The amount of collaboration among MCC shareholders varies more by type of industry than by internal R&D expenditure (Table 4.3.6). While computer and semiconductor firms rank high in R&D spending per employee, there is less of a pattern in terms of total R&D expenditures according to industry groupings. The amount of funds spent on R&D as a percentage of profits for 1989 was 122 percent for aerospace, 113 percent for the computer industry, 129 percent for the semiconductor industry, and 43 percent for an all-industry composite.[3]

Table 4.3.5 Amount of collaboration among MCC shareholders, 1980–1990

	1980–1983	1985–1989	1980–1990	Ranking
GE	30	37	67	1
Boeing	24	13	37	2
Rockwell	17	18	35	3
Lockheed	13	17	30	4
Westinghouse	15	12	27	5
Hewlett-Packard	3	18	21	6
Honeywell	11	8	19	7
Motorola	8	10	18	8
Hughes	13	3	16	9
Martin Marietta	3	13	16	9
DEC	1	12	13	11
Bellcore	NA	12	12	12
Eastman Kodak	7	4	11	13
Harris	3	5	8	14
AMD	3	4	7	15
National Semiconductor	2	5	7	15
3M	3	3	6	17
NCR	5	1	6	17
CDC	1	1	2	19

Source: Gibson, Kehoe, and Lee, 1994.

As shown in Table 4.3.6, research collaboration with MCC (as indicated by SCI data) generally has an inverse correlation with the amount of R&D funds spent per corporate employee—i.e., the more a firm spends on R&D per employee, the less that firm's employees collaborate with MCC researchers in terms of research publications.

Table 4.3.6
Shareholder ranking, based on R&D expenditures, 1989

	Rank—R&D Expenditures per Employee	Total R&D Expenditures (X $1 million)	Rank— Amount of Collaboration
AMD	1	15	15
CDC	2	14	19
Hewlett-Packard	3	3	6
DEC	4	1	11
Eastman Kodak	5	4	13
3M	6	5	17
National Semiconductor	7	13	15
NCR	8	11	17
Motorola	9	5	8
Hughes	10	8	9
Lockheed	11	9	4
Boeing	12	7	2
GE	13	2	1
Rockwell	14	10	3
Honeywell	15	12	7
Martin Marietta	16	16	9
Westinghouse	17	17	5
Bellcore	NA	NA	12
Harris	NF	NF	NF

Source: Gibson, Kehoe, and Lee, 1994.

CONCLUSIONS

Collaborative research among universities, industry, and federal laboratories is being increasingly advocated in the globally competitive marketplace. MCC itself represents a national policy decision to foster collaboration among U.S. corporations. The bibliographic data reported in Appendix 4.3 indicate that MCC as well as the nation's universities play an important intermediary role in fostering such industry collaboration. However, it is emphasized that the types of collaboration discussed in this study center on the joint authorship of research articles—the very front end of the technology transfer process leading to product/process commercialization.

Proximity was an important factor in the degree of collaboration only for The University of Texas at Austin. Proximity is not an important variable in corporate collaboration leading to research publication, nor is MCC membership. Among MCC shareholders, research collaboration varied most by type of industry. International collaboration between MCC researchers and foreign academics is quite frequent given that the consortium is ostensibly closed to foreign membership. Finally, there is an inverse correlation between the amount of funds a firm spends on R&D per employee and the amount of collaboration with MCC researchers.

NOTES

1. Using the Science Citation Index (SCI), Gibson, Kehoe, and Lee (1994) recorded a sample of (1) 195 published research articles authored by MCC researchers from 1984 to 1990 and (2) 166 research articles authored by MCC shareholder scientists from 1980 to 1990. Bibliometric techniques were used to analyze these data. The SCI has a Western bias, and it does not provide an exhaustive list of publications of the researchers in the identified organizations. SCI's focus is on journals considered by its editors to be core to the disciplines represented. Thus, while the analysis does not examine all published, collaborative research, it serves as an indicator of collaborations by researchers that have led to significant publications. Portions of this material are reprinted, with permission, from *IEEE Transactions in Engineering Management,* to be published in March 1994.

2. This analysis is limited to MCC's initial 19 shareholders in order to compare research collaboration before and after the establishment of MCC.

3. SEC data reported in "Statistics: R&D Scoreboard," *Business Week* (June 15, 1990), pp. 192–222.

5

Technology Transfer and MCC

Some companies get in [MCC] and they aggressively pull the technology out. Other companies lean back and sip through a long straw.

Admiral Inman, personal interview, January 26, 1987

Early in the game, there was the feeling that we would deliver ideas, concepts, and prototypes. The companies would then invest to put it to work. That didn't happen.

Grant Dove, personal interview, March 1, 1991

Up front we have technology transfer plans because I believe that it's bad management to wait for the middle or until the end, and then come back and figure out how you're going to transfer it.

Craig Fields, personal interview, March 1, 1991

Technology transfer—from the laboratory to successful process implementation and/or product commercialization—has been a continuing challenge at MCC.[1] One main criticism of R&D consortia in general is that in terms of ROI (return on investment), research results leading to important technology applications have been sparse, especially given the amount of funds and talent invested. As MCC researcher Jeff Conklin commented in a report on technology transfer for Craig Fields (E-mail, August 9, 1990):

The problem with technology transfer is that everyone knows how to do it, but nobody seems to be doing it very well. I suspect we are bringing a flat-earth mentali-

325

ty to the "new world" of technology transfer. In this condition even such widely accepted bits of technology transfer wisdom as "the most effective transfer is in the heads of people" obscure more than they illuminate. Certainly, the result at MCC—the loss, and the risk of loss, of participant funding due to perception of low ROI—can be meaningfully viewed simply as a technology transfer failure.

There are lots of known techniques for technology transfer—volumes have been written. At MCC we have used liaisons, assignees, workshops, training, technical reports, third-party licenses, production and support of products (as opposed to prototypes), and many other techniques. Again, on the basis of the result we may assess the approach reflected by these techniques as having failed. (The alternative, that the technology being developed at MCC was not inherently valuable enough, is also possible, but I believe it to be utterly groundless and in any case irrelevant.)

Consortia in the United States and worldwide are ultimately being judged in terms of technological applications profitably used in the global marketplace. To levy such an evaluation criteria specifically at R&D consortia or federal laboratories and research universities, for that matter, is perhaps inappropriate, in that technology application is a relatively new and much debated mandate for these organizations. Furthermore, technology application has been a continuing challenge even for U.S. business.[2] While the United States has excelled in basic research and in technology development, the nation's firms have not been competitive in getting new technologies to the marketplace in a cost-effective, timely manner. Technology transfer to product/process commercialization is especially difficult when it involves crossing organizational boundaries.

MCC's researchers and potential technology users at the member companies are separated by professional, technological, strategic, cultural, competitive, and distance barriers. Such barriers to technology transfer also exist between firms and corporate R&D, research universities, and federal laboratories. And they exist, although to a lesser degree, within firms (such as among R&D,

manufacturing, and marketing). Although, as noted by one former manager of technology transfer at MCC, "such barriers are as pronounced within the firm as within MCC." He recounted his experiences in one of America's top manufacturers of semiconductors: "We had two labs working side by side on similar projects. When their colleagues from the neighboring lab or others from the firm came into their lab they would take care to cover or otherwise hide their work. There was a fear that someone else would get credit for their ideas." (Werner interview, May 4, 1993)

MCC is an especially rich laboratory in which to study challenges to technology transfer for the following reasons:

- MCC was designed and managed to minimize barriers to successful technology transfer and commercialization, such as bureaucratic, legal, and funding constraints. Technology user companies decided research priorities.
- For over ten years MCC has had a variety of on-site, long-term, and goal-directed research projects that have resulted in a range of software and hardware technologies.
- MCC researchers (including direct hires, shareholder representatives, and visitors) have come from a wide variety of company, academic, and federal laboratory backgrounds.
- Timely and efficient technology transfer has been an ongoing, high-level priority at MCC. Many useful lessons have been learned.

According to Arneson (correspondence, April 8, 1993):

In 1982, it was recognized that the technology transfer problem had never been broadly solved although several institutions (Bell Labs/Western Electric and 3M, notably) had done a lot better than others. One of our MCC planners (Jess Rifkind) had just spent ten years at Xerox PARC unsuccessfully working the technology transfer problem. The notions of independent projects and using consortium members' technical personnel were aimed at attempting a fresh approach to the transfer problem.

THE DIFFICULT NATURE OF TECHNOLOGY TRANSFER

> So from the beginning, technology transfer [at MCC]
> meant: How do you transfer the result of research
> activity that has been done? . . . It's similar to other
> contexts such as having to take the results of research
> done in universities and move that out to the commer-
> cial sector. . . . How do you take research done in gov-
> ernment laboratories, under government contract, and
> move it out to potential users for other purposes? . . .
> Technology transfer involves moving knowledge of
> technology developments into the hands of those who
> have the potential for applying it in a product or
> service. (Inman interview, April 18, 1989)

Two kinds of technology transfer—from research to application—directly influence U.S. industrial competitiveness, as shown in
Figure 5.1: (1) spinning out technologies into start-up companies
(the dashed line) and (2) transferring new technologies from
research organizations to established firms (the solid line). The dot-
ted line indicates spinning technologies into the research activities of
federal laboratories, universities, and consortia. Success in this form
of technology transfer also has important long-term implications for
U.S. industrial competitiveness.

The United States is a successful role model for much of the
industrialized world regarding spin-out technology transfer. Spin-
out companies have been a vitally important if not a dominant factor in the emergence and growth of the United States' two premier
technopoleis or technology centers: Silicon Valley, California, and
Route 128, Boston. An increasing phenomenon in emerging
technopoleis is to have such spin-out companies nurtured in an
incubator (see Chapter 6). America is not as competitive regarding
technology transfer across the organizational boundaries of established firms, a subject we explore in depth in this chapter.

When one of us visited the Fifth-Generation Computer
Project in Tokyo in November 1989, the project's director, Dr.
Kazuhiro Fuchi, would not believe that technology transfer could be
a serious problem for an R&D consortium like MCC: "But the
member companies are paying for the research. Why wouldn't they

be eager to put research results to use?" (Fuchi interview, November 10, 1989)

"It's just damn hard," commented an MCC researcher. "Technology transfer is such a buzzword. People think that you can just tie it [the technology] up in a package, and I could just hand it to you; I would then forget about it, and you would open the package and say 'Wonderful.' It just doesn't happen that way. It's a difficult problem, and it takes dedicated people."

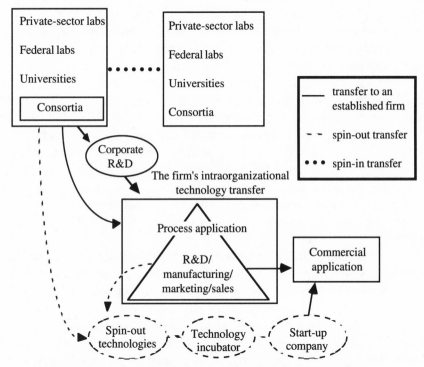

Figure 5.1 Two basic forms of technology transfer to commercial applications

MCC has the longest track record of any privately funded U.S. R&D consortium in dealing with the challenges of commercializing research. Important lessons have been learned, lessons that could improve U.S. industrial competitiveness, but first, this process "technology" (of how to apply research results successfully) must be effectively transferred to other U.S. consortia, corporations, federal laboratories, and universities.

Experienced executives with engineering and technical backgrounds designed MCC. They realized that the transfer of MCC-produced technology to the shareholders was going to be difficult. They designed formal structures such as the technical advisory board (TAB) and research program technical advisory boards (PTABs) in order to facilitate MCC's communication with the member companies. They stressed the importance of shareholder liaisons/representatives as carriers of the technology back to the member companies. A "formal transfer" was to be documented and supported by MCC for a designated period of time. Technology that was turned over to a shareholder company without documentation and support was defined as an "informal transfer."

MCC's shareholder companies also realized that getting technologies from the R&D consortium was going to be a challenge. However, neither the managers nor the researchers at MCC or at the shareholder companies understood just how difficult such technology transfer would be. "One of the fascinating elements of the MCC experience," said Admiral Inman (interview, July 21, 1987), "was to see how different the companies were in dealing with ongoing research . . . the ones that prowl, looking for things that were new, and the majority that waited for you to deliver things to them."

Depending on the perspective of the evaluator, an assessment of MCC's success at technology transfer could be based on a range of criteria. The R&D consortium has published more than 2,400 technical reports, produced more than 400 technical videotapes, "transferred" more than 200 technologies, published numerous research articles, and been issued or assured 117 patents and 182 technology licenses.[3] Such quantifiable measures focus on research productivity, whereas most of the criticism of MCC has focused on research application and how critical MCC's technologies have been to related activities within the shareholder or other member companies.

As a former MCC researcher/manager commented in 1993:

In retrospect, we [MCC] were often not plugged into the ultimate users of our technology: chip and systems designers. In many cases, the "receptors" of our technology within our participant companies had their own internal technology transfer problems. . . . I vividly recall one of our CAD Program managers saying to me: "You know, the problem is that our shareholders don't see us solving their most crucial problems—they don't need MCC."

There are also less tangible and less accepted criteria for judging MCC's success at technology transfer: learning from R&D failures while having costs dispersed; small, incremental wins; support services provided; increased intra- and interfirm communication among MCC's member companies; and learning how to collaborate across organizational boundaries. It would be impossible to specify the ROI from these transferred "technologies," but they may well be among MCC's most significant contributions to U.S. industrial competitiveness.[4]

Learning from failures is sometimes offered as a benefit of R&D consortia. If ten companies invest in a risky technology and it fails, then each company learns what not to do at one-tenth the cost. Such a strategy would certainly seem preferable to a "bet your company" type of investment in cutting-edge R&D. However, MCC researchers and managers soon realized that "learning from failures" was not the way to promote the benefits of belonging to MCC—i.e., member companies were not keen on funding research, on any scale, that produced "failures" as a measure of success.

MCC has engaged in a great many research projects that have led to incremental improvements in member-company technologies and internal processes. The consortium has achieved numerous and often imperceptible transfers of such technologies to its member companies. At times, MCC researchers did not even realize they were transferring important technologies/ideas to member-company engineers, researchers, and managers. Small and continuous transfers were difficult to quantify and shareholder representatives found it difficult to convince their superiors, at their home companies, that such transfers warranted continued support for MCC.

Member companies have looked to MCC for technology support services for particular product or process applications, that the companies could not, or would not, find elsewhere. In late 1986, 3M sent technicians to workshops at MCC's Packaging Interconnect Program to facilitate the debugging of its own tape-automated bonding assembly line. With this expert assistance, 3M had its own line adjusted in 60 days rather than the predicted 12 months or more. MCC hosted teleconferences on cutting-edge research for its member companies, and it organized seminars on important emerging technology areas. MCC's international liaison office provides valuable competitive information to MCC's member companies. U.S. firms have traditionally done a poor job of monitoring the technological advances of their foreign competition, especially when compared to the technology scanning and utilization capabilities of their Japanese, Korean, and Taiwanese counterparts. Yet it would be difficult to place a value on how such information has helped MCC's member firms compete in the global marketplace.

But perhaps the most significant "technology" transferred from MCC to its member companies concerns increased collaboration among the functions, divisions, and hierarchies within the member companies as well as across company boundaries. From the board of directors and program technical advisory boards to less planned and less formal interactions, MCC has provided a forum for cross-organizational communication on a variety of issues. As a result of increased intra- and interfirm communication, MCC's member companies made significant progress in learning how to collaborate within and among firms while competing in the marketplace.

Despite the importance of the "technologies" described above, in the final analysis, MCC (as well as many other U.S. consortia) is ultimately being judged in terms of its impact on short-term, product commercialization. The main criticism of MCC is that the consortium has absorbed over $500 million of member-company funds with only "thin" results to show for such a large investment: "Where are the significant technological breakthroughs?" "Where are the commercial wins?" "What if the member companies had invested their MCC-dedicated funds in their own R&D?"

TECHNOLOGY TRANSFER DEFINED

Many U.S. managers and researchers think of the technology transfer process as looking something like a barbell. The weight at one end represents R&D, whose task is to create technological advancements. The weight at the other end represents the users of the new technology, who operate in the world of manufacturing and marketing. The technology transfer process consists of moving new technologies from the R&D unit to the technology-using unit. From the consortium's inception, MCC's planners realized that this one-way barbell model was not an accurate way to depict the technology transfer process in which they were engaged. How MCC came to recognize just how complex and difficult a process technology transfer was, and how MCC scientists and managers have evolved in meeting these challenges, is the subject of this chapter.

The concepts of technology and of transfer are defined by both theoreticians and practitioners in many different ways. There is usually agreement, however, that (1) technology is not just a "thing," and (2) transfer is a profoundly human endeavor. Essentially, "technology" is information that is put to use in order to accomplish some task, the knowledge of how to do something. "Transfer" is the movement of technology via some channel from one individual or organization to another. So technology transfer involves the application of knowledge, putting a tool to use.

The transfer of technology is a particularly difficult type of communication, in that it often requires collaborative activity between two or more individuals or functional units that are often separated by a range of barriers. Appreciation for the human component in technology transfer directs us away from thinking of simply moving technology from "point A" to "point B" (as in the barbell analogy described earlier). Instead, we can think of technology transfer as an interactive process with a great deal of back-and-forth exchange among individuals over an extended period of time.

Our communication-based model of technology transfer centers on information exchange between a technology source and a receptor as a two-way process (Gibson and Rogers, 1994). Such information exchange is typically not orderly or unidirectional. It is often chaotic and disorderly. Participants are "transceivers," who exchange ideas simultaneously and continuously, thereby blurring the distinction between senders and receivers. The technology being transferred is often not a fully formed idea that can be neatly packaged and forwarded. It has no inherent meaning or value: meaning is in the minds of the participants. Accordingly, transmitters and users are likely to have different perceptions of the same technology. Feedback helps technology transceivers reach convergence about important dimensions. Technology transfer to product commercialization involves an ongoing, multilevel exchange of information.

There is a serendipitous aspect to technology transfer, in that researchers often make unexpected discoveries.[5] Researchers and users may combine in a synergistic way, one that could be neither predicted nor managed, to produce unexpected results. Such technology transfer is a particular case of the "garbage can model" of decision making (Cohen, March, and Olsen, 1972). A transferred technology results from an unplanned mixture of participants, solutions, choice opportunities, and problems. Both problems looking for solutions (technology pull) as well as solutions looking for problems (technology push) are encountered. In accord with this view, technology users may not even know they have a problem until they see the solution.

"On the technology side," says Admiral Inman (interview, December 12, 1989): "it isn't just a strategic-planning push, because you don't know in advance what's likely to evolve out of the investment in research. You're dealing with an unknown. You may think you know what you're after, but the issue for many companies is, are you prepared to deal with the other events that occur, the accidental discoveries?" Inman offered Xerox PARC (Palo Alto Research Center) as an example of a company unprepared to utilize unexpected findings: "They had gathered an incredible array of talent in California . . . did much of the pioneering work in modern computing. . . . Not only didn't they use their own products, but they didn't put into place the mechanisms to sell that technology to other companies. The technology was ultimately transferred by disaffected employees who took the technology with them." (Inman interview, December 12, 1989)

LEVELS OF TECHNOLOGY TRANSFER

MCC's experiences with technology transfer suggest four levels of collaborative activity and four correspondingly different definitions of technology transfer success (Figure 5.2). At level I, technology R&D, researchers conduct state-of-the-art, pre-competitive research and transfer these results by such varied means as research publications, videotapes, teleconferences, and software computer tapes. Technology transfer at this level is a largely passive process that requires little collaborative behavior among the transceivers, although the researchers may work in teams or across organizational or even national boundaries (see Appendix 4.3).

Level I success is measured by the quantity and quality (usually determined by peer review) of research reports and journal articles. Technology transfer plans and processes are not considered very important. *Research strength* is most important.[6] Traditionally, technology users have not been involved at this level of the transfer process. The belief is that good ideas sell themselves; pressures of the marketplace are all that is needed to drive technology use and commercialization. It could be argued that from the 1950s to the 1970s this "trickle out" method of technology transfer was sufficient to sustain (or at least give the perception of sustaining) U.S. industrial competitiveness.

Figure 5.2 Technology transfer at four levels of involvement

Bob Price emphasized the important role the federal government has played in the nation's technology transfer (interview, May 12, 1993):

> Such [government] market pull was central in the development of synthetic rubber during World War II and the production of semiconductors and the development of Silicon Valley. In 1961 there was no commercial market for semiconductors. Then Kennedy set the vision of putting a man on the moon by the end of the decade. In 1964 the government was 100 percent of the LSI market and the impetus was the space program. The government was an insatiable customer, other spin-off markets developed, and start-up companies became major players and world leaders in the semiconductor and computer industries.

During MCC's early years of operation, the consortium's scientists were measured in terms of level I activity. Indeed, these conceptions of technology transfer reflected (1) the norms and values that MCC scientists brought with them from university, federal, and corporate laboratories and (2) the level of technology transfer mandated in the pre-competitive research limitation of the 1984 National Cooperative Research Act. And this perspective continues to have strong advocates, as Smidt (interview, June 2, 1993) commented: "If the technology is superior, it will be used, I can guarantee you that. If you worry about process, then the technology is weak. MCC's greatest problem with technology transfer is that its technologies were weak and the people doing the research and those who came from the shareholder companies were mediocre. Quality of the technology is key."

Level II transfer, technology acceptance, calls for the beginnings of shared responsibility between technology developers and users. Success occurs when a technology is transferred across personal, functional, or organizational boundaries and it is accepted and understood by designated users. Moving from level I to level II technology transfer is an extremely difficult task for research organizations like MCC, where the organization conducting the research is at "arm's length" from the organization that is the prospective user of the technology. Merely determining the appropriate person to contact is an immense challenge as one looks at a large corporation like Lockheed or General Electric or even a much smaller Advanced Micro Devices. A level II perspective encourages the belief that successful technology transfer is simply a matter of getting the right information to the right people at the right time.

In level III transfer, technology implementation, success is marked by the timely and efficient employment of the technology. For level III success to occur, technology users must have the knowledge and resources needed to implement, or Beta test, the technology. Technology implementation can occur within the user organization in terms of manufacturing or other processes, or it can occur in terms of product development, such as building a prototype or proof of concept for commercial application. *Industrial strength* is required. It is at this stage where the receptor organization provides value-added to the transferred technology.

Level IV transfer, technology application, centers on product commercialization. Level IV builds cumulatively on the successes achieved in attaining the objectives of the three previous stages, but *market strength* is required. Feedback from technology users drives the transfer process. Success is measured in terms of ROI or market share. Here, we take a longer-term view. It is with respect to level IV technology transfer that MCC has been most criticized for its relative lack of success.

Moving from level I to level IV is *not* a linear, step-by-step process. Multidimensional collaboration is required. Complexity increases significantly as the technology and perhaps the technology developers move from level I to level IV.

Overall technology transfer success in terms of levels I to IV is difficult to measure by traditional cost-benefit analyses, since (1) it is often difficult to quantify financial or other impacts of a technology over time, and (2) different persons involved in the process are likely to evaluate costs and benefits differently, depending on their unique perspectives. In the case of MCC, different member companies commonly hold different expectations as to which level of technology transfer they expect. Some member companies are happy with research reports, while others want market-strength products. Even within a member company, different managers (e.g., hierarchically) and functional areas (e.g., R&D, production, marketing, and sales) evaluate MCC's technology transfer activities by different criteria. For example, a CEO might be motivated by a new, bold concept, whereas a line manager in the same company might want technology that is of industrial strength and supported. For a scientist, success might be peer recognition or a journal publication rather than the commercial application of his or her idea.

In a 1985 survey of MCC's board of directors and technical advisory board, respondents were asked to rank the consortium's most difficult task in the coming years: 46 percent emphasized the transfer of technology from MCC to the shareholder companies, 33 percent emphasized the transformation of the transferred technology into successful products, and 21 percent emphasized the creation of useful technology by MCC. (Murphy, 1987, p. 224)

During the consortium's formative years, MCC scientists generally held to a level I perspective of technology transfer. To ensure trust and fairness, it was considered MCC's responsibility to present a new technology (as a standard technology package [STP]) to all the funding shareholders at the same time. Success was defined as (1) conducting high-quality, long-range research and (2) making the results available in a timely fashion to the shareholder companies. MCC's shareholder companies had continual access to the consortium's technology through such means as research reports, personnel transfers, and company visits. The shareholder companies were to use MCC-developed technologies to create products of their own design and to compete in markets of their own choice. Market forces and competitive pressures were expected to drive the process.

Over time, it became apparent to MCC's managers and scientists that level I measures of success, however impressive, would not sustain the consortium. This realization increased in intensity as funding for MCC was pushed down the hierarchies of the member companies. Divisional and group managers increasingly demanded measurable technology benefits. MCC faced a dilemma as technology transfer activities moved from a level I to a level IV perspective: the consortium exercised less control over events leading to successful technology commercialization as more collaboration was required across functional and organizational boundaries from a range of participants, many of which resided in the shareholder company (Figure 5.3).

In some ways MCC had the best of all worlds. It was designed to be free of obstacles that inhibit research. Obstructing bureaucracy was kept to a minimum. Researchers enjoyed high autonomy and state-of-the-art facilities and equipment, and were guaranteed long-term funding to work on research in their areas of expertise. However, in one important way MCC was set up to fail, and this dilemma centered on the consortium's lack of power or control over its member companies' application of MCC-developed technologies.

> MCC can fail by doing research that is irrelevant to the goals its shareholders are pursuing. And it can fail by being late. . . . MCC can also fail due to . . . ineffective, inappropriate, and unskilled management. . . . [But] if we did all the right things in the world, at the right time, we could still fail if the shareholders do not capitalize on the excellent output. (Smidt quoted in Fischelli, 1986, p. 77)

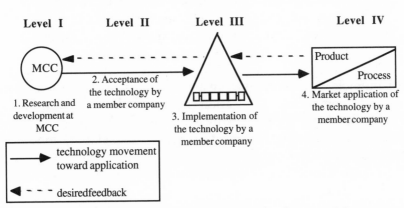

Figure 5.3 Four levels of technology transfer from MCC to a member company

MCC could develop a "silver bullet" technology, but if the member companies chose not to take it to industrial and market strength, MCC would be judged a failure. As one MCC researcher commented:

> We were caught in a paradox that faces many R&D consortia sooner or later: our success depended on how successfully our shareholders adopted MCC technolo-

gy. Yet we had virtually no control once MCC technology was in the hands of the shareholders.

As MCC researcher Jeff Conklin stated in his report to Craig Fields (E-mail, August 9, 1990):

> Clearly the technology transfer problem must be viewed from both the researcher and customer viewpoints. At MCC we have taken every reasonable step to make technology transfer happen except one—we have utterly failed to educate, advise, urge, and coerce the participants into taking the appropriate committed actions that would promote strong and maintained technology transfer "pull" (read "committed" as financial). Most of the participants have been literally wasting their research investment in MCC by failing to put in place effective mechanisms and people for marketing, selling, developing, and supporting MCC technology once it reached the successful prototype stage.

We now offer an in-depth look at one of MCC's earliest and most publicized technology transfer success stories—Proteus, the first major, commercial application (level IV technology transfer) of an MCC-developed technology by a shareholder company. The case highlights the importance of interorganizational collaboration, planning, and serendipity and the high level of effort required by a range of participants over an extended period of time across all four levels of technology transfer.

THE CASE OF PROTEUS

In mid-1987, MCC proudly announced that Proteus, a technology developed in the consortium's Advanced Computer Architecture (ACA) research program, was to be commercialized by NCR Corporation.[7] NCR, one of the founding members of MCC, was using Proteus in a product called DesignAdvisor™.

Proteus was an expert systems development environment, or software systems "shell," that could be loaded with detailed knowledge about a specific problem area. NCR engineers used Proteus to develop an expert system for advising designers of integrated circuits. DesignAdvisor emulated expert knowledge resulting from years of human experience in designing computer microcircuits. Installed on engineering workstations, the product proposed circuit designs and offered advice on how the designs might be improved. DesignAdvisor was considered a significant product advancement, given its ability to (1) incorporate new facts and rules into its existing knowledge base, and (2) be able to revise its "expert thinking" in light of this new information.

The transfer of Proteus technology to NCR's product application in DesignAdvisor provides important lessons. Scientists, product development engineers, and managers had to work very hard as a team in order to effectively transfer the technology across organizational and functional boundaries from MCC's research laboratory in Austin, Texas, through an NCR product division in Fort Collins, Colorado, to NCR's customers.

BIRTH OF THE PROTEUS TECHNOLOGY

Research leading to Proteus was begun at MCC in 1984 by three researchers in the Artificial Intelligence Laboratory of MCC's Advanced Computer Architecture research program. Charles Petrie was the project leader of ACA's Expert Systems Group and was a Ph.D. student in computer science at The University of Texas at Austin. David Russinoff was the principal designer and implementer of the Proteus system. Donald Steiner was a staff researcher. At the time, these three MCC researchers did not have a great deal of experience in developing AI software. But they believed that with their combined expertise and with the hardware and software and other resources available at MCC, they could design a more elegant, state-of-the-art expert systems program than currently existed in the marketplace. Given their relative lack of AI experience, this assumption was rather presumptuous.

AI Program director Woodrow Bledsoe provided early and crucial support for the research team, and MCC's shareholders funding the ACA Program indicated early interest in the Proteus Project. Funding was made available, and Petrie, Russinoff, and Steiner were granted a one-year grace period before being expected to demonstrate some results. Petrie, who had experience in managing advanced development projects in industrial settings, served as the initial interface between the shareholder company representatives and MCC. Despite the agreed-upon one-year grace period, within months, the Proteus researchers felt caught between two seemingly opposing demands: to spend their time and resources in (1) conducting research on Proteus or (2) transferring research results to the shareholder companies.

Each of the different shareholder companies funding the Proteus research had different uses and expectations for the technology. Some shareholders were comfortable with the progress of Petrie's team, while others pressured the MCC researchers to show the usefulness of their work. To help insulate the Proteus design team from shareholder demands, MCC hired Nat Ballou and Shuih-li Liuh to be an interface between the research team and the shareholders that were funding the research.

PROTEUS TO DESIGNADVISOR

Charles (Chuck) Exley, Jr., CEO of NCR Corporation, had helped launch MCC in 1982. He was a strong supporter of the consortium. NCR was a funding shareholder of three of MCC's research programs. In late 1984, he asked his vice president for research, Tom Tang, what technology NCR was obtaining from the consortium. The Proteus research team had recently mailed Tang (and several other individuals at NCR as well as other shareholder companies) an eight-minute videotape about the Proteus technology. Often these tapes were "lost" within the receptor divisions, but in this instance Exley and Tang showed the videotape at the next staff meeting of NCR's senior executives. After viewing the video, Exley discussed the importance of MCC. Then he looked at his senior managers and asked: "How are we going to turn this technology [Proteus] into a product?" (Steele interview, August 20, 1990). With this high-level interest and support, it took just three months for NCR to develop a strategic plan for how the company could use the Proteus technology in a product application.

Ed Krall had worked for NCR for seven years as a senior consultant in corporate R&D. He joined MCC as NCR's liaison to the ACA research program in 1983. Joe Scullion, also from NCR, was deputy director of MCC's artificial intelligence program. Based on their companywide knowledge of NCR's R&D activities, Krall and Scullion believed that the Proteus technology could be applied by NCR's Fort Collins, Colorado, Microelectronics Division. They knew the facility wanted to improve the productivity of its VLSI design process for semiconductor chips. Jack Mullins, NCR's CAD liaison to MCC, also helped Krall and Sullivan champion NCR's use of the Proteus technology.

In response to the recommendations of Krall, Scullion, and Mullins, Dan Ellsworth, manager of advanced development at NCR's Fort Collins division, asked Robin Steele, a senior engineer, to investigate the Proteus technology. It was early 1985, and Steele had been employed at the Fort Collins facility for 18 months. Steele had a master's degree in electrical engineering; she was personable; and she was a world-class triathlete. As it turned out, her professional training, her interpersonal skills, and her athletic stamina would all be needed to successfully pull the Proteus technology out of MCC and turn it into a marketable product for NCR. The transfer of the Proteus technology to DesignAdvisor proved to be much more difficult than anyone at MCC or NCR could have imagined.

In April 1985, Steele presented her plan for using Proteus in a VLSI application to ACA's program managers. As Petrie remembered: "We didn't think the application would work, but we were willing to give it a try" (interview, September 16, 1993). Russinoff and Steiner were not all that enthusiastic about the potential application of their research. As Petrie remembered (interview, September 16, 1993): "They got bogged down in the problems and complications of technology transfer." Fortunately, Nat Ballou and Shiuh-li Liuh were well versed in the Proteus code and they enjoyed working on potential applications. Ballou and Liuh worked closely with Steele. Bolstered by this support, Steele sold the plan to her boss, Dan Ellsworth. As Petrie commented: "Ellsworth was the crucial person at NCR. Without his vision and enthusiasm for the project and without his financial support and the support of his organization, we wouldn't have gotten anywhere." Steele and Ellsworth wrote a proposal about NCR's collaborative advanced development work with MCC. The plan had four main points: (1) NCR's need to learn more about AI, especially given the small size of the company's existing AI program; (2) the value of an NCR/MCC collaborative evaluation of representational approaches in computer software for semiconductor chip design; (3) the importance of technology transfer from MCC to NCR and the identification of this approach as a strategic experiment for NCR; and (4) the resulting boost to NCR's prestige if the technology transfer from MCC were successful.

MCC's Proteus software had been written in LISP on a Symbolics machine, neither of which was used by NCR in Fort Collins. Selling the idea of purchasing a LISP machine was a major barrier that Ellsworth had to overcome with his superiors. He argued that since NCR had already invested over $2 million in MCC, the additional $120,000 for a Symbolics machine was justified. Tang agreed.

In July 1985, several NCR officials visited with Petrie, Russinoff, and Steiner at MCC. Because of NCR's focused attention on the Proteus research, high-level MCC managers were becoming somewhat concerned about the issue of fairness to other shareholder funders of the AI research. There was also concern about protecting NCR's intellectual property. As a result, MCC managers established a visiting scientist position for Steele. This position was made available to all other shareholders that proposed similar joint research and technology transfer efforts with MCC.

MCC arranged for Steele to have an office and a workstation in MCC's Expert Systems Laboratory near the offices of Petrie, Russinoff, and Steiner. To prepare for her technology transfer role, Steele took courses in expert systems and LISP. As Pietre commented (interview, July 27, 1988): "Robin [Steele] was a highly motivated young engineer who had a clear concept in her own mind of how Proteus could be incorporated into a specific NCR product that she was working on." As Krall observed (interview, July 27, 1990): "She came down and interacted with MCC researchers. She grabbed hold of the technology and dragged it out."

Steele knew at the start of the transfer process that any transferred software would have to be rewritten and ported to Apollo and Sun workstations, the main hardware used by NCR's customers at that time. So computer compatibility was a major problem to be overcome in the transfer process (1) from MCC to NCR and (2) from NCR to its customers.

From 1985 to 1986, Steele spent one week in every six in

Austin working with Petrie, Russinoff, and Steiner. The first day of each week's visit was spent in downloading her computer tape, getting it running, and then giving demonstrations of NCR's applications of the Proteus technology to MCC's researchers. A second day was spent learning what had been happening with the Proteus research during the five weeks since her last visit. It took Steele a third day to incorporate these new developments into her software package. On the fourth day, she conducted further demonstrations with MCC researchers based on the new ideas. On the last day of each visit, Steele loaded code on a computer tape for her return trip to Fort Collins.

Once back in Colorado, Steele downloaded the revised version of Proteus and worked with Ballou and other NCR engineers to apply the Proteus technology to DesignAdvisor. Getting the MCC-developed technology to work satisfactorily at NCR was a difficult, time-consuming, interactive process. Proteus was not at industrial strength. As Ed Krall (interview, July 27, 1990) said:

> By sheer dint of will, [Steele] got Proteus to work in a real product setting. It was very poor quality, a very bad interface. But it sort of worked. More importantly, it convinced the [NCR] plant what [it] was possible to do. Proteus continued to be developed, and DesignAdvisor has evolved.

At the start of the collaboration, Petrie, Ballou, and Liuh made one trip to the Fort Collins facility and met with Steele's NCR colleagues who were involved in the Proteus application. However, as Petrie commented: "We just couldn't find the time or funding to make repeated trips to Colorado." Steele's trips between Fort Collins and Austin went on for 12 months. She liked working with Petrie, Ballou, and Liuh and believed in the value of what she was doing. She appreciated the management support she was getting at NCR and from MCC. But it was long, hard work, and the tedium and pressure got to Steele. During her visits to MCC, she would take breaks from staring into a computer screen by changing into her running clothes and jogging for several miles on the track that wound through the cedar trees that surrounded MCC's headquarters.

Initially, Petrie and his research team were leery of the time they spent with Steele. But gradually, they learned to respect her considerable dedication to the Proteus transfer. They also came to realize that Steele made valuable contributions to their research by orienting them to the VLSI applications of the Proteus technology. As Krall explained:

> After visiting with the researchers in Austin, [Steele would] take back a tape [to Fort Collins], spend some time getting it to work, do some data analysis, deal with the problems. . . . Come back with the tape a month later and say: "Hey, guys, this didn't work. . . . Fix this, please." And they [the MCC researchers] would learn from this feedback. (interview, July 27, 1990)

Thus, MCC researchers got timely, useful feedback on the functions they were building into Proteus. In total, Steele and her collaborators worked on the commercial application of Proteus for over two years. The back-and-forth exchange demanded a deep, long-term commitment from both NCR and MCC personnel and management. But by mid-1987, Proteus had been successfully trans-ferred to a market-strength product, DesignAdvisor, at NCR's Fort Collins facility.

BENEFITS FROM THE PROTEUS TRANSFER

In July 1987, MCC and NCR held a national press confer-ence at New York City's Hayden Planetarium. A laser light show featured entwined NCR and MCC logos. Presentations were made by Randall Davis, associate professor of information sciences, MIT; the Honorable Malcolm Baldrige, U.S. secretary of Commerce;[8] Grant Dove, chairman and chief executive officer–elect, MCC; Charles Exley, Jr., chairman and president, NCR Corporation; and James Van Tassel, vice president, NCR Corporation, and general manager, NCR Microelectronics Division. A videotape of DesignAdvisor was shown, and Steele was presented with an award by Exley, who stated, in an NCR news release:

> In 1982, NCR and nine other U.S.-based computer companies decided, like the famous television space travelers, to "boldly go where no one had gone before." Together, we created a consortium to meet some common challenges and to help contribute to sustaining American technological leadership. NCR is proud to be the first to bring a product to market based on MCC research.

Steele (interview, August 20, 1990) was surprised at the attention: "I really had no idea that the product and the synergism between MCC and NCR would be such a hot topic. . . . It really did more for my career than I ever expected." As Ed Krall (interview, July 27, 1990) said admiringly: "She's gained a reputation at NCR as someone that knows all about AI."

For over two years, Steele had been the only dedicated NCR employee working on the Proteus to DesignAdvisor transfer. However, it was not entirely a one-woman show. At least nine other NCR and MCC employees were directly involved in the successful transfer of Proteus. Personal chemistry was the key to maintaining the cooperative support of MCC's and NCR's research teams. Steele was a bridge for the transfer. She benefited from crucial administrative and technical backup from the Fort Collins Microelectronics Division, the support of NCR managers like Tang and Ellsworth, as well as the blessing of NCR's CEO Exley. Organizational incentives at both MCC and NCR sustained the Proteus transfer over time. MCC benefited from the public relations value of the transfer. Unlike other MCC technologies that had previously been transferred in secret, the Proteus transfer to a commercial product was an event that went public in a big way.

This case of successful technology transfer exemplifies the importance of collaboration across hierarchical levels and organizational boundaries by scientists and managers at both NCR and MCC. But without Steele's determination, the transfer would not have happened. The Proteus to DesignAdvisor transfer process is an example of "technology pull" by an aggressive, competent champion who was supported by her company's divisional and corporate superiors, combined with "technology push" by researchers who saw value in the early application of their research results. Steele took MCC's technology and made it her own, while involving both MCC and NCR personnel. The parallel development of Proteus and DesignAdvisor meant that Steele's NCR colleagues could obtain quick answers to their questions about using Proteus in specific VLSI applications. MCC researchers benefited from receiving valuable application feedback from a member company. It was a win-win situation for both technology producers and users.

To what extent did NCR benefit from the transfer? In 1987, DesignAdvisor was considered an important technological advancement. The product was on the leading edge of computer software for semiconductor design. As of 1990, no other vendor had yet developed a comparable product. However, DesignAdvisor was never a "barn burner" for NCR in terms of market share or profits. So was MCC's Proteus research and the transfer to DesignAdvisor considered a success by NCR? As Steele (interview, August 20, 1990) said:

> We don't really sell software as a business. We sell integrated circuits; that's our business. We had never really intended to sell [DesignAdvisor] as a software package. Development decided somewhere down the line that we would sell it if people wanted it. Software sales is a small part of what we consider ROI. The real return was to help our customers be smarter and have cheaper development for their integrated circuits and to produce higher-yielding parts, which helps us in manufacturing and also helps them get higher-quality integrated circuits and reduces our cost and time in the process. DesignAdvisor has been a success, even though I think we are phasing out our software sales of the product. We'll strictly use it as an assist to our customers.

In 1989, Charles Petrie corresponded with his MCC colleagues over E-mail concerning his assessment of the Proteus research project:

> Proteus failed because it should have succeeded so much better. It had a non-novel, useful basis, and its novel elements weren't revolutionary. But the number

of applications were small and most shareholders didn't pick it up at all. . . . In the first three years, when we were pushing Proteus hard, we got only two active collaborators: Honeywell and NCR. Kodak was secretive (and combative) and DEC, CDC, Sperry, and Harris were no-ops. There was some indication that CDC and Sperry might have done something if we had pursued them more. . . . The most successful application [NCR] was tremendously expensive, both for us and the shareholder. . . . And if Proteus was so difficult to transfer, what of more novel technology? What went wrong?

With Proteus, we did visit the shareholders, have many meetings, and produce MCC-supported software. We gave training sessions and identified shareholder contacts. We even put internal contact names and phone numbers on software releases. . . . We did not prospect for opportunities. We did a relatively poor job of showing the applicability of Proteus to business applications.

But there are structural barriers within the shareholders that we could overcome only by luck and great effort a very few times. In general, we could not talk to the people that we should have, or talk to all of the people we knew, often enough. (E-mail, July 18, 1989)

Petrie and his group transferred five versions of Proteus. Each version had multiple and new technologies. Versions 1.0, 1.5, and 2.0 were not standard technology packages (STPs). But 1.0 and 2.0 were used commercially by Honeywell; 1.0 was licensed by CAD participants; and 1.5 was used by NCR. Versions 2 (released in May 1987) and 3.0 (released in February 1989) were STPs. However, little commercial value came from these supported versions (Petrie, E-mail, January 17, 1990). And as Petrie commented later in 1990:

Yes, collaboration is the way and yes there have been successes. . . . We did the collaborator model with NCR in 1985-1987. There have been other ACT "successes." Successes like that will kill us . . . such collaborations are tremendously expensive and unlikely. It also tends to make the shareholders expect us to produce products. It's not that we've done a bad job of pushing. It's that there is no corresponding pull and the pushing is so difficult. How do you search inside these large companies for a good collaborator? Pretty hard. How far does the technology spread from the initial collaboration? Not far. What a waste. (E-mail, August 13, 1990)

The Proteus case leads to such questions as: Why is technology transfer so difficult? What special challenges to technology transfer arise when the R&D function is filled by an organization that is at arm's length at a central R&D lab like MCC?

TECHNOLOGY TRANSFER AT MCC

Over the years, MCC has tried a variety of technology transfer strategies, which are discussed in this chapter (Table 5.1). No one method has been completely effective and in varying degrees most are still being used. One that has been pretty well discarded is the standard technology package.

THE STANDARD TECHNOLOGY PACKAGE

The standard technology package (STP) was a way for MCC to emphasize the fairness issue or equal access to its technology as well as to "start the clock" for determining the three-year period in which the funders of the research had proprietary rights. MCC would announce a technology release date and the shareholder companies that funded the research would be invited to MCC to receive the "package." MCC soon found that effective technology transfer was more of an on-going process. And to have an effective transfer the technology had to be tailored to the needs of individual company receptors or technology users. Furthermore, establishing meaningful release dates was problematic for technology (such as software packages) that has a sequence of upgrades over time. The shareholder receptors were as anxious to get early releases as MCC's researchers were reluctant to give up their still developing technology. As Inman commented (interview, July 21, 1987): "If you wait to transfer the technology until after the researchers are finished with it, you'll have a long wait."

There were several other difficult-to-resolve problems with the STP transfer method. An initial concern was deciding what kind of personnel was needed for the transfer mission. The question was raised whether it was a good use of MCC's resources and to use researchers' and technicians' valuable time on software documentation, transfer, and support. On the other hand, could anyone else do it? If a technician was talented enough to master the software code, MCC researchers wanted to use them in development. A related concern was determining the degree and length of support MCC should provide for the STPs. As one software researcher commented in 1987: "With respect to degree, we need to establish a clear, uniform policy and seek shareholder understanding and agreement on it. Support is clearly more than having a bug fixed. . . . Shareholder support seems much more oriented toward conversion to delivery vehicles and application modeling." As Charles Petrie commented (E-mail, October 24, 1987):

> It is not at all clear to me that we can just end support after six months. We have a special relationship with our shareholders that requires us to continue to support our STPs [Standard Technology Packages] until the next version if there will be one. Such support should naturally tail off. But if we want our deliverables to be used by the shareholders, then we want to do everything we can to promote their use even after the legal obligation to support them has ended. In this sense, support is just another technology transfer issue. But we can't just dump on the shareholders and in many cases, six months is not even enough time for them to get started seriously.

Based on interview, archival, and survey data collected on MCC's first decade of operation (see Appendix A), we now discuss four key issues in achieving successful technology commercialization across organizational boundaries: (1) communication interactivity; (2) physical, cultural, and strategic proximity; (3) technology characteristics; and (4) interpersonal motivation.

Table 5.1
Progression of 17 types of technology transfer
at MCC, 1983–1993

Type 1: Shareholder Representatives

Shareholder companies were to assign high-quality researchers to MCC for a period of two to three years. These shareholder representatives were to transfer MCC-produced technology back to their home companies.

Type 2: The Standard Technology Package

MCC management sought to transfer technology as a "standard technology package" to all research participants at the same time. The technology release date also started the clock for the three-year time period after which MCC could license the technology to nonshareholder companies.

Type 3: Quarterly Meetings

Quarterly meetings were scheduled for shareholder managers and technology specialists to visit MCC and look at work in progress.

Type 4: Written Documentation

Thousands of professionally produced technical and research reports were sent to shareholder companies.

Type 5: Shareholder Visits

MCC arranged shareholder visits to the consortium in order to transfer technologies as they were being developed.

Type 6: Multimedia

MCC made short videotapes in which MCC researchers talked about their research results.

Type 7: Company Days

MCC instituted "company days" when individuals from a single company visited MCC to get acquainted with work under way in the consortium's research laboratories.

Type 8: Videoconferencing

MCC experimented with transferring technology by one-way video teleconferences with audio feedback from the teleconferencing sites.

Type 9: Research Collaboration

MCC emphasized research activities involving collaboration between MCC and shareholder researchers on site at the consortium. Participants were encouraged to begin these project collaborations as early as possible in the research process.

Table 5.1 continued

Type 10: Unbundling

MCC opened up and unbundled its research programs to decrease the cost of company buy-in and to emphasize company-specific technology deliverables on the way to long-term research objectives.

Type 11: Membership Workshops

Membership workshops were instituted that included shareholder and associate MCC companies.

Type 12: Third-Party Licensing and Vendors

MCC actively pursued third-party licensing and vendor-company participation as a means of technology commercialization.

Type 13: Technology Transfer Plans

MCC emphasized technology transfer plans with start and stop dates, business impact assessments, and project management.

Type 14: Spin-Out Companies

MCC began to allow, and then encouraged, spin-out technologies and start-up companies.

Type 15: Vertical and Horizontal Integration

MCC saw value in having wide member (shareholder and associate) diversity to allow for vertical (e.g., vendors) and horizontal (e.g., customers) integration to facilitate technology commercialization.

Type 16: Distributed Research

MCC began to de-emphasize the agglomeration of research talent at its Austin-based headquarters in favor of being a project manager of distributed research activities and searching for technologies to spin into the consortium.

Type 17: PartnerMart

MCC initiated PartnerMart, where member companies, universities, government agencies, and national laboratories exhibited their technology to the consortium's member companies and others.

COMMUNICATION INTERACTIVITY

"Communication interactivity" refers to the richness of exchange between technology transceivers—i.e., developers and users. Interactivity ranges on a continuum from (1) passive, one-way media-based linkage such as technical reports, videotapes, and computer tapes to (2) more interactive face-to-face linkages such as on-site research demonstrations and collaborative research projects. MCC has initiated a range of passive to interactive communication linkages between technology developers and users (Table 5.2).

Table 5.2
Passive and interactive technology transfer mechanisms at MCC

I.   Passive technology transfer
   1. Technical reports, proprietary and nonproprietary
   2. Refereed journal articles
   3. Newsletters
   4. Videotaped overviews/demonstrations
   5. Technical videotapes
   6. Computer tapes

II. Electronic-based technology transfer
   1. Videoconferencing
   2. E-mail consulting

III. Face-to-face technology transfer
   1. MCC/shareholder meetings
      • Technical advisory board (TAB)
      • Program technical advisory board (PTAB)
      • Technology advisory council (TAC)
   2. Shareholder committees/panels
      • Program advisory committees (PACs)
      • Technical requirements panels
      • Manufacturability panels
      • Quality assurance panels
   3. Shareholder assignees/representatives
   4. Visitor programs
   5. Shareholder-site demonstrations
   6. Receptor organizations within shareholders' companies
   7. Shadow research projects within shareholders' companies
   8. Shareholder/MCC collaboration

Initially, MCC emphasized passive modes of communication with its member companies through technical reports and videotapes. Such passive communication demands less time and expense than more interactive modes of communication. Researchers can stay "at home" while transferring technologies to potential users. A large number of individual and organizational receptors can be reached at comparatively little cost. Electronically mediated linkages such as E-mail and videoconferencing can increase interactivity between technology developers and users. All of these forms of communication linkage diminish personal and professional risk for the technology developers, as it can be a challenging experience to go into the field to "sell" one's research. On the other hand, for MCC researchers such passive communication usually did not elicit needed feedback or "technology buy-in" from potential technology users.[9]

A survey of MCC and shareholder scientists and managers documented that the more active and earlier the communication linkages between technology developers and users, the more effective they were in transferring technologies (Figure 5.4).[10] (Please refer to Appendix A for an overview of the survey methodology.) Meetings were most effective when held at the shareholder location rather than at MCC. Technical reports, newsletters, and refereed journal articles (level I) were the least effective means of technology transfer.[11]

As Petrie commented (E-mail, July 18, 1989):

> Our shareholder companies are large. Only a relatively small number of people in them are going to be able to exploit any particular thing we do. We need to find those people. The main tools we have used to do that are sending out tech reports and hosting in-depth reviews at MCC. These methods are clearly inadequate. We have a lot of evidence than in many companies the tech reports and code releases don't go very far past the official receptor who may act passively as a librarian rather than actively as a technology promoter. Even if they get spread around, people don't have time to read them. In-depths don't attract enough people; companies can't afford to send more than a handful of people to any one meeting. We need to expose many more people to our work in order to locate the few who will pick it up.

But there is something else that the shareholders have to do. We simply cannot find all the right people by ourselves. The organizations are large. They change often. They are unwilling to say a lot about themselves to outsiders. We are too far away. In order to make this process work, each shareholder must have some people (I don't know how many) whose job is to find contacts and match up MCC technologies with receptors. These people's performance appraisal should depend on how many successful transfers occur.

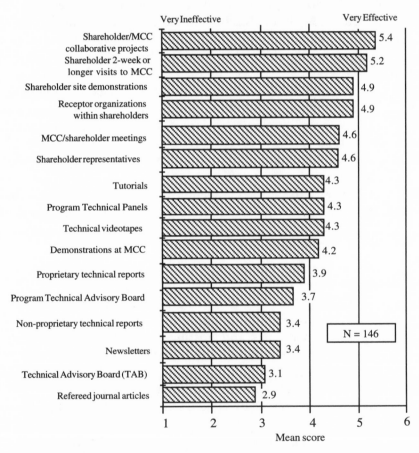

Source: Smilor and Gibson, 1991.

Figure 5.4 Relative effectiveness of technology transfer methods, based on a 1989 survey of MCC and shareholder-company employees

MCC's program technical advisory boards and program technical panels represented formal, structured meetings to facilitate technology transfer between MCC and its member companies. At these meetings, MCC researchers gave formal presentations, tutorials, and demonstrations. However, the *right* information was often not given to the *right* member-company recipient at the *right* time for successful technology transfer to occur. Some member companies did not even send a representative to these technology briefings. As one MCC researcher commented: "This show-and-tell approach failed to gain any real buy-in by those who were to use the technology."[12]

The investment of time and resources increased dramatically as MCC moved from passive to more interactive modes of technology transfer (Figure 5.5). But the evidence was overwhelming that the commercialization of MCC-produced technology required the more interactive forms of communication. However, before such interactive collaborations could occur, the most appropriate technology receptors/users needed to be located.

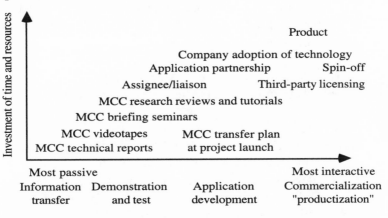

Source: MCC.

Figure 5.5 Passive to interactive modes of technology transfer and the investment of time and resources by developers and users

In 1990, MCC began a newsletter called *The Collaborator,* in an effort to keep MCC and shareholder personnel informed about the consortium's projects, to demonstrate and discuss successful applications of MCC-developed technologies to real-world problems, and to focus on successful collaboration and technology transfer processes in order to determine what worked and what failed. *The Collaborator* featured case histories of shareholder and MCC researchers who were involved with technology transfer. Recognizing the sensitivity of the subject matter, the newsletter was designed to be an in-house document with distribution limited to MCC member companies and employees. As one shareholder representative responded to the announcement of the first issue of *The Collaborator:*

> Although I am almost over run with newsletters, I think *The Collaborator* has a very promising future. I would like to read about how other shareholders overcome the technology transfer barrier. In other words, how do people in my position convince others to become involved with MCC and bring projects into their groups? How do we get middle management to commit to trying the technology from MCC? I have had one very successful transfer since I have been with STP and it was the result of pure luck and persistence more than any specific methodology.

As Craig Fields (interview, March 1, 1991) moved MCC toward more distributed R&D, he was concerned about linking people:

> One of the things we [MCC] are exploring at the moment is a teleconferencing system that links the technology development staffs at the companies with those at MCC. Remember, this is a cooperation among companies; this is not a star network to MCC. I'm trying to get a little different spirit going. It's slowly happening. I don't want to claim any great revolution overnight, but at least the derivation is in the right direction.

In selected cases, passive and active channels of technology transfer have proved to be complementary at MCC. The more passive methods help target appropriate technology receptors by conveying a great deal of information in an inexpensive manner to many receptors at the same time. More active, face-to-face modes of transfer are then employed with the most promising receptor sites, as exemplified by the Proteus case.

COMPUTER-MEDIATED TECHNOLOGY TRANSFER

By 1986, a relatively small, loosely connected and informal group of MCC researchers/managers had been formed by those most knowledgeable and concerned about the consortium's challenges of technology transfer.[13] Members of this group became more formalized as MCC's Technology Transfer Committee in early 1990. Over the years, these individuals thought long and hard about useful ideas for promoting effective technology transfer at MCC and at the shareholder companies. As early as 1987, they discussed such fundamental issues as: What is the unique worth of MCC to its shareholders? Can we do long-range research? How market relevant does our research have to be, and how do we determine that? Or, they would seek to determine the areas they should focus resources on to narrow the time delay between R&D and productization.

One proposal that received some sustained support from these technology transfer activists was E-mail consulting, or an E-mail hot line, with the shareholder companies. As summarized by Petrie (E-mail, May 25, 1990):

> People in the shareholder companies would be given an E-mail address to which they could send questions. The questions should be about anything that we would conceivably know. Examples might be: "What's a free picture drawing utility for Suns?" or "How do I make the ORION FEP files larger?"
>
> The point of this exercise is to increase our visibility within the shareholders and to increase our chances of discovering potential collaborators. One of our main problems is that many folks inside the shareholder companies don't even know we exist and, similarly, we don't know where to prospect because the companies are so large. This is a way of doing passive prospecting by increasing our contacts within the shareholders.
>
> Every question should receive an answer, even if it's: "We don't know." So probably, there should be a

single contact point here at MCC who then farms out the questions and monitors whether an answer is forthcoming. There could even be secondary contacts in each program, and tertiary ones in each project. But one person should monitor responses at the top.

Another researcher commented that such an E-mail system would facilitate the keeping of good records and let the shareholders know how much they are using the service. It was also mentioned that some shareholders would probably want to channel all questions through a central point of contact so that they could retain some control of the process.

Meg Wilson responded (E-mail, May 25, 1990):

Charles, it is a good idea. Do you realize what good communications we have with our associates because there is one point of contact (Susie)! They call us with questions, for advice, for appointments, for information. If we haven't heard from them for a while, we call and say, "What's up, can we do anything for you?" There is no real equivalent single contact for shareholders.

Sandy Dochen, Director of Communications, 1988–1990, a period during which Bill Stotesbery worked for Admiral Inman at Westmark, commented (E-mail, May 29, 1990):

Charles, we've been talking about your shareholder contact person all day. It's a good idea. . . . Interestingly, it's a function we already do on an ad hoc basis. For instance, just today, Jon Paul received a call from a Rockwell person in AUSTRALIA wondering about something with gIBIS. Here's the rub/problem . . . it took Jon Paul 10 minutes just to track someone down in STP to talk to the guy. We frequently get calls that could be marketing leads or general inquiries that depend upon us routing correctly and rapidly. However, with our present staffing levels, I don't think Cynthia's [Communication Coordinator] or anyone else's sanity would survive if the whole MCC world were encouraged to call her for specific information or routing. So, I wouldn't want to implement this tomorrow. Maybe if the programs chipped in to create a corporate clearinghouse position/shareholder relations person, we could do this. Until then, ad hoc is probably the best (but not really the most adequate) way.

Petrie responded (E-mail, May 30, 1990):

Sandy, there are some important differences between what happened and what I proposed.
1. I proposed E-mail rather than phone calls. Response time would be measured in days, not minutes.
2. I proposed a hierarchy of contacts. Given that it was an STP inquiry, Cynthia would simply forward the E-mail inquiry to the STP contact, say Jim Babcock. Jim, recognizing the inquiry, would forward it to the gIBIS contact, perhaps Jeff Conklin. Cynthia's role would be to log the inquiry and ensure that some sort of dialogue ensued within a few days. These two points attempt to show that it can be done now, better than ad hoc. Phone calls should be handled as they are now, although the E-mail technical inquiry system would help that too.

Jim Babcock (technology transfer coordinator for STP) stated that he liked the idea of an E-mail hot line. Indeed, he was named the STP contact switchboard operator for such a service. However he had one question (Babcock, E-mail, June 1, 1990):

How do we handle the problem that only 50 percent of the shareholders have external gateways to any net? As you know STP has a "LEOnet" facility whereby we send "netnews" newsgroups to some of the shareholders. . . . This service "dials up" each night to a shareholder gateway machine and dumps "news" in a specific file . . . then looks thru the shareholder MCC news file and "retrieves" technical topics . . . .

BUT . . . DEC won't let us "dial-in," and Motorola
has a strict policy on not letting external companies
access their net. . . . At Rockwell we have a bootleg-type
connection whereby a manual intervention is required
to take our info and then forward it. . . . LEOnet works
well at Bellcore, CDC, and NCR.

EGS is a very weak solution we think, since that
requires a shareholder to buy a modem, and dial into a
long-distance number for access. . . . Other consortia
who have this service are displeased because the access
is not smoothly integrated into the user's environment.

MCC's management told Petrie that they could not assign the
resources to support the E-mail project. Undeterred, Petrie and a
group of volunteers decided to go ahead with an informal grassroots effort that lasted for about two years.

IDENTIFYING TECHNOLOGY RECEPTORS

In reference to moving from level I to level II technology
transfer (see Figure 5.2), MCC researchers and managers emphasized the difficulty of locating appropriate shareholder recipients for
a particular technology and obtaining meaningful feedback from
these receptors (Figure 5.6). They called it the "black hole" phenomenon: when technical reports, videotapes, and computer tapes
were "transferred" and subsequently lost in the member company's
broad and deep bureaucracy without the MCC scientists' knowing
who, if anybody, received the message. As a result, MCC scientists
did not get the feedback they needed to monitor the technology
transfer process and validate their research activities.

During the 1980s, MCC's shareholder community included
roughly 1.5 million people in 22 companies with divisions located
worldwide. Combined sales were around $200 billion per year. In
the 1990s, this diversity has been augmented by over 50 associate
members and increasing university and federal government participation. This tremendous range of possible technology receptors—
and potential technology producers—makes it extremely challenging
for MCC researchers to locate the appropriate users, or developers,
for any given technology. "In spite of all our efforts," commented

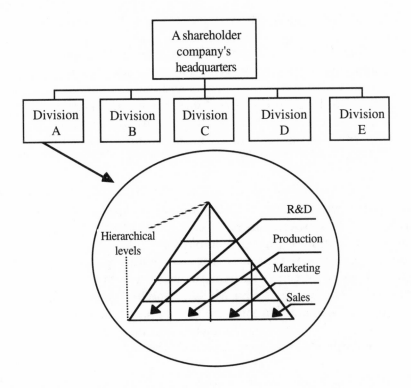

Figure 5.6 Potential division-based receptors for MCC-developed technologies

Laszlo Belady (1992, p. 14), research program director for STP, "we could not build a bridge to our real customers; we could not even find them in the maze of the large organizational bureaucracies of our participants." As an MCC researcher stated:

> It's extremely difficult to locate a [technology] receptor because it [the member company] is just so huge. DEC has 50,000 employees. How do you go about finding the person who might be interested in a particular technology? They'll send 5 representatives to a meeting. You may miss an organization completely that would be just the perfect place to transfer a technology.

And Petrie commented:

> I just came back from Bellcore, and in addition to
> applying my own research to one of their problems, I
> talked with some other people and had fun working on
> their problems too. It struck me that we are starved for
> problems down here. We don't know who to talk to
> in the companies and they don't know we're here.
> (E-mail, May 2, 1990)

MCC researchers also soon realized that even if a supportive
champion were located at a shareholder company, there was the
problem of a "movable target." The concept of technology champions at MCC and receptor sites implied an individual and organizational commitment that was often difficult to sustain over the
required period of time—perhaps two to three years for technology
transfer to take place. As an MCC researcher noted: "As soon as
someone is located and a 'pipeline' is set up, the person gets moved.
You'd like to think that the contact would be there for a few years
and would talk to—you know, train—his replacement."

Personnel assignments and individual career decisions in
shareholder companies usually took precedence over maintaining a
particular technology transfer relationship. Furthermore, even if an
MCC research team was fortunate enough to locate a committed
technology champion, and even if the key individuals involved did
not depart during the period of the transfer process, MCC
researchers often had a rude awakening, perhaps a year into the
transfer process, when they discovered that the targeted champion
lacked the political, resource, or prestige clout needed to get the
MCC-developed technology implemented in the shareholder organization. As Werner commented (interview, May 4, 1993):

> When Grant Dove took over the reigns of the CAD
> program in 1988, he immediately said that we would
> not continue any programs that did not have *champi-
> ons*—shareholder people who were committed to *using*
> the deliverables from the research. So at every CAD
> PTAB after that, we showed a list of champions
> "attached" to each of the ongoing projects.

Unfortunately, after a while that list included mostly CAD developers in the companies who would not be the ultimate users of the tools. . . . Because in many cases MCC did not have a direct line to champions, MCC's researchers were responsible for both defining the problem and devising the solution—in some cases that scenario led to "solutions in search of problems." The individuals installed by member companies as research advisers to consortia often are not qualified to speak for their corporation as a whole, and they may create the mistaken impression that a given research effort is in line with their parent company's needs.

In 1989, Petrie sent an E-mail message to Jim Babcock as they and others prepared a strawman board proposal on technology transfer:

Jim, I want to get together with you [face to face] for greater bandwidth, but one quick public remark on your comment that they [the shareholder technology receptors] do perform a service for us to navigate within a corporation as we look for collaborators.

I just want to say briefly how bad it's been. The ACT receptors generally have been worse than passive. In most cases, the receptors pretended to be prospecting for us, but we discovered that, for various reasons, they were actually sitting on the technology, and not only not prospecting or even notifying others about reports and tapes, but they were actually restricting dissemination, even when it was specifically requested by other divisions.

The receptors have not even been good starting places for active searches. In the case of DEC, for instance, we were specifically instructed not to make contact *except* through the receptor who consistently failed to provide contacts upon request. (Only catastrophic failure has forced revision of this policy.) Other receptors were not this extreme, but were of negligible help in finding collaborators. I continue to think that one way of preventing this horrible state of affairs is to ask the shareholders to measure (somehow) the performance of the receptor based upon "success" of technology transfer. (E-mail, November 27)

Expanding on MCC's difficulty with shareholder technology receptors, Petrie sent the following E-mail message to Jerry Werner on April 19, 1990:

Here's another anecdote for your proposed book. There are several stories I know of where shareholders made it very difficult for MCC technology to be transferred. But I just found out about this one and I think it's the most extreme example.

One Kodak division heard about Proteus and requested it from the official Kodak/MCC contact. It took them six months to get a tape. And then the contact insisted that the tape be only a loan. Not only had it to be returned, but the contact insisted that the disks be wiped. This, I think, could be classified as technology suppression.

In 1991, Petrie again commented on the issue of centralized technology receptors in the shareholder companies (E-mail, April 16):

One common lesson bears repeating. Only through grassroots collaborations do the shareholders "get" anything. All of our suggestions about how the shareholders and we ought to do things differently have to do with opening up the bandwidth between MCC researchers and shareholder engineers.

Highly interactive linkages, while beneficial to technology transfer, also led to communication overload for MCC scientists interacting with numerous clients. Werner (1993) emphasized MCC's "wide-bandwidth" approach to communication created too many to-dos for the consortium's management without a mechanism to prioritize issues. Beginning in 1988, CAD communication channels focused on strategic direction, near-term technical direction, and feedback on research deliverables. Technical panels were established for each of the five CAD research areas and met every six to ten weeks, essentially replacing the large quarterly PTAB meetings of the past.

> The primary benefit of the new communication approach was to reduce the collective to-do list for CAD program management. However, it put a much higher burden on shareholder receptors and shareholder internal managers to market MCC technology and to foster technology adoption. (Werner, 1993, p. 13)

Communication overload has become more pronounced at MCC as project managers have become responsible for a range of industrial- and market-strength research projects in a range of member companies, as opposed to the days when pre-competitive research could potentially meet the expectations of a range of funding companies, and each company had the responsibility of using the technology in its own unique way. As MCC's projects move closer to product applications, shareholder users increasingly look to MCC for direct access to the consortium's laboratories and researchers/technicians to obtain basic technical assistance.

TECHNOLOGY TRANSFER THROUGH PEOPLE

From its inception in 1982, MCC supported the view that technology transfer was a "contact sport," that people were the best means of transferring technology. Over the years, one of the most highly interactive and institutionalized methods of technology transfer between MCC and its shareholder companies has been the shareholder liaison/representative who was expected to carry MCC know-how back to his or her company.

At the December 4, 1982, MCC board of directors meeting in Denver, when Inman inquired as to how MCC was going to transfer its technologies to the member companies, he was told (interview, July 21, 1987): "You shouldn't worry about that at all. We will send our research people to the consortium, and when a piece of research is done, our people will come back to their home companies and bring the technology with them." This simplification worried Inman a great deal. As he recollected: "From my previous experience with the National Security Agency, I had learned that you had to have an effort to both *push* the technology out from the laboratory and to *pull* the technology from the outside. . . . Creating the technology is easier than getting it used." (Inman interview, July 21, 1987)

During MCC's formative years, shareholder liaisons were assigned for a two- to three-year period to a particular research program at the consortium. These liaisons were expected to participate in MCC research activities and gain an in-depth knowledge of the available technologies. They were also expected to make periodic trips back to—and ultimately/permanently return to—their home company in order to transfer technology. MCC's conception of shareholder liaisons (later to be called shareholder representatives) as the premier means of technology transfer to the member companies has not worked out as planned. Why not?

First (as noted in Chapter 4), MCC did not have the expected number of quality shareholder representatives assigned to the consortium by the member companies. Being assigned to MCC for two to three years was generally not viewed as an attractive career option for a fast-track company technician or researcher. Furthermore, shareholder companies were reluctant to give up their best researchers for a tour at MCC. As a result, shareholder representatives in residence at MCC were often not the most visible and respected company researchers, nor were they the most appropriate receptors for MCC-developed technologies. While MCC exercised control over the researchers it hired, the consortium had little control over a company's selection of shareholder representatives assigned to a research program. As Inman commented in 1992 (interview, October 22), these shareholder representatives frequently (1) knew little about their home company's technology priorities and product development, (2) were unable to contribute to MCC's research, and (3) had little clout in their home company.

As one MCC researcher stated:

> Shareholder companies often do not send the best possible technology receptor [one who has the needed technical knowledge and shareholder power and contacts] to the consortium. Consequently, MCC scientists often wound up spending a lot of time and effort talking with

the wrong shareholder representative about the wrong technologies.

However, as another researcher commented:

This is a cop-out. Blaming liaisons is too narrow a perspective. All of the shareholder people, from the board members on down, needed to help the process.

Some shareholder representatives were hired by the member company for the specific purpose of assigning them to MCC. These new hires lacked any broad and deep understanding of the shareholders' technology needs. Usually, they were evaluated by the shareholder firm on how well they transferred technology/knowledge from MCC to the company. There was less concern with making the transfer a two-way process. Two-way transfer was also intentionally inhibited out of antitrust and secrecy concerns. Antitrust concerns involved the perception of MCC getting too involved in product development with specific shareholder companies.

Secrecy issues concerned proprietary knowledge and competitive advantage for the home company. For example, say that a shareholder representative transferred an MCC technology to his or her home company. The concern was that if that company's research experiences were communicated back to MCC's staff by the representative, other companies might gain valuable information or otherwise benefit from these technological advances. In effect, companies not contributing to the research effort could become "free riders" on the research activities of other companies. Such concerns about protecting proprietary knowledge began to lessen in 1986. In our decade-long study of MCC, we found little meaningful scanning of competitors' technologies for competitive advantage. In fact, the situation described in the Proteus case was the more common scenario: shareholder companies that participated most actively in MCC's research projects benefited the most from the technological advances. As Inman observed: "What you get out of a consortium depends on how much you put into it. . . . Some members have gotten a great deal out of MCC. The remainder were waiting for packages tied with ribbons and were disappointed." (quoted in Rifkind, 1990)

Many of the shareholder representatives sent to MCC were volunteers who, for a variety of reasons, wanted a change of pace from their current career options. At MCC, they found facilities, funding, autonomy, and research opportunities that were generally far superior to those they could obtain at their home company. As one long-time MCC researcher in the Advanced Computing Technology Program said: "The result was the creation of a research environment unparalleled . . . offering wonderful facilities and support, as well as access to the technical resources and facilities of some of the country's leading computer corporations."

Shareholder representatives often "went native," preferring to remain at MCC rather than return to their home company. As one such individual stated:

> Well, I have definite plans to go back, but I would like to stay here as long as possible because it is an exciting environment and it's challenging. The exposure is tremendous—I get to see what other companies are doing and get insights that you can't get if you are just inside one company. . . . It's just a very enjoyable and exciting experience.

Another reason why shareholder representatives did not want to return to their home company was that a shift in job focus was usually required. On their return, the representatives often were not seen as an important resource or as an important link to MCC. Contrary to the stated plan, their technology-learning experiences at MCC were not generally valued or transferred to the companies funding the research. Rather, the researchers were assigned to rather mundane positions, or they had to search on their own for an available position somewhere in their home company.

From MCC's perspective, the relocation of a shareholder representative back to his or her home company meant that a research project would lose a trained researcher, often at a time that was inappropriate for the ongoing research. Furthermore, MCC's budget and head count would be decreased unless a replacement was sent. Typically, months would be required to bring a replacement up to speed in the project. As an MCC researcher said: "That is one of the problems that I believe we are just going to have to live with."

On the other hand, over the years, some very capable share-holder representatives have been assigned to MCC, and they have transferred technologies back to their home companies. But even the most capable representative found it a challenge both to be knowledgeable about MCC's wide range of technologies and to keep abreast of his or her own company's vast research activities that might benefit from such MCC-produced technologies. As an MCC scientist stated in 1988:

> No one is competent enough to understand all of the technologies here anyway. If you sent one guy [to MCC] who was supposed to be your "understander," he'd be a bottleneck. The understanding of the technology has to be accomplished by many people coming here.

Finally, the shareholder representative approach to technology transfer emphasized the importance of the MCC technology-based contacts and de-emphasized the importance of the representative's maintaining strong, ongoing personal contacts with key employees in the shareholder company. MCC soon realized that the longer a shareholder representative stayed in Austin, the more out of contact the representative became with personal networks back in his or her home company. Such contacts were seen to be crucial to speeding the transfer of technology, especially to level IV product commercialization. As an MCC shareholder representative told us in 1988:

> The original philosophy was that what the company needed was someone [a liaison] here [at MCC] who understands the technology and gets it back to the shareholders. That is what I came here for. It wasn't long before I personally, and the rest of MCC, learned that this was not the model that you need. You don't have to be here long before you lose all your contacts, the favors that were owed you, and everything else you had back at your company. Although you are still an employee [of the company], it's not the same. I think a model where you have a champion back there in resi-

dence that spends a considerable amount of time here [at MCC] is a much better model. He continues to maintain his [shareholder] contacts.

In a 1990 communication to Craig Fields, researcher Jeff Conklin stated (E-mail, August 9):

I came to MCC in February of 1984 as RCA's liaison to STP. For nearly four years, I worked to prepare RCA for the stream of technology that STP produced. RCA finally agreed to have a "receptor person" (someone at the Advanced Technology lab who accumulated tech reports and attended PTAB meetings) and to allocate $10K per year for that function. When GE bought RCA they naturally asked, "What have we to show for our MCC investment to date?" And of course the answer was, "some technical reports and software, but no new business areas or even usable tools." The rest is history (I became an MCC direct hire at that point).

Jim Babcock responded to Conklin's E-mail message (August 13, 1990):

Jeff is blind to the past two to two and a half years of technology improvement at [MCC]. The collaborative research model at STP (and growing in ACT and CAD and always true with P/I) has begun to pay off as a technology transfer lever for gaining success. . . . There are 45 serious application, problem-solving-oriented collaborations underway at Bellcore, Motorola, NCR, and Rockwell today. Each is a real problem, a real solution with real shareholder technical people. . . . The violent disagreement I have with Jeff is that he bases his lack of success argument solely on ancient history . . . [1984 through 1986] . . . when there wasn't anything to transfer. Now we have many technologies in various stages of maturity . . . collaborative research began to pay off just this year . . . real breakthroughs are possible.

MCC's experience with shareholder liaisons/representatives shows that while knowledge of a technology is important to successful technology transfer, maintaining personal contacts in the receptor company is perhaps more important. The technology transfer process is as much or more "transfer" than it is "technology." The concept of a "reverse liaison" emerged in the late 1980s at MCC. Under this scenario, which has not been strongly implemented, an MCC employee would spend about half of his or her time in the divisions of the shareholder company in order to maintain important personal contacts at the user end of the technology transfer process.

Fields stated in 1991 (interview, March 1):

So I want more assignees, but I also want reverse assignees. I want MCC staff to physically spend three, six, nine months in the member companies. Now for each of our 34 projects, we have one project manager, and they are really racking up the airline miles trying to keep up, but we vowed that they have to be close to the members.[14]

As Admiral Inman recollected (interview, October 22, 1992):

There has to be a climate that encourages communication. That's the really critical ingredient. I'm not sure that a formalized climate will always work because it may become so stultified that it isn't open to new ideas or people. It's also possible that if you create a formalized communication role for technology transfer, you may get a lot of trivia. People may feel the need to fill the pipeline every week with something new. So my own inclination is to make sure you've got the right climate created but not try to force a rigid schedule when dealing with research. Again, you just don't know when a breakthrough will come.

In our 1984 survey, MCC and shareholder researchers and management emphasized the importance of person-to-person contacts, shareholder pull, product champion at the shareholder com-

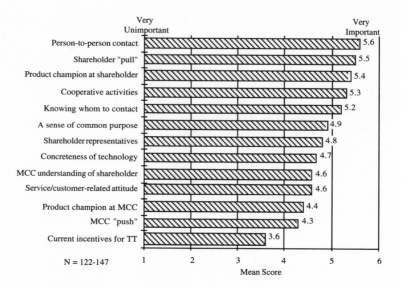

Source: Smilor and Gibson, 1991.

**Figure 5.7 Relative importance of factors facilitating
technology transfer, based on a 1989 survey of MCC and
shareholder-company employees**

pany, cooperative activities and knowing who to contact in facilitating successful technology transfer (Figure 5.7). Shareholder representatives were considered moderately effective. Attempting to push the technology out of MCC was reported to be least effective. Current incentives for technology transfer were not considered adequate at MCC or at the shareholder companies.

PHYSICAL, CULTURAL, AND STRATEGIC PROXIMITY

A relatively small physical distance between individuals (such as different floors of a building or different office locations on the same floor) can decrease the frequency of interpersonal communication, despite distance-canceling technologies such as computer-mediated networking.[15] The worldwide spread of MCC's member-company operations certainly exacerbates the problem of targeting appropriate recipients for MCC-developed technologies. The U.S. headquarters of MCC's shareholders are generally located at a maximum distance from the Austin consortium: in California, New York/New Jersey, St. Paul/Minneapolis, and elsewhere in the United States (as was shown in Figure 2.9). A travel-time analysis commissioned by Craig Fields indicated that the ideal location for MCC (based on this one criterion) was either New York or Washington. "That's the time center, not the geographic center," said Fields (interview, March 1, 1991). "Then there's a third- and fourth-best place, and so on. Austin isn't even in the top ten."[16]

As Fields stated (interview, March 1, 1991):

> I'm into teleconferencing and worknet, but in fact, our location turns out to be quite harmful. . . . Austin has two problems: it's far from supply and far from demand. Researchers would rather be in Boston or San Francisco. For demand, I'd like to be close to our customers. . . . I have to care about that . . . because I want to be close to the members or the talent, but being close to neither doesn't seem to me to be brilliant.

While physical distance exacerbates barriers to timely and efficient MCC–member-company technology transfer, MCC's technology transfer successes have not been correlated with a shareholder's physical proximity to the consortium's research activities in Austin. *Cultural proximity*—the degree of similarity between two individuals, groups, or organizations in their norms and values, especially with respect to technology application—is considered more important than physical distance in influencing successful technology transfer. MCC is staffed by scientists from a range of academic, government, and business institutions. Each of these researchers brought his or her particular research perspectives and styles of work to the Austin-based consortium. Cultural diversity within MCC has remained despite the conscious attempts early in the consortium's existence to build a common MCC culture (see Chapter 4).

MCC initially thought that shareholder researchers of comparable training and technical skill would be the most appropriate receptors for MCC-developed technologies (see Figure 5.6). Effective communication would be facilitated by knowledgeable experts talking with one another. However, such homophilious communication was hindered as MCC and shareholder scientists often competed for research funds and professional prestige.[17] A defensive "not invented here" (NIH) attitude was also a barrier to researcher-to-researcher technology transfer.[18]

As Werner noted:

> I talked to a shareholder receptor (and CAD PTAB) member from one of our shareholder companies after that company had opted out of the CAD program, and asked him: "What are the special problems you faced in heading up the receptor function within your company?" The answer: "It's a no-win situation from my point of view. If we receive CAD Program technology and it turns into a big win, MCC gets the credit. If the technology does not get used within my company, my group gets the blame because MCC has been very effective in marketing its progress to upper-level management." (interview, May 4, 1993)

Another problem with MCC researchers talking to researchers in the shareholder companies (i.e., homophilious communication linkages) was the time it took to get the information to production and marketing people within the firm. As Grant Dove observed (interview, August 15, 1990): "If you have to transfer the technology to a central lab and then to the product units, it's too late. It's all over with." Often MCC researchers were twice removed from the technology users within the shareholders' companies. First, they communicated with the shareholder representatives or MCC's technology transfer personnel who then communicated with technology support groups or researchers within the companies who then communicated with the technology users. There were often weak communication linkages between any two of these sequential groupings, which frustrated the timely transfer of technology. "In short," commented Werner (interview, June 15, 1993), "MCC technologists were dealing with people at the periphery for the shareholder organizations, not with the people who actually had the pain (i.e., problem)." If MCC researchers worked on near-term problems, they would be competing with commercial vendors. If they worked on developing leapfrog technology, they would leave their

customers (e.g., the shareholders) too far behind. The key was finding the right level of technology advancement.

Over the years, it has become increasingly apparent to MCC
that other, more heterophilious receptors (such as shareholder product development managers) may at times be the most appropriate
receptors for an MCC-produced technology. MCC's successful cases
of technology transfer often involved product development, production, and marketing personnel at the shareholder company who
pulled the technology out of MCC. However, such staff were rarely
assigned by the shareholder companies to the consortium,

In 1990, Werner was communicating by E-mail with
Babcock, Conklin, Petrie, and other members of MCC's ad hoc
technology transfer interest group. He was responding to early
drafts of Conklin's technology transfer report to Craig Fields.
Werner added two points to the emerging community of thought
(E-mail, August 14):

> Point 1: Our technology is not ending up in the hands
> of end-users. From my long experience [in the CAD
> Program], that statement is factually and tragically
> true. We deliver technology to CAD people in our par-
> ticipant companies, not end-users. The "receptors"
> who receive our technology ostensibly have the respon-
> sibility to spread the technology to the end-users, but
> don't for one or more of the following reasons:
>
> A. They are developing a competing technology.
> B. They get little credit (if they are successful in
>   spreading the technology, we, that is MCC, get
>   the lion's share of credit).
> C. They don't know how to spread technology. (In
>   the CAD case, the receptors are service-type peo-
>   ple who have "customers" come to them—these
>   receptors are not usually in the mode of market-
>   ing new technology.)
> D. They'd like to spread MCC technology, but don't
>   have the time or resources.
>
> Point 2: The end-users are not aware of MCC technolo-
> gy because that awareness has not spread very deeply

into our shareholder environments. This situation is caused by one or more of the following reasons:

    A. The TAB/PTAB people are not trumpeting MCC technology, either because

      1. They don't have time.

      2. They aren't that familiar with specific technology, and would be embarrassed to try to market it.

      3. They are not well plugged into the end-user community.

    B. We (MCC) aren't collectively doing a very good job of establishing wide-bandwidth communication channels to the participants.

    C. We haven't asked the end-users [about their technology needs], either because:

      1. We don't know who they are.

      2. The "receptors" (in the shareholder companies) say that is their business.

      3. Our technical people already think they know what end-user problems they will be solving, so they think asking the end-users is a waste of time.

    In a nutshell, I think that both points are the essence of our technology absorption problems in CAD, and I suspect that many of the issues generalize to other MCC programs as well. I suggest the following alternative to the way we do business to improve our technology "transfer" (that is, transit to shareholders and absorption by shareholders) effectiveness:

    1. Plug our discussions into the ultimate beneficiaries of our technology from the onset. Going through intermediaries (receptors) at the very beginning is a losing proposition. Only after we know what the end-user problems and possible technical solutions are, should we start to hold discussions with those within the shareholder companies who will be responsible for improving the absorption rate of MCC technology.

    2. Let the technology transfer plan (leading to technology utilization) be the joint responsibility of

MCC and the ultimate beneficiaries. We have responsibility for carrying out our part of the bargain; they have their responsibility. The TAB/PTABs should be partners in the process—high-level "facilitators" if you will. (As far as I'm concerned, the TAB/PTABs are nearly useless today—they love to come in and give advice, but they are very ineffective as facilitators.)

Charles Petrie added to the E-mail dialogue by stating (August 14, 1990):

The main point is that we need a broader bandwidth connection to the shareholders. That's one of the motivations for the E-mail consulting program.

I agree with all of Jerry's comments with the provision that the suggestions about shareholder discussions aren't enough. Finding the "right" people to talk to is one of the hardest problems in technology transfer.

I add to [Werner's] point 1: They (the central receptor) want the credit for the technology and so bottle it up under tight control and dribble it out.

I add to [Werner's] point 2: They don't know that MCC exists, much less that we have any technology to offer.

Yes, things are that bad.

Soon after receiving Petrie's E-mail, Jim Babcock logged onto his terminal since he felt compelled to tone down or qualify what was being said. Babcock did agree that the shareholder end-users were generally unaware of MCC technology, but he adamantly disagreed with the statement that central receptors in the shareholder companies tended to keep MCC-developed technology under tight control. "It just isn't so in many cases" (August 14, 1990).

So I would REALLY hate to see this recent traffic go to the very good and efficient Central Receptor Groups that do exist. . . . In STP's case it is Bellcore (the CTT group), Rockwell (the Info Sys Ctr in Seal Beach),

Motorola (SRD in Schaumberg, IL) and the "new" CDC group in Arden Hills (the DESIRE interface group). These groups move more technology PER DAY than most of us at MCC have ever moved. . . . Using such broad indicting-like remarks that ALL central groups are bad is not healthy dialogue.

The real culprit in all this is the appalling "passivity" of large U.S. corporations who talk out of four or five sides of their mouths at once . . . "give us long-term research, AND tools, AND on all the platforms we use, AND . . . just keep reducing our funding requirements and stop harping that we don't do technology transfer . . . that is someone else's job . . . and so on. . . .

MCC has had to contend with important strategic and cultural differences among its 22 shareholders and numerous associates as potential receptors of MCC-produced technology. In Chapter 2, we discussed the differences among MCC shareholders in terms of company size, the number and location of divisions and their preferred markets, internal R&D expenditures, percentage of company annual sales going to MCC, and the particular industry represented (Table 5.3). The diversity among MCC shareholders has exacerbated the challenges to achieving effective technology transfer.

On the other hand, MCC could be considered a consortium of consortia. At its best, it is a set of interlocking members. As Fields emphasized (interview, March 1, 1991):

The fact is that our members represent about a quarter trillion dollars a year in business, and they spend about eight percent of that on R&D. . . . That's a pretty hefty sum. . . . They employ about a hundred thousand scientists and engineers. That's a large talent pool. Their very highest leverage for getting results and reducing duplication is working with each other. So what I am encouraging is [to] let this happen. One of the things I am doing is giving contracts to MCC's member companies so what in fact happens is that they are working for each other. And that's happening more and more.

That variety I view as strength because we are in the strongest position in the world in terms of our members having a horizontal spread. I'm expanding that spread. You might think it would be nice to adopt a strategy to narrow it down a little to find more commonality. I think we're moving in the other direction, getting broader and including the end-user, the customers.

Andersen Consulting joined us, and I'm tickled pink because they are a great bridge to end-users. . . . Again, it goes back to what does it mean to be an industrial success in the nineties versus an industrial success in the seventies. The link to the customer, the marketing process, reducing the time to market, reducing capital investment, and high quality. That's what's written on the wall in the nineties more so than in the eighties, when the goal was a great new design for a supercomputer.

TECHNOLOGY CHARACTERISTICS

MCC's research programs cover the spectrum from basic research to products and tools. What are the implications of such research and technological diversity for technology transfer? Is it more difficult to transfer basic research? Is software technology more difficult to transfer than hardware and stand-alone products? "Equivocality" refers to the level of concreteness of a technology. Technology that is low in equivocality is less ambiguous and it is hypothesized by some that such technology is easier to transfer (Smilor and Gibson, 1991). MCC's first chief scientist, John Pinkston, contended that "The more a technology can be encapsulated—the more the user only has to deal with the externals (as in the case of a tool)—the easier technology transfer tends to be." (Pinkston, 1989)

MCC's High Value Electronics (HVE) Division (formerly the Packaging/Interconnect Program) has transferred more technologies to its shareholders than all other MCC research programs combined. Most of MCC's patents have been generated in the HVE Division. However, hardware advances have had a longer tradition of

Table 5.3 MCC member companies
by industry sector, as of early 1991

Aerospace
  Aerojet Electronics
  Boeing
  E-Systems
  Fairchild Space and Defense
  GM Hughes
  Lockheed
  LTV
  Martin Marietta
  Northrop
  Rockwell International
  TRW, Inc.
  United Technologies
Consumer Electronics
  Eastman Kodak
Data Management
  Corporate Memory Systems
  EIT
  Itasca
Flat Panel Displays
  Cherry Display (The Cherry Corp.)
  Electro-Plasma, Inc.
  Magnascreen
  OIS (Optical Imaging Systems)
  Photonics Imaging Systems
  Planar Systems
  Plasmatherm
  Projectavision
  Promex
  Standish Industries
Computer-Aided Design
  Cadence Design Systems
Electronics
  Allied-Signal
  Conner Peripherals
  General Electric
  Tektronix
  Teledyne
  Teradyne, Inc.
  Westinghouse
Energy
  Amoco Production
  Occidental Chemical

Computer Systems
  Apple Computer
  Control Data Corp.
  Digital Equipment Corp.
  Hewlett-Packard
  Honeywell
  NCR
  Sun Microsystems
  Tandem Computers
  Unisys
Public Agencies
  Federal Bureau of Investigation
  NASA—Johnson Space Center
  National Security Agency
Research
  Enviro. Res. Institute of Michigan
  Lawrence Livermore National Labs
  MITRE
  SEMATECH
  Software Engineering Institute
Semiconductor Equip. and Materials
  Advanced Packaging Systems
  AMP, Inc.
  Olin Corp.
  Rogers Corp.
  3M
  WT Automation
Semiconductors
  Advanced Micro Devices
  Harris
  Motorola
  Multichip Technology, Inc.
  National Semiconductor
Services
  American Express
  Andersen Consulting
  SAIC
Software
  Microsoft
Telecommunications
  AT&T
  Bellcore
  DSC Communications
  Northern Telecom

patenting than software advances. Packaging/interconnect technologies are generally observable, measurable, and relatively easy to demonstrate. In contrast, the Information Systems Division's technologies (formerly the Software Technology, Computer-Aided Design, and Advanced Computer Architecture programs) tend to be more idea-based, with a variety of possible process and product applications. The superiority of a hardware tool can usually be demonstrated, but the superiority of an idea or software tool is often more difficult to evaluate.

According to Dove (interview, March 1, 1991): "The shareholder mix was important in the P/I Program's success because they had materials, semiconductor, computer, and aerospace companies . . . a good mix to determine what the needs were from their [the customers'] views." Barry Whalen, P/I Program director, had industry experience. He understood the needs and motivations of shareholder group and division managers (i.e., his customers) much better than some of the more academic or research-oriented managers in MCC's other programs. Indeed, Whalen's researchers and technicians were referred to as "blue-collar" types by MCC's researchers in the other program areas.

During MCC's first eight years, each of the consortium's research programs approached the challenge of technology transfer somewhat differently. MCC's management did not try to force the issue and say: "This is the way to do it." The programs that were most successful with level IV technology transfer were the ones that had a steady stream of evolutionary output. The least successful programs delivered concepts and ideas. Grant Dove (interview, March 1, 1991) commented:

> Most companies are in a better position to evaluate hardware, take it, and put it to work. Software is harder because of the large and expensive gap to get to industrial and market strength. In the software world in particular, we were challenged to see if we could take it [the technology] to Beta-test level (which, in technical terminology, means that it is pretty robust, and it does something real, and it will work reasonably well). We learned to fly in the CAD Program by going to open architectures and to robust industrial strength code.

STP was embedded in an essentially microelectronics research environment, observed Program Director Laszlo Belady (1992): "On the surface it looked very progressive and promised interdisciplinary work, but in reality it provided a hardware-flavored management with reduced understanding of, and sympathy for, software." MCC's STP, CAD, and ACA research programs were developing leapfrog, leading-edge technologies, seven to ten years out in front of current user problems. As a researcher in the CAD Program stated: "Packaging was dealing with known problems and known technology. Software was dealing with unknown problems and speculative technology."

In 1989, Petrie commented on how the novelty of MCC's software technology impacted its transfer to the shareholder companies (E-mail, July 18):

> Regardless of the organization, if the technology is too novel, it's not used, and if it isn't sufficiently novel, potential users opt for well-established, supported commercial [software] . . . . Our [MCC] research results are typically going to fall below the state of the art in ordinary features, if only because we don't produce product-quality systems. So if you evaluate a hybrid system like Proteus on its ordinary features, it will lose compared to commercial products. It only wins if its novel features make it worth putting up with less than product-quality level of its ordinary ones. This will only happen if the novelty is real and useful and if that novelty can be successfully communicated.
>
> Communicating the power of novel ideas is hard and we don't know how to do it. . . . If you send a complete Proteus manual, which we did, people may never find the novelty. Novel ideas are rarely picked up the first time they are presented. . . . With Proteus there were several instances where applications were developed in secret. We found out about them later . . . but their developers failed to get the unique benefits of Proteus, while they had to put up with its quirks. They made negative evaluations of Proteus, and based on their [limited] experience, they were right.

MCC's original mission of high-risk, long-term, pre-competitive technology drove staffing and research decisions. As Kay Hammer (former CAD researcher) stated (interview, October 23, 1991):

Much of the first three years of work was conducted on LISP workstations because of the enhanced productivity that the environment provides. There was considerable debate at the time about the choice of this platform, since LISP was not a programming language in commercial use and the cost of LISP workstations ($55,000–$120,000) made them an unlikely choice for a commercial workstation. However, since the research programs did not expect their work to be complete [or asked for] for years out, the pro-LISP forces argued that inexpensive LISP environments would by that time be available, thereby allowing a relatively easy transfer of technology.[19]

MCC researchers were equipped with Sun workstations years before their counterparts in the shareholder companies. While facilitating the recruitment of quality researchers to MCC, these advanced computer technologies also acted as a barrier to the continuous transfer of research results, especially early in the research process before such advanced platforms were available in the user environments of the shareholder companies. The hardware platforms in most MCC shareholders were DEC, IBM, or Apple computers. Even when MCC-developed technologies were compatible with the hardware and software platforms of a particular shareholder, there was usually a lack of commonality of platform technologies among all the shareholders belonging to the same MCC research program.

Throughout our discussion on the effectiveness of technology transfer, we have emphasized the importance of timing, in terms of getting the technology to the receptor at the right time to facilitate adoption. We have also discussed the timing of technology transfer in terms of when to start the transfer process. The general conclusion has been, the earlier the better. As one of MCC's managers of technology transfer commented:

Too often decisions about technology transfer are put off until a project is almost finished. That perspective can be fatal for research consortia, where the disjunction between solutions and problems may not become apparent until it is too late. . . . Much of the current literature (on technology transfer) deals with the process of technology transfer that occurs shortly before research is complete and ends when the technology is in the hands of the recipient organization, sometime called "point hand-off." This perspective is entirely too narrow. While optimizing the point hand-off process can help the overall transfer, it ignores the two most crucial aspects of the process: *technology buy-in* and *technology adoption*. (interview, Werner, May 4, 1993; also see Werner and Bremer, 1991; and Werner 1992)

Technology buy-in refers to having the receptors or ultimate users of the technology, where the "rubber hits the road," be part of the technology development process (Roach, 1992). As several of MCC's technology transfer personnel commented, solving the user problem did not guarantee successful transfer, the user had to own part of the solution.

Some of the most serious impediments to the timely commercialization of MCC-produced technologies resulted from the way in which business decisions were made in the deep hierarchies of MCC's shareholder companies. As Hammer (interview, October 23, 1991) observed, most software projects of any complexity require a team of six to ten people to move from research to market strength: several programmers, a technical writer, a quality assurance person, and product support. To fund such an effort, a manager must command a budget of between $600,000 and $1 million per year. At least a six-month sales cycle is usually required to obtain that kind of budget, as the product manager's reputation rests on bringing the product to market within a projected timeframe. On top of these challenges are concerns about the marketing and sales of the product. To champion a new software process is a lot to ask of a product manager, especially if (1) the management hierarchy is risk-averse, and (2) the product manager knows little about the research environment in which the technology was produced.

Consequently, middle- and upper-level managers, caught between taking a risk that might lead to a real advance for the company and their personal desire to maintain [or improve] their position in the management hierarchy, tend to try to reach a consensus in a large enough group to be able to distribute failure should the decision not prove to be a good one. And all too often, by the time a majority reaches consensus, the market window has been missed, the product fails, and the risk-aversion is reinforced. (Hammer interview, October 31, 1991)

About two years before the program's demise, STP had begun to implement a collaborative model of technology transfer (Babcock, Belady, and Gore, 1990). Essentially the model posits the existence of a dialectical relationship between research and application.

The intense, ongoing researcher/shareholder interaction that occurs in a collaborative project produces a dual movement by the shareholders, toward the incorporation of new ideas and technologies into current development practice; and by researchers, toward the subtle, incremental evolution of the research to meet real and perceived shareholder needs. (Babcock, E-mail, July 10, 1990)

Babcock believed that since STP distinguished the collaborative model in 1989, there had been a gradual growth in the collaborative mind-set—an attitude that would benefit technology transfer but also, ultimately, the successful team-based development of tomorrow's large, complex computer systems. The research-related results of this philosophy revolved around incremental, evolutionary improvements to new technologies. The collaborative mind-set was being implemented in several specific ways at STP, one of which was shared responsibility between the researchers and the shareholder companies for reporting research results. STP's sponsors were to revamp specific tools for use on shareholder hardware (e.g., PCs, NCR Towers, and DEC stations), and STP was reorienting its research toward a Unix/C^{++}/X environment. The concern was whether STP was giving up research flexibility in favor of transferability. However, Babcock noted (E-mail, July 10, 1990) that "[this issue] becomes moot when asked in the context of the collaboration-based research model, because research in this model exists not apart from, but rather hand in hand with, usability. . . . We believe that collaboration lies near the heart of technology transfer, and that this phenomenon is not peculiar to the industrial research consortium."

The timing of technology transfer is also important because of ever shorter product life cycles and increasing worldwide competition. Transfer must not only occur rapidly but it must happen at the right time in the product development cycle for a technology to be of maximum use to a receptor. Central to such timing is researcher awareness of the product-planning strategy of the shareholder companies. For MCC, it has been a significant challenge to get product planners from the member companies to regularly visit MCC. MCC researchers were often shooting in the dark with respect to the shareholder application of their research and the shareholder product development strategies.

Figure 5.8 shows the four stages of idea-to-product formulation. During stage 1, the research strength of a new idea has the greatest likelihood of affecting the process of technology development. MCC pre-competitive technologies would receive less resistance at the user organization at this stage. During stage 2, ideas become more focused, and walls begin to form around a preferred technology. This sorting-out process is driven by product champions and organization power and politics, as well as by technological and

Stage 1	Stage 2	Stage 3	Stage 4

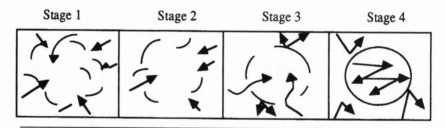

Note: Arrows represent new technology concepts. Solid curved lines represent project institutionalization.

Figure 5.8 Four stages of idea-to-product formulation

bottom-line considerations. Such forces inhibit the absorption or application of new technologies that would call for a new strategic focus. During stage 3, considerable time and effort are invested in building an industrial-strength technology and possibly a prototype. In stage 4, the technology achieves market strength. Psychological, professional, financial, and strategic switching costs increase for the receptor site of an MCC-developed technology as one moves from stage 1 to stage 4.

THE CONTEXT OF TECHNOLOGY TRANSFER

In 1987, Joe Scullion (deputy director of MCC's artificial intelligence program and NCR's liaison to MCC's ACA Program) sent a memo to Grant Dove, Palle Smidt, Gene Lowenthal, and John Pinkston in which he stated that, after a good deal of thought, it appeared clear to him that there were [four] major barriers that inhibited technology transfer from MCC to the shareholder companies (MCC memo, November 3, 1987):

> First, a significant mismatch exists among the experience, education, and intellectual environment of the researchers and that of the receptor organizations. Most MCC researchers have been educated in advanced areas of computer science. Their emphasis is on theorizing and testing. Shareholder developers, on the other hand, are most concerned with the current working environment of computer science including interfaces, documentation, training, and support. This mismatch is evident in differing vocabularies, degrees of understanding concepts, and belief in the value and importance, or applicability, of advanced concepts.
>
> Second, a significant mismatch exists between the researchers' development vehicles (generally LISP-based) and the shareholders' product development environment (usually C-based or other). MCC researchers often require massive amounts of computer memory or specialized processors. The results of their research can only be demonstrated on these specialized systems that are generally unavailable to shareholder personnel. And

there is a lack of standardization across MCC's research activities which require that the shareholder receptors replicate these different (hardware and software) environments in their development organizations. The cost of establishing and maintaining such a range of computer environments (e.g., capital equipment, training and education) is unacceptable.

Third, a lack of a strong demand pull is due to the difficulty of seeing where and how to apply the advanced concepts developed at MCC. Because much of MCC's technology is pre-competitive (e.g., expert systems and truth maintenance systems), it is not clear how or where to apply it in productive applications. MCC is developing solutions in search of a problem, problems which the users often do not know they have. The result is a diminished "demand pull" from the shareholder developers.

Fourth, a resource allocation mismatch exists between MCC and the shareholders. The available resources in the shareholders' development organizations are tightly allocated, for the most part, to the actual development of products. Thus their technology transfer activities are most likely to occur in short bursts, i.e., one day in-depth reviews and short visits to MCC. Compared with the amount of time that goes into the development of new technologies, this time allocation is totally inadequate to successfully transfer any complex concepts into the shareholder's product development cycle. (Scullion memo, November 3, 1987)

In addition, Scullion mentioned that MCC also faced the more immediate problem of how to support and maintain the technologies that had already been transferred. One answer to all of the above challenges was to establish a separate MCC organization dedicated to supporting transferred technology. This group could also serve as a buffer between the researchers and the technology receptors. But, as Scullion emphasized, overlying all the above was the question of cost. If MCC wanted to keep within current budget constraints, then to fund such a proposal, the consortium would have to reduce research expenditures or MCC could try and obtain additional shareholder funding.

Scullion also proposed that the shareholders join with MCC in forming a permanent cadre of personnel, staffed by assignees from the shareholder companies, to provide support and maintenance services to the shareholders as they applied ACA technologies to product development. "Our experience to date has shown that one or two day seminars or in-depth reviews are grossly insufficient mechanisms for effectively transferring highly complex and advanced concepts...extensive training of shareholder personnel is required not only in the new product but also in the underlying technologies...and ongoing support to the customers of those products." (Scullion memo, November 3, 1987)

MCC technicians would instruct this first cadre (personnel from the shareholders' existing development and support organizations) for a period of 12 months. Then as the MCC technicians returned to their research focus, this cadre of students would instruct the second incoming cadre. As this cycle was continually repeated, trained personnel would return to their firms. The net result would be the growth within the shareholders' organizations of a highly trained staff capable of accepting new technologies (from MCC or elsewhere) and using them in the development of competitive new product offerings. The minimum commitment for Scullion's proposal was two and a half years of shareholder support—one year of training, one year of teaching, and six months of transition—for two sets of assignees from the shareholder to be in Austin at any one time.

Scullion's proposal generally received strong support from MCC's researchers and technology transfer personnel who were aware of it. However, members of MCC's board and TAB were uncomfortable with the cost and the commitment required. MCC was not set up to be a training organization. As Petrie commented (interview, September 16, 1993): "It was kind of an internal technology transfer meta-problem: If it's too different it [the technology/process] is not adopted. If it's not different enough, it doesn't do any good." Scullion continued to champion his idea and in late 1988 he sent the following E-mail message to his colleagues at MCC: "Our primary goal (perhaps only some of us agree with this) is to upgrade the technological level of the [shareholders] so that we significantly reduce the chance that their possible failure to compete will be technologically based" (E-mail, December 21, 1988). "We do this," Scullion suggested, "by producing important research results with the complementary approaches of education and technology transfer."

> If more shareholder developers understood inferencing architectures, reasoning, representation issues, knowledge-based approaches to application development, and object-oriented databases, etc., and had the software to experiment with, the shareholders would be better off and at least ACA would have an easier job of technology transfer. MCC can itself be a resource for centralizing that education process. And if MCC had a demonstrable methodology for transferring technology, our research would have enormous added value. (E-mail, December 21, 1988)

Petrie supported Scullion's call for a cadre of experienced technologists to train and upgrade the skills of potential shareholder receptors. He even suggested that MCC make such an activity a revenue center while giving shareholder personnel the best training possible. The training would be divided into two basic groups. One set of courses would focus on such technologies as LISP, PROLOG, search, AI techniques, and computer science fundamentals. Speciality courses would focus on expert systems, object-oriented programming, databases, parallel processing, neural nets, and human interfaces. Once the "students" had progressed through these courses, they could start learning MCC proprietary technology such as NABU, Proteus, ORION, and Cyc. Several training cadres could be operating at once.

The real advantage to such training was seen to be the impact on shareholder cultures. It was to be a "mass approach versus the assignee approach." And then there was the benefit of the transition from training to support, which would overlap with the return of the trained personnel to the shareholder companies. Petrie concluded: "My instinct [in championing Scullion's plan] was to be aggressive as possible and be pushed back reluctantly if we had to retreat in the face of reality" (interview, September 16, 1993). In the end, neither the shareholders nor MCC's management was willing to fund and staff such a training program. As Petrie concluded in 1993:

> We missed a great opportunity by not trying Joe Scullion's Cadre idea. Not only was it novel, but it addressed the heart of the problem. Our goal was to improve the technological base of the shareholders. History shows how unlikely this was to occur by the discovery of a magic bullet. And our experience showed how hard it was to inject even moderately advanced raw technology into the companies. It's more likely that we would have succeeded in spreading the technologies through the waves of industrial engineers trained to support them. Now we will never know. (E-mail correspondence, October 12, 1993)

PROPRIETARY TECHNOLOGY

One important facet of MCC's challenges with technology transfer centered on the lack of commercial interaction with outside vendors and other potential users. Such interaction was inhibited by the consortium's emphasis on making all of its technology proprietary. Several MCC researchers suggested that the shareholders would maximize their value in the consortium's software technology only by making it publicly available. As Petrie emphasized (E-mail May 6, 1991):

> We've shown that making technology proprietary condemns it to being buried. It's worse than that, our shareholders do not incorporate MCC technology internally or in products. They play "dog in the manager:" no one else should have access to it. We have tried to change that model. We can't deliver isolated technologies. It's much harder, but we're going to have to deliver a "technology context" too. One example is the CAD framework initiative that sets standards and methodologies for a large section of the industry.

Another example is Bell and Unix. One way to make new technology standard (even if inferior) is to make it widely and cheaply available. If gIBIS or Proteus or any of several other proven useful technologies had been widely distributed, they would have had the chance to become standards, and our shareholders would have had a chance to make money.

We have to change and our shareholders have to change their model of MCC if we are to be successful. If the new model still includes technology developed here, part of the changed model must include nonproprietary software.

INTERPERSONAL MOTIVATION

Researchers and managers from MCC and the shareholder companies ranked the ways to improve technology transfer (Figure 5.9). At the bottom of the list was delegating responsibility for technology transfer to special committees, programs, or consultants; as with quality control a decade earlier, technology transfer should be everybody's concern. As one long-time manager of technology transfer for the CAD Program commented (Werner, E-mail, August 14, 1990):

We don't need a separate technology transfer office in MCC. To do so would pass off the responsibility to someone else. Everyone in MCC should have an "office" in their brain devoted to technology transfer. In some people's brains, it's a large office with an impressive walnut desk; in most of our researchers' brains it's a telephone booth—but it's there.

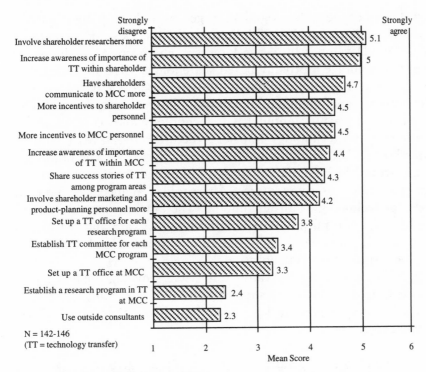

Source: Smilor and Gibson, 1991.

5.9 Ways to improve technology transfer from MCC, based on a 1989 survey of MCC and shareholder-company employees

MCC and shareholder respondents generally agreed that to improve technology transfer, it was most important to (1) increase interpersonal communication while focusing on involving the shareholder researchers more with the developers at MCC, (2) increase motivation by rewarding those involved in the technology transfer processes at both the shareholder companies and MCC, and (3) change the culture or context of the reward structure and increase awareness of the importance of technology transfer. Enacting such cultural and structural changes within MCC and the shareholder companies has proved to be a significant challenge.

While involving shareholder researchers more with MCC research was seen as a good thing, the general feeling among personnel responsible for technology transfer at MCC was that the developers of the technology had to get more directly involved with the technology users. In 1989, Petrie and Babcock came up with the idea for "Developer Initiative Grants." The purpose of the grants was to encourage a broadly based shareholder/MCC flow of people to facilitate research collaboration—to "open wider the channel between 'us' and 'them' and to stimulate interest among shareholder engineers in learning about MCC technology and to establish the beginning of a technology transfer structure between MCC and the shareholders" (Petrie, E-mail, November 29, 1989). The grant program would be advertised broadly within the shareholder companies to create grassroots interest. Shareholder engineers would compete for technology transfer funding. The amounts would be small and for specific purposes such as needed software and travel support. Participants would be required to document and collect data on the results of the collaboration.

The immediate response from MCC's management was that there were no funds for such a program. The funds that were available were needed to keep the researchers employed. As Petrie commented:

> We've got to spend resources on technology transfer or we won't succeed. But to do this some of us must go and we won't have the manpower to succeed. . . . The only answer is going back to the well to suggest that the shareholders fund their own grant initiative program. . . . I don't like being reduced to suggesting stuff to the shareholders. It almost never works. (E-mail, November 29, 1989)

Another concern raised by chief scientist John Pinkston was whether such a program would distract the researcher from his/her primary mission: "We would need to position it clearly as an incentive for technology transfer, not as an entrepreneurial sideline" (E-mail, November 29, 1989). And the concern was also raised that it would be important to make it clear to the shareholder engineer that his or her career would not suffer by participating in such a program. In the end, the lack of funds doomed this attempt to broaden MCC's technology transfer mission.

According to Craig Fields (interview, March 1, 1991): "In

R&D, we do not have objective performance measures [of research quality], so every researcher thinks they're as good as, or better than, every other one, and as a consequence of that, you get a tremendous amount of negativity among R&D staff in a company toward supporting a consortium outside the company. . . . That's not going to change." The lack of support for, or valuation of, the tasks of others involved in the transfer or technology application process is a serious inhibitor. Researchers are usually at the top of the status pecking order with the most theoretical researchers on the top rung of the prestige ladder. An MCC researcher commented in 1992:

> Frequently, there is a lack of appreciation for the importance of the work of other groups within an organization and the difficulties encountered by these groups. Engineers think corporate management is brain dead and marketing is full of know-nothings and liars. Researchers too often believe that development people are not theoretically equipped to solve interesting problems, and in turn, developers think that researchers don't know anything about the real world. These attitudes further complicate creating the kind of cooperation required for effective technology transfer.

Laszlo Belady (1992, p. 14) emphasized the difficulty of finding a motivated researcher/receptor of MCC-produced technologies:

> Many [shareholder] participants had their own research or at least their own advanced development groups in software technology. These people were not friendly to STP. Instead, they lobbied to channel funds intended for MCC into their own organizations. And all this in the face of shrinking funds available for any longer-term research.

Despite the arguments for the importance of motivating technology developers and users to collaborate in the transfer process, such motivation (from levels I through IV) is not sufficient in itself to achieve technology utilization. While highly motivated technology transfer participants can overcome passive or infrequent communication; physical, cultural, and strategic distance; and technology barriers, they are not a panacea for successful technology transfer. During MCC's formative years, the consortium's scientists were initially elated to locate receptive shareholder-based technology champions. However, they often spent considerable time and resources transferring technologies to these receptors, only to find that these individuals, while being extremely well-intentioned and motivated, lacked the political and resource clout to effectively implement the MCC technology within their company.

According to MCC's charter, it was not the concern of MCC researchers to identify real-world applications of their technologies. During MCC's early years, MCC's researchers in STP, ACA/ACT, and CAD were most academic in their orientation and many were not particularly interested in whether the technology they developed was used by MCC shareholders. They preferred to be left to their research activities. Research that did achieve successful commercial application (e.g., Proteus) was actually looked down upon and discouraged. It was not thought to be world-class science, indeed it probably wasn't. Researchers in the P/I Program, the blue-collar folks, were closest to their customers (the shareholders) in terms of technology development and application.

Many of the most talented researchers who joined MCC did so because it afforded them the opportunity to pursue their research goals in a supportive setting. They generally did not look forward to the visits of shareholder personnel who asked "uninteresting" questions about technology application. As one shareholder respondent commented: "Many of MCC's researchers were just incapable of thinking application." And there was also resistance on the part of the shareholders. As Admiral Inman stated (interview, December 12, 1989):

> There's a certain arrogance that builds up, particularly in large corporations. They presume that they are the best and therefore anything new coming out will come from their research. . . . And on the other hand, I've run across [at MCC] a sense that commercializing is almost dirty. That we should be purists. . . . It's our job to create. It's not our job to get it used.

MCC researchers who were interested in product applications of their work were often rebuffed by shareholder researchers and management. Inman thought back to several instances when he asked representatives of the shareholders companies about specific product applications of MCC-produced technology; he was told in so many words: "It's none of your damn business" (interview, December 12, 1989). The shareholder companies funding the research did not want MCC or the other shareholder companies informed about how they were using the consortium's technology. The main exception to this situation was MCC's Packaging/Interconnect Program, which was able to demonstrate to the shareholders that it was doing useful things for them.

Leonard R. Weisberg, an MCC board member and vice president of corporate research at Honeywell, Inc., commented in 1991 that one of the biggest problems at MCC had been the communications gap between the consortium's researchers and the member companies: "You just never knew where they were going and when they were going to get there" (quoted in Richards, 1991). Honeywell scaled back its financial support of MCC after being disappointed in the results obtained from the two projects it had supported.

MCC and shareholder scientists were initially hired and rewarded for their research capabilities, not their skill in technology transfer. Indeed, MCC management questioned whether it was a good use of resources and talent to have highly qualified researchers spend large amounts of time (in some cases, up to 30 to 50 percent) on technology transfer activities. Laszlo Belady (1992) remembered how his software researchers were instructed to market their technologies more aggressively:

> This was a new task for the entire staff. We did not anticipate the huge amounts of time, travel, and effort this marketing venture would require. It became a continuous crescendo, culminating in a sizable professional marketing staff and a huge load on all the senior people: almost daily travel and presentations. Yet it was not successful. Most prospects believed they should be able to join [STP] for just a couple of thousand dollars; they compared us to universities with regard to fund-

ing. When we created individually supported projects [unbundling and projectization] out of the program, the complexity of marketing increased, and we ended up with meager results. . . . We lost many good people who were not willing to spend their creative energies on presentations and salesmanship.

A central question often asked by technology developers and users involved in the technology transfer process was: "What's in it for me?" Frequently, the answer was: "Not much." The transfer of a technology may be viewed by a key individual as requiring too high a personal cost, even if the transfer might be beneficial to that individual's organization or to U.S. industrial competitiveness.[20] Little peer recognition or prestige usually goes to the person who transfers or uses technology that has been developed by others. Indeed, in terms of job security or career development, resistance to a proposed new technology may be a smart move from the point of view of a targeted receptor.

Successful collaboration between MCC and its member companies in the commercialization of technology most frequently occurred in win-win situations, as exemplified in the Proteus to DesignAdvisor case. Frustrating such collaboration is the reality that the criteria for technology transfer success are often markedly different for research, product development, production, marketing, and sales personnel. One well-placed "innovation assassin" can thwart the successful implementation of such collaborative activity.

Over the years, there has been relatively little application of MCC-produced software technologies by researchers in other MCC programs. As one respondent told us: "I tried to get management to start a research program which focused on using MCC-produced technologies in-house, as a Beta test, but I was told that there were no funds for such a program" (Werner interview, March 30, 1992). So from the perspective of MCC as well as the shareholder companies, it was often easier to disregard an MCC-developed technology than to spend the extra effort and money needed to get it to industrial and market strength.

In his 1990 report on technology transfer, Conklin stated that the most critical problem for MCC was the reality that the member-company customer "Only wants to do business and considers bringing in new technology to be somebody else's problem" (E-mail, August 9, 1990). He saw this problem being manifest at two levels: corporate and individual. In his view, MCC's corporate participants had almost uniformly failed to invest either sufficient money or qualified people to bridge the gap and provide technology pull, As he commented: "One participant, who was considering pulling out of MCC confessed recently that [his company] had spent $30 to $40 million at MCC over the years, yet only $500,000 internally to receive MCC technologies" (E-mail, August 9, 1990). MCC's researchers were given the impossible task, by the shareholders, of producing "productized" prototypes, including support and training as well as ground-breaking research while being told not to waste time with refining old research. To counter such barriers, Conklin recommended that it should be a prerequisite to participating in an MCC research project for the member company to (1) provide at least one acceptable assignee to the project, and (2) spend 25 percent of its project investment on a parallel receptor or marketing effort within its own company.

On the individual level, Conklin commented that (E-mail, August 9, 1990):

> The social, organizational, and psychological forces that militate against being a technology champion (for MCC or otherwise) are universal and nearly overwhelming. Why should a participant employee go to the risk and trouble to bring in an MCC technology, particularly when the corporate culture is typically one of putting out fires, low priority on training and education, low commitment to process improvement, etc.? What real incentive is there even for the person who is the official receptor? Just because technology transfer is a part of their job description doesn't equip them with the courage, persistence, pluck, and inventiveness that are required to get research and customer to converse productively and committedly. Six years of trying to make this model work should be enough evidence that it is fatally flawed.

Arneson, one of the founding designers of MCC, commented

on the issue motivating personnel and collaboration in the technology transfer process (correspondence, April 8, 1993):

> The root of the technology transfer problem lies in the well-established U.S. belief that success for individuals and groups stems from successfully competing, not collaborating. Your colleague is also your competitor for the larger office, promotion, raise, or praise. Since the donor and receptor in a technology transfer share this value system, great care must be exercised to eradicate suspicion. The NIH [not-invented-here] syndrome is ubiquitous at all levels of the U.S. industry hierarchy . . . much to the disadvantage of our national productivity.

Incentive policies drive behavior and this impacts what researchers and other personnel consider worthy of their best efforts (Dornbusch and Scott, 1975). Incentives also have a great deal to do with shaping the structure of research activity. As Petrie commented to his MCC peers (E-mail, August 13, 1990): "Making the performance review of someone in the shareholders dependent upon the success of technology transfer from MCC is the single most important change we can make."

Soon after he came to MCC, Fields changed the year-end incentive bonus to reward technology transfer success. As one researcher commented about this change in policy: "Indeed, the problem for some of us now is that we've evolved into great marketers and have forgotten how to do research."

As Fields (interview, February 29, 1991) emphasized:

> There are tremendous problems associated with the incentive structures within companies. Namely, they will advance a person based on the size of their head count as opposed to their output. Thus, I have people from other consortia say to me that "We'd rather have ten people inside than a hundred people leveraged outside the consortium because ten people inside are reporting to me and that's better for my group."

PLANNING FOR TECHNOLOGY TRANSFER

Grant Dove believed that researchers had a proclivity for producing prototypes and demonstration vehicles. That was their degree of maturation of output. "For many of our members, that's just fine. They are totally prepared to take that and make the investment to harden it and support it. But for most, that is not enough. Most want nice, clean, industrial-strength stuff, fully supported, and they don't want to pay the price" (Dove interview, August 15, 1990). Picking up the theme of customer satisfaction, Dove emphasized that MCC had always had a focus on the member companies; it's just that they kept changing their minds. Fields also emphasized the importance of MCC treating the member companies as customers:

> We really try to focus on the customer, who is he and how is he turned on—to make it easier for the customer to implement the technology—to get it to the point where he can put it to work and get fairly immediate and obvious return from it. The big question is not how you do it, but deciding who's going to do it and deciding early enough so that it can be worked out so there is not a big time delay in putting the technology to work. (interview, February 29, 1991)

When MCC was launched, the shareholder companies agreed that they would be responsible for applying MCC-developed technologies. "What's happened as they got closer to it [the technology] was that they changed their modus operandi, particularly in the software world," said Dove (interview, August 15, 1990). "They decided that no, we're not going to take it. We're not going to try to support it. We want a supplier to do that; we want a vendor to do that. We want to help you in the research, but we want to have one of the companies be the vendor, or we want to have companies in the program from the start who can supply it to us at market strength." Figure 5.10 depicts the technology transfer gap as seen by MCC researchers. The gap existed in getting research results from research strength (level I) to market strength (level IV) (see Figure 5.2).

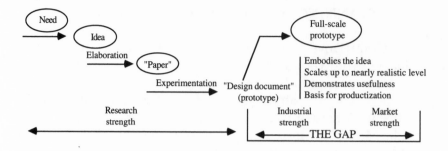

Source: Adapted from Babcock, Belady, and Gore, 1990.

Figure 5.10 The technology transfer gap as perceived by MCC researchers in the software technology program

"We all got frustrated," stated Dove in 1990 (interview, August 15), "when we got up close and then they said: 'No, we're not going to take it. It's going to cost us too much. You guys figure out how you can get it to us and by the way, how are you going to support it?'" As Petrie commented on an E-mail message to Deborah Pederson, Gene Lowenthal, Elaine Rich, and others (April 27, 1989):

> So no one denies that ACT as a whole hasn't reacted to shareholder needs very quickly, or perhaps even listened to them well in the last few years. Or that the shareholders themselves haven't sent consistent explicit messages.
>
> As everyone is now painfully aware, the shareholder model has completely switched from long-range research to industrial R&D. We have at best underestimated the strength of this trend. Thus, as Elaine points out, not only have we not done a particularly good job of technology transfer, we don't have any new deliverables in the stream.
>
> Perhaps our sensitivities were dulled by our history and understanding of MCC's original purpose. Perhaps we should have given up sooner instead of going after new visions. It doesn't matter now.

> Now it's at the point where the TAB is saying that if we can't show them stuff "already" delivered, the game's over. Whoa! When did we miss hearing them say that if we don't give them a plan with concrete deliverables by now, that we're finished?

Gene Lowenthal responded to Petrie (E-mail, April 27, 1989):

> Maybe I'm smoking the wrong stuff, but I believe you are overreacting somewhat, Charles. Now that we have been in business five years, we really can talk about a pipeline model, maturing technology gets transferred (or force fed if necessary) while new stuff is being planned three-plus years out. What the shareholders are complaining about is that we haven't made the technology that is available now tasty enough or we haven't pushed it hard enough, and would [you] please fix it (versus "drop long-range research and do industrial R&D"). Let's make technology transfer success stories out of Orion, LDL, IWS . . . maybe even smaller things like Proteus and Prolog.

As we pursued our study of MCC, we increasingly became curious as to why the founding computer, microelectronics, and aerospace companies had decided to fund such a broad range of pre-competitive research projects in software technology.

Interviewer: [To Bob Price, the chair of MCC's Steering Committee and Interim Board of Directors]: Given the type of companies that made up the Steering Committee, how did you decide on the R&D focus of MCC? Did you really expect the shareholder companies to commercialize software tools?

Price: We were babes in the woods. . . . We were searching. We all needed tools like CAD and we weren't working on them. We all needed building-block technologies like packaging. But our biggest problem was software. We had big discussions about what we could do to increase software productivity—to increase the productivity of systems programmers by a factor of 10 or 100. Gordon Bell [of Digital Equipment Corp.] was somewhat visionary when he noted that what we needed was software that would allow engineers to do their own programming—to get the software closer to the application. But for the most part, the companies thought in terms of hardware, we were a long way from understanding software commercialization.

Under Gene Lowenthal, MCC's data base research efforts were world class, especially their work on object-oriented programming, but nobody wanted to commercialize it. The fact that there is a market need doesn't mean didley—what's required is desire. MCC's companies had the need for CAD and for many of the software technologies developed at the consortium, but what was lacking was the desire to take the technology and commercialize it. (interview, May 12, 1993)

According to Fields, because companies often change their plans: "You can't have things that are endless. You have to have modest-term things, fixed term with schedules, milestones, and deliverables, and somebody in charge." Under Fields, MCC has gone into a project management mode. "Each project has its end point. . . . It's not good management to linger on forever and get disappointing returns," stated Fields (interview, March 1, 1991). However, as one of our MCC respondents observed: "Giving research projects specific end dates sounds good, but the researchers often don't like it, especially if they don't have another project to move into. Near the end of the second year of a three-year project, they will be concerned about what comes next." (Werner, interview, March 30, 1992). As Petrie commented (E-mail, August 13, 1990):

I have a common problem. Travel money is tight (as it is for shareholders). I want to travel and my boss is reluctant to fund it.

The uncommon (unfortunately) part of my problem is that I want to travel to a shareholder, at their invitation, to look at some shareholder problems that will help me formulate a new project.

John [Pinkston], I will come talk to you about this. Now that I've stated my personal interest, put it aside. That's a small problem that'll get solved. Please consider the larger problem. . . .

Old projects in general don't want to spend their meager resources on initiating new projects. Travel to prospect problems is a good example. Who should fund this part of the renewal process? What should be the MCC structure and policy?

Funding for project renewal is important. This came up even at the technology transfer committee meeting Friday. The attending Motorola representative said they resented paying X to start a project and then being asked to pay +e for trips. . . .

P.S. Then there's the issue of funding shareholders to make exploratory trips here, but that's another topic.

Beginning in 1992, each research project manager at MCC had to make a series of technology transfer decisions at the start of a project (see Table 4.1). Such decisions concerned (1) whether the funding companies would use the technology or whether one particular company was going to use it on behalf of the rest, (2) whether vendors were going to be part of the technology transfer process, and (3) whether a spin-out company was needed. "There should be a business impact assessment," Fields emphasized. "It is important to determine who will pick it [the technology] up and whether they have budgeted to take the technology. Have they done a competitive analysis? How are they going to market it? Is it going to decrease internal costs or increase market share?" (Fields interview, March 1, 1991)

In seeming contradiction to Fields, Admiral Inman (interview, October 22, 1992) suggested: "Technology transfer cannot be proceduralized like other tasks. It isn't just a matter of strategic-planning push, because you don't know in advance what's likely to evolve out of investment in research. You're dealing with an unknown. You may think you know what you are after, but the issue for many companies is how prepared they are to deal with the other events that occur, the accidental discoveries." Indeed, MCC-developed technologies have been used in ways that were not, and could not have been, predicted when the research project began. As Les Belady stated: "In many cases in 1990 we were developing applications for our software technologies which we didn't even envision when we began the research in 1984" (interview, March 22, 1993). Such unanticipated market applications were not limited to software technology.

Rob Smith, director of MCC's Experimental Systems Program, did not set out to invent a high-performance connector device for circuit boards. But Smith and his co-workers needed this technology to complete their research on advanced multiprocessor computers. No suitable connector devices were available, so he built his own. Smith patented his connector and licensed the technology to Cinch Connectors, Elk Grove Village, Illinois. The market for the connector consisted of computer and electronics companies that wanted to link high-speed circuit boards while avoiding the distortion of electronic signals. The patent generated a modest stream of royalty payments to MCC, the shareholder companies funding the research, and Smith. But the technology was not planned in terms of a series of *a priori* technology transfer decisions or a business impact analysis.

Dove stated (interview, March 1, 1991): "The problem we have is getting the companies to decide, in consort, how they are going to put the technology to work. . . . Such planning would allow MCC to discard some technology transfer strategies which would not work." But Dove had reservations concerning how much technology transfer planning was possible: "I told him: 'It's not going to work, Craig. . . . You'll probably not be able to figure out exactly what approach you're going to use." (Dove interview, March 1, 1991)

By 1990, in addition to project management, MCC was promoting technology transfer by (1) third-party licensing, (2) vendors, and (3) spin-out companies. For example, CDC, a participant in MCC's packaging program, invested funds to set up a multichip module substrate facility. CDC sold the technology back to MCC's members and to others, but the MCC members that paid for the technology received incentives: (1) time preference, (2) price preference, and (3) royalties. While all three parameters added value, lead time was most important. Cadence, a CAD vendor, was invited to join MCC's CAD Program for the specific purpose of taking MCC's CAD technology to market strength, supporting the technology, and selling it back to MCC's members.

TECHNOLOGY SPIN-OUTS

By 1989, several of MCC's software research programs had been in operation for six to seven years, the point at which technology results were expected. While many MCC scientists believed their research had commercial potential, their technologies were not being brought to market by the member companies. Two initial attempts to spin technology out of MCC to commercial applications in 1988–1989 met with resistance. MCC administrators and shareholder officials were not ready to support such a drastic change in the consortium's mission.

Shortly after his arrival, Fields began to assess shareholder support for MCC's existing research programs and projects. Based on his analysis, research activities were terminated, most of which were in the software program. MCC researchers affected by this downsizing had three options: (1) find another funded research activity at MCC, (2) find employment elsewhere, or (3) become entrepreneurs and spin their MCC-developed technology out of the consortium. So partly as a result of MCC researchers' frustration with the lack of commercialization of their technologies, partly out of a desire to become entrepreneurs and prove the worth of their technologies, and partly out of the need to find new career options, a few of MCC's scientists began to explore the possibility of creating spin-out companies.

THE CASE OF EVOLUTIONARY TECHNOLOGIES, INC.

As MCC's first technology-based spin-out company, Evolutionary Technologies, Inc. (ETI) had to overcome many obstacles at MCC and the shareholder companies. Dr. Katherine (Kay) Hammer was the MCC researcher and entrepreneur who championed ETI's formation. Hammer, as her name suggests, exhibited the fortitude of hardened steel, a trait that served her well as she pursued her entrepreneurial venture.

Hammer received her Ph.D. in linguistics from the University of Iowa in 1973 and taught at the college level for ten years. She made the transition to software development by spending a year as a visiting scholar at the Center for Cognitive Science at The University of Texas at Austin. In 1981, she joined Texas Instruments as a systems programmer for its Digital Systems Group. When Hammer relates her saga in launching and growing ETI, she often draws on her linguistics background by using metaphors and analogies from medieval military strategy.

Hammer was one of MCC's first direct hires into the VLSI/CAD research program. She moved to the ACT Program in 1987. Gazing out her office window in 1993, she described MCC as "a wonderful place for a researcher to work." She remembered the mid-1980s at the consortium as exciting times. The founding executives had high expectations, and MCC researchers believed that they were going to make important technological contributions to the U.S. computer industry. She particularly enjoyed the state-of-the-art facilities and the luxury of being able to work on well-funded, long-term research projects that suited her talents and interests. However, like many MCC scientists who had been with the consortium since its inception, Hammer experienced both emotional highs and lows during her tenure at the R&D consortium. The low periods became more pronounced in the late 1980s as funding problems increased, along with pressures to transfer technologies to the shareholder companies.

In 1987, Hammer got the idea for EXTRACT, a data conversion tool that facilitated the automated translation of computer data from one format to another. She had determined through market research that U.S. business was spending approximately $4 billion per year migrating data between incompatible formats. High-cost computer programmers had to write task-specific translation programs for each conversion. EXTRACT was designed to allow users to migrate data from flat files or older data bases to new structures such as relational data bases, with a considerable savings in time and expense.

Hammer tried to secure research funding to pursue the EXTRACT research but her efforts met with little success until, in February 1988, Gene Lowenthal, the ACT Program director, managed to obtain $300,000 out of his discretionary budget for nine months of exploratory funding. Hammer and her MCC research team worked long hours on EXTRACT. Lack of funding threatened to kill the project, but by September 1988, Hammer managed to convince seven corporate sponsors (most were not primarily software companies, some were shareholders, some were existing associate members, and some were new MCC associates) along with the U.S. navy to provide $2 million in research funds and about $1.5 million in indirect benefits for two more years of support.

As the 1990s approached, Hammer noticed that more and more of her colleagues were leaving the consortium to pursue careers in industry or university settings. Research projects were being terminated, while few MCC-developed technologies—especially software technologies—were being used by the shareholders. Even fewer were being manufactured as products.

Hammer and a team of five researchers had developed EXTRACT to industrial strength. The technology was ready to be developed and marketed as a product. The ETI "tool kit" minimized the effort needed to write computer software programs to move data between incompatible systems, such as from an IBM to a DEC computer. EXTRACT's user-friendly data migration capabilities allowed "point and click" file conversion, used template and grammar editors for experienced users, and had an internal data base of predefined libraries.

Hammer was convinced that EXTRACT was a promising technology that would meet a growing market need. But she was unable to convince the shareholder companies that were funding her research to provide her with additional funding to develop EXTRACT for their internal use or as a product.

Dove commented (interview, March 1, 1991):

> With EXTRACT we had a set of Beta-testable tools,
> and it appeared that a couple of MCC's companies
> would like to use the technology, but they wanted to
> have market-strength tools and support. . . . That gave
> us a heck of a challenge because the users looked at it
> as maybe we're paying twice: we're paying for the
> research, and we're paying for buying the tools and the
> support.

Out of her belief in the technology and frustration at not being able to pursue its commercial potential, Hammer began to explore the possibility of forming a spin-out company. As she stated (interview, March 1, 1993): "I could have shelved the technology and gone on to another project with new funding, but I decided I didn't want to do that." At the time, however, she did not realize just how difficult it would be to launch MCC's first spin-out.

Hammer had the support of several officials in MCC's hierarchy, such as the consortium's chief legal counsel, Tom Kirkland. Others, however, feared that the precedent of a spin-out company would set an inappropriate example for MCC scientists. The idea of entrepreneurial and spin-out activity at MCC also made shareholder TAB and BOD representatives uncomfortable. Grant Dove was cautiously supportive of Hammer. However, with the arrival of Craig Fields came a strong advocate for the spin-out concept. Fields suggested that the start-up might energize MCC and create an environment that would help attract other capable entrepreneurial scientists to the consortium.

Hammer was assisted in her venture by Robin Curle, who currently serves as ETI's executive vice president of sales and marketing. Curle was a veteran of twenty years in software sales and management. Her experience as a vice president in two previous start-ups and a turn around was of enormous benefit to Hammer (interview, April 27, 1993): "As we traveled the country looking for investors, she groomed me to seem like more of a businessperson and less of an academic."

Curle had been recruited to MCC's ACT Program, about one year earlier, to help market the research program and its products. She was not warmly received by many ACT scientists, who were critical of spending "research funds" on a marketing person. When

Hammer's potential spin-out appeared on the horizon, Curle leaped at the opportunity. As she said: "The carrot for me [in coming to MCC] was to get a company spun out." She added: "This was a very high-risk research project that was successful. We [ETI] hit the ground running. The research had already been funded" (Curle interview, March 1, 1991). Along with Curle and Lisa Keeler, a technical contributor, Hammer founded ETI, Inc. It took about a year and a half of "dancing around" for Hammer and Curle to build the trusting relationship that was needed to launch and grow ETI. As Hammer remembered (interview, March 25, 1993): "I kept wondering if she was out for a quick buck and should I watch my back. Robin was worried whether I'd bring in a new V.P."

In April 1990, Hammer received TAB approval for her spin-out venture. She commented that MCC was perhaps the only place where this kind of research and development process could have taken place. The ability to develop the EXTRACT technology in close collaboration with industrial users, sharing the cost and risk of the research, led to a set of products solving real-world problems. In June, Hammer received approval "in principle" from MCC's board of directors to spin out ETI.

Of the seven companies that had funded the EXTRACT research, only one considered taking equity in ETI, but anticipating trouble in obtaining board approval, the company settled for a corporate license. The other research funders declined any further involvement with ETI. Hammer recruited her former research team of eight, including four former Texas Instruments employees from the consortium. "It stung MCC," Hammer acknowledged (interview, March 1, 1991), "but they didn't try to stop me."

Hammer could have remained at MCC's headquarters while she launched her start-up, but instead she opted to be one of the first tenant companies in the newly formed Austin Technology Incubator (ATI). "As MCC's first spin-out, I knew they would want ETI to succeed even if I left the consortium and by going into ATI as one of their first tenants I was gaining the support of a second, highly visible organization." By August, Hammer had developed ETI's business plan and by November the company was accepted into ATI.

ATI had been formed in 1989 as an alliance of public and private interests to nurture technology-based companies for regionally based job growth and economic development. The IC^2 Institute, The University of Texas at Austin, and the Institute's director, Dr. George Kozmetsky, had launched ATI as an experiment in business, academic, and government collaboration. ATI assisted ETI in closing the technology transfer gap by providing subsidized office space; infrastructure support; pro bono legal, accounting, marketing, and other services that came from the Austin business community; and assistance in securing equity funding. As Laura Kilcrease, director of ATI, remembers (interview, October 6, 1992): "When Kay first came to ATI, she was most interested in the 'tangibles' . . . office space, the fax machine, receptionist. Soon, she came to see the value of the 'intangibles' . . . ATI's know-how network, which provided her with business and management expertise and venture funding—the things that really added value." (See Chapter 6 for a more complete description of ATI.)

Hammer worked through an investment banker to raise capital from additional corporate investors, one of which made a bridge loan for EXTRACT. Still, while engaged in the time-consuming process of product development, it was difficult for Hammer to pay bills and meet the company's payroll. When times were especially lean, ETI employees went on half-pay. Hammer invested her own funds in the company and when expenses kept mounting, EXTRACT's employees survived financially by hiring out as software consultants.

By September 1991, Hammer had shipped her first product. In November, she closed her first round of funding ($1.5 million) with Menlo Ventures of California's Silicon Valley and Admiral Inman, who had been encouraged to invest in the venture by George Kozmetsky. Both Inman and Kozmetsky serve on ETI's board. As Hammer emphasized (interview, March 25, 1993): "When it comes to investors and advisers, it's great to have somebody you can trust and not get blindsided by." Other additional EXTRACT shareholders include MCC and the company's founders and employees.

Having the support of ATI and "friendly" investors allowed ETI the ability to structure more favorable financial support while the company developed its products. Graduate students from The University of Texas at Austin, through a course taught at ATI, conducted market research and designed a customer data base for ETI. By early 1992, EXTRACT had 11 employees and $300,000 in sales, with offices in Atlanta and Los Angeles. In August, EXTRACT negotiated reseller agreements with Pyramid Technologies, Bachman Information Systems, and Dun and Bradstreet Software. In December, Hammer and her start-up company graduated from ATI and rented 10,000 square feet of office space in Austin, employed 30 workers, closed about $2 million in sales, and received a second round of funding at $1.5 million. ETI currently has over 20 customers, including Fidelity Investments, Kodak, Motorola, Honeywell, NCR, CDC, and Enron Gas Services.

A WIN-WIN SITUATION

MCC licensed the data extraction tool kit to ETI in exchange for a small equity share in the spin-out and royalties from sales of EXTRACT products. After paying MCC $4 million in royalties, ETI will own the technology. In addition to royalties and a technology licensing fee, MCC got a visible, commercial win in ETI, a win that demonstrated the market value of the consortium's technologies to member companies, MCC scientists, and the public. MCC member companies that supported the EXTRACT research are preferred customers, and as such, they receive substantial price reductions and customer support in implementing ETI's software. "In the future, after ETI is successful and growing, the company will become an associate member of MCC." (Hammer interview, March 1, 1991)

It was a long, difficult road for Dr. Hammer to get from her initial desire to create a spin-out company to ETI's graduation party at MCC, where then-CEO Dove told Hammer that he "felt like a proud grandfather." Fields stated to the local press: "It's good for us, and good for the incubator, and good for the companies. Long before we know whether this particular company is a success, there will probably be some more of these. . . . Each one will have its own peculiarities."[21] In June 1993, Hammer was named Austin Entrepreneur of the Year in the high-tech division by *Inc. Magazine.*

As mentioned in Chapter 4, in addition to Evolutionary Technologies, MCC had spun out three other technology-based companies by 1993: one, Corporate Memory Systems, was accepted into the Austin Technology Incubator in early 1992; the other two, Pavilion Technologies and Tamarack Storage Devices, remained within MCC's headquarters building.

With the spin-out of four companies and the establishment of MCC Ventures (see Chapter 4), MCC had come a long way from its original mandate of being a long-term, goal-directed, research organization that was to transfer pre-competitive technology to the shareholder companies. In certain ways, MCC was beginning to fulfill the expectations of Texans who, back in 1983, had erroneously viewed the consortium as an important center of entrepreneurial spin-out activity in the Austin area.

CONCLUSIONS

Technology transfer from the research laboratory to product commercialization is a time-consuming, complex, and difficult process that requires a high degree of collaborative activity. MCC was formed to conduct long-term, goal-directed research. It was the job of the shareholder companies to convert MCC-produced technologies into products for competitive advantage. By 1987, this level 1 technology transfer perspective (see Figure 5.2) had become unsustainable as MCC's shareholder firms became more short-term oriented and more critical of the consortium's research and operations.

As shareholder support for MCC was pushed down the hierarchies of the funding companies to operating division levels, cost-benefit analysis by shareholder managers was increasingly made in terms of technology transferred, leading to product applications in a timely manner—level IV technology transfer. Bottom-line judgments were made by division managers who funded MCC's research and who were themselves evaluated according to their own short-term performance.

On the one hand, MCC's member-company diversity has complicated the consortium's management and the transfer of its technologies. On the other hand, this diversity can be viewed as a benefit in terms of developing the horizontal and vertical interorganizational alliances that facilitate level IV technology transfer (product/process commercialization). MCC's current emphasis as an R&D consortium is one of enabling technologies, applications, and accelerating the creation of standards by bringing together small and large companies, technology suppliers and users, venture funding, and business expertise. Here it is not the long-term versus short-term orientation of MCC's research that is the significant issue, but whether the consortium can become a new business incubator, while creating value added for its member companies.

MCC's technology transfer success has been measured differently by different evaluators. Some member companies have supported MCC's long-term, pre-competitive mission, while others wanted shorter-term, usable research results. Some company officials have been content to monitor MCC's research by reading documents and attending member-company meetings. Others wanted industrial or market-strength products. Some member company personnel see themselves as full partners with MCC, while others see themselves in competition with the consortium.

MCC-based technology champions have traditionally been far removed from the marketplace. The technology belonged to MCC's member companies and was to be transferred to them for product development. Many of the rewards associated with entrepreneurship could not be attained by MCC scientists or the member-company receptor. As MCC moves to a more entrepreneurial culture, entrepreneurial rewards are being earned, and risks are being borne, by the developers of MCC's technologies.

At least one high-level manager at MCC and several representatives from the shareholder companies argue that the consortium's difficulties with technology transfer rested most with the low quality of research and the lack of capable people involved in the transfer process. In opposition to this view is the realization that many MCC-developed technologies have been applied and commercialized by the member companies. At times a rather modest technology advance (e.g., Proteus) was commercialized as a result of extremely dedicated and capable researchers at MCC and product development people at the shareholder companies. The quality and marketability of MCC's software and hardware technologies are also validated with the success of each spin-out company that survives and prospers.

Timely technology transfer to successful product/process application has become a key factor in determining the success of U.S. consortia and it is becoming an important determinant of the viability of federal laboratories and research universities. MCC's first ten years has provided a rich laboratory in which to assess the barriers and evaluate solutions to interorganizational technology transfer. Managers in technology generating and using organizations can accelerate technology transfer by fostering interactive communication within and across organizational boundaries, providing meaningful rewards for those involved in the transfer process, facilitating cultural and strategic proximity, and emphasizing the importance of problem/market driven research. Technologists and managers that cross functional and organizational boundaries to the benefit of the transfer process need to be nurtured and rewarded as, in the past, technologists have been rewarded for the pursuit of research excellence. However, even with such management actions, there will still exist a technology transfer gap between quality research and successful product/process application. Linking talent, technology, capital and business know-how with market need is the current challenge of MCC Ventures, a subject that we will cover in greater depth in Chapter 6.

NOTES

1. Technological innovation is the total process by which a new idea is generated and transformed into a commercial product. The term has been used predominantly concerning the management of innovation within a firm. The term "diffusion of innovations" generally refers to the movement of an innovation among individuals across organizational and national boundaries. The term "technology transfer" has been used in different ways by scholars and practitioners. Some argue that the phrase conveys the wrong image of the process—i.e., it implies the handing off of an object. We define "technology transfer" as the application of knowledge (Segman, 1989). We use the term "technology transfer" (rather than "technology commercialization," "adoption," "utilization," and so forth) in part because these two words are most commonly used to describe the challenging process faced by R&D consortia and other research organizations like federal laboratories and research universities in getting their technologies transferred across organizational boundaries into market-strength applications.

2. Publications devoted to this subject include Kidder (1981), Leonard-Barton and Kraus (1985), Reich (1989), Smith and Alexander (1988), and Williams and Gibson (1990).

3. The number of patents is often used as a measure of research and technology achievement. The number of patents granted to MCC during its first five years is as follows: 3 in 1987, 5 in 1988, 18 in 1989, 19 in 1990, and 30 in 1991. This total of 75 patents compares favorably with the industry average for computer-related patents (CHI TechLine); see Chapter 4, Appendix 4.2.

4. One of our MCC respondents noted that "while the Japanese would value and

reward the production of such intangibles, Americans would not." This point of view was supported by Toshio Yoko (general manager, Japan Electronic Dictionary), who was quoted in *The New York Times* as defending the Fifth-Generation Computer Project: "I think the side-effect is the main effect." For example, hundreds to thousands of Japanese engineers were trained in advanced computer sciences, and they are now applying these skills in their respective Japanese companies. (Pollack, 1992)

5. The word "serendip" can be traced to the island of Sri Lanka, where, according to Elizabeth Hodges, the author of *The Three Princes of Serendip*, the word was coined by Horace Walpole. He wrote on January 28, 1754, about the princes in this fairy tale: "As their highnesses traveled, they were always making discoveries, by accidents and sagacity, of things they were not in quest of." (Sawhney, 1990, p. 10)

6. The terms "research strength," "industry strength," and "market strength" convey different measures of a technology's success and different degrees of its readiness to be commercialized. Research strength is established through peer review and accepted scientific procedures. Industry strength requires that a company have the internal support needed to take a technology, use it, and perhaps build a prototype. Market strength means that a technology is documented and will stand the test of the marketplace. It is ready to be commercialized as a product.

7. This case analysis is based on published reports and archival documents as well as interviews and correspondence with Robin Steele (August 20, 1990) and Ed Krall (July 27, 1990), both of NCR, and Charles Petrie (July 27, 1988 and April 22 and June 22, 1993), of MCC.

8. Malcom Baldrige played an instrumental role in gaining congressional support for the National Cooperative Research Act, which supported and defined the operation of cooperative research ventures like MCC.

9. An interesting caveat concerning refereed publications is that for MCC researchers, journal articles ranked as being important because of a perceived "halo effect"—i.e., publishing one's research in a prestigious journal vested that research with more credibility. One MCC respondent told us of a case in which a researcher sent memos and reports within MCC and to shareholder companies but failed to get a positive response until his work was published in a noted journal.

10. When we visited the offices of MCC researchers, we were often shown stacks of confidential and nonconfidential research reports that MCC scientists had prepared and that were mailed to research project participants. We visited the offices of these researchers and saw these same reports stacked out of sight and out of mind. MCC researchers could say: "I've fulfilled my obligation. . . . I transferred the technology." Yet the response generated from shareholder scientists was minimal. We know of one high-tech company in Silicon Valley, California, that tried user-friendly video reports to enhance the effectiveness of media-based technology transfer, only to realize that the target audience (the company's sales personnel) did not take the time to view the tapes. Currently, this company is using seemingly less sophisticated audiotapes with technology messages presented in the form of short stories to try to convince the recipients to listen to the tapes while they are "trapped" in their cars during their slow commutes in Bay Area traffic.

11. Articles reporting this survey research on MCC include Smilor, Gibson, and Avery (1990); Smilor and Gibson (1991); and Gibson and Smilor (1991).

12. One of our MCC respondents emphasized: "MCC never saw a product marketer, product planner, or product strategy manager at these [TAB and PTAB] meetings" (Curtis interview, March 21, 1992). MCC researcher, Bill Curtis contended that one of MCC's shortcomings was that the consortium emphasized the engineering and technical side of R&D, and left the marketing and product development responsibilities to the shareholders.

13. Long-term members of this informal ad hoc alliance for improved technology transfer at MCC were Jim Babcock, Jeff Conklin, Charles Petrie, Elaine Rich, and Jerry Werner.

14. In 1993, the concept of a "reverse assignee" had yet to be implemented at MCC. One of the basic challenges of making such bridging roles work is finding capable people who have both technical and people skills and who are willing to travel frequently and spend extended periods of time on site at member-company locations.

15. When 3M built its new multimillion-dollar research facility in Austin, the company went to considerable extra expense to construct a building that would "encourage" personnel from different functional areas to "bump into one another" in hallways or common meeting areas. The 3M facility in Minneapolis, Minnesota, surrounds an open courtyard, and especially in the winter months, this "barrier" is thought to inhibit communication between researchers and product development people. Although it rarely snows in central Texas, 3M wanted to avoid such a barrier in its Austin facility, and it spent extra millions to build a structure which would facilitate cross-functional communication.

16. MCC member companies 3M, Lockheed, and Motorola moved R&D units to Austin shortly after MCC came to town. However, as of 1991, most MCC shareholder and member companies had neither manufacturing divisions nor R&D divisions in the Austin area.

17. Homophilious communication occurs when both the transmitter and the receptor of a message are similar with respect to criteria important to the communication exchange. They may have similar training and research backgrounds, for example. Heterophilious communication occurs when the communicators differ with respect to particular criteria, such as when a researcher and a marketing person try to communciate. While homophilious communication can be facile, a greater amount of new information is often transmitted through the "weak ties" of heterophilious communication dyads. (Rogers and Kincaid, 1981)

18. In their competition with MCC scientists, shareholder-based researchers have distinct advantages in transferring technology to their organization: the shareholder scientists are in closer proximity (both culturally, geographically, and strategically) to their company's management, production, marketing, and salespeople. Shareholder researchers also have greater access to feedback from company employees and customers.

19. LISP allows the development of complex programs in considerably less time than conventional programming languages such as C. However, the choice of the LISP platform meant that the prototype code developed at MCC was

rarely used by the shareholder companies. The LISP stations that the shareholders eventually acquired were housed in their research labs. There was little opportunity to test intermediate prototypes in a production environment. As a result, MCC researchers were generally deprived of concrete feedback that could assist in the evolution of a prototype to product.

20. One case that exemplifies this point involved a researcher from a shareholder company who worked in Dallas, Texas. The researcher read in an MCC report about a technology that he believed would be useful to his company. However, the researcher was unable to obtain the time off or the travel allowance to fly to Austin in order to visit MCC for a few days. The company accountant was maximizing his mandate to cut travel costs. Meanwhile, the shareholder company was paying several million dollars to fund research at MCC. The link to the MCC technology was never made. The reverse scenario also occurred. MCC's policy was that the shareholders should pay for trips by MCC personnel to the shareholder companies. "In fact no one wants to pay for trips to the shareholders. This is especially true for exploratory trips," commented Petrie. (E-mail, August 20, 1990)

21. Indeed, each spin-out has had its own peculiarities. Pavilion is a 1992 spin-out from MCC's neural nets program. In fall 1991, MCC's board became concerned when it learned that this spin-out would largely be funded by Japanese and Korean venture capital. As one shareholder told our MCC informant: "We spent several million dollars in this technology only to see it handed over to the enemy. . . . That is not why we are funding MCC." This shareholder was argued down and outvoted in the board of directors' resolution that allowed the spin-out and the transfer of the license rights.

6

LOSERS AND WINNERS: REGIONAL
IMPACTS OF MCC OVER TIME

The Admiral came to town and the rocket was lit, and
it went straight up.

> Robert Lane, chairman, InterFirst Bank,
> quoted in the *Austin American-Statesman,*
> April 14, 1984, p. C-1

If we were making the MCC site selection in the spring
of 1985 instead of the spring of 1983, I would have to
think very carefully about whether I would recommend
coming to Texas.

> Admiral Inman, in a March 1985 interview

To prepare for the twenty-first century, communities,
corporations, and countries must implement creative
strategies and innovative tactics that take advantage of
changes in globally competitive market systems. The
challenge and opportunity is to effectively link intellect,
technology, capital, and enterprise at the regional level.

> George Kozmetsky, director, IC^2 Institute,
> in a July 1993 interview

MCC's decision to locate its headquarters in the capital city
of the Lone Star State led to important consequences for Austin and
the University of Texas. These impacts spread like ripples in a pool
to other cities and universities, with immediate impacts causing less
direct consequences for the nation's academic, business, and government institutions. This chapter describes MCC's direct and indirect
socio-economic impacts on Austin, on the three other site finalists

(San Diego, Atlanta, and Raleigh-Durham), and on other regions of the United States. We also consider the impact of these larger socio-economic contexts on MCC.

As described in Chapter 3, the national competition for MCC built to a fever pitch by May 1983. When Austin was announced as the winner, the region's public and private leaders were ecstatic. At times the hype was a bit inflated as reported in *The Neal Spelce Austin Letter* (May 17, 1983):

> The decision today by MCC to locate in Austin falls right behind—in economic significance to our community—the decisions to locate the State Capital and the University of Texas here . . . the national economic spotlight will now turn on Austin as the result of MCC's decision to use our city as the location for the effort which many believe will be the reason for the United States's continued domination in the world's new economy.

The national competition for MCC was also seen as a turning point for regional economic development strategies throughout the United States. As Dan Pegg (president, San Diego Economic Development Corporation) commented after learning of Austin's victory (news release, May 17, 1983):

> The intensity of state and municipal competition for MCC is an overall trend we will see repeating over and over in the future. Our experience with MCC's concerns expressed a sense of urgency to our community and the state in taking steps to mitigate the perceived negatives from companies wishing to do business with us.

During the national competition for MCC, the consortium came to be valued not just for its projected annual budget of $75 million and the 500 jobs that would be added to the local economy, but for the many new high-tech firms that were expected to spin out from the state-of-the-art research conducted at the consortium.[1] Furthermore, as the competition gained momentum during spring 1983, it was increasingly believed that the winning site would get a significant boost toward becoming a technopolis, a major world-wide center of computer and microelectronics research. Today, looking back at over a decade of social, political, and economic events, we can now evaluate specific as well as broader, longer-term impacts of MCC on regional economic development and U.S. industrial competitiveness.

A 1985 analysis of the economic impacts of MCC indicated that most of the benefits (about 80 percent) went to local Austin businesses, where wages were spent and supplies and equipment were purchased (Farley and Glickman, 1986). The spread of such impacts beyond the Austin economy to the rest of Texas was relatively slight. This spatially limited effect contrasts sharply with the high hopes for statewide economic benefits when MCC was recruited. Mark White, governor of Texas, wrote (on November 23, 1983) to prospective MCC supporters that:

> The formation of MCC will prove to be, I am convinced, a turning point in the economic history of Texas and the United States. This combined effort of 13 companies represents our country's best effort at maintaining world preeminence in the increasingly critical field of information processing and computer technology. . . . The impact that the presence of this research talent will have on Texas could be immense. The spawning of new companies that could result would serve to broaden Texas' economic base from one which is now vulnerable to the frequent fluctuations in the prices of oil and gas. MCC should add economic vitality to Texas and give additional momentum to our state's engines of growth much the same way Silicon Valley has in California.

The likely effects of MCC on Texas were cited in an interoffice memo from Carol Bennett to Lee Straus (senior vice president and chief administrative officer, Texas Commerce Bancshares, Inc., Houston and organizer of the MCC Leadership Steering Committee) on August 31, 1983, as:

- The creation of 2,000 new jobs in Austin within two years.

- Within five years, the generation of 100 new companies directly related to supplying and servicing the electronics industry. These new businesses will create a further 2,000 jobs directly and an additional 4,000 indirectly.
- Heightened levels of employment will, within five years, result in an increase of $10 million per year in state and local taxes.
- Because manufacturing activity that occurs at the forefront of technology tends to locate close to research activity, some 10,000 new electronics manufacturing jobs will be created in Austin and San Antonio in three to seven years, generating an additional 20,000 jobs in the area.
- The investments in high-technology personnel and research and training facilities at the University of Texas and Texas A&M will immeasurably enhance the existing attractiveness of Dallas–Fort Worth for electronics and defense plants, San Antonio for medical equipment development, and Houston for space and energy technology.
- Within seven to ten years, the increased employment and business activity should result in expanded state and local tax revenues approaching $75 million per year.

In short, it was believed, or propagated, that MCC would turn the state's economy into an information society in a hurry. It was an unrealistic expectation, at least in the short term. During the first few years immediately after MCC's arrival in Texas, 1985–1987, Austin and the state suffered a dramatic economic downturn that was caused by a range of factors, most of which were *not* related to MCC, such as: declining prices for oil, agricultural products, and livestock; a devalued Mexican peso; changing tax laws that negatively influenced real estate investment; and a nationwide economic slowdown. However, MCC was an important catalyst that fueled Austin's real estate boom in 1983–1985, which contributed to the severity of the economic bust that was to follow.

In the long term, it could be argued that MCC largely fulfilled the expectations and pronouncements of Governor White and others who championed bringing the consortium to Texas. Perhaps most important, MCC's location decision immediately caused a dramatic change in the global perception of Austin as an important, emerging U.S. technopolis. The fact that MCC chose Austin also caused U.S. executives and public officials to take a closer look at this capital city and to re-examine their own regional commitments for economic development.

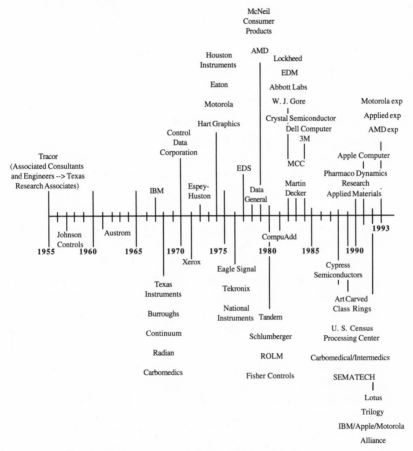

Source: IC^2 Institute, The University of Texas at Austin.

Figure 6.1. Major technology-based company relocations, foundings, and expansions in the Austin area, 1955–1993

HIGH TECHNOLOGY IN AUSTIN PRIOR TO MCC

Austin was a growing Sunbelt city for several decades before MCC came along. The history of high-tech development in Austin goes back about 40 years to the birth of Tracor, the city's first home-grown *Fortune* 500 company. IBM came to Austin in 1967, Texas Instruments in 1969, Motorola in 1974, AMD in 1979, Tandem and Schlumberger in 1980, and Lockheed Missiles and Space in 1982 (Figure 6.1). However, the two main forces driving the city's economy were The University of Texas at Austin (with a resident student population of about 48,000) and state government, including related enterprises such as the state headquarters for many professional associations.

Silicon Valley's rapid high-tech growth was grounded in the creation of the Stanford Industrial Park in 1951, the vision and inspired leadership of Stanford University vice president and engineering professor Frederick Terman, and a high quality of life that was quite affordable in the early 1950s (Rogers and Larsen, 1984). Central to the valley's emergence as the world's preeminent technopolis were two "incubator companies"—Fairchild and Hewlett-Packard—which fostered regional growth through spin-out activity. During the 1960s and 1970s, the most important incubator of high-tech development in Austin was Tracor. The technology base for Tracor was spun out of the Balcones Defense Research Lab and the College of Engineering at the University of Texas, in 1955, by Frank McBee and three colleagues. Producing a wide variety of military avionics and commercial products, Tracor grew to become a *Fortune* 500 defense contractor, employing 2,200 by the mid-1980s. The company had generated at least 15 direct spin-outs by 1983, and these spin-outs fostered many indirect (second- and third-generation) spin-outs employing a total of 6,377 people by 1984 (Figure 6.2).[2]

So by 1983, Austin was well on the way to becoming an emerging technopolis with high-tech employment of 22,800, representing 6.1 percent of the city's labor force, compared to 2.6 percent for Texas and 3.7 percent nationally (Farley and Glickman, 1986). Twenty-eight major high-tech firms employed thousands of Austinites. IBM had 7,000 employees located at its 500-acre Austin site where manufacturing operations began with the IBM Selectric typewriter and moved into communications products and circuit

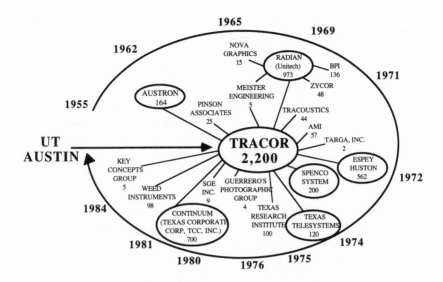

Source: IC^2 Institute, The University of Texas at Austin.

Figure 6.2. First- and second-generation TRACOR technology spin-outs and job creation, 1955–1984

packaging. Motorola employed 5,000 in its microprocessor division, and Texas Instruments data systems group employed 3,000. Lockheed's Austin plant was just beginning work on sophisticated military command and control systems and employed 1,400 by the end of 1983. These companies were headquartered elsewhere in the United States but located their manufacturing plants in Austin largely because of relatively low wages, low taxes, a large and nationally prominent university, and a high quality of life.

Despite this growing concentration of technology-based industries, before MCC's arrival in May 1983, Austin was not generally thought of as a high-technology research center. One of the most important and immediate impacts of MCC's location in Austin was the sudden and dramatic change in national and international perceptions that Austin was an emerging center for computer and microelectronics research. The 400 or so jobs provided by MCC proved to be almost insignificant when measured against the perceptual impact of MCC's picking Austin, Texas, as its world headquarters.[3]

Immediately after the MCC site-selection competition, the U.S. media reported that Austin was poised to become the nation's next Silicon Valley. Southwestern Airlines' in-flight magazine titled its June 1983 cover story: "The Day the Chips Fell on Austin." The October 1984 issue of *Fortune* magazine reported "Austin, Texas: On a High-Tech High." John Watson (interview, January 23, 1987), the Austin real estate developer and head of the governor's and Austin task forces for MCC, observed that MCC was like a "hypodermic needle" that gave Austin's economic growth a shot in the arm:

> Mega, megamillions were made in real estate, finance, and other business activities. . . . Economic development through recruiting companies to Austin was as easy as duck soup. In 1983 and 1984, we were not the hunters. We were like the pretty girl sitting at the side of the dance floor, and when somebody came up that we liked, we kinda winked and flirted a little. But we didn't appear to be looking for companies.

Indeed, soon after MCC came to Austin, major high-tech firms either located in the area or began major expansions there: Lockheed's software R&D operation moved from California to Austin; Motorola committed to a major expansion in Austin; 3M moved an R&D division of 3,000 employees from Minnesota to Austin; and in 1988, after a major national competition, SEMATECH located in Austin (see Chapter 7). By 1993, over 20 major technology-based firms had located in Austin since MCC came to town in 1983 (see Figure 6.1). These companies did not move to Austin or expand their Austin-based operations simply because of MCC's presence but rather because of the same factors that led MCC to pick Austin for its headquarters: the University of Texas; an affordable high quality of life; a growing high-technology infrastructure, including an important research base; and a supportive and relatively inexpensive operating environment.[4]

John Watson, Governor Mark White, and Pike Powers, three key figures in the 1983 Texas campaign for MCC, were central participants in 3M's decision to locate in Austin in 1984. Watson (interview, January 23, 1987) remembers:

They called me because they knew I had been involved in MCC and because I knew the local 3M man [who headed the small 3M unit that was already in Austin]. I got one-on-one with the St. Paul brass [at 3M head-quarters] in convincing them to come to Austin. But it was like a picnic compared to what we did for MCC. There was no real competition. It was just a matter of my trying to communicate with them. All Governor [White] did, although it was very important, was to host a dinner party for five 3M executives, Pike [Powers], and myself one night at the mansion. We sealed it up tight as a drum that night. This was nine months after the MCC announcement, but the MCC competition made it easier. They had good feelings about Austin, MCC, and Texas. 3M joined MCC. They would never have joined otherwise. It [MCC] just wouldn't have gotten into their [3M's] stream of consciousness.

In May 1984, Governor White (always the salesman, he talked from notes written on a Post-it pad—a 3M product) announced at a press conference on the capitol lawn that, for the first time, the Minneapolis-based company would locate a major R&D division in another state. The Austin boom was building. While MCC's location had a major impact on the perception of Austin as an emerging high-tech center, 3M's location decision had a larger direct impact on the escalation of Austin's real estate boom.

In retrospect, in terms of the public at large, just how important was MCC's (or SEMATECH's) coming to Austin and to Texas? In a survey of the most significant events of the 1980s, conducted by the Associated Press of Texas, neither MCC nor SEMATECH was voted as one of the top ten stories of the decade. Toping the list were the failures of Texas' thrift and banking institutions and the steep decline in oil prices.

THE BOOM THAT FUELED THE BUST

From 1980 to 1984, total employment in Austin's metropolitan area increased by 41 percent, the total population of Austin increased by 15 percent, and the metropolitan area's population increased by 18 percent (Table 6.1). From 1982 to 1985, Austin added 10,000 manufacturing jobs, two-thirds of which were in the high-technology research, manufacturing, and service sectors. Such growth set off a two-year housing and building boom, one of the most spectacular booms that has ever occurred in a U.S. city.

In 1983, the average price of a house in Austin was $88,464; two years later, this figure had shot up to $106,177, a striking increase of 21 percent (Table 6.2). During this same period, 1983–1985, 25,000 new apartment units were built in Austin. During 1984 and 1985, 19 new hotels were constructed. From 1982 to 1986, Austin's office space *doubled*. Twelve major office buildings were constructed, creating the highest office vacancy rates (41 percent) in the nation by 1987. Austin had 200 developers and builders in 1982, and more than 800 in 1985, including some of the biggest-name developers in the nation. Austin was a boomtown, caught up in a hysteria of building, speculation, and skyrocketing prices.

Table 6.1 Employment and population growth figures documenting Austin's economic boom, 1980–1984

	1980	1984	Percentage Growth (1980–1984)
Total employment in the Austin metropolitan area	257,000	362,000	+41
Total population of the city of Austin	346,000	399,000	+15
Total population of the Austin metropolitan area	536,000	632,000	+18

Source: Based on Farley and Glickman, 1986.

Table 6.2 Multiple Listing Service (MLS) average home values,
Austin MSA from 1982–1993

Year	Average Home Value in Travis County
1982	$80,347
1983	$88,464
1984	$101,738
1985	$106,177
1986	$110,091
1987	$101,826
1988	$90,587
1989	$85,562
1990	$84,744
1991	$89,391
1992	$106,265
1993 (May)	$115,817

Source: Austin Board of Realtors, Austin MLS.

During 1984–1985, Austin's skyline was changing so fast that local wags declared the building crane to be the new state bird. John Gray (interview, January 22, 1987), the chamber of commerce representative who made Austin's pitch in Chicago, noted:

A tremendous speculative boom happened. Everybody overhyped the fact that MCC was coming to Austin and would attract other business operations here. The uninitiated expected it to happen overnight. Speculators are always looking for something to fuel a boom like that. Any piece of land you could get your hands on, you could sell it even before you closed your contract. Contracts were "flipped" in some instances as much as 20 times before they closed. MCC was just the triggering device to set off this boom.[5]

THE MILLION-DOLLAR TACO STAND

There were some truly incredible real estate deals. One piece of land flipped (that is, was bought and sold) six times in a single day (Wysocki, 1989). Another spectacular land deal involved a million-dollar taco stand. For 24 years, Moses Vásquez operated the Tamale House, selling tacos and other Mexican food for reasonable prices. "You can eat here if you have 50 cents," said Vásquez (Stipp, 1984). The Tamale House was located on West First Street and Congress Avenue, 12 blocks from the state capitol and just across the street from Town Lake. When the post-MCC boom hit Austin, several developers tried to buy Vásquez's 7,000 square-foot lot, but he refused to sell. Finally, in 1984, Vásquez was made an offer that he could not refuse: $1.6 million, about 20 times what he had paid for the place in 1969. The Tamale House was bulldozed and replaced by a 22-story office building, further adding to the overbuilding of Austin. Perhaps more than any of the other real estate transactions that occurred during the 1983–1985 boom, the story of the million-dollar taco stand came to symbolize the dramatic impact of MCC (and related events) on the local economy.

Just after MCC arrived, the most popular skit at the Austin press corps' 1983 Gridiron Show was "Bobby Ray, Superstar," a spoof based on the Broadway play. Disciples carried "Bobby Ray" on their shoulders, singing: "Should we give him land? Willie Nelson's band? A dump on Barton Springs, a co-ed in jeans?" The chorus sang: "MCC, MCC, your microchips will set us free." The song ended: "Time will tell what the price will be" (Northcott, 1987). Indeed, time did tell. In the early 1980s, the rapidly expanding Texas economy was fed largely by growth in the oil business and immigration of people that led to an increase in the absorption of office space and a heightened demand for residential units. "Everyone felt oil was going to $500," said Hugh Caraway, senior vice president of Property Company of America. "Everyone was riding on the top of the world and credit was everywhere" (quoted in Melody and Wagley, 1989, p. 158). The tax act of 1981, the lack of barriers to entry (credit and land were in ample supply), banks and savings and loans (S&Ls) that were uncharacteristically aggressive in lending money, lenient approvals for developers, and the greed and carelessness of some all contributed to Austin's building boom.

The ride up the roller coaster of rising land prices was breathtaking, but this rapid increase was followed by a sickening jolt and a steep plunge. The 1983–1985 boom, in which Austin land values increased by 53 percent (Stipp, 1984), was followed by a spectacular bust in which land prices plummeted to below their pre-MCC levels. In 1982, Austin had 16 million square feet of office space, and an occupancy rate of 95 percent. By 1986, 14 million square feet of office space had been added, and the occupancy rate dropped to 70 percent. By mid-1987, an additional 6 million square feet of office space had been constructed, and occupancy dropped to 60 percent (Walters, 1988). In the early 1990s, many of these office towers, commercial buildings, and other structures stood as empty, forlorn temples to the boom that had passed—markers of unrestrained growth and of fortunes lost.

EROSION OF TEXAS' COLLABORATIVE SPIRIT

"Before the [1983–1984] boom, Austin had the lowest cost of living of any major city in the United States. Now [1987] it is overbuilt, overpriced, and deeply in debt" (Northcott, 1987). Just as suddenly as Austin had shot up the fast escalator of the real estate boom, it dropped back to the ground floor. What happened?

THE BUST

A major factor in Austin's 1985 economic downturn was the collapse of the Texas oil industry. In 1986, the price per barrel of West Texas intermediate crude nose-dived from a high of $39 to $13 soon after OPEC moved to increase market share by increasing production. The number of domestic working rigs declined from a high of 4,520 in 1981 to approximately 700 in 1986. Cheap oil was very bad news for the Lone Star State. For every $1 drop in oil prices, $100 million was lost to the Texas economy (Evans, 1986). About 22 percent of what Texas produced was tied to oil and petrochemicals, making the state five times more dependent on oil and gas than the nation as a whole (O'Reilly, 1985).[6] Oil revenues provided 28 percent of the state's budget in 1982. So when oil prices drop, as they did in the mid-1980s, everyone in Texas groans. The depressed oil market, coupled with a weakened Mexican peso and low farm prices, caused a feeling of gloom and doom in Texas. The shadow of economic decline thoroughly chilled Austin's superheated growth. As the outlook for the agricultural and the oil businesses became bleak, banks began to shift even more of their assets into real estate.

Tax syndication, which enabled developers to pocket money up front and to realize enormous savings, was also an important impetus behind much of the development between 1981 and 1985. "We could get a loan for 90 percent of the project cost and syndicate half of the ownership for an additional 30 percent. We would consistently create a 20 percent profit upon project completion," said Caraway (quoted in Melody and Wagley, 1989, p. 159). Many Texans perceived real estate as the quick and easy path to wealth. "In 1982, we saw the overbuilding and the decline coming," said Louis Sklar, executive vice president of Gerald D. Hines Interests. "However, on a scale of one to ten, we saw a four. What we actually received was a 9.9" (quoted in Melody and Wagley, 1989, p. 159). The Tax Reform Act of 1986 effectively eliminated all the tax-motivated investors from the marketplace, and the weak economic deals had to stand on their own merit, which was often minimal. As Melody and Wagley (1989) concluded, the fact that all of these problems occurred in rapid sequence contributed to the severity of the downturn.

By 1986, the banks and savings and loans that had financed the new homes, the downtown office buildings, and the land deals began to regret their post-MCC go-go decisions. As Texas banks and savings and loans went under, they dragged down other businesses with them. The 1983–1985 Austin boom began to look like a house of cards. One of the best indications of the Austin bust is provided by average home values, which dropped 35 percent from 1986 to 1989 (see Table 6.3). New housing starts dropped from 7,000 in 1984 to a mere 1,800 in 1989. Austin's workforce lost 10,000 construction jobs in the post-1985 bust, as new building slowed to a standstill.[7]

The collaborative spirit that Austin displayed in winning MCC began to fade in the mid-1980s, eroded by the realities of unrestrained growth, greed, and go-it-alone city politics. The public/private segments of the technopolis wheel (see Chapter 3) began to fracture, with cracks of discontent replacing the collaborative spirit that had existed in 1983. As a high MCC official told us in a 1987 interview (Rutishauser, January 23):

> If we were looking at Austin in 1987 as opposed to 1983, we'd have to be concerned about a couple of things we were not concerned about then. Both revolve around one of the original strong appeals of the area in the first place—everybody working together to build a better future for Texas. The first concern is the question we had in California in 1983. Will the state [Texas] continue to fund higher education at the level [at which] it needs to be funded? Everybody says: "Yes, we want to do that." But there are now real budget battles to fight. Second, unfortunately, the relationship between the business community and the city government has deteriorated. The city government is schizophrenic, in that part of the people want Austin to look like it did in the 1950s.

In a little over a year after MCC came to town, and after verifying the importance of the pursuit of educational excellence, the state legislature cut UT's financial appropriations—*before* the sharp decline in oil prices. A noticeable lack of collaboration among Austin's business, academic, and local government/community began to surface. Community leaders argued that Austin was being developed too rapidly, leading to soaring land and housing prices. The city's government became strident about protecting Austin's affordable quality of life. Austin's city council increased electricity rates for corporate users, required a complicated web of permits for the construction of new buildings, and avoided decisions on such projects as relocation and expansion of the city's airport and construction of a convention center.[8] A chilling effect on high-tech development, and on economic growth in general, resulted from the antigrowth movement in Austin. MCC, 3M, and other newcomers to the area began to wonder if the Austin that they were experiencing was the city that they had been promised.

It took 3M two and a half years to obtain a building permit for its massive R&D complex on the outskirts of Austin. The city set electric power rates so that the price per kilowatt was highest for large-volume users. 3M considered the rates exorbitant and elected to build its own power-generating plant. This outcome was hardly an exemplar of public/private collaboration to beat back Japanese competition in high technology.[9]

Enlightened self-interest was surely a motive among the main players in Texas' bid for MCC. For example, John Watson, the real estate developer and head of both the Austin and governor's task forces for MCC, stood to gain new real estate business as a result of MCC's coming to Austin. However, it would be wrong to assume that his dedication to bringing the R&D consortium to Austin was purely a result of such personal objectives. Before the MCC competition, Watson had a well-earned reputation as a highly ethical local developer who engaged in community service activities. Watson's easy charm and sharp mind were important reasons why the governor's and Austin task forces operated as smoothly and efficiently as they did.[10]

Watson was one of the dozen local builders who constructed high-rise office buildings in downtown Austin soon after MCC came to town. In early 1987, we interviewed the developer in his penthouse office atop one of his new buildings—14 stories of shining steel, glass, and stone—constructed during the Austin boom. Watson noted that we were sitting above 13 stories of empty offices, and that he was paying several thousand dollars of interest per day on a multimillion-dollar loan. However, the weight that sank The Watson Group was a deal gone sour with the city of Austin. In 1983, Watson had signed a contract with Mayor Ron Mullen (the progrowth mayor) to build Austin's new city hall. Watson invested heavily in plans and design. In 1985, Frank Cooksey (Austin's antigrowth candidate) defeated Mullen's bid for re-election. Watson and the city council, led by Mayor Cooksey, went through extended legal skirmishes, and finally, the council declared the city's contract with Watson null. In 1988, John Watson's real estate company declared bankruptcy.

One of the best-known Texans to ride Austin's real estate roller coaster was former Governor John Connally. He launched an elite housing development at the height of Austin's boom. The subdivision, named "Estates above Lost Creek," consisted of immense homes ranging in cost up to several million dollars. Targeted customers were high-tech executives who were expected to move to Austin after selling expensive homes in California or New York. Houses were built but few sold. Connally was forced into bankruptcy. Local wags began calling the housing development "Mistakes above Lost Creek" (Northcott, 1987).[11]

Many of the developers involved in the land flipping and rapid overconstruction were not Austin- or Texas-based. They were not attuned to the Austin socio-political scene, and they became frustrated with Austin's no-growth policies. The dilapidated shells of their unfinished construction efforts still mark the hills surrounding Texas' capital city.

PROPONENTS OF NO-GROWTH

To understand Austin's rapid boom-to-bust cycle, it is necessary to understand the city's history and political dynamics. Just as the capital city is bisected by the Colorado River, the city's citizens and politicians are often divided over growth/no-growth issues. In the 1930s, the Colorado was dammed to create Lake Buchanan, Lake LBJ, and Lake Travis, which flow into Town Lake and run through the center of Austin en route to Matagorda Bay on the Gulf of Mexico.[12] Within three miles of the state capitol is Barton Springs, the largest unchlorinated, spring-fed pool in the nation.

Austin residents pride themselves on their city's "laid-back" lifestyle and relaxed pace of living. The city is a live-music center to which Nashville and Los Angeles look for talent. On any given weekend, the city has about 175 live-music venues. The local music scene reaches its peak each spring with the nationally and internationally prominent South by Southwest Music and Media Conference. Austin's indigenous music scene is also widely known through the nationally televised "Austin City Limits." In 1991, Austin formally adopted as its slogan "The Live Music Capital of the World."

In 1983, many Austin residents were *not* pleased that their city was becoming a center for high-tech growth. They remembered the good old pre-MCC days when Austin was a quiet, folksy place;

a university town; a state capital; and not much more. They looked back fondly to when swimming in Barton Springs was not restricted due to polluted run-off from housing and golf course construction and there was no traffic congestion on MoPac or Route 183 (interstate highways running north/south and east/west through Austin).

Escalating real estate prices caused a housing affordability crisis that detracted from the city's overall quality of life. Rising real estate prices forced the closure of live music venues, some of which were demolished for office building construction. No-growth sentiments existed before MCC came to town and they were activated in 1982 when the Armadillo World Headquarters—the Fillmore East of Country Music—was bulldozed for a high-rise office building. Under the guidance of manager Eddie Wilson, the cavernous Armadillo had grown to capture the essence of Austin's inclusive, laid-back lifestyle. Grandparents, parents, and children; students, high school teachers, and professors; politicians and business types; hippies, the culturally elite and bikers all converged on the converted roller-skating rink to drink Lone Star and eat chips and dip served by the "guacamole queen." Depending on the night, the eclectic audience would hear the rock, blues, or country music of such talent as Janis Joplin, B.B. King, Leon Russell, Van Morrison, Arlo Gutherie, Jerry Garcia, Willie Nelson, the Vaughan Brothers, or Lou Ann Barton; enjoy an occasional string quartet; and watch local theater or the Austin Ballet—"Armadillo World Headquarters, where the high and low cultures meet." After the loss of the Armadillo, the arrival of MCC and 3M just added fuel to the no-growth fire.

During the mid-1980s, one of the most visible no-growth representatives on Austin's seven-member city council was Sally Shipman, a former housewife, schoolteacher, and community activist. Shipman was elected because of her strong opposition to Austin's high-tech growth. One of her first actions on the council was to co-author a letter that was sent to *Fortune* 500 companies telling them *not* to come to Austin unless they checked with the council first.

As Austin's unemployment and financial problems (e.g., funds for parks and recreation areas, health services, and education) grew serious, Shipman began to soften her no-growth stance. Still, hers was the only vote against the city council resolution to waive all development fees for SEMATECH (the manufacturing consortium of 14 U.S. semiconductor companies that Austin attracted in 1988; see Chapter 7). Shipman (December 5, 1989) based her opposition to the SEMATECH deal on these grounds:

- The city council was not fully informed about the incentives package that it was asked to approve for SEMATECH. Shipman felt these decisions were made by "good old boys in a smoke-filled room" and the city council was asked to rubber-stamp them after the fact, as was the case with MCC and 3M.[13]
- The microelectronics industry of Austin did not provide enough jobs to the city's underclass, especially blacks and Latinos living in East Austin, where unemployment was highest.
- Austin was encumbered with a huge debt (totaling several million dollars) from building roads, water and wastewater facilities, and electrical improvements for the new high-tech industries that had moved there in recent years. Why should the city's citizens be saddled with such debt so that big business could profit?
- The hype given to Austin's microelectronics industry led to the 1983–1989 boom-bust cycle, and to the business failures in the Texas banking industry, caused by bad loans to builders. Austin did not need another boom-bust cycle.

STEADY GROWTH

A half-dozen years after Austin's rapid and dramatic boom-bust, business and government leaders look back and remember the mid-1980s as a learning experience. Indeed, following the announcement that SEMATECH would locate in Austin in 1988, there was no real estate boom. Not even a boomlet.

As Austin's economic resurgence has been far less dramatic than the mid-1980s boom, the hope is that it is also more stable and sustainable. There is far less real estate speculation, heavy lending by financial institutions, and overly optimistic expansions by local service providers. Technology-based growth is coming from new arrivals, local expansions, and home-grown start-ups. During the early 1990s, Austin's growth rate ranked at the top of Texas' major cities and near the top for the nation (Ladendorf, 1993c). According to Texas' comptrollers office, the number of engineers, software programmers, and other technical jobs more than doubled from 1983 to 1993. The key contributor to Austin's economic recovery was the burgeoning high-tech base (see Figure 6.1). This growth is considered somewhat remarkable because of such inhibitors as the (1) shrinkage of the financial industry and resulting credit crunch, (2) defense slowdown and military base closures, and (3) loss of wealth by much of the investor class in central Texas owing to the past real estate depression.

During the early 1990s, Austin benefited from expansions in large, established high-tech firms such as IBM's advanced worksta-tions and systems division (with about 7,000 employees). Motorola expanded its semiconductor production facilities, adding 2,300 employees since 1991, for a total of 7,300. AMD (with 2,000 local employees) announced plans to build a $650 million chip-making facility in southeast Austin, and Applied Materials (with a $20-bil-lion expansion in the works) plans to employ 2,000 by the end of the decade (see Chapter 7). New arrivals included customer support centers for Lotus Development Corporation and Apple Computer. Austin was selected as the home of the Somerset Design Center, the IBM/Motorola alliance, which began in March 1992 and employed about 300 chip designers from both companies.

Austin's high-tech growth has been fueled by a surge of local start-ups. One of the most visible and successful has been Dell Com-puters, founded in 1985 by Michael Dell, who at the time was a premed student at The University of Texas at Austin. Dell was also a computer hacker who understood personal computer (PC) technolo-gy as well as the wants and needs of PC users. Dell first sold PC clones out of his car and then from his dorm room. By 1988, he employed 400 people and by 1993, Dell Computer Corporation had become Austin's second home-grown *Fortune* 500 company with about 4,000 employees and facility expansions in Austin and the surrounding area. As Tracor had done some 40 years earlier, Dell exemplifies the regionally based economic development impact of high-tech start-ups.

So, ten years after MCC came to town and was quickly followed by a major economic downturn, Austin was fully back on the
road as an emerging technopolis. In 1993, Austin was ranked number one in terms of "Top Cities for Growth" (Alphametrics, an
international consulting firm). Austin posted total growth of 12.2
percent from 1990 to 1993 (the U.S. overall growth for the same
period was .5 percent). Austin was also ranked number one by *The
Wall Street Journal* as the city receiving the most relocations and
expansions from California. As of October 1993, the average price
of an Austin home was $115,800, and the city led the nation in the
increase of multifamily building permits. Occupancy was pushed to
100 percent at most major hotels, and apartment rentals and commercial space were in short supply. The challenge was to have
Austin remain a livable city as it continues to grow. As commented
by Austin Mayor Bruce Todd: "If Austin is to remain at the top of
these lists, it must stress quality growth, not quantity; otherwise,
we'll end up just another large, undesirable place on the map."
(quoted in Breyer, 1993)

QUALITY EDUCATION AND TECHNOLOGY-BASED
ECONOMIC DEVELOPMENT

One major impact of MCC on the nation was to jolt state
governments into funding increases for their educational infrastructure. The governors of many states told Admiral Inman that their
courtship of MCC had caused them to look at education and
economic development in a different way. Inman worked to channel
state leaders' disappointment at losing MCC into efforts to improve
their universities and to create their own "MCCs" (as we detail later
in this chapter). Meg Wilson, then coordinator for the Texas Science
and Technology Council in the Texas governor's office, remembered
that public/private leaders who "lost" MCC called to thank Texas
for helping their state gain higher expenditures for university-based
microelectronics research.

Inman was as devoted to promoting microelectronics research
as he was outspoken in his criticism of state governments for under-
funding public education, particularly at research universities. He
portrayed investment in education as a patriotic strategy that was

crucial to American success in international competition. Bob Rutishauser (interview, January 23, 1987) commented:

> Inman, who is a nut on education and investment in education, used everything he could to get anybody, anyplace in the country, to put more emphasis on education and technology development. . . . I've never seen anyone that has the national interest at heart in so many ways as Inman does. . . . [During the MCC site selection,] he figured here is an opportunity to focus public attention on certain problems and get some resources dedicated to their solutions. So there was undoubtedly a good side and a bad side [for a finalist city] to losing MCC.

In 1984, Texas ranked forty-sixth among the 50 states in the average Scholastic Aptitude Test (SAT) scores of its high school students. Beneath all the hype surrounding MCC and 3M, Governor White knew that something had to be done about raising the quality of the state's primary and secondary education if Texas was to become a meaningful player in the coming globally competitive technology-based economy. White decided to initiate a major push for quality primary and secondary education in Texas. This seemingly noble quest turned into a quixotic adventure.

White was a Democrat; at the time, Ross Perot was a Republican. These two Texas power brokers had not met before the MCC competition. But by working together in the Texas campaign for MCC, they formed a bond of mutual respect. Perot agreed to serve when White asked him to chair a bipartisan commission in 1984 to improve the state's educational system. As was his style, Perot took on the assignment with gusto, traveling the state to interview teachers, parents, and students. The Perot Commission proposed a state law that Perot helped steer through the Texas legislature. The law required that a high school student pass each of his or her major courses or else become ineligible to participate in extracurricular activities. One-fourth of Texas students were promptly suspended from football teams, high school bands, cheerleading squads, and other school activities. Irate parents and athletics enthusiasts bitterly attacked Perot. Bumper stickers appeared such as "Warning—I don't brake for Ross Perot" (O'Reilly, 1985). In late 1986, Texas House Speaker Gib Lewis proposed softening the "no pass, no play" rule by lessening the suspension from extra-curricular activities from six to three weeks. The political fallout from the Perot Commission and the ensuing controversy con-tributed to Mark White's defeat in his 1986 bid for a second term as governor. But the tough state law did improve the quality of public education in Texas.[14]

IMPACTS OF MCC ON THE UNIVERSITY OF TEXAS

During the MCC site competition, public and private leaders made frequent reference to the important role of quality higher edu-cation on technology-based economic development. A memo from Carol Bennett to Lee Straus (November 16, 1983) stated:

> Many prominent observers have attributed the rise of California's Silicon Valley to private funds invested in the University of California and Stanford University. They have differentiated the technological orientation of these universities from the focus on traditional edu-cation of East Coast institutions, and they have found that the location of Silicon Valley in California was not attributable solely to superior weather. The focus on science, the encouragement of entrepreneurship by the universities, and the investments by the private sector into research and training were all vital factors.

Governor White wrote in a November 23, 1983, letter to Howard Creekmore, president of Houston Endowment, Inc.: "These institutions [UT and Texas A&M] have made the commit-ment to grow with MCC and develop into the top concentrations of talent in these fields [computer science and electrical engineering] in the world. MCC will be the magnet to draw approximately 300 Ph.D. scientists to Texas from all sections of the nation." Indeed, about a year after MCC came to Austin, The University of Texas at Austin scored an academic coup that was to have a major impact on faculty recruiting among the nation's prestigious universities. Peter O'Donnell, Jr., a wealthy Texan who lived in Dallas, was impressed with Austin's winning MCC and Texas' drive to become a world competitor in high technology. O'Donnell wanted to make a major financial gift to (1) spur educational excellence in the Lone Star State and (2) have a positive impact on Texas' economic development. He conferred with Admiral Inman and Ross Perot and decided to endow several faculty positions at The University of Texas at Austin.

Originally, O'Donnell had thought of giving $2 million, but he eventually upped the ante to $8 million. O'Donnell's gift was then matched by donations from other private sources from throughout Texas. Then, as part of the university's centennial program, the $16 million was matched again by interest from the Permanent University Fund. The result was 32 endowed chairs in the Colleges of National Science and Engineering, each funded at $1 million, in such fields as electrical engineering, materials, computer science, molecular biology, chemistry, math, and physics. The salary for each of the endowed professorships was around $100,000 per year, a very high figure in 1984. The purpose was to bring additional brainpower to UT in the academic areas that intersected most directly with MCC's research interests.

Finding talented academics to fill these prestigious chairs turned out to be a challenging task. Worldwide, there is only a limited number of such scholars. Furthermore, when offered an opportunity to move to Austin, these elite professors often received counteroffers from the institutions where they were currently employed. The net result was to create major salary increases for microelectronics and computer science professors at Berkeley, Stanford, MIT, Illinois, and elsewhere (Figure 6.3). By 1991, seven years after the O'Donnell gift to UT, about half of the endowed chairs were filled. The addition of these scholars boosted UT's academic rating in electrical engineering and computer science, and the effort had a ripple effect leading to increased research grants and to the recruitment of highly qualified doctoral students to UT.

By 1986, UT's Department of Computer Sciences was receiving three times as many graduate student applications (about 700 per year) as it had before MCC came to Austin in 1983. The department was admitting 30 Ph.D. candidates per year with average Graduate Record Exam scores of 1,400, up from 1,250 before MCC came to Texas. Professor Al Dale (interview, January 22,

1987), chair of the department, believed that the quality of graduate student applicants improved because the University of Texas had improved its academic quality through (1) funding from "The Texas Incentive for Austin," (2) the endowed professorships, (3) state-of-the-art research equipment and doctoral student stipends in the Department of Computer Science, and (4) opportunities for doctoral students and faculty to work part-time at MCC. "The Texas Incentive for Austin" included $750,000 per year for ten years for graduate student aid in computer science and electrical engineering. Inman wanted MCC to have a beneficial impact on UT's ability to attract and keep qualified doctoral students.

THE EYES OF TEXAS ARE UPON US

The University of Texas recently got some impressive new furniture.

32 "chairs" worth a million dollars apiece.

Now they're looking for 32 professors worth a million dollars apiece—to occupy those endowed chairs.

And that's just the tip of the oil well.

In the last 4 years alone, the University of Texas has established over 600 endowed faculty positions, part of an unprecedented effort to attract the finest minds in the country.

How does that affect Cal?

If we're not careful, many of our top scholars may soon be wearing cowboy hats.

And with nearly half of our distinguished faculty retiring in the next decade, we must do everything possible to retain and recruit promising young minds.

There's something you can do, too.

Simply by contributing to the endowment of faculty chairs, you can play an important role in helping Cal reach its goal of 100 new chairs by 1990.

These chairs will provide outstanding professors with equipment, research assistance and many other critical support services. And also ensure that Cal's great tradition of scholarship continues to thrive.

Right here.

Not deep in the heart of Texas.

U.C. Berkeley

It's not the same without you.

Figure 6.3. Ad in *California Monthly*, alumni magazine of the University of California at Berkeley, December 1984

Despite these impressive wins, Texas' momentum for educational and research excellence was not sustained. Shortly after MCC announced that it was coming to Austin, the Texas legislature voted to decrease appropriations for higher education by 3 percent. The economic downturn in Texas' economy in 1984 motivated the state legislature to slash budgets. Texas was the only state in the nation to reduce appropriations for higher education that year. This cut was carried out despite the fact that oil prices were still at $30 per barrel and state revenues had increased by $5.4 billion (17 percent) over the previous year. The University of Texas was whacked by a $22 million cut in 1986–1987. The university began to lose some of the outstanding faculty whom it had acquired in 1983 and 1984. As John Watson (interview, January 23, 1987) stated:

> The state revenue shortfalls were so monumental (in 1984, 1985, 1986, and 1987), and within the legislative process, there has not been a learning curve of the true appreciation of what higher education can do for economic development. The legislature's leadership is as far ahead of the curve as anybody can be, but there are lots of house members that just don't understand. So compromises have had to be made.

Admiral Inman remarked in March 1985, when the Texas legislature was considering further cutbacks in the University of Texas' budget: "If we were making the MCC site selection in the spring of 1985 instead of the spring of 1983, I would have to think very carefully about whether I would recommend coming to Texas." The legislature got Inman's point and lightened its cuts in UT's budget. Then in 1986, faced with a revenue shortfall and the possibility of new state taxes, the House budget writers proposed dipping into Texas' education trust funds: the Permanent University Fund and the Permanent School Fund. Again Inman responded:

> If they proceed with these cuts . . . there will be no more research organizations moving to Texas, I am absolutely sure of that. This runs totally counter to all the promises that were made to me and the companies that formed MCC that this state was going to sustain

the movement to greater investment in its higher education. (quoted in Editorial Opinion, *Austin American-
Statesman*, August 13, 1986, p. A6)

MCC's site-selection team believed it was crucial to locate the
consortium near a strong university with the momentum to become
an academic leader in microelectronics research. Inman wanted to
be at the end of a pipeline of talent, homegrown at a local university.
Over the years, there have been many educational and research links
between MCC and the University of Texas. However, not all of UT's
students, faculty, and administrators regard the university's ties to
MCC as beneficial. Selected groups of UT students see the link as a
cost, not a benefit, to their educational experience. As reported in
the *Daily Texan* (Jenny Lin, a UT student, January 27, 1992, p. 1):

> When [MCC] selected Austin as its base of operations
> in 1983, it got one heck of a deal. . . . Part of the com-
> mitment included building a new $30 million com-
> plex—of which the university paid $14 million—for
> MCC on UT-owned land. Annually UT funds are also
> budgeted for building, grounds, and custodial mainte-
> nance. . . . In return, MCC pays the University an
> annual leasing fee of $2 a year [$1 for the building and
> $1 for the land] in a 10 year lease.

In the same article, UT systems Chancellor Hans Mark estimated the benefits the university received from MCC to be $2 to $3
million per year.[15] William Stotesbery, MCC's director of communications, reported that 15 to 30 UT students worked at MCC in
one capacity or another at any given time. Yet many UT undergraduate and graduate students failed to see the value of MCC to
their educational experience or the value of increased U.S. industrial
competitiveness.

Robert Ovetz, a member of the Graduate Professional
Association, UT-Austin, stated in the *Daily Texan* (January 27,
1992, p. 1):

> MCC is a nice example of using our money and our
> resources to subsidize government research. . . . Even if

you did calculate the returns from MCC, it would be a
lot less than UT's contributions. . . . UT is becoming an
outright business by allowing the University to engage
in using people and public money as a way to subsidize
activity geared toward profit-making orientations. . . .
We're being robbed—not just the students, but the people of Austin.[16]

THE AUSTIN TECHNOLOGY INCUBATOR

When MCC came to Austin in 1983, many of the community's public and private leaders expected the city's economic growth
to be spurred by spin-outs from the R&D consortium, despite the
fact that MCC officials emphasized that this was *not* what the consortium was about. In 1989, when the Austin economy was work-

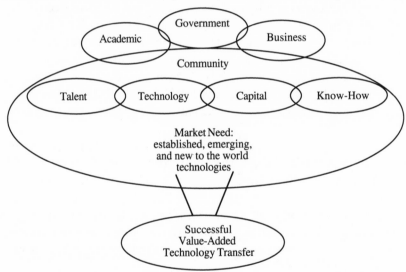

Source: IC[2] Institute, The University of Texas at Austin.

**Figure 6.4. Successful value-added technology transfer by linking
talent, technology, capital, and know-how at the regional level**

ing its way out of the post-MCC bust, the idea of a regionally based technology incubator was being championed by Dr. George Kozmetsky. To Kozmetsky, such an incubator would facilitate public/private collaboration at the regional level and it would spur economic development, fill vacant office space, train entrepreneurs, and create high-value jobs. The facility, which came to be called the Austin Technology Incubator (ATI), would act as a "lightening rod," linking talent, technology, capital, and business know-how to market needs (Figure 6.4).

"The [ATI] alliance is a result of a year-long strategic process among its sponsors to build indigenous home-grown companies in Austin," stated Kozmetsky at a February 1989 press conference inaugurating the ATI. The incubator was funded by the city of Austin ($50,000 per year for three years), the Greater Austin Chamber of Commerce (at $25,000 per year for three years), Travis County (a one-time donation of $70,000), and private funds (primarily, a donation of $50,000 from the Kozmetsky family). In-kind services totaling $163,000 were donated by UT and local firms, including much of the incubator's furnishings and pro bono legal, marketing, financial, and other business services.

Figure 6.5 depicts the overall components of ATI, which seeks to fill the technology transfer gap between research strength and market applications (see Chapter 5). The primary drivers for the incubator are entrepreneurs and technology, which come from the private sector, universities, federal laboratories, and R&D consortia. To be accepted as a tenant company, entrepreneurs have to submit a business plan that is evaluated by seasoned business professionals as well as technologists. The entrepreneurial culture of ATI fosters the linking of cutting-edge research and technology with venture financing and the realities of the marketplace. Whereas technology reports, patents, and technology licenses are often the output of R&D environments, they are considered inputs to the due diligence and business plans required at ATI. The incubator shortens the product development cycle by broadening tenant entrepreneurs' know-how in market research, finance, advertising, quality issues, management, sales, and service. ATI's culture emphasizes the importance of intangibles (e.g., business know-how and learning from each other) over tangibles (e.g., nice office furniture) and it reinforces resource leveraging and spending hard-to-get cash on factors that add value and speed product commercialization.

MCC's first contact with ATI came in 1989, when Donoho Publishing Group (DPG) licensed an MCC-developed technology to manufacture parallel computing hardware and software for desktop workstations. Operating as a tenant company in the incubator, Andrew Donoho's one-person start-up evolved into Fusion Data Systems and received prestigious awards for its CPU accelerators such as the Eddy Award at the Eighth Annual MacUsers Editor's Choice Awards in San Francisco in January 1992. Fusion Data Systems graduated from the incubator in November 1993 with $1 million in revenues, five products, and eight employees.

The evolution of MCC came full circle—from opposing to encouraging spin-out activity—in 1990 when the consortium spun

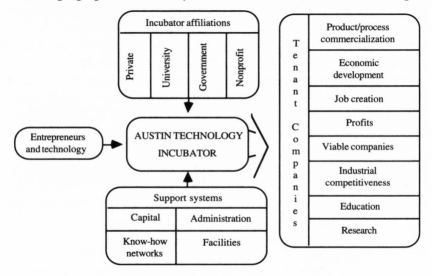

Source: Adapted from Smilor and Gill, 1986.

Figure 6.5. Critical components of the Austin Technology Incubator, IC² Institute, The University of Texas at Austin

out its first company, Evolutionary Technologies Inc., into ATI (as described in Chapter 5). A second company, Corporate Memory Technologies, was spun out of MCC into ATI in 1991, and in 1992,

GEORGE KOZMETSKY

Dr. George Kozmetsky is the kind of first-level influencer (see Chapter 3) who moves freely and with impact in the worlds of academia, government, and business. Kozmetsky makes things happen. He generally keeps a low profile, preferring to work behind the scenes, encouraging others to receive public credit for his ideas and actions. Kozmetsky started his career on an academic track with a Ph.D. from Harvard and an appointment to the faculty at Carnegie Mellon University. He dropped out of academe for a 20-year career in business, first serving as assistant controller at Hughes Aircraft Company and then moving to Litton Industries, where he was a corporate vice president and co-director of the systems division. In 1960, Kozmetsky left Litton to co-found Teledyne, Inc., a producer of consumer electronics and aerospace weapons. Kozmetsky became a multimillionaire and in 1966, he returned to academic life as dean of the College and Graduate School of Business at The University of Texas at Austin.

Within the University of Texas system, Kozmetsky has been instrumental in the creation of new centers and institutes, including the Center for Energy and Economic Diversification at The University of Texas at the Permian Basin, the Advanced Robotics Institute at The University of Texas at Arlington, and the Institute of Biotechnology at The University of Texas at San Antonio. He also helped create the Large Scale Programs Institute, which advanced long-term research, planning, development, and managment of such large-sale programs as a lunar colony and manned exploration of Mars.

In 1977, Kozmetsky founded the IC^2 Institute— Innovation, Creativity, and Capital—which concentrates on scholarly work in unstructured problem domains in a range of academic disciplines. One such area focuses on linking theory and practice in the study of technology-based economic development. The institute performs as a catalytic organization linking talent, networks, and knowledge—regionally, nationally, and internationally. Kozmetsky stepped down as dean of UT's business school in 1982 to work full time as director of the IC^2 Institute, while continuing to serve as executive associate for economic affairs at the University of Texas system.

Dr. Kozmetsky is a founding member and has served as president of The Institute for Management Science (TIMS), chancellor of the American Society of Macro-Engineering, and a fellow of the American Association for the Advancement of Science. As a member of the advisory panel of the Office of Technology Assessment, Kozmetsky was appointed to evaluate the defense technology base in the United States. He has served state and local governments on task forces, commissions, and policy boards.

As an "international technology ambassador," Kozmetsky consulted with the USSR State Committee for Public Education and worked with the USSR Academy of Science to develop programs for economic development and technology diffusion. In the People's Republic of China, he consulted with the Technological Corporation of China and the State Council on Science and Technology. In Japan, he worked with Mitsui & Co., Inc. in venture capital projects on the commercialization of technology and with the Mitsubishi Research Institute on large-scale research projects.

On September 30, 1993, in recognition of his far-reaching influence in technology and education, Kozmetsky was awarded the National Medal of Technology by President Clinton, and in the same month, the MIT Enterprise Forum of Cambridge, Inc. established the Entrepreneurial Leadership Award and designated Dr. Kozmetsky as its first recipient.

Fourth State Technologies was spun out of SEMATECH into the incubator (see Chapter 7). Three years after its founding, ATI was fulfilling Kozmetsky's vision and serving as an important bridging organization to commercialize technologies developed at MCC, SEMATECH, and the University of Texas, thereby creating high-paying jobs, helping to decrease Austin's glut of vacant office space, and contributing to U.S. industrial competitiveness.

Each of ATI's sponsoring organizations has its own motivation for supporting the incubator, and these motivations color how they judge ATI's success. The city of Austin and Travis County are mostly concerned with creating jobs and increasing the region's tax base. The Greater Austin Chamber of Commerce is concerned with accelerating economic development in high-technology industries and increasing chamber membership. The Austin business community, which supplies much of the pro bono expertise, wants to nurture new customers. The University of Texas gains a laboratory of entrepreneurial technology-based companies for research and teaching purposes. Students from a variety of disciplines attend classes taught at the incubator. They work on tenant company tasks as term projects and study the formation and management of fast-growth technology companies as living case studies. Many are hired by the start-up companies as they grow and graduate from ATI. The university earns income from technology-based companies that spin out and are nurtured in the incubator. Most important, however, the university has a visible and dynamic bridging organization that (1) helps students and professors gain real-world experience and research opportunities in technology commercialization and (2) links real-world entrepreneurs, business professionals, and university resources.

Since 1989, under the leadership of Director Laura Kilcrease, ATI has expanded its activities three times to occupy two facilities, a suite of offices, and a light manufacturing facility and wet lab, totaling 60,000 square feet. Twenty-seven high-tech start-ups currently reside in the incubator. The tenant companies are given three years to graduate and launch new businesses in biotechnology, telecommunications, computer, and software industries. Also resident in the incubator is the Texas Capital Network that matches funds from private investors (ranging from $10,000 to $3 million) with entrepreneurial companies. As of late 1993, ATI had graduated 13 firms and generated over 550 technology-based jobs in the Austin area. The graduated companies occupy 151,000 square feet of office, manufacturing, or laboratory space and have attracted more than $200 million in capital investment. In 1993, ATI (under the auspices of the IC^2 Institute, The University of Texas at Austin) received a $5.4 million grant from the National Space and Aeronautics Administration (NASA) to establish "Field Center Based Technology Commercialization Centers" at Johnson Space Center, Houston, Texas, and Ames Research Center, Silicon Valley, California.

WINNING BY "LOSING"

In retrospect, the three cities that lost MCC to Austin in 1983 have, in a certain sense, also won in terms of regionally based economic development. When MCC located in Texas, government, academic, and business leaders in other states envisioned their flagship universities' being stripped of outstanding professors and top gradu-ate students in microelectronics and related computer industries, wooed to UT by the million-dollar endowed professorships and well-paying doctoral student stipends. These leaders also worried that other high-tech companies would follow the lead of Lockheed, 3M, and Motorola in relocating their R&D divisions to Austin. In the long term, losing MCC to Austin looked like a multiple disaster.

UNIVERSITY OF CALIFORNIA BUDGET INCREASES

California did a good bit of soul searching in 1983 after los-ing MCC, especially since "they figured they had it [MCC] in the bag. . . . The news that Austin won really shook them up" (Inman interview, March 1985). After the MCC competition, David Saxon, president of the University of California system, formed a special committee to study San Diego's failure to lure MCC to California. Bruce Darling, assistant chancellor of the University of California at San Diego (UCSD), remarked (interview, July 15, 1986): "The Texas newspapers were crowing about the great success that they had achieved. A lot of those newspaper articles flowed back to California, and a lot of them were directed to the governor's office in California."

At the time of MCC's site visit to San Diego in 1983, Governor Deukmejian's proposed state budget called for a cut in the University of California system's allocation. After San Diego lost MCC, the governor was stung by the criticism of his handing of the Golden State's bid for the consortium. In a dramatic reversal, the UC system's 1984 budget was increased by 30 percent, and in 1985, the budget increased a spectacular 45 percent from its 1983 level! The single-year (1984–1985) budget increase of 30 percent was the largest university budget increase in the history of California—a turnabout that was inspired by California's losing MCC.

The February 1984 issue of the *San Diego Magazine* pub-lished an article by Lt. Governor Leo McCarthy titled, "Have We Been Starving Our Universities and Colleges into Mediocrity: What California Can and Must Do about the Loss of High-Tech University-Related Industry." By March 1984, an estimated one-fourth of the 70 faculty members in microelectronics at UC-Berkeley had been approached by either MCC, UT, or Texas A&M. The UC budget increases included a 16.5 percent raise in faculty salaries, one reason why the University of Texas had difficulty recruiting Berkeley, UCLA, and other California-based professors to the endowed chairs at UT-Austin.

In 1984–1985, the California legislature approved $43 million for a new engineering building at UCSD. This was the first new major facility funded by the legislature for the UC system since 1977. The Department of Electrical Engineering and Computer Science at UCSD had been founded only a year or two prior to the MCC competition. After the consortium went to Austin, this UCSD department was strengthened. So in hindsight, one of the best things to happen to higher education in California was losing MCC.

GEORGIA'S "ALMOST-GOT-IT" STRATEGY

The MCC experience started an era of political pork barreling in the Georgia legislature for various high-technology projects, some wise and some unwise. The almost-got-it strategy set off by the MCC competition led the Peach State to carry out most of the high-tech programs that were originally offered as inducements to MCC. Among the three finalists that lost MCC, Georgia's Governor Harris was most gracious. He told Inman (interview, March 1985): "Well, we've learned so much. You helped us to get organized. It is just the beginning of my administration, and the lessons that we've learned out of this [the MCC site selection] will carry us through the next eight years."

The main lesson that Governor Harris learned from losing MCC was the important role that a research university like Georgia Tech could play in attracting high-tech employment to the state. Harris could see what was happening at Research Triangle next door in North Carolina. Joe Pettit (the president of Georgia Tech, who had wowed MCC officials at the Chicago presentation in 1983) had labored for more than a decade to make Georgia Tech a nationally prominent research university. In 1982, the Georgia Microelectronics Research Center (GMRC) was established on Georgia Tech's campus, but it was largely a paper organization until 1983, when it received $24 million of state funds plus equal matching funds from private companies. Losing MCC was a catalyst that accelerated funding for the GMRC.

Governor Harris used the almost-got-it psychology to convince his legislature to dedicate substantial funds to promote high-tech research and development. Pettit and Harris had promised MCC that they would establish a Georgia Research Consortium (GRC) as an umbrella organization to (1) scout out high-tech growth opportunities and (2) provide funding to establish centers of excellence in Georgia's research universities. Subsequent to the MCC competition, the Georgia legislature allocated $30 million (half from the state and half from private donors) for the GRC. The GRC and the legislature funded the Microelectronics Research Center at Georgia Tech and a Biotechnology Research Center at the University of Georgia at Athens.

An Advanced Technology Development Center (ATDC) at Georgia Tech was created to provide incubator space to start-up companies, facilitate contacts between private industry and Georgia Tech, and assist high-tech start-ups in locating venture capital. The ATDC existed prior to the MCC competition; in fact, it was the ATDC's building on the Georgia Tech campus that was offered to MCC. After Georgia lost MCC in 1983, the ATDC began to play an increasingly important role in facilitating high-technology development in the state.

THE HIGH-TECH REVOLUTION IN NORTH CAROLINA

North Carolina had been trying harder and longer than any other state to develop a regional technopolis. Research Triangle—a large area cornered by the University of North Carolina (UNC) at Chapel Hill, North Carolina State University at Raleigh, and Duke University at Durham—was established as a high-tech science park by Governor Luther Hodges in the 1950s. At that time, Silicon Valley was just a rather hazy vision of Stanford Vice President Frederick Terman. It took 20 years for Research Triangle to reach a critical mass of technology-based companies. Many R&D-minded corporations were recruited through the personal efforts of North Carolina's governors. James B. Hunt, governor in 1983, spent about half of his time recruiting high-tech companies for Research Triangle (Hunt interview, February 19, 1987). So going after MCC fit naturally with the governor's economic development inclinations. Hunt responded to the loss of MCC with a call for a state investment of $46 million for the Microelectronics Center of North Carolina.

Bill Friday, who was chancellor of the North Carolina state university system at the time of MCC's decision to locate in Austin, telephoned Admiral Inman to ask what Texas had offered that North Carolina had not. Inman told Friday that North Carolina did not have a facility to house MCC (at that time, neither did Austin) and that "You've got to bring yourself to pay professors a base salary of $100,000" (Inman interview, March 1985). Friday sent his chief academic officer to Austin. "He came back with stories about 60 endowed professorships and about jet plane travel [the Lear jet]." Friday reported details of the Texas incentive package to the governor and to other high state officials. One result was a new $9 million building for the UNC Department of Computer Science. "Fred Brooks [chair of the department] shepherded the whole process. We have on board our first $100,000 professor, who was brought here from Europe. He's Swiss" (Friday interview, February 19, 1987). In all, seven new faculty positions were added to the UNC Department of Computer Science.

As former Governor James Hunt (interview, February 19, 1987) stated:

> Every single thing that we promised MCC we would do if they came here, we did even though they did not come. . . . I wouldn't say that it helped us by not getting it [MCC], but the involvement with competition and finding out what you had to do to be competitive was very motivating. . . . Losing MCC led to a renewal in strengthening our commitments. . . . We said: "All right, we didn't get MCC, but we're going to do an even better job of making MCNC [the Microelectronics Center of North Carolina] into a world-class facility." And the state legislature was even more generous in appropriations.[17]

Losing the competition also helped convince Governor Hunt of the limitations of microelectronics in North Carolina's development and of the potential for biotechnology. Duke University's excellent medical school, UNC's School of Public Health, and North Carolina State's Agriculture College are leaders in biotechnology research. A Biotechnology Center was established in 1981 in

Research Triangle Park, two years prior to the MCC decision. This organization received a major increase in state funding ($6.5 million per year) after North Carolina lost MCC.

Losing MCC also convinced Hunt that North Carolina had to improve the quality of the technical education that was being provided by its high schools. Hunt convinced the state legislature to fund the North Carolina School of Science and Mathematics, located in Durham. Talented high school students from all over the state, rich or poor, attend the school.

ARIZONA

California, Georgia, and North Carolina were not the only states that were affected by losing MCC. Other states that did not make the final competition were also motivated. Phoenix, for example, reacted with shock to not being selected as one of the four finalists. State leaders concluded that for Arizona to become a high-tech state, it needed a better understanding of what private industry expected in terms of educational excellence, quality of life, and cultural amenities (Wigand, 1987).

Two months after the MCC decision, Bruce Babbitt, then the governor of Arizona, hosted a high-technology symposium attended by 150 of the state's business, academic, and government leaders. Recommendations were formulated for the role of education, worker training, venture capital, and university-industry research partnerships in attracting high-technology industries to Arizona (Wigand, 1987). The loss of MCC led to increased support for Arizona State University's Engineering Excellence Program, supported by funds from state government and private industry. By 1990, this program had approximately doubled the number of faculty in electrical engineering and computer science at Arizona State University and it had greatly increased the amount of research in microelectronics. So although Phoenix was not a finalist for MCC in 1983, the state university, with help from the governor and the legislature, established its own mini-MCC. By 1988, Phoenix was so well established in microelectronics research that it finished as an almost-winner in the SEMATECH competition (see Chapter 7).

CONCLUSIONS

In 1983, the state of Texas and the city of Austin wanted MCC badly, very badly. In the years since MCC came to the capital city, have the high hopes for its economic development impact been fulfilled? The answer is mixed. In the first two years following the location decision, the city of Austin experienced a dynamic period of growth. Real estate prices escalated. Housing and office building construction flourished. The consortium's location in Austin preceded 3M's move in 1984, resulting in several thousand additional jobs, which helped fuel the real estate boom. Motorola, Lockheed, IBM, and AMD moved R&D workers to the area and expanded their Austin-based facilities. The population of the city rose rapidly, with much of this growth driven by the increased number of jobs in microelectronics. However, as much as the boom energized bankers, builders, and speculators, it turned off many old-time Austinites.

During the final two weeks of competition for MCC, regional collaboration among government, the academic community, and business was enormously important to the consortium's fact-finding and site-selection committees. But the Texas collaborative spirit that helped attract MCC to Austin was difficult to sustain. By 1985, the boom was followed by a severe bust. Falling oil prices weakened the Texas economy. The state legislature made budget cuts in the University of Texas' system that put a damper on UT's quest for academic excellence. Newly recruited faculty left the university. Austin's city council increased the cost of doing business in the capital city and generally frustrated business development and inhibited high-tech growth.

Most high-tech companies founded in Austin since 1983, like Dell Computer Corporation, CompuAdd, and National Instruments, were not linked to MCC. The recruitment of high-technology firms to Austin (e.g., Applied Materials, Apple Computer) and the expansion of existing firms (e.g., Motorola, IBM, AMD) occurred independently of MCC, which was downsizing in the early 1990s. The employment impact of relocations, expansions, and start-ups far outweighed MCC's impact on Austin's employment levels, increased office occupancy rates, and U.S. industrial competitiveness. However, Austin's winning the nationwide 1983 site-selection competition for MCC had a very important effect on how the regional high-tech community viewed itself and on how national and international high-tech leaders viewed Austin. MCC was a very important catalyst that accelerated high-tech development in Austin and in many of the other cities that competed for the consortium.

The Austin Technology Incubator forged creative alliances between the University of Texas, the city of Austin, Travis County, and public and private leaders to spur regional economic development, foster entrepreneurial education, and create high-paying jobs. One of ATI's first tenant companies, Fusion Data, was built on technologies licensed from MCC. The first MCC technology spin-out, Evolutionary Technologies, Inc., was taken in by the incubator in November 1990, as was SEMATECH's first company spin-out Fourth State Technologies, in April 1992. With the downsizing of the MCC's on-site software research activities, the consortium's researchers looked for employment alternatives. Some moved out of state, and some remained in Austin to pursue start-up activities, such as Corporate Memory Systems, which became an ATI tenant in September 1991, and Pavilion Technology and Tamarack, which remained housed in MCC's Balcones Research Center building.

After a brief period of disbelief, blame, and criticism, the three finalist cities in the MCC site-selection contest—San Diego, Atlanta, and Raleigh-Durham—actually "won by losing." They launched their own microelectronics research centers and increased their state university and education budgets. The University of California at San Diego received major funding increases from the state, a new $43 million engineering building, and a special legislative appropriation of $1 million to get the Supercomputer Project in 1985. UC–San Diego was on the way to becoming the high-tech university that it was not in 1983. Losing MCC "educated" the then newly elected governor of Georgia about the political and economic importance of high technology. Georgia's state government has since provided Georgia Tech with funding for excellence in microelectronics R&D.

The Department of Computer Science at the University of North Carolina got a new $9 million building, plus seven additional faculty slots. The university lifted the $68,000 faculty salary lid when it hired a world-class computer science professor in the late 1980s. North Carolina, a relatively poor state, invested $100 million of state funds in the Microelectronics Center of North

Carolina. Finally, the loss of MCC caused North Carolina's leaders to steer their state's high-tech thrust toward biotechnology as an alternative to microelectronics. This focus and commitment led to state funding of the Biotechnology Center in Research Triangle Park.

NOTES

1. During MCC's site-selection competition in 1983, MCC officials emphasized that creating technology spin-out companies was not an objective of the R&D consortium. MCC was to transfer its pre-competitive technologies to the shareholder companies that funded the research. If spin-out activity were to result from MCC technologies, the entrepreneurial ventures would most likely be located at the site of the shareholder divisions that were spread nationwide. Such a process would take many years.

2. The life cycle of the birth of Tracor (a child of the University of Texas and $5,000 in federally funded research) and the company's spin-outs came full circle soon after Tracor was purchased (in 1988) in a leveraged buyout by Westmark Systems, the holding company founded by Admiral Inman after he left MCC. In 1990, loaded with a $747 million debt that was compounded by cutbacks in the U.S. defense industry, Tracor was forced into bankruptcy. However, many of Tracor's spin-outs (the grandchildren of UT and federally funded research) and the spin-outs of these spin-outs (the great-grand-children) continued to prosper. After the leveraged buyout, Frank McBee left Tracor in 1989 at age 69. He launched RAI (Research Applications, Inc.), a for-profit firm that provided seed financing for entrepreneurial ventures spinning-out from university research. RAI established a venture fund of $1.6 million and made its first capital investment in a start-up company in 1989. In December 1991, under the leadership of President James Skaggs, Tracor emerged from Chapter 11 with a reported revenue of $262 million. In 1992, the company returned to the national stock exchange and a *Fortune* 500 ranking.

3. Indeed, this perceptual change seemed to be greatest among the business, academic, and government leaders in foreign countries who read about the national competition for MCC. Judging from a distance, it seemed clear that Austin, Texas, had been targeted by U.S. industry to become an important high-tech region.

4. As we discuss in Chapter 7, national politics did play a major role in SEMATECH's 1988 site-selection process.

5. The economic boom even rippled out to John Gray's son, who ran a small printing company in Austin. He made a nice little profit from a popular poster of Austin's downtown skyline at sunset, entitled: "The Secret Nesting Area of the Sky Crane: Austin, 1986."

6. In 1984, Texas produced $290 billion worth of goods and services, approximately 7.5 percent of the gross national product.

7. One of us had an interesting conversation with a local laborer who delivered land fill to an Austin residence in 1986. The truck driver remembered the good times in 1983–1984 when he had owned a land-fill business, including three trucks. Then Austin's bust hit, and his business went bankrupt. He had to lay off his workers, and his trucks were repossessed. He argued loudly against the no-growth city council and against increased taxes. He could not see a connection between (1) MCC (which he had not heard of, nor did he know that it was located in Austin) and a highly qualified workforce successfully competing with Japan in producing state-of-the-art technologies, and (2) his owning a thriving construction business.

8. The construction of a convention center was finally approved by a public referendum in 1989. The issue of moving the city's airport, and where to move it, was debated by Austin until 1993.

9. As a result of this stand-off between the city and 3M, Austin lost a large-volume customer for the city-owned electric utilities, and one of the nation's globally competitive companies was saddled with the responsibility of building a plant to generate its own electric power.

10. The year after MCC came to town, Watson donated land, worth $3.5 million at the time, in downtown Austin for the city's Laguna Gloria Art Museum. Years passed as the museum's committee was unable to agree on the building design, financing, and management. Eventually, the bank foreclosed on the land, and the new museum was never built. So, in this case, a lack of synergy between public and private sectors resulted in a lose-lose scenario for the city.

11. By 1993, there were more than 100 houses in Lost Creek, prices were exceeding the 1983 highs, and available building lots were becoming scarce.

12. During his first term in Congress in the 1930s, Lyndon Baines Johnson was instrumental in getting these flood-control dams built by the U.S. Army Corps of Engineers. The resulting lakes were formed long before anyone could have conceived of their impact on Austin's quality-of-life, an important underlying factor in the city's emergence as a technopolis in the 1990s.

13. It was considered essential to keep Austin's bid for MCC a secret so that other competing sites would not benefit from this information. This norm of secrecy was also highly valued in Austin's bid for SEMATECH.

14. One of us has a nephew who was a high school basketball star in Wichita Falls, Texas, in 1984 when the new state law was passed. Before the new regulation, he played basketball about "ten hours a day" and devoted only indifferent attention to his studies. He was incredulous about the tough new restrictions: "You mean they won't let me play basketball if I don't get at least Cs in my courses?" During his junior and senior years in high school, this athlete excelled academically and earned a 3.0 grade average. He was awarded an athletic scholarship to college.

15. Using Hans Mark's calculations, UT would have been paid in full for its MCC investment within six years (at $2.5 million per year). The university owns MCC's headquarters building, for which it will begin receiving market rent in 1996.

16. These critics fail to see the connection between (1) U.S. excellence in microelectronics research, enhanced U.S. industrial competitiveness, and a healthy, growing U.S. economy and (2) funding for quality education, low tuition pay-

ments, the availability of student loans and research funds, increased prestige of a university, and the creation and maintenance of quality jobs for university graduates.

17. In 1981, the North Carolina legislature appropriated $24.4 million in initial funding for the Microelectronics Center of North Carolina. MCNC was patterned directly after the Center for Integrated Systems (CIS) at Stanford University, a university-based R&D consortium that is funded by private firms in Silicon Valley. Governor Hunt had been impressed with CIS when he visited Stanford in 1980. A major difference between CIS and MCNC is that MCNC mainly represents a state government initiative rather than being founded by private firms, although seven member companies (including GE) help support MCNC. The North Carolina microelectronics consortium was created to attract high-tech industry to the area and facilitate interuniversity collaborative research in North Carolina. The center includes a wafer fabrication plant for manufacturing semiconductors and has a microwave network linking each of the participating universities so that they can receive classroom instruction from researchers at MCNC.

7

THE POLITICS OF R&D CONSORTIA: MCC AND SEMATECH

The semiconductor industry is in serious trouble. If this vital industry is allowed to wither away, the Nation will pay a price measured in millions of jobs across the entire electronics field and in technological leadership in many allied industries such as telecommunications and computers, and the technical edge we depend on for national security.

National Advisory Committee on Semiconductors (1989),
A Strategic Industry at Risk, report to President Bush

America is known for science and technology. Yet something is wrong. We're losing markets and industries. So either our model is wrong or our policy is wrong. The time has come to debate the merits of solutions rather than the source of problems and then encourage action.

Dr. Robert N. Noyce (founding president and CEO of SEMATECH, co-inventor of the integrated circuit, and co-founder of Intel Corporation), IEEE Panel on Imperatives for Effective Utilization of Science and Technology, February 1989

Consortia are formed by people who have lost. They go to the government and say: "We need help," and the government gives them money. It's a form of reverse Darwinism.

T.J. Rodgers, president of Cypress Semiconductor Corporation of San Jose; quoted by Von Tyle (1989)

What is the political process through which (1) the general idea of R&D consortia was legitimized in the United States and (2) public policy decisions were made about consortia like MCC and SEMATECH? Such major socio-political-institutional change inevitably involves politics. While MCC was formed as a privately funded consortium, federal politics were involved because of antitrust concerns. SEMATECH depends heavily upon federal funding. Here we describe the politics behind these two consortia. We also draw some comparisons between MCC and SEMATECH in terms of SEMATECH's formation and site-selection process, objectives, and organization during its first six years of operation; case studies of technology transfer; and the impacts of SEMATECH on the U.S. semiconductor industry and on Austin, Texas.

TEXAS-STYLE POLITICS

Some state and local governments have learned to play the game of Washington-stimulated economic development more proficiently than others. While the goals are economic—jobs and taxable income—the process is political. Texans excelled at winning this high-tech political game in the 1980s, with MCC, SEMATECH, and the superconducting supercollider as the state's biggest victories.[1] Pike Powers emphasized that being involved in the MCC and SEMATECH site-selection processes was a great learning experience for Texas political leaders: "Things have come a long way. Before MCC, the basic state legislator didn't know how to say 'research and development,' much less fund it."[2] (Powers interview by Strain, March 24, 1989)

The American public associates a Texas drawl with political savvy for a very good reason. The art of politics is practiced with consummate skill in the Lone Star State. This perception grows out of a history tracing back to John Nance Garner, Sam Rayburn, and Lyndon Baines Johnson. To Texas' leaders, it is obvious that getting big federal projects for their state is a political process. The seven lakes around Austin are a result of successful political lobbying by LBJ for his congressional district during his first term in Washington in the late 1930s. Each lake lies behind a flood-control dam built by the U.S. Army Corps of Engineers. NASA's huge Johnson Space

Center was located in Houston in 1962, in part, because of LBJ's political power and buttonholing ability in Washington. So when Texas-style politics comes together with multimillion-dollar high-tech undertakings like MCC, SEMATECH, and the Superconducting Supercollider Project, some fascinating history results.

One reason for Texas' power in Washington is congressional seniority. The citizens of Texas loyally re-elect their Washington representatives term after term, and as a result, Texas' politicians rise to high-ranking positions in the U.S. House and Senate. At the time of the SEMATECH decision in 1987–1988, Jim Wright (D-Fort Worth) was Speaker of the House (he resigned from Congress in 1989), Senator Lloyd Bensten was chairman of the Senate Finance Committee, Senator Phil Gramm was a Republican freshman, Jake Pickle (D-Austin) was chair of the Ways and Means Oversight Committee, Jack Brooks (D-Beaumont) was chair of the Government Operations Committee, and George Bush was vice president. Congressman J.J. (Jake) Pickle is an exemplar of Texas politics: 79 years old and a millionaire with more than 30 years in Congress. He represents the Tenth Congressional District, centered in Austin, the same district served by LBJ. Pickle lives on a ranch in Hays County, just south of Austin. He ran unopposed in his last election.

Charles Cook, a noted Washington-based congressional analyst and editor of the *Cook Political Report* commented:

> Absolutely, without a doubt, Texas has the premier delegation in terms of clout and influence . . . . The backfield stars of the Texas team are Wright, Bentsen, Pickle, and Brooks. . . . That stability in the delegation is a major factor in the new rise to power by Texas. (Quoted by Seth Kantor, 1988, D1)

In addition to seniority, why does Texas pack so much clout in high-tech politics? Two fundamental reasons are size and unity. Texas' large population gives it 29 congressional representatives and senators. While California has 47, the Golden State often exercises less influence because its politicians do not work as a team. Decades back, in the days of Sam Rayburn and LBJ, the Texas delegation was almost entirely Democratic and acted with partisan unity. In recent decades, a mixture of Republicans and Democrats (who are actually not that far apart ideologically anyway) continue the tradition of cohesion. On any issue that entails Texas' state interests, the Texas delegation in Washington tends to stand together.

Perhaps the historical roots of Texas' political unity go back to when Texas was a sovereign nation from 1836 to 1845. Texans still express a special pride in the Lone Star State. There is a feeling of "us versus the rest." The "rest" includes the rest of the United States as well as Japan and other nations. As Jack Carter, Houston lawyer and former chairman of Texas' Harris County Democratic party, said at President Clinton's Black Tie and Boots Inaugural Ball: "What links us all is not politics as much as our statehood. Texans, by choice or by birth, like to get together irregardless of party" (quoted by D. McNeely and D. Gamino, "Let the Countdown Begin," *Austin American-Statesman;* January 17, 1993). Such perceived togetherness helps Texas politicians collaborate. In short, it is teamwork that gives Texas its special power in Washington, along with the state's large size, congressional seniority, and political know-how.

THE POLITICS OF MCC'S LOCATION DECISION

The Texas Governor's Task Force understood that a significant plus in attracting MCC to Austin would be to help legitimize the consortium with the U.S. Department of Justice. Texans worked to get state and local political support to stand together for MCC. Texas was the only finalist site to promise political collaboration in resolving MCC's shaky antitrust status.

As Powers (interview, March 27, 1986) explained:

> We got the entire Texas congressional delegation and all the resolutions in both houses of the Texas legislature to unanimously support "The Texas Incentive for Austin." We even got the Austin city council's unanimous support, and on and on. So we were able to show MCC that we had the total, unanimous support of every relevant governmental entity. We were able to show the documents: "Here they are—one, two, three."

We could say: "Nobody is opposed to this. Everybody wants you to come to Texas."

Congressman Jake Pickle played a key role in winning MCC. Daron Butler (interview, January 23, 1987), a member of the Austin Task Force, remembered:

For the MCC people, an important question had to be: "Who can go to Washington and be sure that the antitrust legislation deal is going to get delivered?" Pickle's commitment that he was going to make that legislation his cross I think helped get MCC here in Austin. Having Texas politicians on the committee that writes the legislation meant a commitment to make it happen. That had to be an important factor to Inman and his [site-selection] committee.

The idea of collaborative R&D was not entirely new to the federal government in 1983. The National Science Foundation had funded ten industry-university collaborative research centers, such as the Center for Welding Research at Ohio State University, the Center for Interactive Computer Graphics at Rensselaer Polytechnic Institute, and the Ceramics Research Center at Rutgers University. In each case, NSF provided about $5 million, awarded on a year-by-year decreasing basis, with private companies picking up an increasing share of the funding. Each R&D center was typically located on a university campus with a professor as the center's director. Some centers have been sustained after the five years of federal funding ended. Others have died.

During summer 1983, Senators Paul Tsongas (D-Massachusetts) and Charles Mathias, Jr. (R-Maryland) and other elected officials were working on legislation to permit MCC's form of resource pooling, but the obstacles were many. As reported by one congressional observer: "Severe compromise will be needed to make such legislation acceptable to the staunchest defenders of antitrust law—a process that may be as complex and time-consuming as MCC's research." (Guinn, 1983)

Admiral Inman, Bill Norris, and Bob Price made numerous trips to Washington to testify before committees and subcommittees that were involved with the National Cooperative Research Act. They did a lot of one-on-one lobbying, explaining the importance of R&D consortia—why MCC was good for the country in the long run and why Congress ought to support the proposed law.

MCC provided a real-life model. Inman, Norris, and Price could say: "Here's a company that's trying to get going. We have a mechanism for materially helping the United States. Just clarify the rules for us." Senator Peter Rodino (D-Rhode Island) asked Inman to help him draft the legislation that would eventually be passed as the National Cooperative Research Act. As Inman (interview, July 21, 1987) explained:

> In 1983, various bills were being pushed, but Congress was reluctant. They were worried about what a new law could open up [a weakening of federal antitrust policies]. By 1984, there was a working model that they could examine and see its impact. The ambiguity was gone. They said: "Gee, we can do that!" But the Reagan administration's first reaction was: "We don't need it!" I introduced the bill [the National Cooperative Research Act] in February 1984, and it immediately gained very strong bipartisan support from the committee. It passed the House 411 to 0 in early May. At that point, the administration decided it was a pretty good thing. . . . The assistant attorney general for antitrust, William Baxter, still opposed it. However, MCC companies thought him wrong. Their lawyers thought him wrong. Then the bill moved through the Senate on 31 July 1987 by 97 to 0. . . . The size of those votes silenced critical comments about changing antitrust laws pretty quickly.

Bob Rutishauser accompanied his former boss, President Bob Price of CDC, to Washington in 1984 to testify for passage of the National Cooperative Research Act. Rutishauser (interview, January 23, 1987) explained:

> We went to a subcommittee of the Senate Finance Committee. The chair was very receptive. He said: "What can we do to help? We passed the R&D tax credit. We're trying to stimulate innovation." Bob

[Price] said: "We need to have you folks clarify the rules. It's not that there are rules that we can't live with. It's just that there aren't any rules. Companies are concerned that ten years later, somebody will say this thing [MCC] back in 1982 was illegal [on antitrust grounds] and come up with a few trillion dollars in damages." Too many companies were unwilling to proceed [to join MCC] without some kind of clarification. So that was the basis for the 1984 act.

Prior to the unanimous vote in both houses of Congress, the White House had announced that it would veto the bill. But President Reagan realized that to do so would be an exercise in futility as his veto would be overridden. Palle Smidt (MCC's senior vice president) and George Scalise (AMD executive and member of the MCC site-selection committee) were in the Roosevelt Room of the White House when the president signed the National Cooperative Research Act into law on October 11, 1984. So when MCC came to Texas in 1983, the consortium set in motion a political process in Washington that led to a new law and to the subsequent proliferation of R&D consortia.

SEMATECH

SEMATECH (SEmiconductor MAnufacturing TECHnology initiative) was formed in 1987 as a not-for-profit industry-government consortium. SEMATECH was not intended to design chips or build products for sale. The consortium was to develop the tools and equipment necessary to manufacture semiconductors. SEMATECH's sole product was knowledge. According to Turner Hasty (interview, February 26, 1992), SEMATECH's second chief operating officer, the consortium was to provide the U.S. semiconductor industry with the domestic capability for world leadership in manufacturing.

In 1987, the U.S. semiconductor industry was in bad shape, very bad shape. World semiconductor market share was slipping for U.S. companies as it was rising for the Japanese. The U.S. share of the worldwide DRAM (dynamic random access memory) market had shrunk from nearly 100 percent to less than 20 percent (see Figure 1.1). These trends were attributed, in part, to U.S. integrated circuit (IC) assembly's moving offshore, the VLSI Project, Japanese dumping of semiconductors on foreign markets, and Japan's massive investment in plants and equipment (Figure 7.1).

U.S. semiconductor manufacturers had lost more than $2 billion in earnings and 27,000 jobs (Schneer, 1987). For each 1 percent loss in global semiconductor market share, 5,500 industry jobs are lost, and the U.S. government loses $200 million in tax revenues (Congressional Budget Office, 1987, p. 3). This marketplace disaster represented an incredible defeat for U.S. semiconductor companies, with ominous implications for the U.S. balance of trade, the future of American industrial competitiveness, and national defense. Something had to be done about the continuing and successful Japanese attack on the U.S. semiconductor industry, or it might disappear entirely. Maybe it was already too late.

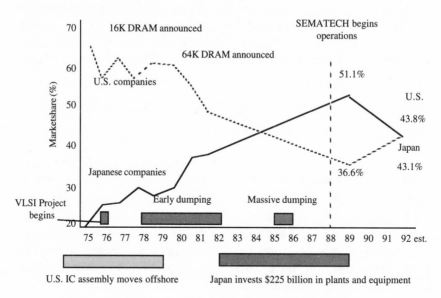

Sources: Prudential-Bache and Dataquest, 1991, and VLSI Research, Inc., 1992.

Figure 7.1. World semiconductor market share, 1975–1992

THE BIRTH OF SEMATECH

One afternoon in 1975, Charles Sporck, CEO of National Semiconductor Company (NSC), Bob Noyce of Intel, and Jerry Sanders of AMD, were sitting at a table in Ming's Restaurant in Palo Alto, eating sweet-and-sour shrimp and worrying about how Japanese competitors were making inroads into their market share (Rogers and Larsen 1984). They created the Semiconductor Industry Association (SIA) as a lobbying group for U.S. semiconductor firms to convince the federal government to intervene on the side of U.S. companies in their economic war with Japan. In 1982, the SIA formed the Semiconductor Research Corporation (SRC), the North Carolina–based consortium that sponsored university research in microelectronics. Now something much bigger and stronger was needed.

In 1985, Sanford (Sandy) Kane, IBM vice president for industrial operations produced an alarming IBM report about the U.S. semiconductor industry. Why was IBM concerned?

> The survival of the U.S. semiconductor industry was critical to us for several reasons. . . . We like to source locally, and we didn't want to lose the option of buying U.S. chips. Besides, since most Japanese companies were both competitors of ours and suppliers of chips, we didn't want to be in a position where we had no choice but to be dependent on our competition. (Kane interview by Strain, March 7, 1989)

Another gloomy report, this one by the Defense Science Board Task Force for the U.S. Department of Defense, appeared in February 1987. It argued that the national security of the United States rested on worldwide technology leadership by U.S. semiconductor companies. The report recommended that: "The DOD should encourage and actively support with contract funding the establishment of a U.S. Semiconductor Manufacturing Institute formed as a consortium of U.S. manufacturers." (Defense Science Board, quoted in Strain, 1989, p. 11)

Dr. Hans Mark, who at the time was chancellor of the University of Texas system (and who was former deputy director of NASA and former U.S. secretary of the air force), described a key event that got SEMATECH under way (interview with Strain, March 8, 1989):

SEMATECH got started in probably late 1986 when somebody pointed out to Caspar Weinberger [U.S. secretary of Defense] that more than half of the piece parts in the fire-control radar of the F-16 [fighter] were built offshore and that we no longer had the manufacturing capability to build these things in this country. He said: "That's an unacceptable situation, and we need to do something about it."

Although government and industry support for SEMATECH was building, there still was considerable opposition to the idea of the nation's largest semiconductor firms pooling their resources with the assistance of a hefty government subsidy. The Office of Management and Budget was opposed to the idea as observed by Dr. Tom Dorsey:

The total aggregate R&D budget for these [14] semiconductor firms is over $4.5 billion. They claim SEMATECH is critical to their success; yet unless government puts in $100 million a year, it won't fly. Where are their priorities? There is a real danger of politicization here, a risk that this won't be done for scientific reasons, but instead will evolve into a giant entitlement program. Government shouldn't be allocating resources and making priorities, the market should. (quoted in Lodge, 1990, p. 83)

Sporck became chairman of the SIA's steering committee on SEMATECH and directed the lobbying effort in Washington. Duality of purpose—commercial and military—marked the passage of SEMATECH's legislation through Congress. Secretary of Commerce Malcom Baldrige liked the idea but thought the program too big. The Department of Commerce, which would have to sponsor a purely commercial SEMATECH, did not have the funds. DOD had the money, the supervisory personnel, and the votes. (Lodge, 1990)

Congressman Pickle was approached by semiconductor industry people, who told him that something like SEMATECH was needed. Then the U.S. Department of Defense told him it was interested:

Charles Wilson from Lufkin, Texas, on the House Appropriations Committee, told me [Pickle] that Defense was concerned that the U.S. was lagging behind in chip technology. We just simply can't depend on the opposition [Japan] to furnish the technology for our military machines. We just couldn't accept that. The Department of Defense, particularly DARPA, said it was critical. . . . When I saw that the money was real, I felt that SEMATECH could be created. . . . It took us some time to work out an agreement between the Defense Department and the semiconductor industry. (Pickle interview by Strain, March 29, 1989)

So, the idea of a U.S.-based semiconductor manufacturing consortium had been around for some years. MCC had pioneered the way and championed the passage of the National Cooperative Research Act. In response to Sandy Kane's 1985 IBM report, the SIA had set up a task force headed by Sporck to devise the framework for SEMATECH. The February 1987 report of the Defense Science Board moved the SIA to action (Figure 7.2). At its March 3, 1987, board meeting, the SIA approved the concept, and the SRC gave SEMATECH $100,000 to get started. At its May board meeting, the SIA approved a five-year plan and appointed Larry Sumney, the president and CEO of SRC, as interim managing director of SEMATECH. A letter was sent to the country's governors, inviting them to make proposals for locating the consortium in their state.

In February 1988, SEMATECH was assigned to DARPA. Deputy Director Craig Fields rejected the consortium's first operating plan. He was concerned over the seeming lack of cooperation among SEMATECH's member companies. As he told Kane, chairman of SEMATECH's executive committee: "As companies, you have submitted advanced research projects for DARPA funding that you haven't shared with each other. You've told us more than you have told each other" (quoted in Lodge, 1990, p. 86-85). By summer 1988, DARPA had gained influence over SEMATECH's research agenda, but had no operational authority. SEMATECH's plans and government funding were to be reviewed annually by Congress.

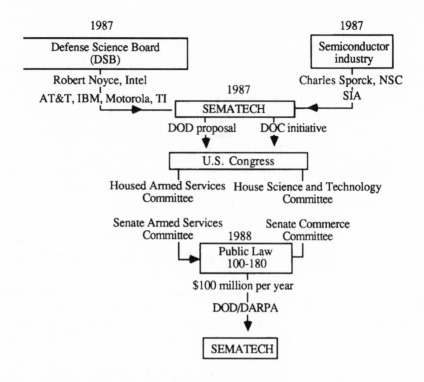

Source: SEMATECH Strategic Overview, 1991.

**Figure 7.2. The genesis of SEMATECH, growing out of two
initiatives in 1987**

SEMATECH'S SITE-SELECTION

In 1987, SEMATECH was in a hurry to begin operations
(Table 7.1).[3] In many ways SEMATECH's headquarters location
process was very similar to the national competition for MCC four
years earlier. SEMATECH's site-selection criteria included the following: the amount and quality of financial incentives; an available
and suitable facility; supportive state and local government; a positive business environment; a high quality of life, including cost of
living, housing, and airport connections; and proximity to a major
university. SEMATECH wanted to attract top-notch scientists to

serve as shareholder representatives from its member companies. Such researchers would be more likely to join the consortium if they could be recruited to an area that had a major research university where they could continue their graduate education. SEMATECH was also looking for synergy with the public and private sectors in the community in which it located.

Table 7.1. Main events in the history of SEMATECH

1987	
February	A report by the Defense Science Board of the U.S. Department of Defense recommends federal funding for a semiconductor manufacturing consortium.
March	The Semiconductor Industry Association approves the concept of SEMATECH.
April	Willis A. Adcock, professor, Department of Electrical and Computer Engineering, UT-Austin, sends a letter to Charles Sporck informing him that he (Adcock) will be heading the initial analysis in the Texas' campaign for SEMATECH.
May	SEMATECH is officially created by 13 members of the Semiconductor Industry Association (NCR joins later).
	Semiconductor Industry Association officials, meeting in Dallas, Texas, approve a $1.5 billion, five-year funding plan.
	Larry Sumney is appointed interim SEMATECH director.
June	SEMATECH receives proposals from 135 sites in 34 states.
July	Texas senators Lloyd Bentsen and Phil Gramm, along with House Speaker Jim Wright, Jake Pickle, and 25 other congressional representatives, send Sandy Kane, chairman, SEMATECH site-selection committee, a letter of support for Texas' bid for SEMATECH.

July	Oral presentations are made to the SEMATECH site-selection committee in Santa Clara, California.
September	A SEMATECH technical team visits Austin to inspect the Data General building and a site near MCC, at Balcones Research Center.
October	The SEMATECH site-selection committee visits Austin to lunch with Governor Bill Clements and tour MCC, the University of Texas, and the Data General building.
November	SEMATECH announces 11 finalist sites.
December	Federal funding of $100 million for SEMATECH is approved by Congress.

1988

January	SEMATECH's board of directors meets in Dallas to select the winning site.
	Austin is announced as the SEMATECH site at a press conference held in the Texas legislature in Austin.
	Turner Hasty, a 30-year veteran of Texas Instruments, serves as SEMATECH's acting chief operating officer, overseeing the critical early stages of clean room construction and staff recruitment.
	IBM and AT&T agree to present to SEMATECH processes for making two computer chips. This agreement is the first such cooperative move for both companies.
February	SEMATECH is assigned to DARPA.
	Construction begins on SEMATECH's clean room in the old Data General building.
	NCR joins SEMATECH.
	President Reagan proposes slashing federal spending for SEMATECH from $100 million to $45 million.

July	Bob Noyce is appointed president and CEO of SEMATECH.
August	SEMATECH's clean room is completed (in 32 weeks). Paul Castrucci, a retired IBM executive, is named chief operating officer.
	Turner Hasty becomes director of external resources.
September	Peter Mills, Greater Austin Chamber of Commerce, vice president of economic development, is hired as SEMATECH's senior vice president for administration.
	A congressional conference committee approves full $100 million funding for SEMATECH. However, $75 million will be withheld until the Department of Defense agrees to the consortium's 1989 operating plan.
October	President Reagan signs a bill calling for full funding ($100 million) for SEMATECH's second fiscal year.
November	SEMATECH officially dedicates its south Austin facility, including a 60,000-square-foot clean room.

1989

February	SEMATECH produces its first semiconductors.
March	Paul Castrucci leaves SEMATECH.
July	Turner Hasty becomes SEMATECH's second chief operating officer.
	SEMATECH reduces the scope of its manufacturing activities and delays some of its technical goals to focus on equipment improvement.

1990

| June | Robert Noyce dies from a heart attack. |
| October | William J. Spencer, formerly of Xerox, becomes SEMATECH's second CEO. |

1991

January | Robert Galvin, Motorola's chief executive for 31 years, is named chairman of SEMATECH's board of directors, replacing Charles Sporck. Galvin also served on MCC's board of directors. Sporck, although retiring as chief executive of National Semiconductor Corporation, remains on SEMATECH's board.

March | William L. (Bill) George of Motorola is named chief operating officer. Turner Hasty retires and becomes an adjunct professor in UT's College of Engineering.

SEMATECH submits a proposal to Congress for another five years of funding and receives $100 million for 1993.

1992

January | Two of SEMATECH's 14 members (LSI Logic and Micron Technologies) drop out of the consortium

1993

January | Harris Corporation leaves SEMATECH.

April | $100 million, five-year cooperative research agreement signed with Sandia National Laboratories.

July | SEMATECH requests $10 million less in funding from Congress as well as its member companies for a total of $180 million support for 1994.

September | James B. Owens, Jr., National Semiconductor executive vice president, is named SEMATECH's chief operating officer, succeeding Bill George of Motorola, whose three-year assignment ended in March.

INTERSTATE COMPETITION

The lure of an estimated 800 high-paying research jobs, a $200 million annual budget, the expected relocation or expansion of semiconductor equipment suppliers, and the prediction of technology spin-offs from SEMATECH's research efforts spurred a nationwide bidding war. By the deadline of June 30, 1987, SEMATECH had received 135 proposals from potential sites in 34 states, including New York, California, Florida, Massachusetts, New Mexico, North Carolina, New Jersey, Missouri, Wisconsin, Arizona, Illinois, Oregon, Colorado, and Texas. SEMATECH officials were flabbergasted at such a high level of nationwide interest. Sandy Kane, chairman of the consortium's site-selection committee, commented: "We figured that we were going to get eight or ten proposals, and about half of them would be worth reading" (interview by Strain, March 7, 1989). Indeed, less than half the proposals were worth reading: for example, one state's proposal offered a defunct state hospital to SEMATECH, misunderstanding what the consortium meant by "clean room."[4]

The competition for SEMATECH was generating more proposals from more states than did the competition for MCC (27 states and 57 cities were initially involved in the MCC competition), and the proposals were usually better organized and quite a bit larger in their financial incentives. Governor Michael Dukakis took time out from his presidential campaign to tout his state's universities and the Massachusetts Microelectronics Center (MMC), a $58 million facility. Massachusetts offered $260 million in financial incentives and a long-term lease on 33 acres adjacent to the MMC. Two dozen engineering schools in the Northeast offered the services of an academic consortium (located near Troy, New York), which was to be led by James Meindl, the provost of Rensselaer Polytechnic Institute. The consortium would be composed of faculty and consultants from such schools as MIT, Carnegie-Mellon, New York University, Columbia, and Cornell.[5] New York State officials offered a $40 million interest-free loan.

California legislative leaders, led by Governor George Deukmejian, valued their package of inducements to SEMATECH at $134 million in direct grants. Five possible sites were offered in the heart of Silicon Valley, where one-third of the nation's semiconductors were manufactured.

North Carolina's general assembly set aside $8 million for SEMATECH and appropriated $18 million for a supercomputer to be shared by North Carolina's research universities and SEMATECH. The state had the added advantage of being the home of the Semiconductor Research Corporation, which was to work closely with SEMATECH. SRC's president and CEO, Larry Sumney, was SEMATECH's interim managing director. Thirteen of the firms forming SEMATECH were members of SRC.

Florida lawmakers initially rejected an appropriation of $20 million for SEMATECH, but in a special October 1987 session, they pledged $35 million for construction of a plant and start-up costs. Colorado offered $50 million in low-interest loans and $3 to $4 million in improvements in engineering-related programs at the University of Colorado. New Mexico's proposal was low on cash incentives but emphasized the research resources available at Sandia and Los Alamos national laboratories. State officials hoped that Congress might opt for an academic retreat atmosphere away from states with large research universities (Copelin, 1987).

Austin's proposal to SEMATECH benefited from the insights and leadership of Dr. Willis A. Adcock and Pike Powers. Adcock was a professor in the Department of Electrical and Computer Engineering at The University of Texas at Austin. He headed the initial analysis in Texas' campaign for SEMATECH. The expertise Powers had gained during the MCC site competition showed in the competition for SEMATECH. Austin did not mail its proposal, as had the other 134 sites. Powers had Peter Mills (vice president for economic development of the Greater Austin Chamber of Commerce) fly to New York and hand deliver it to SEMATECH.[6] "From the start, we were always thinking of ways to do things differently, to give us an edge on the competition," Mills explained. (Wysocki, 1988)

In 1987, Austin was in the economic doldrums of the post-MCC bust period. Average home values had dropped considerably and office vacancy rates were the highest in the United States. Austin really wanted SEMATECH. But what had been successful strategy in the MCC competition often proved difficult to re-enact during Austin's quest for SEMATECH. When the city was engaged in the competition for MCC, it was a new ball game. The players did not have a script from which to work. Public visibility was low for the members of both the governor's and Austin task forces for MCC. Public and private leaders who were involved in the competition for SEMATECH were much more visible, and citizen groups and the press demanded to be privy to the process.

The "SEMATECH Texas Foundation" tried to remain close-mouthed about its proposal. Powers had been paid high compliments by Ross Perot and Admiral Inman for "keeping 'The Texas Incentive for Austin' off the streets" until after MCC's site-selection decision was made. But such a strategy proved to be difficult in the SEMATECH competition. Laylen Copelin, the Austin newspaper reporter covering the site-selection process, argued that details of the Austin incentive ought to be made public. After all, the people of Texas were paying for it. The Austin Task Force for SEMATECH began to refer to Copelin as "the worm." Powers refused Copelin's requests for information and swore everyone to secrecy. "Fortunately, I had sources in the Texas state government, in Washington, California, and in other places. That's where I was getting my stories. I wasn't getting anything from the local [Austin] folks." (Copelin interview by Strain, March 4, 1989)[7]

Most important, from their experience with MCC, many of the states involved in the SEMATECH competition had learned what to do and what not to do in such an interstate contest. Numerous articles appeared in the media. Information was exchanged through personal and professional networks. Participants in Austin's proposal for MCC had visited the losing states to describe key aspects of the Lone Star State's winning strategy. Valuable lessons were learned and throughout the interstate competition for SEMATECH, representatives from the academic, business, and government sectors endeavored to collaborate to compete more effectively with the other potential site locations.

AUSTIN'S DATA GENERAL BUILDING

Attached to Sandy Kane's July 14, 1987, letter to Governor Clements inviting Austin to make a July 28 presentation in Santa Clara, California, was a list of concerns regarding Texas' proposal. All 21 items dealt with the proposed clean room environment, specifications, and building codes, with minor variations on a few subcategories. The main worry about the Austin location was "the plan and timeframe to add the required clean room and support facilities for SEMATECH's initial and ultimate requirements." (interview by Strain, March 7, 1989)

Austin's incentive package to SEMATECH totaled approximately $68 million, the largest component of which centered on facilities incentives (Table 7.2). Constructing a semiconductor clean room is a complicated process, as the facility must not only be airtight but it must have negative air pressure so that dust specks do not contaminate the clean room's environment.

The original Texas proposal offered SEMATECH a choice of two buildings: (1) a vacant building owned by Data General on the south side of Austin, on Montopolis Drive, or (2) a new building to be built to SEMATECH's specifications at the University of Texas' Balcones Research Center northwest of Austin, next to MCC's headquarters building. SEMATECH was determined to move into an existing facility, for the sake of a speedy start-up, so the consortium told Austin to focus on the Data General building. This structure consisted of an office building adjoined by a huge warehouse, which was to be retrofitted as a clean room.

Building a clean room to SEMATECH's specifications, even inside the vacant Data General building, would be a challenging, time-consuming task. Austin's leaders knew that several of the other finalist sites had ready-for-occupancy clean rooms. How could this considerable disadvantage be overcome? Powers and Mills located Al Tasch, a University of Texas engineering professor who had constructed a dozen clean rooms, including facilities for TI and Motorola, two of SEMATECH's members. Tasch assembled a team of 20 specialists who met every morning at 7:30 at Austin's chamber of commerce to plan the clean room's construction. They began meeting in July 1987, and by September, when SEMATECH's technical team visited the Data General plant, Professor Tasch and his people had formulated a detailed plan.

Table 7.2 Austin's incentive package to SEMATECH

Facilities incentives	$50,250,000[*]
Time on supercomputer	1,500,000
Cooperative state-funded research	5,000,000
Community-based incentives:	
Transportation assistance	750,000
Recruitment assistance	50,000
Spouse job assistance	100,000
Mortgage incentives	9,800,000
Children's incentives	75,000
Children's reduced-tuition incentives	312,000
Family sponsors	100,000
Club memberships	100,000
Tickets	<u>40,000</u>
	$68,077,000

[*]Source of funds for facilities incentives:

University of Texas	$50,000,000
City of Austin	<u>250,000</u>
	$50,250,000

Projected use of facilities incentives:

Site acquisition	$12,350,000
Retrofit	25,000,000
Equipment, added space	9,510,000
Interim debt service	<u>3,390,000</u>
	$50,250,000

Led by Ray Tyx, an Austin resident who worked with Tasch, the Texans built a complete clean room mock-up inside the Data General building. Tyx convinced vendors from all over the United States to display their products for SEMATECH: model floors, walls, lights, fans, filters, and other equipment. Otherwise, said Tyx: "You could not expect the SEMATECH people to just come into the Data General site with rose-colored glasses on and imagine what a clean room would look like" (Strain, 1989, p. 72). When SEMATECH's technical inspectors came to Austin they were shown a plan to build the clean room in 32 weeks. Ray Tyx and Al Tasch along with their team worked around-the-clock shifts and completed the clean room on schedule (about one-third the time normally required to build a world-class fab).

THE $50 MILLION TYPO

At the time of SEMATECH's September 1987 visit to the Data General plant, there was one little catch: Texas did not own it, Data General did. While driving out to the plant for Al Tasch's presentation, SEMATECH official Frank Martin asked Pike Powers what he was going to say about financing the building. Powers responded: "Well, Frank, I'm not going to say anything about it today. It's not together yet, and I'm not sure how it's all going to come together" (interview by Strain, March 24, 1989). It was not that Powers had not tried. A bill to provide the $50 million needed to purchase the Data General building and the 90 acres on which it was located had passed the Texas legislature. But on the final day of the July 1987 special legislative session, a typographical mistake was found in the bill's wording, and it was killed on a point of order by a disgruntled politician (Copelin, 1988). The Texas spirit of collaboration came up short at this critical point. How could such a minor error as a typo block a major legislative drive in support of SEMATECH?

Representative Bob Richardson of Austin had proposed the bill to buy and retrofit the vacant Data General plant for SEMATECH's headquarters and semiconductor clean room. The $50 million for the building was considered essential if Texas were to stay in the race with the other leading states that were also raising large amounts of money to offer SEMATECH. The bill was discussed in committee, it was voted out, and it seemed headed for approval by the legislature, but then an unexpected development occurred. Ron Wilson, a legislator from Houston, cited a point of order on the last day of the special session. Wilson had earlier insisted that the SEMATECH funding bill be amended to require the participation of minority-owned companies in the retrofitting of the Data General plant for SEMATECH. Powers had argued that such an amendment would be an inappropriate intrusion into SEMATECH's affairs. While Wilson was forced to give way on his proposed amendment, he remembered this rebuke, and he retaliated by catching the typo, and rising to a point of order, when it was too late to begin the legislative approval process anew. The typo incident was a display of "politics as usual." It seemed guaranteed to sink Austin's chances of winning SEMATECH. Without money for the clean room building, Texas was a sure loser. The state's collaborative public/private effort to win SEMATECH and to help spur U.S. industrial competitiveness was stumbling badly.

Through the support of Hans Mark (chancellor of the University of Texas system), the UT system's board of trustees agreed, in October 1987, to provide $12.3 million from the Permanent University Fund, the oil-financed kitty for Texas universities. Mark had made a cost-benefit analysis of the value that the University of Texas received each year from MCC in graduate student support, adjunct faculty, research grants, and research equipment. By his calculation, the benefits totaled $2.25 million per year. UT had put up $14 million to attract MCC to Austin in 1983. So the payoff period was about six years. "SEMATECH is twice as big as MCC, so if we put in $12.3 million, the payback should be in three or four years. Any commercial bank will say that's a helluva good investment. . . . I think that's really what persuaded the regents to go ahead and do it" (Mark interview by Strain, March 8, 1989). That still left $37.7 million to be raised from other sources.

While the additional $37.7 million could not be justified in terms of its educational benefits to UT, Chancellor Mark and the University of Texas system regents were willing to take the risk of providing these additional funds with the understanding that the legislature would reimburse the university for the funds when the legislature was next in session. "We said there will be benefits to Texas that are over and above education, and as public-spirited citizens, we will take the risk and back that loan" (Mark interview by Strain, March 8, 1989). The Texas legislature repaid UT in 1989.[8]

NARROWING THE FIELD

Given the overwhelming number of proposals that they received, SEMATECH officials quickly realized that they were dealing with a political hot potato. The fact that SEMATECH's $100-million-per-year funding package was being steered precariously through Congress in late 1987, while SEMATECH was evaluating and rejecting most of the 135 proposed sites, required very delicate balancing.

SEMATECH narrowed the proposals down to the strongest sites, whose representatives were invited to the headquarters of the Semiconductor Industry Association in Santa Clara, California, to pitch their proposal to a technical team and to the executive committee in charge of site selection. The Texas team included Hans Mark, Admiral Inman, and Robert Farley, an aide to Texas Governor Bill Clements. Both Austin and Dallas, the two Texas sites then in the running, made presentations. Austin was represented by Pike Powers, Peter Mills, and Dr. Ben Streetman, the University of Texas electrical engineering professor who had won the day for Austin in March 1983 at the MCC presentation in Chicago. The Dallas proposal suffered from not having a local, major research university with world-class capability in microelectronics.

A main difference from the MCC site-selection process was the markedly political nature of SEMATECH. For instance, Tampa made a concerted political push to attract SEMATECH. Then-Senator Lawton Chiles (D-Florida) was a member of the Senate Appropriations Defense Subcommittee. Also involved in SEMATECH's federal funding was Representative Bill Chappell (D-Florida), who was chairman of the House Appropriations Defense Subcommittee. During the fall of 1987, getting the $100 million of funding through Congress was a very high priority for SEMATECH. In fact, the site-selection process, originally scheduled to be completed in July 1987, was deliberately slowed until SEMATECH's federal funding was decided. Senator Chiles told SEMATECH that if Florida were not chosen, he would zero out the federal money (Nelson, 1988). Despite such pork-barreling efforts, the Tampa proposal was not considered a top contender by SEMATECH. For one thing, Tampa did not have a semiconductor clean room ready to go (but then neither did Austin).

Madison, Wisconsin, had a great many things going for it in the SEMATECH competition. Incentives offered to SEMATECH totaled $14 million from the state of Wisconsin and the city of Madison. The University of Wisconsin at Madison is an excellent research university, one of the best in the Midwest. Its research on X-ray lithography was on the cutting edge and applied directly to how circuitry is projected onto semiconductor wafers. Madison sits in a jewel of a setting, surrounded by several beautiful lakes. The Wisconsin proposal offered temporary space in a university building for three years, a period during which permanent facilities would be constructed on the university's research park, 15 miles south of Madison. However, the temporary facility lacked a clean room. Wisconsin also used its Washington clout to win SEMATECH. Representative Robert Kastenmeier (D-Wisconsin) had a solid relationship with SIA executives as a result of his having authored a 1984 bill that established intellectual property protection for semiconductor chip designs. Wisconsin Democratic Representative Les Aspin was chairman of the House Armed Services Committee, which authorizes defense funding (including SEMATECH's).

California also was a strong contender in the SEMATECH competition. The proposed site was near San Jose, where several of the consortium's member companies were located. Stanford University and the University of California at Berkeley were close by. But a September 1987 bill to provide state funding for the offer to SEMATECH was shot down in the California legislature. In desperation, a coalition of 18 state legislators wrote a letter to SEMATECH assuring financial support. In the last few days before the site-selection committee's final decision, Governor Deukmejian told SEMATECH that he could promise that a $125 million package would pass the state legislature. The numbers sounded impressive, but SEMATECH doubted that the governor could deliver, given the state's inability to overcome partisan politics. As Sandy Kane remembered: "There was no clear level of consensus that 'We want this, and we're going to go get it together.'" (interview by Strain, March 7, 1989)

In the finger pointing that followed San Jose's inability to make SEMATECH's short list of proposed sites, California legislators and San Jose officials commented that their bid had been crippled by arrogance, disorganization, and the lack of a coherent strategy for pursuing such projects. As Carmel Assemblyman Sam Farr (1989 chairman of the assembly's Economic Development Committee) said: "Part of the problem has been parochialism—we've never been able to pull together in a unified fashion." (Schmitz, 1989)

On December 22, 1987, the first year of SEMATECH funding was approved by the U.S. Congress. This event signaled that the time was ripe to finalize SEMATECH's site selection. On January 5, 1988, the SEMATECH board of directors met in Dallas to select the winning site, Austin, Texas.

WHY DID AUSTIN WIN?

Three main factors proved to be crucial in Austin's winning SEMATECH: political clout, geography, and avoiding "the fatal flaw" during the site-selection competition.

Back in December 1987, the lengthy congressional effort to secure funding for SEMATECH had almost been defeated. Even though both the House and the Senate had already agreed in principle to fund SEMATECH at $100 million annually for five years, a December 4, 1987, report of the Senate Appropriations Committee recommended only $65 million. The House of Representatives had already approved the full $100 million funding for fiscal year 1988, so the bill was sent to a House-Senate conference committee to work out the differences.

Pickle became the signal caller for the Texas delegation when funding for the SEMATECH project was threatened. Pickle helped coordinate each step through the Armed Services, Energy and Commerce, and Appropriations committees with the help of Governor Clements and Bob Inman. More than 140 House members from California and East Coast states formed a coalition to remove SEMATECH from the funding bill for a separate vote that would have killed it. Pickle marshaled support from Les Aspin, Representative Martin Frost (D-Dallas) on the rules committee, Representative Charles Wilson (D-Lufkin), and House Speaker Jim Wright in preventing a breakdown of SEMATECH's proposal (Kantor, 1988).

> A group [of legislators] from California and New Jersey . . . decided that we ought to slow down on SEMATE-CH and send the bill back to the Commerce Committee for study because SEMATECH was an industrial or a business venture, not a matter for defense. They wanted the Rules Committee to grant a separate vote. That would have killed SEMATECH just deader than a doornail because the Commerce Department is not

putting up a nickel of the money. The Defense
Department said that if you pass this amendment, we're
going to withdraw [the $100 million of funding]. But
we convinced the Rules Committee, through the
Speaker of the House [Jim Wright], not to allow a separate vote. SEMATECH went on through then. (Pickle
interview by Strain, March 29, 1989)

Texas senators Lloyd Bentsen and Phil Gramm, along with
Florida Senator Lawton Chiles (who had undergone a change of
heart since his earlier threat to withhold support unless
SEMATECH went to Tampa), pushed through the $100 million of
funding. In response to the concern of some senators that
SEMATECH's specific relationship with Defense was unclear, the
conference committee specified that a SEMATECH–Department of
Defense memo of understanding be signed prior to spending the
funds. Future awards of the $100 million per year were to be reap-
proved in each annual federal budget. Hence, SEMATECH was very
shrewd in selecting a site with a lot of congressional clout (Strain,
1989, p. 96).

Texas has a congressional delegation that . . . will get
together and stand behind [an issue] as one. . . . The
other two states . . . that have comparably sized congressional delegations, one in California and the other
one in New York, do exactly the opposite. They could-
n't get together on the time of day. (Kane interview by
Strain, March 7, 1989)

Copelin, the *Austin American-Statesman* reporter, observed:

SEMATECH used the site-selection process to get all of
the states interested, so everyone in Congress was pushing SEMATECH because they thought it might be coming to their home state. But what SEMATECH had to
worry about was, once they picked the site, who could
deliver the federal money the next year and the next
year and the next year. (Copelin interview by Strain,
March 4, 1989)

Within a month of SEMATECH's January 1988 decision to locate in Austin, the Texas politicians went to bat for the consortium's continued funding. In his budget proposal for fiscal year 1989, President Reagan requested $45 million. Some congressional representatives were concerned that SEMATECH still had not selected a CEO (more on this later in the chapter). Once again, Pickle came through and led the Texas delegation in restoring the full $100 million for the second year of SEMATECH's budget.

> Jake Pickle really believed in SEMATECH, and fought to get its initial appropriation of $100 million, and its second year budget, and go to Charlie Wilson, go to the House, and go to Senator Bentsen, and go to Senator Gramm, and say: "Now, we've got to have this." Getting that full second year of $100 million worth of funding may be the unknown key to making SEMATECH a success. That's when Pickle had to really go in and just twist arms and fight hard to get it back up from $45 million to $100 million. (Hilgers interview by Strain, February 27, 1989)

Pickle was considered a key ally by the SIA, even prior to SEMATECH. He helped pass the R&D tax credit in 1981 and the U.S.-Japan Semiconductor Trade Agreement in 1986. So it was natural for SEMATECH officials to work closely with Pickle in getting their federal funding. "They already knew me, and they kept coming to me. . . . I was holding hands with them, so to speak, on a regular basis." (Pickle interview by Strain, March 29, 1989)

A second major reason why Austin won SEMATECH concerns location. From a geographic point of view, Austin was well situated for SEMATECH.

> That's a critical factor, geography. It's vastly underestimated how important geography is—to be located equivalent distances from the two coasts. . . . You look at every time they [SEMATECH] met to make a major decision, where they brought the corporate board together, it was in Texas. (Powers interview by Strain, March 24, 1989)

Six of the consortium's member companies already had manufacturing operations in Austin: AMD, AT&T, IBM, LSI Logic, Motorola, and Texas Instruments. Seven of SEMATECH's members were also MCC shareholders: AMD, DEC, Harris, Hewlett-Packard, Motorola, National Semiconductor, and Rockwell. In all, 11 of SEMATECH's then 14 members had a presence in Austin; the 11 included all 6 member companies represented on the SEMATECH site-selection committee. Furthermore, no single company was dominant in Austin: AMD had 1,700 employees; IBM, 7,000; Motorola, 5,100; and Texas Instruments, 2,300. So a single SEMATECH member company would not "own" the consortium if it came to Austin. The Missouri proposal lost, in part, because its suggested site at Lee's Summit, about 20 miles from Kansas City, was dominated by a huge AT&T facility.

To those critics who reasoned that Austin and Texas had "bought" MCC, SEMATECH's choice of Austin was counterintuitive. Texas offered SEMATECH a package worth $68 million, much less than Phoenix's offer of $201 million. Massachusetts' financial package was more than double that of any other state. But on close inspection, SEMATECH believed that the amount was inflated: "You could take the Massachusetts offer and hold it up to the window and the sun would shine right through. It wasn't real. A lot of it was puff and fluff." (Powers interview by Strain, March 24, 1989)

Sandy Kane stated:

The biggest problem that the media had, and others had, as they analyzed our selection afterwards, was that they couldn't understand how we could have picked Austin, who offered a package worth $68 million, while other states offered us packages that were two and three and four and, in one case, seven times as much. They said that didn't make any sense. . . . For instance, the Massachusetts proposal was $441 million. . . . But a couple of things deflated it rather rapidly. First, about half of the amount, $200 million or so, was a low-interest loan. A consortium of companies with a very large partner called the U.S. government doesn't really need to borrow money. . . .

> Secondly, if I wanted to borrow $200 million at 1 percent better than prime, that's not worth $200 million. It's worth 1 percent of $200 million, or a couple of million bucks annually. (Kane interview by Strain, March 7, 1989)

There was little "soft money" in the Texas proposal. The cash was on the table, not just a promise to try to pass a bill in the state legislature to provide the funding, as was true in many other states. The Austin proposal was lean, but strong. However, as was true with the competition for MCC, *how* the Austin incentive was presented to SEMATECH may have been as important as *what* the package included. As Powers remembered: "Everybody in the community—business and the public and the university—[was] singing from the same hymnbook in the same pew at the same time and that's a remarkable occurrence in Austin, Texas in recent times." (quoted in Green, 1988)

As in the case of MCC, Austin avoided having a fatal flaw in its proposal. Powers said:

> That's the value of the MCC experience. The overlap of being able to know what it takes to really run hard and compete in one of these national public economic development sweepstakes competitions permitted us to know that you had to address in a very straightforward fashion your weaknesses, and find a solution to them and admit them right up front, and address them before anybody can pull the rabbit out of the hat on you and say: "Voila! What about this?" and lay you on the carpet. (Powers interview by Strain, March 24, 1989)

In November 1988, SEMATECH officials threw a three-hour building dedication party at the consortium's newly refurbished Austin-based facility for top electronics industry executives and Capitol Hill sponsors. More than 1,300 people attended the by-invitation-only morning dedication ceremony and tour of SEMATECH's clean room, as seen through the windows that separated the observers from the state-of-the-art facility. Cameras were forbidden. The ceremony was framed in red, white, and blue bunting and featured the Austin Symphony Orchestra and a fly-over by jets from

Austin's Bergstrom Air Force Base. Charles Sporck, a member of SEMATECH's board of directors, commented that the consortium was a long way from achieving its goal of revamping the U.S. semiconductor process. "This country is full of starters," he said. "There are damn few finishers. That's what SEMATECH is all about, getting good at finishing." (Pope, 1988)

A BREAKDOWN IN PUBLIC/PRIVATE COLLABORATION

Public/private collaboration was the clarion call in Austin's winning SEMATECH in 1987. Economic development officials had included permanent tax exemptions for the R&D consortium as one of the incentives to woo SEMATECH to Austin. SEMATECH leases its land and property from the University of Texas and a county research authority, both of which are tax-exempt. SEMATECH was to pay taxes only on the property it owned. In August 1989, the Travis Central Appraisal District review board voted to reverse the earlier decision and make the consortium pay property taxes. The review board, which was made up of a citizens' appeal group, had final jurisdiction over the taxes set by the district, and in deciding to tax SEMATECH, they overruled the district's chief appraiser.

Review board members argued that the consortium was a business, whose purpose was to make money for its member companies. It was not a public agency. Technology produced by the consortium was to be used in products sold by the consortium's member companies. "In its own lease, SEMATECH talks about the commercialization of research," said Bill Elkins, chairman of the review board. "We just don't think that SEMATECH is devoted exclusively to public programs." (Pope, 1989c)

SEMATECH officials argued that the consortium was not in business to make money. "The principle they have raised is whether we are an entity that serves the public good. . . . We believe we are serving the American people," said Peter Mills, SEMATECH's chief administrative officer (Pope, 1989g). SEMATECH argued that its nonprofit status had been upheld in rulings by several government agencies, including the U.S. Department of Defense, Congress, the state comptroller's office, and the state attorney general's office. SEMATECH's claim to tax-exempt status was supported by the

Greater Austin Chamber of Commerce, UT President William Cunningham, and the deputy director of the Department of Defense, the agency that provided approximately half of SEMATECH's annual budget.

The appraisal district valued SEMATECH's property at $61 million and presented SEMATECH with a $1 million tax bill. The review board voted 9–0 with 2 abstentions, to support the staff proposal. "A million dollars is a lot of taxpayers' dollars that we could be using to spend on our mission," said SEMATECH spokesman Miller Bonner. "That money is a couple more joint projects we could be doing to fight the Japanese" (McCann, 1989). In November 1989, SEMATECH sued the Travis Central Appraisal District for tax-exempt status. Representatives of the consortium stated that they were disappointed that this action was necessary since it distracted them from pursuing their primary mission. On the other hand, the suit pleased Elkins, who said: "Our original motivation was that they go to court. We didn't have the expertise to legally decide this. We didn't want to be the ones to make the final decision." (Pope, 1989g)

In January 1991, SEMATECH reached an out-of-court settlement that saved the consortium $1.9 million in property taxes. In reaching this settlement, the consortium was able to retain most of the tax-exempt status it was offered as an inducement to locate in Austin. In the future, SEMATECH expected to pay property taxes of about 15 percent of the amount due under the review board's initial request. As Bonner stated: "SEMATECH still believes it is totally tax exempt under the Texas constitution and statutes. However, this settlement allows us to refocus our efforts on our national mission rather than on local politics." (*Austin American-Statesman*; January 20, 1991)

SEMATECH'S OBJECTIVES AND ORGANIZATION

Although there were many similarities in the MCC and SEMATECH site-selection processes, these R&D consortia differ from each other in several important ways:

- SEMATECH's annual funding (originally about $200 million per year) comes jointly from (1) the U.S.

Department of Defense as a $100 million congressional appropriation and (2) $100 million paid by the member companies which are assessed an annual membership fee of 1 percent of their semiconductor sales with a maximum of $15 million for any one company. SEMATECH's annual budget is about four times larger than MCC's. The U.S. government is more directly involved in SEMATECH, and so, naturally, are Washington politics.

- SEMATECH seeks to improve the quality of semiconductor manufacturing rather than do basic research on semiconductors. While MCC (at least in its early years) could be characterized as big "R" and little "d" with a five-to-ten-year timeframe to commercialize research, SEMATECH's longest research window is about three years and is more focused on near-term R&D (little "r" and big "D"). SEMATECH is more tightly tied to the rapid cycles of technology evolution within the semiconductor industry. The consortium's longer-term research is channeled through the SRC to universities and national laboratories.

  Thus, SEMATECH pushes back U.S. antitrust limits even further than does MCC, and it illustrates the changing attitude of the federal government toward consortia, from an initial position of tentative permissiveness to one of active support.[9]

- While SEMATECH does not produce semiconductor chips for its member companies, it does operate a semiconductor clean room where advanced semiconductor manufacturing tools are investigated and demonstrated. SEMATECH is therefore a kind of laboratory/demonstration of improved methods for making semiconductors using U.S. technology.

  MCC experienced most success with respect to technology transfer (e.g., patents, technologies licensed and applied) within its Packaging/Interconnect research program, which is most similar to SEMATECH's R&D activities. The majority of the research conducted at MCC focused on software development, which proved to be most difficult to transfer and commercialize.

- SEMATECH also differs from MCC in that it has: (1) a single research program, in which all member companies participated and (2) a specified lifetime—originally five years from the time of legislative funding, although, in 1991, the consortium proposed and was granted a five-year extension.

The following eight SEMATECH member companies were also MCC shareholders at the time that the semiconductor manufacturing consortium was founded:

1. Advanced Micro Devices, Inc. (AMD); Sunnyvale, California
2. Digital Equipment Corporation (DEC); Maynard, Massachusetts
3. Harris Corporation; Melbourne, Florida
4. Hewlett-Packard Company (H-P); Palo Alto, California
5. Motorola, Inc.; Schaumburg, Illinois
6. National Semiconductor Corporation; Santa Clara, California
7. NCR Corporation; Dayton, Ohio[10]
8. Rockwell International Corporation; Pittsburgh, Pennsylvania

Six additional companies joined SEMATECH:

9. American Telephone and Telegraph (AT&T); New York
10. Intel Corporation; Santa Clara, California
11. International Business Machines Corporation (IBM); Armonk, New York
12. LSI Logic; Milpitas, California
13. Micron Technology, Inc.; Boise, Idaho
14. Texas Instruments Corporation; Dallas, Texas

While these 14 companies represented about 85 percent of U.S. semiconductor manufacturing capacity in 1988, the nation had about 200 smaller semiconductor companies. Why didn't more of the smaller firms join SEMATECH? One reason was the cost of membership. Many of the nonmember companies represented smaller and newer custom-design semiconductor firms that were founded during the 1980s. The philosophy and goals of SEMATECH did not generally meet the more entrepreneurial, go-it-alone philosophy of these firms. Examples of such manufacturers are Cypress Semiconductors, Chips & Technologies, Weitek, Altera, and Integrated Device Technology. These companies produce special-purpose, application-specific semiconductors. By filling many small niche markets, many of these companies do not compete directly with IBM, AT&T, National Semiconductor, and Intel nor with the Japanese. So many of the smaller, newer semiconductor firms believed that they did not need SEMATECH, some could not afford to join, and most have not supported the consortium.

LSI Logic Corporation and Micron Technology Incorporated left SEMATECH in 1992, about four years after the consortium began operations in Austin. With $5.1 million in earnings in fiscal 1991 and $2.4 million in annual dues, Micron Technology was SEMATECH's smallest member. Micron CEO, Joe Parkinson, criticized SEMATECH for its heavy investment in semiconductor equipment companies rather than chip-manufacturing processes (Ladendorf, 1992b). LSI Logic, also one of the consortium's smallest members, produced specialized logic chips and microprocessors. The company also wanted SEMATECH to spend more of its resources developing flexible manufacturing processes. After contributing about $16 million ($4 million/year) supporting SEMATECH's broad range of targets, LSI reported that the firm's funds would be better spent on internal research. George Wells, LSI's president and former member of SEMATECH's board of directors, commented: "With tight budgets and an increased emphasis on improving profitability, this decision came down to a matter of getting maximum return on our research investment." (quoted in Ladendorf, 1992a)

Looking on the bright side, SEMATECH's management commented that the loss of LSI and Micron would greatly diminish the cross-company hassles in deciding SEMATECH's research agenda. The two departing companies were described as "thorns in the side" of SEMATECH because they continually contested the consortium's change in research goals.

Harris Corporation left SEMATECH in 1993. Harris' dues were .7 percent of sales, or an estimated $5 million annually. A fourth member, NCR Corp., was purchased by AT&T. As of 1993, SEMATECH was funded by the following member companies: the five largest U.S. chipmakers—Intel, Motorola, Texas Instruments, National Semiconductor, and AMD; three giant computer makers that also make chips—IBM, Digital Equipment, and Hewlett-Packard; the communications giant, AT&T; and Rockwell International, a military and space contractor. These 11 companies represent the overwhelming majority of the U.S. chip-making capacity.

During its first six years, 1987–1993, SEMATECH experienced difficulty in maintaining its annual funding commitment of $100 million from the Department of Defense's Advanced Research Projects Agency (ARPA). (In 1993, the Pentagon's research arm dropped the word "Defense" from the beginning of its name and generally increased its funding for the commercial applications of R&D.) As noted, several of SEMATECH's member companies left, which resulted in the 11 remaining companies each having to pay a larger share to meet the $100 million private-sector funding contribution.

The Bush administration recommended $80 million for the government's support of SEMATECH in 1993. As part of the political campaign to restore full funding, in late January 1992, a group of Austin's leading politicians, academic leaders, and high-tech executives courted a group of visitors from the Congressional Competitiveness Caucus, a bipartisan group aimed at bolstering key U.S. industries. The group, hosted by Congressman Jake Pickle, made its pitch for continued federal support of SEMATECH. The local anthem was that "partnership between private industry, government, and a topflight university can make a difference in technology research with national consequences." (Landendorf, 1992d)

Governor Ann Richards stated that

> [Government] has been investing in private business all along, we just did it in the name of defense. Now we have to do it in the name of jobs; now we've got to do it in the name of the economy. This is the future of the United States of America and I firmly believe that it is

in your valuable hands and that you'll do the right thing. (quoted in Ladendorf, 1992d)

SEMATECH's management saw the writing on the wall and in their budget requests for 1994, asked for $90 million from ARPA and $90 million from the member companies. The $180 million budget was justified by SEMATECH as proactively reducing its requirements for federal and private money through such cost-saving operations as (1) using computer models to simulate factory operations, (2) working more closely with national laboratories and federally funded university research programs, (3) reducing administrative overhead from 18 to 13 percent, and (4) transferring responsibilities to other organizations. As William J. Spencer (SEMATECH's second CEO) commented: "Our plan to do more for less reflects today's economic realities: tough spending constraints for Congress and leaner times for SEMATECH's corporate members." (*SEMATECH Update*, September/ October, 1993)

SEMATECH'S GOVERNANCE

SEMATECH is a relatively flat organization largely governed by the member companies. A board of directors is composed of SEMATECH's CEO, a CEO from each member company, a representative from SEMI/SEMATECH (the Semiconductor Equipment and Materials Institute), and a representative from ARPA—each representative has one vote. An Executive Technical Advisory Board (ETAB) makes decisions about the overall technical/research focus of the consortium. ARPA and the member-company board members each have one vote on the ETAB. Each area of technical concentration is governed by a Focused Technical Advisory Board (FTAB) and Project Technical Advisory Boards (PTABs), the members of which often overlap. Vendor firms may have membership on the PTABs, but not on the higher-level decision-making groups.

Decisions about what general technical areas and specific projects SEMATECH will pursue are mostly member driven. But the decision-making process is problematic even though there is, unlike the case of MCC, a common focus on the semiconductor industry. For example, DOD is most concerned with chip flexibility and reliability, while the member companies are generally most interested in cutting costs and increasing their technological competitive edge through advancements in chip capacity.

Member companies have diverse motivations for joining SEMATECH. Motorola, Intel, and Texas Instruments are most concerned with increasing chip capacity through such means as narrower line widths. NCR, Hewlett-Packard, and Rockwell are more concerned with incremental cost savings in their manufacturing processes. Harris produces chips for the defense industry and is most concerned with reliability. Such variety is demonstrated when an FTAB attempts to compile a list of possible projects, only to have one or two companies express an interest in each project. (Morrison et al., 1993)

In some cases, the technical thrust areas, which are designated by the ETAB, have become organizationally entrenched. The managers of these "little kingdoms" tend to choose projects that perpetuate their area's mission rather than those actually needed by the member companies (Morrison et al., 1993). Furthermore, some member companies complicate the decision-making process by emphasizing second- and third-tier projects, realizing that SEMATECH's other member companies will push for top-tier projects. In this way a member company will have a broader range of its research interests represented at the consortium.

There are also conflicts in priorities and expected ROI to be sorted out between the consortium's member-company chipmakers and the equipment suppliers represented by SEMI/SEMATECH. There is a move toward a more "robust planning methodology" and "integrated planning" to bring equipment supplies closer into the project-selection process. Under the emerging plan, evaluation of prospective projects will be based on business viability as well as technical feasibility (a direction also being pursued by MCC).

SEMATECH'S RESEARCH

The original five-year plan for SEMATECH called for three overlapping stages. In the initial three-year phase, the consortium was to develop manufacturing technology for semiconductors with a minimum feature size of 0.8 micron. (A micron is one-thousandth of a millimeter, about one-hundredth the width of a human hair.) Phase 2 was to concentrate on 0.5 micron, which was expected to create parity with foreign competitors as well as to define the standards and specifications for chemicals and equipment. Phase 3, which began in 1989, targeted semiconductors of 0.35 micron (or one seventy-two thousandth of an inch) to regain worldwide leadership in semiconductor manufacturing for U.S. companies. Phase 3 objectives were met in 1993, a year ahead of schedule and on budget.

SEMATECH's original mission was "to provide the U.S semiconductor industry with the domestic capability for world leadership in manufacturing." In 1993, the consortium's mission was broadened as follows: "[To] solve the technical challenges required to keep the United States number one in the global semiconductor industry."

The R&D focus of SEMATECH has progressed through three basic phases. The first R&D focus, which lasted about one year, was on semiconductor manufacturing development. Shortly after its founding, SEMATECH devoted more of its resources to assisting the troubled U.S. semiconductor equipment industry with infrastructure development. This phase lasted about three years. As noted, both LSI and Micron Technology disagreed with this emphasis. SEMATECH's most recent research effort is on computer-integrated manufacturing. This last phase got off to a slow start. As Frank Squires, CAO, stated in 1992: "Finding people with [computer] systems skills in our industry is hard. We've had to stumble with that . . . pull ourselves together again and launch a new, redirected effort" (Ladendorf, 1992c). Advanced computer software is considered crucial to automate chip manufacturing and provide quick shifts to new manufacturing processes. As SEMATECH places more emphasis on software development to automate the factory floor, we are reminded of MCC's struggles with software development and application in a hardware-dominated world.

The Semiconductor Industry Association in collaboration with ARPA, the SRC, universities, and national laboratories has produced a semiconductor technology road map, a comprehensive plan for the U.S. semiconductor industry. It details who is responsible for different areas of research and it broadens SEMATECH's role in semiconductor R&D and flexible manufacturing methods, even as the consortium's annual budget has shrunk to $180 million. One looming concern is in the environmental area, specifically the release of ozone-depleting substances by the electronics industry. SEMATECH is devoting double the congressionally directed $10 million to environmental, safety, and health R&D programs.

Another pressing concern is how the consortium might gain more control over the SEMI/SEMATECH companies that entered into cooperative agreements, only to be purchased by Japanese or European companies. SEMATECH is beginning to explore the possibility of taking equity positions in (as well as increased control over) the technological advancements achieved through its cooperative agreements.

SEMATECH has essentially five levels of activities: (1) joint development programs (JDPs), which occur at the member companies and at SEMATECH; (2) equipment improvement programs (EIPs), which focus on using semiconductor tool manufacturers as Beta sites; (3) SEMATECH internal programs/projects, which concern enabling technologies to help meet the goals of the other research and development activities; (4) SEMATECH centers of excellence (SCOEs); and (5) national laboratories. SEMATECH funds research projects at 31 universities identified as centers of excellence. Proposals for research are solicited by and submitted to the Semiconductor Research Consortium (SRC), which administers the SCOE program for SEMATECH. These university-based centers have two measures of success: outstanding research and well-educated employees. The distribution of these centers throughout 14 states nationwide reflects both the location of research excellence and the political nature of SEMATECH's funding (Figure 7.3).

SEMATECH has a tradition of funding external R&D activities at federal laboratories, and by the early 1990s, that trend was increasing. In April 1993, SEMATECH agreed to spend $100 million over the next five years (about 10 percent of the consortium's budget) in a cooperative research program with the Department of Energy's (DOE) Sandia National Laboratories, in Albuquerque, New Mexico. This is the largest cooperative research project ever formed between DOE and a private-sector partner. Most of the research will be conducted at Sandia and will focus on the performance and costs of chip-making equipment, contamination-free manufacturing, equipment and software reliability, and materials analysis.

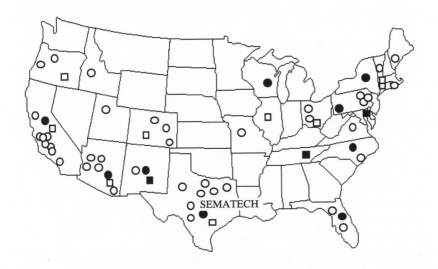

O   Member plant sites (40 fabrication sites in 17 states)

●   (SCOE): SEMATECH centers of excellence: 31 universities and
         federal laboratories in 14 states

□   (JDP/EIP): Joint Development and Equipment Improvement
         Projects: 51 contracts with 45 companies in 17 states

■   National labs in 3 states

Source: SEMATECH annual report, 1991.

**Figure 7.3 SEMATECH is an R&D consortium with wide
geographical/political involvement**

SEMATECH'S CEOs

As SEMATECH was being formed in 1987–1988, the consortium's member companies conducted an extensive search for a CEO. The selection committee wanted someone of high national stature and credibility, much like MCC's Admiral Inman. However, SEMATECH also needed someone who had a deep and broad knowledge of the semiconductor industry. The CEO was to have been selected by August 1987. As the search dragged on into the summer of 1988, the consortium was perceived by Washington politicians and industry observers to be in trouble. The lengthy search implied that the member companies could not agree on this fundamental matter. Congress threatened to reduce or withhold the next year's funding. During this period of indecision, the best possible leader was right in front of the executive search committee all along. Dr. Robert N. Noyce was one of SEMATECH's founders, and he was a member of the search committee. Early on, Noyce had been asked about heading SEMATECH, but he had declined, saying that at age 60, he was too old for the job.

Noyce was born a preacher's son in Burlington, Iowa, on December 12, 1927. He graduated from Grinnell College with a Phi Beta Kappa key and a bachelor's degree in physics and mathematics. He went on to earn his Ph.D. in physical electronics at MIT. Noyce—who held 16 patents for semiconductor devices, methods, and structures—was a co-inventor (with Jack Kilby of Texas Instruments) of the integrated circuit. He was a researcher at the Philco Corporation in Philadelphia in 1956, when Dr. William Shockley (co-inventor of the transistor) phoned from Palo Alto to invite him to join Shockley Semiconductor Laboratory, the first of the many semiconductor companies that were to spring up in Silicon Valley. Noyce accepted the job, moved to northern California, stayed for 32 years, founded two semiconductor companies (Fairchild Semiconductor Corporation in 1957 and Intel Corporation in 1968), and became a multimillionaire. As a co-founder of the Semiconductor Industry Association, Noyce was a strong and vocal advocate of enhancing the competitiveness of U.S. industry. When Noyce received the first international Charles Stark Draper Award given by the National Academy of Engineering in 1989, he donated his $175,000 prize to improve science and math education in the nation's public schools.[11]

In July 1988, Noyce left California (where many considered him the unofficial mayor of Silicon Valley) and Intel to become president and CEO of SEMATECH. He came reluctantly but immediately began to immerse himself in a work regimen of 14- to 16-hour days, six to seven days a week. The old warhorse was starting up yet another new company. Noyce really didn't need that. But the U.S. semiconductor industry needed SEMATECH. And SEMATECH needed Bob Noyce.

Miller Bonner, a SEMATECH official who worked closely with Noyce, observed (interview, November 16, 1990):

> Why did he come to the party? His place in history was secure. His personal fortune was made. He had good health. But he had to join SEMATECH because of the feeling of responsibility for losing the battle on his watch. . . . The only thing driving him was: "Let's bring America back."

Getting Bob Noyce on board was a tremendous shot in the arm for SEMATECH. Paul Hilgers, Congressman Jake Pickle's assistant, commented:

> Most crucial was getting Bob Noyce. All of a sudden, just as SEMATECH gave Austin clout, Bob Noyce gave SEMATECH clout. It was getting bad. That's why President Reagan had only approved $45 million [for SEMATECH's second-year budget]. People said: "Hell, you can't even find anybody to run this damn thing." SEMATECH not only found somebody to operate it, they found the very best in the business. (Hilgers interview by Strain, February 27, 1989)

Noyce had an immediate impact on the consortium:

> The first year of SEMATECH's existence, through summer 1988, was a set of board meetings that I could best describe as chaotic. . . . There was no real leadership. . . . There was just a raging debate and no focus and no direction out of the board. Then we hired Bob Noyce. The first couple of board meetings after he came on board were euphoric. . . . Nowdays, I feel like I am sitting on a real board. We are reviewing plans, talking strategies, and having intelligent debates. . . . That change has been a dramatic one. (Kane interview by Strain, March 7, 1989)

Bob Noyce died from a heart attack at the age of 62 in June

1990. Two months earlier, he had asked SEMATECH's board of directors to begin searching for someone to replace him as president. When President George Bush telephoned Noyce's wife, Ann Bowers, to express his condolences, he asked if there was anything that he could do. Spontaneously, Bowers told the president that he could continue to provide the $100 million per year to SEMATECH.

Charles Sporck was key to the hiring of Noyce to head SEMATECH, and he was also central to the hiring of Noyce's successor, William J. Spencer, age 60, who came from Xerox. Born in Raytown, Missouri, Spencer earned a bachelor's degree from William Jewell College and a master's in math and a Ph.D. in physics from Kansas State University. He began his career in semiconductor research at AT&T's Bell Laboratories in 1959 and later worked at Sandia National Laboratories in Albuquerque, New Mexico, and Livermore, California. In 1981, Spencer joined Xerox, where he became a manager of the company's integrated circuit laboratory at its Palo Alto (California) research center (PARC). Spencer later became group vice president and senior technical officer for Xerox in Stamford, Connecticut, where he managed the company's worldwide research activities. Spencer was noted for turning technology into products, such as Xerox's DocuTech Production Publisher, a blend of computer and copier technology. He was thus a veteran of semiconductor R&D. He was also a close friend of Bob Noyce.

SEMI/SEMATECH

To improve U.S. semiconductor manufacturing, SEMATECH works with U.S. companies that supply manufacturing equipment and raw materials with which semiconductors are made. These companies were hit hard by Japanese competitors during the 1980s, even worse than the U.S. semiconductor manufacturers (Figure 7.4). The trade association for these companies is called SEMI, which includes both U.S. and foreign member companies.

SEMI has over 900 members, including 700 U.S. and 200 Japanese companies. In light of SEMATECH's focus on national competitiveness, an independent organization, SEMI/SEMATECH was formed of U.S. member companies, 142 as of November 1993. SEMI/ SEMATECH is a separate corporation that is represented as a single member company representative who sits on SEMATECH's board of directors. SEMI/SEMATECH has its headquarters offices in SEMATECH's building in Austin and interacts with the consortium on a project-by-project basis. When SEMATECH decides that a new item of equipment or a new type of material is needed for semiconductor production, SEMI/SEMATECH works to ensure that a U.S. company gets the contract. In 1991, more than 60 percent of SEMATECH's total budget of $200 million went to equipment-supplying companies. So SEMATECH and SEMI/SEMATECH are decidedly pro-American.

1980	Sales in Millions		1991	Sales in Millions
Perkin-Elmer	$151		Tokyo Electron	$764
GCA	$116		Applied Materials	$654
Applied Materials	$115		Nikon	$616
Fairchild	$105		Advantest	$448
Varian	$90		Canon	$360
Teradyne	$83		Varian	$328
Eaton	$80		Hitachi	$316
General Signal	$57		Teradyne	$263
Kulicke & Soffa	$47		General Signal	$243
Takeda Riken	$46		SVG	$235
Totals	$890			$4,227

Source: VLSI Research, April 1992.

Figure 7.4 Semiconductor equipment suppliers' worldwide sales, 1980 and 1991

Once SEMATECH got going, it was important for the consortium to purchase U.S.-manufactured equipment. Early in the consortium's operation, one highly visible exception, which highlighted the lack of domestic capability, occurred when SEMATECH bought a Nikon stepper for its wafer fabrication plant. As Miller Bonner (interview, November 16, 1990) of SEMATECH related:

> We got a lot of heat for putting in the Nikon stepper. "Here you are, innovating for America's future, and you're buying a Nikon stepper." We put the Nikon stepper in a room with opaque plastic in the windows, so that you couldn't see through. The Nikon service people came in and did preventive maintenance. We watched them like hawks. . . . When we put the new GCA prototype in, we made the glass clear again.

As noted, SEMATECH commissions semiconductor equipment suppliers/vendors (Semi/Sematech members) to produce specialized manufacturing equipment, and it commissions centers of excellence to conduct research on tasks targeted by SEMATECH's funding companies. This process has been criticized as empowering the consortium to pick winners and unfairly penalizing vendors and research activities not funded by SEMATECH.[12] Criticism of this aspect of SEMATECH's operations was heightened when the chosen companies failed or when Japanese or other U.S. competitors bought the companies that SEMATECH's funds and expertise had benefited.

THE CASE OF SEMI-GAS SYSTEMS, INC.

One of the equipment supplier companies which SEMATECH picked to win was Semi-Gas Systems, Inc., which designed, assembled, and installed gas systems used in making semiconductors. Based in California, the rather small company had 122 employees and $21 million in annual sales in 1988–1990 when it provided SEMATECH with specialized gas systems to produce the superclean environment needed to manufacture smaller, faster, and more powerful chips. As Peter Mills (the consortium's chief administrative officer) stated: "We've worked very much as a team . . . to develop leading technology. . . . Through a joint development project with SEMATECH, Semi-Gas has been able to improve its purity levels by tenfold . . . giving them a world leadership position." (Kantor, 1990)

In April 1990, Hercules, Inc., of Wilmington, Delaware (a major chemical producer that had purchased Semi-Gas in 1987 for about $5 million) announced its intention to sell Semi-Gas to Nippon Sanso K.K. for $23 million. Hercules rejected a leveraged buyout offer by Semi-Gas management in favor of a higher offer from the Japanese competitor. Nippon Sanso was a world leader in gas purification and distribution equipment, but according to Mills the technology of Semi-Gas was at least two years ahead of the Nippon Sanso technology and probably any other technology in the world. SEMATECH stressed that the sale would give the Japanese confidential information about its 14 member companies. Management lobbied to block the proposed sale of this "American technological jewel" by saying it would breach national security and run afoul of antitrust laws.

Taking a laissez-faire attitude, the Bush administration said that it would not intervene in the sale of Semi-Gas Systems to Nippon Sanso. The White House and the Interagency Committee on Foreign Investment in the United States (which is composed of representatives from eight federal agencies) argued that the sale was not vital to U.S. security interests. Then Senator Albert Gore (D-Tennessee), chair of the Science, Technology, and Space Subcommittee, called the Bush administration's action outrageous: "a kind of electronic Teapot Dome scandal. . . . The White House decision [pending final approval by the Justice Department] just gives away an incredible list of assets to the very people that SEMATECH was set up to compete against" (quoted in Kantor, 1990). "We built a partnership with these [Semi-Gas] people," said Miller Bonner of SEMATECH. "They have access to the keys to the kingdom." (quoted in Ladendorf, 1990b)

In reaction to adverse publicity, a Bush administration official was quoted as saying that Nippon Sanso would have to isolate the five Semi-Gas technicians working at SEMATECH and that these technicians would report to a separate corporation that would be governed by a board of U.S. citizens and would act as a subsidiary to deal directly with SEMATECH. Nippon Sanso said that it was prepared to sign a confidentiality agreement with the Interagency Committee on Foreign Investment in the United States. SEMATECH, which was not involved in writing the proposed confidentiality agreement, announced that it would not allow Semi-Gas personnel on the premises and that the consortium would use every legal means to "protect our intellectual property. . . . We sort of feel like we're in an economic war right now" (Rothschild, 1990). SEMATECH's management argued that the sale of Semi-Gas would force the consortium to implement a costly and time-consuming switch to a new supplier for the "gas cabinet" system needed to distribute and monitor the ultra-pure gas SEMATECH used in chip production. It stated that the Semi-Gas sale would ultimately cost the consortium and the American taxpayers up to $100 million. Robert White, undersecretary of commerce for technology, testified at Gore's Senate hearing that the United States was "not operating on all cylinders" with regard to the international electronics marketplace. (Kantor, 1990)

By the end of 1990, taking a somewhat revolutionary stance, the U.S. Justice Department moved to block the sale of Semi-Gas Systems to Nippon Sanso on antitrust grounds. Justice was somewhat aggressive in applying the antitrust ruling to a foreign company's acquisition of a U.S. company. With ownership of Semi-Gas, Nippon Sanso would control 43 percent of the U.S. and 52 percent of the world market share in gas purification and distribution equipment. Although semiconductors were argued to be crucial to both military and economic security, the threat to national security—from an economic point of view—was not used by Justice. After the ruling, SEMATECH commented that the consortium could now move forward with the technological advances it had made in gas purification, advances that were crucial to the manufacturing of state-of-the-art microchips. Semi-Gas management commented that it was pleased to continue being part of SEMATECH. Believing that the antitrust claims had no merit, Hercules, Inc., intended to fight the lawsuit.

In April 1991, Semi-Gas Systems was sold for $23 million to the New Jersey-based subsidiary of Nippon Sanso. The transaction was completed a few weeks after a federal judge in Pennsylvania rejected the U.S. Justice Department lawsuit that claimed the Semi-Gas sale would violate antitrust prohibitions. SEMATECH officials reported that they did not expect any disruptions in their programs as they maintained that the consortium owned the rights to the technological advances made with Semi-Gas.

THE CASE OF GCA

Straining to retain a U.S. presence in advanced photolithography manufacturing equipment—one of the most crucial processes in making chips—SEMATECH made another important bet by investing tens of millions of dollars in a company called GCA. The company was one of five semiconductor equipment businesses owned by General Signal Corporation, a manufacturer of equipment and instruments for the process control, electrical, and industrial technology industries. GCA's three business segments were worldwide service and maintenance operations, manufacturing lenses for wafer steppers and instrumentation, and a wafer stepper product line (chip-printing machines). The company had pioneered wafer stepper technology in 1979 with the introduction of an opto-mechanical electronic system to optically pattern integrated circuits.

The U.S. market for microlithographic machinery is relatively small (about $300 million), but the technology is a critical link in the technological food chain of the $31 billion semiconductor industry, which in turn supports the $310 billion U.S. electronics industry (Carey and Port, 1992). If Japan cornered the lithography business, Japanese chipmakers might get favored treatment on new steppers.[13] Japanese computer companies could then have a cost and performance advantage over their U.S. counterparts.

By 1990, with SEMATECH's assistance, GCA had developed a line of photolithography products that were among the best in the world. However, GCA introduced its technology to the marketplace about a year late, after leading U.S. chipmakers had already committed to other suppliers. By 1991, it was apparent that GCA had missed its "window of opportunity" to gain substantial sales for its equipment. SEMATECH cut back on its product support for the company, and GCA began shutting down its once-formidable research and manufacturing complex in Andover, Massachusetts, in May, 1993.

According to Malcolm S. Forbes Jr. (editor in chief, *Forbes*): "by placing its biggest bet on [GCA], SEMATECH hurt other American companies that wanted to compete against [that company]. The subsidies were for naught; GCA couldn't cut it" (Forbes, 1993, p. 25). Forbes went on to argue that SEMATECH's failure with GCA demonstrated that government involvement was not a guarantee of success and may even retard the development of alternative technologies. ASM, a company financed by N.V. Philips (a multinational conglomerate headquartered in the Netherlands), was the leader in photolithography. The Philips connection, in the eyes of SEMATECH, made ASM a threat, commented Forbes. Hence, the decision was made to subsidize GCA. Forbes concluded: "Technology is global; by its very nature it can't be the monopoly of one company, one nation or one race."

In a March 26, 1993, fax sent by SEMATECH's division of technology transfer to SEMATECH's board (and copied to the consortium's technical advisory boards, member companies, Washington representatives, directors, senior assignees, SEMI/SEMATECH, the SIA, and the SRC), contingency questions and answers were posed about the sale of GCA.

Question:	Doesn't this mean failure for one of SEMATECH's critical programs?
Answer:	We lost a battle, but certainly not the war. The concept behind a consortium is to share the costs and share the risks. SEMATECH has devoted significant time and effort in lithography and GCA is not the only company with which we are working.
Question:	Could SEMATECH have done anything to prevent the announcement?
Answer:	We feel we did everything we could do to assist GCA. The reality is that technical success does not necessarily equate to business success.
Question:	How could SEMATECH assure business success?
Answer:	SEMATECH cannot and should not. SEMATECH's mission is to focus on semiconductor manufacturing technologies.
Question:	Why did GCA fail?
Answer:	We feel it failed to meet the timetable for the marketplace.

Question:	If GCA is sold to a foreign firm, does that mean that SEMATECH's investment—and the investment of the American taxpayer—will go to a foreign competitor?
Answer:	Not necessarily. Under the provisions of SEMATECH's contract, we have protected our intellectual property investment in GCA. SEMATECH could share its GCA knowledge base with another American firm should GCA be sold to a foreign firm.

THE CASE OF SVG

SEMATECH also funded Silicon Valley Group Lithography Systems, Inc. (SVGL) in Wilton, Connecticut. The technology, called Micrascan II, could print millions of transistors on the 256-megabit chip, and it was winning plaudits from analysts and customers by summer 1992. IBM had purchased 13 of the first-generation scanners produced by SVGL and was planning to purchase dozens of Micrascans. Toshiba, Intel, and Motorola were also expressing interest in purchasing the advanced etching equipment. As of June 1992, it seemed that SEMATECH's bet would pay off by making it possible for U.S. chipmakers to produce cutting-edge chips using American-made equipment. "The revival has been five years in the making, but the U.S. may finally be about to retake some ground in the technological war with Japan. . . . Such performance catapults the U.S. back into the technological lead," stated a *Business Week* article. (Carey and Port, 1992)

In May 1993, SVGL announced that the company would share its industry-leading technology with Japan-owned Cannon to jointly develop new equipment designs. Spencer commented:

The heat we're getting is based on a lack of understanding . . . as to what the alternatives were. . . . I'm delighted with what SVGL is doing. Their chances of surviving are 100 times greater than they were before this arrangement. [The lesson from GCA, is that good technology is not enough.] If you don't have a viable business plan and credible management, you're not going to succeed with just technology. . . . We made a good attempt [with GCA] and it didn't work. (Spencer quoted in Ladendorf, 1993d, p. D-1)

Papken Der Torossian, chairman of the Silicon Valley Group, commented:

We couldn't succeed without Cannon. My company is not big enough, where people like Motorola and Intel and others can bet their billion-dollar factories on it. . . . We [now] have a chance to be a global leader in the market. . . . If we were not strong, Cannon would not have talked with us. . . . Bottom line, I'm depending on SEMATECH to stand by me to maintain my leadership. If I'm weak, I'm dead. (Torossian, quoted in Ladendorf, 1993d, p. D-2)

SEMATECH will work with both Cannon and SVGL to improve and perfect existing technology. As Spencer observed,

If SVGL is going to be a player, they have to learn to manufacture better. We're going to have to help them in the future to make sure that Cannon does not swallow them up and spit them out as an empty shell. . . . We'll have some people in Japan working with Cannon as well as some people in Connecticut [working with SVGL]. . . . I suspect our friends in Washington will be unhappy. (Spencer quoted in Ladendorf, 1993d, p. D-2)

Noyce stated in 1988: "SEMATECH is for the benefit of American industry and American tax payers" (Sanger, 1988). Yet even as the R&D consortium was being formed, international alliances and cooperative agreements by U.S. chipmakers—many of them SEMATECH members—were under way. And there were pervasive, informal ties and communication networks among Japanese and American researchers and technicians. Motorola and Toshiba were sharing proprietary technology. Texas Instruments and IBM were making one-megabit chips in plants located in Tokyo that were being managed by Japanese engineers. NEC was operating a chip-fabrication plant near Sacramento, California, and had expressed an early interest in joining SEMATECH. NEC's stated motive sounded like a page from SEMATECH's public relations literature: "To ensure that a healthy network of equipment makers and supplies remains in the United States, where NEC is building more and more of its manufacturing capacity" (Sanger, 1988). So from SEMATECH's earliest days, the U.S. chip industry and the Pentagon were faced with a difficult choice: weighing the benefits and politics of using a combination of public and private funds to support only American-owned chip companies versus the increasing reality of international alliances and the potential benefits of leveraging resources and gaining technological know-how from Japan's most skilled chipmakers.

Efforts to keep new chip technologies within national borders is proving to be an increasingly futile exercise. As John P. Stern (executive director of United States Electronics Industry Japan) observed: "There is a flow of technology to foreigners no matter what we do. People move between these companies all the time. And these days, the Japanese acquire an interest in American electronics companies about once a week" (Sanger, 1988). "We are able to cooperate in the military arena. Why can't we do it in the semiconductor area?" asked Tomihiro Matsumura, head of NEC's $3 billion-a-year semiconductor division. (Sanger, 1988)

In September 1991, SEMATECH and JESSI (the Joint European Submicron Silicon—SEMATECH's European counterpart) agreed to formally share information. The objective of the accord was to make the member companies of both consortia more competitive—with Japan. Collaboration was to be conducted on a project-by-project basis to share resources and talent and to speed development in such areas as equipment standards, competitive analysis, and equipment qualification. Complementary projects were also cited as a motive for collaboration. European companies had been making advances in materials research that might benefit SEMATECH's members since most U.S. materials companies had been purchased by Japanese and European competitors. Industry analysts were skeptical of the alliance. Will Strauss (Forward Concepts, Tempe, Arizona) commented:

> Both organizations were formed to fight the tidal wave
> of Japanese companies becoming dominant in the semi-
> conductor business. JESSI has proved to be a huge cash

sink for the Europeans. On SEMATECH, the jury is still out, but everything they've got is no better than what the Japanese have right now. (quoted in Ladendorf, 1991b)

While Spencer acknowledges the increasing globalism of U.S chip manufacturers, he also realizes that it complicates the approval process for SEMATECH's annual appropriation from Congress. As Ladendorf (1993c) summarized, the old SEMATECH believed that the United States must slug it out with the Japanese for control of every segment of the semiconductor industry that appeared to be slipping away from America's grasp. The new belief is that SEMAT-ECH must help U.S. companies gain sufficient technical muscle to join international partnerships and to pursue global competition from a position of strength.

THE CASE OF FOURTH STATE TECHNOLOGY

SEMATECH researcher Terry Turner, an assignee from Texas Instruments, was convinced that his work on sensor-based manufacturing could save millions of dollars for semiconductor producers. No other company was making a tool that would allow chipmakers to bypass the time-consuming measurement steps required to make sure silicon wafers were being processed correctly. However, none of SEMATECH's members wanted to fund the research to market strength and support it as a product. So, Turner created SEMATECH's first spin-out, Fourth State Technology, wrote a business plan, and was accepted into the Austin Technology Incubator in April 1992. ATI is assisting the business venture by providing flexible and relatively inexpensive office space, phone, and other support services as well as less tangible, but perhaps more important, access to professional and financial networks.

By making minute voltage and current measurements in the plasma used in etching, Fourth State's product monitors silicon wafers as they are being processed into semiconductor devices. SEMATECH has no ownership rights in Fourth State Technology. Congressman Pickle (who attended the ceremony when Fourth State was admitted into ATI) commented: "The integrated circuit was invented in America by pioneers in the electronics field who were willing to take the risk to do something different. SEMATECH as a consortium encourages its assignees and employees to do things differently. As a result, new technology was developed and we have a new business that will create new jobs and help make America more competitive." (quoted in Ladendorf, 1992c)

In September 1993, Fourth State Technology announced that it had generated sales of more than $250,000 in the six months since the introduction of its RF Metrology System, which enables chipmakers to improve production yields by detecting flaws in the semiconductor manufacturing process. Fourth State's customers include AMD, Micron Technology, Texas Instruments, Hewlett-Packard, and SEMATECH.

TECHNOLOGY TRANSFER

Since SEMATECH was launched in 1988, the consortium's governance and technology transfer activities have been somewhat similar in form and process to MCC's early years under Admiral Inman and Grant Dove. However, SEMATECH placed a much heavier emphasis on shareholder assignees as the primary means of technology transfer to the member companies. Assignees make up about 60 percent of the consortium's professional staff. SEMATECH has an Office of Technology Transfer that traditionally has had two objectives: to market possible projects to member companies and to document the work done at the consortium. Over time the technology transfer office has become more customer-based rather than document-based.

During its formative years, SEMATECH's management generally believed that it would have less difficulty with technology transfer than MCC had experienced. SEMATECH did not have the diverse mix of shareholder support for separately funded research programs that characterized MCC. All of SEMATECH's member companies were collaborating on a common research program that targeted semiconductor manufacturing. New technology would be tested in the clean room or designated beta sites before it was transferred to the funding companies for high-volume use. So by means of targeted industry participation, focused research activities, and an emphasis on tested prototypes, SEMATECH, it was suggested, would be more successful than MCC in transferring technology to its member companies. (Novak, 1989)

By 1992, as a result of continued frustration with technology transfer, SEMATECH's Office of Technology Transfer emphasized the importance of the "old lessons" that

- Technology transfer is a participative sport.
- SEMATECH's members have common needs at the highest customer-requirements levels but tend to diverge into customer niches when the requirements are developed in depth, in terms of between- and within-company activities.
- Customer satisfaction must be monitored at least quarterly.

SEMATECH's researchers are suppose to ask themselves: (1) What is my output?, (2) Who receives (benefits from) my output?, (3) What are my customers' requirements?, (4) How can we work together for a win-win outcome?, and (5) Is my customer satisfied? (Pankratz interview, July 17, 1992). SEMATECH's emerging technology transfer philosophy stresses that each of the various consortium functions should be actively involved in understanding specific customer requirements, which need to be mapped rigorously into an annual strategic-planning process. Emphasis is placed on the involvement of SEMATECH, member companies, SEMI/SEMATECH, universities, and federal labs. Technology transfer activities are to evolve into a "member-company needs approach" that focuses on how the technology will actually be used. Member-company commitment to a new technology is seen as a phased process (Figure 7.5). As a SEMATECH memo on technology transfer stated:

> We have to be first in the market with best-of-breed equipment. Market windows are crucial. We can develop the best tools and technologies in the world, but if they are late, they will be of little use to our member companies. In consultation with our member companies and [ARPA], we have to be on target in our decisions on which technologies to pursue.
>
> We are dedicated to working together with each other, our customers and suppliers, following the BEST principles: Build a supportive environment; Encourage open communication; Share a common purpose and direction; and Treat individuals with respect.

THE QUALITY ASSIGNEE PROGRAM

When MCC was formed, emphasis was placed on liaisons for achieving timely and effective technology transfer to the shareholder companies. When SEMATECH was formed, assignees were expected to transfer the consortium's technologies to the member companies. Both consortia have experienced significant challenges with this method of technology transfer (see Chapter 5 for a discussion of MCC's experience with shareholder liaisons/ representatives).

In 1992, SEMATECH had a total of 755 employees—525 full-time hires, 213 assignees, and about 15 temporaries. When assignees arrive at SEMATECH, they are given a one-week orientation on such matters as safety and hazardous chemicals, human relations, travel requirements, E-mail, career managers and the role of senior assignees, and re-entry into the member company. The orientation also stresses cultural values for assignees such as being on time [with technology transfer], on target, and together.

Source: SEMATECH, April 1993.

Figure 7.5 Technology transfer as a phased process

On April 22, 1992 (almost four years after the consortium began operations), SEMATECH hosted a meeting at the Dallas–Fort Worth Airport Hyatt to establish a task force of member-company staff responsible for assignees.[14] The task force was to improve various aspects of the quality assignee program (QAP), such as assignee selection, integration into SEMATECH, smoothness of return to member companies, and tracking the careers of assignees after re-entry to their home companies. The emphasis was on people—having the right assignees at SEMATECH to transfer technology back to the member companies (Figure 7.6).

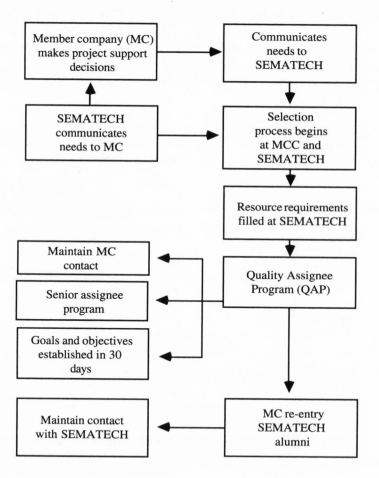

Source: SEMATECH, 1992.

Figure 7.6 Overview of technology transfer and the assignee program at SEMATECH

As did MCC, SEMATECH initially experienced difficulty in attracting qualified assignees. SEMATECH argued that it needed to increase the likelihood that such an assignment would enhance the assignee's professional career. Participants at the Dallas–Fort Worth meeting discussed the "we" versus "you" phenomenon that occurred when assignees came to SEMATECH. It was felt that there was a sense of displacement for the assignee, which could best be handled by (1) close contact with the member company, (2) a carefully planned career path, and (3) the initial selection process.

SEMATECH's 1992 Annual Report stated that the consortium would "train tomorrow's leaders—major emphasis would be on filling critical positions with assignees from member companies and returning them to member companies with the expertise for senior management roles." Member-company representatives at the Dallas–Fort Worth meeting believed that (1) the statement set expectations too high, (2) there would be disappointment if no management position were available for returning assignees, and (3) lateral assignments were more prevalent than promotions.

SEMATECH representatives wanted to give the assignee program more visibility and publicity in order to attract higher quality assignees. They wanted a way to determine the most qualified applicants by such means as a questionnaire, a reference check, or a check of the employees' previous performance review. These ideas were considered unacceptable to the member-company representatives, who expressed concern about whether SEMATECH's management was sufficiently skilled to ensure that assignees were adequately managed. As one company representative said: "It would be unfair to assignees to be improperly managed and have it reflect on their review or for them to not receive the knowledge expected."

Lengthy discussion centered on whether to use SEMATECH's or the member-companies' employee evaluation processes. Member companies wanted to be in on the decisions about promotion or change of assignments for the assignees. They wanted a standard procedure whereby they could review proposals and agree on placement before the assignees were approached.

An additional concern expressed at the meeting was whether assignee assignments should be tied to project length rather than a set calendar term (the current practice). It was not considered effective technology transfer to have trained assignees leave and new ones arrive in the middle of a project. Another concern was getting assignees into the SEMATECH culture rapidly enough to make them effective early on in their assignments.

SEMATECH representatives asked: "What can we do to get assignees back to their respective companies with the technology they have developed at SEMATECH?" As of June 22, 1992, 289 assignees from the 14 member companies had completed their SEMATECH assignment, and of this total, 51 (18 percent) did not return to the member companies or were not retained for the first year (Table 7.3). For example, of 20 AMD assignees, 7 chose not to go back to or remain employed by AMD. Of all those employees not returning to the member companies, some went to work for competitors (some of which were members of SEMATECH and some of which were not), some went to work for supplier companies that were part of SEMI/SEMATECH, some became consultants, and a few became permanent SEMATECH employees. The motivations most often cited for such career moves were to obtain a better job, stay in Austin, pursue an education, take early retirement, or start a SEMATECH spin-off.

Member companies used three approaches to ensure an assignee's return: (1) a legal approach, (2) a bonus approach, and (3) a career aproach. For example, in summer 1992, SEMATECH's legal department considered how to keep member companies from hiring SEMATECH assignees away from other member companies for a period of two years. Harris Corp. had a deferred compensation plan for returning assignees, in which they received a bonus equal to one year's salary—50 percent for staying two years and 50 percent for applying skills they learned at SEMATECH. One of the most effective ways to ensure the return of assignees was to have a career manager personally involved with the assignee at the member-company site so the assignee continued to view himself or herself as part of that organization.

One factor hindering implementation of any number of the above-mentioned policies was the lack of financial resources. Another was corporate restructuring and downsizing which was occuring at member companies such as Harris, LSI Logic, Micron, and Rockwell. SEMATECH's member companies had the right to waive the employment of a returning assignee if the firm did not want to rehire the individual or did not have a position open.

Indeed, as with MCC, many of the assignees who wanted to return to their former companies were not assigned or given positions that took advantage of the knowledge they had gained during their stay at SEMATECH.

Table 7.3 Returning assignee information, as of June 1992

Member Company	Number Completing Assignment	Number Not Retained*	Percentage Turnover
Advanced Micro Devices	20	7	35
AT&T	30	4	13
Digital Equipment Corp.	6	2	33
Harris Corp.	17	7	41
Hewlett-Packard	11	0	0
IBM	41	5	12
Intel	26	1	4
LSI Logic Corp.	7	2	29
Micron	8	3	38
Motorola	28	3	11
NCR	17	3	18
National Semiconductor	32	4	13
Rockwell International	12	5	42
Texas Instruments	<u>34</u>	<u>5</u>	<u>15</u>
	289	51	18

* The definition of this count includes assignees not returned to their member company and those who leave their member company within one year or less.

Source: SEMATECH, 1992.

IMPACTS OF SEMATECH

In 1980, U.S. companies held three-quarters of the $2.1 billion global market for chip-making equipment (see Figure 7.4). In 1988, the U.S. market share was half of an $8.2 billion worldwide market. The Japanese had increased their market share from 24 to 39 percent (Hayes, 1990). In 1990, the number of domestic companies eligible to compete for SEMATECH contracts was down to 130. Of that group, more than 100 had sales of $25 million or less. Most of these companies had little cash to invest in costly research. Given such realities, SEMATECH's mission soon became one of providing money and guidance to help U.S. equipment and material suppliers meet the consortium's standards for chip-making equipment.

In September 1990, the General Accounting Office (GAO) issued a report stating that SEMATECH needed to do a better job of bolstering the equipment and material suppliers that served the U.S. computer chip industry. In the survey, supplier-company executives ranked two factors as being most important in the decline of their industry: (1) the high cost of investment capital in the United States, and (2) relatively poor relations among U.S. chipmakers. Respondents believed that Japanese chipmakers gave their suppliers far more support than did their U.S. counterparts. In response to such criticism, SEMATECH implemented Partnering for Total Quality, a program to improve supplier-semiconductor company relationships. The plan called for a sharing of strategic goals and plans, performance information, and cost information.

In July 1991, a Capitol Hill House panel reviewed the funding of SEMATECH for the next five years. Spencer and Congressman Pickle testified that the consortium offered U.S. semiconductor companies the chance to pool resources, finances, and expertise to solve common problems providing a unique competitive advantage for the entire industry. But executives of the nation's smaller, independent firms criticized SEMATECH as "'an exclusive country club' that stifled competition and creativity." As commented by T.J. Rodgers, president and chief executive officer of Cypress Semiconductor: "SEMATECH and its members are not supporting [the] new innovative arm of the U.S. [semiconductor] industry" as represented by chip design houses (Moore, 1991). More helpful than renewing government support for the industry's biggest fish, Rodgers commented, would be restructuring capital gains to encourage long-term investment, revising banking law to improve the availability of venture capital financing, and a permanent R&D tax cut.

By the end of 1991, U.S. semiconductor equipment manufacturers had captured 48 percent of the world market, and by 1992, they had increased their market share to 53 percent. In early 1993, Applied Materials, Inc. (a SEMI/SEMATECH company and a beneficiary of SEMATECH grants), was ranked first (by VLSI Research of San Jose, California) among world suppliers of advanced equipment for making microchips. Applied Materials, with estimated 1992 sales of $794 million, passed Tokyo Electron, which had ranked first in 1991 (see Figure 7.4).[15]

Figure 7.7 shows how the rankings of the world's largest semiconductor companies have shifted from 1980 to 1993. In 1980, Texas Instruments, Motorola, and Philips were ranked above NEC, Japan's top semiconductor producer. By 1990, NEC, Toshiba, and Hitachi topped the list. In 1993, Intel was on top, followed by NEC and Motorola, and then Toshiba. Overall, the market share of North American semiconductor companies increased 3 percent in 1992, while the market share of Japanese companies fell by almost 4 points (Dataquest, 1993). In 1993, three of the world's ten largest chipmakers were American, while six were Japanese, and one was Korean.

In August 1992, a U.S. General Accounting Office report concluded that the consortium was on schedule and that the U.S. chip industry appeared to have reached parity with its Japanese competitors in manufacturing know-how. Six of SEMATECH's members—AMD, Hewlett-Packard, IBM, National Semiconductor, NCR, and Motorola—reported that they were either breaking even or receiving greater returns from SEMATECH's research. Two companies—AT&T and Texas Instruments—reported that they broke even or had a positive return from SEMATECH for the first time in 1991. Three other companies—Intel, Rockwell International, and DEC could not quantify their return on investment (Ladendorf, 1992e).

In 1993, SEMATECH announced that the consortium had proved that the United States was building all the tools needed to produce integrated circuits with device widths as small as .35 micron (one seventy-two thousandth of an inch) and that the U.S. semiconductor industry had, with the consortium's assistance, achieved at least parity with Japanese competitors. As Bill George, SEMATECH's chief operating officer, stated:

> When SEMATECH was created in 1987, we made a commitment to re-establish the U.S. semiconductor industry at the forefront of world manufacturing with the advancement of .35 micron technology. It's my pleasure to announce [that] we accomplished that feat [on time and on budget]. (Ladendorf, 1993a)

Charles Sporck, commented:

> Clearly things have been reversed. I don't think any one of us can claim that SEMATECH caused that reversal, but we damned well better take some credit for it. [The U.S. chips industry] is in a better position today because we learned a lot more over the last five years [about] how to work together effectively. (Ladendorf, 1993a)

Sales in millions 1980			Sales in millions 1990			Sales in millions 1993*		
	TI	$1,580		NEC	$4,952		Intel	$7,842
	Motorola	$1,110		Toshiba	$4,905		NEC	$6,436
	Philips	$935		Hitachi	$3,927		Motorola	$6,007
	NEC	$787		Motorola	$3,692		Toshiba	$5,873
	National	$747		Intel	$3,135		Hitachi	$4,740
	Toshiba	$629		Fujitsu	$3,019		TI	$3,842
	Hitachi	$622		TI	$2,574		Fujitsu	$3,298
	Intel	$575		Mitsubishi	$2,476		Samsung	$3,092
	Fairchild	$566		Matsushita	$1,945		Mitsubishi	$3,039
	Siemens	$413		Philips	$1,932		Matsushita	$2,430
Totals		$7,964			$32,557			$30,286

Source: Dataquest, 1993, VLSI Research Inc.   *estimated 1993

Figure 7.7 Top ten semiconductor suppliers' worldwide sales, in 1980, 1990, and 1993

IMPACTS ON AUSTIN

Compared to the 1983–1985 Austin boom which followed the arrival of MCC, the post-1988 impact of SEMATECH was hardly a boomlet in terms of residential and office building construction. Perhaps Texas' real estate developers and lending institutions had learned a lesson from the late-1980s bust, or perhaps they were broke. Since SEMATECH's arrival, building construction and job expansion in the Austin area has been slower, steadier, and more technology-based. As with MCC, winning SEMATECH focused world attention on Austin; however, SEMATECH proved to be a more important catalyst for the relocation and expansion of semiconductor equipment suppliers in central Texas.

Perhaps the most telling relocation/expansion example of SEMATECH's extended impact is Applied Materials Incorporated, which drew numerous additional semiconductor equipment and parts manufacturers to the Capital City. Applied Materials came to Austin to be near SEMATECH as well as two major and growing customers (Motorola and AMD), and because of the University of Texas and the availability of skilled workers. In summer 1990, Applied began construction of a $21 million facility that began operation in 1992 and employed about 250. By summer 1993, the company was beginning construction of a second Austin-based manufacturing plant at a cost of $20 million. By the year 2000, Applied plans to have an eight-building campus in Austin with roughly 1 million square feet and as many as 2,000 workers.

In summer 1993, Applied Materials' Austin-based facility gave credit to SEMATECH for assistance in producing the company's latest generation of advanced etch equipment. The product line was improved during a three-year joint development program with SEMATECH and several of the consortium's member companies. David Wang (group vice president for Applied's chemical vapor deposition and etch technologies division) said: "The new systems breakthrough technology would make it the etch standard into the next century." (quoted in Ladendorf, 1993e)

During its relatively short residence in Austin, Applied Materials has attracted and spawned a network of about 30 businesses that supply crucial goods and services that have helped vertically integrate the city's semiconductor manufacturing infrastructure. Such businesses include Photronics Inc., a Connecticut-based company that manufacturers photomasks, high-precision photographic plates made from glass or quartz; Lonestar Surface Technologies Inc., a subsidiary of Anodizers, Inc. of Redwood City, California; CDS Leopold, a San Carlos, California-based precision-machining company; Pro Fasteners, a San Jose, California-based supplier of nuts and bolts; Touche Manufacturing, a San Jose, California-based manufacturer of precision metal enclosures; and Serra, Inc., a Silicon Valley-based firm that manufacturers metal frames and sheet-metal parts. And Applied has facilitated the expansion of local companies such as AMP Packaging Systems, which produces printed circuit boards, and Briggs-Weaver Inc., which makes tools, safety equipment, and packaging materials.

In 1989, The University of Texas at Austin committed to a $22-million construction project that would double the school's computer chip research operations and provide students with 12,000 square-foot clean room laboratories as sophisticated as those found in private industry. The Microelectronics and Engineering Research Building was built at the Balcones Research Center in North Austin, across the street from MCC. As Ben Streetman, the Center's director, said: "Our interest is in looking at processes that are beyond what is currently used in industry. We want to look at new ways of growing and processing materials." (quoted in Pope, 1993)

Motorola, the pioneer of semiconductor manufacturing in Austin, built its first MOS (metal oxide semiconductor) plant in the city in 1974, followed by MOS 3 in 1975 and MOS 8 in 1980. While these were relatively small (25,000-square-foot) facilities, in 1991, using SEMATECH's prototype clean room as a model, Motorola began construction of its Austin-based MOS 11 (an $800 million, 76,000-square-foot facility). Noteworthy was the fact that the facility was equipped using more than 80 percent U.S.-manufactured tools.

In 1992, IBM, Apple, and Motorola announced they would form an Austin-based alliance to create a new computing standard. The Power PC was to use reduced instruction set computing (RISC) and was to be a major challenge to Intel's popular Pentium chip. The IBM-Apple-Motorola alliance, called Somerset, was staffed by 340 engineers and required a massive investment in hardware and software research and technology. Somerset's first product was the 601 microprocessor.

Momentum was building for Austin's emergence as a major semiconductor manufacturing center. In summer 1993, Motorola announced it would build another new chip laboratory and factory in Austin. MOS 14 was to cost upward of $1 billion, occupy nearly 800,000 square feet, and add 700 jobs to Motorola's Austin employment base of 7,700. The new facility was to be the home of Motorola's Advanced Products R&D Laboratory (APRDL), which would employ 400 scientists, engineers, and technicians who would create the advanced materials and manufacturing processes required for future generation of microchips. Also in summer 1993, AMD began construction of its new chip factory called "Fab 24." The 700,000-square-foot state-of-the-art facility will cost upward of $1 billion when fully equipped and by 1997 will add 1,000 workers to AMD's Austin-based work force of 2,500.

According to SEMATECH's records, more than 300 of the consortium's direct-hire employees were recruited from within Texas, and nearly all of the 100 manufacturing technicians were recruited from Texas schools. Residents of east Austin (where many blacks and Hispanics live) represented 22 percent of SEMATECH's workforce, taking home about $4.8 million annually. SEMATECH's procurement of goods and services pumped more than $13 million into east and south Austin businesses between June 1990 and February 1992.

U.S. MEMORIES

The brief, ill-fated history of U.S. Memories, Inc., also provides certain insights into the political process involved in the formation of a multicompany consortium. U.S. Memories was formed on January 21, 1989, in order to manufacture computer memory chips, the type of semiconductor that U.S. companies had almost lost to their Japanese competitors. Dynamic random-access memory chips were considered the most important single product in the semiconductor industry. The U.S. share of world production of DRAMs had dropped to only 20 percent in 1986, while Japanese market share had climbed to 70 percent (see Figure 1.1). U.S.

Memories was formed to regain U.S. market share by constructing a manufacturing plant to produce 4-megabit DRAMs by 1991.

Seven companies were behind the founding of U.S. Memories: IBM, AT&T, Hewlett-Packard, Intel, AMD, National Semiconductor, and LSI Logic. All were members of SEMATECH, and three were also members of MCC. The purpose of this consortium was to produce memory chips, not to conduct research; thus, it did not fit under the provisions of the 1984 National Cooperative Research Act. Antitrust regulations would have to be loosened further in order for such a manufacturing consortium to be exempted from federal prosecution. But given the sorry state of the U.S. semiconductor memory chip industry, the White House seemed inclined to relax U.S. antitrust policy even to this degree.

U.S. Memories was headed by Sandy Kane, the IBM vice president who had chaired the SEMATECH site-selection committee. Plans for U.S. Memories were very grand: the manufacturing consortium was planned as a $1 billion joint venture of the member companies, with about half of the funding to come from the Department of Defense. The consortium would employ 3,000 workers in a $500 million plant. Fifty-seven communities in 15 states competed for this rich prize.

U.S. Memories' 1989 site-selection process was conducted in a way that was reminiscent of MCC and SEMATECH. By late 1989, Austin was one of the four finalist sites being considered, along with Phoenix, Colorado Springs, and Middletown, New York (a site near IBM headquarters). Austin's incentive package of $125 million was the highest of the four finalist cities. Once again, it was Pike Powers, as chair of the Austin Chamber of Commerce, who headed the Austin effort.

It turned out that U.S. Memories was aptly named, since as the site-selection process neared its conclusion, the consortium failed to attract the needed funding. The effort to form the consortium was abandoned in early 1990. The main reason given for the demise of U.S. Memories was the apparent lack of a crisis in DRAM cost and availability. By late 1989, the United States was practically awash in computer memory chips, and the price of a 1-megabit DRAM had dropped to only 15 percent of its 1988 peak.

CONCLUSIONS

The location and formation of R&D consortia are intimately political processes, especially when federal funding is involved, as in the case of SEMATECH. A key factor in MCC's decision to locate in Austin was the promise of help by powerful Texas legislators in Washington. Indeed, the Texas delegation, along with Admiral Inman and MCC's member companies, played an important role in the unanimous passage of the 1984 National Cooperative Research Act, which removed antitrust restrictions on R&D consortia in the United States.

The fact that SEMATECH depended on an annual appropriation of $100 million from the U.S. Department of Defense complicated the consortium's site-selection process. As the original 134 proposed sites were narrowed down to a small number of finalists, SEMATECH tried not to alienate congressional members from the rejected sites. These votes were needed in order to obtain the first year's $100 million from the Department of Defense. This delicate balancing act ended in early January 1988 with the selection of Austin. Two factors stand out as key to Austin's winning SEMATECH: political clout and geographic location. The power of the Texas congressional delegation, in terms of both its unity and its seniority, was a major factor in the SEMATECH decision. The semiconductor-manufacturing consortium would need a great deal of political support in order to continue to receive the necessary federal funding. Austin's central geographic location was also an important factor in its winning SEMATECH. However, the public/private collaboration exhibited by the key sectors of Texas and Austin also favorably impressed SEMATECH's site-selection committee. As was the case with MCC, once the site-selection competition was narrowed to a few qualified sites, academic, business, and local government support and a lack of "fatal flaws" became critical decision-making criteria.

Like MCC, SEMATECH was launched with a flash of national publicity and very high hopes as to how the consortium would improve the global competitiveness of its member firms. Following is a list of transitions that have faced both MCC (during its first ten years) and SEMATECH (during its first five years).

Over time, both consortia have become less concerned with the Japanese threat that inspired their founding. U.S. semiconductor equipment suppliers and merchant companies are in better shape in 1993 than they were in 1988. For MCC's members, the threat of the Japanese fifth-generation computer never materialized. While attempting to draw specific cause and effect relationships as to the impact of MCC or SEMATECH would be problematic, it seems generally accepted that SEMATECH has been most successful in galvanizing the relevant industry of its member companies.

Both consortia pushed against antitrust law. MCC motivated the passage of the National Cooperative Research Act and established the legality of pre-competitive R&D. SEMATECH extended the weakening of antitrust as it applied to R&D collaboration leading to the production and testing of semiconductor manufacturing equipment.

Both consortia experienced the loss of their smallest members during the first few years of operation and both have experienced the strain of decreased financial support as they have explored alternative forms of revenue generation (e.g., technology licensing, leasing clean room space). An interesting difference is that while MCC seeks to increase government funding, SEMATECH is faced with declining government support.

Both consortia have experienced a change in their research priorities and culture due to operational constraints, changes in member companies priorities, and changes in leadership. Both Admiral Inman and Bob Noyce were inspirational leaders of exceptional capability, credibility, and visibility—qualities that were needed to launch their respective organizations. Both Grant Dove and Bill Spencer came from industry backgrounds and both applied mid-course corrections to their organizations. After seven years, MCC's leadership changed most significantly. Will SEMATECH's third CEO find it necessary to usher in dramatic structural and management change as Fields has done with MCC?

Both consortia have struggled with the challenge of technology transfer. Because SEMATECH's member companies were funding a common research program that was quite applied (similar to MCC's Packaging/Interconnect Program) and since member company assignees were a central part of SEMATECH's operations, it was expected that SEMATECH would be more successful in transferring its technologies. However, both consortia have experienced a similar movement away from relying on published reports and formal meetings toward a more personalized and customized approach to technology transfer. As MCC experienced problems with its liaison/shareholder representative program, SEMATECH experienced challenges with its Quality Assignee Program. As MCC fostered spin-out companies, so has SEMATECH. As MCC has been frustrated by limited control over the acceptance and application of its technology by its shareholders, so has SEMATECH been frustrated by its limited control over its SEMI/SEMATECH members.

Both consortia are becoming more open to foreign collaboration. MCC has come to accept foreign company participation in selected technology activities. SEMATECH has had to deal with the international alliances of its member companies as well as SEMI/SEMATECH companies.

Both consortia are concerned with how they are measured. External evaluators of both MCC and SEMATECH have often expected too much too quickly in terms of the impact of these consortia on U.S. industrial competitiveness. Both consortia have come to realize that volumes of technical reports and numerous patents and technologies licensed provide limited measures of what they have accomplished. For example, the members of both consortia have benefited from learning how to communicate and collaborate within and across organizational boundaries in ways not thought possible when they founded their respective organizations.

Both consortia have received assistance from the community in which they located and from local, state, and federal government. Both consortia have had a profound impact on accelerating the development of Austin's high-tech industry as well as the enhanced national and worldwide perception of Austin as a developing technopolis. Both consortia have contributed to educational excellence within the state and the nation. Both consortia have experienced setbacks and both are evolving and learning.

NOTES

1. Just two weeks prior to SEMATECH's January 1988 decision to locate in Austin, Texas landed another plum—the Superconducting Supercollider Project, funded by the U.S. Department of Energy at $238 million for fiscal year 1989. After a major national competition, the project's $8.5 billion 53-mile underground atom-smashing track was to be constructed in Waxahachie, Texas, south of Dallas. As with MCC and SEMATECH, Texas won the supercollider in the face of intense competition from other states. In October 1993,

a House-Senate conference committee ordered the superconducting supercollider shut down and allocated $640 million for dismantling the project.

Budget cutting pressures and politics were intense in the decision to cut off funding for the supercollider, but there were other more subtle issues involved, as commented by Lobbyist John White: "Very few people, including this fellow, ever knew what the damn thing would do. You can't sell something you can't explain" (quoted in "SSC Fall Linked to Its Complexity," A. Reifenberg, Washington Bureau, *The Dallas Morning News* (October 27, 1993). Tokyo had earlier declined financial and technical assistance for the Supercollider, but in late October, Japanese scientists vowed to push ahead with their own high-energy physics research by starting to build an accelerator in 1994. As commented by Shinroku Saito, chairman of the Kanagawa Academy of Science: "International cooperation is important, but we should build up our own facilities" (quoted in *The Nikkei Weekly*, October 25, 1993).

2. Powers was one of the key members of the governor's and Austin task forces for MCC in 1983. In 1987, during the SEMATECH site-selection process, Powers served as vice chairman for economic development of the Greater Austin Chamber of Commerce.

3. It is interesting that the Japanese threat was a main motivation for both MCC and SEMATECH and that the organizers of both consortia felt rushed to get their operations under way: weeks and even days were counted. Yet after impressive starts, both of the consortia got bogged down operationally, and the Japanese threat proved to be less of a concern than predicted.

4. Another proposal that particularly tickled Kane and his site-selection committee was from a certain midwestern state. The proposal's authors said that they had searched their state far and wide to find just the right facility for SEMATECH. The proposed building was a mental sanatorium. As Kane remembered: "The next line in their proposal was priceless. It stated: 'The current mentally retarded residents are being moved to other facilities so that the sanatorium will be ready for your occupancy in September'" (interview by Strain, March 7, 1989). Kane had this page of the proposal framed, for display on his office wall.

5. James Meindl was a key figure in the building of Stanford University's semiconductor research program.

6. Prior to coming to Austin, Mills had earned an engineering degree from MIT and had worked for DEC in Boston. In 1988, Mills became SEMATECH's senior vice president for administration and chief administrative officer. After leaving the consortium in 1991, Mills became president of the U.S. Display Consortium that was formed in the summer 1993 with $20 million from the Defense Department's Advanced Research Projects Agency. The company group is headed by AT&T and Xerox. Flat-panel displays are argued to be one part of high-tech's "holy trinity," the others being software and semiconductors.

7. As we discussed in Chapter 6, this norm of secrecy also caused problems when Sally Shipman and other Austin city council members used the "behind closed doors" and "old boys' network" aspects of the SEMATECH and MCC proposals to fuel their no-growth campaign.

8. The $37.7 million was actually used by the University of Texas to guarantee bonds of the Travis County R&D Authority, which was set up to buy the land and plant from Data General for the University of Texas, which then retrofitted the building as a clean room. The university rents the facility and grounds to SEMATECH for $2 per year. Jim Crowson, general counsel of the University of Texas system, came up with the idea of creating the Travis County R&D Authority, the first to be established under a new state law.

9. An even more daring consortium from an antitrust point of view was the attempt to launch U.S. Memories, Inc., which was initiated on January 21, 1989, to manufacture computer memory chips. In early 1990, the proposal for U.S. Memories was abandoned.

10. NCR paid the minimum participation fee of $1 million to join SEMATECH in February 1988 and will pay that amount each year that the company remains a member of the consortium.

11. Noyce was awarded the National Medal of Science by President Carter in 1980 and the National Medal of Technology by President Reagan in 1987. He was inducted into the National Inventors Hall of Fame in 1983 and elected to the U.S. Business Hall of Fame in 1989.

12. In SEMATECH's boardroom there is a large picture of five puppies nestled in a field of bluebonnets (Texas' state flower). At times, SEMATECH's managers were reminded that when they picked certain equipment suppliers to support, the rest of the "litter" was likely to fail. Spencer's retort to such concerns was: "At times you have to kill the puppies."

13. With the old stepper technology, light is projected through a stencil-like mask of a chip's circuitry onto a silicon wafer. Each exposure "burns in" the pattern for two or three of the scores of chips that will be made from the wafer. Then the wafer moves, or "steps" for the next exposure. The new step-and-scan method "prints" a much larger area, making it cheaper to produce finer circuit lines for faster chips. The mask moves between a lens and a light, scanning the chip pattern and projecting it onto the wafer, which also moves. Then the wafer shifts for the next strip exposure. (Carey and Port, 1992)

14. The statements and quotes in this section are based on the May 18, 1992, minutes of a Quality Assignee Program Task Force meeting, which was held at the Dallas–Fort Worth Airport Hyatt, April 22, 1992. At the meeting were two representatives from SEMATECH and representatives from AMD, AT&T, DEC, Harris, Hewlett-Packard, Motorola, Intel, National Semiconductor, Rockwell, and Texas Instruments.

15. Applied Materials was founded in 1967 in Mountain View, California, by a 28-year-old chemical engineer, Michael McNeilly, and five others. In a little over 20 years, the company had become a world leader in designing and manufacturing equipment for depositing fine layers of coatings on silicon wafers and for etching microcircuits on wafers. The companies total revenues grew from about $190 million in 1984 to close to $800 million by 1992. In late 1993, Applied Materials, the world's biggest manufacturer of semiconductor production equipment, broke through the $1 billion mark in revenues.

8

LESSONS LEARNED

Looking back over the past ten years, I see remarkable progress in technological collaboration . . . and community based public/private collaboration for economic development . . . considering that we are a highly individualistic society, more prone to compete among ourselves than to work together. Ten years ago, the environment for collaboration overall might be best characterized, in a word as inhospitable.

Remarks by William C. Norris,
at the tenth anniversary of MCC,
May 11, 1993, Austin, Texas

The rapid increase in and diversity of new technologies is changing the nature of economic competition. How communities, regions, and nations anticipate and respond to this competitive environment will largely determine the health and viability of economies and the quality of life that is sustainable.

George Kozmetsky
IC^2 Institute

To critics, the Microelectronics and Computer Technology Corporation (MCC) is faulted for not producing "silver bullet" technologies to beat back Japanese competition. However, as we have emphasized, MCC was not designed (or even legally allowed) to produce products. The consortium was to be an experiment in R&D collaboration, focusing on pre-competitive (or pre-production) research in areas judged to be critically important by its shareholder companies. MCC-developed technologies could be world class, but if they were not successfully adopted and/or sold in the marketplace by the consortium's members, MCC would be judged a failure.

No one organization should be expected to "save" a threatened U.S. industry—especially a relatively small and experimental organization like MCC. Enhanced U.S. industrial competitiveness involves problems that are broad and deep, including both regional and national concerns such as governmental policies, the cost of capital, quality of education and training, manufacturing capability, health care costs, environmental concerns, crime, and poverty. MCC's founding fathers thought the nation's first for-profit R&D consortium would have its greatest impact in helping U.S. computer and electronics industries compete with Japan in computer architecture, design tools, software, and technology cooperation (see Table 2.1). MCC was not expected to have much of an impact on quality issues, cost of capital, or government encouragement. By 1993, it has become clear that in terms of technological contributions, MCC has had its greatest impact through the transfer and application of its packaging/interconnect technologies. MCC's contributions in computer architecture and design tools has not lived up to initial expectations. The application of MCC-developed software would have to be judged an overall disappointment except for the companies that have spun-out of the consortium and, possibly, research and applications in progress.

It is in learning about the process of technology collaboration where MCC may have its greatest impact on the member companies in particular and enhanced U.S. industrial competitiveness in general. MCC has served as an important real-life laboratory to study the barriers and facilitators of collaborative R&D leading to technology application and commercialization. MCC has been an important stimulus and model to R&D consortia and alliances that have followed.

So the answer to whether MCC can be judged a success depends largely on the perspective of the evaluator and on how well U.S. public and private leaders apply its lessons (i.e., the "technology" of consorting and the processes of technology commercialization). Public and private leaders should not dismiss consortia because of disappointing results, but should work to improve on this important new organizational form. The Japanese have a long history in learning how to manage alliances, and they continue to work at improving the effectiveness of their consortia.

LEARNING ABOUT COLLABORATION

MCC's formation, site-selection process, operation, and impact have provided a basis for drawing a number of useful lessons about collaboration across organizational boundaries.

First, a credible vision inspired by first-level influencers is an important motivator in the formation and operation of new organizational forms that collaborate across organizational barriers. Capable second-level influencers are required to enact such visions at the operational level. Such collaboration is facilitated by a commonly accepted and supported goal, physical and cultural proximity, interactive communication, and motivated participants.

Second, while the fear of not surviving the global economy has been an important motivator for public/private collaboration, such motivation does not sustain the cooperative/synergistic activity required to make such alliances work effectively over the long term. Sustaining such collaboration (among companies in a consortium or between public/private sectors in a community) is a major challenge. In marketplace economies, such collaboration does not come easily; it must be learned and reinforced.

Third, individuals who facilitate cross-organizational collaboration (e.g., boundary spanners) need to be rewarded. As demonstrated in the case of Austin and MCC, the "social memories" of communities and organizations are often short about the motivations for, and benefits of, such boundary spanning and networking activity. Such benefits are often subtle and long-term, but can have tremendous impact.

Fourth, a high degree of heterogeneity among the members of an R&D consortium (or a community) can be a barrier to collaboration, but if cross-organizational and resource leveraging is achieved, it may lead to important competitive advantages. As diversity increases, the challenge to initiating and sustaining collaboration increases, but so do the potential rewards of such collaborative activity.

Fifth, great initial success in collaborative activity can put in motion forces that later lead to cross-sector conflict and dissension.

MCC enjoyed a successful launch that generated unrealistic expectations concerning criteria for success. Soon after the consortium came to Austin, Texas, collaboration among state and city leaders, academic institutions, and private business became fractured. Unrestrained economic development and greed decreased the qualities that Austin residents prized most in their community.

Sixth, collaborative activities on specific projects often lead to unplanned and unexpected gains. R&D consortia founded to conduct joint research for technological advancements often make their most important contributions in other, unplanned and more subtle ways. The act of forming MCC, and of having managers and technicians from competing U.S. companies meet regularly at the consortium, caused these companies to learn new ways to coordinate activities within each firm as well as to collaborate across organizational and institutional boundaries.

The 1990s is argued to be the era of boundaryless, virtual corporations that are composed of networks of independent companies linked by advanced information technology. The objective is to share skills and costs and to access one another's technology and markets. Such collaborations are to be temporary and responsive to rapid changes in the global marketplace. A communication superhighway is to permit far-flung units of different companies to quickly locate suppliers, designers, and manufacturers through an information clearinghouse. Once connected, these virtual corporations are expected to sign "electronic contracts" to speed linkages without legal headaches. Advanced technology is predicted to make the creation of these boundaryless enterprises as straightforward as connecting components for a home audio and video system by different manufacturers. MCC's first ten-years demonstrates how significant the organizational challenges are to establishing and maintaining such "technologically sophisticated" collaborative alliances. Advanced technology will not cause organizations, communities, and strategic regions to become more cooperative. Advanced technology is merely an additional tool that can facilitate the process. The real challenges are behavioral and managerial.

LEARNING FROM MCC

MCC has survived for over ten years by being a very adaptable organization. Through three eras of management, the consortium has faced key challenges that include dealing with constituencies at regional, state, and federal levels; a complex mix of member companies; and national and international competitors and collaborators from business, academia, and government. When MCC was formed in 1982, its founders were constrained by political, social, economic, and legal conditions. These constraints caused MCC's management to endorse the cafeteria approach to funding research; hire research talent that did not come from the shareholder companies; support the concept of a standard package to facilitate equitable technology transfer; mount a concerted effort to keep MCC's technologies secret; and rely on formal structure, technical reports, and shareholder liaisons to achieve effective technology transfer. Key management decisions that seemed reasonable at the time contributed to challenges in effectively managing the consortium over the long term.

The MCC story is filled with paradoxes that highlight the complexities faced by the nation's first major R&D consortium.

- MCC was to be a cooperative R&D activity, yet it was made up of highly competitive computer, semiconductor, and aerospace firms. The consortium's management and technology transfer challenges centered on how to achieve and sustain meaningful collaboration with one's competitors.
- MCC shareholders funded research that was targeted to help beat the Japanese threat, yet few managers and scientists within the shareholder firms aggressively worked to commercialize MCC-produced technologies to enhance their competitiveness.
- MCC was initially championed by "kings" (that is, high company executives) as an important source of long-term (five to ten years), pre-competitive research. Yet in order to survive, MCC was forced to respond to pressures from "dukes and barons" (middle management) and to focus on specific research

projects with relatively short-term (one to three years) objectives.

- MCC's original organizational structure and resource allocation focused on research excellence while minimizing obstructing bureaucracy. World-class technological advancement was the goal. It was to be the responsibility of the funding companies to commercialize the pre-competitive research results. To maintain support from the member companies, the consortium added staff in such functional areas as marketing, public relations, and technology transfer.

- MCC's desire to get off to a fast and impressive start encouraged the recruitment of a decidedly heterogeneous mix of shareholder companies. While such diversity initially led to problems with secrecy and collaboration, it also became valued as a potential benefit in terms of the horizontal and vertical integration needed for successful product commercialization.

- In 1982, MCC was formed to be a centralized research facility to facilitate the leveraging of collaborative research efforts. By 1992, the consortium was moving toward becoming a project coordinator of distributed activities.

- Efforts to facilitate the creation of a state-of-the-art research facility (such as recruiting top-notch scientists, equipping them with advanced technology, and giving them research autonomy), contributed to behavioral and technological barriers between MCC and its member companies that frustrated the transfer of results.

- MCC was organized, funded, and to some degree staffed by U.S. companies that were themselves struggling to effectively compete with Japan, yet the consortium was criticized for doing little to quickly counter the Japanese threat.

- MCC was formed in 1982 to transfer pre-competitive technologies to member companies, yet by the

1990s, the consortium was commercializing its technology through entrepreneurs and spin-out
companies.

In many ways arguments for R&D consortia are stronger in
1993 than in 1983. MCC and SEMATECH were formed to increase
the competitiveness of their member firms in terms of the Japanese
threat. Over the past decade, the number of nations and strategic
regions that are global competitors for U.S. industry has increased
considerably, and this trend will continue. Federal and corporate
budgets for long-term R&D are shrinking, world-class science is
increasingly expensive and in short supply, advanced technologies
are proliferating, product development life cycles continue to shrink,
and national and international alliances abound. The comfort level
has changed for U.S. corporations, national laboratories, and
research universities as these organizations face severe budget
reductions while striving to become more quality conscious and productive. Consortia are viable organizations for leveraging resources
as well as facilitating interorganizational collaborations. Consortia
allow participants to share the up-front cost of pre-production
research and standards setting while being able to concentrate
scarce resources on those value-added efforts that will make the
member organizations more competitive.

LEARNING ABOUT TECHNOLOGY TRANSFER

During its first ten years, MCC faced two fundamental challenges: (1) creating a centralized research environment, funded by a
diverse group of highly competitive companies, in order to produce
significant technological breakthroughs; and (2) successfully transferring these technologies to the member companies in a timely
manner. MCC was most successful in building a state-of-the-art
research environment and attracting high-quality scientists to work
in Austin, Texas. The consortium's greatest challenge has been getting MCC-produced technologies used.

Effective technology transfer leading to successful commercial applications is an increasingly important challenge for U.S.
firms, federal laboratories, and research universities. The challenges
are accentuated as R&D organizations attempt to move technologies across organizational boundaries. In interorganizational tech-

nology transfer, spatial and cultural distance impedes effective communication, which involves confidential information about complex tasks often involving high levels of competition, uncertainty, and risk. Technology transceivers who communicate across technology-producing and -receiving organizations are often not meaningfully rewarded for their boundary-spanning collaborative activities. Knowledge creators, not users, are the ones celebrated in the technology transfer process.

Important technologies have been successfully transferred from MCC to process and product applications. However, such transfers have been relatively few in number, and they have been difficult and time-consuming. A technology transfer gap existed between MCC's research and achieving the industrial and market strength needed to successfully bring the technologies to commercial application. Partly as a result of MCC's frustration in getting its member companies to commercialize its research results, by 1990, the consortium began to foster technology use through entrepreneurship and spin-out activity.

Even with highly motivated champions, a critical gap in technology transfer from quality research to the commercial application is know-how—the ability to find and apply expertise in areas (e.g., manufacturing, marketing, finance, distribution, sales, and management) central to successful technology commercialization. The challenge is to effectively leverage the nation's academic, government, and business resources at the community level by linking talent, technology, capital, and business know-how with markets. Such value-added technology transfer can help sustain established firms, and it can foster the growth of new firms for increased economic competitiveness.

The resources of R&D organizations lie more within the technologists and researchers than any particular set technologies that are currently available—the most valuable technology to be transferred is in the researcher's head, not sitting on the shelf. The vast array of advanced and not-so-advanced technologies that MCC developed could not simply be pushed out through superior outreach attempts and marketing. Technological capabilities had to be linked to existing and vital problems at the user level, and for new-to-the-world technologies, markets had to be developed.

The entrepreneurs that successfully spun technologies out of MCC were product champions who had a clear vision of a problem that they were trying to solve and its market potential as well as an intimate knowledge of the technology they were developing. Still, they had to be adaptable and listen to business, financial, and legal advisors as they took their technologies to market strength. To achieve technology transfer from the laboratory to successful commercial/process applications through the development of new firms requires sustained public/private collaboration at the regional level in a supportive context guided at the national level. In Austin, regional public/private collaboration made possible the recruitment of MCC and the formation of the Austin Technology Incubator, which commercialized the first technologies to spin out of MCC.

From the research facilities in the nation's universities and colleges to those under federal and state jurisdiction, there is a great concern with metrics—the measuring of performance and return on investment (ROI). Such concerns increase as budgets are slashed, jobs are on the line, and established and new research missions are subject to external scrutiny. While the measures of success of R&D organizations vary considerably with the perspective (i.e., institutional affiliation and organizational position) of the evaluators, a common tendency is to emphasize only what can be counted in the short-term (e.g., technical reports, journal articles, copyrights, patents, and amount of funding generated).[1]

It would be a mistake to rely on traditional management metrics to evaluate the processes of technology creation, transformation, and application. W. Edwards Deming (1993) stated that the current system of management in the United States crushes motivation and the eagerness to learn as it ranks people on the basis of annual appraisals, production quotas, and incentive pay. The resulting corporate culture encourages competition, not collaboration.

> We are living under the tyranny of the prevailing style of management [which is] a modern invention, a trap that has led us into decline. The workers are handicapped by the system, and the system belongs to management. Transformation is required . . . transformation to a new kind of economics where everyone comes out better. [The current] I win only if you loose mentality needs to be replaced. . . . Business survival in the

western world is dependent on transformation to the new economics of cooperation, a win-win attitude. And once the transformation is made, the course of western industry will move forward and upward. (Deming, 1993)

The Japanese tend to place a higher value on the less quantifiable and long-term benefits of R&D consortia such as information sharing and education, raising the level of an emerging industry, and standards setting. They work at learning from past events to improve future attempts whether it be refining a product, managing consortia, or building a science city. The Japanese credit such process technologies as being fundamentally important to their successes in competing in the global marketplace.

SCIENCE AND TECHNOLOGY COMMERCIALIZATION

Washington's concern with military security—not economic security—provided the call to action in the formation of MCC and SEMATECH. When it became clear that the U.S. microelectronics industry was threatened, the Department of Defense became alarmed, which in turn, alarmed the White House and Congress. The 1984 National Cooperative Research Act was passed and the U.S. launched one major R&D effort after another. Federal and state research funds and tax credits have traditionally been provided for companies that invest in research and experimentation. Much less concern and funding has been directed toward understanding and facilitating technology commercialization to (1) improve the competitiveness of established firms, (2) launch and grow new firms, and (3) establish new industries. Managing technology transfer has been seen as someone else's job and relatively unimportant in the scheme of things. The traditional orientation has been that doing good science ought to be enough.

With the formation of each new major research project the federal government suggests that the way for the United States to win in global high-tech competition is big-expenditure R&D projects, plus financial incentives like tax breaks for R&D investment by private companies. We do not question the value of basic R&D, the "seed corn" of U.S. industry. Indeed, U.S. research universities and federal laboratories are the envy of the industrialized world. These knowledge resources may well constitute the best hope for increased U.S. industrial competitiveness. However, following the lead of the nation's secretary of labor and former Harvard professor Robert Reich (1989), we label these incentives the "loud path" to international competitiveness.[2] We recommend that more attention, research, and funding be targeted toward the "quiet path" of successful technology commercialization. The most direct route to restoring America's international competitiveness centers on improving technology transfer processes through which R&D results are rapidly transformed into high-quality, competitive products and manufacturing processes.

MCC was formed by successful, experienced, and committed executives, managers, and technicians from the electronics industry. It was designed to be free of obstacles that were known to inhibit the pursuit of research excellence and technology transfer. Research direction and buy-in came early from the funding companies. Capable researchers were hired from leading U.S. research universities, federal laboratories, and corporations. These researchers were provided with sustained financial support and state-of-the-art laboratories. Bureaucratic and legal obstacles were kept to a minimum. Despite such advantages, the R&D consortium experienced major barriers in getting its research used in commercial applications. Management, cultural, financial, bureaucratic, and legal constraints are much greater in the nation's federal laboratories and research universities. Participants and observers should not expect immediate and successful results as these institutions are called on to shift from long established research missions to be more responsive to market forces and the demands of technology commercialization.

Businesses and governments are operating in an era where there are no national technologies, products, corporations, or industries. There are global markets for capital, labor, and technology. Regional wealth comes from world-class science and technology being quickly linked to product/process application—the timely commercialization of cutting-edge research wherever it is developed. No longer always the teacher, the United States and its technologists and managers need to be better students of global R&D capabilities so that advanced technologies flow into as well as out of the United States.[3]

The United States' failure to compete effectively with Japan does not involve technological invention but technology application. The United States has led the world in the quantity and quality of its research and development, but this lead has not produced sufficient commercially competitive products and processes to maintain U.S. industrial strength. The importance of effectively utilizing the nation's existing research base—cutting-edge technologies and research personnel at R&D consortia, federal laboratories, and research universities—will only increase. National laboratories provided the technologies for the U.S. military to win the cold war and for NASA to send astronauts to the moon and bring them safely back to earth. U.S. research universities are the best in the world. Students from Japan, Taiwan, South Korea, China, Singapore, and Europe overcome strong competition and cultural barriers for the opportunity to study at these centers of educational and research excellence. The challenge is to see that America's research base is more effectively and efficiently used for shared prosperity at home and abroad.

NOTES

1. During its first 10 years, MCC has been awarded 117 patents. SEMATECH has received 23 patents over a five year period. Japan's four-year VLSI Project generated about 600 patents. SEMATECH has about four times the budget of MCC and the total VLSI budget for four years was a litttle more than half the funds spent on MCC. So what does this comparison mean? Is it a measure of research quality or market potential? Some R&D organizations up their patent count simply by providing organizational and financial support and by rewarding those who file. The Japanese flood the U.S. Patent and Trademark Office with applications for minor innovations, many of which would be dismissed by U.S. inventors and organizations. In semiconductors, U.S. inventors have been awarded the most significant underlying patents. A recent National Science Foundation patent-citation analysis designed to measure the importance of patents, found that between 1980 and 1987, Japanese patents were cited most often and with increasing frequency while U.S. patents were second and Canadian patents third. Historically the U.S. has filed many more patents than the Japanese while the island nation dominated in new product developments and increased market share in key industires. When a company enters the Austin Technology Incubator, a patent is just one aspect of a quality business plan that also includes a competitive analysis, market and financial projections, and an assessment of the management team.

2. Historically the commercial return on investment for major research efforts (i.e., the loud path) has not been all that impressive. Since 1955, the govern-

ment has spent more than $1 trillion on R&D for nuclear arms and other weaponry. According to the National Science Foundation, this figure represents 62 percent of all federal research expenditures. In addition, large amounts of funds went into related efforts such as the civilian space program's $90 billion race with the Soviet Union to land men on the moon (Broad, 1992). Many of the missions assigned these spectacular research efforts have been successfully completed bringing credit to all involved and indeed bring the U.S. to the point where we can work toward and compete in a post-cold war economy. However, other loud path research efforts have not yielded such impressive mission oriented results, such as the Air Force's Manned Orbiting Laboratory (cost $1.3 billion), the A-12 attack plane (projected cost $62 billion), synthetic fuels (cost $20 billion), and the Strategic Defense Initiative (cost $30 billion). The main point is that greater effort and resources need to be devoted to choosing research efforts based on commercial payoff so that U.S. industrial competiveness is enhanced along with the nation's military strength and the search for the unknown.

3. In another kind of trade gap, in 1988 the Japanese had 52,224 scientists working in the United States while there were only 4,468 U.S. scientists working in Japan (Japanese Ministry of International Trade and Industry). At present, because of foreign language deficiencies, the United States is largely flying blind in its technological competition with Japan and many other Asian and European countries.

APPENDIX A
GATHERING THE DATA

Our objective in writing *R&D Collaboration on Trial* is to document the formation, site-location process, operation, and impact of MCC's first ten years (with some comparisons made to SEMATECH) and to draw useful lessons about collaborative R&D. Our research is based on data collected by us and our research colleagues from 1983 to 1993. This lengthy period of data gathering allowed us to investigate change in (1) MCC's structure and process through three eras of management, (2) the relationships between MCC and its member companies, (3) the barriers and facilitators to technology transfer and the emergence of an entrepreneurial culture at MCC, and (4) the relationship of MCC to other institutions and organizations in Austin as well as to other regions in the United States.

Implicit in our analysis of the formation and management of MCC are three perspectives on action that depict individual behavior as being (1) purposive and rational, or goal directed; (2) externally constrained, or situationally determined; and (3) more random and dependent on an emergent, unfolding process with rationality being constructed after the fact to make sense of behavior that has already occurred (Van de Ven and Astley, 1981; Pfeffer, 1982; Weick, 1984).

For a variety of reasons, such as the philosophical underpinnings of much of American life and culture, the perspective that views action as being rational, foresightful, and value maximizing has dominated theories of decision making and organization behavior (Pfeffer, 1982; Scott, 1982). This perspective is evident in many of the recollections of our respondents. The second perspective on behavior, also evident in our chronicle, has little to do with the values or preferences of actors taking action, but instead reflects the limiting forces of external factors. Action results from the time-dependent pattern of constraints, contingencies, or demands confronting social units. The third perspective evident in *R&D Collaboration on Trial* stresses the sequential, unfolding nature of activity. Preferences are viewed as emerging from action, rather than guiding action. Action is governed by the systems of meaning that emerge and develop within the social structure (March, 1978). Stability and cohesion occur through shared perspectives and negotiated order. This perspective views influencers/leaders as having an important, symbolic, legitimating, sense-making role that enhances the development and maintenance of a shared vision. This third perspective is best studied through case analysis and natural language, the methodology most prominent in our description of MCC. (Daft and Wiginton, 1979)

Communities and the organizations and individuals within them are, in many important respects, composed of and driven by relational networks, and they need to be observed and analyzed as such (Rogers and Kincaid, 1981; Pfeffer, 1982). In *R&D Collaboration on Trial,* we emphasize the important role played by relational networks that exist within and among communities, and within and among organizations. We describe how informal communication networks were established and re-activated across academic, business, and government sectors when Austin and Texas competed for MCC and SEMATECH. In both instances, a "community of actors" with a common purpose was formed. We also exemplify the power of communication networks in the formation and operation of MCC, especially concerning interorganizational technology transfer.

We look at the determinants of different network structures as well as decision outcomes and the effects of structural and contextual factors (Rogers and Kincaid, 1881; Pfeffer, 1982; Weick, 1984). We assess the positions and the reputational or attributional measures of those who were the more influential or more central participants in regional and organizational networks (Tichy and others, 1978). We assess different perceptions of decision criteria and outcomes over time. And we examine real-life decisions by describing who was actually involved, to what degree, and at what points in various parts of different decision processes. From this analysis, we describe the critical importance of networks of interaction around specific decisions and the variety of perceptions concerning the consequences of those decisions.

When assessing the composition of communication networks described in *R&D Collaboration on Trial,* the reader may want to explore the characteristics of individual actors and the various networks under consideration. (Table A.1)

We document the formation, site-location process, operation, and impact of MCC's first ten years through a grounded-theory approach, collecting multiple forms of data: interviews, a survey, archival data and publications, E-mail correspondence, and observation (Glaser and Strauss, 1967; Argyris, 1972; Mintzberg, 1973, 1979; Scott, 1981; Lincoln and Guba, 1985; and Eisenhardt, 1989).

INTERVIEWS

More than 150 interviews, most of which were from one-to-two-hours' duration, were conducted with key respondents knowledgeable about MCC's formation, location decision, operation, and impacts. (A smaller set of interviews was collected on SEMATECH.) Most interviews were conducted by two researchers and were tape-recorded and transcribed. Initially, interviews were open-ended, allowing the respondent to inform the interviewer about what he or she considered most important and interesting concerning MCC's formation and operation. Over time, and especially in the case of repeated contact with the same informant, the interviews became more focused. Transcripts allowed the researchers to retrieve information and quotes, the importance of which was not fully appreciated at the time of data collection. Respondents could request that the tape recorder be temporarily shut off during particularly sensitive points of the discussion; however, this happened rarely. We found the informants to be remarkably open and candid in telling us of their accounts of MCC.

Table A.1 Dimensions and properties of communication networks

Property	Definition
A. Transactional content	Type of exchange in network: expression of effect, influence, exchange of information, exchange of resources or goods and services
B. Nature of the links	
1. Intensity	Strength of the relationship
2. Reciprocity	Degree to which relationship is commonly perceived by all parties
3. Clarity of expectations	Degree of clearly defined expectations
4. Multiplexicity	Degree to which individuals are linked by multiple relations
C. Structural dimensions	
1. Size	Number of people in network
2. Density or connectedness	Number of actual links in network as a proportion of total possible links
3. Clustering	Number of dense regions or groupings in network
4. Centrality	Degree of hierarchy and restriction on communication in network
5. Stability	Degree to which network pattern changes over time
6. Reachability	Average number of links between any two individuals in network
7. Openness	Number of actual external links as a proportion of total possible external links
8. Star	Individual with highest number of network links
9. Bridge	Individual who is a member of multiple clusters in a network
10. Gatekeeper	A star who also links the network to external networks
11. Isolate	An individual with few (or no) links to others in the network

Source: Tichy, Tushman, and Fombrun, 1979, p. 508; Rogers and Kincaid, 1981; Pfeffer, 1982, p. 274.

LOOKING BACKWARD

Many of our interviews were retrospective. For such back-ward-looking data gathering to provide useful information, it should center on an event that has left a deep and detailed impression on the mind of the respondent. Several of our informants told us that their involvement with MCC (i.e., its formation, location decision, or operation) was one of the most memorable events in their lives. MCC represents high drama, involving big money; executives of major U.S. firms; local, state, and national political leaders; and noted researchers from academia, federal laboratories, and business.

Informants may recollect an event in ways suggesting greater rationality and self-importance than was in fact the case. We countered such potential biases by:

- Asking multiple respondents about the same event. Respondents did not always agree, but their disagreements were informative.
- Checking a respondent's answers against archival materials whenever possible. Several of our informants kept rather complete files on MCC, and they permitted us to review and cite these documents.
- Nurturing long-term relationships of rapport and trust with our informants and contacts. The scholarly nature of our research helped in this regard, in contrast to the sometimes inaccurate and sensationalized treatment of MCC in the mass media.
- Conducting a "member check" by providing all, or a portion, of our book to individuals who served as key respondents in our research.

While the retrospective nature of our data collection caused some difficulty, advantages also accrued. Several of our informants were no longer in their MCC-related position at the time we interviewed them and thus felt freer to share feelings about sensitive topics and views that they had not previously divulged. Also, with the passage of years came a strong desire on the informants' part to help us create an accurate historical record of MCC's first decade of operation.

SURVEY

In 1989, in conjunction with the IC² Institute and its Executive Director, Raymond W. Smilor, we administered a survey on technology transfer to MCC and shareholder personnel. Likert-scale survey questions were constructed from interview and archival data. The focus of the survey was on the effectiveness of different methods of technology transfer, factors facilitating technology transfer, the importance of barriers to technology transfer, and ways to improve technology transfer between the research consortium and its shareholder companies. The survey had a targeted population of 430 respondents, including MCC researchers and managers as well as shareholder representatives and assignees who worked at MCC and who served on MCC's board of directors and advisory panels.

One hundred and forty-seven respondents completed and returned the survey, for a response rate of 34 percent. Seventy-one of the respondents were MCC employees, and 76 were employees of the shareholder companies. The respondents were divided almost equally among the consortium's four research programs: Advanced Computer Architecture, Computer-Aided Design, Software Technology, and Packaging Interconnect. For published articles on this research, see Smilor, Gibson, and Avery, 1990; Smilor and Gibson, 1991; and Gibson and Smilor, 1991.

OBSERVATION AND ARCHIVAL RECORDS

Unobtrusive data collection removes the observer(s) from the events being studied. Over the past ten years, we attended many MCC functions and made numerous visits to the consortium's offices. We kept detailed notes of our on-site observations of MCC, which added a useful complement to our other forms of data collection. With research colleagues Cynthia A. Kehoe and Sun-Yoon Lee, we conducted a bibliographic search of MCC co-authored published research articles (Gibson, Kehoe, and Lee, 1994).

Much has been written about MCC in the local, national, and international press; in trade publications; and in scholarly journals. Over the years, we have built an extensive library of these clippings and articles. Often, these published accounts and archival documents reflected biases that were useful to our understanding of how MCC was perceived and judged by different constituencies. Several of our informants also kept extensive files on MCC, which they shared with us. Finally, a small group of MCC researchers and managers allowed us to review and cite their E-mail correspondence covering a period from 1986 to 1991.

Appendix B

List of Interviewees

Cal Adkins, July 26, 1990**(M)
Keith M. Andren, March 9, 1990**(M)
Marshall Andrews, August 8, 1988***; June 8, 1990**(M)
Angelos Angelou, March 17, 1989*; March 22, 1993(L)
Phillip W. Arneson, September 28+ and October 6, 1992+; and February 1;+ April 8,+ June 15,+ July 19,+ and September 24, 1993+(M)
James D. Babcock, January 12 and November 16, 1990; March 13, 1992(M)
Laszlo A. (Les) Belady, March 22, 1993(M)
Chuck Bieber, February 9, 1990**(M)
George D. Black, May 5, 1986(M/L)
Miller Bonner, November 16, 1990(S)
Ron Borgstahl, June 18, 1990**(M)
Mark Bower, August 17, 1990**(M)
Ron Bracken, July 26, 1990**(M)
K.C. Burgess-Yakemovic, August 20, 1990**(M)
Daron (Dan) Butler, January 23, 1987(L)
Narcisso Cano, February 16, 1987(L)
Henry G. Cisneros, February 16, 1987(L)
Terry Clas, July 27, 1990**(M)
Andy and Alison Cohen, May 4, 1993(S)
Peter G. Cook, May 8, 1990+**(M)
Lee Cooke, December 18, 1985; March 29, 1989(L)
Laylen Copelin, March 4, 1989*(L)
Bob Cottoi, June 11, 1990**(M)
James Crowson, February 28, 1993+(L)
Robin L. Curle, February 23 and March 1, 1991(M)
Bill Curtis, March 21, 1992(M)
Al Dale, January 22, 1987(L)
Bruce Darling, July 15, 1986(L)

James W. Dearing, June 3, 1993+
Sandy Dochen, May–August, 1988***(M)
Grant Dove, August 15, 1990; March 1, 1991**(M)
Clif Drummond, March 26 and May 5, 1986(L)
Mark Eaton, August 5, 1993(M)
Howard D. Falkenberg, March 27, 1986(L)
Robert Farley, March 10, 1989*(L)
Craig Fields, August 15, 1990; February 29, and March 1,
    1991**(M)
Mark Fowler, April 18, 1990**(M)
Bill Friday, February 19, 1987(L)
Kazuhiro Fuchi, November 10, 1989
Mohammed Ghazi, January 30** and June 18, 1990**(M)
Kunio Goto, summer 1992
Johannes Grande, April 26, 1990**(M)
John H. Gray, January 22, 1987(L)
Douglas Green, August 24, 1984(L)
Katherine (Kay) Hammer, February 29, March 1, and October 23,
    1991; March 25 and April 27, 1993(M)
Edward J. Hanslik, January 22, 1987(L)
Michael A. Harper, April 28 and November 5, 1993(S)
Bert Haskell, May 18, 1990**(M)
Turner Hasty, February 26 and March 16, 1992(S)
George Herbert, February 19, 1987(L)
Dennis Herrell, August 8, 1988***(M)
Paul Hilgers, February 27, 1989*(S)
James Hollan, July 27, 1988***(M)
James Hunt, February 19, 1987(L)
Bobby Ray Inman, March, 1985; January 26 and July 21, 1987;
    April 18 and December 12, 1989; October 22, 1992(M/L)
Becky Joos, May 18, 1990**(M)
Sanford (Sandy) Kane, March 7, 1989*(S/L)
Laura J. Kilcrease, October 6, 1992
George Kozmetsky, December 5, 1989; October 12, 1993
Mary Kragie, July 27, 1988***(M)
Ed Krall, 1988***; July 27, 1990**(M)
Ben F. Love, August 10, 1992+(L)
Gene Lowenthal, July 22, 1988***(M)
Niek Luijtjes, August 8, 1988***(M)

Bill McDermott, October 6, 1988
Hans Mark, March 8, 1989*(L)
Peter Marks, August 17, 1990**(M)
Jack Mayo, July 15, 1986(L)
John Mendel, March 5, 1990**(M)
Susan Millea, April 21, 1993(M)
Ann Miller, June 6, 1990+**(M)
Peter Mills, March 10, 1989*(L)
David Misunas, February 27, 1992; April 2,+ March 10, and
    November 9, 1993(M)
Brad Nelson, August 15, 1990(M)
William C. Norris, August 10, 1990(M)
John Pankaratz, July 16 and 17, 1992(S)
Louis R. Paradiso, July 26, 1990**(M)
Deborah Pedersen, July 27, 1988***; March 26, 1992(M)
Daniel (Dan) Pegg, July 15, 1986(L)
Charles Petrie, July 27, 1988***; April 22, June 22, September 16,
    and October 12,+ 1993(M)
Thomas R. Pian, May 18, 1990**(M)
J.J. (Jake) Pickle, March 29, 1989*(L)
Gene Pierce, July 27, 1990**(M)
John Pinkston, May 5, 1993+(M)
Pike Powers, March 27, 1986; March 24, 1989*; May 11, 1992(L)
Robert M. Price, May 12, 1993(M)
Keith Rathjen, June 1, 1990**(M)
Gail Rein, February 2, 1992(M)
Karl Reissmueller, March 5, 1990**(M)
Jess Rifkind, November 11, 1992;+ February 8, 1993;+ March 14,
    1993;+ June 24;+ and September 26,+ 1993(M)
M. Lea Rudee, July 15, 1986(L)
Martha Russell, February 25, 1993(M)
Robert G. Rutishauser, January 23, 1987; March 11, 1992(M/L)
Toshihiro Sasaki, July 27, 1993
Sally Shipman, December 5, 1989(L)
Baldev Singh, August 17, 1990**(M)
Mel Slater, August 20, 1990**(M)
Palle Smidt, May 5, 1986; June 2, 1993(M/L)
David Smith, April 2, 1992; July 7, 1993(S)
Neal Spelce, December 18, 1985; January 30, 1986(L)

Phil Spletter, June 18, 1990**(M)

Robin Steele, August 20, 1990+**(M)

William (Bill) Stotesbery, December 18, 1985; January 23, 1987;
    November 16, 1990; March 30, 1992, April 8 and June 3,
    1993(M/L)

Noel R. Strader, August 24, 1984(L)

Ben G. Streetman, December 18, 1985; March 13, 1989*(L)

Al Tasch, March 13, 1989*(L)

Chand R. Viswanathan, July 2, 1986(L)

Hank Wardek, February 16, 1990**(M)

Karen K. Ware, September 18, 1988(L)

John P. Watson, January 23, 1987(L)

Jerry Werner, September 26, 1991; February 21, March 30 and
    December 4, 1992; May 4 and June 15, 1993(M)

Barry Whalen, August 8, 1988***; August 15, 1990(M)

Harden H. Wiedemann, May 27, 1986(L)

Cynthia Williams, November 16, 1991**(M)

Meg Wilson, December 18, 1985; November 30, 1989; November
    16, 1990; April 8, June 3, and November 15, 1993(M/L)

Darrell Woelk, July 27, 1988***(M)

Herbert (Herb) H. Woodson, May 5, 1986; April 24, 1992(L)

Elias Zachos, May 7, 1993(S)

+ Phone interviews and correspondence

* Interviews conducted by Mark Strain

** Interviews conducted by/with Nan Muir

*** Interviews conducted by/with
    Christopher Avery

General topic of interview

(M)= Microelectronics and
Computer Technology
Corporation (MCC)

(S)= SEMATECH

(L)= Site-Location Decision
(MCC and/or SEMATECH)

Appendix C
The Main Characters[1]

Raymond W. Allard, vice president and program director, Human Interface Research Program, director International Marketing, director High Value Electronics Division, MCC

Angelos Angelou, chief economist, Austin Chamber of Commerce

Phillip W. Arneson, head of the CDC team that worked on the technology and business plans for MCC

Del Asmussen, CDC employee selected to work on the fact-finding team at the time of MCC's 1983 location decision

Richard Atkinson, chancellor, University of California at San Diego

James D. Babcock, STP technology transfer manager, MCC

Robert Baldwin, vice chairman, University of Texas regents

Donald S. Beilman, director, MCNC (Microelectronics Center of North Carolina)

Laszlo A. Belady, vice president and program director, Software Technology Program and Advanced Computing Technology Program, MCC

George D. Black, vice president for human relations, MCC

Woodrow W. Bledsoe, vice president and program director, Artificial Intelligence/Knowledge-Based Systems Program, MCC

Henry G. Cisneros, mayor of San Antonio

Bill Clements, governor of Texas

James Crowson, vice chancellor and general council, The University of Texas System

Robin Lea Curle, vice president for marketing and sales, Evolutionary Technologies, Inc. (ETI), Austin

Grant Dove, chairman and chief executive officer, MCC

Clif W. Drummond, director, Energy Studies Center, College of Engineering, University of Texas at Austin; executive assistant to Texas Governor Mark White

George Deukmejian, governor of California

Charles E. Exley, Jr., chairman and CEO, NCR

Harold Falkenberg, president, Neal Spelce Communications, Austin

Robert Farley, aide to Texas Governor William Clements; deputy director of research and planning, Texas Department of Commerce

Craig Fields, president, chief executive officer, and chairman, MCC

Peter T. Flawn, president, University of Texas at Austin

Gerhard J. Fonken, vice president for research and academic affairs, University of Texas at Austin

Joe Friday, president, University of North Carolina

John Gray, manager, economic development, Austin Chamber of Commerce

Katherine (Kay) Hammer, researcher, Computer-Aided Design, MCC; president and CEO, Evolutionary Technologies, Inc. (ETI), Austin

John R. Hanne, vice president and program director, VLSI/CAD, MCC

Arthur E. Hansen, chancellor, Texas A&M University system

Ed Hanslik, Austin Chamber of Commerce vice president for economic development

Joe Frank Harris, governor of Georgia

Ben T. Head, president, Austin Chamber of Commerce, chairman and CEO RepublicBank Austin

George Herbert, director, Research Triangle Institute, North Carolina

Paul Hilgers, district administrator for Congressman Jake Pickle, Austin

James Hunt, governor of North Carolina

Bobby Ray Inman, chairman and cheif executive officer, MCC

Sanford (Sandy) Kane, vice president for industrial relations, IBM; chair of the SEMATECH site-selection committee; president, U.S. Memories, Inc.

George Kozmetsky, director, IC^2 Institute, The University of Texas at Austin

John W. Lacey, executive vice president, Control Data Corporation

Ben Love, chairman and CEO, Texas Commerce Bancshares, Houston

Eugene I. Lowenthal, vice president and program director, Data Base Research Program and Advanced Computer Architecture, MCC

Stephen F. Lundstrom, vice president and program director, Parallel
    Processing, MCC
Leo McCarthy, lieutenant governor of California
Hans Mark, chancellor, The University of Texas System
Peter H. Mills, senior vice president and chief administrative officer,
    SEMATECH
David Misunas, HVE business development manger, MCC
Jon Newton, chairman, University of Texas regents
William C. Norris, chairman, Control Data Corporation; visionary
    behind the formation of MCC
Robert Noyce, president and chief executive officer, SEMATECH
Daniel (Dan) Pegg, president, San Diego Economic Development
    Corporation
H. Ross Perot, chairman of the board, EDS (Electronic Data
    Systems), Dallas
Charles Petrie, ACA researcher, MCC
Joseph M. Pettit, president, Georgia Institute of Technology
Bum Phillips, Texas businessman
J.J. (Jake) Pickle, U.S. Congressman, Tenth Congressional District,
    Austin
John T. Pinkston, vice president and chief scientist, MCC
Arthur (Skip) Porter, director, Texas Engineering Experiment
    Station, Texas A&M University system
Pike Powers, executive assistant to Texas Governor Mark White
Robert Price, president, Control Data Corporation; chairman of
    MCC's steering committee and interim board of directors
Robert Price (technical Bob Price), member of the team that worked
    on the technology and business plans for MCC
Jess Rifkind, member of the team that worked on the technology
    and business plan for MCC
Robert G. Rutishauser, vice president for finance and administra-
    tion, MCC
Palle Smidt, member of MCC's interin board of directors, and
    senior vice president for Plans and Programs, MCC
Neal Spelce, chairman and CEO, Neal Spelce Communications,
    Austin
William D. (Bill) Stotesbery, director of government and public
    affairs, MCC
Ben Streetman, Janet S. Cockrell Centennial Professor, Department
    of Electrical Engineering, University of Texas at Austin

Al Tasch, Professor, Department of Electrical Engineering,
 University of Texas at Austin
Frank Vandiver, president, Texas A&M University
E. Donald Walker, chancellor, University of Texas system
John Watson, real estate developer, Austin
Jerry Werner, CAD technology transfer manager, MCC
Barry H. Whalen, vice president and program director,
 Semiconductor and Packaging and Interconnect research
 program, MCC
Mark W. White, governor of Texas
Harden H. Wiedemann, director, Governor's Office of Planning and
 Intergovernmental Relations
Meg Wilson, Governor's Office of Planning and Intergovernmental
 Relations; Center for Technology Development and Transfer,
 University of Texas at Austin; director, MCC Membership
 Services Office
Herb Woodson, professor, Department of Electrical Engineering,
 University of Texas at Austin
Andrew Young, mayor of Atlanta

NOTE

1. Titles indicate the relevant position(s) of the person at the time of the events
    described in *R&D Collaboration on Trial*.

References

Aldrich, Howard E., and Toshihiro Sasaki (1993). "R&D Consortia in the United States and Japan." Working paper, Department of Sociology, University of North Carolina at Chapel Hill.

Aldrich, Howard E., and Mary Ann von Glinow (1992). "Personal Networks and Infrastructure Development." In *The Technopolis Phenomenon: Smart Cities, Fast Systems, and Global Networks*, edited by D. Gibson, G. Kozmetsky, and R. Smilor. Savage, MD: Rowman & Littlefield, pp. 125–145.

Allison, Graham T. (1969). "Conceptual Models and the Cuban Missile Crisis." *The American Political Science Review*, (September) Vol. 18, No. 3, p. 689.

_____ (1971). *Essence of Decision: Explaining the Cuban Missile Crisis*. Boston: Little, Brown.

Anderson, Paul A. (1983). "Decision Making by Objection and the Cuban Missile Crisis." *Administrative Science Quarterly*, Vol. 28, pp. 201–222.

Argyris, Chris (1972). *The Applicability of Organizational Sociology*. London: Cambridge University Press.

Arneson, Phillip W. (1982). Personal notes and documents from the meeting to launch MCC, Orlando, Florida.

Avery, Christopher M. (1989). "Organizational Communication in Technology Transfer Between an R&D Consortium and Its Shareholders: The Case of MCC." Ph.D. dissertation. College of Communication, The University of Texas at Austin.

Babcock, James D., Laszlo A. Belady, and Nancy C. Gore (1990). "The Evolution of Technology Transfer at MCC's Software Technology Program: From Didactic to Dialectic." Nice, France: Proceedings of the 12th International Conference on Software Engineering (March 26–30), pp. 290–299.

Baker, Stan (1991). "MCC Sets Tech Plan for '90s. *Electronic Engineeering Times* (March 11), pp. 1, 150.

Barnett, John (1987). "Executive at Texas Instruments Selected To Head MCC in Austin." *Houston Chronicle* (March, 22), p. 4.

Barney, Clifford (1983). "R&D Co-Op Gets Set to Open Up Shop." *Electronics* (March 24), pp. 89, 90.

Belady, Laszlo A. (1992). "Seven Years of MCC's Innovative Technology Program." *The American Programmer* (January), Vol. 5, No. 1, pp. 11–15.

Benningfield, Damond (1989). "Chipping In." *Austin Magazine*, 31 (1): pp. 21–24.

Bower, Joseph L., and Eric A. Rhenman (1985). "Benevolent Cartels." *Harvard Business Review*, 85 (4): pp. 124–132.

Bozzo, Umberto, and David Gibson (1990). "Italy: Technopolis Novus Ortus and the EEC." In F. Williams and D. Gibson (eds.), *Technology Transfer: A Communication Perspective*, edited by Newbury Park, CA: Sage, pp. 226–239.

Breyer, R. Michelle (1993). "Spotlight: Austin's Rankings in 1993." *Austin American-Statesman* (November 28), p. F1.

Broad, William J. (1992). "What Path Will the U.S. Follow Now?" New York Times News Service, *Austin American-Statesman* (March 15), p. D1.

Butler, K.S., and Dowell Myers (1984). "Boomtime in Austin, Texas: Negotiated Growth Management." *Journal of the American Planning Association,* 50: pp. 447–458.

Bylinsky, Gene (1990). "Turning R&D into Real Products." *Fortune* (July 2), pp. 72–77.

Carey, John, and Otis Port (1992). "One Stepper Forward for SEMATECH." *Business Week* (June 8), pp. 110, 112.

Chen, Ying–Chung Annie (1987). "The Diffusion of Cable Television Systems in the United States." Ph.D. dissertation. University of Southern California, Los Angeles.

Coggins, Cheryl (1983). "Texas-Size News." *Austin American-Statesman* (May 22), p. C–1.

Cohen, Michael D., James G. March, and Johan P. Olsen (1972). "A Garbage Can Model of Organizational Choice." *Administrative Science Quarterly*, 17 (1, March): pp. 1–25.

Cole, Joe (1988). "Austin's Chamber of Commerce Was Sure that Phoenix Had Won SEMATECH's Heart." *Arizona Republic* (February 3), p. C1.

Congressional Budget Office (1987). "The Benefits and Risks of Federal Funding for SEMATECH." Washington, DC.

Connolly, Ray (1982). "U.S. R&D Consortium Takes Shape." *Electronics* (March 10), pp. 97–99.

Copelin, Laylen (1987). "Austin Called a Finalist in SEMATECH Sweepstakes." *Austin American-Statesman* (November 19), pp. A1, A10.

_____ (1988). "Moxie vs. Money." *Austin American-Statesman* (January 6), p. A1.

Crudele, J. (1990). "U.S. Can't Afford to Lose Technology War." *Austin American-Statesman* (February 5), p. 14.

Cude, Roger L. (1987). "The Uses of Argument in Deciding Whether to Relocate a Municipal Airport." Paper presented at the Summer Conference on Interpretive Approaches to Organizational Study, Alta, Utah (August 13–16).

Cunnington, Bert, and David V. Gibson (1991). "Mangerial Competencies for the 21st Century: Collaborative Individualism and the Networked Organization." Unpublished manuscript, IC^2 Institute, University of Texas at Austin.

Curtis, Bill, Herb Krasner, and Neil Iscoe (1988). "A Field Study of the Software Design Process for Large Systems. *Communications of the ACM* (November), Vol. 31, No. 11, pp. 1268–1287.

Daft, Richard L., and John C. Wiginton (1979). "Language and Organization." *Academy of Management Review*, 4: pp. 179–191.

Daft, R. L. and R. H. Lengel (1986). "Organizational Information Requirements, Media Richness, and Structural Design." *Management Science*, 32 (5), pp. 554–571.

Davis, Dwight B. (1985). "R&D Consortia." *High Technology* (October), pp. 42–47.

Day, Kathleen (1984). "MCC Places Hopes on Long-Range Strategy." *Los Angeles Times* (September 10), pp. 1, 6.

Dearing, James W. (1989). "Communication among Researchers in a Science City: Tsukuba, Japan." Ph.D. dissertation. Annenberg School for Communication, University of Southern California, Los Angeles.

_____ (1991). "In Search of Radical Creativity: Large-Scale Planned Science in Japan." Paper presented at College on Innovation Management and Entrepreneurship, Institute of Management Sciences, Vol. V, Nashville, TN (May 12–15).

Defense Science Board Task Force (1987). "Defense Semiconductor Dependency." Washington, DC: U.S. Department of Defense.

Deming, W. Edwards (1993). Quoted in *Focus,* published by the National Center for Manufacturing Sciences (March), p. 1.

Dineen, Gerald P. (1988). "R&D Consortia: Are They Working?" *Research and Development,* pp. 63–66.

Dobyns, Lloyd (1990). "Ed Deming Wants Big Changes and He Wants Them Fast." *Smithsonian* 21 (5, August).

Dornbusch, Sandy M., and W. Richard Scott (1975). *Evaluation and the Exercise of Authority.* San Francisco: Jossey-Bass.

Dove, Grant A. (1989). "Cooperative Research at MCC: A Focus on Semiconductor-Related Efforts." *IEEE Special Issue on Collaborative Semiconductor Research* (September), Vol. 77, No. 9, pp. 1363–1375.

_____ (1990). Address to the Plenary Session of the Semiconductor Research Corporation, Washington, DC (February 27).

Dowler, R.H., and Adam Watson Brown (1991). "The Impact of European Collaborative and National Research and Development Programs." In D. Gibson (ed.), *Technology Companies and Global Markets: Programs, Products, and Strategies to Accelerate Innovation and Entrepreneurship.* Savage, MD: Rowman and Littlefield, pp. 313–334.

Eaton, Mark (1988). "MITI and the Entrepreneurial State: The Future of Japanese Industrial Policy." Technical report, MCC.

_____ (1993). "Cooperative Research Management Issues." Document, MCC.

Eisenberg, Eric M. (1990). "Jamming: Transcendence through Organizing." *Communication Research* 17 (2): pp. 139–164.

Eisenhardt, Kathleen M. (1989). "Building Theory from Case Study Research." *Academy of Management Review,* 14: pp. 532–550.

Evan, William M. and Paul Okl (1990). "R&D Consortia: A New U.S. Organizational Form." *Sloan Management Review* (Spring), pp. 37–46.

Evans, Peggie I. (1986). "Social Impact of Oil Bust Is Devastating." *Arizona Republic* (August 17), p. C-1.

Farley, John, and Norman Glickman (1986). "R&D as an Economic Development Strategy: The Microelectronics and Computer

Technology Corporation Comes to Austin, Texas." *Journal of the American Planning Association,* 52: pp. 407–418.

Farnsworth, Clyde H. (1990). "Report Warns of Decline of U.S. Electronics Industry." *New York Times* (June 9), pp. 17–18.

Feibus, Michael, and David M. Kutzman (1988). "Austin's Go-Get-'Em Attitude Got SEMATECH." *San Jose Mercury News* (January 7), p. 1A.

Fischetti, Mark A. (1986). "A Review of Progress at MCC." *IEEE Spectrum* (March), pp. 76–82.

Forbes, Malcolm S., Jr. (1993). "Fact and Comment." *Forbes* (May 10), p. 25.

Fox, Karen F.A., and Philip Kotler (1980). "The Marketing of Social Causes: The First Ten Years." *Journal of Marketing,* 44: pp. 24–33.

Fusfeld, Herbert I., and Carmela S. Haklisch (1985). "Cooperative R&D for Competitors." *Harvard Business Review* (November–December), pp. 60–76.

Geisler, E. and A. H. Rubenstein (1993). "The Role of the Firm's Internal Technical Entrepreneurs in Commercializing Technology from Federal Laboratories." Paper presented at the From Lab to Market, University of New Mexico, Santa Fe, MN (March).

Gellhorn, Ernest (1981). *Antitrust Law and Economics in a Nutshell,* 2d ed. St. Paul, MN: West.

General Accounting Office (1990). "GAO Study Finds SEMATECH Falls Short in Helping Industry." Wire reports in *Austin American-Statesman* (September 28).

Gentsch, Eric L. (1990). "The Consortium: Cooperation versus Competition." Report IR004R1, Bethesda, MD: Logistics Management Institute, (February).

Gerstner, Richard L. (1985). "MCC Participant Technology Readiness Assessment." MCC Proprietary Report (June).

Gibson, D., ed. (1991). *Technology Companies and Global Markets.* Savage, MD: Rowman & Littlefield Publishers.

Gibson, David V., Cynthia A. Kehoe, and Sun-Yoon K. Lee (1994). "Collaborative Research as a Function of Proximity, Industry, and Company: A Case Study of an R&D Consortium." *IEEE Transactions on Engineering Management,* forthcoming.

Gibson, David V., George Kozmetsky, and Raymond W. Smilor (eds.) (1992). *The Technopolis Phenomenon: Smart Cities, Fast Systems, and Global Networks.* Savage, MD: Rowman & Littlefield.

Gibson, David V., and Everett M. Rogers (1988). "The MCC Comes to Texas." In Frederick Williams (ed.), *Measuring the Information Society.* Newbury Park, CA: Sage, pp. 91–115.

_____ (1994). "A Communication-Based Model of Technology Transfer." Working paper in progress.

Gibson, David V., and Raymond Smilor (1991). "Key Variables in Technology Transfer: A Field-Study Based Empirical Analysis." *Journal of Engineering and Technology Management,* 8 (December): pp. 287–312.

Gibson, David V., Raymond W. Smilor, and George Kozmetsky (1991). *Austin Technology-Based Industry Report,* IC^2 Institute, Austin, Texas.

Glaser, B.G., and A.L. Strauss (1967). *The Discovery of Grounded Theory.* New York: Aldine.

Granovetter, Mark S. (1973). "The Strength of Weak Ties." *American Journal of Sociology,* 78: pp. 1360–1380.

Green, Tim (1988). "Austin on SEMATECH: 'Yeeow.'" *Austin Business Journal* (January 11–17), pp. 1, 12.

Guinn, Jeffery M. (1983). "Consortia Is Sampling All of Its Chips." *Fort Worth Star-Telegram* (June 26), p. 10A.

Hasty, Turner (1990). Paper presented to IEE Committee on Industrial Competitiveness, Mayflower Hotel, Washington, DC (October 20).

Hays, Constance L. (1990). "An Inventor of the Microchip, Robert N. Noyce, Dies at 62." *New York Times* (June 4), pp. A1, B16.

Hiatt, F., and M. Shapiro (1990). "In Japan, a Fear of Being America's Enemy No. 1." Washington Post Service in *International Herald Tribune* (February 13), p. 5.

"High-Tech's Fickle Helping Hand" (1989). *Time* (December 4), p. 68.

Hilts, Philip J. (1984). "Interview Bobby Ray Inman," *OMNI* (November), pp. 100–122.

Huxley, Aldous (1941/1969). *Grey Eminence.* New York: Harper & Row.

Inman, Bobby R. (1984). "The Microelectronics and Computer Technology Corporation." In Robert Lawrence Kuhn (ed.), *Commercializing Defense-Related Technology*. New York: Praeger, pp. 149–152.

Inman, B.R., and Daniel F. Burton, Jr. (1980). "Technology and Competitiveness: A New Policy Frontier." *Foreign Affairs*, pp. 116–134.

Ishihara, Shintaro (1981). Japanese legislator and co-author of *The Japan That Can Say No*, quoted in *Time* (November 20), pp. 81–82.

Kahn, Joseph (1983). "The Isosceles of Texas is Upon Us." *Inc.* (October), pp. 155–158.

Kantor, Seth (1988). "Teamwork Makes for a Powerful Texas Delegation." *Austin American-Statesman* (February 14), pp. D1, D7.

_____ (1990). "Uproar over Proposed Semi-Gas Sale." *Austin American-Statesman* (August 2), pp. F1, 2.

Kehoe, Cindy (1993). "Unobtrusive Measures of Research Collaboration: The Case of MCC." Research dissertation in progress, Graduate School of Library and Information Science, University of Texas at Austin.

Kidder, Tracy (1981). *The Soul of a New Machine*. Boston: Atlantic-Little, Brown.

Kotler, Philip, and Gerald Zaltman (1971). "Social Marketing: An Approach to Planned Social Change." *Journal of Marketing*, 35 (3): pp. 3–12.

Kozmetsky, George (1988). "The Challenge of Technology Innovation: The New Globally Competitive Era." In *Technology Companies and Global Markets*, pp. 3–15.

_____ (1989). "Tomorrow's Transformational Managers." In K. D. Walters (ed.), *Entrepreneurial Management: New Technology and New Market Development*. Boston: Ballinger, pp. 171–176.

Krishnan, Harihar (1987). "First Product Strengthens MCC Credibility." *San Antonio Light* (July 26).

Kurozumi, Takashi (1992). "Outline of the Fifth-Generation Project and ICOT." In *Technology Transfer in Consortia and Strategic Alliances*, pp. 173–191.

Ladendorf, Kirk (1983a). "Ex-Spy Shifts Gears for Top Job at MCC." *Austin American-Statesman* (May 22), p. C–1.

_____ (1983b). "The Anticipation Ends." *Austin American-Statesman* (September 12), p. C-1.

_____ (1984). "MCC." *Austin American-Statesman* (May 13), p. D14.

_____ (1990a). "MCC to Launch Research on 'Multi-Chip Modules.'" *Austin American-Statesman* (June 13).

_____ (1990b). "Rebooting: Consortium Ponders High-tech Mission, Future." *Austin American-Statesman* (August 16), p. A12.

_____ (1990c). " SEMATECH Objects to Sale of Supplier." *Austin American-Statesman* (October 11), p. B5.

_____ (1991a). "Chipping Away: U.S. Semiconductor Industry's World Market Share Still Slipping.'" *Austin American-Statesman* (January 28).

_____ (1991b). "SEMATECH to Cooperate with European Group." *Austin American-Statesman* (September 21).

_____ (1992a). "Chip Firm Withdraws from SEMATECH." *Austin American-Statesman* (January 7), pp. D1, D8.

_____ (1992b). "Micron is 2nd Firm to Cash in Its Chips at SEMATECH." *Austin American-Statesman* (January 11), pp. E1, E4.

_____ (1992c)."Research Spins Off from SEMATECH." *Austin American-Statesman* (April 15), pp. D1–D2.

_____ (1992d). "Computer History Program Tunes into Lenant." *Austin American-Statesman* (April 25), p. E1.

_____ (1992e)."SEMATECH Officials Feel Chipper about Future." *Austin American-Statesman* (August 24), pp. C1, C5.

_____ (1993a). "SEMATECH Celebrates Tiny Milestone in Microchip Race." *Austin American-Statesman* (March 5), p. D1.

_____ (1993b). "MCC Creates Discount Memberships." *Austin American-Statesman* (March 5), p. D1.

_____ (1993c). "High-Tech Industry Spurs Jobs, Economy." *Austin American-Statesman* (April 18), pp. A1, A7.

_____ (1993d). "SEMATECH: Egg on Its Face." *Austin American-Statesman* (June 14), pp. D1, D2.

_____ (1993e). "Applied Materials Gives Credit to SEMATECH for Circuit Help." *Austin American-Statesman* (July 14), p. B6.

_____ (1993f). "MCC Partnership to Develop Flat-Panel Display." *Austin American-Statesman* (September 9), pp. F1–F2.

Laffitte, Pierre (1988). "Sophia-Antipolas and the Movement South in Europe." In Raymond W. Smilor, George Kozmetsky, and David V. Gibson (eds.), *Creating the Technopolis: Linking Technology, Commercialization, and Economic Development.* Cambridge, MA: Ballinger, pp. 91–97.

Lardner, James (1987). *Fast Forward: Hollywood, the Japanese, and the Onslaught of the VCR.* New York: W.W. Norton.

Ledeboer, William, and Tjerk R. Gorter (1992). "The ESPRIT of a European R&D Program." *International Journal of Technology Management,* forthcoming.

Leibowitz, Michael R. (1990). "U.S. Consortia: How Do They Measure Up?" *Electronic Business* (January 22), pp. 46–51.

Leonard-Barton, Dorothy (1988). "Implementation as Mutual Adaptation of Technology and Organization." *Research Policy,* 17, pp. 251–287.

Leonard-Barton, Dorothy, and W.A. Kraus (1985). "Implementing New Technology." *Harvard Business Review,* 63 (6): pp. 102–110.

Lewis, Peter H. (1992). "Barring the Door to the Ivory Tower." *New York Times* (October 11).

Lincoln, Yvonne S., and Egon G. Guba (1985). *Naturalistic Inquiry.* Newbury Park, CA: Sage.

Lodge, George C. (1990). *Perestroika for America.* Boston: Harvard Business School Press.

McCann, Bill (1989). "Sematech Tax Bill May Hit 41 Million." *Austin American-Statesman* (September 23), p. D1.

McCarthy, John (1987). "First Product Strengthens MCC Credibility." *San Antonio Light* (July 26).

McCullar, Michael (1988). "Clean Room Awaits Plans of SEMATECH's Team." *Austin American-Statesman* (January 24), p. D1.

Mandell, Mel (1990). "The Consortium: An Idea Whose Time Has Come (Or Gone)?" *Issues in Science and Technology* (June), pp. 31–35.

March, James G. (1978). "Bounded Rationality, Ambiguity, and the Engineering of Choice." *Bell Journal of Economics,* 9: pp. 587–608.

Marks, Dena (1983). "Computer Dating: The Wooing of MCC. *Third Coast* (July), p. 34.

Melman, Seymour (1983). *Profits without Production.* New York: Alfred A. Knopf, pp. 164, 165.

Melody, Thomas J., and James F.P. Wagley (1989). "Texas Developers Recount 'Boon To Bust' Period; How and Why Becomes Clear in Cyclical Industry." *National Real Estate Investor* (October), pp. 158–162.

Metzenbaum, Shelley (1992). "Making the Most of Inter-state Bidding Wars for Business." Ph.D. dissertation. J.F. Kennedy School of Government, Harvard University.

Mintzberg, Henry (1973). *The Nature of Managerial Work.* New York: Harper & Row.

———— (1979). "An Emerging Strategy of Direct Research." *Administrative Science Quarterly,* 24: pp. 580–589.

Mintzberg, Henry, Duru Raisinghani, and André Théôrét (1976). "The Structure of 'Unstructured' Decision Processes." *Administrative Science Quarterly,* 21: pp. 246–275.

Moore, Jonathan (1991). "SEMATECH under Fire on Capital Hill." *States News Service* (July 24), p. D1.

Morita, Keisuke, and Hiroshi Hiraoka (1988). "Technopolis Osaka: Integrating Urban Functions and Science." In *Creating the Technopolis,* pp. 23–50.

Morrison, Anne, Nina Shetty, Jason Webb, and Cecil Way (1993). "SEMATECH: A Case Study." In *Assessment of Technology Transfer Strategies.* A class project, The Heinz School, Carnegie-Mellon University, Pittsburgh, PA (forthcoming).

Muir, Nan Kanoff (1991). "R&D Consortium Technology Transfer: A Study of Shareholder Technology Strategy and Organizational Learning." Ph.D. dissertation, University of Texas at Arlington.

Murphy, William J., and Joseph L. Bower (1986). "Cooperation for Competition: U.S. and Japan." Harvard Business School Case 9-386-181.

Murphy, William Joseph, III (1987). "Cooperative Action to Achieve Competitive Strategic Objectives: A Study of the Micro-electronics and Computer Technology Corporation." DBA dissertation, Harvard Business School.

Myers, Dowell (1987). "Internal Monitoring of Quality of Life for Economic Development." *Economic Development Quarterly,* 1 (3): pp. 268–278.

Narin, F., and D. Olivastro (1988). "Technology Indicators Based on Patents and Patent Citations." In A.F.J. Van Raan (ed.), *Handbook of Qualitative Studies of Science and Technology.* New York: Elsevier Science Publishing.

National Advisory Committee on Semiconductors (1989). "A Strategic Industry at Risk." Arlington, VA: National Advisory Committee on Semiconductors, Report to the President and the Congress.

Nelson, Mark (1988). "Texans Flexed Political Muscle to Save SEMATECH Funding." *Dallas Morning News* (January 7).

New York Times News Service (1989). "High-Tech Funding Is Crucial to Future of U.S., Studies Say." *Austin American-Statesman* (November 21), pp. C15–C16.

Norris, William (1982). "Keeping America First." *Datamation*, pp. 282–287.

_____ (1985). "Cooperative R&D: A Regional Strategy." *Issues in Science and Technology* (Winter), pp. 92–102.

Northcott, Kaye (1987). "Tex Mess: Austin Finds Its City Limits." *The Progressive*, pp. 36–39.

Okimoto, Daniel I. Takuo Sugano, and Franklin B. Weinstein (1984) *Competitive Edge: The Semiconductor Industry in the U.S. and Japan.* Stanford, CA: Stanford University Press.

Onda, Masahiko (1988). "Tsukuba Science City Complex and Japanese Strategy." In *Creating the Technopolis*, pp. 51–68.

O'Reilly, Brian (1985). "Texans Look Away from Oil." *Fortune* (July 8), pp. 41–47.

_____ (1986). "What's So Great About Admiral Bobby Inman?" *Fortune* (November 10), pp. 106–107, 112.

Ouchi, William G. (1984a). *The M-Form Society: How American Teamwork Can Recapture the Competitive Edge.* Reading, MA: Addison–Wesley.

_____ (1984b). "Political and Economic Teamwork: The Development of the Microelectronics Industry of Japan." *California Management Review*, 26, No. 4 (Summer), pp. 8–34.

Ouchi, William G., and Michele Kremen Bolton (1988). "The Logic of Joint Research and Development." *California Management Review* (Spring) 30, pp. 9–33.

Peck, Merton J. (1986). "Joint R&D: The Case of Microelectronics and Computer Technology Corporation." *Research Policy*, 15: pp. 219–231.

Peck, Merton J., and Akira Goto (1981). "Technology and Economic Growth: The Case of Japan." *Research Policy*, 10: pp. 222–243.

Petit, Michael J. (1987). "Industrial Research and Development Consortia: An Analysis of Survey Results." Professional Report, Graduate School of Business, University of Texas at Austin.

Petri, Amy Elizabeth (1992). "Information Sharing Within R&D Consortia: An Exploratory Case Study of the Microelectronic Computer Technology Corporation (MCC)." Masters thesis, Georgia Institute of Technology.

Pfeffer, Jeffrey (1982). *Organizations and Organization Theory.* Marshfield, MA: Pitman.

Pine, Art (1990). "U.S. Leadership in Electronics at Risk, Congress Warned." *Los Angeles Times* (June 9), pp. D1, D4.

Pinkston, John T. (1988). "From Visionary Ideas to Products." *Future Generations Computer Systems,* 3: pp. 233–243.

_____ (1989). "Technology Transfer: Issues for Consortia." In K. Walters (ed.), *Entrepreneurial Management: New Technology and New Market Development.* Cambridge, MA: Ballinger, pp. 143–149.

Pollack, Andrew (1992). "Fifth Generation Became Japan's Lost Generation." *New York Times* (June 5), p. D1.

Pope, Kyle (1988). "SEMATECH Opens with High Hopes." *Austin American-Statesman* (November 16), pp. A1, A11.

_____ (1989a). "MCC Puts Technology into the Marketplace." *Austin American-Statesman* (February 9), p. B1.

_____ (1989b). "MCC Unveils Optics Research." *Austin American-Statesman* (June 24).

_____ (1989c). "Tax Ruling Goes Against SEMATECH." *Austin American-Statesman* (August 8), pp. A1, A14.

_____ (1989d). "MCC Revamps Offerings." *Austin American-Statesman* (August 22), pp. A1, A9.

_____ (1989e). "Texas Superconductivity Center to Share Work with Defense Labs." *Austin American-Statesman* (August 24), p. F1.

_____ (1989f). "MCC Technology Going into Digital Mainframe." *Austin American-Statesman* (August 29).

_____ (1989g). "SEMATECH to Sue Appraisal District Over Tax Bill." *Austin American-Statesman* (November 14).

_____ (1989h). "MCC Comes Out of the Shadows." *Austin American-Statesman* (December 11), pp. 1, 19.

Porter, Michael E. (1990). "Japan Isn't Playing by Different Rules." *New York Times Forum* (July 22), p. F13.

Prestowitz, Clyde V., Jr. (1988). *Trading Places: How We Allowed Japan to Take the Lead.* New York: Basic Books.

Preuss, Gil, Dorothy Leonard-Barton, Marco Iansiti, and David Gibson (1990). "MCC: The Packaging and Interconnect Program." Harvard Business School Case N9-691-036.

Reed, Ted (1987). "MCC Makes Itself Known." *The Sacramento Bee* (August 24).

Reich, Robert B. (1989). "The Quiet Path to Technological Preeminence." *Scientific American*, 261: pp. 41–47.

Richards, Evelyn (1989). "Adrift: Despite Overseas Threats, High-Tech Unable to Form Strategy for the '90s." *Washington Post Service* (November 26), pp. H1, H4.

_____ (1991)."Transforming an Ivory Tower in Texas: Technology Broker Fields Revamps Research Consortium to Speed Innovations to Market." *Washington Post* (April 21).

Rifkin, Glenn (1990). "R&D Group Finds Shoes It Can Fill." *ComputerWorld,* Vol 24, No. 39 (September 24), pp. 1–9.

Roach, Thomas W. (1992). *"Effective Systems Development in Complex Organizations: A Field Study of Systems Development and Use in the United States Army Medical Department."* Ph.D. dissertation, College and Graduate School of Business, University of Texas at Austin.

Rogers, Everett M. (1983). *Diffusion of Innovations.* New York: Free Press.

Rogers, Everett M., and D. Lawrence Kincaid (1981). *Communication Networks: A New Paradigm for Research.* New York: Free Press.

Rogers, Everett M., and Judith K. Larsen (1984). *Silicon Valley Fever: Growth of High-Tech Culture.* New York: Basic Books.

Rothschild, Scott (1990). "SEMATECH Blasts Bush For Letting Japan Buy Chip-Related Company." *Austin American-Statesman,* Associated Press (July 28).

Russell, Bill, and T. Branch (1979). *Second Wind: The Memories of an Opinionated Man.* New York: Random House.

Sakakibara, Kiyonori (1983). "From Imitation to Innovation: The Very Large Scale Integrated (VLSI) Semiconductor Project in Japan." Working Paper 1490–83, Sloan School of Management, MIT.

———— (1989). "R&D Cooperation among Competitors: Lessons from the VLSI Semiconductor Research Project in Japan." Department of Economics. Hitotsubashi University, Tokyo, Working Paper # 8906.

Sanger, David E. (1984). "Rivalries Split U.S. Project." *New York Times* (September 5), pp. D1, D5.

———— (1988). "Japanese Firm Wants to Join SEMATECH." *New York Times Service* (August 16).

———— (1991). "Japan Asks Aid on Next Computers." *New York Times* (March 15).

Sawhney, Harmeet (1990). "Serendipity Is Happening All the Time." In *The Synectic*, newsletter of the Technology Transfer Research Group, IC^2 Institute, University of Texas at Austin, p. 10.

Saxenien, Anna Lee (1989a). "In Search of Power: The Organization of Business Interests in Silicon Valley and Route 128." *Economy and Society*, 18 (1): pp. 25–70.

———— (1989b). "Regional Networks and the Resurgence of Silicon Valley." Paper presented at the Association of Collegiate Schools of Planning, Portland, OR.

Schaffer, Jan (1983). "Too Little Too Late: Philadelphia's Ill-fated Attempt for MCC." *Philadelphia Inquirer* (May 29), p. 10-F.

Schmitz, Tom (1989). "California Thinks It Learned Something from SEMATECH Loss." *San Jose Mercury News* (August 21).

Schneer, George (1987). Quoted in Laylan Copelin (1987). "Austin Called a Finalist in SEMATECH Sweepstakes." *Austin-American-Statesman* (November 19), pp. A1–A10.

Schrage, Michael (1989). "Admiral Inman in Command at Consortium." *Washington Post* (July 28), p. D1.

———— (1990). "Applying Zaibatsu Principles in the U.S." *Los Angeles Times* (March 8), pp. D–1, D–17.

Science (1991). "Britain Picks the Wrong Way to Beat the Japanese." (May) Vol. 252 .

Scott, Bruce R., and George C. Lodge (eds.) (1985). *U.S. Competitiveness in the World Economy*. Boston: Harvard Business School Press.

Scott, W. Richard (1981). *Organizations: Rational, Natural, and Open Systems*. Englewood Cliffs, NJ: Prentice-Hall.

Segal, N.S. (1988). "The Cambridge Phenomenon: Universities, Research, and Local Economic Development in Great Britain." In *Creating the Technopolis*, pp. 81–90.

Segman, Ralph (1989). Roundtable on Technology Transfer sponsored by the Technology Transfer Research Group, IC^2 Institute, University of Texas at Austin, July.

SEMATECH (1991). Annual Report.

Senda, Atsushi (1993). "The Challenge of Soft Information Processing." *Nikkei Computer* 4 (5), translated report.

Sigurdson, John (1986). "Industry and State Partnerships in Japan: The Very Large Scale Integrated Circuits (VLSI) Project." Lund, Sweden: Research Policy Studies Discussion Paper 168, Research Policy Institute.

Singhal, Arvind, Everett M. Rogers, Harmeet Sawhney, and David Gibson (1990). "Bangalore: India's Emerging Technopolis." In *Technology Transfer: A Communication Perspective*, pp. 240–257.

Smilor, Raymond W., and David V. Gibson (1991). "Technology Transfer in Multi-Organizational Environments: The Case of R&D Consortia." *IEEE Transactions on Engineering Management,* 38 (1, February): pp. 3–13.

Smilor, Raymond W., David V. Gibson, and Chris Avery (1990). "R&D Consortia and Technology Transfer: Initial Lessons from MCC." *Journal of Technology Transfer,* 14 (2): pp. 11–22.

Smilor, Raymond W., David V. Gibson, and George Kozmetsky (1988). "Creating the Technopolis: High-Technology Development in Austin, Texas." *Journal of Business Venturing*, Vol. 4, pp. 49–67.

Smilor, Raymond W. and Michael D. Gill, Jr. (1986). *The New Business Incubator: Linking Talent, Technology, Capital, and Know-How*. Lexington, MA: Lexington Books.

Smilor, Raymond W., George Kozmetsky, and David V. Gibson (eds.) (1988). *Creating the Technopolis*. Cambridge, MA: Ballinger.

Smith, Douglas K., and Robert C. Alexander (1988). *Fumbling the Future: How Xerox Invented, Then Ignored, the First Personal Computer*. New York: William Morrow.

Smith, Lee (1989). "Can Consortiums Defeat Japan?" *Fortune* (June 5), pp. 245–254.

Stanley, Dick (1991). "Intelligent Computer More Than a Dream." *Austin American-Statesman* (April 29), p. A1, A5.

Stipp, David (1984). "Austin, Texas, Keeps Courting High Tech, Irking Some Residents." *The Wall Street Journal* (September 11).

Strain, Mark P. (1989). "The Decision of SEMATECH to Locate in Austin: A Case Study of Synergism among Government, Industry, and the Local Technopolis." Senior honors' thesis, University of Texas at Austin.

Sullivan, Kathleen (1986). "Fund Drive for MCC Lacks Cash." *Austin American-Statesman* (December 11), pp. K1, K5.

———— (1987). "MCC Chairman Closes the Door to Foreign Membership." *Austin American-Statesman* (October 24), p. C1.

Tatsuno, Sheridan (1986). *The Technopolis Strategy.* Englewood Cliffs, NJ: Prentice-Hall.

———— (1988). "Building a Japanese Technostate: MITI's Technopolis Program." In *Creating the Technopolis,* pp. 3–22.

Taylor, Paul (1984). "Development Boom Shakes Austin." *Washington Post* (November 25), pp. A–4, A–5.

Tichy, Noel M., et al. (1978). "A Network Approach to Organizational Assessment." In E. Lawler et al. (eds.), *Organizational Assessment: Perspectives on the Measurement of Organizational Behavior and the Quality of Working Life.* New York: Wiley-Interscience.

Tichy, Noel M., Michael L. Tushman, and Charles Fombrun (1979). "Social Network Analysis of Organizations." *Academy of Management Review,* 4: pp. 507–519.

Torstendahl, Rolf (1989). "Industrial Research and Researchers in Sweden 1880–1940." *Social Science Information,* 19 (3): pp. 641–661.

Tyson, Kim (1988a). "MCC Members Force Change in CAD Project." *Austin American-Statesman* (April 22), p. E1.

———— (1988b). "MCC Wins Contract to Fund Superconductor Project." *Austin American-Statesman* (February 3).

U.S. Congress, House Subcommittee on Trade, Committee on Ways and Means (1980). *U.S.-Japan Trade Report* (September 5), p. 5.

Uttal, Bro (1982). "Here Comes Computer Inc." *Fortune* (October 4), pp. 82–90.

Van de Ven, Andrew H., and W. Grahan Astley (1981). "Mapping the Field to Create a Dynamic Perspective in Organization Design and Behavior." In A.H. Van de Ven and W.F. Joyce (eds.), *Perspectives on Organizational Design and Behavior9.* New York: Wiley-Interscience, pp. 427–468.

Von Tyle, Sherrie (1989). "Sorting Out the Consortia." *Electronics,* pp. 79–82.

Wakasugi, Ryuhai (1988). "A Consideration of Innovative Organizations: Joint R&D of Japanese Firms." Tokyo: Ministry of International Trade and Industry, Staff Paper Series 88–05.

Walsh, John (1983). "MCC Moves Out of the Idea Stage." *Science* (June 17), p. 1257.

Walters, Donna K.H. (1986). "MCC under Pressure to Turn R&D into Products." *Los Angeles Times* (November 2), pp. 1, 4.

Warsh, David (1983a). "High-Tech Gets Even Smarter." *Boston Globe* (April 10), pp. A18–A19.

_____ (1983b). "The MCC Gamble." *Austin American-Statesman* (April 17), pp. C-1, C-15.

_____ (1986a). "Texas-Size Hopes for MCC's Effect on Austin Economy Quickly Deflated." *Los Angeles Times* (November 2), pp. 4–5.

Weber, Jonathan (1991)."Chip-making Partnership Suffering Growing Pains." *Los Angeles Times* (October 27), pp. A1, A22.

Weick, Karl (1984). "Theoretical Assumptions and Research Methodology Selection." In F.W. McFarlan *(ed.), The Information Systems Research Challenge.* Boston: Harvard Business School Press, pp. 111–132.

Werner, Jerry (1980). "Department of Justice: Co-Op R&D Not Necessarily Illegal." *Electronic Engineering Times* (March 31), p. 178.

_____ (1992)."Technology Transfer in Consortia: Challenges and Opportunities." *Research Technology Management,* May–June, pp. 38–43.

Werner, Jerry, and Jack Bremer (1991). "Hard Lessons in Cooperative Research." *Issues in Science and Technology,* VII (3), pp. 44–49.

White, Lawrence J. (1985). "Clearing the Legal Path to Cooperative Research." *Technology Review* (July), pp. 39–44.

Whittington, Dale, ed. (1985). *High Hopes for High Tech: Microelectronics Policy in North Carolina.* Chapel Hill: University of North Carolina Press.

Wigand, Rolf T. (1987). "Taming the Desert: High-Technology Development in the Phoenix Area." In *Creating the Technopolis,* pp. 185–202.

Williams, Frederick, and David V. Gibson (eds.) (1990). *Technology Transfer.* Newbury Park, CA: Sage.

Worthy, James C. (1987). *William C. Norris: Portrait of a Maverick.* Cambridge, MA: Ballinger.

Wysocki, Annette (1988). "Community Teamwork, Chamber Leadership Vital to Successful SEMATECH Effort." *Skyliner* (February), Austin Chamber of Commerce newsmonthly.

———— (1989). "Austin Is on the Rise Again." *Austin* (October), pp. 12–20.

Zimel, Norman S. (1992). "Cooperation Meets Competition: The Impact of Consortia for Precompetitive R&D in the Computer Industry, 1982–1992." Program on Information Resource Policy, Center for Information Policy Research, Harvard University.

Zonana, V.F. (1988). "U.S. Companies Prefer to Go It Alone." *Austin American-Statesman* (February 28), p. D4.

Zorpette, Glenn (1990). "Electronic Consortia to Impact Products for Generations." *IEEE Spectrum,* special issue on R&D, Vol. 27, No. 10 (October), pp. 25–84.

INDEX

589

ABOUT THE AUTHORS

David V. Gibson is a senior research fellow at the IC^2 Institute, The University of Texas at Austin. Dr. Gibson is co-director of the Multidisciplinary Technology Transfer Research Group at the university and chair of the College on Innovation Management and Entrepreneurship (COLIME), The Institute of Management Sciences. Dr. Gibson's research and publications focus on cross-cultural communication and management, regional economic development, and the management and application of technology. His current research is on science and technology commercialization at federal laboratories, technology incubator operations, and the management of fast-growth technology firms. His most recent publications include: *The Technopolis Phenomenon: Smart Cities, Fast Systems, and Global Networks* (Rowman and Littlefield, 1992); *Technology Transfer in Consortia and Strategic Alliances* (Rowman and Littlefield, 1992); and *Technology Transfer: A Communication Perspective* (Sage, 1990).

Everett M. Rogers is professor and chair of the Department of Communication and Journalism at the University of New Mexico and senior research fellow at the IC^2 Institute. For 35 years he has been conducting research on the diffusion of innovations and has written a series of books on this topic, including *Diffusion of Innovations* (Free Press, 1983). Dr. Rogers studies the role of technology transfer in high-technology industry. His research on this topic includes *Silicon Valley Fever: Growth of High-Technology Culture,* co-authored with Judith K. Larsen (Basic Books, 1984) and *India's Information Revolution,* co-authored with Arvind Singhal (Sage, 1989). His most recent book is *A History of Communication Study: A Biographical Approach* (Free Press, 1994). Dr. Rogers is presently involved in conducting research on the development and transfer of microcomputer user-interface technologies, and on technology transfer from federal labs.

607